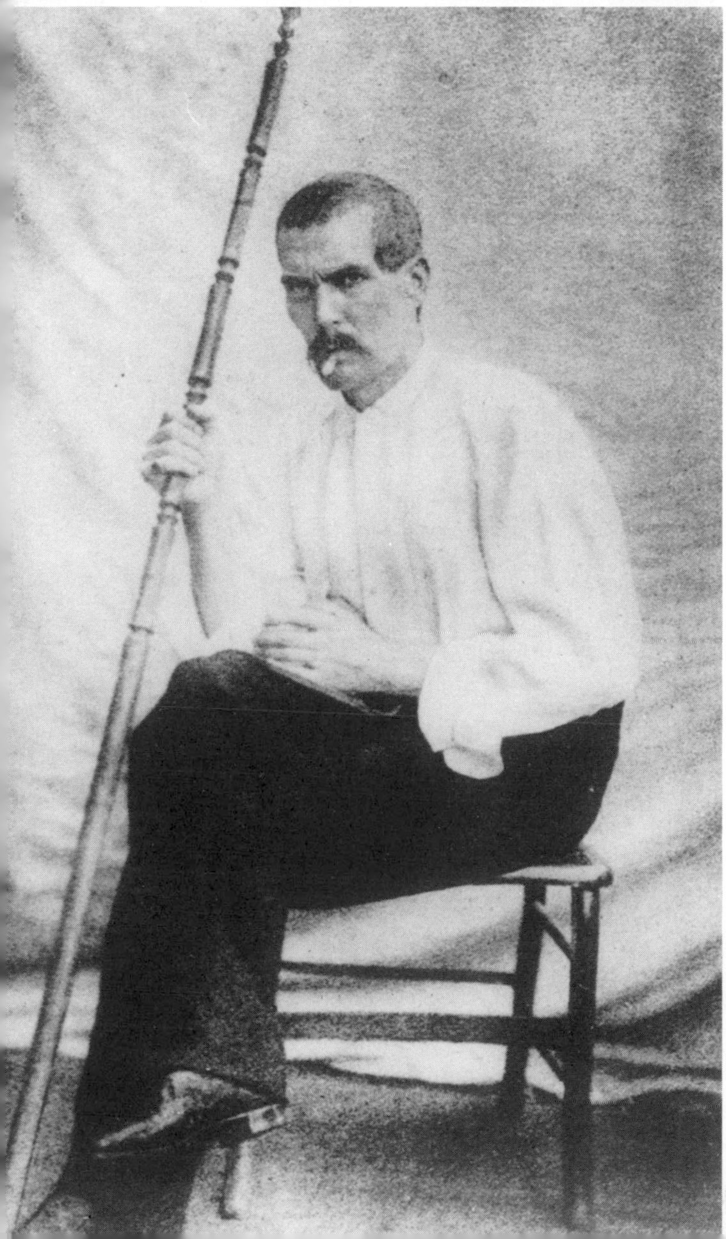

Dictionary of Literary Biography • Volume Fifty-five

Victorian Prose Writers Before 1867

Dictionary of Literary Biography

1: *The American Renaissance in New England*, edited by Joel Myerson (1978)

2: *American Novelists Since World War II*, edited by Jeffrey Helterman and Richard Layman (1978)

3: *Antebellum Writers in New York and the South*, edited by Joel Myerson (1979)

4: *American Writers in Paris, 1920-1939*, edited by Karen Lane Rood (1980)

5: *American Poets Since World War II*, 2 parts, edited by Donald J. Greiner (1980)

6: *American Novelists Since World War II*, Second Series, edited by James E. Kibler, Jr. (1980)

7: *Twentieth-Century American Dramatists*, 2 parts, edited by John MacNicholas (1981)

8: *Twentieth-Century American Science-Fiction Writers*, 2 parts, edited by David Cowart and Thomas L. Wymer (1981)

9: *American Novelists, 1910-1945*, 3 parts, edited by James J. Martine (1981)

10: *Modern British Dramatists, 1900-1945*, 2 parts, edited by Stanley Weintraub (1982)

11: *American Humorists, 1800-1950*, 2 parts, edited by Stanley Trachtenberg (1982)

12: *American Realists and Naturalists*, edited by Donald Pizer and Earl N. Harbert (1982)

13: *British Dramatists Since World War II*, 2 parts, edited by Stanley Weintraub (1982)

14: *British Novelists Since 1960*, 2 parts, edited by Jay L. Halio (1983)

15: *British Novelists, 1930-1959*, 2 parts, edited by Bernard Oldsey (1983)

16: *The Beats: Literary Bohemians in Postwar America*, 2 parts, edited by Ann Charters (1983)

17: *Twentieth-Century American Historians*, edited by Clyde N. Wilson (1983)

18: *Victorian Novelists After 1885*, edited by Ira B. Nadel and William E. Fredeman (1983)

19: *British Poets, 1880-1914*, edited by Donald E. Stanford (1983)

20: *British Poets, 1914-1945*, edited by Donald E. Stanford (1983)

21: *Victorian Novelists Before 1885*, edited by Ira B. Nadel and William E. Fredeman (1983)

22: *American Writers for Children, 1900-1960*, edited by John Cech (1983)

23: *American Newspaper Journalists, 1873-1900*, edited by Perry J. Ashley (1983)

24: *American Colonial Writers, 1606-1734*, edited by Emory Elliott (1984)

25: *American Newspaper Journalists, 1901-1925*, edited by Perry J. Ashley (1984)

26: *American Screenwriters*, edited by Robert E. Morsberger, Stephen O. Lesser, and Randall Clark (1984)

27: *Poets of Great Britain and Ireland, 1945-1960*, edited by Vincent B. Sherry, Jr. (1984)

28: *Twentieth-Century American-Jewish Fiction Writers*, edited by Daniel Walden (1984)

29: *American Newspaper Journalists, 1926-1950*, edited by Perry J. Ashley (1984)

30: *American Historians, 1607-1865*, edited by Clyde N. Wilson (1984)

31: *American Colonial Writers, 1735-1781*, edited by Emory Elliott (1984)

32: *Victorian Poets Before 1850*, edited by William E. Fredeman and Ira B. Nadel (1984)

33: *Afro-American Fiction Writers After 1955*, edited by Thadious M. Davis and Trudier Harris (1984)

34: *British Novelists, 1890-1929: Traditionalists*, edited by Thomas F. Staley (1985)

35: *Victorian Poets After 1850*, edited by William E. Fredeman and Ira B. Nadel (1985)

36: *British Novelists, 1890-1929: Modernists*, edited by Thomas F. Staley (1985)

37: *American Writers of the Early Republic*, edited by Emory Elliott (1985)

38: *Afro-American Writers After 1955: Dramatists and Prose Writers*, edited by Thadious M. Davis and Trudier Harris (1985)

39: *British Novelists, 1660-1800*, 2 parts, edited by Martin C. Battestin (1985)

40: *Poets of Great Britain and Ireland Since 1960*, 2 parts, edited by Vincent B. Sherry, Jr. (1985)

41: *Afro-American Poets Since 1955*, edited by Trudier Harris and Thadious M. Davis (1985)

42: *American Writers for Children Before 1900*, edited by Glenn E. Estes (1985)

43: *American Newspaper Journalists, 1690-1872*, edited by Perry J. Ashley (1986)

44: *American Screenwriters*, Second Series, edited by Randall Clark, Robert E. Morsberger, and Stephen O. Lesser (1986)

45: *American Poets, 1880-1945*, First Series, edited by Peter Quartermain (1986)

46: *American Literary Publishing Houses, 1900-1980: Trade and Paperback*, edited by Peter Dzwonkoski (1986)

47: *American Historians, 1886-1912*, edited by Clyde N. Wilson (1986)

48: *American Poets, 1880-1945*, Second Series, edited by Peter Quartermain (1986)

49: *American Literary Publishing Houses, 1638-1899*, 2 parts, edited by Peter Dzwonkoski (1986)

50: *Afro-American Writers Before the Harlem Renaissance*, edited by Trudier Harris (1986)

51: *Afro-American Writers from the Harlem Renaissance to 1940*, edited by Trudier Harris (1987)

52: *American Writers for Children Since 1960: Fiction*, edited by Glenn E. Estes (1987)

53: *Canadian Writers Since 1960*, First Series, edited by W. H. New (1987)

54: *American Poets, 1880-1945*, Third Series, 2 parts, edited by Peter Quartermain (1987)

55: *Victorian Prose Writers Before 1867*, edited by William B. Thesing (1987)

Documentary Series

1: *Sherwood Anderson, Willa Cather, John Dos Passos, Theodore Dreiser, F. Scott Fitzgerald, Ernest Hemingway, Sinclair Lewis*, edited by Margaret A. Van Antwerp (1982)

2: *James Gould Cozzens, James T. Farrell, William Faulkner, John O'Hara, John Steinbeck, Thomas Wolfe, Richard Wright*, edited by Margaret A. Van Antwerp (1982)

3: *Saul Bellow, Jack Kerouac, Norman Mailer, Vladimir Nabokov, John Updike, Kurt Vonnegut*, edited by Mary Bruccoli (1983)

4: *Tennessee Williams*, edited by Margaret A. Van Antwerp and Sally Johns (1984)

Yearbooks

1980, edited by Karen L. Rood, Jean W. Ross, and Richard Ziegfeld (1981)

1981, edited by Karen L. Rood, Jean W. Ross, and Richard Ziegfeld (1982)

1982, edited by Richard Ziegfeld; associate editors: Jean W. Ross and Lynne C. Zeigler (1983)

1983, edited by Mary Bruccoli and Jean W. Ross; associate editor: Richard Ziegfeld (1984)

1984, edited by Jean W. Ross (1985)

1985, edited by Jean W. Ross (1986)

Dictionary of Literary Biography • Volume Fifty-five

Victorian Prose Writers Before 1867

Edited by
William B. Thesing
University of South Carolina

A Bruccoli Clark Layman Book
Gale Research Company • Book Tower • Detroit, Michigan 48226

Matthew J. Bruccoli and Richard Layman, *Editorial Directors*
C. E. Frazer Clark, Jr., *Managing Editor*

Manufactured by Edwards Brothers, Inc.
Ann Arbor, Michigan
Printed in the United States of America

Library of Congress Cataloging-in-Publication Data

Victorian prose writers before 1867.

(Dictionary of literary biography; v. 55)
"A Bruccoli Clark book."
Includes index.
1. English prose literature—19th century—History and criticism. 2. English prose literature—19th century—Bio-bibliography. 3. Authors, English—19th century—Biography—Dictionaries. I. Thesing, William B. II. Series.
PR781.V53 1987 828'.808'09 [B] 86-25837
ISBN 0-8103-1733-8

For Amy

Contents

Plan of the Series

... Almost the most prodigious asset of a country, and perhaps its most precious possession, is its native literary product—when that product is fine and noble and enduring.

Mark Twain*

The advisory board, the editors, and the publisher of the *Dictionary of Literary Biography* are joined in endorsing Mark Twain's declaration. The literature of a nation provides an inexhaustible resource of permanent worth. It is our expectation that this endeavor will make literature and its creators better understood and more accessible to students and the literate public, while satisfying the standards of teachers and scholars.

To meet these requirements, *literary biography* has been construed in terms of the author's achievement. The most important thing about a writer is his writing. Accordingly, the entries in *DLB* are career biographies, tracing the development of the author's canon and the evolution of his reputation.

The publication plan for *DLB* resulted from two years of preparation. The project was proposed to Bruccoli Clark by Frederick G. Ruffner, president of the Gale Research Company, in November 1975. After specimen entries were prepared and typeset, an advisory board was formed to refine the entry format and develop the series rationale. In meetings held during 1976, the publisher, series editors, and advisory board approved the scheme for a comprehensive biographical dictionary of persons who contributed to North American literature. Editorial work on the first volume began in January 1977, and it was published in 1978.

In order to make *DLB* more than a reference tool and to compile volumes that individually have claim to status as literary history, it was decided to organize volumes by topic or period or genre. Each of these freestanding volumes provides a biographical-bibliographical guide and overview for a particular area of literature. We are convinced that this organization—as opposed to a single alphabet method—constitutes a valuable innovation in the presentation of reference material. The volume plan necessarily requires many decisions for the placement and treatment of authors who might properly be included in two or three volumes. In some instances a major figure will be included in separate volumes, but with different entries emphasizing the aspect of his career appropriate to each volume. Ernest Hemingway, for example, is represented in *American Writers in Paris, 1920-1939* by an entry focusing on his expatriate apprenticeship; he is also in *American Novelists, 1910-1945* with an entry surveying his entire career. Each volume includes a cumulative index of subject authors and articles. The final *DLB* volume will be a comprehensive index to the entire series.

With volume ten in 1982 it was decided to enlarge the scope of *DLB*. By the end of 1985 twenty-one volumes treating British literature had been published, and volumes for Commonwealth and Modern European literature were in progress. The series has been further augmented by the *DLB Yearbooks* (since 1981) which update published entries and add new entries to keep the *DLB* current with contemporary activity. There have also been occasional *DLB Documentary Series* volumes which provide biographical and critical background source materials for figures whose work is judged to have particular interest for students. One of these companion volumes is entirely devoted to Tennessee Williams.

The purpose of *DLB* is not only to provide reliable information in a convenient format but also to place the figures in the larger perspective of literary history and to offer appraisals of their accomplishments by qualified scholars.

We define literature as the *intellectual commerce of a nation:* not merely as belles lettres but as that ample and complex process by which ideas are generated, shaped, and transmitted. *DLB* entries are not limited to "creative writers" but extend to other figures who in this time and in this way influenced the mind of a people. Thus the series encompasses historians, journalists, publishers, and screenwriters. By this means readers of *DLB* may be aided to perceive literature not as cult scripture in the keeping of cultural high priests but as at the center of a nation's life.

DLB includes the major writers appropriate to

*From an unpublished section of Mark Twain's autobiography, copyright © by the Mark Twain Company.

each volume and those standing in the ranks immediately behind them. Scholarly and critical counsel has been sought in deciding which minor figures to include and how full their entries should be. Wherever possible, useful references are made to figures who do not warrant separate entries.

Each *DLB* volume has a volume editor responsible for planning the volume, selecting the figures for inclusion, and assigning the entries. Volume editors are also responsible for preparing, where appropriate, appendices surveying the major periodicals and literary and intellectual movements for their volumes, as well as lists of further readings. Work on the series as a whole is coordinated at the Bruccoli Clark editorial center in Columbia, South Carolina, where the editorial staff is responsible for the accuracy of the published volumes.

One feature that distinguishes *DLB* is the illustration policy—its concern with the iconography of literature. Just as an author is influenced by his surroundings, so is the reader's understanding of the author enhanced by a knowledge of his environment. Therefore *DLB* volumes include not only drawings, paintings, and photographs of authors, often depicting them at various stages in their careers, but also illustrations of their families and places where they lived. Title pages are regularly reproduced in facsimile along with dust jackets for modern authors. The dust jackets are a special feature of *DLB* because they often document better than anything else the way in which an author's work was launched in its own time. Specimens of the writers' manuscripts are included when feasible.

A supplement to *DLB*—tentatively titled *A Guide, Chronology, and Glossary for American Literature*—will outline the history of literature in North America and trace the influences that shaped it. This volume will provide a framework for the study of American literature by means of chronological tables, literary affiliation charts, glossarial entries, and concise surveys of the major movements. It has been planned to stand on its own as a vade mecum, providing a ready-reference guide to the study of American literature as well as a companion to the *DLB* volumes for American literature.

Samuel Johnson rightly decreed that "The chief glory of every people arises from its authors." The purpose of the *Dictionary of Literary Biography* is to compile literary history in the surest way available to us—by accurate and comprehensive treatment of the lives and work of those who contributed to it.

The *DLB* Advisory Board

Foreword

This volume, *Victorian Prose Writers Before 1867,* and its forthcoming companion, *Victorian Prose Writers After 1867,* are designed to complement the previously published *DLB*s—18, 21, 32, and 35—that treat Victorian novelists and poets. Although some of the figures discussed in the earlier volumes are necessarily covered again here, the emphasis in the present work is on writings of nonfiction prose. This genre has been defined broadly to include letters, journals, diaries, sermons, speeches, reviews, biographies, autobiographies, and travel writings, as well as historical, philosophical, political, critical, and scientific books and essays.

Twenty-eight figures are covered in *DLB 55: Victorian Prose Writers Before 1867*. Five have been judged worthy of extended treatment as major figures—Thomas Carlyle, Thomas Babington Macaulay, John Stuart Mill, John Henry Newman, and John Ruskin. The barometer of literary taste, however, fluctuates from decade to decade. As Matthew Arnold said in discussing the literary reputation of Macaulay, "while the number of those who are delighted with rhetoric such as Macaulay's is always increasing, the number of those who are dissatisfied with it is always increasing too." The reputations of some of these writers have changed during the eight decades of the twentieth century. Carlyle, for example, was linked unfavorably with fascism in the 1930s and Mill was linked favorably with the liberal causes of the 1960s. Although predictions are hazardous, it seems that Macaulay's status as a major figure is the most likely to be challenged in the remaining years of this century. In 1968 George Levine, in his *The Boundaries of Fiction: Carlyle, Macaulay, Newman,* sounded the warning: "Macaulay, perhaps, did stand at the center of the Victorian experience, but Carlyle and Newman, Arnold and Ruskin, Pater and Morris, represent more sophisticated and critical responses to that experience." Although the 1970s and early 1980s saw publication of the six-volume collected letters of Macaulay and computer strategies were applied to the study of his rhetoric and stylistics, such efforts have not curtailed the feeling that he is often too complacent and naive in his views and opinions.

The writers treated in this volume worked within the historical context bounded by the years from 1830 to 1867. Although the key events of these four decades of rapid progress are well-known to students of the period, a few of the most significant developments should be mentioned here. Important advancements in the industrial and communications revolutions occurred: the opening of the Manchester and Liverpool Railway in 1830; the enactment of the first effective Factory Act in 1833; the inauguration of regular Atlantic steamship service in 1838; the establishment of commercial telegraph service in 1846; and the completion of the transatlantic cable in 1866. Not until the 1870 Franco-Prussian War did another country—Germany—emerge to rival Great Britain as the world's leading industrial power. Innovative technologies also affected the way print sources were circulated to Victorian readers. In 1832 the first cheap mass-circulation weeklies, *Penny Magazine* and *Chambers's Edinburgh Journal,* were founded. The ban on unstamped radical papers ended in 1836 and the penny post was established in 1840. With an unstamped press, there was a dramatic increase in the printed propaganda produced by the Owenites, the Chartists, the Anti-Corn Law League, and other radical groups. In 1843, for example, nine million pamphlets were distributed by the Anti-Corn Law League. In 1842 Charles Edward Mudie's "Select Circulating Library" was founded. Mudie was responsive to the demands of his thousands of reader-subscribers in Great Britain: for example, he purchased 2,400 copies of the third and fourth volumes of Thomas Babington Macaulay's *History of England.* The abolition of the newspaper tax in 1855 quickly led to the founding of the first mass-circulation daily paper, the *Daily Telegraph.*

During this early and middle Victorian period, the democratic revolution progressed: from the passage of the First Reform Bill in 1832, which gave the vote to a portion of the urban middle class, to the adoption of the Second Reform Bill in 1867, which extended the vote to the remainder of the middle class and to most town workers. The year 1867, then, can be considered a landmark date in British social and political history, as the nation faced the implications of a significantly broadened franchise. Indeed, the Victorian sage Thomas Carlyle dramatically compared the Second Reform Bill to "shooting Niagara" in his polemical and conservative essay "Shooting Niagara: and After?" (*Macmillan's Magazine,* 1867). Matthew Arnold's response to the July 1866 Hyde Park Riots that were part of the agitation preceding the bill's passage led to the publication of his *Culture and Anarchy* in the *Cornhill Magazine* beginning in July 1867. The year 1867 also marked the thirtieth anniversary of Queen Victoria's ascension to the throne. At the periphery of British society in 1867, other latent challenges to the democratic system appeared as Fenian agitators went on trial at Manchester, Karl Marx produced the first volume of his *Das Kapital,* and trade unions established a commission.

Many of the writers covered in this volume continued to be engaged in literary activity after 1867. Thus, the task of deciding whether an author belongs to the period before or after the Second Reform Bill has often been a challenging one. Both quality and quantity of the writing produced have been considered. Were an author's most significant works published before 1867? Were most of his or her works written before that dividing-line date?

Although the year 1867 serves as a dividing line in British social and political history, the entire decade of the 1860s should be viewed as the key period of transition in the style and outlook of Victorian prose writing. David J. DeLaura writes in the introduction to his *Victorian Prose: A Guide to Research* (1973) of "the literary climate of the long period" between 1830 and 1870; he sees new and different directions in "the emergence in the sixties of such authoritative critical voices as those of Arnold, Swinburne, and Pater." Likewise, Kenneth Allott—in his introduction to the anthology that he edited with Miriam Allott, *Victorian Prose 1830-1880* (1956)—delineates a shift in emphasis in prose writing from broad, homogenized social prophecy to individual and diversified self-consciousness in the 1860s. After Carlyle's *Sartor Resartus* was published in *Fraser's Magazine* (1833-1834), the effect on other prose writers of his Romantic matter and manner is pervasive. As Allott points out, "It is scarcely possible to exaggerate his influence on the prose of the forties and fifties." New tastes and sensibilities are worked out in the remaining years of the nineteenth century: "There is more to be said in favour of eclecticism when we look at the later Victorian prose-writers, and this is consonant with the view that a critical, self-conscious temper is widespread in the late sixties and the seventies and develops strength as the century advances." Clearly by the 1860s, the first-generation voices of Victorian prose writers—Macaulay, Carlyle, Mill, Thomas Arnold, and others—were fading as the second-generation figures—Morris, Pater, Matthew Arnold, and others—began to offer their own distinctive prose writings.

The sparkling diversity of writings produced during the period 1830-1867 bodes well for the current revival of interest in Victorian studies. It is encouraging that each year increasing attention is being paid to previously neglected authors of the period such as Jane Welsh Carlyle, John Clare, E. S. Dallas, Alexander William Kinglake, Harriet Martineau, Samuel Smiles, and Queen Victoria. The worlds explored by these and other Victorian prose writers were many and various. John Clare wrote about a vanishing rural England and the torments of the human mind isolated in a mental asylum. Henry Mayhew recorded the human spectacle from the slums and streets of London. Dr. Thomas Arnold worked to reform the English public schools. Many writers, such as E. S. Dallas, George Eliot, and George Henry Lewes, worked as journalists or reviewers. Some, such as Walter Bagehot, focused on the everyday realities of the Victorian Age; others—John Stuart Mill, for example—worked for the causes of individual or minority rights, including women's suffrage. Richard F. Burton, George Borrow, and Alexander William Kinglake were explorers, and often through their travel writings they caused Victorian readers in England to perceive their own customs, traditions, and attitudes from a fresh, illuminating perspective. To help place writers' achievements into a broader context, at the end of this volume there is a selected bibliography for further reading in the field.

The contributors of the essays for this volume deserve special gratitude for their efficient and conscientious efforts. Geographically, they are located in diverse places: within the borders of the continental United States, from Washington State to Maine and from Indiana to Texas; outside the United States, from England, Scotland, and Canada. Thus, the gathering of this volume has not only been a "Victorian" effort, but also one of national and international scope. Many of the contributors made valuable suggestions for illustrating their essays. Jerold J. Savory was especially helpful with the photographic reproduction of several *Vanity Fair* prints. Special thanks are due also to the Lilly Library, Indiana University, and appreciation should be extended to Jill Reid, who, as a graduate assistant, gathered many suggested illustrations.

—*William B. Thesing*

Acknowledgments

This book was produced by Bruccoli Clark Layman, Inc. Karen L. Rood is senior editor for the *Dictionary of Literary Biography* series. Margaret A. Van Antwerp was the in-house editor.

Art supervisor is Patricia M. Flanagan. Copyediting supervisor is Patricia Coate. Production coordinator is Kimberly Casey. Typesetting supervisor is Laura Ingram. The production staff includes Rowena Betts, David R. Bowdler, Mary S. Dye, Kathleen M. Flanagan, Joyce Fowler, Pamela Haynes, Judith K. Ingle, Judith E. McCray, Janet L. Phelps, Joyce Rogers, Joycelyn R. Smith, and Lucia Tarbox. Jean W. Ross is permissions editor. Joseph Caldwell, photography editor, and Joseph Matthew Bruccoli did photographic copy work for the volume.

Walter W. Ross and Rhonda A. Marshall did the library research with the assistance of the staff at the Thomas Cooper Library of the University of South Carolina: Lynn Barron, Daniel Boice, Connie Crider, Kathy Eckman, Michael Freeman, Gary Geer, David L. Haggard, Jens Holley, Marcia Martin, Dana Rabon, Jean Rhyne, Jan Squire, Ellen Tillett, and Virginia Weathers.

Dictionary of Literary Biography • Volume Fifty-five

Victorian Prose Writers Before 1867

Dictionary of Literary Biography

Thomas Arnold

(13 June 1795-12 June 1842)

Clinton Machann
Texas A&M University

Thomas Arnold, circa 1820

BOOKS: *The Effects of Distant Colonization on the Parent State* (Oxford: Privately printed, 1815);
The Christian Duty of Granting the Claims of the Roman Catholics (Oxford: Printed by J. Rivington for J. Parker, 1829);
Sermons, 3 volumes (London: Rivington, 1829-1834);
Thirteen Letters on Our Social Condition (Sheffield: Printed by J. C. Platt, 1832);
Principles of Church Reform (London: Fellowes, 1833);
History of Rome (3 volumes, London: Fellowes, 1838-1843; 2 volumes, New York: D. Appleton/Philadelphia: G. S. Appleton, 1846);
On the Divisions and Mutual Relations of Knowledge (Rugby: Printed by Combe & Crossley, 1839);
Two Sermons on the Interpretation of Prophecy (Oxford: Parker, 1839);
Christian Life; Its Course, Its Hindrances, Its Helps (London: Fellowes, 1841; Philadelphia, 1852);
Introductory Lectures on Modern History (Oxford: Parker, 1842; New York: D. Appleton/Philadelphia: G. S. Appleton, 1845);
Christian Life; Its Hopes, Its Fears, and Its Close (London: Fellowes, 1842; Philadelphia: Lindsay & Blakiston, 1856);
Fragment on the Church (London: Fellowes, 1844);
Sermons Chiefly on the Interpretation of the Scripture (London: Fellowes, 1845);
Sermons Preached in the Chapel of Rugby School (London: Fellowes, 1845; New York: D. Appleton/Philadelphia: G. S. Appleton, 1846);
History of the Later Roman Commonwealth (2 volumes, London: Fellowes, 1845; one volume, New York: D. Appleton/Philadelphia: G. S. Appleton, 1846);
The Miscellaneous Works of Thomas Arnold (London: Fellowes, 1845; enlarged, New York: D. Ap-

pleton/Philadelphia: G. S. Appleton, 1845); *Sermons*, 6 volumes, edited by Mrs. W. E. Forster (London: Longmans, Green, 1878).

OTHER: Thucydides, *The History of the Peloponnesian War*, translated by Arnold, 3 volumes (Oxford: Collingwood, 1830-1835).

Thomas Arnold is remembered today chiefly as a reformer of the English public schools and as the father of major Victorian poet and critic Matthew Arnold. His reputation as an educator is based less on his published works than on the legend of his headmastership at Rugby created by influential former students and by works such as A. P. Stanley's adulatory biography (1844) and Thomas Hughes's enormously popular fictionalized account of his Rugby days, *Tom Brown's School Days* (1857). Arnold himself wished to be known primarily as a historian and social and religious reformer. In fact, his appointment as regius professor of modern history at Oxford in 1841 signaled his increasing recognition as a historian, but he died of a heart attack the next year, on the day before he would have turned forty-seven.

He was born at Cowes, on the Isle of Wight, the son of William and Martha Delafield Arnold. His father, a customs official, died when Thomas Arnold was only six. Arnold went to school at Winchester and Corpus Christi College, Oxford. He became a fellow of Oriel in 1815 and in that same year won the English Prize for *The Effects of Distant Colonization on the Parent State*. The essay, in which Arnold demonstrated a marked interest in social issues, became his first publication, printed at Oxford in 1815. He was ordained a deacon in 1818, took up his first teaching duties at Laleham in 1819, and married Mary Penrose in 1820. He was appointed headmaster at Rugby School in 1828, and he remained there for the rest of his life, although he became a public figure to a much greater extent than did his contemporaries in similar positions. In the year after his appointment, Arnold published a pamphlet entitled *The Christian Duty of Granting the Claims of the Roman Catholics*, which supported Catholic rights in Ireland on historical and moral grounds, despite his generally negative view of the Catholic faith. Throughout his career as a social critic, Arnold adopted consistently controversial positions.

His published collections of sermons delivered from the pulpit at Rugby show his intensely emotional commitment to a belief in Christ and his obsession with sin. He defines his mission as that of overcoming the basic wickedness of young boys in order to give them a Christian education and instill in them high principles and a devotion to duty that they could carry into social life. In order to accomplish these goals, in Arnold's view the transition from childhood to manhood must be hastened. In a representative sermon, he observes, "The besetting faults of youth appear to me to arise mainly from its retaining too often the ignorance, selfishness, and thoughtlessness of a child, and having arrived at the same time at a degree of bodily vigour and power, equal, or only a very little inferior, to those of manhood."

His fusion of secular and religious elements in education was related to his insistence on the inseparability of Church and State in his social criticism, and he argued strongly for both religious and secular reform. With the exception of the New Testament, no source of authority or institution was exempt from Arnold's critical eye. In politics, he was a Radical and argued for social reform in thirteen letters to the *Sheffield Courant* prior to and following passage of the Reform Bill in 1832. He found the conditions of laborers in his society to be appalling and intolerable, and by drawing analogies with classical Greek society Arnold adopted the position that free men must become property owners before they can become responsible citizens. He saw two possible solutions to the problem: "home colonies" or emigration. Arnold's missives to the *Courant* were published together as *Thirteen Letters on Our Social Condition* (1832).

In the next year, he called for a complete revision of the Church of England in his *Principles of Church Reform*. For Arnold, Church institutions and traditions in themselves were meaningless, and the various Christian sects could be reconciled in a new Church-State where only a fundamental belief in God and Jesus Christ was universally recognized. It is easy to understand why Arnold made many enemies among conservative Church leaders and Tories, both on the national scene and in the Rugby area. His views were diametrically opposed to those of fellow Oxonian John Henry Newman and the Tractarians, and he became a bitter enemy of the Oxford Movement. Perhaps he expressed his most extreme views in an unsigned article entitled "The Oxford Malignants and Doctor Hampden" (*Edinburgh Review*, April 1836), in which he compared his opponents to those who stoned to death the early Apostles. (Dr. R. D. Hampden was a liberal theologian whose appointment as regius professor of divinity was being opposed by the Tractarians.) It is possible that Arnold's reputation as an outspoken controversialist cost him advancement to a bishopric on more than one occasion.

Arnold was a staunch classicist in his approach to the educational curriculum at Rugby and was himself a translator of Thucydides, producing three volumes of *The History of the Peloponnesian War* in the period 1830-1835. Furthermore, as a historian he concentrated on classical subjects and took great pride in his three-volume *History of Rome* (1838-1843), which had grown out of a series of articles on Roman history commissioned by the *Encyclopaedia Metropolitana* in 1822, and which he was planning to expand when he died. (The posthumously published *History of the Later Roman Commonwealth*, 1845, was also taken from his *Encyclopaedia* articles.) For him, however, there was no conflict between this classicism and his involvement in current social and religious issues. The classics, he held, represented the high point of civilization and thus were timeless. He taught his students that classical ideas and attitudes were directly applicable to modern problems, and he acted upon the same principle in his own work. In fact, the ability of the classical to elucidate the modern offered the only justification of classical studies for Arnold. His view of the classics helps to explain apparent contradictions in his life and work. On the one hand, he welcomed technological progress, symbolized chiefly by the railroad in his day, and he believed that scientific methods, including statistical studies, should be applied to social problems. On the other, Arnold practically excluded natural science from the curriculum at Rugby (although there is some evidence that he was beginning to see this policy as a mistake toward the end of his life), and he left very little room for mathematics.

Since the middle of the twentieth century, scholars have increasingly clarified the assumptions which underlie Arnold's overall vision of history and the development of society. At Oxford, Arnold was associated with a small group of scholars known as the Noetics—including Richard Whately, Connop Thirlwall, and Hampden—who sought to revitalize English historiography by studying the work of the German historian Barthold Niebuhr

School House, the Rugby building where the Arnold family had their quarters during Arnold's tenure as headmaster from 1828 until his death in 1842

and the Italian theorist Giovanni Battista Vico. Although Arnold never wrote a comprehensive statement of his theory of history, two principal sources of his ideas are usually cited: his "Essay on the Social Progress of States," initially published as an appendix to his translation of Thucydides, and his *Introductory Lectures on Modern History* (1842), a collection of addresses delivered toward the end of his life. Following Vico and Niebuhr, Arnold developed an organic concept of the nation and its society, by which the nation is analogous to a person and the nation's history must be told in terms of its developing mental and moral personality or spirit. The national spirit develops from its infancy, passing through a youthful, romantic age to a mature, philosophical one. Unlike the Saint-Simonian "march of mind," which occurs once in the history of mankind, Arnold's developmental scheme applies to the history of each nation. Arnold believed that "States, like individuals, go through certain changes in a certain order and are subject at different stages of their course to certain peculiar disorders."

Arnold was convinced that he lived in a civilization that was similar to the classical civilizations of Greece and Rome. For him, "there is in fact an ancient and a modern period in the history of every people." Much "ancient" history of Greece and Rome is really "modern" because it describes society in a stage that is analogous to that of the present. Thus, he describes Thucydides' work as "modern" and in his *History of Rome* cites the characteristics that link contemporary England to the Greece of Thucydides and the Rome of the Antonines: a spirit of free inquiry, skepticism, proliferation of theories on all subjects, and superficiality of feeling. In a 1982 article entitled "Thomas Arnold and the Mirror of History," A. Dwight Culler sees Arnold as the "chief purveyor" in England of the early-nineteenth-century view of itself as an age of inquiry and skepticism following an age of faith. Arnold's theory of translation was also related to his concept of national histories. It was an error to translate a writer who lived at one stage of a nation's development into the language appropriate to another stage. As Charles R. Moyer has pointed out in "The Idea of History in Thomas and Matthew Arnold" (1969), this theory led Arnold to the extreme of retelling Roman myths in a biblical idiom.

In spite of his progressive, cyclical concept of history and his acceptance of the general view that man not only makes but is made by history, Arnold's historical writings, like those of Carlyle and other contemporaries, are better described as "moral" and "literary" than as "scientific" or "objective." As Rosemary Jann has shown in "Changing Styles in Victorian Military History" (1982), in describing military tactics in the *History of Rome,* Arnold is more concerned with moral than with strictly military evaluations of men and actions. He derives moral lessons from history and sees the hand of Providence at work there.

Arnold was an activist who sought to reform the world, and there was little of the cloistered scholar in him. Appropriately for a man whose works exude a muscular Christianity and social activism, Arnold was full of nervous energy, restless and ambitious. Although he had powerful friends, such as Edward Stanley, the Bishop of Norwich, he also had enemies. His tenure at Rugby was turbulent, marked by several public scandals over the years concerning charges of his mismanaging the school. Arnold was by and large a traditional disciplinarian, and he defended the practices of flogging and fagging in an 1825 article, "On Discipline in the Public Schools," published in the *Quarterly Journal of Education* and later collected in *The Miscellaneous Works of Thomas Arnold* (1845). His religion-based views toward corporal punishment and expulsion were particularly stern and occasionally led to excesses, while his lack of tact and unwillingness to compromise often made even his friends uncomfortable.

Arnold, however, was a loving father to his nine children, and he allowed a great deal of freedom (some would argue, too much) to members of his sixth form and was extremely generous to them. Also, in addition to increasing his own salary and prestige as headmaster, he consistently improved the salary and status of his teaching staff. Arnold's most recent biographer, T. W. Bamford, claims that Arnold made no real reforms in school curriculum, however, and that he was really somewhat reactionary in that regard. In general, Bamford observes, Arnold and the "Arnold legend" were largely responsible for improving the status of the English public schools, but Arnold's reputation as a reformer in education is somewhat questionable. Although Arnold published very little on the subject of education during his lifetime, in his 1970 book *Thomas Arnold on Education* Bamford included a selection of passages culled primarily from the *Quarterly Journal of Education* article and from Arnold's letters and sermons.

Because Arnold was a multifaceted man, the various aspects of his career must be evaluated separately in order to achieve a balanced view of his continuing influence today. As an educator, his

Queen Adelaide at Rugby in October 1839, with Dr. Arnold and two of his sons, Matthew and Thomas. The drawing is by Arnold's oldest daughter, Jane.

name is inseparably linked to the tradition of the English public school as it developed in the nineteenth century. His reputation as the legendary headmaster of Rugby, rather than his pedagogical writings, accounts for his continuing fame. As a religious and social critic, Arnold acknowledged Samuel Taylor Coleridge as his master, and his notions of a Church-State certainly owe something to this earlier figure. Arnold never attached himself to a specific reform movement or school of thought, and his critical writings were not widely read after his death. However, he is considered to be one of the founders of the Broad Church Movement, which is associated with his students A. P. Stanley and Thomas Hughes, as well as with such religious and cultural figures as Frederick Denison Maurice and Charles Kingsley. In Bamford's view, Arnold's social and religious criticism would repay further study today; it is, however, still largely ignored.

Arnold was a noted historian in his own time, known primarily for his *History of Rome,* and his work will undoubtedly continue to be of interest to scholars who study the development of historiography in nineteenth-century England. Arnold's ambitions as a scholar and writer lay primarily in this area, and his opening lectures as regius professor of history at Oxford suggest that he would have continued to develop as a historian if his career had not been cut short by his sudden and early death.

Overall, Arnold's literary works suffer from a style that reflects haste and lack of polish. Bamford has noted Arnold's apparent lack of concern for revision, illustrated by the fact that only minor stylistic differences are discernible among his hastily written letters, his sermons, and his other works. However, although Arnold himself is not remembered primarily as a literary figure, much of the recent scholarship about him is in fact the work of literary critics. This apparent anomaly is explained by Arnold's profound influence on the work of his son (and student) Matthew Arnold, who helped fashion posterity's image of his father in the well-known elegiac poem "Rugby Chapel." Although Matthew Arnold's earliest critics saw that he owed much to his father's influence, recent scholars have shown in increasing detail the son's intellectual debt to the father. While Matthew Arnold did not inherit his father's apparently unquestioning Christian faith, there is little doubt that the father's views of history, the classics, and morality were central to the son's work, as they were to British secondary education in the nineteenth century.

Biographies:

Arthur P. Stanley, *The Life and Correspondence of Dr. Arnold,* 2 volumes (London: Fellowes, 1844);

Arnold Whitridge, *Dr. Arnold of Rugby* (London: Constable, 1928);

Norman Wymer, *Dr. Arnold of Rugby* (London: Hale, 1953);

T. W. Bamford, *Thomas Arnold* (London: Cresset Press, 1960).

References:

T. W. Bamford, *Thomas Arnold on Education* (Cambridge: Cambridge University Press, 1970);

Reginald J. Campbell, *Thomas Arnold* (London: Macmillan, 1927);

A. O. J. Cockshut, "Arnold, Hook, Ward: A Wiccamical Sidelight on Nineteenth-Century Religion," in *Winchester College: Sixth-Centenary Essays,* edited by Roger Custance (Oxford: Oxford University Press, 1982), pp. 375-402;

A. Dwight Culler, "Thomas Arnold and the Mirror of History," *Browning Institute Studies,* 10 (1982): 15-25;

Duncan Forbes, *The Liberal Anglican Idea of History* (Cambridge: Cambridge University Press, 1952);

J. Gathorne-Hardy, *The Public School Phenomenon* (London: Hodder & Stoughton, 1977);

Rosemary Jann, "Changing Styles in Victorian Military History," *CLIO,* 11 (Winter 1982): 157-164;

Jonathan Middlebrook, " 'Resignation,' 'Rugby Chapel,' and Thomas Arnold," *Victorian Poetry,* 8 (Winter 1970): 291-297;

Charles R. Moyer, "The Idea of History in Thomas and Matthew Arnold," *Modern Philology,* 67 (November 1969): 160-167;

D. Newsome, *Godliness and Good Learning* (London: Murray, 1961);

Rose E. Selfe, *Dr. Arnold of Rugby* (London: Cassell, 1889);

Julia A. Smith, "Thomas Arnold and the Genesis of Past and Present," *Arnoldian,* 3 (Winter 1976): 14-16;

Lytton Strachey, *Eminent Victorians* (London: Chatto & Windus, 1918);

John O. Waller, "Doctor Arnold's Sermons and Matthew Arnold's 'Rugby Chapel,' " *Studies in English Literature 1500-1900,* 9 (Autumn 1969): 633-646.

Papers:

Arnold's papers are at the British Library, the British Transport Commission Archives, and the Brotherton Library at the University of Leeds.

Walter Bagehot

(3 February 1826-24 March 1877)

Michael Shelden
Indiana State University

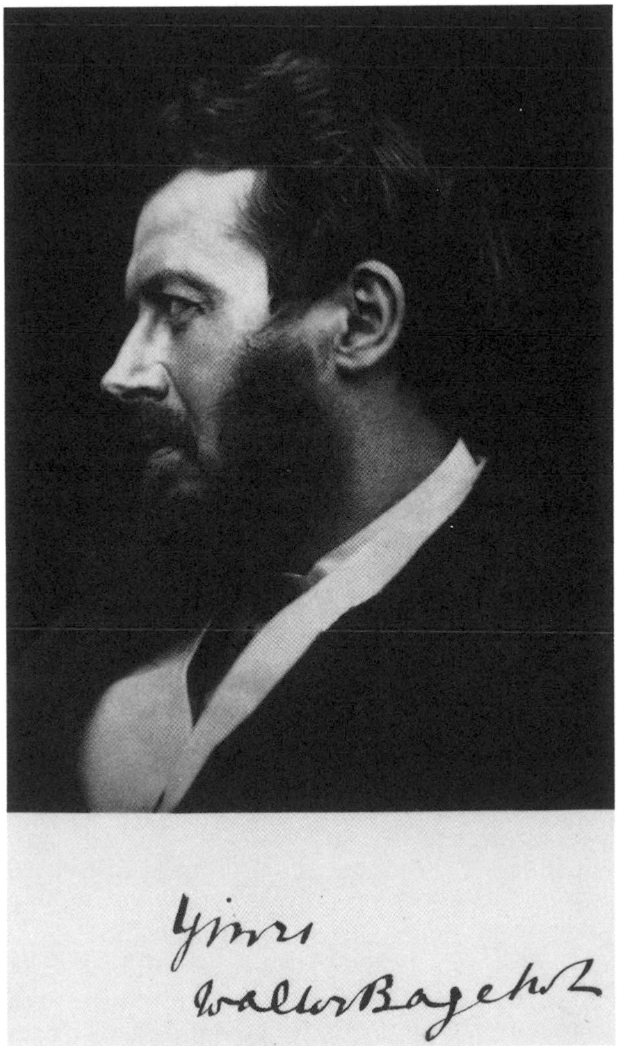

BOOKS: *Estimates of Some Englishmen and Scotchmen* (London: Chapman & Hall, 1858);

Parliamentary Reform: An Essay (London: Chapman & Hall, 1859);

The History of the Unreformed Parliament, and Its Lessons: An Essay (London: Chapman & Hall, 1860);

Memoir of the Right Hon. James Wilson (London: H. Bale, 1861);

Count Your Enemies and Economise Your Expenditure (London: Ridgway, 1862);

The English Constitution (London: Chapman & Hall, 1867; enlarged, London: King, 1872; revised, Boston: Little, Brown, 1873);

A Practical Plan for Assimilating the English and American Money, as a Step Towards a Universal Money (London: Longmans, Green, Reader & Dyer, 1869);

Physics and Politics; or, Thoughts on the Application of the Principles of "Natural Selection" and "Inheritance" to Political Society (London: King, 1872; New York: Appleton, 1873);

Lombard Street: A Description of the Money Market (London: King, 1873; New York: Scribner, Armstrong, 1873);

Some Articles on the Depreciation of Silver and on Topics Connected with It (London: King, 1877);

Literary Studies, edited by Richard Holt Hutton, 2 volumes (London: Longmans, Green, 1879; London & New York: Longmans, Green, 1891);

Economic Studies, edited by Hutton (London: Longmans, Green, 1880; London & New York: Longmans, Green, 1888);

Biographical Studies, edited by Hutton (London: Longmans, Green, 1881; London & New York: Longmans, Green, 1895).

Collection: *The Collected Works of Walter Bagehot,* edited by Norman St. John-Stevas (15 volumes, London: Economist Publications, 1965-1986; volumes 1-11, Cambridge: Harvard University Press, 1965-1974).

Walter Bagehot's modern reputation rests primarily on his authorship of *The English Constitution,* a masterpiece of political journalism which has long been regarded as the best introduction to the great age of Victorian parliamentary democracy. A highly respected essayist and editor, Bagehot wrote *The English Constitution* in order to dispel some of the mystery surrounding the inner workings of the political system of his day. The work which he produced is not a philosophical treatise or a sensational exposé but a straightforward, uncompromisingly honest description of the way in which mid-Victorian England was governed. As such, it is a remarkable historical document; but its appeal is not merely historical, for Bagehot's keen insights into the essential nature of English political life raise important questions about parliamentary democracy that are still relevant today. As long as that form of government continues to function, in England or elsewhere, Bagehot's brilliant study will remain politically significant. It is, in any case, an eminently readable work, and an eminently quotable one as well. Bagehot was one of the most accomplished prose stylists of his generation, and the easy elegance and dry wit of his style give his political commentary a surprising freshness and charm. In spite of the formidable complications of its subject, *The English Constitution* is never dull or ponderous, and over the years it has become a popular source of wise political sayings for politicians of all persuasions.

Bagehot's writing, however, is not limited to political topics. As an editor of the *National Review* and the *Economist,* Bagehot took an interest in a wide range of subjects—history, biography, science, religion, finance, and literature—and the many essays that he wrote for his two journals reflect this variety of interests. Outside of his political essays, the best of his periodical work can be found in his writings on literary subjects. Most of these originally appeared in the *National Review* from 1855 to 1864, and several of them are still considered to be among the finest examples of Victorian literary criticism. His approach to literature was not systematic or scholarly, but his essays are filled with sharp flashes of insight into the works of many of the great English authors—Shakespeare, Milton, Swift, Scott, Keats, Shelley, and Dickens. What most distinguishes Bagehot's literary criticism, however, is the vitality of his prose, which is given freer rein than in his political writing. To the modern reader, many of Bagehot's literary opinions may seem commonplace, but his prose style is never so.

Bagehot was born on 3 February 1826 in Langport, Somersetshire. The son of Thomas Watson Bagehot, a prosperous country banker, and Edith Stuckey Bagehot, he was raised in a solid middle-class environment where the virtues of hard work, perseverance, and thrift were kept constantly before him. At the age of sixteen he was sent to University College, London, where he excelled as a student of intellectual and moral philosophy. He took his degree in 1846, with a double first, and was given a scholarship to pursue a graduate degree. He was awarded an M.A. two years later and was called to the Bar in 1852. At the last moment, however, he turned away from a career in the law, settling instead for a position with his father's bank in the town of Langport. In September 1852 he began what would become a long and very successful career as a banker, a profession which he would later describe as "a watchful but not laborious trade."

During his final year as a graduate student at University College, Bagehot launched his career as an essayist by contributing a long article on Philip Bailey's *Festus* (1839) to the *Prospective Review* (November 1847). Now a largely forgotten poem, *Festus* was a very popular work among Victorian readers, and though Bagehot makes the mistake of overrating the poem's literary significance, his article is an impressive production for a student of twenty-one. His style is smooth, his tone confident, and his range of literary knowledge wide. In 1848 he had two more articles published in the *Prospective Review*—which was edited, in part, by one of his friends from college, William Roscoe—and then for the next four years he put his career as a writer on an indefinite hold while he read for the Bar. He had strong literary ambitions as a young man, but he was much too practical and responsible to stake his future on a risky career as a full-time writer. He needed a solid, secure profession, and for a time the law seemed to him the best choice. When it finally became apparent to him, however, that a legal career would not leave him enough time or energy for his writing, he abandoned it in favor of banking, and within a few months of taking up his new job in his father's bank, he was once again writing essays for the *Prospective Review.*

Among his early efforts as an essayist his long article entitled "Shakespeare—The Individual" stands out as the best. It appeared in the *Prospective Review* in July 1853 and was written entirely in Bagehot's spare time after his banking duties were taken care of. The essay is not so much a work of literary criticism as it is an imaginative piece of biographical speculation. Working almost exclusively from his knowledge of the plays, Bagehot tries to arrive at a few basic conclusions about the nature of Shakespeare's life. At the outset of the essay he confidently asserts that no great writer can avoid revealing important clues about his life in his work, and that any reasonably intelligent reader should be able to pick out these clues without much difficulty. "A person who knows nothing of an author he has read," Bagehot declares, "will not know much of an author whom he has seen." Based on what he has read, Bagehot concludes that Shakespeare's life must have been particularly rich in experience. Shakespeare achieved greatness as a writer, we are told, because he possessed "a first-rate imagination working on a first-rate experience." Bagehot is especially impressed with Shakespeare's keen awareness of the practical affairs of everyday life, and he argues that Shakespeare must have spent a good deal of time closely observing the lives of ordinary people, not as an outsider but as one who shared many of the daily hardships and concerns of the common man. "He was not merely with men, but of men," Bagehot writes; "he was not a 'thing apart,' with a clear intuition of what was in those around him; he had in his own nature the germs and tendencies of the very elements that he described. He knew what was in man, for he felt it in himself."

Bagehot's essay on Shakespeare is, in large part, an attempt to come to terms with the whole question of how a writer should live if he is to further the best interests of his work. Bagehot strongly objects to the notion that a good writer must distance himself from the turmoil of daily life in order to devote more of his attention to his writing. The work of writing is, by its very nature, solitary, and if carried to an extreme, the solitude will leave the writer nothing to inform his work except books and his own imagination. To the writer who boasts that he has devoted his life to his work, Bagehot offers the reply, "Then you have taken the best way to prevent your making anything of it." For Bagehot, a good writer must know not only how a sentence works but also how the world works. "The reason why so few good books are written," he states, "is that so few people who can write know anything. In general an author has always lived in a room, has read books, has cultivated science, is acquainted with the style and sentiments of the best authors, but he is out of the way of employing his own eyes and ears. He has nothing to hear and nothing to see." Bagehot admires Shakespeare not simply because he was a great poet but because he was also, in Bagehot's view, a knowledgeable man of the world who could describe, in sharp detail, what he had seen and heard in the great world outside his room. As a country banker who wrote literary essays in his spare time, Bagehot understood only too well how the demands of daily life could interfere with a writer's work, but apparently he was convinced that an active life could ultimately prove more beneficial than harmful to his writing career. In the example of Shakespeare's life he found what he believed to be reassuring confirmation of that belief.

In 1855 Bagehot was secure enough in his banking career that he felt able to take on an ambitious new literary project. With his close friend Richard Hutton, he founded a new quarterly in London, the *National Review.* Hutton was given the title of editor, but Bagehot was, in effect, his co-editor, for he took part in almost every major editorial decision, in spite of the fact that he continued to live and work in Langport. Bagehot also put up a good part of the capital needed to produce the handsome 200-page issues of the journal, and during the first few years of its operation he was a frequent contributor. One of the supporters of the *National Review,* James Martineau, wrote that its primary purpose was to serve as a forum for the "unrepresented feeling and opinion between the heavy Whiggism and decorous Church-latitude of the *Edinburgh* [*Review*] on the one hand and the atheistic tendency and refugee politics of the *Westminster* [*Review*] on the other." It was, simply put,

Bagehot's wife, Eliza Wilson Bagehot. The couple met in January 1857 when Bagehot visited her father, James Wilson, editor of the Economist. *They were married on 21 April 1858.*

a journal of moderate political and religious opinion, neither very conservative nor very radical. Its peak circulation was 1,500, a respectable figure for journals of its type, and it appeared regularly until 1864, when Bagehot decided to discontinue publication following Hutton's move, two years earlier, to the editorship of the *Spectator.*

Bagehot's first article for the *National Review* appeared in the very first issue (July 1855) and was devoted to a critical appraisal of the work of the eighteenth-century poet William Cowper. Bagehot praises Cowper as a "common-sense poet," one capable of speaking directly and honestly to his readers in "a free, working, flowing picturesque garb of words adapted to the solid conduct of a sound and serious world." In response to the charge that Cowper's style is bland and his subjects dull, Bagehot answers that Cowper's dullness has a special charm to it, especially for English readers. Cowper is a master at depicting "the trivial course of slowly-moving pleasures, the petty detail of quiet relaxation"; and for the English—"a settled and practical people . . . in favour of heavy relaxations," as Bagehot puts it—the world of Cowper's poetry is immensely appealing. Bagehot fully recognizes Cowper's shortcomings as a poet—his complete lack of "the higher and rarer excellences of poetical expression"—but he cannot help admiring a poet whose work manages to convey so well the traditional nature of the English character. In any case, Bagehot makes it clear that he has a weakness in his own heart for a life of simple, modest pleasures beside a cozy English fireside, "where the tea-urn hisses so plainly, the toast is so warm, the breakfast so neat, the food so edible."

After the publication of his article on Cowper, Bagehot produced a long essay for each of the next five issues of the *National Review.* Every three months he turned out an article of approximately 15,000 words on subjects as diverse as Shelley's poetry, Sir Robert Peel's politics, the early years of the *Edinburgh Review,* Gibbon's history of Rome, and Macaulay's history of England. The essay on Shelley (October 1856) is particularly interesting because it provides a fascinating glimpse of the romantic strain in Bagehot's generally down-to-earth, practical character. Bagehot disapproved of most of Shelley's idealistic views on religion, politics, and love, but he could not deny the lyrical beauty and imaginative power of Shelley's best work, and in his essay he shows considerable admiration for Shelley's inspired descriptions of dreamlike visions. To some extent, Bagehot—the cautious, orderly banker—is envious of Shelley's "pure impulsive character." After long hours of methodical work in the bank, Bagehot must have longed occasionally for the physical and mental freedom that Shelley professed to enjoy. Rather fondly, Bagehot describes Shelley's "mind placed in the light of thought with pure subtle fancies playing to and fro. On a sudden an impulse arises; it is alone, and has nothing to contend with; it cramps the intellect, pushes aside the fancies, constrains the nature; it *bolts* forward into action." Though he finds such impulsiveness tempting, Bagehot is too responsible and realistic to be seduced completely by it. The proper Victorian gentleman in him will simply not allow it. Nevertheless, it is characteristic of his own good nature and generous spirit that he does not begrudge Shelley the pleasure of pursuing a way of life far different from his own.

Just a few months before the appearance of his Shelley essay, Bagehot published his first important political essay in the *National Review*—"The Character of Sir Robert Peel" (July 1856). It is written in the form of a biographical sketch, but essentially Peel's life provides Bagehot with a convenient way of discussing some of his own ideas about political leadership. At age thirty Bagehot was beginning to formulate the political opinions that would remain with him for the rest of his life, and his essay on Peel is a remarkably accomplished first effort at explaining some of those opinions. In Bagehot's view Peel's service as prime minister in the 1840s set the pattern for effective political leadership within the Victorian system of parliamentary democracy. Bagehot does not believe that Peel was an original or advanced thinker, but he recognizes that he was a very able administrator who carried out efficiently the necessary business of government. Peel was not one to shape public opinion or undertake innovative reforms on his own; he listened instead to what the public wanted, Bagehot says, and then he expertly used the machinery of government to give the people what they had asked for. The example of Peel's successful style of leadership leads Bagehot to conclude that the best "constitutional statesman is the one who most felicitously expresses the creed of the moment, who administers it, who embodies it in laws and institutions, who gives it the highest life it is capable of, who induces the average man to think: 'I could not have done it any better, if I had had time myself.' " In a democracy it is dangerous for a leader to strike out on his own course of action without regard to public opinion; political freedom, Bagehot argues, must always rely on government by consensus. "When we speak of a free government," he writes, "we mean a government in which the sovereign power is divided, in which a single decision is not absolute, where argument has office." Although bold, independent leaders may excite the imagination, they do not ultimately serve the best interests of a free people, according to Bagehot.

At the beginning of 1858 the highly respected London firm of Chapman and Hall published a collection of some of Bagehot's best essays from the *Prospective Review* and the *National Review*. Entitled *Estimates of Some Englishmen and Scotchmen*, the collection contains Bagehot's essays on Shakespeare, Cowper, Shelley, and Peel, as well as five other essays on Hartley Coleridge, Bishop Butler, the *Edinburgh Review*, Gibbon, and Macaulay. It was Bagehot's first book, and as fate would have it, this was the only collection of Bagehot's essays to appear in his lifetime. Unfortunately, the book was not widely read when it first came out, though it was certainly well received among the small but influential group of readers who subscribed to the *National Review*. One such reader was Matthew Arnold, who was so taken with Bagehot's literary essays, especially the one on Shelley, that he wrote a personal letter to him praising his work. The article on Shelley "and one or two others," Arnold wrote, "seem to me to be of the very first quality, showing not talent only, but a concern for the *simple truth* which is rare in English literature as it is in English politics and English religion." Arnold's comments pleased Bagehot immensely, but even before publication of the book of essays, it did not seem likely to Bagehot that his first collection would attract wide notice. He was modest about his talent and did not hold out much hope for fame. In a letter written shortly before his book appeared, Bagehot remarked: "Posterity cannot take up little people, there are so many of them. *Reputation* must be acquired at the moment and the circumstances of the moment are matters of accident. In my case I have had a good deal of newspaper praise for these essays, at least for some of them—when they first came out, and I must expect very little more."

For Bagehot, the most important event of 1858 was not the publication of his first book but his marriage to Eliza Wilson, the daughter of James Wilson, editor of the *Economist* and financial secretary to the Treasury. Bagehot first met Eliza on a visit to her father's country home outside Bath in January 1857. It did not take long for Eliza to draw out the romantic streak in the young banker's character, and by autumn he had proposed marriage and she had accepted. They were married on 21 April 1858 and shortly afterward set up their household in a large home with a pleasant country view near Bristol. A branch of the family bank was located in Bristol, and Bagehot commuted there by train to manage it.

The year 1858 also saw the appearance, in the *National Review*, of Bagehot's two most important literary essays—one on Sir Walter Scott and one on Bagehot's great contemporary Charles Dickens. Of all Bagehot's literary essays, these two remain the most widely read and respected. Entitled "The Waverly Novels" (April 1858), the article on Scott is particularly good at explaining Scott's genius for combining realistic and romantic elements in his novels. Scott gives readers great love affairs between men and women, Bagehot says, but he astutely surrounds the romantic action with events of great social or historical importance, thus providing his fiction with much greater range, authority, and substance than might otherwise be possible in novels of pure romance. Scott had a refined touch for realistic detail as well as romantic sentiment: "The hero and the heroine walk among the trees of the forest according to rule," Bagehot notes of Scott's lovers, "but we are expected to take an interest in the forest as well as in them." Bagehot has especially high praise for Scott's tendency to describe the world as he saw it, without imposing any doctrine of behavior on it. "Sir Walter had no *thesis* to maintain," Bagehot remarks approvingly. In this respect Scott ranks in the same class as Shakespeare—a writer who, in Bagehot's view, can be relied on to portray faithfully all the varied shapes of everyday reality.

Given the realistic descriptions of ordinary lives in Dickens's novels, one might assume that Bagehot would hold Dickens in the same high regard as Scott, but this is not the case at all. In his essay "Charles Dickens" (October 1858) Bagehot has uncharacteristically harsh criticism for the most popular novelist of his day. Objecting to the great emphasis on social reform in Dickens's fiction, Bagehot says that the ultimate effect of this emphasis "is to make men dissatisfied with their inevitable condition, and what is worse, to make them fancy that its irremediable evils can be remedied, and indulge in a succession of vague strivings and restless changes." Bagehot was not opposed to social reform, but he disapproved of what he calls Dickens's "sentimental radicalism," by which he means unrealistic, abstract doctrines for social change. As Bagehot's essay on Peel indicates, he did not have much tolerance for independent spirits who wanted to rock the ship of state; once such rocking starts, it might not end, Bagehot feared, until the ship of state was in ruins. Bagehot was one of the first in a long and distinguished line of critics to point out that Dickens's fondness for caricature caused him to reduce complicated issues to comic simplicities. Bagehot is willing to laugh at Dickens's caricatures until they are turned against the state; for Bagehot, the business of governing a complex democracy was not something to be made fun of, and he cannot forgive Dickens for using his popularity as a novelist to indulge in satiric attacks on parliament and other institutions of government.

By the time that Bagehot wrote his essay on Dickens, political matters were beginning to exercise an increasing importance on his life and work. Thanks to his father-in-law's extensive contacts in government, Bagehot began to secure introductions to influential politicians and to make a place for himself in the social life of the capital, which he frequently visited in connection with his banking business and the operation of the *National Review.* As the editor of the *Economist,* James Wilson was also able to give his son-in-law an important forum for expressing political and financial opinions; beginning in 1857, Bagehot contributed articles frequently to the *Economist,* and in 1859, when Wilson went to India for an extended stay on government business, Bagehot was appointed managing director of the weekly paper in his father-in-law's absence. Burdened with heavy journalistic and banking responsibilities, Bagehot had little time left for writing articles of literary criticism, and thus in large part his career as a critic was over. His last major literary essay appeared in the final issue of the *National Review* at the end of 1864.

When James Wilson suddenly died in 1860, the management of the *Economist* was left entirely to Bagehot. By the spring of 1861 he had resigned his banking post in Bristol and had moved to London to assume the editorship of the paper, a job which he continued to perform until his death sixteen years later. Under Bagehot's guidance the prestige and authority of the *Economist* increased considerably. In his weekly editorials for the paper, Bagehot quickly established a name for himself as one of the most astute political and financial commentators in the country. Government leaders and important businessmen began to seek his advice; no less a figure than William Gladstone, the future prime minister, became one of his greatest admirers. He consulted frequently with Bagehot on government fiscal policy, and in later years came to rely so heavily on his advice that he once referred to him as "a sort of supplementary Chancellor of the Exchequer."

Bagehot's position at the *Economist* allowed him to acquire a detailed and intimate knowledge of the daily workings of government. Politics held a deep fascination for him, and by the middle of the 1860s he was ready to undertake a book-length examination of the English system of government. Chapman and Hall agreed to publish the book after first arranging to have it appear in serial in a new journal which the firm was establishing in cooperation with Anthony Trollope. Over a period of eighteen months—from May 1865 to January 1867—the *Fortnightly Review* ran installments of

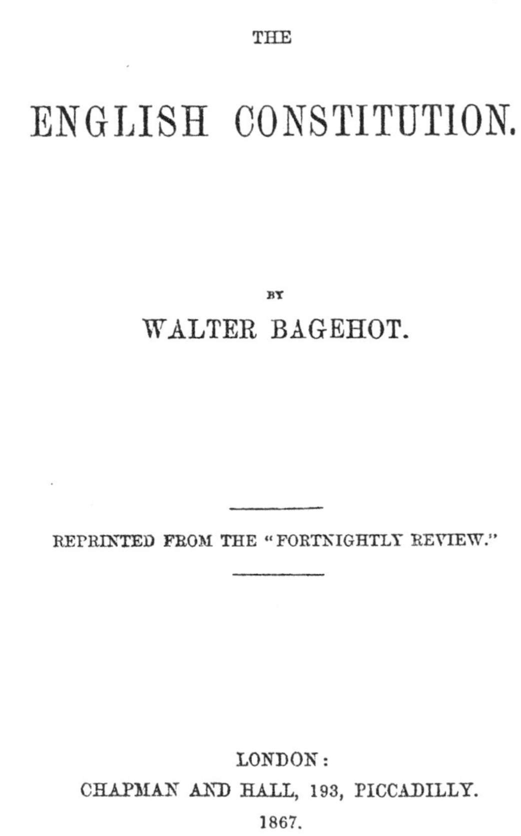
THE

ENGLISH CONSTITUTION.

BY

WALTER BAGEHOT.

REPRINTED FROM THE "FORTNIGHTLY REVIEW."

LONDON:
CHAPMAN AND HALL, 193, PICCADILLY.
1867.

Title page for Bagehot's study of the British political system, originally published in the Fortnightly Review *from May 1865 to January 1867*

Bagehot's *The English Constitution.* The work was a great success and won Bagehot widespread praise for his straightforward approach to a difficult and confusing subject. In his *Introduction to the Study of the Law of the Constitution* (1885), A. V. Dicey wrote that "Bagehot was the first author who explained in accordance with actual fact the true nature of the Cabinet and its real relation to the Crown and to Parliament." Before *The English Constitution,* there was more myth than fact in most accounts of the constitutional system. In characteristic fashion Bagehot swept aside all the textbook theories about the functions of the government and focused instead on the everyday practice of those functions as he had observed them in his own experience. The fresh approach and engaging prose style of Bagehot's work pleasantly surprised his Victorian readers, who had come to expect nothing but clichés and abstractions where descriptions of the government's organization and powers were concerned.

One by one *The English Constitution* methodically examines the major centers of power within the government—the prime minister and his cabinet, the monarch, the House of Lords, and the House of Commons. But Bagehot perceived that perhaps the best way to explain the actual nature of these various centers of power was to distinguish between the "dignified" exercise of constitutional authority and the "efficient" use of that authority. The pomp and circumstance of the monarchy and the aristocracy provide the visible symbols of power—they present the dignified, ceremonial aspects of rule; but the real work of governing the country—the efficient use of its state power—is in the hands of the politicians working quietly behind the theatrical scenery of the monarch's court and the House of Lords. Until Bagehot openly stated the true limitations on royal authority, the myth that the queen still retained considerable power had rarely been questioned publicly. For more than a century royal power had been steadily on the decline; Bagehot was simply the first important writer to reveal the fact without any attempt to disguise its full impact on the body politic. Indeed, *The English Constitution* makes the rather startling but accurate point that the House of Commons had become so dominant that the queen was completely at the mercy of its will. "She must sign her own death-warrant," Bagehot declares, "if the two Houses unanimously send it up to her."

Despite its greatly reduced status from an "efficient" force in the government to a merely "dignified" one, the monarchy is still vitally important to the nation, Bagehot argues. It provides, for one thing, a necessary sense of continuity and stability within the volatile political structure of a free society, where power frequently shifts back and forth between rival parties. The monarch can stand apart from party strife and help to unify the country in times of crisis. More important, the monarchy can provide a symbol of governmental authority that the average man and woman can readily comprehend and accept. "The best reason why Monarchy is a strong government is that it is an intelligible government," Bagehot writes. "The mass of mankind understand it." Carrying out the actions of government in the queen's name gives those actions a sense of power and purpose that is immediate and real to common people, who require, Bagehot believes, visible symbols of authority on which to fix their emotions. In politics most people are guided by their hearts rather than their minds, Bagehot observes, and therefore royalty will always have a certain appeal for the masses.

In general *The English Constitution* presents a condescending view of the masses. Bagehot's concept of democratic government did not include direct representation of the lower classes. It was his feeling that the responsible middle and upper classes should have charge of the government until the lower classes were sufficiently educated to act as intelligent voters. As matters stood during the time in which Bagehot wrote his study of the political system, the lower classes were still largely excluded from parliamentary representation, and Bagehot did not want that arrangement to change for the forseeable future. He believed the system was working very well just as it was, and that the great majority of the lower classes were content with their place in that system. Only opportunistic politicians, he argued, were intent on reforming the system in order to win favor with newly enfranchised voters. Bagehot believed that England was, in general, a "deferential" nation in which "the numerical majority . . . is ready, is eager to delegate its power of choosing its ruler to a certain select minority. It abdicates in favour of its *élite,* and consents to obey whoever that *élite* may confide in." In centuries past that select group was the aristocracy, but now, Bagehot says, it is more often than not the active business and professional men of the middle classes. Whether the upper or lower classes were fully aware of the fact or not, England was essentially under the rule of the average middle-class gentleman—"the bald-headed man at the back of the omnibus," as Bagehot refers to him. *The English Constitution* is, in part, a tribute to the triumph of middle-class power in mid-Victorian England. It sets a seal of approval on middle-class values and aspirations, as they manifest themselves in the slow but steady progress of constitutional government.

Bagehot's faith in the gradual improvement of society, as opposed to radical transformations of it, led him to adopt some of the beliefs of social Darwinists like Herbert Spencer. The notion that patterns of evolutionary development could be traced in society as well as in biology appealed strongly to Bagehot's fondness for order and logic. A few months after *The English Constitution* was completed, Bagehot began writing a series of long essays for the *Fortnightly Review* on the question of how societies reach advanced stages of development. In 1872 the essays were brought together for publication as the book entitled *Physics and Politics*. The book traces the rise of three basic types of social order. One type belongs to what Bagehot calls the "preliminary age," when primitive humans first joined together to create social bonds outside the immediate family circle. The second type belongs to the "fighting age," when protective states were formally established, each with its own fixed set of national interests, laws, and customs. And, finally, the third type belongs to the "age of discussion," when nations began to recognize the need for political freedom and tolerance, both within and without their territorial boundaries. The key to real social progress, Bagehot observes, lies in a nation's ability to evolve sophisticated political and social outlets for free and open discussions of national concerns. In that way progress can occur in a moderate and reasonable fashion, without violent social upheavals or dark reactionary periods. Government by discussion makes it possible for change to take place within, Bagehot writes, "a kind of selective conservatism, for the most part keeping what is old, but annexing some new but like practice—an additional turret in the old style." This concept is the social equivalent of the biological principle of natural selection, and Bagehot clearly believed that the give-and-take of government by discussion in the English parliamentary system represented the highest form of political life yet achieved by mankind.

The imposing title and scientific aspects of *Physics and Politics* obscure the fact that the book is essentially a restatement of many of the political ideas that Bagehot had already expressed in previous works. Bagehot's fascination with evolutionary theory allowed him to give a new slant to his long-standing belief in political moderation, but it also blunted the impact of his style and confused issues which were handled so clearly in his earlier, less theoretical works. Although Bagehot may have hoped that *Physics and Politics* would enhance his reputation as a serious political thinker, it did not enjoy anything like the critical and popular success of his other major book on politics, *The English Constitution*. In that earlier work Bagehot's talent for inspired journalistic observation is not undercut by too much political theorizing, but in *Physics and Politics* Bagehot allows the journalist in him to be overshadowed by the theorist.

By the end of the 1860s Bagehot's enormous workload as a writer and editor began to take its toll on his health. At Christmas 1867 he became quite ill, apparently from an attack of pneumonia, and for the next three years he suffered a general decline in health, unable to recover fully from his initial illness. *Physics and Politics* took five years to complete because, in large part, Bagehot's delicate health kept him from working on it steadily. In 1871 he regained some of his strength and began working on a new book, *Lombard Street*, a study of the London money market. It was finished in less than two years and was very well received on its publication in 1873 as a lively and authoritative account of English financial systems. The book helped to strip away some of the mystery surrounding the country's complicated banking arrangements, just as *The English Constitution* had helped to shed light on the political system. Published in a period of economic depression, *Lombard Street* contained valuable suggestions for improving the Bank of England's effectiveness as a force for stability in the money markets. The book won Bagehot renewed respect as an economist, and although *Lombard Street* is not often read today, it remains one of the best contemporary accounts of Victorian finance.

Lombard Street was the last of Bagehot's books to be published in his lifetime. Four years after its publication, Bagehot came down with another serious chest cold and after a short illness died on 24 March 1877. He was fifty-one. Shortly after his death, Richard Hutton set to work collecting some of Bagehot's essays for publication in a three-volume series of books, in the hope of salvaging many of Bagehot's best works from the obscurity of the journal issues in which they originally appeared. The publication of *Literary Studies* (1879), *Economic Studies* (1880), and *Biographical Studies* (1881) helped to establish Bagehot's reputation as one of the best essayists of his time. Since his death Bagehot has come to be regarded as one of the most congenial and honest spokesmen for established Victorian society. He was not an original thinker, but he had the talent to express the conventional opinions of his age in an original way. For that reason, in an essay collected in *Today and Yesterday* (1948), the historian G. M. Young praised Bagehot as the "greatest Victorian," in the sense that he represents Victorian ideas and hopes in their most engaging form. Bagehot's name may not rank as high on other scholars' lists of eminent Victorians, but certainly it can be said with confidence that there were very few Victorians who understood the daily realities of their age as well as Walter Bagehot.

Letters:

The Love Letters of Walter Bagehot and Eliza Wilson, edited by Mrs. Russell Barrington (London: Faber & Faber, 1933).

Biographies:

Mrs. Russell Barrington, *Life of Walter Bagehot* (London: Longmans, Green, 1914);

Alastair Buchan, *The Spare Chancellor: The Life of Walter Bagehot* (London: Chatto & Windus, 1959).

References:

Jacques Barzun, "Bagehot, or the Human Comedy," in his *The Energy of Art: Studies of Authors Classic and Modern* (New York: Harper, 1956), pp. 195-225;

Asa Briggs, "Trollope, Bagehot, and the English Constitution," in his *Victorian People: A Reassessment of Persons and Themes, 1851-1867* (Chicago: University of Chicago Press, 1970), pp. 87-115;

R. H. S. Crossman, Introduction to Bagehot's *The English Constitution,* Fontana Classics edition (London: Fontana, 1963);

Francis Davis, "Walter Bagehot: Follower of Edmund Burke," *CLA Journal,* 21 (December 1977): 292-303;

Gertrude Himmelfarb, "Walter Bagehot: A Common Man with Uncommon Ideas," in her *Victorian Minds* (New York: Knopf, 1968), pp. 220-235;

William Irvine, *Walter Bagehot* (London & New York: Longmans, Green, 1939);

Harold Orel, "Walter Bagehot," in his *Victorian Literary Critics* (New York: St. Martin's, 1984), pp. 31-57;

Norman St. John-Stevas, *Walter Bagehot: A Study of His Life and Thought Together with a Selection from His Political Writings* (Bloomington: Indiana University Press, 1959);

Charles Sisson, *The Case of Walter Bagehot* (London: Faber & Faber, 1972);

Leslie Stephen, "Walter Bagehot," in his *Studies of a Biographer* (London: Duckworth, 1902), III: 155-187;

Harry R. Sullivan, *Walter Bagehot* (Boston: Twayne, 1975);

Woodrow Wilson, "A Literary Politician," in his *Mere Literature, and Other Essays* (Boston: Houghton Mifflin, 1896), pp. 69-103;

G. M. Young, "The Greatest Victorian," in his *Today and Yesterday: Collected Essays and Addresses* (London: Hart-Davis, 1948), pp. 237-243.

Papers:

Many of Bagehot's papers were destroyed. Some of his letters have survived and are located chiefly at the British Library, London, and at the Bodleian Library, Oxford.

George Borrow

(5 July 1803-26? July 1881)

Stephen Pulsford
University of South Carolina

See also the Borrow entry in *DLB 21, Victorian Novelists Before 1885.*

SELECTED BOOKS: *The Zincali; or, An Account of the Gypsies of Spain* (2 volumes, London: Murray, 1841; 1 volume, New York: Wiley & Putnam, 1842);

The Bible in Spain; or, The Journeys, Adventures, and Imprisonments of an Englishman, in an Attempt to Circulate the Scriptures in the Peninsula (3 volumes, London: Murray, 1843; 1 volume, Philadelphia: Campbell, 1843);

Lavengro; The Scholar, the Gypsy, the Priest (3 volumes, London: Murray, 1851; 1 volume, New York: Putnam's, 1851);

The Romany Rye; A Sequel to Lavengro (2 volumes, London: Murray, 1857; 1 volume, New York: Harper, 1857);

Wild Wales: Its People, Language, and Scenery (3 volumes, London: Murray, 1862; 1 volume, New York: Putnam's, 1868);

Romano Lavo-Lil: Word-Book of the Romany, or English Gypsy Language (London: Murray, 1874; New York: Putnam's, 1905);

Celtic Bards, Chiefs, and Kings, edited by H. G. Wright (London: Murray, 1928).

Collection: *The Works of George Borrow: Norwich Edition,* edited by C. K. Shorter, 16 volumes (London: Constable, 1923-1924; New York: Wells, 1923-1924).

OTHER: *Celebrated Trials and Remarkable Cases of Criminal Jurisprudence, from the Earliest Records to the Year 1825,* compiled by Borrow, 6 volumes (London: Printed for Knight & Lacey, 1825).

TRANSLATIONS: Friedrich Maximilian von Klinger, *Faustus: His Life, Death and Descent into Hell* (London: Simpkin & Marshall, 1825);

Romantic Ballads, Translated from the Danish; and Miscellaneous Pieces (Norwich: S. Wilkin, 1826);

National Portrait Gallery

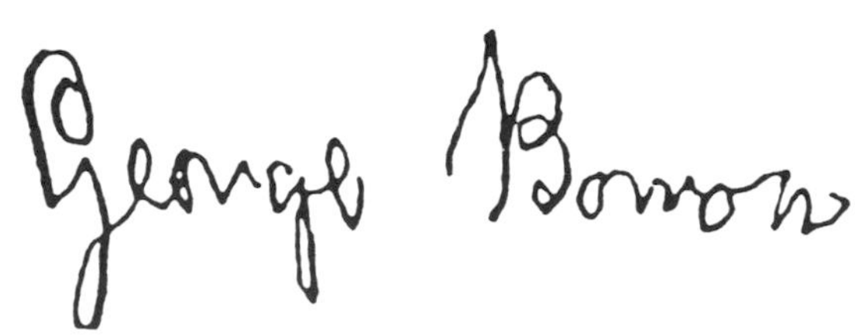

Targun; or, Metrical Translations from Thirty Languages and Dialects (St. Petersburg: Schulz & Beneze, 1835);

Alexander Pushkin, *The Talisman* (St. Petersburg: Schulz & Beneze, 1835);

Embéo e Majaró Lucas, The Gospel according to St. Luke, translated into Spanish Gypsy (Madrid, 1837);

Elis Wyn, *The Sleeping Bard; or, Visions of the World, Death, and Hell* (London: Murray, 1860);

The Turkish Jester; or, The Pleasantries of Cogia Nasr Eddin Effendi (Ipswich: W. Webber, 1884);

The Death of Balder from the Danish of Johannes Ewald (London: Jarrold, 1889);

Ballads of All Nations, edited by R. B. Johnson (London: Alston Rivers, 1927).

George Borrow rose to international fame by writing about himself. His three-volume travelogue, *The Bible in Spain,* was probably the best-selling book of 1843. John Murray sold nearly 20,000 copies in a year, while 30,000 pirated copies were sold within six months of the work's appearance in America. The book had much to recommend it to a wide audience—humor, adventure, and travel (Dickens's *Pickwick Papers* had been another best-seller only a few years previously); a lively, though erratic, style; interpolated passages of moralizing; and a fervent sense of English nationalism. Most of all, it impressed upon the popular imagination the eccentric and extrovert personality of its author-hero, who combined the roguery of the picaro with Evangelical good works and professions of piety. To his admirers Borrow was a morally acceptable Byron: a handsome and brave, but chaste and temperate, wanderer who could revel in the company of disreputable characters, under cover of his mission to spread Protestantism to the Catholic and heathen Spaniards.

Yet Borrow never repeated the success of *The Bible in Spain.* It took him eight years to produce the follow-up, the novel *Lavengro; The Scholar, the Gypsy, the Priest* (1851), which described his childhood and early adventures in London in similar picaresque form. This book was a critical and commercial flop. In the year of the Great Exhibition, and to a public taste that had recently elevated itself to such social works as *Vanity Fair* (1847-1848), *David Copperfield* (1849-1850), Kingsley's *Alton Locke* (1850), and Carlyle's *Latter-Day Pamphlets* (1850), *Lavengro* was an anachronism, without social purpose or moral message. It was twenty-one years before the first edition of 3,000 copies was replaced by a second.

The three later books published in Borrow's lifetime were equally unpopular. Yet though he died forgotten in 1881, Borrow's career has remained fascinating to twentieth-century commentators, inspiring a score of book-length biographies. His father, Thomas Borrow (1758-1824), married Ann Perfrement (1772-1858) while he was a sergeant in the West Norfolk Militia (he later attained the rank of adjutant-captain). George Henry, the second of their two sons, was born in Norfolk on 5 July 1803 and began his traveling career almost immediately as his father's regiment was posted around the country. His early education was sporadic and unconventional. He was sent to school in almost every town where the regiment halted, often for as little as a few weeks at a time. Most substantially he attended schools in East Dereham, Huddersfield, Edinburgh, Norwich, and Clonmel, Ireland, for periods of from three months to a year, before finally reentering Norwich Grammar School for the three years 1816-1819. The features of his childhood that were to shape his later career—love of the outdoors, association with gypsies, and an extraordinary facility for languages—came from the periods between schools. When he was seven he began learning Latin from a friend of his father. He began Greek when he was eleven, picked up some Irish in Clonmel in 1815 and 1816, studied French and Italian with a priest in Norwich, and by the time he was twenty had also taught himself an inaccurate but effective working knowledge of Spanish, Low Dutch, Welsh, German, Romany, Hebrew, Arabic, and Danish. Borrow eventually developed a working knowledge of more than fifty languages and dialects. As a young man looking for work, he once advertised himself thus: "Mr. George Borrow, Willow Lane, St. Giles, Norwich. Gives instructions in German and in any other European language. Hebrew taught, if required." Rather than study at school, however, Borrow preferred to box or ride. He dreamed of traveling and in 1818 persuaded three younger boys to run away with him. They were caught within a day, and Borrow was publicly horsewhipped.

After leaving school, when he was nearly sixteen, Borrow was articled for five years to a prominent Norwich solicitor, William Simpson. Yet though he served the full term of this apprenticeship, he remained more dedicated to his own pursuits than to formal study. He taught himself more languages and met two men who encouraged his writing. William Taylor, at fifty-five, had traveled in Europe, read German philosophy, defended the French Revolution, was a friend of Southey, and, most appealing of all, made his living as a journalist. John Bowring, still in his twenties, was a linguist and had traveled in Russia, Spain, and Scandinavia. These two friends awoke Borrow to the possibility of a literary career. At the end of his apprenticeship in 1824, and after the death of his father, Borrow headed for London to try, fairly unsuccessfully, to publish his translations of Welsh and Danish po-

National Portrait Gallery

Two men who encouraged the young Borrow to write: William Taylor, in an 1821 portrait by J. Thomson, and John Bowring, depicted in 1826 by John King

etry. He made a living in Grub Street, contributing articles and reviews to the *New Monthly Magazine* and the short-lived *Universal Review,* and by compiling the six-volume (4,000-page) *Celebrated Trials and Remarkable Cases of Criminal Jurisprudence, from the Earliest Records to the Year 1825.* According to Borrow, the compilation of this last work taught him how to write. It undoubtedly did much to develop his concise, reportorial, and fluent prose style, and to interest him in the characters of low life that fill his work.

Borrow was busy during his first two years in London. He worked on more verse translations and on preparing for the press a translation of Friedrich Maximilian von Klinger's *Faustus,* which appeared in 1825. His activities between 1826 and 1832, however, are largely a mystery. He was based in Norwich and seems to have traveled extensively in England and perhaps France. Michael Collie, in his 1984 biography of Borrow, suggests that he may have traveled much more widely to countries all around the world. All he published was *Romantic Ballads, Translated from the Danish* (1826). Although this work was eventually published with three different title pages, it was hardly noticed by the critics. At the beginning of 1833 he was introduced to the British and Foreign Bible Society, which gave him £10 to cover expenses while he learned the Manchu language (it took him six months), before they sent him abroad. In St. Petersburg, Russia, from mid 1833 to 1835, he worked on a Manchu translation of parts of the Bible, for distribution in China. He eventually published 1,000 copies, at a cost to the Society of £2,600, but he was unable to get permission from the czar to move them eastward and had to ship them back to London.

The Bible in Spain (1843) describes his three later excursions for the Bible Society, to Portugal and Spain between 1835 and 1840. His mission was to leave tracts and Bibles with influential people he met, and with booksellers. In Madrid he had to obtain permission from an uninterested and constantly changing series of politicians to print Spanish New Testaments. On several occasions permission was revoked, Bibles were seized, and Borrow was jailed for illicit distribution of them. Adapted from the letters he wrote home explaining and justifying his movements, *The Bible in Spain* is an episodic account, unified only by the constant purpose of the expedition. The odds are stacked against the hero because of corruption in the Catholic Church, bureaucracy in the Spanish government, and the dangers of a country in civil war. The narrative is filled out with vivid descriptions of the Iberian landscape, and of the variety of characters met along the way—thieves, revolutionaries, Gypsies, soldiers, politicians, and priests. Borrow also takes time out to moralize and thank his Creator, to rail against "the foul stains of Popery" responsible for most of Spain's problems, and to reflect on the glories of the English nation.

The appeal of Borrow's book is due partly to the persona he creates for himself. He has an infectious self-confidence. Not only can he handle himself in a fight (he was 6′ 3″ tall), but he can also use his brains. He is good at everything, moving freely from one level of society to another, from the prison cell to the houses of the nobility; making a profit from a horse dealer as skillfully as he persuades the Spanish prime minister to bend legal restrictions on his publishing activities. And he communicates effortlessly in all languages. His behavior was justified to a Victorian Evangelical audience (as it was to his employers) by his eventual moderate success at distributing Bibles. Nevertheless, much of his piety rings false. Within a page of professing the faith that moderates his life, Borrow reports losing his temper and getting into a fight. Though he says he trusts in God, in practice he relies mostly on his own wit. His tirades of obsessive patriotism and anti-Catholicism are countered by his real-life fascination for interesting characters of all religions and nationalities.

Throughout his time in Spain, Borrow was writing and translating. In Madrid in 1837 he published *Embéo e Majaró Lucas,* his own Spanish Romany translation of the Gospel of St. Luke. And by 1839 he was gathering material for a book on the languages of the Spanish Gypsies. His research included a brief visit to North Africa. He was also corresponding with an old friend, Mrs. Mary Clarke, the widow of Lt. Henry Clarke, who had died twenty years previously. By June 1839 she and her daughter, Henrietta, had accepted his invitation to join him in Seville, where the three of them took a house together for the last nine months of Borrow's Iberian adventures. At the same time, the local authorities were becoming particularly antagonistic to Borrow's activities, and the Bible Society was dissatisfied with his progress. He left Spain for the last time and returned to London with the Clarkes in April 1840.

George Borrow and Mary Clarke were married on 23 April 1840, exactly a week after their arrival in England. They settled on her estate at Oulton Broad, Norfolk, where Borrow was to live and write for the last forty-one years of his life. His first book, which he began immediately, was a combination of his philological notes, descriptions of Gypsy life, and some of his personal experiences. Published in two volumes in April 1841, *The Zincali; or, An Account of the Gypsies of Spain* was favorably reviewed as entertaining and original. The first edition of 750 copies sold in a few months, and a second edition was printed in March 1843, after the early success of *The Bible in Spain.* Though its scholarship is now seen as inaccurate, *The Zincali* gave Borrow a reputation as an authority on Gypsy life and language. The favorable reception of the autobiographical parts of this book encouraged Borrow in his writing of *The Bible in Spain*—which sold much more rapidly, particularly after its appearance in one volume as the first of John Murray's innovative Colonial and Home Library series. In four years Borrow earned about £1,400 from *The Bible in Spain.*

But at Oulton Borrow was becoming restless and finding it difficult to write creatively. During most of 1844 he went off on his own, touring Eastern Europe. On his return he suffered attacks of fever, possibly recurrent from the malaria he had picked up in Spain. *Lavengro* was not finished until the end of 1850, and when it failed to sell well Borrow blamed the critics (whom he later attacked vociferously in the extraordinary appendix to its 1857 sequel, *The Romany Rye*). For a time he thought of abandoning literature, though he already had many of the notes for his next book. He was still fit, and he still traveled. In 1853, at the age of fifty, he rescued a man from drowning at sea in a storm at Great Yarmouth, an act of heroism reported in many newspapers. Struggling with his writings, he sought release in long walking tours. Out of these tours came *Wild Wales: Its People, Language, and Scenery* (1862), similar in form to *The Bible in Spain,* but more leisurely and reflective.

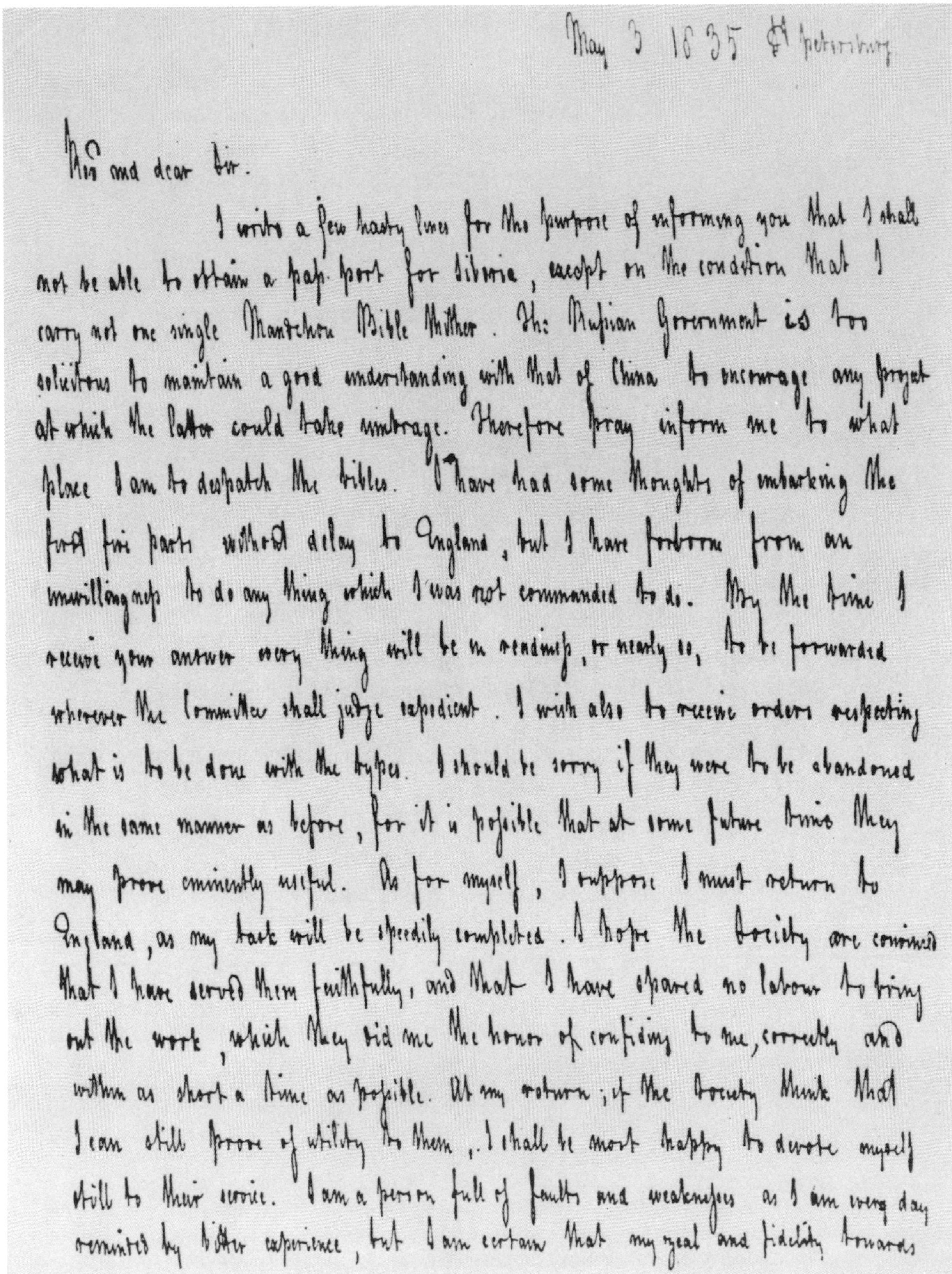

May 3 1835 St Petersburg

Rev. and dear Sir.

I write a few hasty lines for the purpose of informing you that I shall not be able to obtain a pass-port for Siberia, except on the condition that I carry not one single Mandchou Bible thither. The Russian Government is too solicitous to maintain a good understanding with that of China to encourage any project at which the latter could take umbrage. Therefore pray inform me to what place I am to despatch the bibles. I have had some thoughts of embarking the first five parts without delay to England, but I have forborne from an unwillingness to do any thing which I was not commanded to do. By the time I receive your answer every thing will be in readiness, or nearly so, to be forwarded wherever the Committee shall judge expedient. I wish also to receive orders respecting what is to be done with the types. I should be sorry if they were to be abandoned in the same manner as before, for it is possible that at some future time they may prove eminently useful. As for myself, I suppose I must return to England, as my task will be speedily completed. I hope the Society are convinced that I have served them faithfully, and that I have spared no labour to bring out the work, which they did me the honor of confiding to me, correctly and within as short a time as possible. At my return, if the Society think that I can still prove of utility to them, I shall be most happy to devote myself still to their service. I am a person full of faults and weaknesses as I am every day reminded by bitter experience, but I am certain that my zeal and fidelity towards

Letter to the Reverend Joseph Jowett written while Borrow was in St. Petersburg, Russia, working on a Manchu translation of parts of the Bible (British and Foreign Bible Society)

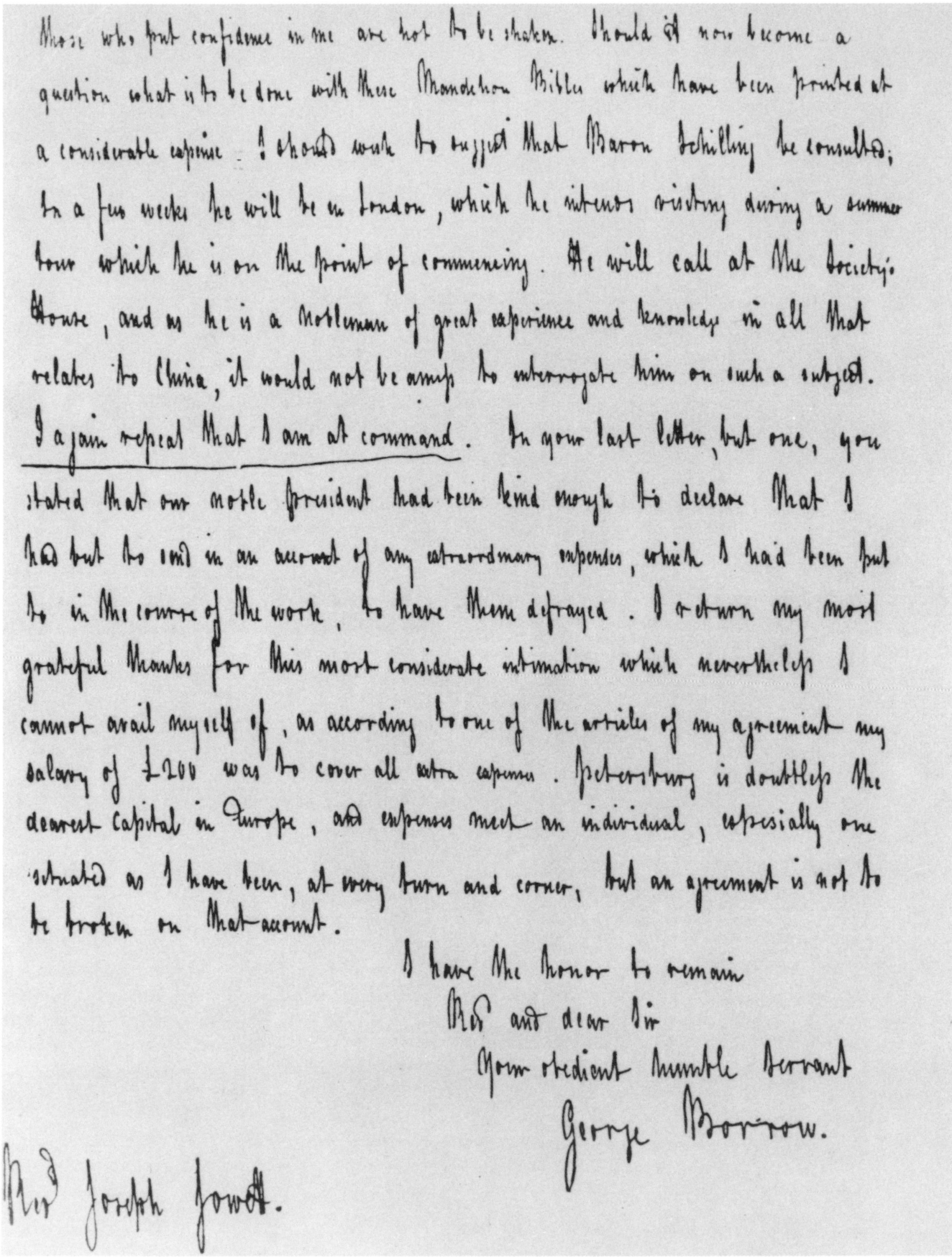

those who put confidence in me are not to be shaken. Should it now become a question what is to be done with these Mandchou Bibles which have been printed at a considerable expense – I should wish to suggest that Baron Schilling be consulted; In a few weeks he will be in London, which he intends visiting during a summer tour which he is on the point of commencing. He will call at the Society's House, and as he is a Nobleman of great experience and knowledge in all that relates to China, it would not be amiss to interrogate him on such a subject. I again repeat that I am at command. In your last letter, but one, you stated that our noble President had been kind enough to declare that I had but to send in an account of any extraordinary expenses, which I had been put to in the course of the work, to have them defrayed. I return my most grateful thanks for this most considerate intimation which nevertheless I cannot avail myself of, as according to one of the articles of my agreement my salary of £200 was to cover all extra expenses. Petersburg is doubtless the dearest capital in Europe, and expenses meet an individual, especially one situated as I have been, at every turn and corner, but an agreement is not to be broken on that account.

I have the honor to remain
Revd and dear Sir
Your obedient humble Servant
George Borrow.

Revd Joseph Jowett.

Though it is in many ways his best book, and perhaps his best liked today, in the 1860s it sold poorly. In his lifetime Borrow earned only £275 from the book.

Each of Borrow's books contains episodes that make good anthology pieces, but overall they are marred by an irregularity of style. At his worst Borrow lapses into pedestrian verbosity, ineffective ornateness, or unnecessary imitation of Biblical rhythms and diction. His dialogue is particularly erratic, shifting within a few lines from realistic colloquialism to artificial and improbably elegant stylization. He describes the strengths and weaknesses of his style—indirectly and unwittingly—in *Lavengro,* when he recalls his early experiences editing the volumes of *Celebrated Trials:* "What struck me most with respect to these lives was the art which the writers, whoever they were, possessed of telling a plain story. It is no easy thing to tell a story plainly and distinctly. . . . People are afraid to put down what is common on paper, they seek to embellish their narratives, as they think, by philosophic speculations and reflections; they are anxious to shine, and people who are anxious to shine can never tell a plain story." Borrow's weaknesses show when he is moralizing or reflecting, when he is too eager to impress. But at his best he is colloquial and plain as few other Victorian prose writers ever are. In fact, he looks not to contemporary writers for his model, but to eighteenth-century writer Daniel Defoe. Like Defoe, he attempts to convince the reader of the truth of his narrative through unobtrusive, but realistic, detail and description. He can describe a scene economically, as background to a story, or for its own interest, as if it were an entry in a guide book. He is at his best when depicting natural scenery, as he was aware when he described *Lavengro* as "a series of Rembrandt pictures interspersed here and there with a Claude." Charlotte Brontë admired him for his "athletic simplicity."

Throughout his life Borrow consciously isolated himself from the literature of his own time and country. Oblivious to the works of such widely read writers as Dickens, Tennyson, Carlyle, and Browning, he preferred instead to translate and praise obscure Scandinavian, Welsh, and Danish poets. He was as independent in his art as he was in his life, on his journeys across Europe, or in his last years alone at Oulton. Mary Clarke Borrow died in 1869, but he continued to write. In 1874 his notes yielded *Romano Lavo-Lil,* a study of English Gypsy language, which failed because it was outdated. By this time there were other, more scholarly, students of the Gypsies. When George Borrow died in July 1881 he had been forgotten. He was buried beside his wife in Brompton Cemetery.

Letters:

T. H. Darlow, ed., *Letters of George Borrow to the British and Foreign Bible Society* (London: Hodder & Stoughton, 1911).

Bibliography:

Michael Collie and Angus Fraser, *George Borrow: A Bibliographical Study* (London: St. Paul's Bibliographies, 1984).

Biographies:

W. I. Knapp, *The Life, Writings, and Correspondence of George Borrow,* 2 volumes (London: Murray, 1899);

Herbert Jenkins, *The Life of George Borrow* (London: Murray, 1912);

Edward Thomas, *George Borrow: The Man and His Books* (London: Chapman & Hall, 1912);

C. K. Shorter, *George Borrow and His Circle* (London: Hodder & Stoughton, 1913);

René Fréchet, *George Borrow (1803-1881): Vagabond polyglotte—Agent biblique—Ecrivain* (Paris: Didier, 1956);

Michael Collie, *George Borrow: Eccentric* (Cambridge: Cambridge University Press, 1982);

David Williams, *A World of His Own: The Double Life of George Borrow* (Oxford: Oxford University Press, 1982).

Papers:

The largest collections of Borrow's papers are at the Huntington Library, San Marino, California; the Berg Collection, New York Public Library; Humanities Research Center, University of Texas at Austin; the Symington Collection, Rutgers University; the Brotherton Collection, University of Leeds; the Scott Library, York University, Toronto; the Fales Library, New York University at Washington Square; and the Ashley Collection, British Library.

Richard F. Burton

(19 March 1821-20 October 1890)

Joan Corwin

SELECTED BOOKS: *Goa, and the Blue Mountains; or, Six Months of Sick Leave* (London: Bentley, 1851);

Scinde; or, The Unhappy Valley, 2 volumes (London: Bentley, 1851);

Sindh, and the Races that Inhabit the Valley of the Indus (London: Allen, 1851);

Falconry in the Valley of the Indus (London: Van Voorst, 1852);

A Complete System of Bayonet Exercise (London: Clowes, 1853);

Personal Narrative of a Pilgrimage to El-Medinah and Meccah (3 volumes, London: Longman, Brown, Green & Longmans, 1855-1856; 1 volume, New York: Putnam's, 1856);

First Footsteps in East Africa; or, An Exploration of Harar (2 volumes, London: Longman, Brown, Green & Longmans, 1856; 1 volume, London: Dent/New York: Dutton, 1910);

The Lake Regions of Central Africa (2 volumes, London: Longman, Green, Longman & Roberts, 1860; 1 volume, New York: Harper, 1860);

The City of the Saints and Across the Rocky Mountains to California (London: Longman, Green, Longman & Roberts, 1861; New York: Harper, 1862);

Abeokuta and The Cameroons Mountains. An Exploration, 2 volumes (London: Tinsley, 1863);

Wanderings in West Africa, From Liverpool to Fernando Po, as a F.R.G.S., 2 volumes (London: Tinsley, 1863);

A Mission to Gelele, King of Dahome, 2 volumes (London: Tinsley, 1864);

The Nile Basin, part 1 by Burton, part 2 by James M'Queen (London: Tinsley, 1864);

The Guide-Book. A Pictorial Pilgrimage to Mecca and Medina. (Including Some of the More Remarkable Incidents in the Life of Mohammed, the Arab Lawgiver) (London: Printed for the author by William Clowes, 1865);

Stone Talk . . . Being Some of the Marvellous Sayings of a Petral Portion of Fleet Street, London, to One Doctor Polyglott, Ph.D., as Frank Baker (London: Hardwicke, 1865);

The Highlands of Brazil, 2 volumes (London: Tinsley, 1869);

Letters from the Battle-fields of Paraguay (London: Tinsley, 1870);

Unexplored Syria, Visits to The Libanus, The Tulúl el Safá, The Anti-Libanus, The Northern Libanus, and the 'Aláh, by Burton and Charles F. Tyrwhitt-Drake, 2 volumes (London: Tinsley, 1871);

Zanzibar; City, Island, and Coast, 2 volumes (London: Tinsley, 1872);

Ultima Thule; or; A Summer in Iceland, 2 volumes (London & Edinburgh: Nimmo, 1875);

Etruscan Bologna: A Study (London: Smith, Elder, 1876);

A New System of Sword Exercise for Infantry (London: Clowes, 1876);

Two Trips to Gorilla Land and the Cataracts of the Congo, 2 volumes (London: Low, Marston, Low & Searle, 1876);

Scind Revisited: With Notices of the Anglo-Indian Army; Railroads; Past, Present, and Future, Etc., 2 volumes (London: Bentley, 1877);

The Gold-Mines of Midian and The Ruined Midianite Cities. A Fortnight's Tour in Northwestern Arabia (London: Kegan Paul, 1878);

The Land of Midian (revisited), 2 volumes (London: Kegan Paul, 1879);

The Kasîdah (couplets) of Hâjî Abdû El-Yezdî a Lay of the Higher Law, Translated and Annotated by His Friend and Pupil F. B. (London: Privately printed, 1880; Portland, Maine: Mosher, 1896);

Camoens: His Life and His Lusiads. A Commentary, 2 volumes (London: Quaritch, 1881);

A Glance at The "Passion-Play" (London: Harrison, 1881);

To the Gold Coast for Gold. A Personal Narrative, by Burton and Verney Lovett Cameron, 2 volumes (London: Chatto & Windus, 1883);

The Book of the Sword (London: Chatto & Windus, 1884);

The Jew, The Gypsy, and El Islam, edited by W. H. Wilkins (London: Hutchinson, 1898; Chicago & New York: Stone, 1898);

Wanderings in Three Continents, edited by Wilkins (London: Hutchinson, 1901; New York: Dodd, Mead, 1901);

Selected Papers on Anthropology, Travel and Exploration, edited by Norman M. Penzer (London: Philpot, 1924; New York: McBride, 1924);

Love, War and Fancy: The Customs and Manners of the East, From Writings on the Arabian Nights, edited by Kenneth Walker (London: Kimber, 1964; New York: Ballantine, 1964).

Collection: *The Memorial Edition of The Works of Captain Sir Richard F. Burton,* edited by Isabel Burton, 7 volumes (London: Tylston & Edwards, 1893-1894).

TRANSLATIONS: *The Lands of Cazembe. Lacerda's Journey to Cazembe in 1798,* translated and annotated by Burton in a volume that also includes translations by others (London: Royal Geographical Society, 1873);

Kama Shastra; or the Hindoo Art of Love (Ars Amoris Indica), translated from the Sanskrit by Burton as B. F. R. and F. F. Arbuthnot as A. F. F. (N.p.: Privately printed, 1873); republished as *Ananga-Ranga; (Stage of the Bodiless One) or, The Hindu Art of Love (Ars Amoris Indica)* (Cosmopoli: Printed for the Kama Shastra Society, 1885);

Luiz de Camoëns, *Os Lusiadas (The Lusiads),* 2 volumes (London: Quaritch, 1880);

The Kama Sutra of Vatsayana, seven parts (London & Benares: Printed for the Hindoo Kama Shastra Society, 1883);

Camoëns, *The Lyricks. Part 1, Part II (Sonnets, Canzons, Odes, and Sextines)* (London: Quaritch, 1884);

A Plain and Literal Translation of the Arabian Nights' Entertainments, Now Entitled The Book of the Thousand Nights and a Night, 10 volumes (Benares: Printed for the Kama Shastra Society, 1885);

Supplemental Nights to the Book of The Thousand Nights and a Night, 6 volumes (Benares: Printed for the Kama Shastra Society, 1886-1888);

J. M. Pereira da Silva, *Manuel de Moraes, A Chronicle of the Seventeenth Century,* translated by Burton and Isabel Burton, bound with Isabel Burton's translation of *Iraçéma, The Honey-lips,* by J. de Alencar (London: Bickers, 1886);

The Perfumed Garden of the Cheikh Nefzaoui, A Manual of Arabian Erotology, translated from the French by Burton (7[?] parts, Cosmopoli: Printed for the Kama Shastra Society, 1886);

The Behâristân (Abode of Spring) By Jâmi. A Literal Translation from the Persian (Benares: Printed for the Kama Shastra Society, 1887);

The Gulistân or Rose Garden of Sa'di (Benares: Printed for the Kama Shastra Society, 1888);

Priapeia or the Sportive Epigrams of divers Poets on Priapus: the Latin Text now for the first time Englished in Verse and Prose (the Metrical Version by "Outidanos") with Introduction, Notes Explanatory and Illustrative, and Excursus by "Neaniskos," translated by Burton as Outidanos and Leonard C. Smithers as Neaniskos (Cosmopoli: Privately printed, 1890); Burton is responsible for the poetry translation;

Giovanni Battista Basile, *Il Pentamerone; or, the Tale of Tales,* 2 volumes (London: Henry, 1893);

The Carmina of Caius Valerius Catullus, Now first completely Englished into Verse and Prose, translated by Burton and Smithers (London: Privately printed, 1894).

OTHER: Randolph B. Marcy, *The Prairie Traveller, A Handbook for Overland Expeditions. With Il-*

lustrations, and Itineraries of the Principal Routes between the Mississippi and the Pacific, and a Map, edited by Burton (London: Trübner, 1863);

Wit and Wisdom from West Africa; or, A Book of Proverbial Philosophy, Idioms, Enigmas, and Laconisms, compiled by Burton (London: Tinsley, 1865);

Vikram and the Vampire, or Tales of Hindu Devilry, adapted by Burton (London: Longmans, Green, 1869);

The Captivity of Hans Stade of Hesse, in A.D. 1547-1555, Among the Wild Tribes of Eastern Brazil, translated by Albert Tootal, annotated by Burton (London: Printed for the Hakluyt Society, 1874);

Arthur Leared, *Marocco and the Moors: Being an Account of Travels, with a General Description of the Country and Its People,* second edition, revised and edited by Burton (London: Low, Marston, Searle & Rivington/New York: Scribner & Welford, 1891).

Sir Richard F. Burton, one of the most widely traveled, best read, and most fascinating of Victorian adventurers, was a prolific writer who left enduring accounts of his journeys in India, Arabia, Africa, and North America. He brought to his scholarship and explorations a sophisticated detachment unmatched by his peers and made significant contributions to anthropology, ethnology, archaeology, and geography. His educated curiosity extended to botany, geology, meteorology, medicine, architecture, and the study of religions. A superb swordsman, he began this extraordinary career as a soldier in India and ended it in Trieste, at his fourth consular post. The avenue for Burton's curiosity and ambition was his linguistic talent: he mastered forty languages and dialects, and produced sixteen translations. The most famous of these is his definitive translation of *The Arabian Nights* (1885), but he also tackled materials as diverse as Portuguese poetry and Sanskrit erotica.

Translations account for only a part of Burton's prodigious literary output. He wrote two long poems, *Stone Talk* (1865) and *The Kasîdah* (1880), but his best original writings are his volumes on travel and exploration, his notes and appendices to the *Arabian Nights,* and his more than one hundred articles, most of them written for the journals of organizations such as the Anthropological Society, which he helped to found, and the Royal Geographical Society, which awarded him a gold medal in 1859. Norman M. Penzer's sampler of Burton's *Selected Papers on Anthropology, Travel and Exploration* (1924) reveals the startling range and diversity of Burton's interests.

In spite of Burton's many achievements, his life can be seen as a record of accumulated disappointments. His mother, Martha Beckwith Burton, virtually cheated him of formidable wealth by preventing the disinheritance of her prodigal brother, Burton's uncle. In a single gallant gesture, his father, Joseph Netterville Burton, threw away a promising military career by refusing to testify against Queen Caroline in the divorce case brought by George IV in 1820, the year before Richard Burton's birth. Reduced to half pay as a result of this act of defiance, Burton's father resigned his commission and moved his family to the Continent. In this way, Joseph Burton was largely responsible for making his son a stranger to his own country. Richard Burton's unconventional upbringing abroad alienated him from British society, while his fierce egotism and personal integrity made him many enemies among British officialdom. His outspokenness, exercised repeatedly in the face of authority, proved an obstacle to his success in more than one career. He was continually passed over for the awards, promotions, and appointments he deserved, and as he watched these prizes go to less talented rivals, he nursed an increasingly bitter sense of injury.

Burton, born on 19 March 1821, at Torquay, Devonshire, was raised, from his first year, on the Continent. Because Joseph Burton moved his family frequently, the three Burton children, Richard, Edward, and Maria, suffered from a lack of discipline and formal schooling. The lack of discipline is reflected in Burton's life and writing (he once called himself "a blaze of light, without a focus"), but also conspicuous are a breadth of experience and worldly sophistication attributable to his unusual childhood. From his perspective at a remove from the English society, he became an important critic of his countrymen's hypocrisy. Another result of Burton's upbringing was his taste for the romantic. He became the swashbuckling "Ruffian Dick," even to his friends. But though he reveled in shocking society with his deeds and disguises, he longed to be accepted and lionized by those he scorned, and in spite of his fierce individualism, he became an uncompromising imperialist.

Burton spent the first nine years of his life in Tours at a charming château on the banks of the Loire. The setting fed and gratified his romantic nature, as did the legend that he was descended, though illegitimately, from Louis XIV. He was extremely fond of Beauséjour, his château home, but

Burton disguised as a Moslem pilgrim on his way to Mecca

when Burton was nine the family entered a period of wandering, making fourteen moves in ten years. Although Burton's appetite for knowledge was prodigious, his haphazard education allowed him to indulge exclusively in those subjects which interested him. He applied himself to swimming, dancing, and, especially, fencing—eventually he would become one of the best swordsmen in Europe—and he gained a precocious expertise in European art and architecture. This cosmopolitanism extended to matters of pleasure. Burton familiarized himself with drink and prostitutes at the age of fifteen. His escapades of this period were early explorations into the secrets of life—and death. A characteristic adventure of his adolescence, combining truancy with ghoulish curiosity, was his masquerade as an undertaker's assistant in Naples during a devastating cholera epidemic. This impersonation foreshadowed later, mature explorations, also undertaken in disguise, in India, Arabia, and Africa, and, like the later expeditions, was motivated by a combined spirit of adventure and scientific inquiry.

During a brief acquaintance with public school, Burton had found England shabby and ignoble. Ten years later, when Edward was jailed after a drunken debauch with a group of medical students in Pisa, Joseph Burton packed the brothers off to university in England to study for the clergy. Richard Burton's experience of Oxford reinforced his early judgment of England. His first distinguishing act was to challenge a bewildered upperclassman to a duel for laughing at his mustachios. Nevertheless, Burton's wit, boxing prowess, and capacity for drink made him popular among the undergraduates. In his first bitter disappointment at the hands of authority, he was denied a fellowship in classical languages. Burton, who went on to become one of the Western world's leading authorities on the Arabs and their language, consoled himself by learning Arabic without the benefit of class or tutor. His last act at Oxford was to have himself sent down by deliberately provoking the college authorities. Joseph Burton finally acquiesced to the inevitable and bought his son a commission in the Indian army.

Burton's military career in India was his first contact with the exotic East. He was terribly disappointed with the squalor he found on his arrival in Bombay in October 1842. Nevertheless, he threw himself into the study of native languages and passed examinations in a variety of dialects. Knowledge of languages offered two advantages: special access to the lives and minds of native Indians and an avenue to promotion as translator for chief staff officers. He left India having mastered Hindustani, Sanskrit, Gujarti, Marathi, Persian, Sindi, Punjabi, Teluga, Pashto, Multani, Armenian, and Turkish, and was well on his way to becoming one of the greatest linguists of his time.

Contemptuous of the insulated English community in India, Burton mingled with the native population, thereby earning himself the sobriquet "the white nigger" from his fellow officers. In 1844 he was sent with the 18th Native Infantry to the northern province of Sind, now part of Pakistan, where he was assigned as a field surveyor to Captain Walter Scott, who became a devoted friend. In Sind, Burton's linguistic talents came to the attention of his chief, Sir Charles Napier, who recruited the young officer as a translator and intelligence officer. In the latter capacity, Burton infiltrated native society to report on such subjects as infanticide, wife-killing, homosexual prostitution, and the hiring of substitutes for execution. Burton's assignments generated the first of his legendary successes with disguise. As the half-Persian, half-Arab cloth merchant Mirza Abdullah, he passed freely through the bazaar and into the homes of Moslem Indians. Such an impersonation required an intimate knowledge of Islam, and with characteristic thoroughness he became a Master Sufi. Islam remained throughout his life the religion most congenial to his tastes.

India was also the scene of Burton's first career "disgrace," involving the emergence of a fascination with the sexually curious that would attend all of his later researches. As an anthropologist, Burton felt that sexual customs were an essential part of cultural identity. He often used what he found, particularly the Eastern appreciation of female sexuality, as a springboard for his criticism of Victorian prudery, and, at times, particularly early in his literary career, editors felt compelled to delete from his manuscripts what they considered "unpleasant garbage." In India Burton was commanded by his superior Napier to investigate the homosexual brothels in Karachi. Burton's clinically graphic report fell into unsympathetic hands on Napier's retirement, and Burton found his military career permanently hindered.

Although broken in body and spirit when he returned to England on sick leave, Burton produced four books on India within two years. Burton had contracted cholera during an epidemic in Sind in 1846. While recuperating, he collected material for *Goa, and the Blue Mountains; or, Six Months of Sick Leave* (1851), which includes accounts of the peoples of Goa, a district located south of Bombay on India's west coast; of the Malabar Hindus; and of the mountain-dwelling Todas who, because they practiced polyandry, appealed to Burton's unorthodox curiosity. The publication of his next book, *Scinde; or, The Unhappy Valley* (1851), a narrative of the journey he made with Scott in the northern province, marks Burton's debut as a capable anthropologist. His skill in anthropology reaches its apex in *Sindh, and the Races that Inhabit the Valley of the Indus* (1851), which, as Fawn M. Brodie notes in the 1967 biography *The Devil Drives,* has been evaluated as a "brilliant ethnological study." The volume on Sindh reveals the astonishing scope and diversity of Burton's interests. Its topics include the province's history, topography, commercial and military value, agriculture, crime and criminal law, literature, occult sciences, and social customs, especially the sensitive subjects of birth, nuptial, and death rites and circumcision. Although Burton's fourth work of the period, *Falconry in the Valley of the Indus* (1852), is primarily a handbook of the sport, like all of the Indian books, it contains a variety of matter. It is also extremely valuable, like the others, for its wealth of autobiographical detail. In *Falconry in the Valley of the Indus* Burton describes his masquerade as Mirza Abdullah; in *Scinde; or, The Unhappy Valley* (1851) he offers an account of his affair with a Persian girl; and in *Goa, and the Blue Mountains* he relates his attempted abduction of a beautiful young nun.

The books were fresh and perceptive, far in advance of their time in their detachment and objectivity. But they bewildered the press and sold badly. Burton's excesses, which proved characteristic of all his writings, were the result of his indiscriminate curiosity. Hastily written from his voluminous notes, his books are too encyclopedic; they lack proportion and are marred by digressions and displays of knowledge that violate their coherence. The lack of selectivity extends to his style. Critics have complained of his prolixity. Allusions, archaisms, foreign phrases, and coined words make many passages inaccessible to the general reader. But Burton's weakness is also his strength. In his introduction to a 1961 edition of Burton's *Lake Regions of Central Africa* (1860), Alan Moorehead calls Burton "a natural writer. Similes, witticisms, flights of imagination, scientific speculations and historical theories pour out of him in a bubbling irrepressible stream. . . . On a journey he sees more than other people because he knows more about the world." Burton had simply read more and done more than other travel writers, living with an intensity that gave tremendous vitality to his prose.

The Indian books contain all of the significant themes of Burton's writing. The most important of these is the clash of cultures precipitated by travel and residence abroad, an inevitable feature of English imperialism. Burton felt that the heart and mind of a people were accessible through their language and customs. As he claimed in "Proverbia Communia Syriaca," published as an appendix to his 1871 collaboration with Charles F. Tyrwhitt-Drake, *Unexplored Syria,* through proverbs "each people speaks out the truth or the half-truth which is in it." Because he believed that good government was based on knowing about the people, he saw the British brand of insulated colonialism as misrule.

For Burton, getting to know a people meant recognizing ways in which a foreign culture was superior to his own. He was fond of comparing

Drawing of El-Medinah by Burton, from his Personal Narrative of a Pilgrimage to El-Medinah and Meccah *(1855-1856)*

cultures in his writing, often to the disadvantage of the English. In India he admired native sensitivity to female sexuality; in the Arabian desert he envied the Bedouin lack of self-consciousness. In both cases, he suggested that his own society could draw lessons from these virtues. If he found much to emulate in other cultures, however, he never relinquished a sense of the difference between Western civilization and less "advanced" societies. Often this consciousness took the form of racism masquerading as social Darwinism. Burton *was* an imperialist, an attitude that may simply have been an extension of his immense personal egotism. Ironically, in his later life, his conviction of white superiority led him to argue against colonial expansion in Africa, where the natives, he felt, were incapable of being civilized; England would be wasting her time on such infertile soil.

From his earliest writing in India, Burton's researches into the nature of a people involved an exploration of the inner man, especially the secret, darker side of human nature. He examined, described, and experimented with the forbidden, hoping to penetrate the mysteries of thought and behavior. A forerunner of modern anthropologists and psychologists in his approach to sexuality, he fumed against his society's "immodest modesty," arguing that the act of love was normal and healthy. His interest in the erotic was part of a crusade to educate a prudish Victorian society about its own sexuality. But Burton's obsession with such subjects as castration and homosexuality has led many critics to suspect him of more than a scientific interest. In any case sensational topics, usually presented with clinical detachment, form a large part of his prose writings.

Burton was democratic in his condemnation of hypocrisy and incompetence and dealt his blows with heavy irony against both the Victorian establishment and the barbarism he witnessed abroad. His apparent objectivity seems to have had its roots in Burton's confusion about his own identity, to which both the variety of his vocations and his passion for disguise attest. He has often been described as a dual man, at once an individualist and an imperialist, both sympathetic and superior to the native Arab or Indian, both contemptuous and envious of British respectability. He raged at religious superstition, for instance, but embraced that mystic form of Islam, Sufism. The duality takes shape in Burton's writing in his strange combination of swashbuckling adventure story and detached presentation of scientific observation. Burton created of himself two heroes: the romantic adventurer and the serious scholar in whose writings storytelling is punctuated by erudite annotation.

From this period, too, dates Burton's *A Complete System of Bayonet Exercise* (1853), the first detailed instruction on the use of that weapon. With this thirty-six-page pamphlet, Burton hoped to make the British soldier a more efficient killing machine. He was criticized for his efforts, and the war office ignored the pamphlet until, sobered by the poor performance of British troops in the Crimea, they recognized the book's value and had it republished sending Burton permission to draw one shilling for service to the Crown. In a characteristic gesture of contempt, Burton collected his shilling and handed it to the first beggar he met.

In 1852 Burton approached the Royal Geographical Society with a plan that appealed to both his love of adventure and his scientific curiosity. Disguised as a Moslem pilgrim, he would penetrate the forbidden holy cities of Mecca and Medina. Burton's successful *hajj* earned him immediate notoriety as "Burton of Arabia" and generated his best-known, highly praised, three-volume travel book *Personal Narrative of a Pilgrimage to El-Medinah and Meccah* (1855-1856). Granted a year's leave of absence by the East India Company and funded by the Royal Geographical Society, he left for Alexandria in the spring of 1853. Disguised as a Pathan, or Indian Moslem of Afghan parentage, he remained in Alexandria to perfect his Arabic before boarding a Nile steamer for Cairo. From there, a desert crossing brought him to Suez and to the pilgrim ship *The Golden Wire,* on which he made the twelve-day voyage on the Red Sea to Yenbo. Another more taxing desert journey ended in Medina, where Burton remained for a month before leaving for Mecca.

Fastidious in the details of impersonation, which included having himself circumcised, he weathered many confrontations without detection. Confident in his disguise, he did not avoid contact with the Arabs, but made friends wherever he stayed and collected an entourage of colorful attendants and fellow travelers. The result of this bold undertaking was a classic adventure story, whose highlights include Burton's accounts of the grueling desert travel, a drunken debauch at a Cairo caravansary, a brawl aboard ship, and attacks by robber Bedouins. The book climaxes with Burton's dramatic entrance into the Kaaba, or the innermost chamber of the Great Mosque at Mecca.

Appendices account for almost a quarter of Burton's volume and often chapters of detailed discussions of architecture, religious ritual, and other topics interrupt the narrative flow. Yet the *Personal Narrative of a Pilgrimage to El-Medinah and Meccah* is Burton's most coherent travel book and may be his smoothest integration of experience and knowledge. Burton's primary objective had been to "see with my eyes Moslem inner life in a really Mohammedan country," and his book is remarkable for its wealth of information on the Islamic world and its insight into the Moslem culture and character. Reflecting Burton's moment of singular triumph, the style is exuberant and self-assured. The book contains some of his most memorable and eloquent prose, including the evocative passages on desert travel and on the voluptuous enjoyment of Arab *kayf,* or hemp-smoking.

After his Arabian adventure, Burton returned to duty in India, where he completed the *Personal Narrative.* Even before the book's publi-

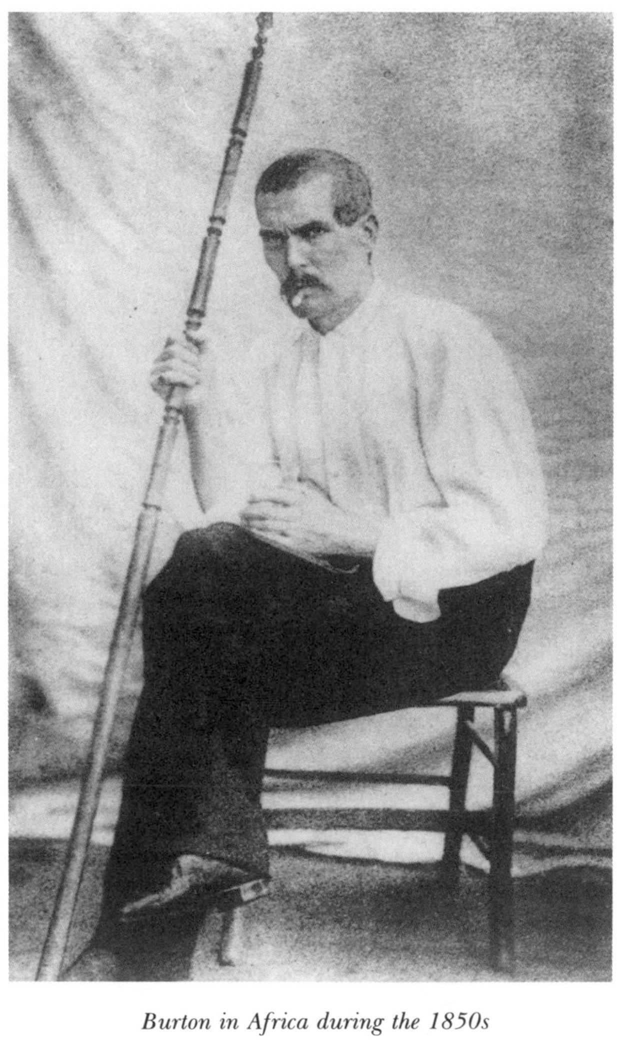

Burton in Africa during the 1850s

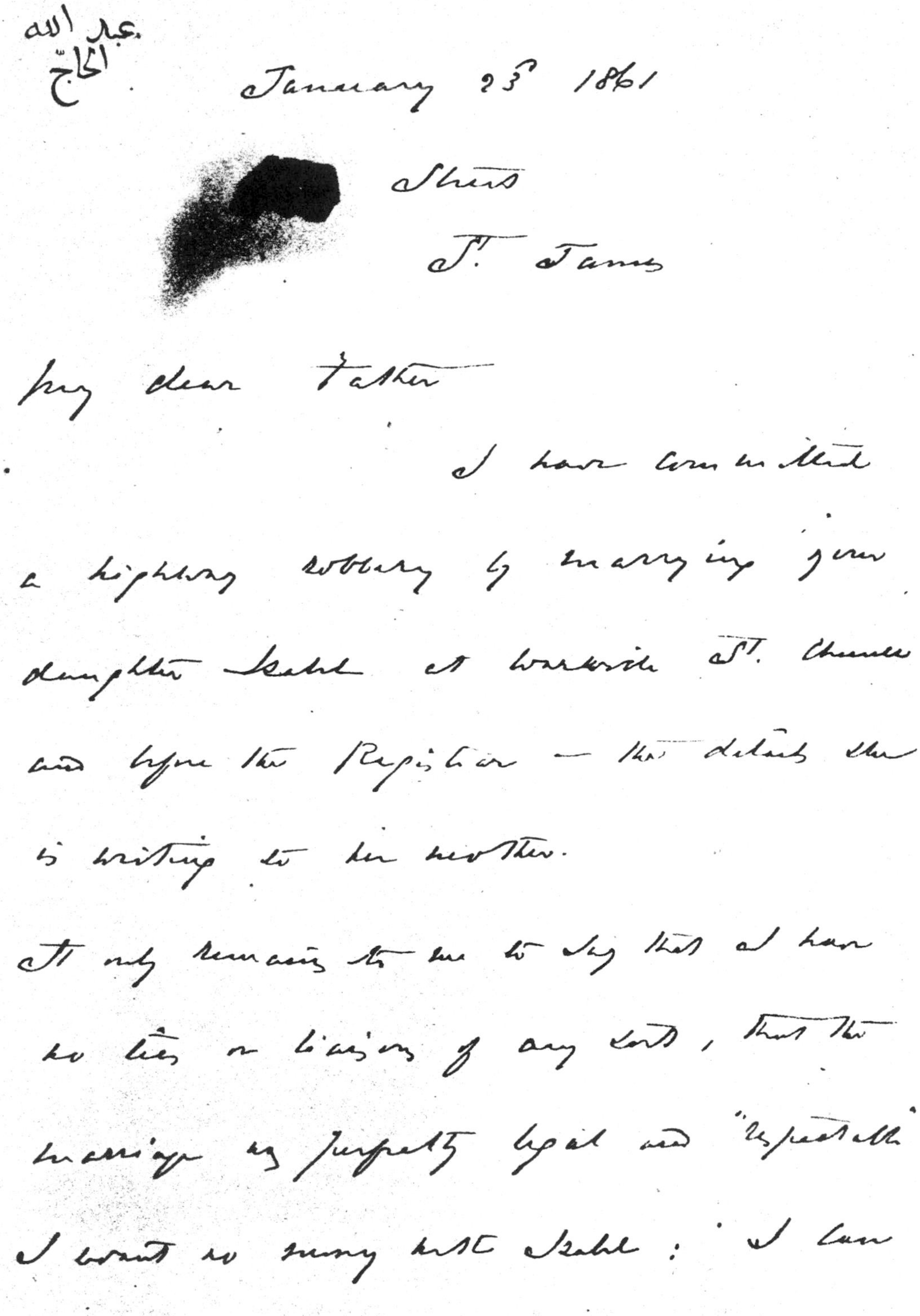

عبد الله
الحاج

January 23rd 1861

Street

St. James

My dear Father

I have committed a highway robbery by marrying your daughter Isabel at Warwick St. Church and before the Registrar — the details she is writing to her mother.

It only remains for me to say that I have no ties or liaisons of any sort, that the marriage is perfectly legal and "respectable." I want no money with Isabel: I can

Letter from Burton to Henry R. Arundell, announcing his recent marriage to Arundell's daughter, Isabel (Isabel Burton, The Life of Captain Sir Richard F. Burton, *1893)*

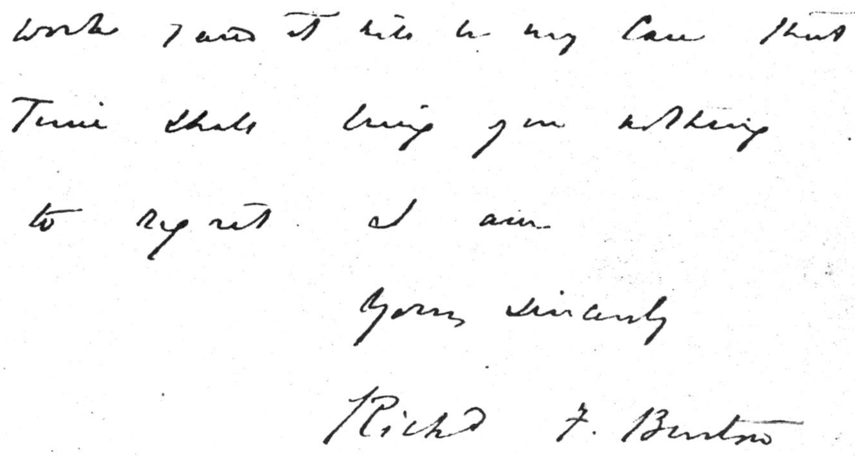
work [illegible] it lies in my case that
Time shall bring you nothing
to regret. I am
Yours sincerely
Richard F. Burton

Isabel Arundell Burton

cation, he had embarked on an exploration in East Africa to determine the value of Somaliland's productive resources. This expedition involved another dangerous journey, again in disguise, to the Moslem city of Harar. Burton chose three Indian army officers to assist him in this enterprise, surveyor and geologist Lt. G. E. Herne and two friends from the survey in Sind, Lt. William Stroyan and Assistant Surgeon J. E. Stocks. Stocks, the "universal favourite" as Burton called him, died before the expedition began, and Burton recruited as a replacement Lt. John Hanning Speke of the Bengal Native Infantry, who had come to Aden on leave to shoot specimens for his hunting collection. Burton assigned his assistants to explorations in Berbera and the gold-bearing region Wadi Nogal, reserving Harar for himself.

He left Aden on 29 October 1854, landing at Zayla, where he remained for twenty-six days before pushing on to Harar, accompanied on this journey by a party of native guides and attendants, who, like Burton's companions in Arabia, play an important role in his account of the adventure, published as *First Footsteps in East Africa* in 1856. Before entering Harar, Burton decided to abandon his disguise and approach the dreaded emir of the forbidden city as an emissary of the British political agent at Aden. To his great relief he was received graciously. On his return to rendezvous with his subordinates at Berbera, he took a shortcut across the desert which almost proved fatal. Burton's description of this leg of the journey provides one of the book's most tense and exciting episodes. *First Footsteps in East Africa* is one of his most entertaining books. The style is crisp and economical, lacking the bravado of the *Personal Narrative.* In addition, the footnotes are lively and anecdotal, with less of the ponderous scholarship Burton used in documenting later works. Because it was overshadowed by interest in the Crimean War, *First Footsteps in East Africa* did not receive the attention it deserved.

In *First Footsteps in East Africa* surfaces Burton's capacity for making enemies of important people, what he called his "impolitic habit of telling political truths." Having already outraged his superiors in the Bombay government by accurately predicting that their misrule would lead to an Indian mutiny, now, in an explosive preface, he attacked the British East India Company's timid African policy and advocated a ruthless imperialism. He also alienated Speke. Shortly after the four officers were reunited in Berbera, their camp was attacked by Somalis. Stroyan was killed, Speke was seriously wounded, and Burton received a javelin through the jaw. Burton consigned his account of the attack to a short chapter at the end of the book, choosing to devote the bulk of the narrative to his success at Harar. He minimized Speke's suffering and, in condescending fashion, rewrote as an appendix the diary Speke kept during the Wadi Nogal exploration.

Having recovered from his wound, Burton sought active duty in the Crimea, where he spent a frustrating year during which he was subject to his commander in chief Lord Raglan's prejudice against Indian army officers. In addition he was forced to watch with impotent rage as the incompetence of his superiors cost the lives of many British soldiers. The experience of the Crimea fueled his despair over his career and his contempt for authority.

Ignorant of Speke's rising hatred, Burton enlisted him for an exploration of Central Africa, which began in June 1857. Enduring great hardship and illness, in February 1858 they discovered Lake Tanganyika. While Burton recuperated among Arab friends in the village of Kazeh, Speke pushed on to discover the Victoria Nyanza, which he rightly proclaimed the source of the Nile. Burton's disbelief at Speke's assertion sparked a controversy between the two men that accelerated until 1864, when Speke died, the day before they were to debate the issue before the British Association for the Advancement of Science. In *The Lake Regions of Central Africa,* published in 1860, Burton ignored Speke's participation in the expedition, though he attacked him in the preface. In addition one of Burton's most surprising prejudices crystallized in this work. Whereas in earlier works he had been ambivalent toward native Indians, Arabs, and Somalis, all of his African books after *The Lake Regions of Central Africa* were distorted by a blinding contempt for the black race. Nevertheless, the book enjoyed a favorable press, and after a slow start in sales, demand increased significantly. *The Lake Regions of Central Africa* was admired for its accuracy and detail and served as an essential guide for the explorers who followed in Burton's wake.

Too ill to return home, Burton convalesced in Aden, reassured by Speke's promise to remain silent on their discoveries until Burton could join him in England. Speke betrayed his promise, going immediately to the Royal Geographical Society to proclaim the Victoria Nyanza the source of the Nile. He was lionized by the Society, which offered to fund a new expedition under his command. In May 1859, decimated by attacks of fever, Burton returned to a cool reception from the Society and to Speke's venomous accusations. The anguish he felt over this turn of events was compounded by the tragedy of his brother's mental illness, the result of a beating received during a native attack in Ceylon.

In 1860 Speke was preparing for a return to Africa. The only salve for Burton's wounded ego was a new expedition—another pilgrimage, in fact—this time to the Mormon capital, Salt Lake City, which had become a requisite tourist stop on the stagecoach ride from Missouri to California. In 1860 that journey was still fraught with the kind

"Capt. Burton, Traveller," 1863 portrait by Ernest Edwards (Collection of Mrs. Christopher Wood)

of hardships and dangers that Burton enjoyed. In addition, because previous travelers had condemned the Mormon practice of polygamy, Burton was able to use his observations in Utah to challenge conventional attitudes toward two of his favorite subjects, religion and sex. Integrating seven hundred pages of notes with his usual formidable reading, he produced one of his finest travel books, *The City of the Saints and Across the Rocky Mountains to California* (1861).

A special strength of the book is the appealing objectivity with which Burton approaches potentially sensational subjects, such as Mormon domestic life and the Indian mutilation of victims. In Salt Lake City Burton met the Mormon prophet Brigham Young and was favorably impressed. The famous polygamist was not at all the profligate his critics described. The Mormon "harem" appeared to Burton to be an arrangement beneficial to both the health of the woman and the morals of the man. In fact, Burton found the Mormon practice of polygamy almost too puritanical because it replaced love with a sense of communal responsibility.

Richard and Isabel Burton with Burton's personal physician, Dr. F. Grenfell Baker

Burton returned from his journey through the American West to marry Isabel Arundell. He had first met his wife in France in 1850 during the sick leave that followed the Karachi report. Although Isabel secretly determined to marry him, they did not enter into a serious courtship until 1856, the year after Burton's return from the Crimea. In the eyes of most British matrons, Burton was a demonic figure and hardly a suitable choice for a son-in-law. His behavior in society—he could be willfully rude and loved to shock—did little to soften the image conveyed by his controversial reputation. Not surprisingly, Isabel Arundell's mother forbade the match. Although Burton had proposed marriage before leaving on the Nile expedition, Isabel was still equivocating when he returned half dead from fever to face Speke's betrayal. This additional burden must have sorely tried him, for he gave her an ultimatum before leaving for America: she must choose between him and her mother. He would expect a firm decision either way on his return. Back in London in January 1861, he found Isabel resolved to marry him, and a secret wedding was held on the twenty-second of the month.

Isabel Arundell was a devout, convent-bred Roman Catholic. Although a mature twenty-nine at the time of her marriage, she was, by most reports, fatuous, superstitious, and cloyingly sentimental. Burton's exploits and bearing fulfilled her naive fantasies about love and adventure. She idolized him, but was never reconciled to the dark side of his romantic nature, that is, his preoccupation with the erotic and the grotesque; and she was distressed by his scorn for her religion. Burton's marriage was a turning point in his career, heralding the decline of his powers as both an explorer and a travel writer. He became a diplomat, an anomalous career for so outspoken a man, and spent most of his remaining years at unremarkable consular posts abroad. Friends complained that Isabel had "tamed" Burton, but his decline is attributable to other influences as well, particularly his history of accumulated disappointments, culminating, perhaps, in the loss of his army commission. Instead of honoring Burton's request that he remain on half pay while serving as consul to Fernando Po, the Indian office struck him from the list in retaliation for Burton's having published correspondence which made the office look incompetent. This incident was one of many in which Burton's irreverent disregard for rank and rules cost dearly. In these circumstances, Isabel Burton's devotion, however smothering and unrealistic, became an important refuge.

Burton spent most of his final twenty-nine years in four consular posts abroad. Although his literary efforts during this period produced weak original work, they did much to establish his reputation as one of his century's greatest linguists. He was a polyglot whose versatility was revealed in the extraordinary variety of texts he translated, including Hindu devil legends, African proverbs, Indian sexual manuals, and Portuguese poetry. In 1865 Burton had published pseudonymously his first attempt at poetry, the political and social diatribe *Stone Talk,* only to have the copies bought and destroyed by the prudent Isabel, who feared damage to his career. His second and last poetic production was *The Kasîdah (couplets) of Hâjî Abdû El-Yezdî a Lay of the Higher Law* (1880). A much more successful work than *Stone Talk, The Kasîdah,* in fact, became one of Burton's most popular books. Although essentially an imitation of the *Rubáiyat of Omar Khayyám,* it has appeared in many editions since its first publication.

Burton alleviated the intolerable boredom and frustration of consular duty with frequent travel. Of his first appointment, from 1861 to 1864, as consul to the disease-ridden island off Africa's west coast, Fernando Po, he maintained, "They want me to die." He refused to take his new wife to live in "the white man's grave," as the island was known. The travel books of the consular years suffered from Burton's increasing contempt for most of humanity and for the African in particular; for once, a native population did not inspire his genius. Also, he tried less and less in his later books to maintain coherence among the varied materials he incorporated into his work.

The journal he kept of his trip along the coast to Fernando Po became his narrative *Wanderings in West Africa, From Liverpool to Fernando Po* (1863), which he signed simply with the initials F. R. G. S., Fellow of the Royal Geographical Society. This two-volume work touches on a tremendous variety of topics, on anything, it seems, that he saw and experienced, as he put it, "during the few hours allotted to him [a traveler] by the halts of the mail packet." He also wrote three travel accounts of his excursions into the interior of the continent. In *Two Trips to Gorilla Land and the Cataracts of the Congo* (1876), the last-published of the three, he debunks the myth of the indomitably ferocious gorilla and minimizes the horrific reputation of the Fan cannibal tribe. *Abeokuta and The Cameroons Mountains. An Exploration* (1863) is a high-spirited adventure narrative. *A Mission to Gelele, King of Dahome* (1864) is possibly the best of Burton's West African books. It describes his attempt to dissuade the notorious African King Gelele from the custom of human sacrifice and the practice of slave-trading. Dahome was also the home of the "Amazon army" of 2,500 trained women warriors. Burton found the reports of both the number of sacrifices and the prowess of the women soldiers, though based in fact, to have been exaggerated. He was disgusted in general by the Dahoman people, whom he considered degraded; nevertheless, his book has been praised for its anthropological detail and certainly makes for entertaining reading.

Burton's consulship in Brazil from 1865 to 1869 generated both travel and writing, but *The Highlands of Brazil* (1869) is a mediocre production; more successful is *Letters from the Battle-fields of Paraguay* (1870), a keen firsthand analysis of the war between Paraguay and the three allies Brazil, Argentina, and Uruguay, which had begun in 1864 and was four years old at the time of Burton's observation.

Release from the soul-deadening Brazilian consulship came with Burton's appointment to Damascus, a post for which his temperament and qualifications were ideally suited. One of the happiest periods of his life, the Damascus consulship (1869-1871) almost evolved into an illustrious term. Despite Burton's devotion and skill as administrator, however, his uncompromising sense of fair play and his wife's proselytizing earned them enemies among influential Jews, Moslems, and Greek Christians. The efforts of the Turkish governor of Syria and the British ambassador to Constantinople, which often misrepresented Burton's attempts to maintain peace among the many Damascene religious factions, resulted in Burton's being recalled from the only post he had enjoyed for many years.

Damascus kept Burton busy, but not writing. Only *Unexplored Syria* (1871), an archaeological study coauthored with Charles F. Tyrwhitt-Drake, emerged from his experiences there. Isabel Burton, however, produced the lively, gossipy *Inner Life of Syria, Palestine, and the Holy Land* (1875), which sold better than any of her husband's travel books.

From 1872 until his death in 1890, Burton fulfilled the dull and insignificant position of consul to Trieste. Although his duties there lacked challenge, he was comfortable and able to make frequent trips far afield. His unsuccessful gold-mining expeditions to the Midian desert in Egypt (1877-1880) and to the African Gold Coast (1881-1882) resulted in some weak travel writing, *The Gold-Mines*

Burton in Trieste three weeks before his death (Royal Anthropological Institute)

of Midian and The Ruined Midianite Cities (1878), *The Land of Midian (revisited)* (1879), and *To the Gold Coast for Gold* (1883), the third book a collaboration with Verney Lovett Cameron. Two notable prose works do date from this period. *Etruscan Bologna: A Study* (1876), a guidebook to archaeological ruins, is an admirable piece of scholarship, though it lacks originality. The 300-page *The Book of the Sword* (1884), in contrast, is an imaginative presentation of a wealth of socio-historical research on the weapon.

Trieste did allow Burton the leisure to complete his masterpiece, ten volumes of *A Plain and Literal Translation of the Arabian Nights' Entertainments* (1885). Burton had long wanted to publish an "uncastrated" translation of the ribald tales. A "labour of love," in Burton's words, that occupied more than twenty-five years, the translation epitomized his role as interpreter of East to West, for Burton was his era's foremost Orientalist. Burton's remains the most complete version, and Burton alone captures the flavor of the original by rendering the tales, he notes in the foreword, "as the Arab would have written [them] in English." Despite archaisms and coinages, the prose is one of exotic beauty. It is also exuberant, earthy, and unembarrassed. The notes and appendices are as bold as the text. While much of the famous discussions of sex education for women, castration, circumcision, and homosexuality appears to bear no relation to *The Arabian Nights,* the scholarship on which they are based illuminates the Eastern mentality Burton meant to convey.

Aware of the potential for lawsuits, Burton had only 1,000 copies printed at his own expense, naming as publisher the Kama Shastra Society, which he had fabricated in the winter of 1882-1883 with F. F. Arbuthnot to produce their joint translations of Indian sexual manuals. Although *The Arabian Nights* elicited almost universal praise for its beauty and integrity, the few exceptions were violent. Henry Reeve concluded in the *Edinburgh Review,* "Burton for the sewers." Burton had prepared for such a response. In his "Terminal Essay" for the translation, and later in an appendix to the six-volume *Supplemental Nights* (1886-1888), he argued that *The Arabian Nights* might be crude, but only the debased would find them titillating. The sixteen volumes of *The Arabian Nights* and the *Supplemental Nights* were Burton's first financial successes, bringing him a profit of 10,000 guineas. He had no illusions about the appeal of his "doubtful book": "Now that I know the tastes of England, we need never be without money."

Apart from his translation of *The Arabian Nights,* Burton's books did not sell well, but they exercised considerable influence on the English perception of the countries he visited. After 1861 the travel books declined in quality because of Burton's bitter irony and lack of focus. In the 1960s and 1970s several of the travel books appeared as modern reprints. *The Arabian Nights* continues to enjoy popularity and is occasionally republished. In 1964 the notes and appendices to the translation were extracted and published separately in an edition by Kenneth Walker entitled *Love, War and Fancy: The Customs and Manners of the East, From Writings on the Arabian Nights.*

The Burtons' tomb at Mortlake, England

Glenn S. Burne's *Richard F. Burton* (1985) is the only book-length critical study of Burton's writing. Norman M. Penzer's annotations to his bibliography are valuable. The two best modern biographies, by Fawn Brodie and Byron Farwell, contain brief, helpful evaluations of the books, and articles by Jonathan Bishop and M. E. Bradford deal with Burton's writing. Introductions to the modern republications of Burton's travel books and translations, Alan Moorehead's *The White Nile,* and Thomas J. Assad's *Three Victorian Travellers* are also useful sources.

Burton's final disappointment was the government's refusal to appoint him to the consulship in Morocco, for which he would have been ideally suited. As had happened often in his career, a much-less-qualified candidate was given the post. In 1886 he received a knighthood, long overdue in the opinion of many. In Trieste, Isabel Burton grew increasingly alarmed by Burton's translations of erotic texts and by his resistance to her efforts to convert him to Catholicism. After his death, she closeted herself with his voluminous notes, diaries, and manuscripts and, horrified, burned them.

Burton has been described as a Renaissance man, and it is true that he shone in three distinct areas of human endeavor. As an explorer, he took his place among other legends in their own time, David Livingstone, John Hanning Speke, Henry Morton Stanley, and Samuel White Baker. As a scientist, he joined the company of "inspired amateurs" such as Charles Darwin in revolutionizing the way Victorians looked at themselves: the anthropologist Burton has been seen as a forerunner of his twentieth-century counterparts in his approach to human sexuality. Finally, Burton the writer contributed among his many volumes and articles several classic travel accounts and his brilliant translation of *The Arabian Nights.* Contemporaries and later biographers, however, have consistently asserted of Burton that the man was greater than his writings or his other accomplishments. It was the personality of Burton that exercised the greatest influence on the imagination of his era, as well as on his closest friends, including the poets Algernon Swinburne and Richard Monckton Milnes. Although a contradictory man, insecure about his own identity, he embodied a combination of courage, intellect, and exoticism that thrilled his society. In his effort to bring East and West together, he came to represent the Orient to Victorians. More than anyone else, Burton created the image of the East for his time. Although he held a fundamentally imperialistic perspective, he drew a picture of the Arab people that was fuller and more sensitive than any that had come before.

Bibliographies:

Norman M. Penzer, *An Annotated Bibliography of Sir Richard Francis Burton, K.C.M.G.* (London: Philpot, 1923);

B. J. Kirkpatrick, *A Catalog of the Library of Sir Richard Francis Burton, K.C.M.G., Held by the Royal Anthropological Institute* (London: Royal Anthropological Institute, 1978).

Biographies:

Frances Hitchman, *Richard F. Burton,* 2 volumes (London: Low, Marston, Searle & Rivington, 1887);

Isabel Burton, *The Life of Captain Sir Richard F. Burton,* 2 volumes (London: Chapman & Hall, 1893);

Georgiana Sisted, *The True Life of Capt. Sir Richard F. Burton* (London: Nichols, 1896);

Thomas Wright, *The Life of Sir Richard Burton,* 2 volumes (London: Everett, 1906);

Walter Phelps Dodge, *The Real Sir Richard Burton* (London: Unwin, 1907);

Byron Farwell, *Burton* (London: Longmans, 1963; New York: Holt, Rinehart & Winston, 1963);

Fawn M. Brodie, *The Devil Drives: A Life of Sir Richard Burton* (London: Eyre & Spottiswoode, 1967; New York: Norton, 1967);

Michael Hastings, *Sir Richard Burton* (New York: Coward, McCann & Geoghegan, 1978).

References:

Thomas J. Assad, *Three Victorian Travellers: Burton, Blunt, Doughty* (London: Routledge, 1964);

Jonathan Bishop, "The Identities of Sir Richard Burton: The Explorer as Actor," *Victorian Studies*, 1 (December 1957): 119-135;

M. E. Bradford, "Sir Richard Francis Burton and the Literature of Travel," *Sewanee Review*, 72 (October-December 1964): 720-724;

Fawn M. Brodie, Introduction to Burton's *City of the Saints* (New York: Knopf, 1963);

Glenn S. Burne, *Richard F. Burton* (Boston: Twayne, 1985);

Stanley Lane-Poole, Introduction to Burton's *Personal Narrative of a Pilgrimage to El-Medinah and Meccah* (London: Bell, 1898);

Alan Moorehead, Introduction to Burton's *The Lake Regions of Central Africa* (New York: Horizon, 1961);

Moorehead, *The White Nile* (New York: Harper, 1961);

C. W. Newbury, Introduction to Burton's *A Mission to Gelele* (London: Routledge, 1966);

Norman M. Penzer, Introduction to Burton's *Selected Papers on Anthropology, Travel and Exploration* (London: Philpot, 1924);

Kenneth Walker, Introduction to Burton's *Love, War and Fancy: The Customs and Manners of the East, From Writings on the Arabian Nights* (London: Kimber, 1964);

Gordon Waterfield, Introduction to Burton's *First Footsteps in East Africa* (London: Routledge, 1966).

Papers:

Manuscripts and letters by Burton are at the Royal Anthropological Institute, the British Library, and the Royal Geographical Society. The Trinity College Library, Cambridge, and the Huntington Library, San Marino, California, have collections of letters.

Jane Welsh Carlyle

(14 July 1801-21 April 1866)

Ian Campbell

University of Edinburgh

WORKS: *Letters and Memorials of Jane Welsh Carlyle,* prepared for publication by Thomas Carlyle, edited by James Anthony Froude (3 volumes, London: Longmans, Green, 1883; 2 volumes, New York: Scribners, 1883);

Early Letters of Jane Welsh Carlyle, Together with a Few of Later Years and Some of Thomas Carlyle, edited by David G. Ritchie (London: Sonnenschein, 1889);

New Letters and Memorials of Jane Welsh Carlyle, annotated by Thomas Carlyle, edited by Alexander Carlyle, 2 volumes (London & New York: John Lane/Bodley Head, 1903);

The Love Letters of Thomas Carlyle and Jane Welsh, edited by Alexander Carlyle, 2 volumes (London & New York: John Lane/Bodley Head, 1909);

Jane Welsh Carlyle: Letters to her Family, 1839-1863, edited by Leonard Huxley (London: Murray, 1924; Garden City: Doubleday, 1924);

Letters of Jane Welsh Carlyle to Joseph Neuberg, 1848-1862, edited by Townsend Scudder (London & New York: Oxford University Press, 1931);

Jane Welsh Carlyle: A New Selection of her Letters, edited by Trudy Bliss (London: Gollancz, 1949; New York: Macmillan, 1950);

The Collected Letters of Thomas and Jane Welsh Carlyle, edited by Charles Richard Sanders, K. J. Fielding, Clyde de L. Ryals, and others, volumes 1- (Durham: Duke University Press, 1970-);

I Too Am Here: Selections from the Letters of Jane Welsh Carlyle, edited by Alan and Mary McQueen Simpson (Cambridge: Cambridge University Press, 1977);

Thomas and Jane: Selected Letters From the Edinburgh University Library Collection, edited by Ian Campbell (Edinburgh: Friends of Edinburgh University Library, 1980).

Jane Welsh Carlyle, 1843 portrait by Gambardella

Because Jane Baillie Welsh Carlyle did not write for publication, she is most often remembered as the wife of the great Victorian Thomas Carlyle. Witty, liberated in her time, highly gifted, warm, intense, she might have smiled wryly at the idea of being recalled mainly as the wife of her famous husband, much as she loved and admired him—even in the dark later years of their marriage, when a combination of continued ill-health, on her part, and thoughtless fascination with Lord and Lady Ashburton and their set, on his, led to fits of depression and despair which caused her to destroy her journals and much of her other written work. Some writing does survive—most notably the incomparable expanded letter which forms an account of her visit to her native Haddington in 1849. Part diary, part confessional letter to her husband as the scenes of her childhood crowded in on her, it is written with keen observation and a strong sense of controlled emotional loss, and it makes the reader wish that more works from this sharp, witty mind had been preserved.

Jane Baillie Welsh, the daughter of John Welsh, a physician, and his wife, Grace ("Grizzie") Welsh, was born in Haddington, a small town near Edinburgh. She was an only child, clever, precocious, admired. Her mother was elegant and high-strung, her father hardworking and set for professional success until his early death in 1819 after catching a patient's infection. Jane Welsh never really recovered from the loss. Throughout her life she referred to "Him," not to her husband but to her father. (Oddly, after Jane had died, it was Carlyle who was to refer, obliquely but emotionally, to "Her.") Dr. Welsh's death meant straitened circumstances for his widow and daughter, and the story of Jane Welsh's girlhood is one of genteel restriction, chafing at the limitations of Haddington society relieved only by visits, most often to Edinburgh, and illuminated already by girlhood letters which show that a conventional exterior concealed a brilliant mind.

That mind found stimulation and development in the early 1820s when Jane Welsh met and slowly gravitated toward Thomas Carlyle. Already she had gained the attention of one of Scotland's most notable intellects, the charismatic Edward Irving, then at the threshold of his hectically brief preaching career at the Caledonian Chapel in London. But Irving was promised elsewhere, and, despite a strong mutual attraction between him and Jane, Irving introduced her to his closest friend, an unemployed, self-financing, restless, clever, socially graceless young writer and translator called Thomas Carlyle. Mrs. Welsh, dismayed, took a long time to approve the match, and, indeed, Jane Welsh had higher social ambitions than she thought Carlyle could fulfill. But an initial fascination with his intellectual abilities (which led her to overlook his gaucherie) slowly turned to love. In Thomas Carlyle she had found a correspondent to match her own talents, and their love letters, published in 1909, constitute one of the most remarkable records of the century. The multi-volume publication of *The Collected Letters of Thomas and Jane Welsh Carlyle,* in progress since 1970, is revealing fully the stature each achieved in that difficult art.

Jane Welsh married Thomas Carlyle on 17 October 1826, and there followed happy years in suburban Edinburgh until 1828 and increasingly difficult and lonely ones at their remote hill-farm, Craigenputtoch, in Dumfriesshire, until 1834, when they cut their links with Scotland and moved to London, settling in Chelsea to a new metropolitan life and, as it soon turned out, popularity. With *Sartor Resartus* published by the time the couple set up their home in Cheyne Row, Carlyle had added to the reputation already gained from his critical essays, and he became known in a small circle, but *The French Revolution* (1837), *Chartism* (1839), and *On Heroes, Hero-Worship & the Heroic in History* (1841) made him famous by the early 1840s. Fame brought society, and since the Carlyles were for many years too poor to make much of a figure

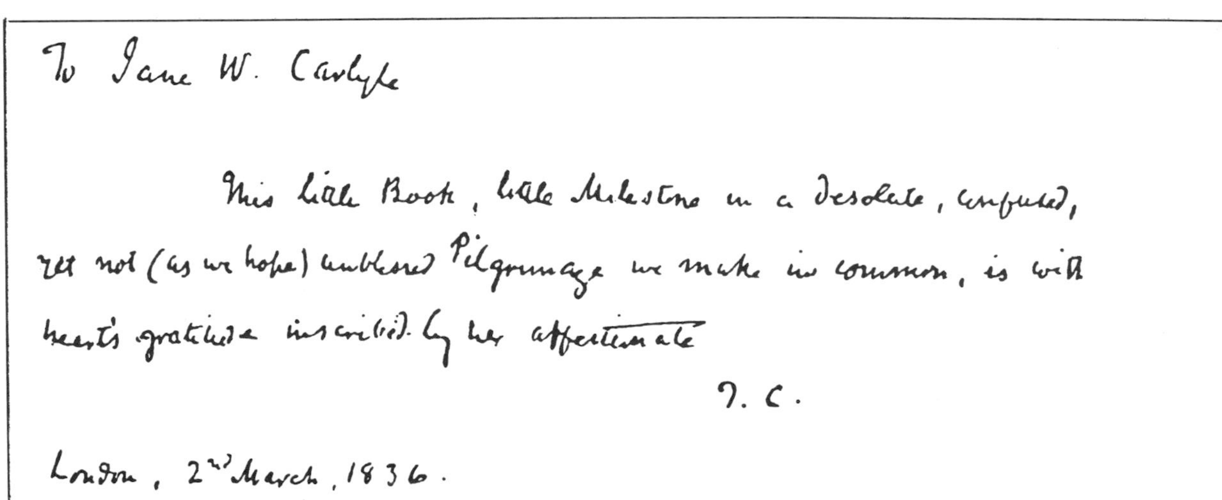
To Jane W. Carlyle

This little Book, little Milestone in a desolate, confused, yet not (as we hope) unblessed Pilgrimage we make in common, is with heart's gratitude inscribed by her affectionate

T. C.

London, 2d March, 1836.

Thomas Carlyle's inscription to his wife in Sartor Resartus

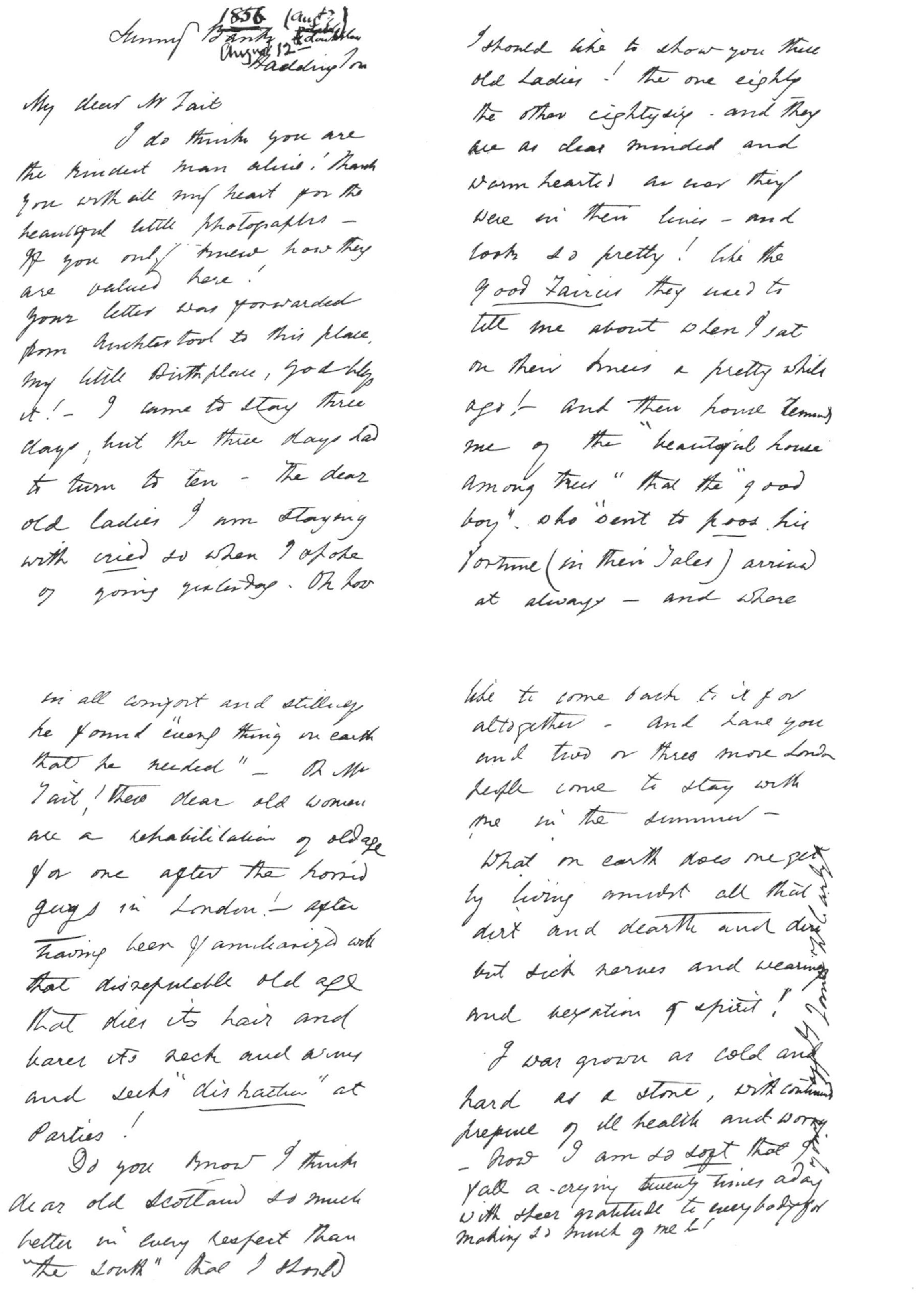
1856 (Augt?)
Sunny Bank, Haddington
August 12

My dear Mr Tait

I do think you are the kindest man alive! Thank you with all my heart for the beautiful little photographs — If you only knew how they are valued here!

Your letter was forwarded from Auchtertool to this place, my little Birthplace, God help it! — I came to stay three days, but the three days had to turn to ten — The dear old ladies I am staying with cried so when I spoke of going yesterday. Oh how I should like to show you these old Ladies! the one eighty the other eighty six — and they are as clear minded and warm hearted as ever they were in their lives — and look so pretty! like the Good Fairies they used to tell me about when I sat on their knees a pretty while ago! — And their house reminds me of the "beautiful house among trees" that the "good boy" who went to seek his fortune (in their Tales) arrived at always — and where in all comfort and stillness he found "every thing on earth that he needed" — Oh Mr Tait! these dear old women are a rehabilitation of old age for me after the horrid guys in London! — after having been familiarized with that disreputable old age that dyes its hair and bares its neck and arms and seeks "dissipation" at Parties!

Do you know I think dear old Scotland so much better in every respect than "the South" that I should like to come back to it for altogether — and have you and two or three more London people come to stay with me in the summer —

What on earth does one get by living amidst all that dirt and dearth and din but sick nerves and weariness and vexation of spirit!

I was grown as cold and hard as a stone, with continued presence of ill health and worry — Now I am so soft that I fall a-crying twenty times a day with sheer gratitude to everybody for making so much of me!

Yours affly
Jane Carlyle

Letter from Jane Carlyle to London painter Robert S. Tait, who had sent her some photographs of her mother. The letter, published in Reginald Blunt's The Carlyles' Chelsea Home *(1895), is dated in Tait's hand.*

"Thomas and Jane Carlyle in the Drawing Room of their House in Cheyne Row," painting by Robert S. Tait that hangs in Carlyle House, London (The Marquis of Northampton)

in London, they early found their forte in welcoming people to Cheyne Row for tea and conversation. Each of them excelled in conversation as they did in correspondence, with the same individual talents. Carlyle's was a thunderous monologue which mystified, enraged, and exalted. Jane Carlyle provided the witty underlay which set Carlyle's topics for him, which punctured his pretensions, which added a human warmth often missing when the Sage, as he was known, was in a denunciatory mood. Alone, she commanded the stage effortlessly, being possessed of a fluent tongue and a sharp one. Her friends found her sometimes too fluent, sometimes too sharp, but there is a wealth of evidence—the diaries of William Allingham and Francis Espinasse, occasional comments in scores of Victorian correspondences and biographies, the recorded verbal testimony of Charles Dickens—that hers was a magnetic personality and that she exercised a strong influence over her circle (and it was a circle large enough to include Dickens and John Forster, Geraldine Jewsbury and Harriet Martineau, Giuseppe Mazzini and Count d'Orsay, James Anthony Froude and Espinasse and Allingham). Some she found difficult—Ralph Waldo Emerson was one of Carlyle's friends she never could quite accept—and some she mocked openly or quietly: John Stuart Mill for his affair with Harriet Taylor, Harriet Martineau for her scarcely concealed worship for Carlyle.

Jane Carlyle was fiercely unconventional, in small things such as etiquette of street and restaurant behavior; she liked to shock and was not in any way restrained by the quiet pieties her circle and her class might have suggested. When Carlyle's affairs had to be argued before the income tax commissioners it was Jane Carlyle who went and who carried her point. When neighbors had to be tactfully handled, or tradesmen coerced, the work fell not to the thunderous Carlyle, who in truth hated confrontations, but to Jane who efficiently faced up to any domestic unpleasantness. There was, in short, a real and fascinating person behind the façade of the wife of Thomas Carlyle. She read widely, listened to gossip acutely, and held her own when it came to denunciation and nickname coinage, activities at which her husband was considered a master.

Jane Carlyle made a real impact on literary London from the early 1830s to the early 1860s, when her health gave serious cause for concern, but the repeated migraine headaches and neuralgic attacks that reduced her powers never extinguished them. Days before her death, she was the center of a merry party, to all intents and purposes on the road to recovery. But the strain on her heart told, and on 21 April 1866, while Carlyle was in Scotland holidaying after his installation as rector of Edinburgh University, she died suddenly while riding in a coach in Hyde Park. It was a thunderclap to Carlyle, who was scarcely to write another word for public consumption. As he said on the tombstone which he had made for her grave at Haddington, with her death, the light of his life went out.

Although Jane Carlyle burned her journals and notebooks, which must have indeed been startling, in the bitter years when she thought her childless marriage was to be loveless too and she was to lose her husband to Lady Ashburton, she made an important and vivid contribution to Victorian literature in her correspondence. Not all of it survives, and for long periods (for instance, the later Craigenputtoch years) she fell strangely and moodily silent, but many hundreds of her letters do remain, and they are splendid. In their self-revelatory moods (to her husband above all), wit (to her friend Kate Sterling), or tact (to her mother-in-law), in catty asides, in brief sunshine sketches, in domestic and social communications (dashed off to Erasmus Darwin and John Forster, two favorites), they show her extraordinary powers of vividness and insight. Her letters are brief, ungrammatical, unfinished in detail, but have the impetuous energy of good conversation. Through her letters (and many of the replies, for Carlyle and his wife preserved thousands of letters received, to the gratitude of their editors) we have vivid insights into Victorian London, into the émigré world of Mazzini, the liberated-female literary world of Geraldine Jewsbury, and the intense circles of the Darwins, the Sterlings, and the Wedgwoods, in whose company Jane Carlyle delighted.

Another notable feature of Jane Carlyle's achievement is as the inspiration for her husband's most important later work, which he wrote in response to her death. Stricken by loss of her (cruelly, at a time when his history of Frederick the Great was finished and there seemed some chance of semiretirement with Jane), Carlyle came absolutely to a standstill. Unable to produce after a lifetime of nervous self-discipline and haunted by memory and quiet, he turned to the composition of his *Reminiscences* (1881), one chapter of which is entirely devoted to Jane Carlyle. Several other chapters devote large sections to her, so that her witty presence haunts the evocative and painfully spontaneous pages of this great autobiography. When instinct made him stop writing the *Reminiscences* he turned to the gathering of Jane Carlyle's letters and fragments and to the long-term editing of her letters, endeavors which were partially accomplished in such projects as the *Letters and Memorials of Jane Welsh Carlyle* (1883) and *New Letters and Memorials of Jane Welsh Carlyle* (1903), published only after Carlyle's death. Each letter was agonized over, annotated, sometimes usefully, sometimes only with vain regrets, for the elegiac mood settled very fixedly on Carlyle after Jane's death. Sometimes a fragment sparked a reminiscence from Carlyle which is a masterpiece in miniature. It was a task Carlyle never completed, preserving and living up to the memory of his wife, but the posthumous publication of both *Reminiscences* and the letters had the dual effect of making Jane Carlyle famous and embroiling the memory of the Sage in controversy

Jane Welsh Carlyle, July 1854

which darkened his reputation for decades. Carlyle's intense relationship with Jane continued in what he wrote about her after her death, and the writing has a nervous directness which compels. "Am I now right to *leave* it," Carlyle asks, ending the chapter on Jane in *Reminiscences* with an apostrophe to his dead wife, "to take farewell of *Her* a second time? Right silent and serene is *She*, my lost Darling yonder, as I often think in my gloom; no sorrow more for *Her*,—nor will there be long for me."

Jane Baillie Welsh Carlyle deserves a place in literary history as a writer as well as the wife of Thomas Carlyle. She was part of the chemistry of a famous partnership which we only partly understand through surviving letters and papers and chance records of her fascinating conversation. Despite the vividness of her own letters and the brilliance of her husband's *Reminiscences*, a fuller understanding will always elude us.

Biography:

Lawrence Hanson and Elisabeth M. Hanson, *Necessary Evil: The Life of Jane Welsh Carlyle* (London: Constable, 1952).

References:

Reginald Blunt, *The Carlyles' Chelsea Home* (London: Bell, 1895);

James Anthony Froude, *Thomas Carlyle, A History of the First Forty Years of his Life, 1795-1835*, 2 volumes (London: Longmans, Green, 1882);

Froude, *Thomas Carlyle, A History of his Life in London, 1834-1881*, 2 volumes (London: Longmans, Green, 1884);

Henry Larkin, "Carlyle and Mrs. Carlyle: A Ten-Year Reminiscence," *British Quarterly Review*, 74 (July 1881): 15-45.

Papers:

The largest and most important collection of Jane Carlyle's letters is at the National Library of Scotland in Edinburgh. Other substantial collections are at Duke University, the British Library, the University of California, Santa Cruz, the New York Public Library (Berg Collection), and the University of Edinburgh.

Thomas Carlyle

Ian Campbell
University of Edinburgh

BIRTH: Ecclefechan, Annandale, Scotland, 4 December 1795, to James and Margaret Aitken Carlyle.

EDUCATION: Edinburgh University, 1809-1814.

MARRIAGE: 17 October 1826 to Jane Welsh.

DEATH: London, 5 February 1881.

SELECTED BOOKS: *The Life of Friedrich Schiller* (London: Printed for Taylor & Hessey, 1825; Boston: Carter, Hendee, 1833);

German Romance (4 volumes, Edinburgh: William Tait/London: Charles Tait, 1827; 2 volumes, Boston: Munroe, 1841);

Sartor Resartus (Boston: Munroe, 1836; London: Saunders & Otley, 1838);

The French Revolution: A History (3 volumes, London: Fraser, 1837; 2 volumes, Boston: Little & Brown, 1838);

Critical and Miscellaneous Essays, 4 volumes (Boston: Munroe, 1838; London: Fraser, 1839);

Chartism (London: Fraser, 1839; Boston: Little & Brown, 1840);

On Heroes, Hero-Worship & the Heroic in History (London: Fraser, 1841; New York: Appleton, 1841);

Past and Present (London: Chapman & Hall, 1843; Boston: Little & Brown, 1843);

Oliver Cromwell's Letters and Speeches (3 volumes, London: Chapman & Hall, 1845-1846; 2 volumes, New York: Wiley & Putnam, 1846; revised and enlarged, 3 volumes, London: Chapman & Hall, 1846; revised and enlarged again, 4 volumes, London: Chapman & Hall, 1850);

Latter-Day Pamphlets, eight pamphlets bound together (London: Chapman & Hall, 1850; Boston: Phillips, Sampson, 1850);

The Life of John Sterling (London: Chapman & Hall, 1851; Boston: Phillips, Sampson, 1851);

Occasional Discourse on the Nigger Question (London: Bosworth, 1853);

History of Friedrich II. of Prussia, called Frederick the Great, 6 volumes (London: Chapman & Hall, 1858-1865; New York: Harper, 1858-1866);

Inaugural Address at Edinburgh, April 2nd, 1866 (Edinburgh: Edmonston & Douglas/London: Chapman & Hall, 1866); enlarged as *On the Choice of Books*, includes letters by Carlyle (London: Hotten, 1869; Boston: Osgood, 1877);

THOMAS CARLYLE,
ÆT. 58.
Best likeness, known to me:
T. Carlyle (April 1869).

Photograph by Robert S. Tait taken in 1854 and used as the frontispiece for Reginald Blunt's The Carlyles' Chelsea Home *(1895)*

Shooting Niagara: and After? (London: Chapman & Hall, 1867);

The Early Kings of Norway: Also An Essay on the Portraits of John Knox (London: Chapman & Hall, 1875; New York: Harper, 1875);

Reminiscences by Thomas Carlyle, edited by James Anthony Froude (2 volumes, London: Longmans, Green, 1881; 1 volume, New York: Scribners, 1881);

Reminiscences of my Irish Journey in 1849 (London: Low, Marston, Searle & Rivington, 1882; New York: Harper, 1882);

Last Words of Thomas Carlyle, on Trades-Unions, Promoterism and The Signs of the Times (Edinburgh: William Paterson, 1882);

Reminiscences, edited by Charles Eliot Norton, 2 volumes (London & New York: Macmillan, 1887);

Last Words of Thomas Carlyle (London: Longmans, Green, 1892; New York: Appleton, 1892);

Carlyle's Unpublished Lectures: Lectures on the History of Literature or the Successive Periods of European Culture, Delivered in 1838, edited by R. P. Karkaria (London & Bombay: Kurwen, Kane, 1892); also published as *Lectures on the History of Literature, Delivered by Thomas Carlyle, April to July 1838,* edited by J. Reay Greene (London: Ellis & Elvey, 1892);

Wotton Reinfred, A Posthumous Novel (New York: Waverly, 1892);

Montaigne and Other Essays, Chiefly Biographical (London: Gowans, 1897; Philadelphia: Lippincott, 1897);

Historical Sketches of Notable Persons and Events in the Reigns of James I. and Charles I., edited by Alexander Carlyle (London: Chapman & Hall, 1898; London: Chapman & Hall/New York: Scribners, 1898);

Two Note Books of Thomas Carlyle from 23rd March 1822 to 16th May 1832, edited by Norton (New York: Grolier Club, 1898);

Collectanea. Thomas Carlyle, 1821-1855, edited by Samuel Arthur Jones (Canton, Pa.: Kirgate Press, 1903).

Collection: *The Works of Thomas Carlyle,* Centenary Edition, edited by H. D. Traill, 30 volumes (London: Chapman & Hall, 1896-1899; New York: Scribners, 1896-1901).

OTHER: *Letters and Memorials of Jane Welsh Carlyle,* prepared for publication by Carlyle, edited by

James Anthony Froude (3 volumes, London: Longmans, Green, 1883; 2 volumes, New York: Scribners, 1883);

New Letters and Memorials of Jane Welsh Carlyle, annotated by Carlyle, edited by Alexander Carlyle, 2 volumes (London & New York: John Lane/Bodley Head, 1903).

TRANSLATIONS: *Elements of Geometry and Trigonometry; with Notes. Translated from the French of A. M. Legendre,* translated with an introductory chapter by Carlyle, edited by David Brewster (Edinburgh: Oliver & Boyd, 1824); revised edition, edited by Charles Davis (New York: Ryan, 1828);

Wilhelm Meister's Apprenticeship. A Novel. From the German of Goethe, 3 volumes (Edinburgh: Oliver & Boyd/London: Whittaker, 1824; revised edition, London: Fraser, 1839; Philadelphia: Lea & Blanchard, 1840).

Thomas Carlyle was an extremely long-lived Victorian author. He was also highly controversial, variously regarded as sage and impious, a moral leader, a moral desperado, a radical, a conservative, a Christian. Contradictions were rampant in the works of early biographers, and in the later twentieth century he is still far from being understood by a generation of critics awakening to his pivotal place in nineteenth-century Britain. His major works, long out of print and never properly edited, are soon to appear in new editions, thanks to the Essential Carlyle project (University of California Press), under the general editorship of Murray Baumgarten. The staggering correspondence he and his wife conducted with each other and with their formidable circle of friends and acquaintances (a circle which touched Victorian Britain at every point) will further enhance his reputation when the long process of editing and publishing it reaches an end. By 1985 twelve volumes of the Duke-Edinburgh edition of *The Collected Letters of Thomas and Jane Welsh Carlyle* (Duke University Press), edited by Charles Richard Sanders and others, had appeared. Volumes thirteen through fifteen are expected in 1987, and a total of forty volumes is planned. Carlyle is emerging from neglect and obscurity, from the dubious reputation of early fascist (which damned him for many in the 1930s and 1940s) or reactionary, windbag, and sham. Instead he is coming to be seen as innovator and survivor, a man born in the eighteenth century who lived through most of the nineteenth, whose early work predated Victoria's accession, and whose longevity almost matched his monarch's. Alive, he was an enigma; dead, he remains a problematic figure for the literary historian as well as for the critic.

Carlyle was definitely a Scot. Ecclefechan, his birthplace in rural southwest Scotland, was a farming village remote from the cities but on the main routes to the universities of Scotland, and to the burgeoning industrial center of England. Thomas Carlyle was the eldest son of a large family. His intensely pious parents, James Carlyle, a stonemason of extraordinary strength of character, and Margaret Aitken Carlyle, quieter but still intense, intended Thomas Carlyle for the Church, but his personal belief soon outgrew the limitations of their desire. He inherited their verbal gifts, their intense energy, and their will to succeed; he left behind their piety and rural values, passing through high school and Edinburgh University with a precocious interest in literature, in science, and in Scotland, which was enduring the tribulations of the Napoleonic Wars and their aftermath. Carlyle was a voracious reader. He treated Edinburgh University distantly, reading on his own when he could, flinging himself into scientific and mathematical studies (which were his early ambition), restlessly trying out careers and rejecting teaching, the law, the Church, and free-lance translation and reviewing.

Early signs of lifelong dyspepsia date from these years, indicating long nights of reading and writing, a poor diet, and stress. An early affair with Margaret Gordon (Blumine in Carlyle's *Sartor Resartus*) shook his self-confidence, and his social links in Edinburgh became increasingly uneasy, particularly after he broke with his parents' Christian values. Though he never lost the broad outlines of the hierarchical, duty-dominated Calvinist world-picture of his youth, he found it sat uneasily with the new freedom of university reading and friendships, till in the early 1820s he discovered "a new Heaven and a new Earth" in German literature, in Schiller, and in Goethe. The result was electric: a clever but essentially sterile mathematical and scientific curiosity was transformed into the agency of a blazingly original synthesis of Carlyle's remaining Calvinist belief and his half-understood metaphysic and Romantic aspiration. The process of transformation, essentially, is the plot of the philosophical satire *Sartor Resartus* (1836): Carlyle's philosopher Diogenes Teufelsdröckh reflects his creator in his suffering and in the resolution of his life's crisis; happily, he speaks not only for Carlyle but for those many in the nineteenth century who found identification with orthodoxy in society and religion im-

Photograph and inscription published in The Love Letters of Thomas Carlyle and Jane Welsh *(1909), edited by Alexander Carlyle*

possible and who were equally dissatisfied with quiescence. Teufelsdröckh's reaction is protest that saturates *Sartor Resartus* with an energy that is now seen as the book's most brilliant sustained achievement.

The similarities between Carlyle and his philosopher-hero are remarkable, despite Carlyle's later denials that *Sartor Resartus* was autobiographical. While recognition of the work's universality came slowly (*Fraser's Magazine,* where *Sartor Resartus* appeared first, in serial form, was the object of some reader hostility and the book had very few initial comments or reviews), it did eventually surface. In London, in 1831-1832 and after 1834, Carlyle had a circle in which he functioned as spokesman for an intelligent, articulate group with members as diverse as Harriet Martineau and John Stuart Mill—and Ralph Waldo Emerson, as is well known, thought little of crossing the Atlantic to find the author of *Sartor Resartus.* The combination of energy, allusive style, and symbolic layers of manipulation make Carlyle's early message at once seemingly precise and elastic enough to permit a wealth of personal identification; like Tennyson's *In Memoriam, Sartor Resartus* allows a good deal of reader latitude in identifying precise meaning and recognizing personal allusion. The early 1830s were a time for steady, puzzled growth in Carlyle's artistic reputation. His wife, Jane, saw in *Sartor Resartus* a work of genius from the start; slowly, the nineteenth century came to share her opinion.

Carlyle the man found steady resolutions to the crises of early manhood. While he was adjusting his faith in the 1820s, the crisis of loneliness and rejection was steadily lessened by his growing literary success as a translator and then as essayist and by the personal satisfaction of meeting Jane Welsh, whom he assiduously courted through four difficult years of conversation and correspondence. They married on 17 October 1826 and settled in

Craigenputtoch, the hill-farm in Scotland where Carlyle worked on Sartor Resartus *(The National Trust for Scotland)*

an Edinburgh still enjoying the *éclat* of the Age of Scott. Finding it stimulating but too expensive, they moved to their celebrated fastness of Craigenputtoch, an isolated hill-farm in Dumfriesshire where they spent six years which saw the genesis of the essays eventually collected in Carlyle's *Critical and Miscellaneous Essays* (1838) and, more important, of *Sartor Resartus*. He hated the silence, but he found it enabled him to write. Jane Carlyle, a lively and sociable person and brilliant conversationalist and *raconteuse,* had had quite enough by 1834 when a little affluence enabled them to move to London while Carlyle wrote his first major popular success, *The French Revolution* (1837), which has become a celebrated piece of historical writing.

In suburban but inexpensive Chelsea (the house still survives as a museum) the Carlyles established a life-style which changed very little over the years. They were never rich, but became increasingly comfortable. They entertained frugally, but their guests included the wits and thinkers, writers and public figures of their age, who flocked to enjoy the salon and above all the company of two of the century's great conversationalists. Dickens, Forster, Browning, Tennyson, Mazzini, Jewsbury, Martineau—all literary London seemed to enjoy a night with the Carlyles, or an account of one from their friends. Carlyle talked stupendously, often overbearingly, but his conversation was always stimulating. An outsider to much that stamped the English gentleman, lacking the background of public school and English university, he gave a view of his times and his society which often shocked his audience by virtue of its originality (as in the analysis of a "mechanical" society in the 1829 piece "Signs of the Times"), but impressed them nonetheless with its cogent, simple (some would say simplified) message.

Much of what we see now as Carlyle's "message" came from those early Scottish years—a Calvinist obsession with order, with duty, with work, with destiny; a fear of anarchy in the home, in the State, in international relations; an obsessive feeling that the times were morally degenerate; a narrow view of international affairs and an anti-intellectual view of the fine arts; a willingness to oversimplify, often knowingly, in order to make a start at reform, rather than allow visible degeneracy to proceed.

The Sage of Chelsea, or as some called him, the Sage of Ecclefechan, dominated a circle of disciples and cast a long shadow over distinguished contemporaries as various as Dickens and Tennyson, Browning and Forster, Elizabeth Cleghorn Gaskell and George Eliot. Jane Carlyle had her own circle, less famous, still intensely clever and often advanced in particular on the question of woman's rights. In public Jane Carlyle deferred to her famous husband; in private she was a formidable presence, supportive of his creative work, ensuring the domestic order he craved, accepting his increasing eccentricity, and, finally, tolerating with bitterness his indifference to her feelings, his fascination with the aristocracy and particularly with Lady Harriet Ashburton. Jane Carlyle's health weakened steadily in the 1850s and 1860s; with his history of Frederick the Great finally complete in 1865, Carlyle intended to settle back and enjoy domestic retirement with Jane, but by then Jane was exhausted, and in 1866 while Carlyle was absent in Edinburgh, on the occasion of his installation as rector of his alma mater, Jane Carlyle collapsed in London and died.

Jane's death had a remarkable effect on her husband. While he continued his voluminous correspondence and worked in private on a brilliant autobiographical document which was to be published posthumously as his *Reminiscences* (1881), Carlyle was a spent force as a public writer. Without Jane he became lonely, embittered, valetudinarian. He was courted by a large circle of admirers and still respected by many despite his political inclinations, which leaned further and further to the right with advancing age and which, with the polemic that stretched from the publication of his *Occasional Discourse on the Nigger Question* (1853) to *Shooting Niagara: and After?* (1867), finally alienated a whole generation of liberal thinkers including John Stuart Mill. Yet he was there, centrally a figure who had been in the public eye since the late 1820s, an innovator, a publicizer of new ideas, unquestionably an important writer and figurehead. When he died in 1881 there was a distinct sense that an era had ended.

Carlyle's early works, a translation of Goethe's *Wilhelm Meister's Apprenticeship* (1824), a biography of Friedrich Schiller (1825), and the four volumes of translations and biographical and critical notices entitled *German Romance* (1827), introduced to the British public those German writers who had opened new vistas for Carlyle himself. In the Bildungsroman *Wilhelm Meister's Apprenticeship,* Carlyle found that Goethe had given shape to what had seemed frighteningly shapeless in Carlyle's own life—the search for a faith, for an understanding of an apparently hostile and shapeless universe, and for a moral imperative to act on knowledge and self-knowledge. As Wilhelm Meister in his *Wanderjahre* moved away from sterile self-questioning to understanding and to action, and as Schiller resolved his personal problems to act and to produce great art, so Carlyle progressed to the world outside his study, the world of a Great Britain recovering from a major international conflict and grappling with the longer-term conflicts of industrialization, urban poverty, uncertain public and private faith, and a social system visibly ossified, visibly uncertain, yet fiercely resistant to the scale of change which seemed increasingly necessary to avert violence. In translating and studying German writers Carlyle found that personal problems very different from his own, yet clearly analogous, had solutions: in his early essays, Carlyle transferred that knowledge to analysis of his times and his country.

The 1829 essay "Signs of the Times" can be argued to mark the beginning of the Victorian age, even though Victoria was eight years from taking the throne. An original and clever piece of journalism, "Signs of the Times" ironically surveys the fallacies and weaknesses of a decade, sweetening a serious message which was developed two years later in another *Edinburgh Review* piece, "Characteristics." Briefly, that message had to do with the spiritual price to be paid for the industrial success and the onward movement of the early-nineteenth century: the reverberations of Carlyle's analysis were to be felt years later in Dickens's *Hard Times* (1854) and Elizabeth Cleghorn Gaskell's *North and South* (1855). "Mechanical" thinking, in Carlyle's description, accompanies and stultifies mechanical success. Man has moved mountains literally and metaphorically, but suddenly and without consideration. Reducing operatives to cyphers and giving up subtle and centuries-old mechanisms of an interdependent society, mankind has achieved miracles but discarded too much en route. Such, in brief, with amusing anecdotal outworks, is the message of Carlyle's early essays, which by the early 1840s were widely available on both sides of the Atlantic in the volumes entitled *Critical and Miscellaneous Essays.*

Several factors help account for their success. To make his points in these pieces Carlyle drew for illustrative purposes on his knowledge of Germans who wrote creatively (Goethe, Schiller) and philosophically (Kant), as well as on those who combined these functions (Richter, Novalis) to produce work which Carlyle frankly did not understand, but which he did manage to incorporate into his own original ideas (in, for example, "Thoughts on History," an often-reprinted periodical essay) and into the book which increasingly was forcing itself to the surface of his creative processes while he earned a living for Jane and himself with the essays.

Sartor Resartus is in some ways a baffling work. For one thing, its form is daringly experimental, borrowing the layered narrative techniques of Laurence Sterne and (less obviously) Henry Mackenzie and using multiple personae to present a chaotic picture of a chaotic reality. For another, the radicalism of Carlyle's work is cloaked and made oblique by a technique which aims at making impossible direct attribution to Carlyle of the radical premise (that the old clothes are worn out, that new clothes are needed, that violent change is not only desirable but also imminent). For the *source* of the narrative of Teufelsdröckh's life and career is, presumably, his editor, and the *source* of the editor's narrative is the conventional cache of papers, in this case some autobiographical, some analytic, some speculative, divided at random among a number of paper bags. From imperfect sources, with imperfect understanding, a fictional editor pieces together the story of the half-understood German mystic Teufelsdröckh, purportedly translating (seriously and frivolously by turns, as the sense dictated) from German originals and presenting the amalgam in an original and forceful exclamatory style.

Small wonder that the publisher's readers (whose puzzled comments Carlyle gleefully included in later editions) found it hard to cope with *Sartor Resartus*: genuinely original in form and content, it combines biography, autobiography, essay, and political commentary with a layered structure and avoidance of final meaning which makes it seem well in advance of its time. Its narrative thrust is to tell the story of a protagonist whose academic setting suggests that he should be taken seriously, though readers who possess a smattering of German can easily interpret both his name (Devil's Excrement) and his university (Nowhere in Particular) as obvious jokes. Teufelsdröckh follows a familiar path from struggling beginning and self-doubt to awakening sensitivity to a supernaturally alive universe, from the terrible "Everlasting NO" and "centre of indifference" to the explosion of energy and affirmation in the "Everlasting YEA" which marks the turning point of the book.

Typically, Carlyle mixes the serious with the almost farcical. In setting, name, manipulation of German for a largely ignorant readership, and manipulation of persona to hide overstatement, the book is clever tomfoolery. In passionate recollection of a personal descent into Hell reversed by a new, Goethean affirmation, in painfully oblique reminiscence of earlier rejection in love, society, and career, and in the undoubted frankness of a young man's renunciation of what is rotten in his society in favor of a juster and more egalitarian system, *Sartor Resartus* is unquestionably in deadly earnest. Jane Carlyle, a perceptive voice among early readers, pronounced it "a work of genius," and others took it as such (notably, Emerson) at a time when it was greeted with indifference or hostility. James Munroe of Boston had the honor of publishing *Sartor Resartus* in book form two years before it was published in London. The appearance of the three volumes of *The French Revolution,* in 1837 better acquainted readers with Carlyle's passionate style and his passionate belief in the need for society's rebirth, so that the seriousness of *Sartor Resartus* was more readily received, and now it is taken for a masterpiece, and rightly. To have conceived it on the Dumfriesshire moors was a major achievement: to have completed it made him ready to mix with his intellectual equals in London.

Settled in London, Carlyle found his environment changed and, with it, the process by which he wrote. Instead of the isolation of the Dumfriesshire hills, he had the stimulus of a major capital, its libraries (much as Carlyle execrated them as places to work), its personalities, its excitement. His thin nerves were no match for the noise and the pollution overtaking Chelsea even in 1834, but as an author he needed London. *The French Revolution* (1837) was the outcome of the first contact with the city and its riches. The libraries gave him resources for his scrupulous research. John Stuart Mill and his set gave him many ideas, either in serious discussion or in the verbal jousting they engaged in. The stream of visitors to Chelsea also gave Carlyle an audience. The loneliness of the creative process (Carlyle wrote with difficulty, revising endlessly) gave him a focus for the chaotic input of his very full life.

While writing *The French Revolution,* Carlyle suffered a severe setback—the loss of the handwritten draft for volume one. Though the episode is among the most famous in Victorian history, exactly what happened is not clear. It is known that the manuscript, messy and much rewritten in the course of Carlyle's hesitant creative process, was borrowed by Mill and that somehow it was mistaken for wastepaper and burned. Speculation as to how, when, and why the accident happened is impossible to corroborate: what is interesting is that, though

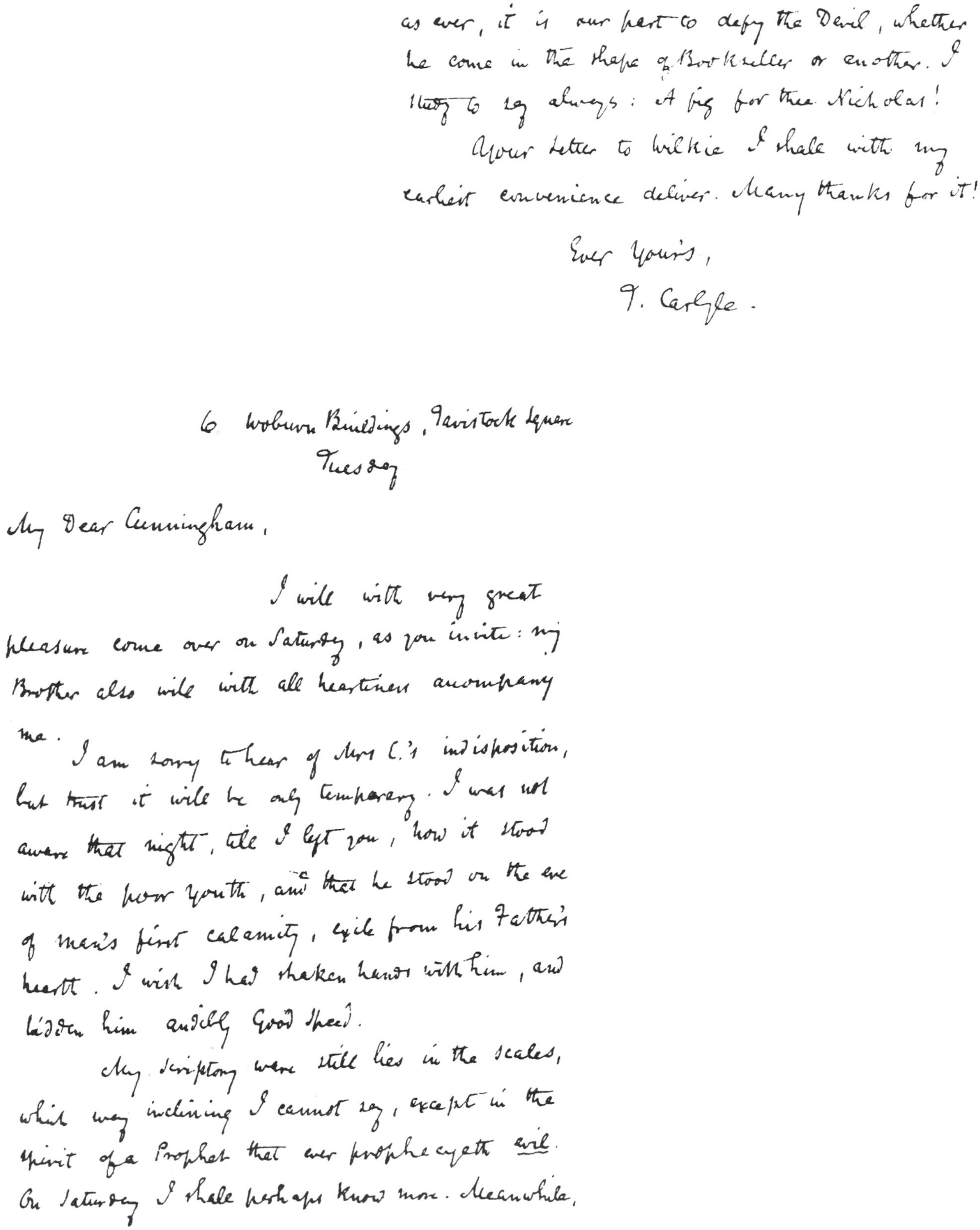

as ever, it is our part to defy the Devil, whether he come in the shape of Bookseller or another. I study to say always: A fig for thee Nicholas!

Your Letter to Wilkie I shall with my earliest convenience deliver. Many thanks for it!

Ever Yours,
T. Carlyle.

6 Woburn Buildings, Tavistock Square
Tuesday

My Dear Cunningham,

I will with very great pleasure come over on Saturday, as you invite: my Brother also will with all heartiness accompany me. I am sorry to hear of Mrs C.'s indisposition, but trust it will be only temporary. I was not aware that night, till I left you, how it stood with the poor Youth, and that he stood on the eve of man's first calamity, exile from his Father's hearth. I wish I had shaken hands with him, and bidden him audibly God speed.

My scriptory ware still lies in the scales, which way inclining I cannot say, except in the spirit of a Prophet that ever prophecyeth evil. On Saturday I shall perhaps know more. Meanwhile,

April 1831 letter from Carlyle to Dumfriesshire "mason-poet" Allan Cunningham, published in Reginald Blunt's The Carlyles' Chelsea Home *(1895). According to Blunt, " 'scriptory ware' no doubt refers to 'Sartor Resartus,' which was just then going the hopeless rounds of London publishers. . . ."*

Carlyle claimed to have kept no notes and to have rewritten volume one completely, fragments which survived the destruction tally very closely with the final published version. Although he may have kept some notes, the energy and courage Carlyle required to overcome his loss should not be underestimated. Perhaps it was inevitable that the warmest review of *The French Revolution* should have come from Mill. Others shared his enthusiasm: passionate, immediate, persuasive, *The French Revolution* touched events in the memories of many readers, and immediate in the history of many more. Fame and financial security followed this first major success, though not immediately.

While historians today have discredited much of the emphasis and interpretation Carlyle gave history in the volumes on France (and in the later works on Oliver Cromwell and Frederick the Great), few deny the power of Carlyle's view of the revolution. The historical research and annotation bespeak careful preparation, and the artistic impulse behind the finished work orders and selects, to orchestrate a pattern clearly of the author's choosing and to highlight his message of the inevitability of revolution in a France rotten with abused social privilege, skeptical freethinking, and human exploitation.

The French Revolution clearly articulates basic Carlylian principles: the king must rule, and the nobles effectively manage their estates; failing this, these orders of society must be put down. That a society based on bankrupt, mechanical, repetitive values will inevitably fail is taken for granted, and the magnificently described scenes of carnage and horror are presented not as aberration but as inevitable, tragic harvest after years of bad government. The Feast of Pikes, when blood ran in the streets of Paris, the storming of the Bastille, long enjoyed in isolation as bonbons of Victorian prose, should be seen in context as parts of Carlyle's argument that the French Revolution was history in action, the climax of a long and tragic plot, the letting-loose of the hounds of anarchy and popular revolution which could have been contained by strong and wise government, spiritual values, and good planning. Carlyle brought the conflict vividly to life for an audience who, in 1837, could remember uncomfortably the anarchy of Napoleonic war or Reform disturbance. The power of Carlyle as historian was not just to recreate the past but also to use his historical works to disturb the present.

Affluence came slowly. To eke out his early royalties, Carlyle had to give annual lectures, a process he detested and feared, yet which he seemed to perform with great public success, his normally impressive conversational and monologuing skills sharpened by nervousness and by the sense of occasion. His lectures on heroes, given in May 1840, were excellent. Published in 1841 as *On Heroes, Hero-Worship & the Heroic in History,* they pick up some of the main concerns of the volumes on the French Revolution.

The lectures, as Carlyle's title makes clear, are about heroes. Carlyle considered his own father a hero who had bred in him the view that heroes were necessary for both the individual and society as figures of support and guidance in morally difficult times. In *On Heroes,* Carlyle goes through history to select different great men in literature and in religion, in war and in peace, in the far past and in the recent past, but not—significantly—in Victorian Britain, which held few heroes for a man like Carlyle. He asks what each hero did for his age, and in every case he gives it shape, form, direction, values, coherence: often destructive, Carlyle's heroes prevented bloodshed, prevented anarchy, which even in the 1830s was a nightmare to many thinkers. Carlyle himself was becoming a hero to many. The ideas in *On Heroes, Hero-Worship & the Heroic in History* became some of his most widespread and influential. The lectures were republished many times, excerpted and made available to the new millions of literate poor. Their message was simple, clear, undemanding. Find your hero, give him your loyalty and your obedience. The times are dangerous, but follow your hero and fulfill your obligation to your creator. Christian and skeptic alike found in this clear and simple message a resonant faith, and Carlyle became more and more widely discussed.

Carlyle's 1839 work, *Chartism,* is about the Chartist movement seeking worker representation and rights for the industrious (and often starving) poor. *Past and Present,* published in 1843, is about the same contemporary problem, but Carlyle contrasts the nineteenth-century situation with that of the medieval monastery of St. Edmundsbury, in whose ordered community Carlyle found much to offer his age as a formula for improvement and reform.

In *Chartism* and *Past and Present* there is no spectacle of distinction comparable to that of the villainous aristocrats in *The French Revolution.* Instead the specter of anarchy and collapse is always in the wings, overtaking society not openly (as the phoenix is consumed at the end of *Sartor Resartus*), but implicitly, should the aristocracy not take their duties of government seriously, should social planners not wake up to the enormity of current problems, should the managerial class not buckle down to the duties of true management, should all society not redirect its social and ethical concerns to the whole complex framework of industrial Britain, its impoverished Irish and its impoverished urban and rural poor, its growing pollution, its increasing population, its emptying churches, its shaky educational ideals. The past of St. Edmundsbury was not pastoral idyll. In fact, the monastery had been revealed in historical records (the publication of which by the Camden Society in 1840 had spurred Carlyle) as corrupt and weakly governed, needing a new leader, who is found in Abbot Samson, to put things right sternly, inflexibly, unpityingly, heroically. Such a man, clearly, is needed for the Britain described in *Chartism,* and the need is pressingly conveyed by Carlyle's insistent rhetoric that makes use of repetition, questions, unusual syntax, and coinages to convince, to hector, to wheedle. Carlyle often annoyed his readers, but he was hard to ignore. He believed, overwhelmingly, in the wrongness of his society and rightness of his message. While people might dispute his message—they did in the 1830s, and many more did by the 1860s—they found it difficult to ignore the problems he cited. Something plainly was wrong when Chartist protest was necessary. Mrs. Gaskell's *Mary Barton* (1848) explores the problem from ground level in working-class Manchester: *Chartism* takes the aerial view, dizzying, the details blurred, the excitement unmistakable. And Carlyle the historian warns that the problem is not new, and the result has been terribly visible in recent European history.

By the early 1840s Carlyle's works were selling well, and each new book conveyed an original mind at the peak of its powers. *Oliver Cromwell's Letters and Speeches*—two volumes (1845) and a supplement (1846)—is a case in point. The civil war fascinated Carlyle for decades, and the personality of its great hero (and he certainly saw the Protector in this light, as the strong leader who saved the country from collapsing into anarchy) gave him the focus for a historical work which blends narrative with letters and documents of the period and intersperses all with the author's addresses to the figures he treats, especially Cromwell. It is an extraordinary history, almost a dialogue with a dead hero. It was provocative, original, fiercely contested at the time of its publication and more so when Carlyle was deceived by patent forgeries of Cromwellian letters—the celebrated "Squire Letters"—offered him after he had completed the basic writing of his history. Carlyle accepted the letters uncritically and stubbornly clung to his belief in their authenticity after they had been revealed to the reasonable as forgeries. Just such a weakness makes it easy to criticize Carlyle's method and his conclusions: his method was intuitive, and his admiration for character (often on apparently inconsequential grounds) overrode many critical mechanisms which could have ensured greater objectivity. Carlyle's primary aim was to present a point of view, an analysis of past events, which could be read and understood by his contemporaries and applied to his own time *mutatis mutandis.* Cromwell's methods were direct and crude; they violated human rights—but they saved a country which was tearing itself apart in civil war. Carlyle's unambiguous stand on this issue (which hardened throughout the remainder of his life) shaped his following, steadily alienated liberal thinkers, sparked public argument, and made many politicians and thinkers uneasy.

In private life, paradoxical Carlyle could monologue for hours about the virtues of Cromwell and benign force, of the need for radical disciplined reform, yet reconcile these views with the delightful sense of humor and self-deprecatory ridicule which made him magnificent company. The public persona he put forth in his writing hardened in this period into that of a largely inflexible analyst of his times. He did, however, produce the whimsical, affectionate, autobiographically revealing *The Life of John Sterling* in 1851. Sterling was an essayist and poet who shared an intense friendship with Carlyle despite his anguished attempts to get Carlyle to state his religious position clearly and without pretense. (This Carlyle would not—perhaps by this time could not—do, being at the same time a great symbol of public Christian faith and conformity, and a private nonchurchgoer and at best a partial believer.) Carlyle's tribute to Sterling is one of the most approachable of his works, rich in interesting reminiscences, including Carlyle's recollection of Coleridge of Highgate Hill, which tells much about Coleridge in his old age, but even more about Carlyle in his early years.

The *Latter-Day Pamphlets* (1850), *Occasional Discourse on the Nigger Question* (1853), and *Shooting Niagara: and After?* (1867) are late Carlyle, and they share a set of ideas which had developed over the years and which, for many, colored the character of the sage of Chelsea. To be sure, they are the work of a man well into his maturity, in his sixties and seventies increasingly set in his ways and impressed by the accelerating chaos he perceived around him. They represent bitter, unyielding op-

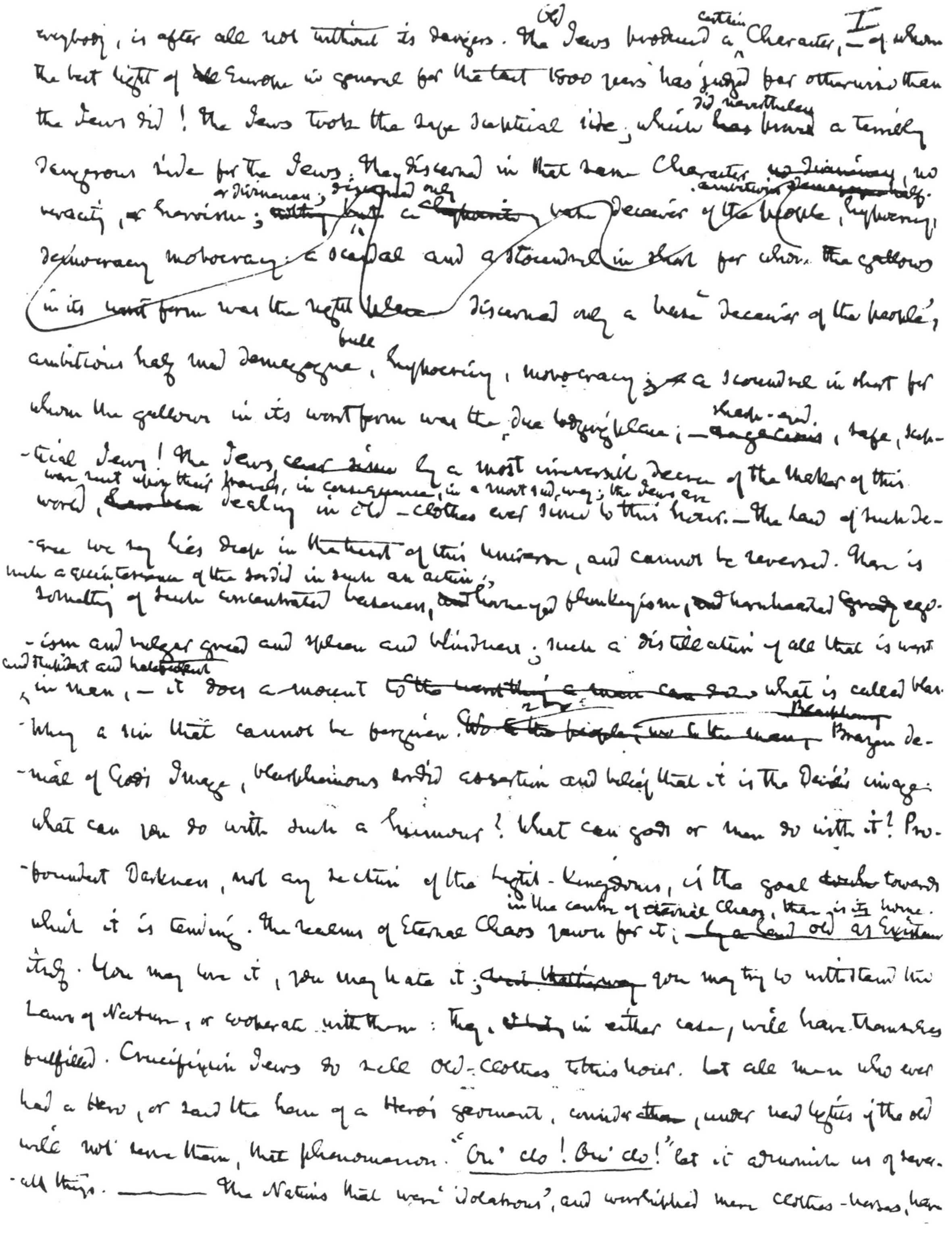
everybody, is after all not without its dangers. The old Jews produced a certain Character, — of whom the best light of Europe in general for the last 1800 years has judged far otherwise than the Jews did! The Jews took the safe sceptical side, which did nevertheless prove a terribly dangerous side for the Jews. They discerned in that same Character no divineness, no veracity, or heroism; discerned only a base deceiver of the people, ambitious half-mad demagogue, bully, hypocrisy, mobocracy, a scoundrel in short for whom the gallows in its worst form was the due lodging-place; — sharp-eyed, safe, sceptical Jews! The Jews, ever since, by a most universal decree of the Maker of this world, wander without any their proper country, in consequence, in a most sad way; the Jews are dealing in Old-clothes ever since to this hour. — The law of such decree we say lies deep in the heart of this universe, and cannot be reversed. There is such a quintessence of the sordid in such an action; something of such concentrated baseness, hard-eyed flunkeyism, and hard-hearted greedy egoism and vulgar greed and spleen and blindness; such a distillation of all that is worst and stupidest and malevolent in men, — it does amount to what is called Blasphemy, a sin that cannot be forgiven. Brazen denial of God's Image, blasphemous sordid assertion and belief that it is the Devil's image: what can you do with such a humour? What can gods or men do with it? Profoundest Darkness, not any section of the Light-Kingdoms, is the goal towards which it is tending. The realms of Eternal Chaos yawn for it; in the centre of Eternal Chaos, there is its home. You may love it, you may hate it; you may try to withstand the Laws of Nature, or cooperate with them: they, in either case, will have themselves fulfilled. Crucifying Jews do sell Old-clothes to this hour. Let all men who ever had a Hero, or saw the hem of a Hero's garment, consider under new lights of the old well-nigh [illegible] that phenomenon. "Old clo'! Old clo'!" let it admonish us of several things. —— The Nations that were 'Idolatrous', and worshipped mere Clothes-horses, have

Page from the manuscript for one of the Latter-Day Pamphlets, *Carlyle's series of eight booklets surveying British public institutions and lambasting them for their inefficiency and irrelevance to the needs of the time (The Norman and Charlotte Strouse Collection of Thomas Carlyle, at the University Library, University of California, Santa Cruz)* position to liberal views on human rights (particularly for Negroes), on individual liberty, on prison reform, and on international relations, particularly with less-developed nations. The eight *Latter-Day Pamphlets* systematically survey the public institutions of the time and lambaste them for their lazy inefficiency, their dangerous, soft-bellied liberalism, and their lack of relevance to the crying needs of the time. The *Occasional Discourse on the Nigger Question* is addressed to the emancipated slaves of the West Indies sugar plantations and questions their right to strike or demand better conditions when there is sugar to be grown. *Shooting Niagara: and After?* apocalyptically sees the weaknesses of home and abroad, foreigners and British alike, combining to push British society over the brink of an unguessable future which threatens the collapse of Western civilization. This is not empty overstatement; Carlyle believed that collapse was a real, imminent possibility, but his readers polarized. Increasing numbers gave up their sage as an embittered and authoritarian old man; others believed him right, on balance, or altogether.

In the early 1850s Carlyle began working in earnest on his monumental history of Frederick the Great of Prussia. He, like Cromwell, was a ruler who earned Carlyle's approval for a job well done. Like Cromwell, too, he violated most of the civilized rules of freedom and justice to keep the machine of society running. The end, for Carlyle as for Frederick, clearly justified the means.

Researching and writing the six huge volumes of the history of Frederick almost killed Carlyle and did much to kill Jane. The work grew as he learned more about Frederick's time and about the complexity of the Prussian politics that trapped Frederick and to which he tried to respond. Carlyle grimly traced Frederick's life, decade by decade, as Frederick, grimly, kept his view of life and society and did his job by his own lights. Carlyle, locked in his attic study in Chelsea. increasingly saw Frederick's way as one which might work for his own times. Perhaps when Carlyle emerged, exhausted, from his labor in 1865 he had lost sight of how much the age was changing, had changed. But there are two sides to this coin: Carlyle was now in his late sixties, and he was not the sardonic and witty writer of "Signs of the Times." He had achieved an immense oeuvre, thirty volumes in the Centenary Edition of 1896-1899, many more volumes of miscellanea, and thousands and thousands of letters. He had seen Queen Victoria ascend the throne and reign for thirty years over an age which changed each half-decade almost beyond recognition. The history of Frederick is an older man's impatience and an older man's certainty.

It is the product, too, of years which had seen Jane Carlyle's health go from valetudinarianism to downright collapse (a collapse often little heeded by her husband, wrapped up in the task of *Frederick*), and years in which Carlyle had alienated public opinion by his unyielding conservatism, while he alienated friends and (especially) wounded his wife by his intense fascination with the Ashburton set of brilliant and titled aristocrats. The Ashburtons' Bath House came to represent for Jane Carlyle the graveyard of her marriage—even if Carlyle almost certainly had no more than a platonic and naive fascination with a world he had never known—and the bitterness of these years is visible even in the relatively few surviving letters and tantalizing scraps of Jane Carlyle's diary. Had Jane's confidential letters to Geraldine Jewsbury survived we might know more: but they were destroyed by prior arrangement, and we can judge only by the violence of Carlyle's remorse at Jane's death.

Certainly the period from the early 1850s to the mid 1860s was a period of crisis, of deteriorating health and marital security, of the "Valley of the Shadow of Frederick," of gradually polarizing opinion among admirers and former admirers. An interesting touchstone was the controversy provoked by Governor Edward Eyre in 1865: Carlyle, with little firsthand knowledge but a strong overall sense of the importance of strong government at a time of crisis, applauded a brutal overreaction to a Jamaican rebellion as consistently as he came to admire Frederick the Great's unconstitutional but effective martial law. Once committed, he was unshakable: and he was supported by Dickens, Tennyson, Charles Kingsley, Ruskin, and Tyndall. Those outraged by Eyre's actions included Charles Darwin, T. H. Huxley, Charles Lyell, Herbert Spencer, Frederick Harrison, and Leslie Stephen. Clearly, by 1865, the author of the history of Frederick could no longer command liberal and youthfully radical support from the whole sweep of British intellectual life. Yet the list of names supporting Eyre, and supporting Carlyle's very public defense of Eyre, was a very strong one.

Carlyle's book on Frederick marked the end of an era. After Jane's death, Carlyle simply ceased to write effectively for public consumption, his hand shaky, his spirits shakier, dictation useless, and his wish to communicate (beyond occasional letters to the *Times* and generally ineffective later works on Scandinavian and Scottish history) dulled. The work of these lonely years is still remarkable

Carlyle in his attic study, Chelsea, 1857

in literary terms, in the correspondence he still conducted on a large scale, in the collecting and editing of his wife's letters and papers, and in the very private *Reminiscences* (1887) which, apart from an early chapter on his father composed in 1832, is the intense product of the first year or so of loneliness after Jane Carlyle's death. Driven almost beyond endurance by loneliness and hypochondria, he solaced himself by reliving the happier years of his youth. In so doing he revealed a photographic memory and an ability to organize and juxtapose that brought incidents from his life vividly into focus. Probably he never fully thought out the fate of these *Reminiscences,* which were meant to keep his mind occupied while he grew to live with the idea of life without Jane. Their posthumous publication reveals a new Carlyle, one far removed from the wooden repetitions and feeble arguments of *The Early Kings of Norway* or *An Essay on the Portraits of John Knox,* two works published together in a single volume in 1875. In these two late volumes Carlyle strives to revive a public persona which is effectively dead. From the mid 1860s to his death in 1881 Carlyle was Grand Old Man to many who knew perhaps only *On Heroes, Hero-Worship & the Heroic in History* and *Sartor Resartus,* who knew something about the old man's political vagaries or who knew them well but perhaps overlooked them in admiration for his achievement. While the procession of the famous and the young aspirants continued to Chelsea, the old man grew bored, lonely, feeble. All Britain held its breath as he lay dying in Chelsea; the newspapers recorded the end as a major national loss, and it was.

Several works published after Carlyle's death had a profound effect on his reputation. His confidant and executor was James Anthony Froude, a young historian and longtime admirer of Carlyle to whom his literary remains and papers were entrusted. Froude took his position seriously and was hard at work on biographical materials long before Carlyle's death. Hence the *Reminiscences* appeared soon after Carlyle's death, followed by four magnificent but badly flawed volumes of biography by Froude (1882, 1884) and *Letters and Memorials of Jane Welsh Carlyle* (1883), which had been partly annotated by Carlyle in the 1860s and 1870s.

The effect of Froude's work in the years following Carlyle's death was extraordinary. Almost overnight, it seemed, Carlyle plunged from his position as Sage of Chelsea and Grand Old Victorian to the object of puzzled dislike, or even of revulsion. The *Reminiscences* had been published, warts and all, by an editor who thought his duty to give them to the public rather than to polish away the irritations, the thin-skinned sarcasms against contemporaries (many of whom had died recently or had living relatives), the asides of a man recently bereaved but possessed still of such verbal gifts that a passing remark could make a very visible mark. The *Reminiscences* gain much of their effect from the immediacy of the emotion which produced them. In 1881, however, they seemed harsh, intolerant, bitter, unjustified often: to a readership that wanted the Olympian reminiscences of a Great Man of Letters, they offered instead evidence that Carlyle was an ordinary human being with sensitive nerves and a gift of speech which made his utterances memorable, even those his admirers might prefer to forget.

This process of Carlyle's decline was merely accelerated by the *Letters and Memorials* (with Carlyle's extensive and passionate annotations) and by Froude's *Thomas Carlyle, A History of the First Forty Years of His Life, 1795-1835* (1882) and the subsequent *Thomas Carlyle, A History of his Life in London, 1834-1881* (1884). Carlyle was revealed as a man of temper and tantrum, of bitter exaggeration in speech and in letter (though not as the man of self-deprecation and humor who emerges from so many other accounts). Froude plainly worshipped Jane Carlyle, and found Carlyle's attitude to her insufficiently respectful and neglectful in the decades of her poor health. Froude's writing, though vivid, is clearly flawed and biased, and his manipulation of evidence and documents high-handed. The family reacted with outrage: Charles Eliot Norton's 1887 edition of the *Reminiscences* is a new book, an attempt to rescue Carlyle's memoirs by proper editing (and delicate censorship) from notoriety. The volumes of letters and papers edited by Norton and by Carlyle's new champion, his nephew Alexander Carlyle, in the late-nineteenth and early-twentieth centuries attempted to right the balance. To some, Carlyle had been revealed as a wife-beater, a reactionary, a pig-headed, narrow, sharp-tongued man of double standards who advocated high morals and lived by low ones. To others, this portrait was an impossible travesty and in the arguments back and forth about who said what, who edited which manuscript with how much fidelity, and even over whether Carlyle ever beat his wife (or indeed consummated his marriage, for the argument gained grotesque momentum once

Carlyle with Louisa Ashburton, Jane Carlyle, and an unidentified woman, 1865 (courtesy of the Rare Book and Manuscript Library, Columbia University)

it had started), Carlyle's work, his positive contributions to his age, became blurred and almost forgotten. And time moved on: what had been revolutionary in 1829 faded in the 1880s and 1890s.

The 1930s saw some revival of Carlyle's fortunes thanks to new biography (above all the completion of David Alec Wilson's six-volume life) and solid scholarly attention on both sides of the Atlantic, but the subject of fascism in the 1930s and 1940s again drove Carlyle out of fashion, despite the very dubious links people made between his later work and the National Socialism of Hitler, who may have enjoyed reading Carlyle's history of Frederick the Great, but who hardly lived up to the demands Carlyle made of a real hero. No matter: Carlyle remained a neglected writer till the mid 1950s; since then critical awareness of his work and its importance has risen steadily. With the publication of scholarly editions of his works, and above all of his letters, the reader stands a better chance than ever before of making an accurate and fair estimation of his importance.

Any critical estimation of Carlyle must take into account the sheer scale of his work, not only in quantity but also in range. It is hard not to credit Carlyle's industry. He was adept at several different kinds of writing, he changed his ideas over decades, he had the courage to innovate when he could have repeated formulae of previous successes. He responded freshly and memorably to the Victorian industrial urban scene when he first settled in London in the 1830s; by the 1860s he *was* part of the Victorian urban scene, even if he still thought as an outsider, an observer. Much as he deprecated the greater part of public life and most public figures in his time, he was part of that time, and an important man who enjoyed the attention he received, while paradoxically requiring much peace, privacy, and freedom to walk the streets alone at night, like Dickens seeking inspiration and strength from the power of slumbering London. He advocated a universe of hard work and dedication to ideals, and certainly he practiced what he preached.

But what exactly did he practice? First, Carlyle practiced an incisive, satirical, perceptive journalism. He had the power to see weakness and to give it grotesque shape—in the color of the complexion of the famous "sea-green Robespierre" (an indicator of character); as the fatuous "Morrison's Pill," in *Past and Present,* promising a patent wonder cure for an ailment too deep-seated and complex to be cured ever (by extension a rejection of political panaceas of every kind); in the Hebrew "Old Clothes," conflating the Jewish moneylenders and parasites of society which Carlyle personally execrated with the central image in *Sartor Resartus* of the tattered and outworn intellectual garments of a society that desperately needed a new set; and finally, in purely invented characters, such as "Sir Jabesh Windbag" of *Past and Present,* empty political orators offering endless iteration instead of incisive analysis, or better still *action.* By skillful and repetitive use of essentially deflationary tactics, Carlyle alerted his readers to much that was degenerate. He taught them distrust of the facile and the glib; indeed, he taught them to distrust leaders of almost every hue, even while striving to inculcate hero worship. Samuel Butler's bitter gibe that "Carlyle led us into the wilderness, and left us there" has a good basis in fact, for Carlyle's reductive political analysis was seductive in that it did much to sweep aside sham (a favorite term in his vocabulary), but it also undermined confidence in all public figures. Lacking heroes in his own time, Carlyle satisfied himself with revering heroes of the past and puncturing would-be heroes of the present. It was a dangerous, but, for many decades, a successful political stance.

Second, Carlyle practiced a form of history in which carefully documented past events were to reveal a hidden construct, a deeper truth, a movement of the inevitable and the supernormal. He visited battlefields, always seeking the truth and the flavor of historical experience. The past became real to Carlyle in the privacy of his attic study, after he had tramped the Prussian battlefields, the villages that figured in the history of Cromwellian England. In his study he surrounded himself with likenesses (as he thought—often very questionably) of the people he was studying, with pictures of their homes and of the places where they fought, with firsthand accounts of battles and of everyday reality. In the study Carlyle tried to re-create reality as it was for his subjects and attempted to see life vividly through their eyes. For him, this was reality. Further, there was another deeper reality, a Garment which he had glimpsed through his reading of German Romanticism, a mystery neither understood nor controlled by clumsy humanity, but visible in glimpses to the patient historian who could interpret the mystery to the reader. Carlyle took this responsibility seriously. There was an enormous amount of chaff to be sifted and winnowed for the essential aspects of such history to be glimpsed, and the convolutions with which Carlyle wrote, revised, and proofread his work (he drove printers to despair with his proof changes) are an

Carlyle's attic study at the time he was writing the history of Frederick the Great. The maps and portraits on the walls are those he chose to represent the era he was seeking to re-create.

index of the extent to which he worked at his history and perfected the art of looking at the past from the present, somehow bending the shaft of that regard back toward the present. He lived in troubled and reforming times and, in highlighting the weaknesses and the bloodshed of the past, he tried to contribute a sense of order and structure to a process still going on, and imperfectly under control.

Third, Carlyle perfected a style which had a notable effect on his times. "Carlylese" became fashionable and was frequently (and grotesquely) imitated by lesser writers. Its constituents are various. He drew on his early study of German for syntax and some verbal items. An early admiration of Elizabethan and Puritan authors was, by his own admission, a powerful stimulus to his style. His peasant Scottish ancestors he also credited with a strong formative power, and it is notable that family friends spoke of the Carlyle facility for coining nicknames, which Thomas Carlyle used to devastating effect in such works as *Latter-Day Pamphlets.* Carlyle was, openly, a hectoring author. The suavity of earlier works such as "Signs of the Times" was replaced by infectious energy in such scenes as the storming of the Bastille in *The French Revolution:* the overwhelming desire to make vivid, to capture the imagination and visualizing power of the reader sweep through the pages and command attention, captivate, and compel.

Carlyle's vividness operated powerfully to command assent, both assent to long-vanished history and assent to a new vision of the present (the dingy slums surrounding the Model Prisons of the *Latter-Day Pamphlets,* the Irish needlewoman of *Past and Present*). Carlyle's creation was spurred by a single item of reported news, by a single artifact (a jawbone from a Cromwellian battlefield), by a single picture. His imaginative involvement was such that it demanded a like effort from the reader, and his style is very much involved in eliciting that response.

If the mind's eye is affected by the power of Carlyle's descriptive writing, so is the ear. Carlyle's verbal manipulations are those of elaboration, but the actual sentences and repetitions are such as to assault the senses. Rhetorical punctuation, repetition, orchestrated effects of imagery and symbolism suggest pictures and elicit assent more through the effect of a "mighty line" than through philosophical or logical progression; it was easy, many felt too easy, to be swept away by such passages as that describing the fall of the Bastille in *The French Revolution,* to mistake style for sense.

A related point was sharply made by Anthony Trollope in his celebrated satirical portrait of "Dr Pessimist Anticant" in *The Warden* (1855). There Carlyle, thinly disguised, is welcomed as a Teufelsdröckh-figure satirizing things *in general:* but when he becomes specific, Trollope remarks, the "charm is spoiled"—and in life this was so. Carlyle's *Past and Present* is a case in point. Clearly, he advocates moral improvement, mental bracing, order, duty, hero worship: these are not easy doctrines to translate to practice, and Carlyle lost many adherents when they found that the general prescriptions which had seemed compelling when presented with all Carlyle's skill, seemed unworkable in the less ordered and more ambiguous light of everyday. This difficulty was sensitively treated in Mrs. Gaskell's *North and South:* Carlylian ideas obviously inform every part of this novel, yet the characters who try to implement Carlylian ideas in their unrefined form (Thornton, Margaret) find that some flexibility and some modification are required. Those who were able to adapt and adjust Carlylian principles continued to revere him as a potent influence on their thinking. Those who could not, distrusted his writing and his ideas.

What, finally, are these ideas? First, order is a central theme. Carlyle grew up in a home dominated by a system which stressed order and submission. He survived adolescent identity crisis by imposing order on his own life, and he went on to produce a critique of his times based on an awareness that disorder was threatening to overtake and destroy the advances of the Victorian age and the industrial successes it had achieved. In his adult life Carlyle lost no chance to show his particular brand of order in action (Cromwell, Frederick, Abbot Samson) and the chaos that followed loss of order. Trapped between a warm personality (he gave, generously, to various objects of charity) and an urgently, overwhelmingly pressing view of order, Carlyle found himself torn in his private life and, increasingly, in his public writing—torn between a vision of a freer humanity (in his early works) and a vision of collapsing anarchy in society (in all his later ones). Only order could stand between his society and that anarchy. Second, the energy which Carlyle saw in the world around him, whether as a result of his early scientific studies in physics or

Carlyle in 1874

of his fascination with the German Romantics and their sense of life's Mystery, was an abiding concern. In "Signs of the Times" he saw that energy in the machines which were taking over his world; by *Chartism* and *Past and Present* the worth of those machines had become ambiguous indeed, and the dystopian vision of a world where people surrendered moral autonomy to their machines was a real nightmare for him. Only such a surrender of oneself, he argued, could lead to the asinine lack of priorities he set about revealing in the *Latter-Day Pamphlets,* the general breakdown he saw around him. His rallying call to "Work and despair not," from *Sartor Resartus* onward, seeks to give shape to a vision of directed energy, directed to production in an ordered society, guided by a yet higher energy that is not seen and not understood, yet that is clearly there in Carlyle's world pattern. As God or as Creator, that energy pulses through Carlyle's world, and man responds by working. The problem, always, is to channel and to understand energy, to keep control without stifling creativity.

Third, Carlyle gave his age a vision of structure. His own religious position, carefully vague in its exposition, allowed readers to find in it a workable position for themselves. Injunctions to work, to obey, to reverence heroes, to fear God found echoes in many people who wished to believe, and who were captivated by the style with which Carlyle delivered these injunctions. That they were not specifically Christian did not prevent Christians from accepting them sincerely; like Tennyson, Carlyle found the artistic means to project a message in a carefully unfocused state which suited the diverse needs of his readership. Behind his public stance lay a private world of doubt, rarely communicated, only occasionally hinted at in stray remarks that have been preserved by those who heard Carlyle make revealing comments in conversation. The overall structure of his view of the world held firm: God at the head, planning and controlling; mankind at ground level, understanding little and requiring to understand still less, but owing reverence and obedience in the long run to a creator and in the short run to hero figures sent by that creator to give impulse to the unfocused energies of the age. In private and in public, Carlyle remained deeply skeptical of his age's achieving such a structure as he longed for, which does much to explain his growing preoccupation with forcible guidance of an apparently wayward society. Carlyle would not have put into practice the fiercely intolerant measures he proposed for recalcitrant Negro workers in the West Indies. Faced with the reality of human suffering, he always responded with human warmth; only in the privacy of his study did abstract ideas work him into righteous frenzy, and his style made that mood the memorable one. In private life in Chelsea, he kept a much more secure balance, but this is not the side of Carlyle that survives in the public eye.

Thus, the Carlyle we have seen is a mass of contradictions, and his self-doubts in old age, and his growing impatience with his era, must be linked to the fact that he was not one single individual with a clear, unchanging "message." Carlyle was a complex, continually evolving, highly intelligent and original thinker who witnessed many decades of change, developed formidable powers of self-expression which helped mold these decades, and lived into an era in which many regarded his work as inflexible, out of date, often irrelevant. He did, however, retain a following; even in old age, he was still to many a figure of hope. In *Sartor Resartus* and in *On Heroes, Hero-Worship & the Heroic in History,* his two most popular works, he showed his readers that it was possible for a man to be assaulted with the doubts and self-doubts common to the century and to find a workable philosophy to overcome them. Teufelsdröckh, in the peroration to *Sartor Resartus,* and the author-figure apostrophizing the worker-heroes both give hope to the common Victorian that a workable solution is within reach. That intellectuals should find Carlyle's solution oversimplified or crude and that the long-term appeal of his actual prescriptions has been at best patchy does little to detract from his real achievement—his original and abrasive critique of Victorian society, his emphasis on the importance of spiritual values in history and in the present, his inspiration of his contemporaries toward a world view in which the individual has a place, and with that place duties and the possibility of dignity in a fulfilled existence.

From the perspective of the late-twentieth century Carlyle can be seen without the outrage that greeted his originality. His ideas are undoubtedly oversimplified, his tolerance levels for others' ideas far too low. His vivid style can be abused, particularly in indiscriminate attack. His stubborn iteration of one point can be dangerous when that point is a weak or indefensible one.

Against these weaknesses, Carlyle has survived the scrutiny of the years as an original critic of his time and as a skillful, though uneven, writer/stylist who understood the needs of a generation. After his death his reputation suffered a remarkable eclipse. Happily, he has been rehabilitated as an important representative Victorian, and, as the discovery of his work and above all his correspondence continues, so too does the rehabilitation of his reputation. We have passed beyond the need to venerate him as sage, of Chelsea or of Ecclefechan. Rather we see him as an emblem of the complexity, contradiction, and sometimes absurdity of the era. As the Victorian Age was untidy and contradictory, so were the original minds which responded to its needs and shaped their writing to its complex demands. In his contradictions Carlyle challenges us to a new formulation by which to judge his success, and he leaves behind an achievement sufficiently large and sufficiently diverse, as to ensure that the process of evaluation will be a long and critically challenging one.

Letters:

The Correspondence of Thomas Carlyle and Ralph Waldo Emerson, 1834-1872, 2 volumes (Boston: Osgood, 1883; London: Chatto & Windus, 1883); supplementary volume (Boston: Ticknor, 1886);

Early Letters of Thomas Carlyle, edited by Charles Eliot Norton, 2 volumes (London & New York: Macmillan, 1886);

Correspondence between Goethe and Carlyle, edited by Norton (London: Macmillan, 1887);

Letters of Thomas Carlyle, 1826-1836, edited by Norton, 2 volumes (London & New York: Macmillan, 1888);

Letters of Thomas Carlyle to His Youngest Sister, edited by Charles Townsend Copeland (Boston & New York: Houghton, Mifflin, 1899; London: Chapman & Hall, 1899);

New Letters of Thomas Carlyle, edited by Alexander Carlyle, 2 volumes (London & New York: John Lane/Bodley Head, 1904);

The Love Letters of Thomas Carlyle and Jane Welsh, edited by Alexander Carlyle, 2 volumes (London & New York: John Lane/Bodley Head, 1909);

Letters of Thomas Carlyle to John Stuart Mill, John Sterling and Robert Browning, edited by Alexander Carlyle (London: Unwin, 1923; New York: Stokes, 1923);

Letters of Thomas Carlyle to William Graham, edited by John Graham (Princeton: Princeton University Press, 1950);

Thomas Carlyle: Letters to His Wife, edited by Trudy Bliss (Cambridge: Harvard University Press, 1953);

The Correspondence of Emerson and Carlyle, edited by Joseph Slater (New York: Columbia University Press, 1964);

The Letters of Thomas Carlyle to His Brother Alexander, edited by Edwin W. Marrs, Jr. (Cambridge: Harvard University Press, 1968);

The Collected Letters of Thomas and Jane Welsh Carlyle, edited by Charles Richard Sanders, K. J. Fielding, Clyde de L. Ryals, and others, volumes 1- (Durham: Duke University Press, 1970-);

Thomas and Jane: Selected Letters From the Edinburgh University Library Collection, edited by Ian Campbell (Edinburgh: Friends of Edinburgh University Library, 1980);

The Correspondence of Thomas Carlyle and John Ruskin, edited by George Alan Cate (Stanford: Stanford University Press, 1982).

Bibliography:

Isaac Watson Dyer, *A Bibliography of Thomas Carlyle's Writings and Ana* (Portland, Maine: Southworth, 1928).

Biographies:

R. S. Shepherd, with the assistance of C. N. Williamson, *Memoirs of the Life and Writings of Thomas Carlyle* (London: Allen, 1881);

James Anthony Froude, *Thomas Carlyle, A History of the First Forty Years of His Life, 1795-1835,* 2 volumes (London: Longmans, Green, 1882);

Froude, *Thomas Carlyle, A History of his Life in London, 1834-1881,* 2 volumes (London: Longmans, Green, 1884);

David Alec Wilson, *Life of Thomas Carlyle,* 6 volumes (London: Kegan Paul, 1929-1934);

Ian Campbell, *Thomas Carlyle* (London: Hamilton, 1974);

Fred Kaplan, *Thomas Carlyle* (Ithaca: Cornell University Press, 1983).

References:

John Clubbe, ed., *Carlyle and his Contemporaries: Essays in Honor of Charles Richard Sanders* (Durham: Duke University Press, 1976);

Francis Espinasse, *Literary Recollections and Sketches* (London: Hodder & Stoughton, 1893);

K. J. Fielding and R. L. Tarr, eds., *Carlyle Past and Present: A Collection of New Essays* (London: Vision, 1976);

T. W. Reid, ed., *The Life, Letters and Friendships of Richard Monckton Milnes, First Lord Houghton* (London: Cassell, 1890);

J. P. Seigel, ed., *Thomas Carlyle: The Critical Heritage* (London: Routledge & Kegan Paul, 1971);

Hill Shine, *Carlyle's Early Reading to 1834* (Lexington: University of Kentucky Libraries, 1953);

G. B. Tennyson, *Sartor Called Resartus: The Genesis, Structure, and Style of Thomas Carlyle's First Major Work* (Princeton: Princeton University Press, 1966).

Papers:

The major collection of Carlyle's papers is at the National Library of Scotland in Edinburgh; other collections are at the Edinburgh University Library and the British Library. In the United States there are important collections at Harvard, Duke, the University of California, Santa Cruz, and at the New York Public Library (Berg Collection).

John Clare

(13 July 1793-20 May 1864)

R. K. R. Thornton
University of Newcastle upon Tyne

The only known photograph of Clare, taken in 1864 by William Wilby Law of Northampton (Northampton Public Library)

SELECTED BOOKS: *Poems Descriptive of Rural Life and Scenery* (London: Printed for Taylor & Hessey and E. Drury, Stamford, 1820);

The Village Minstrel and Other Poems, 2 volumes (London: Printed for Taylor & Hessey and E. Drury, Stamford, 1821);

The Shepherd's Calendar; with Village Stories, and Other Poems (London: Published for John Taylor by James Duncan, 1827);

The Rural Muse, Poems by John Clare (London: Whittaker, 1835);

The Life and Remains of John Clare, edited by J. L. Cherry (London: Warne/Northampton: Taylor/New York: Scribner, Welford & Armstrong, 1873);

Poems by John Clare, edited by Norman Gale (Rugby: Over, 1901);

Poems by John Clare, edited by Arthur Symons (London: Frowde, 1908);

John Clare: Poems Chiefly from Manuscript, edited by Edmund Blunden and Alan Porter (London: Cobden-Sanderson, 1920; New York: Putnam's, 1921);

Madrigals and Chronicles, edited by Blunden (London: Beaumont Press, 1924);

Sketches in the Life of John Clare, Written by Himself, edited by Blunden (London: Cobden-Sanderson/New York: Oxford University Press, 1931);

The Poems of John Clare, edited by J. W. Tibble, 2 volumes (London: Dent/New York: Dutton, 1935);

Poems of John Clare's Madness, edited by Geoffrey Grigson (London: Routledge & Kegan Paul, 1949);

The Prose of John Clare, edited by J. W. Tibble and Anne Tibble (London: Routledge & Kegan Paul, 1951);

The Later Poems of John Clare, edited by Eric Robinson and Geoffrey Summerfield (Manchester: Manchester University Press/New York: Barnes & Noble, 1964);

The Shepherd's Calendar, edited by Robinson and Summerfield (London & New York: Oxford University Press, 1964);

John Clare: Selected Poems, edited by J. W. Tibble and Anne Tibble (London: Dent/New York: Dutton, 1965);

Clare: Selected Poems and Prose, edited by Robinson and Summerfield (London & New York: Oxford University Press, 1966; enlarged, 1967);

John Clare: Selected Poems, edited by Elaine Feinstein (London: University Press, 1968);

The Midsummer Cushion, edited by Anne Tibble and R. K. R. Thornton (Ashington & Manchester: Mid Northumberland Arts Group/Carcanet Press, 1979);

The Journal, Essays, The Journey from Essex, edited by Anne Tibble (Manchester: Carcanet New Press, 1980);

John Clare's Birds, edited by Robinson and Richard Fitter (Oxford & New York: Oxford University Press, 1982);

The Rural Muse, revised edition, edited by Thornton (Ashington & Manchester: Mid Northumberland Arts Group/Carcanet Press, 1982);

John Clare's Autobiographical Writings, edited by Robinson (Oxford & New York: Oxford University Press, 1983);

The Natural History Prose Writings of John Clare, edited by Margaret Grainger (Oxford: Clarendon Press, 1983);

John Clare, edited by Robinson and David Powell (Oxford & New York: Oxford University Press, 1984);

The Later Poems of John Clare, 1837-1864, edited by Robinson and Powell, 2 volumes (Oxford: Clarendon Press, 1984);

The Parish, edited by Robinson (Harmondsworth & New York: Viking, 1985).

A discussion of John Clare's prose writings must be as much an account of the reception and publishing history of his work as it is a biographical sketch of the man himself. His life was a struggle from a disadvantaged peasant background to achieve recognition as a poet, and an equal struggle to achieve and retain his own sense of identity. His poems, despite a remarkable growth of interest in Clare's work, have still not been fully published, although Eric Robinson and David Powell have made a substantial start on a projected eight-volume complete edition with *The Later Poems of John Clare* (2 volumes, 1984), which includes all of the extant poems from the period 1837 to 1864. The prose has been even longer in reaching publication and is only now beginning to receive the attention which it deserves. There has been continued interest in the prose as evidence of the raw material from which the poetry emerged or as a biographical resource for compiling the life, but there is increasing recognition now of its intrinsic merits and of the light that it can shed on a wide array of subjects including early-nineteenth-century natural history (particularly the distribution and history of birds and flowers) and the nature of village experience in that period.

John Clare was born to peasant parents in the village of Helpston (spelled Helpstone in Clare's day) in Northamptonshire on 13 July 1793: his mother, Ann Stimson, was the daughter of a shepherd, and his father, Parker Clare, was a flail thresher, the illegitimate son of an itinerant teacher called John Donald Parker. In the *Sketches in the Life of John Clare,* begun for his friend and first publisher John Taylor in 1821 (but unpublished until edited by Edmund Blunden in 1931), Clare describes his parents as "illiterate to the last degree," but though Clare's mother "knew not a single letter," his father could read the Bible and had a large repertoire of ballads, a suggestion of the importance folk culture was to have in Clare's experience. John Clare was one of twins and more weakly than his sister in appearance at birth, but it was the girl who died after a few weeks. Of the four children born to the family, only Clare and a sister six years his junior survived infancy, which meant that the family's meager resources did not have to spread far.

Clare's education was fragmentary but effective; he wrote that "as to my schooling, I think never a year passd me till I was 11 or 12 but 3 months or more at the worst of times was luckily spared for my improvment." He began at the age of five in a local dame school run by Mrs. Bullimore, and two years later went to Mr. Seaton's class conducted in the church vestry at nearby Glinton. Clare's account in his *Sketches* indicates both his ambition to succeed and his desire to impress his publisher that he was a diligent and deserving worker: "soon as I began to learn to write, the readiness of the Boys always practising urgd and prompted my ambition to make the best use of my abscence from school, as well as at it, and my master was always supprisd to find me improved every fresh visit, instead of having lost what I had learned before for which to my benefit he never faild to give me tokens of encouragment." Clare so impressed his teachers that James Merrishaw, who took over as schoolmaster in 1803, encouraged him by allowing him to use the books in his fairly extensive library. While at Glinton school Clare met and fell in love with Mary Joyce, the daughter of a local farmer. She was four years younger than he but his passion for her was lifelong; family pressure on her was probably the cause of the breakup of their relationship, but she remained Clare's ideal woman, in many ways his muse, and in his mind his "first" wife.

After the age of twelve, except perhaps for some evenings at Glinton, Clare educated himself through books, through a limited number of friendships, and through observation of the world around him. He discovered early the reciprocal truths that no knowledge from books can take the place of knowledge of the world and that no knowledge of the world can be meaningful without an understanding of its relationship to what has been thought and written. The intimate connection between literature and life became a familiar subject of Clare's work, in which he often linked book and nature, art and life. For example, his account of the composition of the first poem he committed to paper tells of returning with a copy of James Thomson's *The Seasons* and reading it in Burghley Park: "the Scenery around me was uncommonly beautiful at that time of the year and what with reading the book and beholding the beautys of artful nature in the park I got into a strain of descriptive ryhming on my journey home." The connection is central to his prose too, as is evident from the very beginning of the *Sketches:* "There is a pleasure in recalling ones past years to reccolection . . . and I think a double gratifycation is witness'd as we turn to a repetition of our early days by writing them down on paper."

His early discovery of Thomson's poem indicates his love of poetry and suggests an important tradition from which and indeed out of which his work developed; but he also had a living to earn, though he could not afford the expense of an apprenticeship. He considered employment as shoemaker's apprentice, stonemason's apprentice, signpainter, and clerk in the office of his uncle's master, but his usual employment was manual labor, as thresher or ploughboy or gardener. In 1805 he entered service (for the only year in his life) with Francis Gregory, the next-door neighbor who kept the Blue Bell public house. Then he found employment as gardener's boy at Burghley House, the nearby seat of the Marquis of Exeter, but, frightened by the fierce head gardener, he soon fled to look for work elsewhere. He tried gardening again, made an abortive attempt to join the militia, and returned home where he began to compose more freely. Family necessity—his father's crippling rheumatism was threatening to drive him on the parish—and the opportunity of a national emergency persuaded him to volunteer for the militia (the alternative to volunteering was not to get the bounty of two guineas but to "be forcd to be drawn and go for nothing").

He was an awkward soldier, recording later that "I was never wonderful clean in my dress at least not clean enough for a soldier for I thought I took more then nessesary pains to be so I was

John Clare in an 1820 painting by William Hilton (National Portrait Gallery)

not very apt at learing my exercise for I then was a rhymer and my thoughts were often absent when the word of comand was given and for this fault I was terribly teazd by a little louse looking coporal who took a delight in finding fault with me and loading me with bad jests on my awkardness as a soldier as if he had been a soldier all his life." Clare's fiery sense of justice and indignation at this corporal's taunts led him on one occasion to throw down his rifle, seize the man by the throat, twist him to the ground and kick him, for which Clare served extra guard duty. But "the fellow threw a mortified eye on me ever after and never found his tounge to tell me of a fault even when I was in one." Service in the militia was not a permanent job but it made a laborer less employable since employers did not like the disturbance of having a man who could be called for training at any time. Clare took on the unattractive work of lime-burning at Bridge Casterton and Pickworth, with two important consequences: first, he met and fell in love with Martha ("Patty") Turner (born 3 March

1799), whom he later married; second, he earned enough money to make the first step toward publication.

He had been composing tales and verse since his days at the Blue Bell and in 1814 was looking for a book of blank paper into which to copy his poems. To abbreviate what was, like all Clare's publication ventures, a long and involved story, he made contact with a bookseller of Market Deeping named J. B. Henson, who printed some prospectuses of Clare's work. The project came to the notice of another bookseller, Edward Drury, who was sufficiently impressed by the poems to contact his London cousin John Taylor, the publisher (most notably of Keats); Taylor and his partner James Hessey arranged to publish the poems. The book was a great success; *Poems Descriptive of Rural Life and Scenery* came out in January 1820 and the first edition of 1,000 copies sold out quickly, as did the second, requiring a third edition in May and a fourth the following year. The title (much more so than the one earlier proposed, "Pastoral Sketches in Songs, Ballads and Sonnets") suggests the type of rural and descriptive poetry for which the vogue was just beginning to decline.

The publication made a reputation for Clare and he married Patty Turner, already pregnant, on 16 March 1820. The first of their eight children, Anna Maria, was born on 2 June, and Clare's prospects seemed to be thriving. In response to the publication Lord Radstock started a subscription fund to help Clare. This soon reached nearly £400 which was invested in the Navy Five Per Cents. Together with £10 a year from Earl Spencer and £15 a year from the Marquis of Exeter, Clare thus received about £43 a year. In later years the interest (in both senses) waned, and Clare ironically could not get at the capital since it had been secured from creditors by allowing him only the interest. Money pressures were always to plague him, though in 1820 he felt newly rich and the poetry-reading public was interested in him. He paid the first of his four visits to London in March 1820 just before his marriage, and there he met literary men, including Charles Lamb, Allan Cunningham, Henry Francis Cary and William Hazlitt; the painters Thomas Griffiths Wainewright and William Hilton, the latter of whom painted his portrait; and two people who were to be important patrons, Lord Radstock and the caring, if sentimental, Mrs. Eliza Emmerson. Clare also saw the great actors Edmund Kean and William Charles Macready, but Clare himself was the center of much attention.

His poems had revealed him as an exact observer of the countryside, though at this stage his clarity and exactness of observation were often qualified by too great a willingness to be influenced by conventional pastoral and popular sentimentality. The development of his poetry was a process of learning confidence in his own vision and his own vocabulary while recognizing what could be learned from the traditional pastoral. Somewhat less hampered by a public demand but still shaped both by convention and their immediate purpose were Clare's *Sketches in the Life of John Clare*, in which he began to give Taylor an accurate account of his life and which he continued fragmentarily for some years. The intimate mixture of experience of life with his own developing range in reading and skill in writing accounts for the vivacity of the sketches which re-create with sharp immediacy the daily life of a child and young man at the turn of the century and the curiosity of his own development. Clare is acutely aware of which details will tell and is never unwilling to include facts and anecdotes which do not redound to his credit. He straightforwardly acknowledges that his father was a bastard, "one of fates chance-lings who drop into the world without the honour of matrimony," but, rather than depict his grandmother as a deserted and fallen woman, he lightens the tone by the comment that "her love was not that frenzy which shortens the days of the victim of seduction, for she liv'd to the age of 86." Clare's sense of shape is such that near the end of his autobiographical narrative he returns to another seduced woman in his account of his marriage to the already pregnant Patty Turner and to his nostalgic affection for Mary Joyce.

It is not clear whether the *Sketches* were ever finished; there are signs in the manuscripts that the parts we now have and the various autobiographical fragments edited by J. W. and Anne Tibble and by Eric Robinson had been transcribed in a lost fair copy. There is, however, a different tone in the autobiographical notes, where the shift from formal autobiography to personal jottings allows Clare a greater freedom and a more open criticism of the middle classes. The ambiguous attitude to enclosure and other social change also emerges; the sense of being displaced and disadvantaged while at the same time being intensely interested in new learning—"everything in my hours of leisure that came in my way Mathematics Astronomy Botany and other things"—even land-surveying, the effects of which threatened his rural Eden. Many books, on subjects as diverse as flowers, philosophy and fishing, are mentioned in the prose,

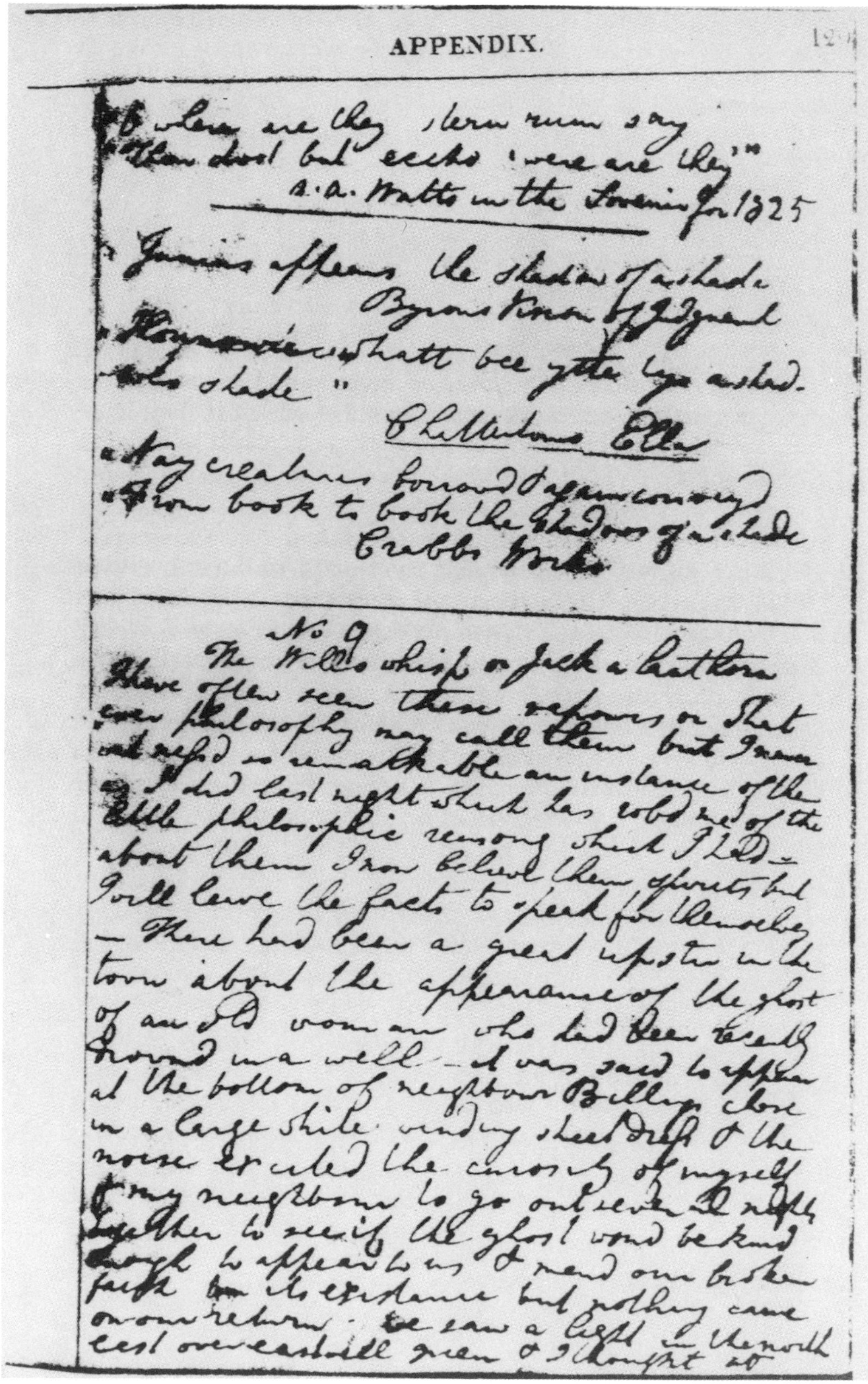
APPENDIX. 124

"O where are they stern men say
"Then doth but echo 'where are they'"
A. A. Watts in the Souvenir for 1825

"Junius appears the shadow of a shade
Byrons Vision of Judgment

"[illegible] shall be yette the lyfe a shad-
-ows shade"
Chattertons Ella

"Nay creatures borrowd & again conveyd
"From book to book the shadows of a shade
Crabbs Works

No 9
The Will o whisp or Jack a lanthorn
I have often seen these vapours or what ever philosophy may call them but I never witnessd so remarkable an instance of them as I did last night which has robd me of the little philosophic reasoning which I had about them I now believe them spirits but I will leave the facts to speak for themselves — There had been a great upstir in the town about the appearance of the ghost of an old woman who had been recently drownd in a well — it was said to appear at the bottom of neighbour Billings close in a large white winding sheet dress & the noise excited the curiosity of myself & my neighbours to go out seven of us together to see if the ghost woud be kind enough to appear to us & mend our broken faith in its existence but nothing came on our return we saw a light in the north east over eastwell green & I thought it

Page from Clare's journal on which he began writing "The Will o Whisp or Jack a lanthorn," a report of his encounters with ghosts or "vapours or whatever philosophy may call them . . . which has robd me of the little philosophic reasoning I had about them . . ." (Northampton Borough Council and Northampton Central Library) and indeed the accounts give valuable insights into what was available and of interest to the village reader. More particularly Clare's autobiographical writings show the vast range of his own reading, from the predictable Bible and "the superstitious tales that are hawked about a sheet for a penny, such as Old Nixons Prophesies, Mother Bunches Fairey Tales, and Mother Shiptons Legacy" to Thomson, Pope, Milton, Fielding, Defoe, and many of the authors of his own day. One must also add to Clare's reading many classical and contemporary books on natural history, the extent of which is evident in the 440 volumes in Clare's library listed in David Powell's *Catalogue of the John Clare Collection in the Northampton Public Library* (1964; Supplement, 1971).

The success of *Poems Descriptive of Rural Life and Scenery* encouraged the publication of a second volume, though it was too soon for much real development to have been possible in Clare's verse. *The Village Minstrel and Other Poems* was published in 1821 (with a second edition in 1823) and received mixed reviews. It was, however, taken seriously and not so much as a literary curiosity. Clare was extremely active in this period and the preponderance of his prose comes from the 1820s. He began three prose pieces, "The Two Soldiers," "The Stage Coach," and "The Parish Register," but all are mere fragments. Fragmentary also is the projected novel whose subject he described in a letter to Taylor of 31 January 1822: "I have at last pitchd upon a subject for a 'novel' it is 'Cares & Comforts' or 'Notes from the Memoirs of Uncle Barnaby & family as written by himself.' " The most substantial surviving fragment of this project is a passage entitled "The Bone and Cleaver Club," and Clare's suggestions of the novel's shape suggest why it did not get far: it was to be episodic and, if not completely unstructured, shaped more by the accidents of experience than by the exigencies of plot: "I shall write it in Chapters & confine myself to no mechanical plot but go on just as things jump at the moment."

This faith in accident is typical of Clare in both prose and verse, as if accident would provide insight into the shape and structure of things more effectively than a theory of the picturesque or a system like Linnaeus's. Clare always preferred discovery to system-learning and his gut reaction could prove right. Margaret Grainger points out in the general introduction to *The Natural History Prose Writings of John Clare* (1983) that: "Whilst he struggled for a time with the Linnaean or Sexual System, in which plants are classified according to the number and arrangement of male and female organs inside the flower, all his life Clare continued to prefer the old herbalists. He was more at home in working a 'natural' rather than an 'artificial' system; and his instinctive choice was vindicated by the gradual return, in the 1820s and 1830s, to the essential correctness of [John] Ray's tentative and cumbersome attempts at a natural classification." Clare was far from hostile to the detailed study of nature, and, in 1823 or 1824, at the prompting of Hessey, he began his Natural History Letters. Hessey seemed at this time more in sympathy with Clare's aims than Taylor did, even suggesting passages from the poets, including the one from Chaucer which Clare used in his third Natural History letter. Clare's project, an obvious choice for him and one whose loss as a completed piece is a source of regret, grew until he could write in his journal on 11 March 1825: "Intend to call my Natural History of Helpstone 'Biographys of Birds & Flowers' with an Appendix on Animals & Insects"; the reference indicates the conscious link with Gilbert White's 1789 work known as the *Natural History of Selborne.* Clare shared White's knowledge, curiosity, and humane interest in natural and rural life and added his own distinctively poetic observation, but his publishers did not appreciate the qualities of his prose and never took up his suggestion of a "Pastorals in Prose," made in a letter of 3 January 1821.

From September 1824 to September 1825 Clare kept a journal into which went a medley of records and natural observations, opinions on literature, everyday life in the village, and news and events. The same lively curiosity marked his various essays, and his sure literary discrimination shows, for example, in his notes on Keats, to whose genius he had immediately responded.

Clare's poem *The Parish,* a satire of over 2,000 lines, was written during the first half of the 1820s and voiced the growing sense of anger against cant which had begun to show in the autobiographical notes and in the "Bone and Cleaver Club" fragment; but the poem was never printed in his lifetime. Left uncompleted, or at least unpolished, versions or selections have been edited by J. W. Tibble in *The Poems of John Clare* (1935), in J. W. Tibble and Anne Tibble's *John Clare: Selected Poems* (1965), in Elaine Feinstein's *John Clare: Selected Poems* (1968), and in Eric Robinson's *The Parish* (1985). While Clare worked on *The Parish,* he was also struggling with *The Shepherd's Calendar.* Taylor had suggested the idea in 1823 and the poem was indeed advertised in January 1824, but its publi-

The front of Clare's cottage at Northborough, where he settled with his family in 1832. At Clare's request the cottage, built by Lord Milton, had its door in the back so that he could escape unnoticed when unwelcome visitors approached from the road.

cation was delayed while Clare tried to amend and alter—even substituting verses on a whole month—to satisfy what seem now to be unsympathetic and unperceptive demands of the publisher. The effect was that (according to Eric Robinson and Geoffrey Summerfield in the introduction to their 1964 edition of the poem) "the sequence as a whole was reduced from 3,382 lines (i.e. excluding the second version of *July*) to 1,761 lines (excluding the second version of *July*) and *July* was replaced by a completely new poem." Impressive as the achievement now seems, especially to a modern audience who can read what Clare wrote and not the "Taylored" text, the book sold only 400 copies between its publication in April 1827 and 1829.

Clare, often ill, often having difficulty in supporting his growing family and his aging parents, also had the problem of moving uneasily between the incompatible demands of the life of the peasant and the life of the literary man. The hassle with *The Shepherd's Calendar* and its ultimate lack of success intensified the problems from which he tried to extricate himself in the 1830s with a new project, to publish by subscription a book of poems entitled "The Midsummer Cushion." This undertaking also met difficulties. While he was engaged in securing subscribers he moved from the cottage of his birth to a cottage in Northborough, some two or three miles distant. When his projected book finally appeared in 1835 in a truncated form and under the more formal title *The Rural Muse,* his sense of deracination and disorientation was evident in the poem he called "The Flitting," which had been retitled more formally "On Leaving the Cottage of my Birth." He had proved unable to publish his own book—it was published by Whittaker and Company, though the editing was done by Mrs. Eliza Emmerson and Taylor—and the response to it, though not unfavorable, was not wide. The edition failed to sell out, though his situation had eased a little with a grant of £50 from the Literary Fund in January 1835. The full four-hundred-odd pages of fair copy Clare had prepared for this project did not appear in print until 1979, when they were published as *The Midsummer Cushion.*

The pressures, the illnesses, the dissatisfactions, the disappointments culminated in a breakdown in 1837, and Clare went as a voluntary patient

Drawing, signed by Clare, made while he was an inmate of the Northampton General Lunatic Asylum. A label on the drawing, which was published for the first time in Edward Storey's 1982 biography, reads "Pen and ink portrait of John Clare, sketched about six months before his death by a Maniac an inmate of the Asylum. G. B. Berry of Bristol Artist."

to the asylum run by Dr. Matthew Allen at High Beach in Epping Forest. Clare was able to work there and composed "Child Harold" and "Don Juan," but, as those Byronic titles suggest, his grasp of his own identity had become a struggle. Allen, an acquaintance of Tennyson who at this time lived nearby, was enlightened in his treatment of the insane, but Clare, dissatisfied with what he considered incarceration and longing for his home ground, escaped in July 1841 (since he was not locked up and nobody pursued him it might be fairer to say he left) and walked back to Northborough. The account of his journey (first published in 1865 in Frederick Martin's *The Life of John Clare*) is a poignant picture of his determination and a touching emblem of his heroic independence; expecting no charity, grateful for help, he was self-reliant in the most fundamental way. This reliance on the self stresses his dependence on the mind to structure an alternative world. His poetry had always structured this alternative in images of childhood, of Eden, of love for an Eve in the shape of Mary Joyce or an ideal woman, and in his narrative of the journey he ends by disbelieving the facts told to him that Mary is dead. In prosaic terms it is his wife Patty who greets him and takes him home, but he is "homeless at home." He had begun to live in the mind and seemed to have a confused idea of himself, a confusion which mixes strangely and revealingly with a scrupulously unself-pitying clarity of description.

Though Patty made attempts to keep him at home, he became impossible, and he was finally removed in late December 1841 to Northampton General Lunatic Asylum, where he spent the rest of his life. He still wrote poetry, often harking back to the traditional songs and ballads he had known in his youth, and much of it was transcribed by the attendants. Only fragments of his prose were transcribed, and there is much less prose than poetry in this period, though enough to show Clare's brightness of response to his experience. His last extant letter, written on 8 March 1860, indicates the collapse of his abilities to use words to name, communicate and tell, know and say:

> Dear Sir, I am in a Madhouse & quite forget your Name or who you are you must excuse me
>
> for I have nothing to communicate or tell of & why I am shut up I dont know I have nothing to say so I conclude
>
> yours respectfully John Clare[.]

He died in 1864.

The struggle for recognition of Clare's work was not over with his death. Clare had always had to defend his integrity and individuality against a variety of conformities, social, literary, linguistic, cultural, and it was a long time before the unmediated Clare became available. Taylor had adapted and punctuated Clare's texts right from the beginning with *Poems Descriptive of Rural Life and Scenery*, and the process was almost always to take away some of the distinctiveness of the writing. Dialect words were occasionally allowed but often "corrected"; even more frequently, dialectal forms of syntax, such as subject-verb concord, and particularly spelling were "corrected" and punctuation supplied. But just as Clare was almost constitutionally incapable of keeping to the rules as a soldier, he was unhappy to accept the subordinations implied in grammar: "do I write intelligable I am generally understood tho I do not use that awkward squad of pointings called commas colons semicolons &c & for the very reason that altho they are drilled hourly daily weekly by every boarding school Miss who pretends to gossip in correspondence they do not know their proper exercise for they even set grammarians at loggerheads and no one can asign them their proper places." Subordination and a conventional idea of proper place were notions which Clare reacted against. In *The Idea of Landscape and the Sense of Place* (1972) John Barrell has pointed out the lack of subordination in the syntax and viewpoint of Clare's poems; Timothy Brownlow, in *John Clare and Picturesque Landscape* (1983), has shown Clare's reaction against the implications of status in the language of the picturesque; in an appendix for the 1982 edition of *The Rural Muse,* Barbara M. H. Strang has revealed the important content in the idiosyncracies of Clare's writing, syntax, dialect, spelling and indicated how much Clare tells us about the actual language of his place, time, and class. During Clare's lifetime all his texts were tidied up for publication, either by Taylor alone or with (in the case of *The Shepherd's Calendar*) Harry Stoe Van Dyk or (in the case of *The Rural Muse*) Mrs. Emmerson. After Clare's death, J. L. Cherry's *The Life and Remains of John Clare* (1873) continued the pattern, which was preserved by editions of the poems prepared by Norman Gale in 1901 and Arthur Symons in 1908. Symons touched on but did not thoroughly explore two of the three important developments that would expand Clare's reputation in the twentieth century. First, he noticed the amount of unpublished material, which Edmund Blunden began to bring to the notice of the public in 1920 (*John Clare: Poems Chiefly from Manuscript*), 1924 (*Madrigals and Chronicles*), and 1931 (*Sketches in the Life of John Clare*). This renewed interest prompted the biography *John Clare: a Life* by J. W. Tibble and Anne Tibble in 1932 and the two-volume edition of *The Poems of John Clare* in 1935. The editions by Blunden and the Tibbles made a great deal more material available but did not respond to Symons's second point, the need to go back carefully to Clare's own text. The importance of reproducing Clare's own spellings, punctuation, language, and syntax was most firmly established by Eric Robinson and Geoffrey Summerfield's editions of *The Later Poems of John Clare* and *The Shepherd's Calendar* in 1964, is now accepted as essential for any serious reading, and is the practice in all good recent editions.

The third development has been the growing interest in Clare's prose, sometimes as a necessary adjunct to the poetry but increasingly for its intrinsic merits. During his lifetime, Clare's prose was read by very few—Taylor, for whom he wrote the autobiographical sketches, and Hessey, for whom he wrote the Natural History Letters, and a few friends—but its merits have come to be recognized by a wider audience. Blunden's edition of *Sketches in the Life of John Clare* made strong claims that the *Sketches* contained "Fresh information and thoughts of a poet of the purest kind; originality of judgment, bold honesty; illuminating and otherwise unobtainable observations of intricate village life in England between 1793 and 1821; a good narrative—nearly as good as Bunyan—and plenty of picturesque expression. It will be a long time before a voice again speaks from a cottage window with this power over ideas and over language." More and more prose has emerged into print from the manuscript collections, mainly in Peterborough and Northampton: in the Tibbles' editions of *The Prose of John Clare* (1951) and *The Letters of John Clare* (1951) and, subsequently, in scrupulously edited versions in Margaret Grainger's *Natural History Prose Writings of John Clare* (1983) and Eric Robinson's *John Clare's Autobiographical Writings* (1983). A new edition of *The Letters of John Clare,* edited by Mark Storey, was published in 1985. Like the prose, Clare's letters have the immediacy of his impassioned desire to set things down: "Letter writing is a thing I give no brush of correction or study too—

Sketch by Clare for his gravestone

tis just set down as things come to my 'tongue's end.' "

The fragmentariness of his prose is not as much of a problem as it might be for an author with a different view of the world. For Clare, all observation had to begin with detail and the immediate response. So, although the natural history of Helpstone was never completed, though the journal ends at no conclusion, though the *Sketches in the Life of John Clare* take his story only to 1821 and are supplemented by fragments thereafter, the prose accumulates in impact on similar lines to the poetry by the amassing of detail, fresh, vital, and known to so few. In fact one of Clare's great merits as a writer is not simply the clarity and honesty of description, but his perception that some of the things he notes need observing at all. As George Deacon writes in *John Clare and the Folk Tradition* (1983), "From no other source can we so clearly appreciate the content and nature of the tradition of rural England." As an observer of what it was like in England in the early nineteenth century, not only for the peasant but also from the peasant point of view, he is irreplaceable. All the observations, all the fragments, all the letters, all the autobiographical pieces cohere in the single vision of one man, and demand attention. We see in his prose the record of the growth of a poet's mind, but we also see reflected there in sharp clarity the very essence of a period, a place, a language, a culture, and a time.

Letters:

The Letters of John Clare, edited by J. W. Tibble and Anne Tibble (London: Routledge & Kegan Paul, 1951);

The Letters of John Clare, edited by Mark Storey (Oxford: Clarendon Press, 1985).

Bibliographies:

David Powell, ed., *Catalogue of the John Clare Collection in the Northampton Public Library* (Northampton: Northampton Public Libraries, Museums and Art Gallery Committee, 1964; Supplementary volume, 1971);

A Descriptive Catalogue of the John Clare Collection in Peterborough Museum and Art Gallery (Peterborough: Peterborough Museum Society, 1973);

H. O. Dendurent, *John Clare: A Reference Guide* (Boston: G. K. Hall, 1978);

Barbara Estermann, *John Clare: An Annotated Primary and Secondary Bibliography* (New York & London: Garland, 1985).

Biographies:

Frederick Martin, *The Life of John Clare* (London: Macmillan, 1865); republished with introduction and notes by Eric Robinson and Geoffrey Summerfield (London: Cass, 1964);

J. W. Tibble and Anne Tibble, *John Clare: a Life* (London: Cobden-Sanderson, 1932; revised, London: Joseph/Totowa, N.J.: Rowman & Littlefield, 1972);

June Wilson, *Green Shadows* (London: Hodder & Stoughton, 1951);

J. W. Tibble and Anne Tibble, *John Clare: His Life and Poetry* (London: Heinemann, 1956);

Edward Storey, *A Right to Song* (London: Methuen, 1982).

References:

John Barrell, *The Idea of Landscape and the Sense of Place, 1730-1840* (Cambridge: Cambridge University Press, 1972);

Timothy Brownlow, *John Clare and Picturesque Landscape* (Oxford: Clarendon Press, 1983);

Tim Chilcott, *'A Real World & Doubting Mind'* (Hull: Hull University Press, 1985);

Greg Crossan, *A Relish for Eternity: the Process of Divinization in the Poetry of John Clare* (Salzburg: Universität Salzburg, 1976);

George Deacon, *John Clare and the Folk Tradition* (London: Sinclair-Browne, 1983);

William Howard, *John Clare* (Boston: Twayne, 1981);

John Clare Society Journal, nos. 1-5, ongoing (1982-);

Mark Storey, ed., *Clare: the Critical Heritage* (London & Boston: Routledge & Kegan Paul, 1973);

Storey, *The Poetry of John Clare: A Critical Introduction* (London: Macmillan, 1974);

Janet M. Todd, *In Adam's Garden* (Gainesville: University of Florida Press, 1973).

Papers:

The major collections of Clare's papers are at the Northampton Public Library and the Peterborough Museum and Art Gallery. The Egerton manuscripts at the British Library include important letters to Clare.

E. S. Dallas

(?1828-17 January 1879)

Winifred Hughes

BOOKS: *Poetics: An Essay on Poetry* (London: Smith, Elder, 1852);

The Gay Science, 2 volumes (London: Chapman & Hall, 1866).

OTHER: *Kettner's Book of the Table,* ghostwritten by Dallas (London: Dulau, 1877).

PERIODICAL PUBLICATIONS: Review of *Maud and Other Poems,* by Alfred Tennyson, *Times* (London), 25 August 1855, p. 8;

"Currer Bell," *Blackwood's Magazine,* 82 (July 1857): 77-94;

Review of *Adam Bede,* by George Eliot, *Times* (London), 12 April 1859, p. 5;

"Anthony Trollope," *Times* (London), 23 May 1859, p. 12;

Review of *Essays on Fiction,* by Nassau William Senior, *Times* (London), 18 May 1864, p. 11;

Review of *Our Mutual Friend,* by Charles Dickens, *Times* (London), 29 November 1865, p. 6.

E. S. Dallas

E. S. Dallas, journalist and speculative critic, remains best known to scholars and literary historians as the author of *The Gay Science* (1866), a pioneering work in the field of psychological criticism which was either ignored or resoundingly misunderstood at the time of its publication. In his own day, Dallas achieved considerable if anonymous public influence in his role as a leading reviewer of biography and fiction for the London *Times.* During the 1850s and 1860s he led the life of an elegant, gregarious man about literary circles, member of the Garrick Club, friend of John Ruskin, dinner guest of George Eliot and George Henry Lewes.

Eneas Sweetland Dallas was born in Jamaica of Scottish parents, Elizabeth Baillie McIntosh Dallas and John Dallas, variously identified as a colonial planter or a physician. Brought to Scotland when he was four years old, Dallas was educated at the University of Edinburgh, where he studied philosophy under Sir William Hamilton and appears to have prepared for the ministry in the Church of Scotland. For reasons which remain obscure—one obituary mentions "an unfortunate personal defect"—he neither became a clergyman nor took his degree but instead surfaced in the early 1850s as a founder and staff reviewer of the *Edinburgh Guardian.* His most important apprentice work consisted of a series of reviews of Ruskin's lectures in Edinburgh and his first book, brashly entitled *Poetics: An Essay on Poetry* (1852). Before leaving Scotland permanently, Dallas met and fell in love with the well-known tragic actress Isabella Glyn, five years his senior. He married her first according to the Scottish form in December 1853 and again in an English ceremony at St. George's, Hanover Square, on 12 July 1855.

Dallas's *Poetics* offers a challenge to Aristotle's from the standpoint of Romantic aesthetic theory, as practiced by Samuel Taylor Coleridge and his German predecessors, and of post-Kantian metaphysics, as interpreted by Hamilton and other members of what John Stuart Mill contemptuously labeled "the Intuitive school." Rejecting both Aristotle's definition of poetry in terms of truthful imitation and Sir Francis Bacon's definition in terms of lies or invention, Dallas followed Coleridge in identifying pleasure as the definitive element in poetic experience. Pleasure is both the source and the aim of art, which should therefore be evaluated by critics as "the record of pleasure, . . . intended to produce pleasure in the reader's mind." Unlike the Romantic theorists, Dallas shifted the focus of his inquiry from the poet's power of creation to the reader's power of enjoyment. Poetry in the broadest sense, he argues, is a state of mind or emotion shared by both artist and audience; it is not the exclusive privilege of genius but a universal human possession.

Pleasure itself is to be defined as "*the harmonious and unconscious activity of the soul.*" While pain is inherently self-conscious—in fact the inevitable result of too much introspection—pleasure is spontaneous and self-forgetting. Deriving his earliest ideas from traditional religious mysticism, Dallas in *Poetics* sees pleasure in terms of ecstasy, or a going out of self into unself, ultimately in terms of the soul's merging with the divine. The ecstasy transmitted by poetry can neither be consciously sought nor rationally explained; it is the province not of reason or understanding but of imagination, which Dallas portrays as "the grand harmonist of life . . . the interpreter and peacemaker between mind and matter." In this context Dallas suggests an important revision of the typical Romantic distinction between imagination and fancy, describing them not as two separate faculties but as higher and lower degrees of unconsciousness on the part of both poet and audience: "According as the imagination is weak or strong, its consciousness will be strong or weak. When imagination is at its height, then is consciousness at its lowest ebb; and as the tide of the latter rises, the spirit of the former vanishes." Dallas's theory of the poetic impulse is radically intuitionist and primitivist, finding in the child or the dreamer a flash of divine inspiration denied to the rational philosopher.

In *Poetics* the young Dallas is most effective when he undertakes to convey the sense of mystery at the heart of poetic experience, much less so when he descends to practical application in his extended treatment of the genres and the language of poetry. Here the weaknesses of his methodology are all too obvious: he is obsessed with arbitrary schemes of classification; he has no use for empirical evidence or induction; he is finally unable to demonstrate any convincing relation between abstract principles and specific works of art. Given the abstruse nature of Dallas's speculation, it is perhaps less remarkable that the *Poetics* attracted little public attention than that it was reviewed at all in a handful of contemporary periodicals. Although the critic for the *Athenaeum* admonished Dallas for "too rigorous an adherence to a kind of *a priori* method, which seeks to deduce the laws of poetry from certain preassumed laws of the human mind," the reviews on balance were mildly favorable, expressing approval of Dallas's bold attempt to systematize critical theory, if not of his actual achievement.

Not long after the publication of *Poetics,* Dallas's arrival on the London literary scene was decisively confirmed by his stunning debut in the *Times* in August of 1855. His first published review, which set the town buzzing with curiosity about its anonymous author, launched a sharp attack on the poet laureate as a leader of the so-called spasmodic school of poetry. A reader of *Poetics* would not have been surprised by Dallas's objection to the morbid self-analysis of the narrator of Tennyson's *Maud.* For Dallas, as for Matthew Arnold, the essence of true poetry was action, not diseased introspection, and he blamed Tennyson for misusing his public position to foster an entire generation of "poets hiding themselves in holes and corners, and weaving interminable cobwebs out of their own bowels."

Although he later softened his criticism of Tennyson, finding more to praise in the first installment of *Idylls of the King* (1859) and *Lucretius* (1868), over the next fifteen years Dallas managed to uphold a high standard of consistency and independent judgment while operating as a staff reviewer in the fast-paced, politically charged atmosphere of John T. Delane's *Times.* His authoritative review of *Adam Bede* (1859)—"There can be no mistake about *Adam Bede.* It is a first-rate novel, and its author takes rank at once among the masters of the art"—firmly established George Eliot's reputation before either her identity or her sex was publicly known and led to a succession of perceptive essays on her novels as they appeared. Even when he expressed qualms about her unorthodox choice of fictional materials, particularly in *The Mill on the Floss* (1860), Dallas was moved by the detailed truthfulness of her psychological studies of character and the all-encompassing sympathy of her narrative ethic. The modern decline of heroism, which Dallas elsewhere lamented, became in Eliot's hands a lesson in the dignity and oneness of humanity: "It is the grandest of all lessons . . . the most consoling of all creeds—that real greatness is within the reach of the poorest and meanest of mankind."

George Eliot was not alone in recognizing the extraordinary power that accompanied Dallas's position and the crucial effect of a few columns of print in the *Times* on both sales and critical standing. After years of being savaged by Dallas's predecessors, Charles Dickens was so grateful for a favorable notice of *Our Mutual Friend* (1864-1865) that he presented his reviewer with the handsomely bound original manuscript. Not even Anthony Trollope, who questioned the propriety of such a gift in his *Autobiography* (1883), could deny that Dallas's lengthy review of his travelogue *The West Indies and the Spanish Main* (1859) had "made the fortune of the book," nor did he neglect to commend the general quality of Dallas's work. Numerous contemporary accounts emphasize the unusual depth of learning and scholarship, as well as the graceful and readable style, which characterized this prominent literary voice of the daily press in mid-Victorian England.

Versatility became a Dallas trademark in the heyday of his journalistic career. In addition to his regular reviewing, Dallas turned his hand to everything from writing obituaries to recommending city dining spots and served brilliantly as a special correspondent from Paris during the Exhibition of 1867 and again during the siege of 1870. He supplemented his profitable connection with the *Times* by joining the initial staff of William Makepeace Thackeray's *Cornhill Magazine* and by contributing both occasional pieces and more substantial articles to such current publications as *Blackwood's, Macmillan's,* the *World,* the *Daily News,* and the *Pall Mall Gazette.* In 1868 and 1869 he was able to command a yearly salary of £800 and a front-page byline as editor of the illustrated miscellany *Once a Week.* The price for his undeniable success was to be exacted in the scattering of his energies and of his formidable talents among the fragmentary labors of anonymous journalism. Dallas himself was well aware, as he once wrote in the *Times,* that "not many reviews are worthy of review," for "it is the very nature of criticism—at least, that sort of criticism which takes the form of reviews—to be of fugitive interest."

It was undoubtedly with the desire to produce something of more than fugitive value that Dallas returned in his second book, *The Gay Science,* to his earlier project of establishing a systematic basis for criticism. By 1866 that basis was no longer metaphysics but modern psychology. If criticism was to take its proper place as a science of human behavior, Dallas argued, it must consist of "the science of the laws and conditions under which pleasure is produced," in other words a psychology of imaginative pleasure. In his attempt to construct a scientific foundation for Romantic theories of involuntary poetic inspiration, Dallas became the first English critic to draw upon the work of mid-Victorian experimental psychologists and physiologists, who were then only beginning to collect empirical evidence and derive conclusions that would ultimately lead to the Freudian model of the unconscious. It was Dallas's essential insight—and his most valuable contribution to modern critical theory—to locate the working of the imagination, as well as the pleasure it transmits, in the unconscious or in what he himself termed "the Hidden Soul."

Dallas's exposition of the nature of the hidden soul is quite remarkable for its time and only seems less striking today because it so accurately anticipated developments in Freudian psychoanalysis. For Dallas, the unconscious is nothing less than the elemental ground of being, which exists in vital relation to the conscious self and which carries on in secret the same activities of reason, memory, and emotion. "This unconscious part of the mind is so dark, and yet so full of activity; so like the conscious intelligence and yet so divided from it by the veil of mystery, that it is not much of a hyperbole to speak of the human soul as double; or at least as leading a double life." With this fully naturalistic theory of the unconscious, Dallas no longer had to look to mystical ecstasy or divine inspiration in order to explain the aesthetic powers of creativity and enjoyment. The imagination, with its extraordinary capacity for integrating parts into wholes and reconciling discord, was no longer to be regarded as a special faculty but as a function, as "the automatic action of the mind or any of its faculties. . . . the entire mind in its secret working." The life of the imagination, Dallas proposes in *The Gay Science,* is neither restricted to the poet nor cut off from ordinary experience; its energies and delights are both essential and accessible to all.

The deep and universal pleasure aroused by works of art results from the artist's irresistible appeal to the unconscious minds of his audience. The true artist can be recognized by his ability to touch the imagination of the ordinary man, "to establish a connection with the unconscious hemisphere of

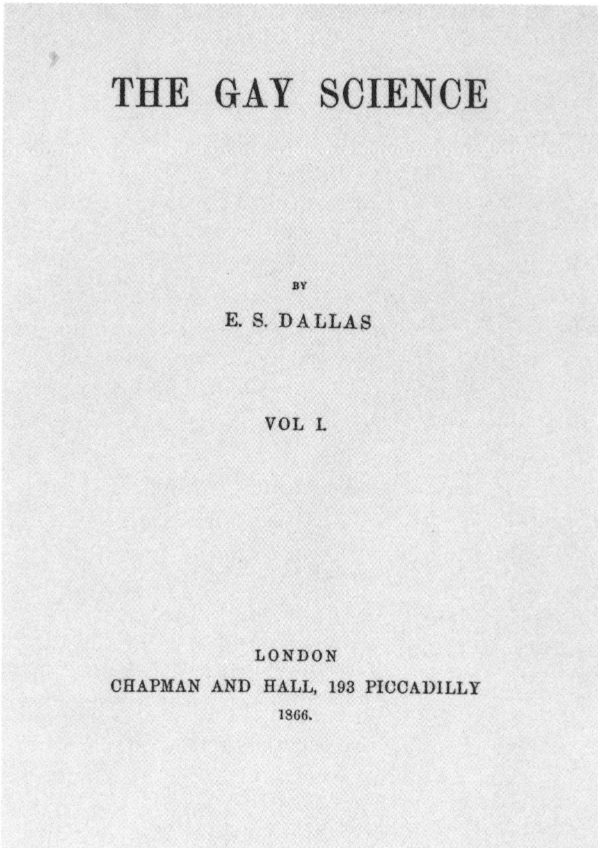
THE GAY SCIENCE

BY

E. S. DALLAS

VOL I.

LONDON
CHAPMAN AND HALL, 193 PICCADILLY
1866.

Title page for the first volume of Dallas's pioneering book based on his insight that the working of the imagination, as well as the pleasure it transmits, is a function of the unconscious mind, or "Hidden Soul"

the mind, and to make us feel a mysterious energy there in the hidden soul." By defining pleasure as inherently unconscious, Dallas was able to resolve Coleridge's antithesis—potentially damaging to the credibility of art—between pleasure as the object of poetry and truth as the object of science. Dallas contends that both art and science embody truth, the former for the sake of giving pleasure and the latter for the sake of imparting knowledge. "To say that the object of art is pleasure in contrast to knowledge, is quite different from saying that it is pleasure in contrast to truth": pleasure and truth need not be seen as conflicting. What art communicates is not falsehood but "the unknown and the unknowable"; its pleasure consists in "a sensible possession or enjoyment of the world beyond consciousness."

In *The Gay Science,* as in his previous work, Dallas unflinchingly advocated "the pursuit of pleasure as pleasure" and "the gratification of impulse" as necessary conditions of art. Placing himself in deliberate opposition to the prevailing mid-Victorian climate of opinion, he openly combated the Ruskinian moral aesthetic and proposed to separate art conclusively from the realm of ethics. In Dallas's view, "all questions as to the moral right or wrong and good or bad of pleasure-seeking are nothing to the point." The unconscious has its own imperatives, related to pleasure rather than to knowledge or morality, which art seeks to fulfill. The moral tendency of art must always remain inherent rather than explicit. In his emphasis on the autonomy and amorality of aesthetic pleasure, Dallas can be considered an early forerunner of the art-for-art's-sake movement that would become dominant in its turn before the end of the century. At the same time, however, he continued to insist on the larger, social dimensions of art and its connection with the cultural life of its age. Unlike the later aesthetes, Dallas rejected an elitist notion of art for one that is thoroughly democratic. "The pleasure of art is a popular pleasure," he wrote in *The Gay Science.* "The fit are not few, and the few are not fit. The true judges of art are the much despised many. . . . The great artist will command high and low alike."

Looking for "the master current" of his own era, Dallas found it in the democratizing influence of a burgeoning mass culture. In the concluding section of *The Gay Science,* as in many of his reviews for the *Times,* he offers some acute analysis of the historical and economic causes behind what he identifies as a gradual but revolutionary "change in the relation of the individual to the mass," a trend reflected on the literary scene in the prominence of biography and the novel. While in Dallas's view the heroic individual of classical literature has suffered an irrevocable decline, the ordinary man, with his private and domestic concerns, has replaced him as the focal point of art: "If individuals fail as heroes, still they flourish and are of more account than ever as men." Dallas responded to these signs of the times with ambivalence, lamenting the confusion of values and the propensity to morbid self-involvement but welcoming the broader extension of artistic sympathies. Although he correctly predicted the major problems that would come to be associated with a modern mass culture, he remained committed to his own unique and democratic form of aestheticism.

The contemporary reception of the ambitious and genuinely original theorizing set forth in *The Gay Science* can only have been discouraging to its author. Even the reviews that were not overtly hostile showed little comprehension of what Dallas was trying to do. There were objections to everything from the title itself—inspired by *el gai saber,* the art of the troubadours, and presumably intended to oppose the "dismal science" of political economy—to the democratic slant of his aesthetic standard. Most unsettling of all to his fellow critics was Dallas's linking of the idea of the unabashed pleasure-seeking of the imagination with a modern empirically based theory of the unconscious. His argument was judged morally and socially dangerous in its tendencies to undermine the power of the conscious will and to threaten a whole society's devotion to unpleasant duties and to the Christian work ethic. Pleasure, for Dallas's critics, was not to be endorsed as an end in itself but only as an artistic means to the higher and more utilitarian purposes of moral instruction and spiritual elevation. The *London Quarterly Review* even included a nasty ad hominem attack on Dallas's qualifications as a leader of public taste, gratuitously mentioning his wife's "unblemished social reputation" despite her eminence on the popular stage before taking a swipe at the general reluctance of other journalists to criticize a reviewer for the powerful *Times.* Only his friend G. A. Sala, writing for the *Illustrated London News,* came to his defense with a cogent and well-informed account of the current state of experimental psychology. It is little wonder that Dallas never completed the further volumes of practical criticism promised in his preface to *The Gay Science.*

In a memoir for the *Illustrated London News,* Sala remembered Dallas at the height of his brief career as "a Prince among journalists," offering a rare glimpse of his attractive personal qualities: "How he was courted, and flattered, and caressed! Strikingly handsome in person, graceful in mien, gentle in manner, with a melodious voice and a winning smile, he had almost everything in his favour." But his final decade was marked by increasing decline, both private and professional. "The shadow of a cypress, as it were," Sala quaintly wrote, "was drawn across his life-path." After separating from his wife in 1867, Dallas went through scandalous and well-publicized divorce proceedings in 1874. He eventually pleaded no contest to her charges of adultery and desertion but was forced to sue her for recovery of property, including some of his manuscripts. Around the same time his health began to deteriorate, and there were rumors of addiction to opium and alcohol as well as excessive gourmandism. His latter-day trouble with meeting deadlines may have been responsible for the end of his association with the *Times* after 1871. In his last years he degenerated to the level of composing food columns for lesser newspapers and ghostwriting a popular cookbook, *Kettner's Book of the Table* (1877), ironically his only best-seller. According to an obituary notice in the *Illustrated London News,* he died in lodgings of "a painful and malignant disease of the liver" at the age of fifty-one. He was buried at Kensal Green.

Although *The Gay Science* had no perceptible influence in its own time, since the early part of the twentieth century there have been sporadic attempts, in the *Times Literary Supplement* and various scholarly journals, to revive interest in the book, which is now considered E. S. Dallas's most important work. Modest as it is, and limited to academic circles, Dallas's reputation as a serious speculative critic has probably never stood higher. In fact, Alba H. Warren, Jr., in *English Poetic Theory* (1950), describes Dallas as "the best abstract theorist of his period." *The Gay Science,* reprinted in 1969, still makes for witty and provocative reading and attests to its author's significance as an unjustly neglected precursor of twentieth-century psychological criticism.

References:

John Drinkwater, "Eneas Sweetland Dallas," in his *The Eighteen-Sixties* (Cambridge: Cambridge University Press, 1932), pp. 201-223;

R. A. Forsyth, " 'The Onward March of Thought' and the Poetic Theory of E. S. Dallas," *British Journal of Aesthetics,* 3 (October 1963): 330-340;

Wendell V. Harris, *The Omnipresent Debate: Empiricism and Transcendentalism in Nineteenth-Century English Prose* (DeKalb: Northern Illinois University Press, 1981), pp. 293-301;

The History of "The Times": The Tradition Established 1841-1884 (London: The Times, 1939);

Derek Hudson, "What Happened to E. S. Dallas?," *Review of English Literature,* 8 (January 1967): 95-106;

Winifred Hughes, "E. S. Dallas: Victorian Poetics in Transition," *Victorian Poetry,* 23 (Spring 1985): 1-21;

Michael Roberts, "The Dream and the Poem: A Victorian Psychoanalyst," *Times Literary Supplement,* 18 January 1936, pp. 41-42;

Francis X. Roellinger, "E. S. Dallas on Imagination," *Studies in Philology,* 38 (October 1941): 652-664;

Roellinger, "E. S. Dallas: A Mid-Victorian Critic of Individualism," *Philological Quarterly*, 20 (October 1941): 611-621;

Alba H. Warren, Jr., *English Poetic Theory 1825-1865* (Princeton: Princeton University Press, 1950), pp. 126-151.

Charles Dickens

(7 February 1812-9 June 1870)

James Diedrick
Albion College

See also the Dickens entry in *DLB 21, Victorian Novelists Before 1885.*

BOOKS: *Sketches by Boz, Illustrative of Every-Day Life and Every-Day People* (first series, 2 volumes, London: Macrone, 1836; second series, London: Macrone, 1937); republished as *Watkins Tottle and Other Sketches Illustrative of Every Day Life and Every Day People,* 2 volumes (Philadelphia: Carey, Lea & Blanchard, 1837) and *The Tuggs's at Ramsgate and Other Sketches Illustrative of Every Day People* (Philadelphia: Carey, Lea & Blanchard, 1837);

The Village Coquettes: A Comic Opera in Two Acts, as "Boz," with music by John Hullah (London: Bentley, 1836);

The Posthumous Papers of the Pickwick Club, Edited by "Boz" (20 monthly parts, London: Chapman & Hall, 1836-1837; 5 volumes, Philadelphia: Carey, Lea & Blanchard, 1838);

The Strange Gentleman: A Comic Burletta, in Two Acts, as "Boz" (London: Chapman & Hall, 1837);

The Life and Adventures of Nicholas Nickleby (20 monthly parts, London: Chapman & Hall, 1837-1839; 1 volume, New York: Turney, 1839);

Sketches of Young Gentleman, Dedicated to the Young Ladies (London: Chapman & Hall, 1838);

Memoirs of Joseph Grimaldi, Edited by "Boz," 2 volumes (London: Bentley, 1838; Philadelphia: Carey, Lea & Blanchard, 1838);

Oliver Twist; or, The Parish Boy's Progress, by "Boz" (3 volumes, London: Bentley, 1838; 2 volumes, Philadelphia: Carey, Lea & Blanchard, 1839);

Sketches of Young Couples, with an Urgent Remonstrance to the Gentlemen of England (Being Bachelors or Widowers), on the Present Alarming Crisis (London: Chapman & Hall, 1840);

The Old Curiosity Shop (2 volumes, London: Chapman & Hall, 1841; 1 volume, Philadelphia: Lea & Blanchard, 1841);

Barnaby Rudge: A Tale of the Riots of 'Eighty (London: Chapman & Hall, 1841; Philadelphia: Lea & Blanchard, 1841);

Charles Dickens in New York, December 1867, photographed by Mathew Brady (National Archives, Brady Collection, No. B-2216)

American Notes for General Circulation (2 volumes, London: Chapman & Hall, 1842; 1 volume, New York: Wilson, 1842);
The Life and Adventures of Martin Chuzzlewit, 20 monthly parts (London: Chapman & Hall, 1842-1844);
A Christmas Carol, in Prose: Being a Ghost Story of Christmas (London: Chapman & Hall, 1843; Philadelphia: Carey & Hart, 1844);
The Chimes: A Goblin Story of Some Bells That Rang an Old Year Out and a New Year In (London: Chapman & Hall, 1845; Philadelphia: Lea & Blanchard, 1845);
Pictures from Italy (London: Bradbury & Evans, 1846); republished as *Travelling Letters Written on the Road* (New York: Wiley & Putnam, 1846);
The Cricket on the Hearth: A Fairy Tale of Home (London: Bradbury & Evans, 1846; Boston: Redding, 1846);
The Battle of Life: A Love Story (London: Bradbury & Evans, 1846; Boston: Redding, 1847);
Dombey and Son (20 monthly parts, London: Bradbury & Evans, 1846-1848; 1 volume, New York: Burgess, Stringer, 1847);
The Haunted Man and the Ghost's Bargain: A Fancy for Christmas Time (London: Bradbury & Evans, 1848; Philadelphia: Althemus, 1848);
The Personal History of David Copperfield (20 monthly parts, London: Bradbury & Evans, 1849-1850; 2 volumes, New York: Harper, 1852);
A Child's History of England (3 volumes, London: Bradbury & Evans, 1852-1854; 1 volume, Boston: Jenks, Hickling & Swan, 1854);
Bleak House (20 monthly parts, London: Bradbury & Evans, 1852-1853; 1 volume, New York: Harper, 1853);
Hard Times: For These Times (London: Bradbury & Evans, 1854; New York: McElrath, 1854);
Little Dorrit (20 monthly parts, London: Bradbury & Evans, 1855-1857; 1 volume, Philadelphia: Peterson, 1857);
A Tale of Two Cities (London: Chapman & Hall, 1859; Philadelphia: Peterson, 1859);
Great Expectations (3 volumes, London: Chapman & Hall, 1861; 2 volumes, New York: Harper, 1861);
The Uncommercial Traveller (London: Chapman & Hall, 1861; New York: Sheldon, 1865);
Our Mutual Friend (20 monthly parts, London: Chapman & Hall, 1864-1865; 1 volume, New York: Harper, 1865);
Hunted Down: A Story, with Some Account of Thomas Griffiths Wainewright, The Poisoner (London: Hotten, 1870; Philadelphia: Peterson, 1870);
The Mystery of Edwin Drood (6 monthly parts, London: Chapman & Hall, 1870; 1 volume, Boston: Fields, Osgood, 1870);
A Child's Dream of a Star (Boston: Fields, Osgood, 1871);
Is She His Wife? Or, Something Singular: A Comic Burletta in One Act (Boston: Osgood, 1877);
The Life of Our Lord (New York: Simon & Schuster, 1934);
The Speeches of Charles Dickens, edited by K. J. Fielding (Oxford: Clarendon Press, 1960);
Uncollected Writings from Household Words, 1850-1859, 2 volumes (Bloomington: Indiana University Press, 1968; London: Allen Lane, 1969);
Charles Dickens' Book of Memoranda: A Photographic and Typographic Facsimile of the Notebook Begun in January 1855, transcribed and annotated by Fred Kaplan (New York: New York Public Library; Astor, Lenox and Tilden Foundations, 1981).

Collections: *Cheap Edition of the Works of Mr. Charles Dickens* (12 volumes, London: Chapman & Hall, 1847-1852; 3 volumes, London: Bradbury & Evans, 1858);
The Charles Dickens Edition, 21 volumes (London: Chapman & Hall, 1867-1875);
The Works of Charles Dickens, 21 volumes (London: Macmillan, 1892-1925);
The Works of Charles Dickens, Gadshill Edition, 36 volumes (London: Chapman & Hall/New York: Scribners, 1897-1908);
The Nonesuch Edition, edited by Arthur Waugh and others, 23 volumes (London: Nonesuch Press, 1937-1938);
The New Oxford Illustrated Dickens, 21 volumes (Oxford: Oxford University Press, 1947-1958);
The Clarendon Dickens, edited by Kathleen Tillotson and others, 6 volumes, ongoing (Oxford: Clarendon Press, 1966-).

Charles Dickens had one thing in common with his creation Thomas Gradgrind, the heartless utilitarian in *Hard Times:* a love of facts. Along with fourteen novels, many of them rich in topical allusion, Dickens produced a body of work as reporter, essayist, correspondent, and editor that constitutes a lifelong account of the facts of Victorian life as he knew them. However, this nonfiction is anything but a mere collection of Gradgrindian data. In his reporting and commentary, Dickens is often an outraged reformer, uncompromising in his attacks on privileged interests.

In the early sketches, he is a writer trying to achieve a synthesis of art and social criticism. The surviving letters, some 14,500 of which the editors of the ongoing Pilgrim Edition have collected, reveal a man of astonishing energies, who attempted to impose an artist's vision of order on every aspect of his life and work. In the late essays, Dickens emerges as a restless, poetic wanderer who masterfully blends observation, autobiography, and allegory. Much of this prose is valuable as a window on the novelist's attitudes and preoccupations, but most of it stands on its own, the work of an acute observer and dedicated craftsman.

The experiences that nourished this prodigious talent began in Portsmouth, where Dickens was born on 7 February 1812 to John and Elizabeth Barrow Dickens. John Dickens was a clerk in the naval pay office, a job that took him and his family to London in 1814, to Chatham in 1817, and back to London in 1822. In Chatham the young Charles Dickens spent the happiest years of his childhood. He loved the sights and sounds of the busy shipbuilding center, and both his parents encouraged his early devotion to such eighteenth-century prose masters as Henry Fielding, Oliver Goldsmith, and Tobias Smollett. But his father's inability to live within his means, coupled with the growth of the Dickens household (Charles Dickens had four brothers and sisters by 1822), brought an early end to this happiness that coincided with the family's second move to London. Just two days past his twelfth birthday, Dickens was sent to work pasting labels on shoe-blacking pots in a blacking warehouse to supplement the family income; eleven days later his father was arrested for debt and taken to the Marshalsea debtor's prison. The double blow of his family's fall from fortune and his own banishment into drudgery and humiliation constituted an abrupt loss of innocence whose ache never fully subsided. Although a bequest freed his father from the Marshalsea after three months, and Dickens's own warehouse tenure lasted only four, the sense of insecurity and injustice these events instilled lasted a lifetime. At the same time, the experience benefited the future writer, broadening his scope, deepening his insight, and contributing to the astonishing energy and resolve with which he subsequently pursued his vocation.

Less than a month after his father removed him from the blacking warehouse, Dickens was enrolled as a day student at the Wellington House Academy in London. Here, between the ages of twelve and fifteen, he was already trying his hand at the kind of writing that would launch him on his professional career. He submitted what was called "penny-a-line stuff" to his father's employer, the *British Press:* information about fires, accidents, or police reports missed by the regular reporters. Several years later, constrained by his work as a clerk in a law office, he set himself the difficult task of mastering shorthand so as to return to journalism in earnest. In 1828, during his sixteenth year, he became a free-lance reporter in the London law courts. For several years he alternated reporting, exploring the London streets, and reading avidly at the British Museum. Already devoted to the essays of Joseph Addison, Oliver Goldsmith, and Samuel Johnson, he now read the major nineteenth-century essayists: Leigh Hunt, William Hazlitt, Charles Lamb, Walter Savage Landor, and Thomas DeQuincey.

In his twentieth year, Dickens secured a job as a parliamentary reporter for the *Mirror of Parliament,* founded by his uncle John Henry Barrow. He worked there from 1832 to 1834. The reputation he made for himself would be the envy of any aspiring journalist. A contemporary of Dickens, James Grant of the *Morning Advertiser,* claimed that Dickens "occupied the very highest rank, not merely for accuracy in reporting, but for marvellous quickness in transcript." Despite his youth, he quickly won the respect of his older colleagues. "There never *was* such a shorthand writer!" de-

Dickens in an 1830 portrait by Janet Borrow, his maternal aunt (Suzannet Collection, Dickens House Museum, London)

clared one of them. Dickens's observations of parliament during and after the heady days of the Reform Bill debates constituted the liberal education neither he nor his parents could afford to finance. It also committed him to reform while making him suspicious of many reformers. The only problem with the *Mirror of Parliament* was that it did not pay its staff members when parliament was not in session, which forced Dickens back to free-lance court reporting. Thus when the liberal daily newspaper the *Morning Chronicle* was reorganized and expanded, Dickens jumped at the chance of becoming one of its regular staff members. His thoroughness and speed helped the *Chronicle* provide serious competition to its conservative rival the *Times.* The ambition that drove Dickens during these apprenticeship years, he later admitted to his friend and biographer John Forster, "excluded every other idea from my mind for four years, at a time of life when four years are equal to four times four." He added that he "went at it with a determination to overcome all difficulties, which fairly lifted me up into that newspaper life, and floated me away over a hundred men's heads."

Dickens's reputation as a reporter was soon eclipsed, however, by his growing fame as "Boz," the name under which he wrote a series of tales and sketches published in the *Monthly Magazine, Bell's Weekly Magazine,* the *Morning Chronicle,* the *Evening Chronicle,* and *Bell's Life in London and Sporting Chronicle.* He later collected these pieces in two hardcover volumes titled *Sketches by Boz* (1836), adding additional material and revising the originals. Many of the sketches are in fact essays, possessing a colloquial immediacy that vividly captures the lower- and middle-class street life he observed firsthand. In them Dickens introduced many of the scenes and much of the subject matter that later appeared in his fiction. For example, the sketch "Gin-Shops," besides demonstrating Dickens's knowledge of the lower reaches of Victorian society, is an early instance of the reformer's anger at those who condemn the symptoms of poverty without addressing its causes: "Gin-drinking is a great vice in England, but wretchedness and dirt are greater; and until you improve the homes of the poor, or persuade a half-famished wretch not to seek relief in the temporary oblivion of his own misery, with the pittance which, divided among his family, would furnish a morsel of bread for each, gin-shops will increase in number and splendor."

When *Sketches by Boz* was published contemporary reviewers were impressed. The critic for the *Morning Post* said that the "graphic descriptions of 'Boz' invest all he describes with amazing fidelity." The *Sunday Herald* hailed the collected sketches as "inimitably accurate." Many years later, during a banquet in his honor given by the New York press on 18 April 1868, Dickens attributed the verisimilitude of his writing to "the wholesome training of severe newspaper work." Recently, increased attention has been paid to the importance of the *Sketches by Boz.* Of the many reassessments the best is Duane DeVries's *Dickens's Apprentice Years: The Making of a Novelist* (1976), which shows how these short pieces allowed Dickens to develop the technical skill necessary to his later achievements.

The origins of *The Posthumous Papers of the Pickwick Club* (1836-1837), later known simply as *The Pickwick Papers,* suggest that Dickens the novelist is often difficult to separate from Dickens the journalist. The success of *Sketches by Boz* brought Dickens to the attention of Edward Chapman and William Hall, booksellers and publishers of periodicals who had recently begun producing books. They proposed that Dickens provide a series of Boz-like sketches to accompany the illustrations of Robert Seymour, one of England's leading comic artists. Dickens would write and edit twenty monthly installments to be sold for one shilling apiece. As reported by biographer Edgar Johnson, Dickens's friends warned him that the shilling number was a "low, cheap form of publication" that would prevent him from rising to the rank of respectable writer, but to no avail. Dickens began writing a few days after his twenty-fourth birthday, and before the end of March 1836, he had written 24,000 words, enough for the first two installments. With the twenty-nine pounds he received in payment Dickens was able to marry Catherine Hogarth (1815-1879) on 2 April, leaving on a short honeymoon before the first installment was published. The couple's first child, Charles, was born nine months later; over the next fifteen years came nine more children, several named after writers for whom Dickens had a special affinity: Mary, Kate, Walter Landor, Alfred Tennyson, Sydney Smith Haldemand, Henry Fielding, Dora Annie, and Edward Bulwer-Lytton.

The first number of *The Pickwick Papers* sold only 400 copies, but when the last number was printed in October 1837 the run was 40,000. In his preface to the first cheap edition of *The Pickwick Papers,* Dickens ironically recalled the warning of his friends, concluding: "how right my friends turned out to be, everybody now knows." The phenomenal success that resulted from this venture

Cartoon published in London's comic journal Mephystopheles *in January 1846, three days after Dickens's debut as founding editor of the radical* Daily News

created an entirely new approach to the publication of novels. Previously, serial publication of literature was restricted to cheap reprints of classics or ephemeral nonfiction turned out by poorly paid hack writers. Readers bought or checked out novels in three-volume hardback editions. Dickens's gamble wedded the serial appeal of journalism to the emotional engagement of fiction. All of his subsequent novels were published in installments, and many other novelists adopted this mode.

The Pickwick Papers turned Dickens from an obscure reporter into a celebrity, but it did not diminish his journalistic energy. While writing *The Pickwick Papers,* in fact, he found that he could occasionally blend his journalism into his fiction. In May, with only two installments of *The Pickwick Papers* in print, Dickens, using the pseudonym Timothy Sparks, wrote a pamphlet fiercely attacking a bill that would prohibit all work and recreation on Sundays. The pamphlet, *Sunday Under Three Heads: As It Is; As Sabbath Bills Would Make It; As It Might Be Made,* argued that without this day of recreation and enjoyment, increasing numbers of poor would resort to the gin shops, just the result that "your saintly law-givers" are supposedly trying to avoid as they "lift up their hands to heaven, and exclaim for a law which shall convert the day intended for rest and cheerfulness, into one of universal gloom, bigotry, and persecution." In the pamphlet Dickens created a Nonconformist preacher whose hypocrisy anticipates that of the red-nosed minister Stiggins, who appeared in the December number of *The Pickwick Papers.* And on 22 June, on assignment for the *Morning Chronicle,* Dickens attended a divorce case in which Lord Melbourne was accused of adultery with the wife of the Hon. George Norton; some of this material found its way into the farcical trial of Bardell vs. Pickwick, which appeared in the July installment. It is likely that the monthly praise Dickens received as Pickwick's adventures unfolded convinced him of the advantages of maintaining regular contact with his readers, as journalism allowed him to do. He did sever his connection with the *Morning Chronicle* in November 1836, but he continued to submit articles and letters to newspapers for the remainder of his life. He even agreed to become founding editor of a new radical paper, the *Daily News,* in

January 1846, but he was not suited for the role of daily-newspaper editor, and his tenure lasted a short seventeen issues. His editorial ambitions, however, were not confined to newspapers.

January 1837 saw publication of the first issue of *Bentley's Miscellany,* a monthly collection of fiction, biographical notes, verses, and humor edited by Dickens and published by Richard Bentley. *Oliver Twist,* the first of Dickens's novels to be published as part of a magazine, was serialized in the *Miscellany* beginning with the second issue and published in three volumes by Bentley in 1838. The novel was partly inspired by Dickens's hatred of the New Poor Law, which he heard debated in Parliament and which he viewed as a subordination of the needs of the poor to institutional control and efficiency. *Oliver Twist* was a huge success for both Dickens and Bentley, but financial and editorial disputes between the two men became increasingly bitter. In a move that foreshadowed subsequent dealings with his publishers, Dickens resigned his position at the magazine in February 1839 in a disagreement over editorial control. At the end of an otherwise judicious and moderate farewell address published in the March issue, Dickens told his readers that the magazine had "always been literally 'Bentley's Miscellany,' and never mine."

Seeking greater editorial autonomy, Dickens arranged with Chapman and Hall to bring out a new weekly periodical, and *Master Humphry's Clock* was born on 4 April 1840. Conceived in the spirit of Addison's *Spectator* papers, *Master Humphry's Clock* began as a blend of sketches, essays, and tales but quickly faltered when readers discovered there was no engrossing novel by Dickens to hold their interest. Before the decline Dickens had discussed with Forster a short pathetic tale he would write for the magazine; when trouble arose he responded with a characteristic adaptability, turning the tale into a novel. Thus was *The Old Curiosity Shop* produced, one of many cases of Dickens's journalism fostering his fiction. *The Old Curiosity Shop* brought the circulation of *Master Humphry's Clock* up to 100,000, and Chapman and Hall published the novel in two volumes in 1841. But after *Barnaby Rudge* (1 volume, 1841) had also appeared in its pages, Dickens arranged with Chapman and Hall to discontinue the magazine in November 1841 and return to publishing his novels in monthly parts.

For Dickens, editing (or "conducting" as he later described it) a magazine was a way of maintaining close contact with his audience, something he learned to value during the publication of *The Pickwick Papers.* When he decided to make his first trip to America, he used the preface to *Master Humphry's Clock* to announce his impending separation from his readers: "I have decided, in January next, to pay a visit to America. The pleasure I anticipate from this realization of a wish I have long entertained . . . is subdued by the reflection that it must separate us for a longer time than other circumstances would have rendered necessary." Dickens and his wife left England on 4 January 1842, arriving in Boston on 22 January and returning on 7 June.

Their itinerary was ambitious, taking them from the eastern seaboard to the southern slave states and west to St. Louis, then back via Ohio, Toronto, Montreal, and New York by way of Lake Champlain. The process whereby Dickens's infatuation with most things American turned to disillusionment is chronicled in a series of increasingly caustic letters he wrote home to friends and in books seven through thirteen of *The Life and Adventures of Martin Chuzzlewit* (published 1842-1844, in twenty parts). In much of *American Notes for General Circulation,* published in two volumes in October 1842, Dickens replaces this vituperation with shrewd journalistic analyses of American institutions in light of their English counterparts: asylums, factories, prisons. His accounts of New York's Tombs prison and the Philadelphia penitentiary are especially powerful, recalling "A Visit to Newgate" in *Sketches by Boz.* In his account of touring the Tombs, Dickens applies the mordant wit of the satirist to his description of an exchange he had with a prison guard. The guard had explained that the boy in one cramped cell had been locked up for "safe keeping" because he was a witness in the upcoming trial of his father. Dickens asked if this was not hard treatment for the witness, and the guard replied: "Well, it ain't a very rowdy life, and *that's* a fact!"

Despite the generally moderate tone of *American Notes for General Circulation,* certain U.S. papers reacted violently. The *New York Herald* reviewer called Dickens "that famous penny-a-liner," with "the most coarse, vulgar, imprudent, and superficial" mind, whose view of America was that of "a narrow-minded, conceited cockney." English readers were generally unimpressed and longed for another novel. Twentieth-century opinion ranges from high praise for the book's social criticism to disappointment at its lack of "personality" in comparison with Dickens's other travel book, *Pictures from Italy* (1846). A richly detailed account of the response to *American Notes for General Circulation* is provided in Michael Slater's introduction to *Dickens*

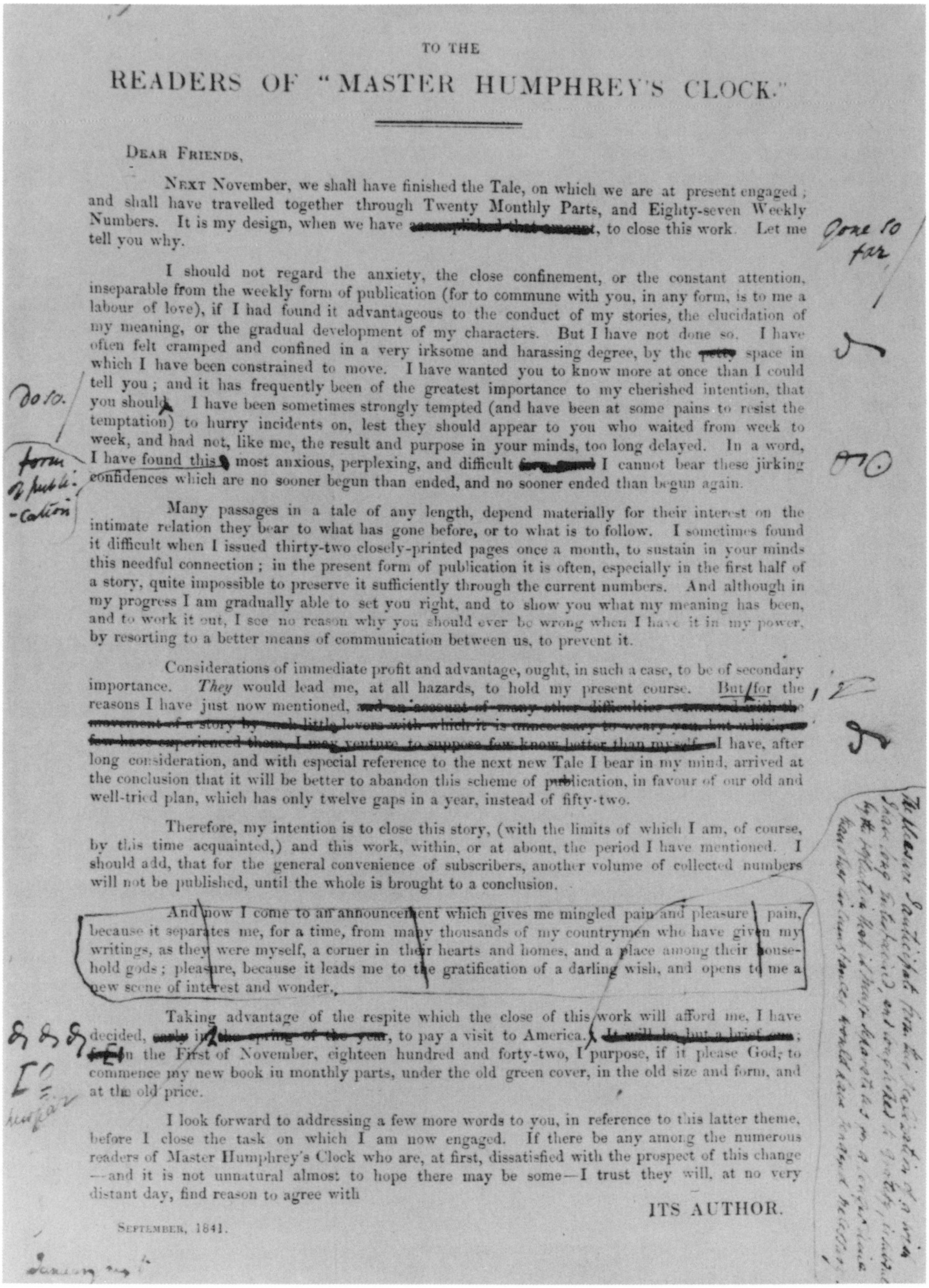

TO THE

READERS OF "MASTER HUMPHREY'S CLOCK."

DEAR FRIENDS,

NEXT November, we shall have finished the Tale, on which we are at present engaged; and shall have travelled together through Twenty Monthly Parts, and Eighty-seven Weekly Numbers. It is my design, when we have ~~accomplished that amount~~, to close this work. Let me tell you why.

I should not regard the anxiety, the close confinement, or the constant attention, inseparable from the weekly form of publication (for to commune with you, in any form, is to me a labour of love), if I had found it advantageous to the conduct of my stories, the elucidation of my meaning, or the gradual development of my characters. But I have not done so. I have often felt cramped and confined in a very irksome and harassing degree, by the ~~petty~~ space in which I have been constrained to move. I have wanted you to know more at once than I could tell you; and it has frequently been of the greatest importance to my cherished intention, that you should. I have been sometimes strongly tempted (and have been at some pains to resist the temptation) to hurry incidents on, lest they should appear to you who waited from week to week, and had not, like me, the result and purpose in your minds, too long delayed. In a word, I have found this most anxious, perplexing, and difficult ~~[illegible]~~ I cannot bear these jerking confidences which are no sooner begun than ended, and no sooner ended than begun again.

Many passages in a tale of any length, depend materially for their interest on the intimate relation they bear to what has gone before, or to what is to follow. I sometimes found it difficult when I issued thirty-two closely-printed pages once a month, to sustain in your minds this needful connection; in the present form of publication it is often, especially in the first half of a story, quite impossible to preserve it sufficiently through the current numbers. And although in my progress I am gradually able to set you right, and to show you what my meaning has been, and to work it out, I see no reason why you should ever be wrong when I have it in my power, by resorting to a better means of communication between us, to prevent it.

Considerations of immediate profit and advantage, ought, in such a case, to be of secondary importance. *They* would lead me, at all hazards, to hold my present course. But for the reasons I have just now mentioned, ~~and on account of many other difficulties [illegible] the movement of a story by [illegible] little levers with which it is unnecessary to weary you, but which few have experienced them, I may venture to suppose few know better than myself.~~ I have, after long consideration, and with especial reference to the next new Tale I bear in my mind, arrived at the conclusion that it will be better to abandon this scheme of publication, in favour of our old and well-tried plan, which has only twelve gaps in a year, instead of fifty-two.

Therefore, my intention is to close this story, (with the limits of which I am, of course, by this time acquainted,) and this work, within, or at about, the period I have mentioned. I should add, that for the general convenience of subscribers, another volume of collected numbers will not be published, until the whole is brought to a conclusion.

And now I come to an announcement which gives me mingled pain and pleasure: pain, because it separates me, for a time, from many thousands of my countrymen who have given my writings, as they were myself, a corner in their hearts and homes, and a place among their household gods; pleasure, because it leads me to the gratification of a darling wish, and opens to me a new scene of interest and wonder.

Taking advantage of the respite which the close of this work will afford me, I have decided, ~~early in the spring of the year~~, to pay a visit to America. ~~It will be but a brief one~~; ~~[illegible]~~ on the First of November, eighteen hundred and forty-two, I purpose, if it please God, to commence my new book in monthly parts, under the old green cover, in the old size and form, and at the old price.

I look forward to addressing a few more words to you, in reference to this latter theme, before I close the task on which I am now engaged. If there be any among the numerous readers of Master Humphrey's Clock who are, at first, dissatisfied with the prospect of this change—and it is not unnatural almost to hope there may be some—I trust they will, at no very distant day, find reason to agree with

ITS AUTHOR.

SEPTEMBER, 1841.

Proof corrected by Dickens for an issue of Master Humphry's Clock, *the weekly he began for Chapman and Hall in April 1840 (Victoria and Albert Museum). The "Tale" to which Dickens refers is his* Barnaby Rudge, *and in the revised passage at the bottom of the page he announces plans for his first visit to the United States.*

on America and the Americans, a collection that attests to the continuing appeal of Dickens's nonfiction.

Unlike the two travel books, most of Dickens's journalism in the 1840s was strident and outspoken. On 25 June 1842 a fiery letter from Dickens appeared in the *Morning Chronicle* supporting Lord Ashley's Bill to bar women and girls from working in the mines. On 7 July he sent a circular letter that continued his criticisms of American publishers who pirated English books. In June 1843 he lashed out against the High Church movement in an unsigned piece for the *Examiner,* where some of his best reporting appeared in the late 1840s, writing to its editor Albany Fonblanque about how misguided it was "to talk in these times of most untimely ignorance among the people, about what Priests shall wear and whither they shall turn when they say their prayers!"

Dickens began writing *A Child's History of England* at about this time, he told a friend, so his son Charley would not "get hold of any conservative or High Church notions." *A Child's History of England,* published in *Household Words* beginning in 1851 and in three volumes from 1852 to 1854, is an ill-informed and often astonishingly slapdash production, but even here Dickens's radical opinions give rise to powerful imagery, as when he refers to Henry VIII as "a blot of grease and blood upon the History of England." In March 1846 he wrote a long and carefully reasoned attack on capital punishment for the *Daily News,* the editorship of which he had recently resigned. This attack was echoed in a 13 November 1849 letter to the *Times* on the evening of a public hanging. "I do not believe that any community can prosper where such a scene of horror and demoralisation as was enacted this morning outside Horsemonger Lane Gaol is presented at the very doors of good citizens, and is passed by unknown and forgotten." Another campaign for reform had begun on 20 January 1849, with the appearance of the first of Dickens's four articles for the *Examiner* on the Tooting scandal, involving the deaths of 150 children at a child-farm outside of London. The article ends with a scathing indictment in the form of a characteristic peroration: "The cholera, or some unusually malignant form of typhus assimilating itself to that disease, broke out in Mr. Drouet's farm for children, because it was brutally conducted, vilely kept, preposterously inspected, dishonestly defended, a disgrace to a Christian community, and a stain upon a civilized land."

Following the failed *Daily News* experiment, Dickens's next major journalistic project was *Household Words.* Having broken with Chapman and Hall over their response to the poor sales of *Martin Chuzzlewit,* Dickens contracted with his new publishers, William Bradbury and Frederick Evans, to bring out the first issue of the twopenny weekly on 30 March 1850. This time Dickens was half-owner, assuring him editorial control, and for eight years he directed *Household Words* with an unerring sense of what would succeed. He also devoted extraordinary energies to every aspect of the magazine's production, from soliciting manuscripts to directing revisions to acting as a sort of silent collaborator on most of the articles. As Harry Stone has shown in his introduction to Dickens's *Uncollected Writings from Household Words* (1968), Dickens made certain that every contribution to the magazine was consistent with his views. Central to these views was a belief in the restorative power of the imagination. In "A Preliminary Word" to the first issue of the magazine, Dickens proclaimed that *Household Words* would teach "the hardest workers at this whirling wheel of toil, that their lot is not necessarily a moody, brutal fact, excluded from the sympathies and graces of imagination." He added that the magazine would show that "in all familiar things, even in those which are repellant on the surface, there is Romance enough, if we will find it out." This clothing of fact in the fabric of fancy is evident in "Valentine's Day at the Post Office," an article that details the workings of London's central postal office. W. H. Wills wrote the bulk of the article, but Dickens's improving hand is evident in many sections, including the following passage, describing the scene as the deadline for posting newspapers approaches: "By degrees it began to rain hard; by fast degrees the storm came on harder and harder, until it blew, rained, hailed, snowed, newspapers. A fountain of newspapers played in at the window. Water-spouts of newspapers broke from enormous sacks, and engulphed the men inside. . . ."

Dickens published a great many of this kind of essay in *Household Words* (he called them "process" articles), on subjects ranging from the production of plate glass to the editing and printing of *Household Words* itself. He also made room for a series of major novels, from Elizabeth Cleghorn Gaskell's *North and South* to his own *Hard Times.* In addition, the magazine often became the voice of Dickens the radical moralist. The 4 January 1851 issue, for instance, contained an article that presented a very different image of England from that promoted by the Great Exhibition of that year. Titled "The Last Words of the Old Year," the article

"The story of our lives from Year to Year."—SHAKSPEARE.

EVERY SATURDAY, FROM THE 30th APRIL, 1859,

PRICE TWOPENCE,

ALL THE YEAR ROUND,

A WEEKLY JOURNAL,

DESIGNED FOR

The Instruction and Entertainment of all Classes of Readers, and to assist in the Discussion of the Social Questions of the Day

Conducted by CHARLES DICKENS.

ADDRESS.

Nine years of HOUSEHOLD WORDS, are the best practical assurance that can be offered to the public, of the spirit and objects of ALL THE YEAR ROUND.

In transferring myself, and my strongest energies, from the publication that is about to be discontinued by me, to the publication that is about to be begun, I have the happiness of taking with me the staff of writers with whom I have laboured, and all the literary and business co-operation that can make my work a pleasure. In some important respects, I am now free greatly to advance on past arrangements. Those, I leave to testify for themselves in due course.

That fusion of the graces of the imagination with the realities of life, which is vital to the welfare of any community, and for which I have striven from week to week as honestly as I could during the last nine years, will continue to be striven for, "all the year round." The old weekly cares and duties become things of the Past, merely to be assumed, with an increased love for them and brighter hopes springing out of them, in the Present and the Future.

I look, and plan, for a very much wider circle of readers, and yet again for a steadily expanding circle of readers, in the projects I hope to carry through "all the year round." And I feel confident that this expectation will be realised, if it deserve realisation.

The task of my new journal is set, and it will steadily try to work the task out. Its pages shall show to what good purpose their motto is remembered in them, and with how much of fidelity and earnestness they tell

THE STORY OF OUR LIVES FROM YEAR TO YEAR.

CHARLES DICKENS.

Published also in Monthly Parts, and in Half-Yearly Volumes,

AT THE OFFICE, 11, WELLINGTON STREET NORTH, STRAND, W.C.:

ALSO BY CHAPMAN & HALL, 193, PICCADILLY, LONDON, W.

THE FIRST NUMBER OF **ALL THE YEAR ROUND**

WILL CONTAIN THE FIRST PART OF

A TALE OF TWO CITIES,

BY CHARLES DICKENS,

CONTINUED FROM WEEK TO WEEK.

On Saturday, 28th May, 1859, MR. CHARLES DICKENS will **CEASE TO CONDUCT HOUSEHOLD WORDS**; that Periodical will be **DISCONTINUED** by him; and its partnership of Proprietors dissolved.

Handbill announcing the journal Dickens began in 1859 after a feud with William Bradbury and Frederick Evans, his partners in publishing Household Words catalogued the legacy of 1850: dispossessed and hungry children, desperate farmers, crowded slums, sewers that spread disease throughout the country. He "bequeathed" to the new year "a vast inheritance of degradation and neglect in England, a general mismanagement of all public expenditure, revenues and property." To urge reform of these "brutal" facts, Dickens regularly employed *Household Words* to campaign for improvements in sanitation, slum housing, popular education, and workplace safety, and for the right workingmen to form trade unions. This blend of information, art, and radical polemic produced a lively hybrid, something like a cross between the *New Yorker* and the *Nation* but with a broader appeal than either.

On 30 April 1859 Dickens brought out the first issue of *All the Year Round,* a magazine that had its origins in a feud with Bradbury and Evans. Dickens had begun to make reference to his marital troubles in several letters of the early 1850s; in April 1857 he met the actress Ellen Ternan, who was twenty-seven years his junior. His infatuation with Ellen made him determined to establish Catherine in a separate household, a move that was accompanied by ill-conceived public announcements, including a front-page address to the readers of the 12 June 1858 issue of *Household Words.* Bradbury and Evans disapproved of this publicity and were critical of the stories that were circulating about Dickens's affair with Ternan. Dickens's anger over their response, coupled with his desire for total control over publication, drove him to sever his relations with the publishers, begin *All the Year Round,* and buy *Household Words* in order to close it down. The last issue of *Household Words* was published on 28 May 1859. Dickens was the publisher and editor of *All the Year Round* until his death, and in most ways it was a continuation of the successful formula of its predecessor. But Dickens did break with the tradition of unsigned articles in 1860 when he was announced as the author of a series of essays narrated by The Uncommercial Traveler. Employed by the "great house of the Human Interest Brothers," the Traveler wanders through a variety of London landscapes and rural scenes. In evocative, memorable images, Dickens describes workhouses, cheap theaters, churches, tramps, merchants, émigrés, and, at times, himself. The reminiscences, many of them recollections of childhood, supplement the autobiographical fragment Dickens wrote (published in Forster's 1905 *The Life of Dickens*) and provide insight into a childhood more famously evoked in *The Personal History of David Copperfield* (20 parts, 1849-1850) and *Great Expectations* (1861). The latter novel, first published in *All the Year Round* beginning 1 December 1860, was in fact initially conceived as a sketch for The Uncommercial Traveler series. Many of the essays in this series incorporate current events, but unlike the polemical journalism of the same period, they are more clearly literary productions. In an otherwise limited formulation, John Forster aptly characterized Dickens's approach in this kind of essay: "In his character of journalist Mr. Dickens has from the first especially laboured to cultivate the kindly affections and the fancy at the same time with the intellect." More recently, Gordon Spence has analyzed the literary qualities of several of these essays in *Charles Dickens as a Familiar Essayist* (1977).

During the last months of his life, while writing *The Mystery of Edwin Drood* (6 parts, 1870) and concluding a final series of phenomenally successful but physically punishing public readings, Dickens remained faithful to the profession that first nurtured his talent. In the spring of 1870 he made several trips to London to supervise his son Charley

Caricature by Leslie Ward of Dickens in 1870, the year of his death (Collection of Jerold J. Savory)

in the offices of *All the Year Round.* At the end of April he officially installed him as subeditor. On 5 April he gave a speech at the annual dinner of the Newsvendors' Benevolent Association, a group which aided the ragged boys and discharged servicemen who peddled newspapers in the streets. On 2 June, seven days before his death, he added a codicil to his will which gave his son his interest in *All the Year Round.* In his journalism as in his fiction, he remained a consummate professional to the end.

Letters:

The Letters of Charles Dickens, Pilgrim Edition, edited by Madeline House, Graham Storey, and Kathleen Tillotson, 5 volumes, ongoing (Oxford: Clarendon Press, 1965-).

Biographies:

John Forster, *The Life of Dickens,* 2 volumes (New York: Scribners, 1905);

Edgar Johnson, *Charles Dickens: His Tragedy and Triumph* (2 volumes, New York: Simon & Schuster, 1952; 1 volume, revised and abridged, New York: Viking, 1977; London: Lane, 1977);

Norman MacKenzie and Jeanne MacKenzie, *Dickens: A Life* (New York: Oxford University Press, 1979).

References:

A. W. C. Brice and K. J. Fielding, "Dickens and the Tooting Disaster," *Victorian Studies,* 12 (December 1968): 227-244;

Philip Collins, "Charles Dickens," in *Victorian Fiction: A Second Guide to Research,* edited by George H. Ford (New York: Modern Language Association, 1978), pp. 34-114;

Collins, *Dickens and Crime* (London: Macmillan/ New York: St. Martin's, 1962);

Collins, *Dickens and Education* (London: Macmillan/ New York: St. Martin's, 1963);

Collins, ed., *Dickens: The Critical Heritage* (London: Routledge & Kegan Paul, 1971);

Duane DeVries, *Dickens's Apprentice Years: The Making of a Novelist* (Hassocks, U.K.: Harvester Press/New York: Barnes & Noble, 1976);

K. J. Fielding, *Charles Dickens* (London: Longmans, Green, 1963);

George H. Ford, *Dickens and His Readers: Aspects of Novel Criticism* (Princeton: Princeton University Press, 1955);

Ford and Lauriat Lane, Jr., eds., *The Dickens Critics* (Ithaca: Cornell University Press, 1955);

John Greaves, *Dickens at Doughty Street* (London: Hamilton, 1975);

John Gross and Gabriel Pearson, eds., *Dickens and the Twentieth Century* (London: Routledge & Kegan Paul, 1962);

Humphry House, *The Dickens World* (London: Oxford University Press, 1941);

Harland S. Nelson, *Charles Dickens* (Boston: Twayne, 1981);

S. J. Newman, *Dickens at Play* (New York: St. Martin's, 1981);

Ada Nisbet, "Charles Dickens," in *Victorian Fiction: A Guide to Research,* edited by Lionel Stevenson (Cambridge: Harvard University Press, 1964), pp. 44-153;

Nisbet and Blake Nevius, eds., *Dickens Centennial Essays* (Berkeley: University of California Press, 1971);

Robert Partlow, ed., *Dickens the Craftsmen* (Carbondale & Edwardsville: Southern Illinois University Press, 1970);

Robert Patten, *Dickens and His Publishers* (Oxford: Clarendon Press, 1978);

Michael Slater, *Dickens and Women* (London: Dent, 1983);

Slater, Introduction to *Dickens on America and the Americans,* edited by Slater (Hassocks, U.K.: Harvester Press, 1978; Austin: University of Texas Press, 1978);

Gordon Spence, *Charles Dickens as a Familiar Essayist* (Salzburg: University of Salzburg Press, 1977);

Alexander Welsh, *The City of Dickens* (Oxford: Clarendon Press, 1971);

Angus Wilson, *The World of Charles Dickens* (New York: Viking, 1970).

Papers:

Major collections of the surviving manuscripts of Dickens's sketches and essays are at the Beinecke Rare Book and Manuscript Library, Yale University; the Huntington Library, San Marino, California; and the Free Library of Philadelphia, which also has a substantial collection of Dickens's letters. The most extensive collection of letters is housed at the Pierpont Morgan Library in New York, which has some 1,360 autograph letters by Dickens. Other important repositories for the correspondence are the Dickens House in London and the Berg Collection at the New York Public Library. The Berg Collection also includes several manuscripts and one of Dickens's notebooks.

Benjamin Disraeli

(21 December 1804-19 April 1881)

Carolyn Matalene
University of South Carolina

See also the Disraeli entry in *DLB 21, Victorian Novelists Before 1885.*

SELECTED BOOKS: *An Inquiry into the Plans, Progress, and Policy of American Mining Companies* (London: Murray, 1825);

Lawyers and Legislators; or, Notes on the American Mining Companies (London: Murray, 1825);

The Present State of Mexico: As Detailed in a Report to the General Congress by the Secretary of State for the Home Department and Foreign Affairs, at the Opening of the Session in 1825 (London: Murray, 1825);

Vivian Grey (5 volumes, London: Colburn, 1826-1827; 2 volumes, Philadelphia: Carey, Lea & Carey, 1827);

The Voyage of Captain Popanilla (London: Colburn, 1828; Philadelphia: Carey, Lea & Carey, 1828);

The Young Duke, 3 volumes (London: Colburn & Bentley, 1831; New York: Harper, 1831);

England and France; or, A Cure for the Ministerial Gallomania (London: Murray, 1832);

Contarini Fleming: A Psychological Autobiography (4 volumes, London: Murray, 1832; 2 volumes, New York: Harper, 1832);

The Wondrous Tale of Alroy. The Rise of Iskander (3 volumes, London: Saunders & Otley, 1832; 2 volumes, Philadelphia: Carey, Lea & Blanchard, 1833);

"What Is He?" (London: Ridgway, 1833);

The Revolutionary Epick, 2 volumes (London: Moxon, 1834);

A Year at Hartlebury; or, The Election, by Disraeli and Sarah D'Israeli as Cherry and Fair Star (London: Saunders & Otley, 1834);

The Crisis Examined (London: Saunders & Otley, 1834);

Vindication of the English Constitution in a Letter to a Noble and Learned Lord (London: Saunders & Otley, 1835);

The Letters of Runnymede, The Spirit of Whiggism (London: Macrone, 1836);

Henrietta Temple: A Love Story (3 volumes, London: Colburn, 1836; 1 volume, Philadelphia: Carey & Hart, 1837);

Venetia; or, The Poet's Daughter (3 volumes, London: Colburn, 1837; 2 volumes, Philadelphia: Carey & Hart, 1837);

The Tragedy of Count Alarcos (London: Colburn, 1839);

Coningsby; or, The New Generation (3 volumes, London: Colburn, 1844; 1 volume, New York: Colyer, 1844);

Sybil; or, The Two Nations (3 volumes, London: Colburn, 1845; 1 volume, Philadelphia: Carey & Hart, 1845);

The Speech of Mr. Disraeli, in the House of Commons, Friday, 15th May, 1846 (London: Olliver, 1846);

Tancred; or, The New Crusade (3 volumes, London: Colburn, 1847; 1 volume, Philadelphia: Carey & Hart, 1847);

England and Denmark: Speech of Mr. Disraeli in the House of Commons, the 19th April, 1848, on the Danish Question (London: Ridgway, 1848);

The New Parliamentary Reform. Mr. Disraeli's Speech. In the House of Commons, on Tuesday, June 20, 1848 (London: Painter, 1848);

The Parliament and the Government. Mr. Disraeli's Speech on the Labours of the Session: Delivered in the House of Commons, on Wednesday, August 30, 1848 (London: Painter, 1848);

Financial Policy: Speech of Mr. Disraeli on the Financial Policy of the Government, Made in the House of Commons. June 30, 1851 (London: Lewis, 1851);

Lord George Bentinck: A Political Biography (London: Colburn, 1852; New York: Routledge, 1858);

Parliamentary Reform: The Speech of the Right Honourable Chancellor of the Exchequer, in the House of Commons, on Thursday, the 25th March, 1852 (London: Olliver, 1852);

Ixion in Heaven: The Infernal Marriage; Popanilla; Count Alarcos (London: Bryce, 1853; New York: Seaside Library, 1881);

Disraeli at twenty-eight, sketched by C. Martin (The National Trust)

Parliamentary Reform: Speech of the Chancellor of the Exchequer, Delivered in the House of Commons Feb. 28, 1859 (London: Routledge, Warne & Routledge, 1859);

Public Expenditure: A Speech Delivered in the House of Commons on Mr. Stansfeld's Motion, June 3, 1862 (London: Hardwicke, 1862);

Mr. Gladstone's Finance, from His Accession to Office in 1853 to His Budget of 1862 (London: Saunders & Otley, 1862);

Speech Delivered by the Right Hon. B. Disraeli, M.P., at a Public Meeting in Aid of the Oxford Diocesan Society for the Augmentation of Small Benefices, on Thursday, October 30th, 1862 (London: Rivington, 1862);

Church Policy: A Speech Delivered by the Right Hon. B. Disraeli, M.P., at a Meeting of the Oxford Diocesan Society for the Augmentation of Small Livings, in the Sheldonian Theatre, Oxford, Nov. 25, 1864 (London: Rivington, 1864);

"Church and Queen." Five Speeches Delivered by the Rt. Hon. B. Disraeli, M.P. 1860-1864 (London: Palmer, 1865);

Constitutional Reform: Five Speeches . . . (1859-65), edited by John F. Bulley (London: Saunders & Otley, 1866);

The Chancellor of the Exchequer in Scotland; Being Two Speeches Delivered by Him in the City of Edinburgh on 29th and 30th October, 1867 (Edinburgh & London: Blackwood, 1867);

Parliamentary Reform: A Series of Speeches on That Subject Delivered in the House of Commons by the Right Hon. Benjamin Disraeli (1848-1866), edited by Montagu Corry (London: Longmans, Green, 1867);

The Prime Minister on Church and State: Speech of the Right Hon. B. Disraeli, M.P., at the Banquet to Her Majesty's Ministers, in the Hall of the Merchant Taylors' Company, June 17th [1868] (London: Hunt, 1868);

Speeches on the Conservative Policy of the Last Thirty Years, edited by Bulley (London: Hotten, 1870);

Lothair (3 volumes, London: Longmans, Green, 1870; 1 volume, New York: Appleton, 1870);

Mr. Osborne Morgan's Burial Bills. Speech of the Right Hon. Benjamin Disraeli, M.P., in the House of Commons, March 26, 1873, on Moving the Rejection of the Bill in its Second Reading (London: Church Defense League, 1873);

Inaugural Address Delivered to the University of Glasgow, November 19, 1873 (London: Longmans, Green, 1873; Glasgow: Maclehose, 1873);

Endymion (3 volumes, London: Longmans, Green, 1880; 1 volume, New York: Appleton, 1880);
Selected Speeches, edited by T. E. Kebbel, 2 volumes (London: Longmans, Green, 1882);
Tales and Sketches (London: Patterson, 1891);
Whigs and Whiggism: Political Writings, edited by William Hutcheon (London: Murray, 1913);
Rumpal Stilts Kin: A Dramatic Spectacle, by "B. D." and "W. G. M.," by Disraeli and W. G. Meredith, edited by Michael Sadleir (Glasgow: Printed by Maclehose, for the Roxburghe Club, 1952);
Disraeli's Reminiscences, edited by Helen M. Schwartz and Marvin Schwartz (New York: Stein & Day, 1976).

Collections: *Hughenden Edition of the Novels and Tales,* 11 volumes (London: Longmans, Green, 1881);
The Works of Benjamin Disraeli, Earl of Beaconsfield, Embracing Novels, Romances, Plays, Poems, Biography, Short Stories, and Great Speeches, edited by E. Gosse, 20 volumes (London: Dunne, 1904-1905);
The Bradenham Edition of the Novels and Tales of Benjamin Disraeli, 1st Earl of Beaconsfield, edited by P. Guedella, 12 volumes (London: Davies, 1926-1927; New York: Knopf, 1927).

OTHER: *The Life of Paul Jones,* edited by Disraeli (London: Murray, 1825).

The life of Benjamin Disraeli, later Lord Beaconsfield, is a useful reminder to students of Victorian England that most generalizations about the period are worth questioning. It seemed impossible that a middle-class Jew given to endless debts, messy affairs, and outlandish costumes, possessing a messianic ambition and a Byronic sensibility should have become the grave frock-coated statesman of the Conservative party and the adored minister of Queen Victoria. Yet, there he was, leader of the opposition, chancellor of the Exchequer, and finally "at the top of the greasy pole" as prime minister. Lacking all of the usual requirements for power and influence, he achieved both through his stunning verbal gifts. Novelist, satirist, journalist, pamphleteer, political thinker, biographer, letter writer, and orator par excellence, he was, as even those who despised him had to admit, a rhetorical genius.

That Disraeli should have been highly literate is not surprising. Born in London into a cultivated and comfortable Jewish family, he was the son of Maria Basevi D'Israeli and Isaac D'Israeli, a quiet scholar who spent most of his life in his study. Isaac D'Israeli's *Curiosities of Literature* (1791-1834) was a popular and often republished collection of anecdote and history which earned him the respect and friendship of the literary figures of his day. His clever eldest son, though given hardly any formal education, was raised in a household of books and talk about books, a household in which reading and writing were the central activities.

The life of either scholarly or literary creation, however, was too confining and too quiet for the young Disraeli, whose ambitions—like his ego—were limitless. As he wrote in his diary, "I am only truly great in action. If ever I am placed in a truly eminent position I shall prove this. I could rule the House of Commons. . . . Poetry is the safety valve of my passions, but I wish to *act* what I *write.*" Disraeli's early years and early writings were marked by a powerful urge to live out the heroics of Byronism. All he needed was a genre.

After two unhappy years as a law clerk, he decided against a career as a solicitor and began involving himself in literary, political, and financial ventures, each of which, he was certain, would lead to greatness. By the time he was twenty-one, he had written his first novel ("Aylmer Papillion"), asked the publisher John Murray to burn it (only two chapters survive), edited *The Life of Paul Jones* (1825), written three promotional tracts on Mexican mining ventures, met Sir Walter Scott, and been associated with the *Representative,* a short-lived Tory newspaper. He had also lost a good bit of money when the mining stocks he touted collapsed, an early start to a lifetime of avoiding creditors.

Disraeli's early nonfiction was written to get into office, but his early fiction was almost always written to get out of debt. Thus, he wrote *Vivian Grey,* published anonymously in five volumes in 1826 and 1827. This novel, in the "silver fork" mode, is a veiled account of the machinations involved in starting the *Representative.* Vicious personal attacks followed the discovery that the author of *Vivian Grey* was a young outsider with the effrontery to write about the high life.

To recover, Disraeli began traveling, and most of the next six years, 1826 to 1832, were spent on the Continent and in the Middle East. In 1828 he produced *The Voyage of Captain Popanilla,* a political satire on Benthamism, and in 1831 another potboiler, *The Young Duke,* appeared. But Disraeli's best writing during this period is found in his letters. "By the bye," he wrote in 1831 to his perpetual creditor Benjamin Austen, "I advise you to take care of my letters, for if I become half as famous as I intend to be, you may sell them for ten guineas a piece. . . ." His audacity, his effrontery, his way with language made his prediction come true.

Although Disraeli is one of the most quoted men in history, his letters—over ten thousand of them—are only now being collected and annotated in a complete edition. The first two volumes of Disraeli's correspondence, covering the periods 1815-1834 and 1835-1837, have been edited by members of the Disraeli Project at Queen's University, Kingston, Ontario, and published by the University of Toronto Press. Volume three, covering 1838-1841, is scheduled to appear in 1987.

The young Disraeli's letters from the Grand Tour are wonderfully readable; Disraeli always approached experience with an eye for detail, a sense of the ridiculous, a taste for the dramatic, and the imagination and literary sensibility of a novelist. To his sister Sarah, he wrote from Gibraltar, "suddenly our guide informs us, that he hears a trampling of horse in the distance. Ave Maria! A cold perspiration came over me. Decidedly they approached—but rather an uproarious crew. We drew up out of pure fear, and I had my purse ready. The band turned out to be a company of actors travelling to Cordova. There they were, dresses and decorations, scenery and machinery, all on mules and donkeys, for there are no roads in this country. The singers rehearsing an Opera—the principal Tragedian riding on an ass, and the Buffo most serious looking as grave as night with a segar and in greater agitation than them all. . . . All this irresistibly reminded me of Cervantes!"

Although Disraeli was a serious traveler, reading guidebooks and histories as he went and writing his best perceptions home to his father, his ruling trope was always hyperbole. He enjoyed creating outlandish characters for himself and watching their effects. "I have also the fame of being the first who ever passed the Straits with two canes, a morning and an evening cane. I change my cane as the gun fires, and hope to carry them both on to Cairo. It is wonderful the effect these magical wands produce. I owe to them even more attentions than to being the supposed author of—what is it—I forget." And there is Disraeli's ever-present wit, as sparkling as Oscar Wilde's, "Yesterday at the racket court sitting in the Gallery among strangers, the ball entered, slightly struck me, and fell at my feet. I picked it up, and observing a young rifle man excessively stiff, I humbly requested him to forward its passage into the Court, as I really had never thrown a ball in my life. This incident has been the general subject of conversation at all the messes to day." And there is always a well-turned maxim to sum up the situation: "To govern men you must either excel in their accomplishments—or despise them."

When Disraeli returned from his travels, he engaged in all of the excesses necessary for a fashionable young man in society, affairs, debts, and socializing. He also wrote, feverishly and prolifically. Just as his studies were never limited—or directed—by an academic discipline, so his writing was never limited by genre. During the 1830s Disraeli wrote novels: *Contarini Fleming* (1832), *The Wondrous Tale of Alroy* and *The Rise of Iskander* (published together in 1832), *A Year at Hartlebury* (a pseudonymous collaboration with his sister, published in 1834), *Henrietta Temple* (1836), and *Venetia* (1837). He also wrote a thoroughly unsuccessful poem, *The Revolutionary Epick* (1834); a drama in blank verse, *The Tragedy of Count Alarcos* (1839); two satires, serialized in the *New Monthly Magazine, Ixion in Heaven* (1833), and *The Infernal Marriage* (1834); as well as a number of tales and sketches that appeared in *New Monthly* and *Court Journal.*

But that was not all. In 1832 the year in which he was defeated twice in elections for the House of Commons, *England and France; or, A Cure for the Ministerial Gallomania* was published anonymously; Disraeli apparently coauthored this attack on pro-French policy with a mysterious figure named Haber. Disraeli's many voices as a writer as well as his changeable politics made it necessary to write a pamphlet explaining his position. *"What Is He?,"* which appeared in 1833, ultimately confused as much as it enlightened because here he suggested an alliance between Tories and Radicals. But in *The Crisis Examined* (1834), a published version of his address to the electors of High Wycombe, Disraeli allied himself clearly with the Conservative party. He also revealed for the first time his potential as a master of invective. "And then Lord Melbourne says that the King turned them out. Turned them out. Gentlemen; why, His Majesty laughed them out! The truth is that this famous Reform Ministry, this great 'united' Cabinet, had degenerated into a grotesque and Hudibrastic faction, the very lees of ministerial existence, the offal of official life. They were a ragged regiment compared with which Falstaff's crew was a band of regulars." Thus began the brilliant attacks on the Whigs which were to make his name.

Lacking political office, Disraeli next served Lord Lyndhurst as a private secretary, and at his request wrote a series of editorials for the *Morning Post.* They are all haranguing attacks on important political leaders, the sort that libel laws now forbid. Much given to image-construction, Disraeli realized that the time had come to create a more serious public image for himself if he was ever to be taken seriously as a candidate. He did so in a pamphlet published in 1835, *Vindication of the English Constitution in a Letter to a Noble and Learned Lord.* Here Disraeli makes clear his belief in the aristocratic principle, in precedent and antiquity. Examining the cultural roots of political freedom, he insists that contributions cannot be transported and imposed but must arise from each country's traditions of governance. Disraeli's powers as a rhetorician are evident; he presents his case clearly and cogently, often arguing by comparison, often depending upon his favorite scheme, parallel structure and antithesis. "An English revolution is at least a solemn sacrifice; a French revolution is an indecent massacre." The *Vindication of the English Constitution* made his reputation as a serious political thinker, and it also attracted the attention of Thomas Barnes, the powerful editor of the *Times.* Disraeli's next journalistic efforts were published there, from January to May 1836, another series of violent (and pseudonymous) political attacks entitled "The Letters of Runnymede." To the modern reader the level of invective is surprising, but to contemporaries, these addresses to Whig leaders probably seemed just a continuation of that epidictic genre popular in earlier centuries, the Theophrastan character. Although Disraeli later denied writing them, they were republished in 1836 in a volume that also included the pamphlet *The Spirit of Whiggism.* All of these writings are available in the 1913 volume edited by William Hutcheon, *Whigs and Whiggism.*

In 1837, after five elections in five years, Disraeli at last succeeded in his longstanding ambition and was elected to the House of Commons. His political career had finally begun; perhaps at last he could put his heroic and poetic principles into action. But in his maiden speech, something went terribly wrong, and he was shouted down and ridiculed. "I will sit down now, but the day will come when you will hear me," he concluded. This seems to have been an occasion when Disraeli entirely misread his audience, trying for elaborate cajolery with a group that would have none of it. The mistake was seldom repeated.

When his day did come not very many years later, Disraeli looked and acted differently. The rings and chains and brocaded waistcoats were gone; the attire was somber black and gray; and the manner was always deadpan, a face so impassive that listeners could never be sure if the right honorable gentleman was being serious or ironic. Disraeli's private life had changed too. Gone were the mistresses; in August 1839 Disraeli married Mary Anne Lewis, a wealthy widow twelve years his senior. Mary Anne Lewis was by all accounts a rattle, but clearly an amusing one, and though Disraeli might have married her to ease the strain of over twenty thousand pounds of debts, he came to love her, too. In a life not marked by consistency, his genuine devotion to his wife cannot be doubted.

Portrait by J. G. Middleton of Mary Anne Lewis, whom Disraeli married in August 1839 (The National Trust)

In 1841 Queen Victoria asked Sir Robert Peel to form a government—which he did, but he did not offer Disraeli an office in it. Disraeli, enraged and mortified, allied himself with a group of young aristocrats committed to the spiritual regeneration of England; known as Young England, they stood for a strong monarchy, a benevolent and responsible aristocracy, a happy peasantry, and in general a kind of rosy feudalism. Disraeli's most serious novels, a trilogy, resulted from his involvement with the Young England movement. They were *Coningsby* (1844), *Sybil* (1845), and *Tancred* (1847). *Coningsby* and *Sybil* have earned Disraeli critical acclaim as the inventor of the English political novel.

When Peel reversed on the issue of protective tariffs for agriculture, Disraeli saw his opportunity, left off romanticizing, and began the attack. His

Hughenden Manor, the Buckinghamshire country home purchased by Disraeli in 1852 (The National Trust)

brilliant speeches against free trade and especially against Peel rendered the Tory leader speechless, established Disraeli as the greatest conservative orator, and soon made him leader of his party, though it was now a split party, in the House of Commons.

To catalogue Disraeli's techniques as a speaker is almost to define rhetorical effectiveness. Careful to let his audience know at the start what he would argue and how, Disraeli made certain that his listeners could follow his remarks and that journalists were able to report his speeches with ease. His favorite argumentative techniques were those recommended by Aristotle, and he depended upon the common topics of definition, comparison, precedent, and antecedence and consequence. Surely, the Aristotelian rule which he understood most profoundly—he had learned it the hard way—was the injunction "Know your audience." Reading his speeches, one senses a very immediate relationship with his audience, a keen understanding of what would impress and move them, a sense of what information they had and what they needed, an unfailing ability to entertain and amuse, as well as a willingness to make any subject colorfully present with elegant hyperbole. "Why if protection had never existed, Lincolnshire might still be a wild wold, a barren heath, a plashy marsh." His most dazzling talents, however, were for invective, sometimes ironic, sometimes painfully direct. "His [Robert Peel's] life has been one great Appropriation Clause. He is a burglar of others' intellect. Search the index of Beatson from the days of the Conqueror to the termination of the last reign, there is no statesman who has committed political petty larceny on so great a scale."

But Disraeli could also praise. When his father died in 1848, Disraeli wrote a memoir for a new edition of *Curiosities of Literature*. The conclusion amply illustrates Disraeli's pride and affection and gratitude as well as his ability to make the English sentence do his bidding: "On the whole, I hope—nay I believe—that taking all into consideration—the integrity and completeness of his existence, the fact that, for sixty years, he largely contributed to form the taste, charm the leisure, and direct the studious dispositions, of the great body of the public, and that his works have extensively and curiously illustrated the literary and political history of our country, it will be conceded, that in his life and labours, he repaid England for the protection and the hospitality which this country accorded to his father a century ago."

Just as Lord Lyndhurst in the 1830s had realized that Disraeli was the best writer available for the Tory cause, so did Lord George Bentinck in the 1840s see that Disraeli was the best speaker. Bentinck and his family helped Disraeli purchase a small country estate, Hughenden Manor, so that their spokesman would have proper landed credentials. When Bentinck died suddenly, Disraeli expressed his gratitude by writing *Lord George Bentinck: A Political Biography* (1852). As a biography it reveals that Disraeli had no understanding of the genre; his subject never comes alive because Disraeli is bent on eulogy and little inclined to provide real biographical information or analysis. But as a political diary covering the years 1845 to 1848, it is an extraordinary record of the workings of Parliament by an insider privy to the intrigues of the day. The twenty-fourth chapter caused considerable offense at the time because here Disraeli unaccountably inserted his own strange theology in which Christianity was viewed as the historical completion of Judaism. "If the Jews had not prevailed upon the Romans to crucify our Lord, what would have become of the Atonement?" Had Disraeli not been baptized as a child he could never have entered parliament when he did, yet he was always both proud and vocal about his Jewishness. His unusual synthesis seems to have allowed him to keep both faiths.

In Lord Derby's government of 1852, Disraeli—in one of history's greatest ironies—was made chancellor of the Exchequer. He presented his first budget in a five-hour speech and defended it two weeks later in a speech filled with personal attacks. In reply, at one in the morning, William Gladstone rose to speak and point by point demolished Disraeli's budget. Thus Disraeli had met his political if not his rhetorical equal, and their duels—the master of hyperbole squaring off against the master of detail—provided the political polarities of the next three decades and made skill at debate seem the essence of statesmanship.

Disraeli was in parliament for forty-four years, but the Conservative party was in power for only eleven of those years, and Disraeli was prime minister for only six (1868, 1874, 1876-1880). The rest was opposition, and Disraeli made it clear that the business of the party in opposition was to oppose. His favorite method of attack, whatever the issue, was to reveal the Whig view of history as factious and erroneous and to replace it with his own, superior Tory version, a version always proving the value of the aristocratic principle. Thus all problems, past and future, were the fault of the Whigs, all successes the result of Tory policies. That outright lies and major reversals were sometimes necessary—Disraeli went, for example, from anti- to pro-French, from protectionist to free trade, from support of very limited to very extensive suffrage—was simply part of staying in office. Sometimes Disraeli even opposed the principles of the party he led; from 1853 to 1858 he wrote anonymously for a progressive Tory newspaper, the *Press*.

Disraeli made many speeches during his long political career. Some were published separately, in pamphlet form, shortly after they were delivered, and the major ones were collected in two volumes edited by T. E. Kebbel in 1882. A few of the more famous are the Maynooth speech of 11 April 1845, with its attack on Peel; the Speech on Address of 22 January 1846, another attack; the Aylesbury speech of 26 June 1847, notable for its plain speaking; the Second Reading of the Reform Bill, 26 March 1867; the Manchester and the Crystal Palace speeches of 3 April 1872 and 24 June 1872 on Conservative Principles; and a speech on the Afghan War of 10 December 1878. Sometimes his speeches are hard to follow without considerable historical background. One that reveals him at this best, rewriting history and attacking Whigs along the way with witty literary allusions, is the speech on the Labours of the Session, 30 August 1848. That speech, in Disraeli's opinion, solidified his leadership of the party in the House of Commons.

Although Disraeli was again chancellor of the Exchequer in 1858-1859, the government soon fell; Disraeli spent more years in opposition and had more time for enjoying his estate. "I have a passion for books and trees. I like to look at them. When I come down to Hughenden I pass the first week in sauntering about my park & examining all the trees, & then I saunter in the library, & survey the books," he wrote in his *Reminiscences*. These memoirs, written during the years 1862 to 1866, were not published until 1976. Here is vintage Disraeli, a sparkling collection of his favorite tales of the rich and famous and their eccentricities and indiscretions, a healthy correction to middle-class versions of Victorian life-styles. Here too Disraeli reveals much about his own highly refined tastes in entertainments and companions and letters. "There used to be well understood rules in the House of Commons, in old days respecting quo-

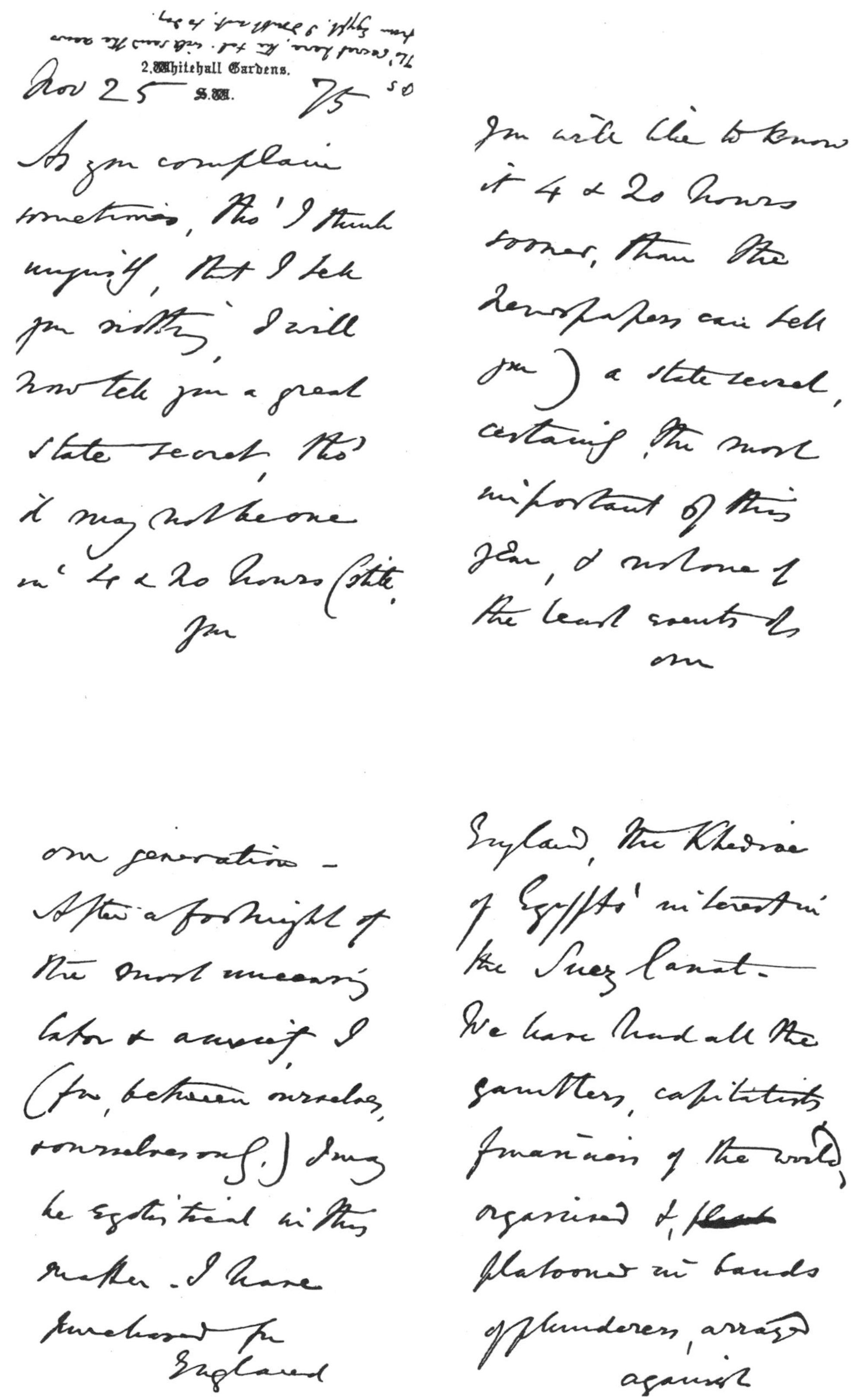
2, Whitehall Gardens.
Nov 25 S.W. 75

As you complain sometimes, tho' I think unjustly, that I tell you nothing, I will now tell you a great State secret, tho' it may not be one in 4 & 20 hours (still you will like to know it 4 & 20 hours sooner, than the newspapers can tell you) a state secret, certainly the most important of this year, & not one of the least events of our generation — After a fortnight of the most unceasing labor & anxiety, I (for, between ourselves, ourselves only,) I may be egotistical in this matter — I have purchased for England the Khedive of Egypt's interest in the Suez Canal. We have had all the gamblers, capitalists, financiers of the world, organised & [illegible] platooned in bands of plunderers, arrayed against

Disraeli's letter to Lady Bradford revealing the "great State Secret" that "I have purchased for England the Khedive of Egypt's interest in the Suez Canal." On page seven Disraeli refers to "The Faery"—Queen Victoria—"in ecstasies about 'this great and important event' " (by permission of The National Trust, courtesy of the Earl of Bradford)

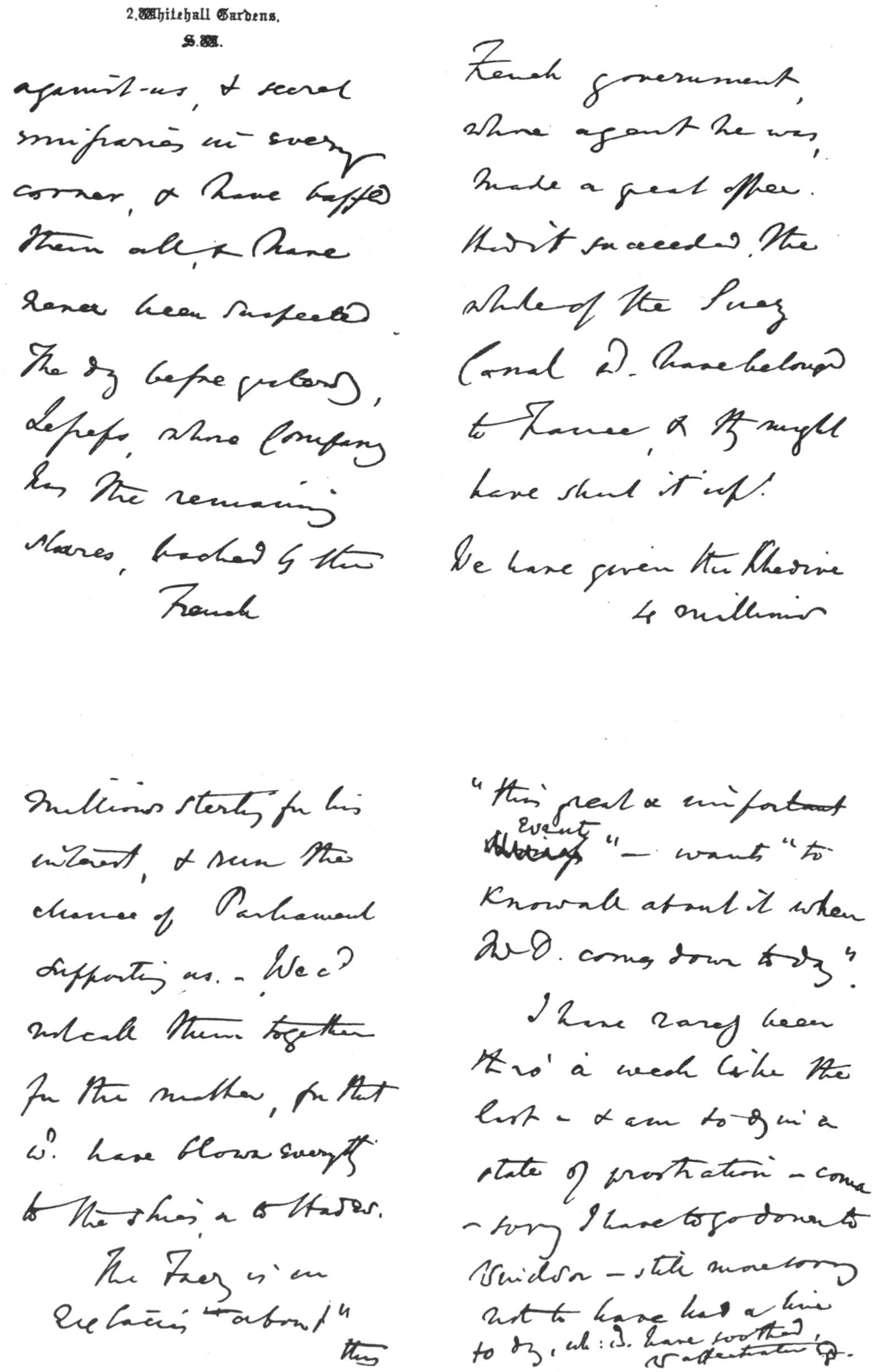
2, Whitehall Gardens.
S.W.

against us, & secret emissaries in every corner, & have baffled them all, & have never been suspected. The day before yesterday, Lesseps, whose Company has the remaining shares, backed by the French

French government, whose agent he was, made a great offer. Had it succeeded, the whole of the Suez Canal wd. have belonged to France, & they might have shut it up!

We have given the Khedive 4 millions

millions sterling for his interest, & run the chance of Parliament supporting us. – We cd not call them together for the matter, for that wd. have blown everything to the skies, or to Hades.

The Faery is in ecstasies "about" this

"this great & important event" – wants "to know all about it when Mr. D. comes down today".

I have rarely been thro' a week like the last – & am today in a state of prostration – coma – sorry I have to go down to Windsor – still more sorry not to have had a line today, wh: wd. have soothed & sustained me.

Queen Victoria with Disraeli at High Wycombe station, 15 December 1877, on her visit to Hughenden

tations. No English poet to be quoted, who had not completed his Century. Greek & French never under any circumstances: Latin as you liked: Horace & Virgil by preference; then Juvenal. Now quotation is what we are most deficient in. . . . It is not merely, that they quote Byron & Tennyson before they have completed their quarantine. But Bright & Cobden, & all those sort of people, are always quoting Dickens & *Punch* &c. Our quotations are either tawdry or trashy. The privilege of quotation should not be too easy. It should be fenced in."

Along with his speeches, the major literary creations of Disraeli's middle years are undoubtedly his letters. Those to his sister Sarah, to Frances Anne, Marchioness of Londonderry, and those of his later years to Lady Bradford and Lady Chesterfield, have been published, though sometimes badly edited, in separate volumes. But those to his elderly Jewish friend Sarah Brydges Williams and those to his sovereign are available only in excerpts in the six-volume biography by W. F. Moneypenny and G. E. Buckle (1910-1920) and in collections of the correspondence of Queen Victoria. When the Disraeli Project edition with its careful dating of the letters is complete, it will be possible to appreciate fully Disraeli's genius as a correspondent, to hear him radically change voice and tenor according to his correspondent, to watch him alter the explanation of an event according to his own purposes with the recipient. It will also be possible to experience firsthand the most unexpected courtship of the century, Disraeli charming Queen Victoria; with outrageous flattery but exquisite sensitivity he turned her hardened contempt into gushing adoration. And all the while, to his other correspondents he was referring to her as "The Faery," to the Crown Prince as "Prince Hal," and to chilly Windsor Castle as "the cave of the winds."

Disraeli's letters deserve reading, not just because they provide an insider's view of the politics of half a century, not just because they are filled with colorful descriptions of the social life of the ruling class, not just because they contain the most accurate portraits there are of the aristocracy, but because Disraeli was, as his biographer Robert Blake concluded in 1966, one of the wittiest men who ever lived. To read the letters of his mature years is to experience a sensibility never taken in by cant, always bemused by the human comedy, always able to puncture pretense with a phrase. "No," he said on his deathbed, "Don't let the Queen come to see me. She would only ask me to take a message to Albert."

Disraeli's preferred correspondents as well as his preferred dinner companions were always women. The gallantry which charmed them is well documented, and in fact a recurrent theme in all of his writing is the essential role played by aristocratic women in the conduct of matrimonial, social, and political affairs. Certainly Disraeli benefited throughout his life from the friendship of women, both titled and obscure, and his recognition of their intellectual gifts appeals to modern readers. His last two novels, *Lothair* (1870) and, especially, *Endymion* (1880), satirize the effete weariness of aristocratic men as they pay tribute to the social and political energies of noble women.

Disraeli's years of greatest political influence occurred late in his life. His success in getting the Reform Bill of 1867 passed and his ability to make political capital out of the idea of Tory democracy ensured his place as Derby's successor. In 1868 he was at last prime minister, though only for a year, then again in 1874, and from 1876-1880, he governed from the House of Lords as Lord Beaconsfield. These were the years of Beaconsfieldism, years during which Disraeli was one of the most prominent statesmen in Europe. Disraeli committed England to empire with Queen Victoria's new title, Empress of India, purchased the Suez Canal, and came home triumphant from the Congress of Vienna in 1878. "In spite of his fantastic novel-writing," said Bismarck, "he is a capable statesman. . . ." When he turned down a dukedom from the grateful Victoria, did he remember his father's withering question about his novel, *The Young Duke*, "What does Ben know of dukes?"

It was a remarkable career, the career of a great rhetorician, whose genius lay in his ability to adapt his voice or his pen to the times, to the audience, to the goal. He could be ironic, sarcastic, serious, grave, baroque, witty, emotional, literary, playful, and even plain speaking. Sometimes he was turgid, repetitive, and excessive; more often he was structured, elegant, and incisive. But all agreed that he could wear many hats and could even create new hats for others to wear—and his only medium was his mastery of words. When Queen Victoria, whose intellect is often underestimated, had a quotation from Proverbs inscribed on his memorial, "Kings love him that speaketh right," she revealed that she indeed knew her man.

Portrait of Disraeli by von Angeli (The National Trust). Queen Victoria presented a copy of this portrait to Disraeli when she visited Hughenden.

Letters:

Home Letters Written by the Late Earl of Beaconsfield in 1830 and 1831 (London: Murray, 1885; New York: Harper, 1885);

Lord Beaconsfield's Correspondence with His Sister 1832-1852 (London: Murray, 1886);

The Letters of Disraeli to Lady Bradford and Lady Chesterfield, edited by the Marquis of Zetland, 2 volumes (London: Benn, 1929; New York: Appleton, 1929);

Letters from Benjamin Disraeli to Frances Anne Marchioness of Londonderry 1837-1861, edited by the Marchioness of Londonderry (London: Macmillan, 1938);

Benjamin Disraeli Letters, 2 volumes, ongoing; volumes 1 and 2, edited by J. A. W. Gunn, John Matthews, Donald M. Schurman, and M. G.

Wiebe (Toronto: University of Toronto Press, 1982-).

Bibliography:

R. W. Stewart, *Benjamin Disraeli: A List of Writings by Him, and Writings about Him, with Notes* (Metuchen, N.J.: Scarecrow Press, 1972).

Biographies:

J. A. Froude, *The Earl of Beaconsfield* (London: Low, Marston, 1890);

Wilfrid Meynell, *Benjamin Disraeli: An Unconventional Biography*, 2 volumes (London: Hutchinson, 1903);

W. F. Moneypenny and G. E. Buckle, *The Life of Benjamin Disraeli*, 6 volumes (London: Murray, 1910-1920);

Cecil Roth, *Benjamin Disraeli* (New York: Philosophical Library, 1952);

B. R. Jerman, *The Young Disraeli* (Princeton: Princeton University Press, 1960);

Robert Blake, *Disraeli* (London: Eyre & Spottiswoode, 1966);

Christopher Hibbert, *Disraeli and His World* (London: Thames & Hudson, 1978);

Sarah Bradford, *Disraeli* (New York: Stein & Day, 1982).

References:

Paul Adelman, *Gladstone, Disraeli, and Later Victorian Politics* (London: Longman, 1970);

Stephen R. Graubard, *Burke, Disraeli and Churchill* (Cambridge: Harvard University Press, 1961);

John Holloway, *The Victorian Sage* (New York: Macmillan, 1953);

Richard Levine, *Benjamin Disraeli* (New York: Twayne, 1968).

Papers:

The Disraeli papers are at the Bodleian Library, Oxford University.

George Eliot
(Mary Ann Evans)
(22 November 1819-22 December 1880)

Kathleen McCormack
Florida International University

See also the Eliot entries in *DLB 21, Victorian Novelists Before 1885,* and *DLB 35, Victorian Poets After 1850.*

BOOKS: *Scenes of Clerical Life* (2 volumes, Edinburgh & London: Blackwood, 1858; 1 volume, New York: Harper, 1858);

Adam Bede (3 volumes, Edinburgh & London: Blackwood, 1859; 1 volume, New York: Harper, 1859);

The Mill on the Floss (3 volumes, Edinburgh & London: Blackwood, 1860; 1 volume, New York: Harper, 1860);

Silas Marner: The Weaver of Raveloe (Edinburgh & London: Blackwood, 1861; New York: Harper, 1861);

Romola (3 volumes, London: Smith, Elder, 1863; 1 volume, New York: Harper, 1863);

Felix Holt, The Radical (3 volumes, Edinburgh & London: Blackwood, 1866; 1 volume, New York: Harper, 1866);

The Spanish Gypsy: A Poem (Edinburgh & London: Blackwood, 1868; Boston: Ticknor & Fields, 1868);

How Lisa Loved the King (Boston: Fields, Osgood, 1869);

Middlemarch: A Study of Provincial Life (8 parts, Edinburgh & London: Blackwood, 1871-1872; 2 volumes, New York: Harper, 1872-1873);

The Legend of Jubal and Other Poems (Edinburgh & London: Blackwood, 1874; Boston: Osgood, 1874);

Daniel Deronda (8 parts, Edinburgh & London: Blackwood, 1876; 2 volumes, New York: Harper, 1876);

Impressions of Theophrastus Such (Edinburgh & London: Blackwood, 1879; New York: Harper, 1879);

Essays and Leaves from a Note-Book, edited by C. L. Lewes (Edinburgh & London: Blackwood, 1884; New York: Harper, 1884);

Quarry for Middlemarch, edited by Anna T. Kitchel (Berkeley: University of California Press, 1950);

Essays of George Eliot, edited by Thomas Pinney (New York: Columbia University Press, 1963; London: Routledge & Kegan Paul, 1963);

Some George Eliot Notebooks: An Edition of the Carl H. Pforzheimer Library's George Eliot Holograph Notebooks, Mss. 707, 708, 709, 710, 711 [the *Daniel Deronda* notebooks], edited by William Baker (Salzburg: Universität Salzburg, 1976);

George Eliot's Middlemarch Notebooks: A Transcription, edited by John Clark Pratt and Victor A. Neufeldt (Berkeley: University of California Press, 1979);

A Writer's Notebook, 1854-1879, and Uncollected Writings, edited by Joseph Wiesenfarth (Charlottesville: University Press of Virginia, 1981).

Mary Ann Evans as sketched by Caroline Bray, circa 1842 (Collection of W. H. Draper)

Collection: *The Works of George Eliot,* Cabinet Edition, 24 volumes (Edinburgh & London: Blackwood, 1878-1885).

OTHER: David Friedrich Strauss, *The Life of Jesus, Critically Examined,* translated by Evans from the fourth German edition, 3 volumes (London: Chapman, 1846);

Ludwig Feuerbach, *The Essence of Christianity,* translated by Evans from the second edition, *Chapman's Quarterly Series,* no. 6 (London: Chapman, 1854).

George Eliot wrote nearly all of her nonfiction prose during two widely separated periods in her life. As Marian Evans, in her mid thirties, she produced more than sixty critical essays that appeared in Victorian organs of heterodoxy such as the *Westminster Review* and the *Leader.* As the aging sibyl, after twenty years as a brilliant novelist and a mediocre poet, she wrote *Impressions of Theophrastus Such* (1879), largely a set of reflective character sketches. Although Eliot's famous novels most often evoke the daisied fields of her provincial childhood, both her early journalism and her late sketches are urban in tone, for, the novel settings notwithstanding, Eliot lived in or near London for most of her adult life.

George Eliot, preliminary sketch for a portrait by Samuel Laurence (Girton College Library, Cambridge). The 1857 date on the sketch is in error; it was drawn circa 1860.

Eliot, born Mary Ann Evans, was the youngest child of Robert Evans, agent for the estate of Sir Francis Newdigate, and Christiana Pearson Evans, his second wife. She grew up at Griff House, whose red-brick-and-ivy exterior and prominent location overlooking the fields and canals of Warwickshire made it a notable sight along the coach road between Coventry and Nuneaton. She began school at five years old, and, like her brothers and sisters (two of the four half-siblings from her father's first marriage), she was a boarding student. Her fiction suggests that the most important relationships of her childhood were with her full brother Isaac, prototype of the difficult-to-please Tom Tulliver in *The Mill on the Floss* (1860), and her father, often described as a model for Adam Bede and Caleb Garth as well as for Mr. Tulliver, who is always willing to take his daughter's part in her emotional struggles.

By the time she was twenty-one, Evans's mother had died and her brothers and sisters were married and scattered. Mary Ann and Robert Evans left Griff and moved into a neat semidetached house on the Foleshill Road in Coventry. There the young woman who had been formed as an Evangelical by her favorite governess, Maria Lewis, made friends and read books that led her first to question and then to renounce her strict religious beliefs. Charles and Caroline Hennell Bray and Sara and Charles Hennell helped introduce her to a freethinking literary/intellectual milieu in which she eventually took her place as translator of David Friedrich Strauss's *Das Leben Jesu* (1835) and contributor to the "Literature and Science" column of the *Coventry Herald and Observer.* Partly because of her friendship with Charles Bray, who had bought the paper in June 1846, Evans wrote some short reviews and essays for the *Herald* the following winter, pieces that, along with a religious poem written in 1839, became her first publications.

The reviews and essays attributed to Evans by twentieth-century scholars Thomas Pinney, Joseph Wiesenfarth, and Gordon S. Haight form a conservative list which includes only works whose authenticity is supported by references in journals, letters, or notebooks. Although this list almost certainly omits some pieces, the ones it includes indicate that in 1846 Marian Evans (as she now called herself) was already reflecting on ideas she would, as George Eliot, embody in her novels. For example, her review (*Coventry Herald and Observer,* 30 October 1846) of a translation of Jules Michelet's *Priests, Women, and Families* considers the place of religion in family life, a theme Eliot engages in the novels *The Mill on the Floss* and *Middlemarch* (1871-1872) in the characters of Maggie Tulliver and Dorothea Brooke, whose intense piety puts them at odds with friends and family. "Prose and Poetry from the Notebook of an Eccentric" (*Coventry Herald,* 4 December 1846-19 February 1847) is a series of reflections by a self-described supersensitive observer named Macarthy that also contains hints of the novels. Constance Fulmer, in a 1974 article on Eliot's heroines, describes the hamadryads in "A Little Fable with a Great Moral" (*Coventry Herald,* 12 February 1847) as early studies for several pairs of contrasting women characters in the fiction.

Evans wrote little prose during the next few years, which she spent keeping house and nursing her father as he endured his last illness. Until she began writing for the *Westminster Review* in 1851, apparently her only publication was a review of James Anthony Froude's *The Nemesis of Faith* (1849), a rave whose appearance was followed by a romantic but fruitless matchmaking plot by Charles and Caroline Hennell Bray. Their plan backfired when Froude failed to show up at the rendezvous point and announced his engagement to another in his note of regret.

Having spent the winter after her father's death alone in Geneva, Evans returned to England and soon made the move by which she left behind the provinces, except as settings for her fiction, permanently. Recruited by John Chapman to edit his newly acquired pet project, the *Westminster Review,* she moved into his publishing, bookselling, and lodging establishment at 142 Strand and became a member of London's lively literary/intellectual set. Among her new acquaintances was George Henry Lewes, who contributed articles on philosophical, scientific, and literary topics to the *Westminster Review* and other London periodicals. Despite his thoroughly failed but still legal marriage to Agnes Jervis, Lewes and Evans began in 1853 a mutually supportive intellectual, sexual, and emotional partnership that endured until his death in 1878.

When they eloped to Germany in 1854 Evans and Lewes set a lifelong pattern by which they interspersed periods of hard work in London with travel that was part vacation, part field trip. On the initial trip to Weimar and Berlin, Lewes was completing his biography of Goethe while Evans gathered material and background for articles. Her need to supplement the small income from her father's legacy resulted in the following two years of intense journalistic productivity during which she wrote dozens of reviews, most of them for the *Westminster Review* and the *Leader.* Her German travel, together with the extensive religious reading of her Evangelical days, equipped her to write especially rapidly and well on books pertaining to these areas. The linguistic ability she had developed as a translator was an asset of equal value: by 1855 she had translated Feuerbach and Strauss, as well as Spinoza, though her rendering of the Dutch philosopher's *Ethics* never appeared in print. Often, as when she reviewed J. M. D. Meiklejohn's translation of Kant's *Critique of Pure Reason* for the *Leader* in October 1855, she drew on several of her areas of expertise at once.

Evans's reviews range from slender notices eked out by long quotations to substantial philosophical essays in which the literary criticism serves mainly as a point of departure. As editor of the *Westminster Review* from 1852 to 1854, she had put together a series of formidable numbers whose authors included Froude, John Stuart Mill, Herbert Spencer, and Harriet Martineau. Nevertheless she considered its quality uneven and often complained of the difficulties of lining up good writers and recent publications that would provide a "peg for an article." As she produced her own articles for the *Westminster Review* and the *Leader* in 1855 and 1856, she tended to increase the proportion of article to peg. A review of Peter von Bohlen's *Introduction to the Book of Genesis* (*Leader,* 12 January 1856) contains a summary that Thomas Pinney describes, in his introduction to the *Essays of George Eliot* (1963), as an excellent "dispassionate and informed description of the grounds for the mid-nineteenth-century intellectual's heterodoxy." Similarly, her review of Thomas Keightley's *Account of the Life, Opinions and Writings of Milton* (*Leader,* 4 August 1855) is largely a plea for more liberal attitudes toward divorce.

Part of the interest of Evans's journalism from this period lies in her estimates of her contemporaries: Charles Dickens's novels are criticized for their sentimental characterizations of children; Alfred Tennyson's *Maud* is far beneath his usual standard. Of the Americans, she expresses admiration for the writing of Harriet Beecher Stowe, Margaret Fuller, William Cullen Bryant, Edgar Allan Poe, and Henry Wadsworth Longfellow (especially *Hiawatha*), but her review of Rufus Wilmot Griswold's 1855 anthology *The Poets and Poetry of America* (*Leader,* 1 March 1856) concludes that the

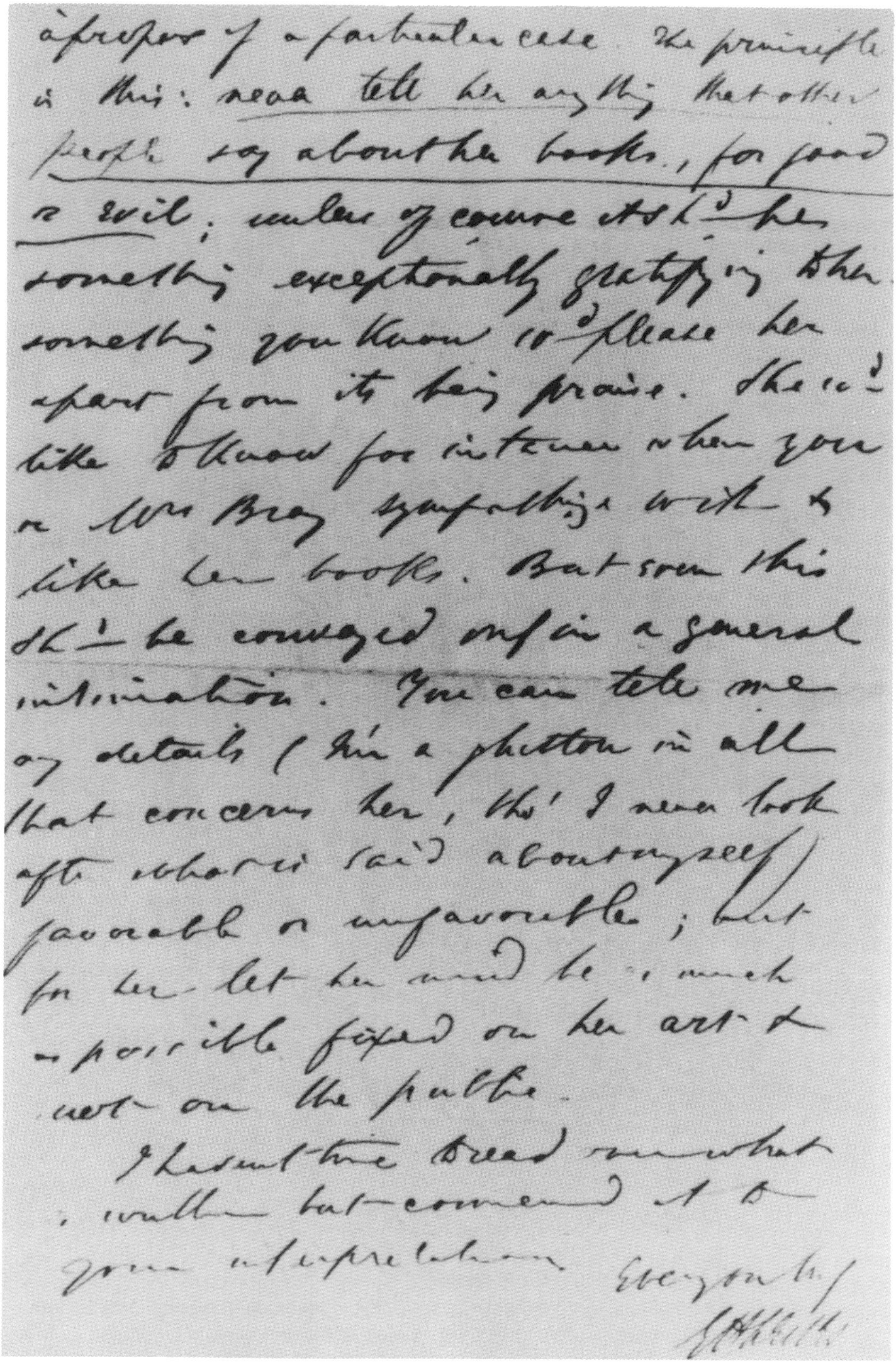
à propos of a particular case. The principle is this: never tell her anything that other people say about her books, for good or evil; unless of course it sh^d be something exceptionally gratifying to her — something you know w^d please her apart from its being praise. She w^d like to know for instance when you or Mrs Bray sympathize with & like her books. But even this sh^d be conveyed only in a general intimation. You can tell me any details (I'm a glutton in all that concerns her, tho' I never look after what is said about myself favorable or unfavorable; but for her let her mind be as much as possible fixed on her art & not on the public.

I haven't time to read over what is written but commend it to your interpretation. Ever yours truly

G.H.Lewes

From a September 1862 letter to Sara Hennell from George Henry Lewes: "never tell her," *he writes, referring to Eliot,* "anything that other people say about her books, . . . *unless of course it sh^d be something especially gratifying to her"* *(Coventry City Libraries)*

volume contains many poems that are "hard to read and easy to forget."

In her reviews of fiction Evans bases her judgments on the theory of artistic realism for which she praises John Ruskin's *Modern Painters* series. She attacks Charles Kingsley's *Westward Ho!*, Geraldine Jewsbury's *Constance Herbert*, Julia Kavanaugh's *Rachel Gray*, and, as the title of an 1856 piece indicates, most of the "Silly Novels by Lady Novelists" on the basis of improbable oversimplification and false morality. In 1856, the summer just before Evans gave up journalism for fiction, she and Lewes spent two months at Ilfracombe collecting zoological specimens for Lewes's *Sea-Side Studies at Ilfracombe, Tenby, the Scilly Isles & Jersey* (1858). The trip coincided with Evans's reading of the first two parts of Wilhelm Heinrich von Riehl's *Die Naturgeschichte des Volks* in preparation for one of her longest articles, "The Natural History of German Life" (*Westminster Review*, July 1856). When she began "The Sad Fortunes of the Reverend Amos Barton" the following fall, she attempted to incorporate as fictional technique the method of scientifically exact observation of reality she praised in Riehl and practiced as a habit in the searches for specimens along the shore at Ilfracombe.

Much of the value of Evans's journalism for contemporary critics lies in its articulation of ideas that reappear in the novels written under the pseudonym George Eliot. The political conservatism of *Felix Holt, The Radical* (1866) is manifested in her support for Riehl's arguments against both bureaucracy and revolution. The religious humanism implied by the novelist's choice of fellow feeling as a major virtue appears in the journalist's reservations about the moral value of an abstract divinity. In "Evangelical Teaching: Dr. Cumming" (*Westminster Review*, October 1855), she argues, "The idea of God is really moral in its influence—it really cherishes all that is best and loveliest in man—only when God is contemplated as sympathizing with the pure elements of human feeling, as possessing infinitely all those attributes which we recognize to be moral in humanity." The essays also help clarify Eliot's fictional responses to nineteenth-century feminism. "Woman in France: Madame de Sablé" (*Westminster Review*, October 1854) expresses ideas about women intellectuals that illuminate Dorothea Brooke's housewifely fate in the "Finale" to *Middlemarch*. As hostess and wife of Will Ladislaw, M.P., Dorothea might resemble "the women whose tact, wit, and personal radiance, created the atmosphere of the *Salon*, where literature, philosophy, and science, emancipated from the trammels of pedantry and technicality, entered on a brighter stage of existence." "Silly Novels by Lady Novelists" (*Westminster Review*, October 1856) and "Margaret Fuller and Mary Wollstonecraft" (*Leader*, 13 October 1856) help place Eliot in a Wollstonecraftian feminist tradition based on the fact that the current condition of women was inferior and that equal access to education and jobs was the remedy.

It is not only the major themes of the novels that the reviews illuminate, for here and there a detail of character, plot, or imagery crops up as well. Pinney picks out the mentally inferior yet powerful wife described in "Margaret Fuller and Mary Wollstonecraft" as a prototype for Rosamond Vincy of *Middlemarch*. "Story of a Blue-Bottle," an April 1856 review of Léon Gozlan's *La Folle du Logis* for the *Leader*, excerpts an argument about water rights that recalls Mr. Tulliver's litigation in *The Mill on the Floss*. Indeed the famous web metaphor that dominates *Middlemarch* appears as a peculiarly female metaphor of determinism in a quotation used in the very first essay attributed to Evans, the *Coventry Herald* review of Michelet's *Priests, Women, and Families*.

Equally interesting are the differences between the reviews and the novels, especially the shift in tone from the occasionally biting irony with which Evans mounts her most severe critical attacks in the reviews to the more sympathetic irony of the novel narrators. Although the reviews nearly always give some praise to authors, Evans occasionally displays what Pinney, in the introduction to his edition of Eliot's essays, calls a "fierce gusto in denunciation." In "Worldliness and Otherworldliness: The Poet Young" (*Westminster Review*, January 1857), she observes, "Other poets, besides [Edward] Young, found the device for obtaining a Tory majority by turning twelve insignificant commoners into insignificant lords, an irresistible stimulus to verse; but no other poet showed so versatile an enthusiasm—so nearly equal an ardour for the honour of the new baron and the honour of the Deity." Summarizing the history of the persona in Tennyson's *Maud* for an October 1855 *Westminster Review* piece, she comments, "These family sorrows and mortifications the hero regards as a direct result of the anti-social tendencies of peace, which he proceeds to expose to us in all its hideousness; looking to war as the immediate curative for unwholesome lodging of the poor, adulteration of provisions, child-murder, and wife-beating—an effect which is as yet by no means visible in our police reports." The sharp wit of these critical attacks cre-

The drawing room at The Priory in London where Eliot and Lewes established permanent residence in 1863

ates an impression of the author that is missing from reverent portraits of the sympathetic sibylline novelist.

Evans gave up journalism almost completely when she began writing fiction in the fall of 1856, and soon, for fear of finding negative comments on her own work, she stopped even reading book reviews. The excellent income from the novels freed her from financial need, and, unlike her journalism, her fiction could conveniently be written away from London. During the next twenty years, despite their permanent residence at The Priory near Regent's Park beginning in 1863, she and Lewes often fled the fog, the noise, and the air of London. Eliot (who had assumed her pseudonym in 1857) wrote much of her fiction while traveling on the Continent or on holiday at the seaside. At home she and Lewes were occupied with settling his three growing sons in suitable professions, taking care of each other's feeble health, and maintaining the literary social life that they developed as the fame of the novels increased.

In the twenty-year period during which she produced her seven novels, Eliot produced only a few odd pieces of straight prose. For the *Pall Mall Gazette* she wrote a series of four short essays, including "A Word for the Germans," "Servants' Logic," "Futile Falsehoods," and "Modern Housekeeping," the last two notable as her only use of an identifiably female persona. "Felix Holt's Address to the Working Man" (*Blackwood's Magazine,* January 1868) responded to John Blackwood's request for an essay in the character of the hero from her 1866 novel. Reviews of William Lecky's *History of the Rise and Influence of the Spirit of Rationalism in Europe* and of Owen Jones's *The Grammar of Ornament* (both in the *Fortnightly Review,* 15 May 1865), together with some brief passages published posthumously in 1884 as "Leaves from a Note-Book," completed her nonfiction prose output until *Impressions of Theophrastus Such* appeared in 1879.

By the late 1870s Eliot's success as a novelist had brought her not only wealth and fame but also the simple social acceptance denied her since she and Lewes had begun living together openly. At The Priory they entertained friends and fans on Sunday afternoons, and they began a series of regular visits to the universities at Oxford and Cambridge.

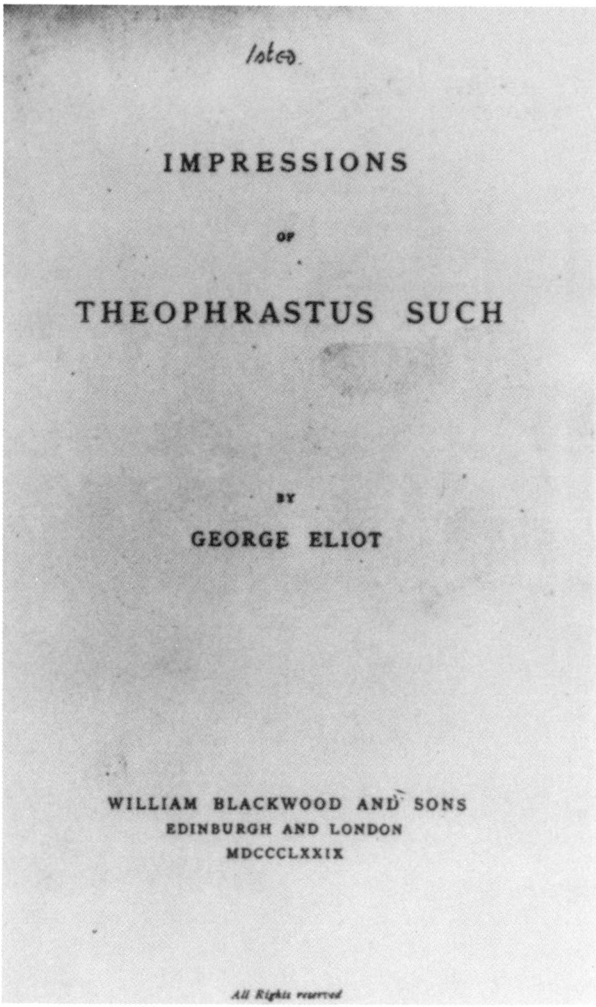

IMPRESSIONS

OF

THEOPHRASTUS SUCH

BY

GEORGE ELIOT

WILLIAM BLACKWOOD AND SONS
EDINBURGH AND LONDON
MDCCCLXXIX

All Rights reserved

Title page for Eliot's 1879 volume of essays and character sketches

Whereas the early essays and reviews depend on an urban literary milieu and achieve their tone through an occasional reference to the Crystal Palace or the railway stations, the urban tone of *Impressions of Theophrastus Such* depends on the personal essay form and on its club/salon settings. The collection contains eighteen essays, many of them character sketches, all written from the viewpoint of a remote observer similar to the Macarthy of the early *Coventry Herald* essays, but, as Rudy V. Redinger has observed in *George Eliot: The Emergent Self* (1975), "tougher" and more "world-weary." The allegorically named characters (Merman, Vorticella) move in a literary social world of research, articles, and periodical reviews, and their self-deceptive follies often involve the vanities of authorship. As in "Leaves from a Note-Book" and other fragments from the later period, metaphors of writing as disease, drug, poison, and cure often represent literary efforts in *Impressions of Theophrastus Such.* A number of allusions to remote tribes (Fuegans, Eskimos, Hottentots) emphasize Theophrastus's ineffectiveness and alienation: his single published work is a romance enjoyed only in its Cherokee translation. Although her affirmation of the moral purpose of art survives both in *Impressions of Theophrastus Such* and in the late fragments such as "Notes on Form in Art" and "On Versification," Eliot's increasingly complex theory of realism and increasing emphasis on artistic organicism result in her intensified preoccupation with the problems of authorship. More and more, toward the end of her career, Eliot was writing about the problems of writing.

The sketches succeed best when their techniques are most novelistic, as in "Diseases of Small Authorship" with its lively dialogue and detailed characterization of young Theophrastus. In "Moral Swindlers," on the other hand, Theophrastus's weak voice and the lack of dramatic scenes dull the effect of the quite reasonable point that the word *moral* is too exclusively applied to sexual conduct: following the method of analysis she describes in several of the essays, that of progressing from generalizations to finer and finer distinctions, Eliot tends to exhaust her argument. Although the last two essays in the group—"Shadows of the Coming Race" and "The Modern Hep! Hep! Hep!"—take shrewd looks at the future (the first anticipating a computerized society and the second warning against anti-Semitism), the nearly complete disappearance of Theophrastus himself deprives them of the personality of the earlier essays "Looking Inward" and "Looking Backward," both of which are often taken as autobiographical.

Contemporary reviews of the book were mixed, most of them combining respect for the novelist with the disappointment that Eliot herself anticipated when she expressed concern that a nonnarrative work would startle her public. Although it sold briskly for four editions totaling 6,000 copies, sales dropped off in the beginning of 1880. Early-twentieth-century readers found that the sketches contained all the ponderous morality against which their own age rebelled. Consequently, *Impressions of Theophrastus Such* helped seal Eliot's reputation for didactic dullness, a reputation that persisted until the critical revival of the mid twentieth century. Recent readers generally find the volume of sketches both ponderous and perplexing, but provocative as well, especially when read in conjunction with the novels.

Because Lewes died shortly after he forwarded the manuscript of *Impressions of Theophrastus Such* to John Blackwood, Eliot saw its publication as a sacred mission. After his death she struggled with her grief for more than a year, then astonished her friends and her public by marrying John Walter Cross, a banker twenty years younger than she. They honeymooned on the Continent and leased a new house in London, but only seven months after her wedding Eliot died suddenly in December 1880. The beloved novelist was buried in Highgate Cemetery on the north edge of London, a city she seldom represented in her novels but evoked consistently in her nonfiction prose.

Back in the *Westminster Review* days Marian Evans and John Chapman had planned a philosophical prose work entitled "The Idea of a Future Life" as her first book. The entire novel-reading world can be grateful that it was, instead, the *Scenes of Clerical Life* (1858) that began her career in fiction. Nevertheless, the early essays and *Impressions of Theophrastus Such* reveal Eliot as a professional journalist with a sharp eye and a sharp tongue and as a moral essayist in the tradition of Jean de La Bruyère. Reading her nonfiction prose helps define her as Victorian critic and literary theorist and enriches the experience of reading her novels.

Letters:

John W. Cross, ed., *George Eliot's Life as Related in Her Letters and Journals*, 3 volumes (Edinburgh & London: Blackwood, 1885);

Gordon S. Haight, ed., *The George Eliot Letters*, 9 volumes (New Haven: Yale University Press, 1954-1955, 1978);

Haight, ed., *Selections from George Eliot's Letters* (New Haven & London: Yale University Press, 1985).

Bibliographies:

Constance M. Fulmer, *George Eliot: A Reference Guide, 1858-1971* (Boston: G. K. Hall, 1977);

David Leon Higdon, "A Bibliography of George Eliot Criticism, 1971-1977," *Bulletin of Bibliography*, 37 (April-June 1980): 90-103.

Biography:

Gordon S. Haight, *George Eliot: A Biography* (Oxford: Clarendon Press, 1968).

References:

K. K. Collins, "Questions of Method: Some Unpublished Late Essays," *Nineteenth-Century Fiction*, 35 (December 1980): 385-405;

Constance Fulmer, "Contrasting Pairs of Heroines in George Eliot's Fiction," *Studies in the Novel*, 6 (Fall 1974): 288-294;

Gordon S. Haight, *George Eliot and John Chapman: With Chapman's Diaries* (New Haven: Yale University Press, 1940; London: Oxford University Press, 1940);

Darrel Mansell, Jr., "Ruskin and George Eliot's Realism," *Criticism*, 7 (Summer 1965): 203-216;

Thomas Pinney, Introduction to *Essays of George Eliot*, edited by Pinney (New York: Columbia University Press, 1963; London: Routledge & Kegan Paul, 1963);

Ruby V. Redinger, *George Eliot: The Emergent Self* (New York: Knopf, 1975);

James D. Rust, "The Art of Fiction in George Eliot's Reviews," *Review of English Studies*, new series 7 (1956): 164-172;

G. Robert Stange, "The Voices of the Essayist," *Nineteenth-Century Fiction*, 35 (December 1980): 312-330;

Joseph Wiesenfarth, Introduction to George Eliot, *A Writer's Notebook, 1854-1879, and Uncollected Writings*, edited by Wiesenfarth (Charlottesville: University Press of Virginia, 1980).

Papers:

Important collections of George Eliot's papers are located at the British Library, the Bienecke Rare Book and Manuscript Library at Yale University, the New York Public Library, the Pforzheimer Library, the Folger Shakespeare Library, and the library of Princeton University.

W. R. Greg

(1809-15 November 1881)

Sidney Coulling
Washington and Lee University

BOOKS: *An Enquiry into the State of the Manufacturing Population, and the Causes and Cures of the Evils Therein Existing* (London: Ridgway, 1831);

Sketches in Greece and Turkey: with the Present Condition and Future Prospects of the Turkish Empire (London: Ridgway, 1833);

Social Statistics of the Netherlands (Manchester: Harrison & Crosfield, 1835);

Past and Present Efforts for the Extinction of the African Slave Trade (London: Ridgway, 1840);

Agriculture and the Corn Law. Prize Essay. Showing the Injurious Effects of the Corn Law upon Tenant Farmers and Farm Labourers (Manchester: Printed by J. Wilson, 1842);

Not Over-production, but Deficient Consumption, the Source of Our Sufferings (London: Hooper, 1842);

The Creed of Christendom: Its Foundations and Superstructure (London: Chapman, 1851; New York: Blanchard, 1855);

Essays on Political and Social Science, Contributed Chiefly to the Edinburgh Review, 2 volumes (London: Longman, Brown, Green & Longmans, 1853);

The One Thing Needful (London, 1855?; second edition, London: Ridgway, 1855);

The Way Out (London: Ridgway, 1855);

Literary and Social Judgments (London: Trübner, 1868; Boston: Osgood, 1873; enlarged, 2 volumes, London: Trübner, 1877);

Political Problems for Our Age and Country (London: Trübner, 1870);

Enigmas of Life (London: Trübner, 1872; Boston: Osgood, 1873);

Rocks Ahead; or, The Warnings of Cassandra (London: Trübner, 1874; Boston: Osgood, 1875);

Mistaken Aims and Attainable Ideals of the Artizan Class (London: Trübner, 1876);

Miscellaneous Essays (London: Trübner, 1881).

William Rathbone Greg, a prolific essayist on literary, social, political, and religious subjects, was born in 1809 in Manchester. There is no published record of the exact date of his birth. His father, Samuel Greg, was an astute businessman of Scotch-Irish descent who had made a fortune from the cotton mill he had built at Wilmslow, in Cheshire, and his mother, Hannah Lightbody Greg, was a cultivated, energetic woman who had compiled a book of maxims and written a manual on nursing. Much of the son's character was shaped by his parents, Unitarians who nurtured in their thirteen children, of whom Greg was the youngest, the love of a simple life devoted to intellectual pursuits and humanitarian service.

After being taught at home by an elder sister and then at schools in Leeds and Bristol, Greg in 1826 entered the University of Edinburgh, where he remained through the 1828 session. He was a bright and industrious student, capable of prolonged periods of work in which he immersed himself as an escape from melancholy, but despite his professed desire to explore every branch of human knowledge he left Edinburgh with neither a degree nor a clear plan for the future.

For the next two years he managed one of his father's mills at Bury, north of Manchester. It was a time of unrest preceding passage of the 1832 Reform Bill, and Greg became so concerned that he wrote a pamphlet, *An Enquiry into the State of the Manufacturing Population, and the Causes and Cures of the Evils Therein Existing* (1831), addressed, he explained, "to the higher classes on the present state of public feeling among the lower, urging them to moderate and direct it if they can." Following another period of depression he spent a year abroad, traveling from France to Switzerland, Italy, and Sicily, then through Greece and Asia Minor to Constantinople, and from there through Hungary to Vienna. On his return he wrote an account of the most exciting part of his travels, published in 1833 as *Sketches in Greece and Turkey: with the Present Condition and Future Prospects of the Turkish Empire.*

The next two decades were the most eventful of Greg's life. He entered business on his own and at the same time, having already supported the

Reform Bill, worked actively for further political and social improvements. In 1837 he stood, though unsuccessfully, for representation of the corrupt borough of Lancaster, and five years later he contributed to the eventual repeal of the Corn Laws with an essay (*Agriculture and the Corn Law,* printed at Manchester in 1842), which won a prize offered by the Anti-Corn Law League. Meanwhile, in 1835, he had married Lucy Henry, daughter of a Manchester physician recognized for his discoveries in the chemistry of gases, and when her health failed they moved to the Lake District. There Greg began and completed the book that brought his name before the public at large, *The Creed of Christendom: Its Foundations and Superstructure,* first published in 1851 and in its ninth edition before the end of the century.

Its thesis, as the subtitle implies, is that popular Christianity is not the religion of Jesus. Whereas the one is based largely on untenable doctrines such as belief in miracles and the inspiration of Scripture, Greg argues, the other rests firmly on great truths that unintelligible creeds have obscured. Greg adopts a moderate tone throughout and reaches a more positive conclusion than is alleged by such critics as Fitzjames Stephen, who compared him to a disciple who had heard the Sermon on the Mount but died before the Resurrection. On the contrary, Greg devotes a long and eloquent passage to extolling the beauties of the universe, affirming God's plan for it, and insisting that, absolute certainty being neither possible nor intended, it is the responsibility of each person to help unfold that plan. John Morley, who praised Greg's "intellectual courage and independence" in a sketch collected in his *Critical Miscellanies* (1898), recognized the work's significant place in what he called "the dissolvent literature" of midcentury, and in the decade following the publication in 1873 of Matthew Arnold's *Literature and Dogma,* with which Greg's book was sometimes compared. It went through almost as many editions as Arnold's more famous book.

At the same time that Greg was writing *The Creed of Christendom* his family fortunes were undergoing a disastrous decline. He had not inherited his father's business acumen, and managing from a distance his own mill as well as that of a brother whose health had broken was beyond his ability. When the 1850 crash came he was forced to close both mills and suffer the loss of almost his entire investment of forty thousand pounds. A still heavier blow was the illness of his wife, who by now was hopelessly insane and incapable of being a mother to their four children. Facing at age forty-one the necessity of making a new start in life, Greg began by moving from his house at the foot of Wansfell, near Ambleside, to the Craig at Bowness.

A more important change, however, came through James Wilson, with whom Greg had developed a close friendship in the movement against the Corn Laws and who in 1843 had established the *Economist.* Greg became a regular contributor and soon branched out to write for the four leading quarterlies of the time— the *Edinburgh, Westminster, Quarterly,* and *North British* reviews. In one year alone, 1852, he produced no fewer than a dozen articles, nearly all on political and economic subjects, and the following year he gathered more than twenty of his contributions and republished them in two thick volumes entitled *Essays on Political and Social Science* (1853).

In one of the essays Greg uttered a rare, thinly veiled autobiographical complaint when he poignantly contrasted the life of a man whose "domestic felicity was great, and almost unclouded to the last," with that of a man who labors under "a nightmare of disappointment, anguish, or anxiety; for whom the treasury of hope is empty, and who has no future before him to redeem and compensate the past." Greg's connection with the quarterlies, however, helped relieve the dreary solitude of his life and brought him in touch with literary and political figures outside the narrow world in which he moved. He enjoyed, to be sure, the friendship of neighbors, including the Arnolds, the Speddings, and Harriet Martineau (who had been drawn to him at first by a common interest in mesmerism). But Hartley Coleridge, with whom he felt a bond of sympathy, had died, and Wordsworth, who had once taken up an entire visit talking about the various qualities and virtues of gravel, had never appealed to him. Now he began to make frequent visits to London and through his relationship with the *Westminster Review* met George Eliot, from whom we have one of the few surviving descriptions of his physical appearance. She found him so unprepossessing—short, with a hooked nose and bad teeth—as to make her wonder who had written the books published under his name; but his large head and black, curly hair were, she thought, phrenologically reassuring, pointing to a strong moral character. Greg also paid annual visits to Paris, spending part of one winter with the Wilson family and becoming acquainted with his future brother-in-law, Walter Bagehot, who had married Wilson's eldest daughter and who later made Greg a special contributor to the *National*

Review, the distinguished Unitarian journal he co-edited with Richard Holt Hutton. From time to time Greg also stayed in Normandy with Alexis de Tocqueville, whom he described, in one of the essays later collected in *Literary and Social Judgments,* as "the purest, noblest, truest gentleman" he had ever known.

Other changes followed. In 1856 Greg reluctantly accepted the offer by the chancellor of the Exchequer, Sir George Cornewall Lewis, of a place on the Board of Customs. The routine duties of the position were repugnant to a man who had been accustomed to independence for most of his life, but the salary (nominally twelve thousand pounds) was irresistible to a writer concerned about the precarious nature of his profession. Because the new work required a change of residence Greg moved his family to Park Lodge, a house on Wimbledon Common, where he lived until his death twenty-five years later. During that period he had but one other move to make, this time (1864) to become comptroller of the Stationery Office, from which he retired in 1877.

Greg continued in these years to contribute to periodicals, sometimes as often as monthly, but more than a decade elapsed before he brought together ten of the essays as *Literary and Social Judgments.* Published in 1868, it became one of his most widely read works and reached a fourth, enlarged edition in 1877.

Nowhere else in his writings are Greg's virtues and flaws more sharply juxtaposed. At times he demonstrates a striking breadth of interest, a penetrating critical mind, and a remarkable freedom from conventional thought. As in Arnold's *Essays in Criticism,* published three years earlier, in 1865, French subjects are prominent in his selections, two of which—those on Madame de Staël and Chateaubriand—remain more than a century later readable and informative essays. In an acute comparison of Charles Kingsley and Thomas Carlyle, Greg accurately pinpoints both their individual defects (the superficiality of the one and the gloom of the other) and those they share (pugnacity and love of power); and in "False Morality of Lady Novelists," in which Elizabeth Cleghorn Gaskell's *Ruth* (1853) is cited as a prime example, he judges Victorian prudery and the double sexual standard with satiric force: "The grasping and cruel man is gravely rebuked; on the feeble and erring woman is poured forth a flood of virtuous indignation. The weak flesh is beaten with many stripes; the wicked spirit is gently told to go and sin no more." But other essays betray how indelibly Greg's ideas were tainted by the prejudices of his age. An 1860 review of French fiction becomes a tirade against its alleged morbidity and licentiousness; an article prompted by the controversy over Governor Eyre out-Carlyles Carlyle in its racial views; and an essay on unmarried women in England denounces the "extravagant fantasies" of "wild schemers" in America who "would throw open the professions to women, and teach them to become lawyers and physicians and professors."

The appearance of *Literary and Social Judgments* marked the beginning of the most productive and perhaps the happiest period in Greg's life. During the next ten years he had four books published and saw two earlier ones through a total of eight new editions. Election to the Athenaeum in 1868 was followed by growing recognition of his work, and there was frequent travel. He revisited Greece with Sir Mountstuart and Lady Grant Duff and went to Egypt on another occasion. In 1873 he was finally released from an empty marriage by the death of his wife, and the following year he married Julia, second daughter of his friend Wilson, by whom he had one son.

The central work of this period was Greg's most popular book, *Enigmas of Life,* first published in 1872 and in its twentieth edition by 1905. Its century-old theme, linking the earliest of the Romantics with the last of the Victorians, is human progress and perfectibility, which Greg proclaims to be "the great design of God and the great work of man." He sees progress everywhere and "incalculable" possibilities for more. Already, he says, the nineteenth century has witnessed more material advances than in all previous history, and each advance makes moral and intellectual achievements still more attainable. He predicts medical improvements, the eradication or drastic reduction of disease and crime, and even, within a single generation, the possible elimination of war. Many of these advances, he declares, might long since have occurred had established religion directed its attention toward "the improvement of the moral and material condition of humanity on this earth, instead of towards the promulgation of an astounding scheme for securing it against eternal torments in a future existence"; but Greg's utopian vision embraces the eventual transformation of religion as well. When that has been accomplished, he writes, only three barriers to unlimited progress will remain, and all can be overcome. The Malthusian problem may be solved by dispersing the world's population and by adequately cultivating its land; the tendency of civilization to invert the process of natural selection (by caring for the sick and incompetent, who, according to Greg, are the most fecund) might be counteracted by the longevity and lower mortality rate of superior classes, by restrictions on philanthropy, and by a more equitable distribution of wealth; and the increasing danger of democracy can be checked by preserving the sanctity of private property and by making the working class too prosperous to wish to agitate for political power. John Morley thought *Enigmas of Life* the "most interesting" of Greg's works, and Hugh Walker, in *The Literature of the Victorian Era* (1910), considered it the "most valuable." But both critics wrote during a period when Greg's elitist and reactionary views seemed less offensive than they now do and before his naive dreams of human progress had been forever shattered by events of the twentieth century.

Enigmas of Life was followed two years later by *Rocks Ahead; or, The Warnings of Cassandra* (1874), a book unaccountably repudiating the buoyant hopes of the former volume and issuing in their place dire warnings that gave Greg his reputation as a prophet of doom. It had been partly anticipated by Greg's *Political Problems for Our Age and Country* (1870), in which, said the critic for the *Westminster Review,* Greg had treated "acutely and profoundly, and yet with a rare amount of independence," the "most pressing social and political questions" of the time, including foreign policy, crime, pauperism, and taxation. But whereas it had been positive and constructive, *Rocks Ahead* seemed unduly negative and pessimistic. "The part of Cassandra can never be a pleasant one for any man to play," Greg begins, but because of dangers threatening the future of England—what he calls the political, economic, and religious "rocks ahead" on which the nation might well be wrecked—he feels compelled to play that role. The causes of his anxiety are the political supremacy gained by the lower classes from the Reform Bill of 1867, which shifted power from the propertied to the wage-earning class; the near exhaustion of the supply of cheap coal, making it increasingly difficult for England to remain the workshop of the world and thus foreshadowing its inevitable industrial decline; and the growing enmity between the critical intelligence and the creedal religion of the nation, imperiling the survival of Christianity as a stabilizing force. Greg was more prescient in his economic warnings than he could have known and more moderate in his political and religious views than his critics allowed. But it is nevertheless true that he gloomily predicted "progressive decadence in all the higher elements of national life," the shrinking of England into "a second Holland," and a "possible catastrophe" when the promises of established religion became widely perceived as fraudulent.

Greg struck a more hopeful note, however, in his final volume, *Miscellaneous Essays* (1881), published five years after his *Mistaken Aims and Attainable Ideals of the Artizan Class* (almost all of which has appeared previously in *Essays on Political and Social Science*) and, according to his obituary in the London *Times,* just prior to his death. It is a virtual summing-up of his life as a philanthropist and his career as an essayist, returning to the subjects that had engaged his attention for decades, stressing once again the need to encourage frugality and industriousness, to spread education and property among the working classes, and to promote understanding between capital and labor, and deploring the spread of democracy and the despotism of organized religion.

Though not among the major Victorian figures or even the most significant of the minor ones, Greg was nonetheless an essayist of considerable if limited gifts. He wrote knowledgeably and copiously on a wide range of subjects, in a clear, fluent style. His mind was exceptionally lucid and incisive, relentless in pursuing an argument or exposing shallow and fallacious thinking. He was to a large degree self-educated and showed both the strength and the weakness of being so: independence from conventional thought but isolation, as Benjamin Jowett found in Ruskin, from other minds to rub against. In his religious writings, notably *The Creed of Christendom,* he was ahead of most of his contemporaries in frankly admitting the loss of doctrinal faith to the advances of science and biblical criticism and in finding elsewhere a basis for religion. In his social and political criticism he was essentially a conservative member of the Manchester school, expressing, to be sure, the humanitarian concerns that had been deeply ingrained in him during childhood but decrying interference with the inexorable laws of supply and demand and voicing in almost identical notes of alarm his fears of democracy, French fiction, the power of labor, and woman's rights. He could be prickly with his editors and acerbic in controversy. But his friends testified to his unselfishness and personal charm and to his bearing with equanimity both the loss of a fortune and a calamitous marriage. Under such circumstances it was no small achievement to have produced a series of books which, in Hugh Walker's words, "are among the best adapted to afford a view of the contemporary problems upon which they touch, as these problems appeared to a remarkably keen intelligence."

References:

Alfred William Benn, *The History of English Rationalism in the Nineteenth Century,* 2 volumes (London: Longmans, Green, 1906);

Julia Wilson Greg, Memoir of W. R. Greg, in Greg's *Enigmas of Life,* eighteenth edition (London: Kegan Paul, Trench, Trübner, 1905);

John Morley, "W. R. Greg: A Sketch," in his *Critical Miscellanies,* volume 3 (London: Macmillan, 1898), pp. 213-259;

Bernard M. G. Reardon, *From Coleridge to Gore: A Century of Religious Thought in Britain* (London: Longman, 1971);

Hugh Walker, *The Literature of the Victorian Era* (Cambridge: University Press, 1910).

John Keble

(25 April 1792-29 March 1866)

G. B. Tennyson
University of California, Los Angeles

See also the Keble entry in *DLB 32, Victorian Poets Before 1850.*

BOOKS: *On Translation from Dead Languages: A Prize Essay* (Oxford: Privately printed, 1812);

The Christian Year: Thoughts in Verse for the Sundays and Holydays throughout the Year, anonymous, 2 volumes (Oxford: Parker/London: Rivington, 1827; New York: Dutton, 1827);

National Apostasy Considered in a Sermon (Oxford: Parker/London: Rivington, 1833);

Tracts for the Times by Members of the University of Oxford, numbers 4, 13, 40, 52, 54, 57, 60, 89 by Keble, 6 volumes (Oxford: Parker/London: Rivington, 1833-1841);

Ode for the Encaenia at Oxford, anonymous (Oxford, 1834);

Lyra Apostolica, anonymous, by Keble and John William Bowden, Richard Hurrell Froude, John Henry Newman, Robert Isaac Wilberforce, and Isaac Williams (Derby, U.K.: Mozley, 1836);

Primitive Tradition Recognized in Holy Scripture: A Sermon (London: Rivington, 1836);

The Psalter or Psalms of David in English Verse, anonymous (Oxford: Parker, 1839);

The Case of Catholic Subscription to the Thirty-nine Articles Considered (London: Privately printed, 1841);

De Poeticae vi Medica: Praelectiones Academicae (Oxford: Parker, 1844); translated by Edward Kershaw Francis as Keble's *Lectures on Poetry 1832-1841,* 2 volumes (Oxford: Clarendon Press, 1912);

Lyra Innocentium: Thoughts in Verse on Christian Children, Their Ways, and Their Privileges, anonymous (Oxford & London: Parker, 1846; New York: Wiley & Putnam, 1846);

Sermons, Academical and Occasional (Oxford & London: Parker, 1847);

On Eucharistical Adoration (Oxford & London: Parker, 1857);

The Life of the Right Reverend Father in God, Thomas Wilson, 8 volumes (Oxford: Parker, 1863);

Sermons, Occasional and Parochial (Oxford & London: Parker, 1868);

Village Sermons on the Baptismal Service, edited by E. B. Pusey (Oxford: Parker, 1868);

Miscellaneous Poems, edited by G. Moberly (Oxford & London: Parker, 1869; New York: Polt & Amery, 1869);

Letters of Spiritual Counsel and Guidance, edited by R. F. Wilson (Oxford & London: Parker, 1870);

Sermons for the Christian Year, 11 volumes (Oxford: Parker, 1875-1880);

Occasional Papers and Reviews, edited by Pusey (Oxford & London: Parker, 1877);

Studia Sacra, edited by J. P. Norris (Oxford & London: Parker, 1877).

John Keble, 1844. Engraving based on a lost portrait by George Richmond (Keble College, Oxford)

OTHER: *Works of Richard Hooker,* edited by Keble, 3 volumes (Oxford: Oxford University Press, 1836);

Five Books of St. Irenaeus against Heresies, translated by Keble, in *A Library of the Fathers of the Holy Catholic Church,* edited by E. B. Pusey, 51 volumes (Oxford: Parker, 1838-1885);

Remains of the Late Reverend Richard Hurrell Froude, edited by Keble and John Henry Newman, 4 volumes (London: Rivington, 1838-1839).

More than any other single figure associated with the religious movements of nineteenth-century England, John Keble was regarded by his contemporaries as something close to a saint. John Henry Newman in the *Apologia Pro Vita Sua* (1864) attests to Keble's reputation for learning and sanctity in the Oxford of the second and third decades of the century and honors Keble as the true begetter of the Oxford, or Tractarian, Movement that began in the 1830s. From the mid 1830s on, Keble's vicarage at Hursley in Hampshire was a virtual pilgrimage destination for pious churchmen from Britain and abroad. In an unprecedented tribute, only four years after Keble's death an Oxford college was founded in his name; at least one Anglican church is called the John Keble Church; and numerous busts, portraits, and memorial windows depicting Keble are still to be found in Anglican churches throughout the world, including Westminster Abbey and Salisbury Cathedral. This reverence, now largely faded, was provoked not so much by Keble the prose writer as by Keble the man and poet, but Keble's prose is of a piece with his character and his poetry.

As poet, Keble anticipated the Oxford Movement by at least a half-dozen years with the publication in 1827 of his *The Christian Year,* a two-volume book of verse that had, in fact, been circulating in manuscript among friends for most of the early 1820s. From its first appearance in print Keble's book of poems organized around the traditional Christian ecclesiastical calendar in its Anglican formulation went through ninety-five editions in his lifetime and an unknown number of later editions during the rest of the century and up to the time of World War I. It was almost certainly the single most popular book of verse in the nineteenth century. To the extent that Keble's name survives today, it does so in large measure as that of the author of *The Christian Year* and of several other volumes of devotional poetry that were popular in the Victorian age, most notably the *Lyra Innocentium* (1846).

Keble also survives in literary and ecclesiastical history as a main figure in the Tractarian Movement. In that role he was renowned in his time as one of the triumvirate who founded and guided the movement (the other two being Newman and E. B. Pusey). He participated in all the major activities and publications of the movement, and with Pusey he stood firm for the Church of England when Newman and some of his followers left for the Church of Rome in the 1840s. Beyond his involvement with Tractarianism, Keble was held in high esteem as an example of the pure rural parson who disdained high prelatical preferment to serve as a simple parish priest.

There was yet another dimension to Keble that was widely known in his lifetime, albeit mainly to the clergy and the learned—that of prose writer of religious works and sermons and of literary criticism and theory. By a curious reversal of historical taste, it is as prose writer, especially as a literary theorist, that Keble has begun to come back into literary discussion today.

John Keble was the second child and elder son of five children (two sons, three daughters) born to Sarah Maule Keble and John Keble, Sr., the vicar of Coln St. Aldwyn's, near Fairford in Gloucestershire. Both sons, John and Thomas, were sent to their father's college at Oxford, Corpus Christi, from which John Keble graduated with double first-class honors in 1811, following that achievement the next year with university prizes for Latin and English essays. From the first Keble was associated with most of the leading intellectual figures of the Oxford of his day, including J. T. Coleridge (nephew of the poet) and Thomas Arnold (father of Matthew Arnold), and, after his election in 1812 to a fellowship at Oriel College, with Edward Copleston and Richard Whately and others known as the Oriel Noetics, though Keble's own churchmanship was to lead him in a more orthodox and less speculative direction than that associated with Whately's Broad Church views.

Keble was ordained deacon in 1815 and priest in 1816. In addition to tutoring and serving as fellow of Oriel and in various examination offices at Oxford, he served as curate in two small parishes in Gloucestershire. The death of his mother in 1823 caused him to leave Oxford to be close to his father and two surviving sisters at Fairford. From there he served as curate in nearby Southrop, and it was here during the long vacations that he tutored a number of promising Oxonians, among them several who would later be active in the Oxford Movement, such as Robert Wilberforce, Richard Hurrell Froude, Isaac Williams, and George Prevost. During this period, too, he was writing and privately circulating the poems that would later be published in *The Christian Year*. It was from Keble's Oxford career and the period of his private tutoring that much of the mystique of the saintly Keble originated, strengthened later by his exemplary behavior as Tractarian and his model life as a parish priest.

Concern over his father's ill health persuaded Keble to decline the offer of the archdeaconry of

Keble College at Oxford, founded in Keble's honor four years after his death

The vicarage at Hursley. In 1836, ten years after resigning as curate of Hursley, Keble was appointed vicar. He remained at Hursley until his death in 1866.

Barbados in 1824, but the next year he accepted a post at Hursley in Hampshire, only to resign it in 1826 when his youngest sister died and he felt obliged to return to his father and an invalid sister at Fairford. He then succeeded his father as vicar of Coln St. Aldwyn's, declining an offer to return to Hursley in 1829, remaining instead at Fairford until his father's death at age ninety-one in 1835. In that year he married Charlotte Clarke, a friend since childhood and the sister of his brother Thomas's wife. (The marriage did not produce any children.) The next year, the post at Hursley again being vacant, he accepted the vicarship and remained at Hursley for the rest of his life, continuing to exercise a role in the Tractarian Movement and to influence Anglican churchmanship through his character and his writings. At Hursley he also catechized the future writer Charlotte Mary Yonge, whose many highly popular novels were seen as the application to domestic life of Keble's principles. In his last years he spent the winters in warmer climates along the southern coast of England for the sake of his wife's health. His own health was also deteriorating, and, after a week's illness, he died on 29 March 1866 in Bournemouth. His death was followed six weeks later by that of his wife. Both were buried in Hursley churchyard.

Although Keble first gained widespread public recognition as a poet, he was already known to literary circles as a writer of essays and sermons, and he continued to produce numerous works of prose throughout his life. That prose, while heavily religious, has a more various character than Keble's saintly image might at first suggest. It ranges from literary criticism to biography to biblical and theological commentary. Nor is it lacking in firm expression and even at times in polemic character. It was Keble's Assize Sermon, delivered on 14 July 1833, that Newman hailed as marking the official beginning of the Oxford Movement. In that much-republished piece, which first appeared in pamphlet form as *National Apostasy Considered in a Sermon* (1833), Keble took the British government to task for presuming to decide matters (in this case the allocation of bishoprics for Ireland) better left to the Church itself in its role as a divinely ordained instrument for preaching God's word. The sermon was an anti-Erastian blast from the very heart of Oxford Toryism and helped strike what would become the characteristic Tractarian note of insistence on the special character vouchsafed the Church of England by its preservation of the apostolic succession. *National Apostasy* stands as a brief and concentrated example of what Keble so often did as a person and as a writer: he sounded a revolutionary trumpet by calling his contemporaries back to origins.

Many of Keble's writings on religious matters exhibit the same character as his Assize Sermon: a reaffirmation in a tone of quiet earnestness of old principles that, because they had been forgotten, seemed to be new. Such was in fact Keble's view of the Oxford Movement itself. It had, he claimed, no tenets other than those that he had been taught by his father. The reaffirmation of tradition is always at least an undertone in Keble's religious writings and frequently it forms the theme and substance of them. His separately published sermon *Primitive Tradition Recognized in Holy Scripture* (1836) is a good example of Keble's dealing directly with religious tradition, as is his later sermon *On Eucharistical Adoration* (1857). His many other volumes of sermons exhibit similar concerns: for example, his *Village Sermons on the Baptismal Service* (published posthumously in 1868) deals with one of the two sacraments (the other being the Eucharist) that the Tractarians held in highest esteem as being the bedrock of traditional Catholic sacramentalism. Even when sermonizing on general topics, Keble maintained an emphasis on tradition. It is completely in character for the author of a volume of verse organized around the ecclesiastical year that Keble's major collection of sermons (published posthumously from 1875 to 1880) is the eleven-volume *Sermons for the Christian Year.* As a writer of sermons and religious tracts Keble exhibited some of the characteristics of Newman in that his style exemplifies the Tractarian doctrines of Analogy and Reserve, but Keble's more restrained tone, his greater reverence for the concept of Reserve, and his avoidance of the personal element keep his sermons from having the intense emotional impact of Newman's.

As a biographer and editor Keble also dealt with religious matters. He labored for many years on his eight-volume life of the seventeenth-century Anglican bishop of Sodor and Man, Thomas Wilson. Published in 1863 as *The Life of the Right Reverend Father in God, Thomas Wilson,* the work suffers from excessive detail on ecclesiastical matters, but for Keble it was a work of piety through which he hoped to hold up an example of model churchmanship. His earlier, 1836 edition of the works of the great Elizabethan theologian Richard Hooker was for many years the standard text, as was his translation of St. Irenaeus, published posthumously in 1872 as a volume in *A Library of the Fathers of the Holy Catholic Church* (1838-1885). Less enduring but certainly more incendiary in its time was Keble's coeditorship with Newman of the literary legacy of their recently deceased friend Froude, the volumes known as "Froude's Remains." Published in 1838 and 1839, at the height of the early phase of the Tractarian Movement, the *Remains of the Late Reverend Richard Hurrell Froude* provoked a storm of controversy for its revelations of the romanizing tendencies of Froude. Keble and Newman gained censure, not for any faults in the editing, but for making Froude's private sentiments public and thus fueling suspicions about the direction the Oxford Movement was taking.

During the 1830s and early 1840s Keble contributed eight of the ninety *Tracts for the Times,* the series of pamphlets that Newman inaugurated in 1833 to acquaint churchmen with the views of the Oxford Movement. Keble's contributions are thoughtful and learned pieces, of which the most important is *On the Mysticism Attributed to the Early Church Fathers* (1841), tract number 89. Here Keble's deep learning is admirably displayed, along with the literary and artistic bent of his mind. This pamphlet is the most sustained explanation of the Tractarian concept of Analogy, the idea that God can be known analogically through His works. The tract as it stands is lengthy and detailed and was intended as the first of two parts. The second part, however, was not written because the next tract, Newman's *Remarks on Certain Passages in the Thirty-nine Articles* (1841), caused an outcry that brought the *Tracts for the Times* altogether to a close.

Though Keble's biographies, editions, translations, and above all his sermons and treatises—all of them to a greater or lesser extent religious—were the most prominent aspects of his role as prose writer, it is his literary theory more than his other prose that has been the focus of twentieth-century scrutiny. As early as 1814, in a review of a work by Copleston for *British Critic,* Keble had written on literary matters. That essay, along with his 1825 *Quarterly Review* piece "Sacred Poetry," can be seen as predecessors of his most ambitious work in this field, his series of Oxford Lectures delivered from 1832 to 1841 and published in 1844 as *De Poeticae vi Medica: Praelectiones Academicae.* Keble delivered his lectures in his capacity as the Oxford Professor of Poetry. As was the custom at the time, the lectures were written and delivered in Latin, and it was in Latin that they were published. This

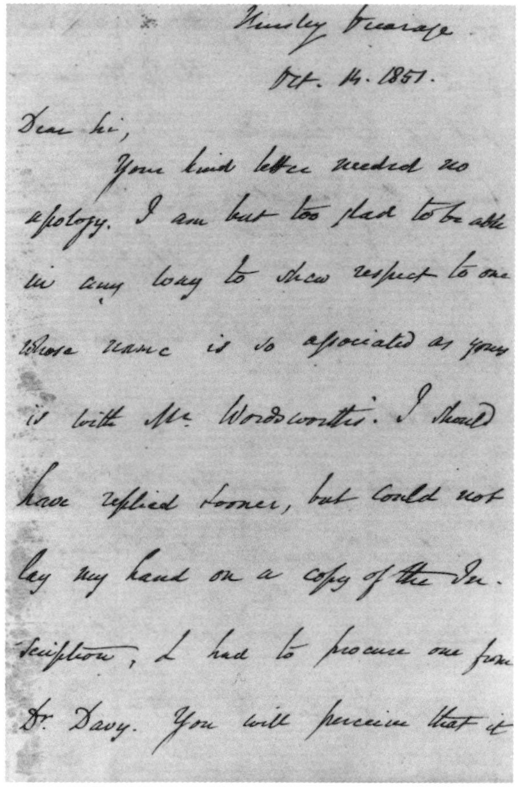

Hursley Vicarage
Oct. 14. 1851.

Dear Sir,

Your kind letter needed no apology. I am but too glad to be able in any way to shew respect to one whose name is so associated as yours is with Mr Wordsworth's. I should have replied sooner, but could not lay my hand on a copy of the Inscription, & had to procure one from Dr. Davy. You will perceive that it

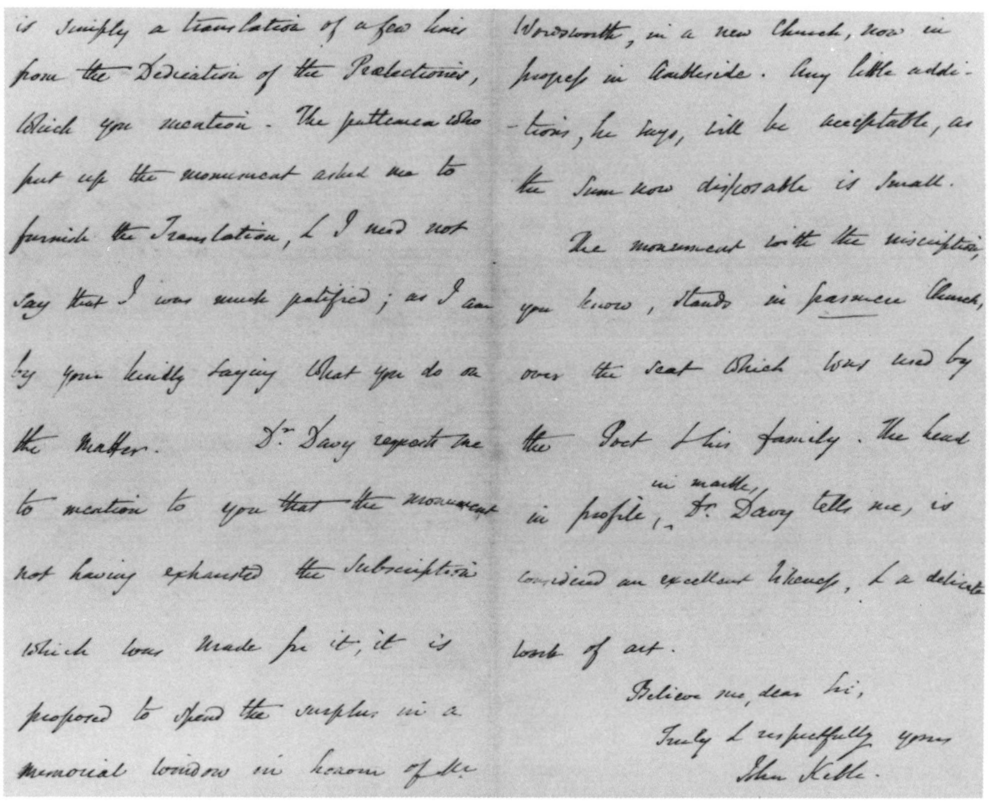

is simply a translation of a few lines from the Dedication of the Praelectiones, which you mention. The gentleman who put up the monument asked me to furnish the Translation, & I need not say that I was much gratified; as I am by your kindly saying what you do on the matter. Dr Davy requests me to mention to you that the monument not having exhausted the Subscription which was made for it, it is proposed to spend the surplus in a memorial window in honour of Mr Wordsworth, in a new Church, now in progress in Ambleside. Any little additions, he says, will be acceptable, as the sum now disposable is small.

The monument with the inscription, you know, stands in Grasmere Church, over the seat which was used by the Poet & his family. The head in profile, in marble, Dr. Davy tells me, is considered an excellent likeness, & a delicate work of art.

Believe me, dear Sir,
Truly & respectfully yours
John Keble.

Letter from Keble to an unidentified correspondent in which he refers to the "Praelectiones," his series of Oxford lectures dedicated to Wordsworth and collected for publication in 1844 (Lilly Library, Indiana University) hindered their accessibility, but they maintained a degree of currency among the academically educated that led Edward Kershaw Francis to translate them into English almost seventy years after the original publication, and they were published under the title *Lectures on Poetry* (1912).

Keble's lectures are the most sustained statement of the Tractarian aesthetic position ever presented. In them Keble envisions art, especially literature, as the outpouring of an essentially religious emotion and hence as a relief to the overburdened spirit. He develops the concepts of Analogy and Reserve at length, he classifies poets as primary or secondary (corresponding to the directness with which they are moved by and express religious feeling), and he discusses extensively the character of nature poetry as especially suited to the expression of religious emotion. His lectures were dedicated to Wordsworth as the supreme nature poet, and they show also, though more subtly, the theoretical influence of Coleridge. In the lectures Keble can be seen as having theologized Romantic aesthetic theory.

Keble's position as a prose writer is certainly minor in terms of the modern popularity or endurance of most of his works, but it is major in terms of the influence it exerted on a large body of nineteenth-century literature, including that of the distinctly major prose writer John Henry Newman. Like the man, Keble's style is self-effacing, but also like the man, that style had a capacity to speak gently but powerfully to his contemporaries and to convey with special authority the ethos of Tractarianism. For the twentieth century the contribution to aesthetic theory of Keble's *Lectures on Poetry* is proving to be his most important intellectual legacy, as critics continue to rediscover the Oxford addresses a century and a half after their presentation and recognize them as a compelling statement of a Christian aesthetic.

Biographies:

J. T. Coleridge, *A Memoir of the Rev. John Keble* (Oxford & London: Parker, 1869);

John Frewen Moor, *The Birth-Place, Home, Churches and Other Places Connected with the Author of "The Christian Year"* (London: Savage & Parker, 1877);

Walter Lock, *John Keble: A Biography* (London: Methuen, 1893);

Charlotte Mary Yonge, *John Keble's Parishes: A History of Hursley and Otterbourne* (London: Macmillan, 1898);

Georgina Battiscombe, *John Keble* (London: Constable, 1963);

Brian W. Martin, *John Keble, Priest, Professor and Poet* (London: Croom Helm, 1976).

References:

M. H. Abrams, *The Mirror and the Lamp: Romantic Theory and the Critical Tradition* (New York: Oxford University Press, 1953), pp. 144-149, 257-261, 318-319, 339;

Willem Joseph Antoine Marie Beek, *John Keble's Literary and Religious Contributions to the Oxford Movement* (Nijmegen, Netherlands, 1959);

J. C. Shairp, *John Keble* (Edinburgh: Edmonston & Douglas, 1866);

G. B. Tennyson, "The Sacramental Imagination," in *Nature and the Victorian Imagination,* edited by U. C. Knoepflmacher and Tennyson (Berkeley: University of California Press, 1977), pp. 370-390;

Tennyson, "Tractarian Aesthetics: Analogy and Reserve in Keble and Newman," *Victorian Newsletter,* no. 55 (Spring 1979): 8-10;

Tennyson, *Victorian Devotional Poetry: The Tractarian Mode* (Cambridge: Harvard University Press, 1981), pp. 1-113, 215-232;

Alba H. Warren, *English Poetic Theory, 1825-1865* (Princeton: Princeton University Press, 1950).

Papers:

The major collection of John Keble's papers is at Keble College, Oxford; Pusey House and the Bodleian Library, both at Oxford, have additional materials.

Alexander William Kinglake

(5 August 1809-1 January 1891)

Ned Toomey
Central Washington University

BOOKS: *Eothen; or, Traces of Travel Brought Home from the East,* anonymous (London: Ollivier, 1844; New York: Colyer, 1845);

The Invasion of the Crimea: Its Origin, and an Account of Its Progress down to the Death of Lord Raglan (8 volumes, Edinburgh & London: Blackwood, 1863-1887; 6 volumes, New York: Harper, 1863-1888).

PERIODICAL PUBLICATIONS: "The Rights of Women," *Quarterly Review,* 75 (December 1844-March 1845): 94-125;

"The French Lake," *Quarterly Review,* 75 (December 1844-March 1845): 532-569;

"The Life of Madame Lafayette," *Blackwood's Magazine,* 112 (September 1872): 361-368.

Though Alexander William Kinglake's ambition was to be remembered for his eight-volume history of the Crimean War, his fame rests on *Eothen* (1844), a classic account of his travels in the Near East in the early 1830s. Kinglake was born in Taunton, Somerset, England, the son of a prosperous attorney-at-law and banker, William Kinglake, whose family had owned land in the area for about four hundred years. His mother, born Mary Woodforde of Castle Cary and Taunton, was a pretty and lively woman, as capable in the household as she was familiar with the world of books and men. Alexander Kinglake was the oldest of six surviving children, four boys and two girls. Under the tutelage of his mother, the pale, delicate boy learned, as he later wrote in *Eothen,* to "find a home in his saddle, and to love old Homer, and all that Homer sung." The heroes of *The Iliad* and *The Odyssey* captured the imagination of the six-year-old child, and though he labored over their adventures line by line, he later claimed that this early acquaintance with the classics was much preferred to the cramming forced upon him in grammar school.

When he was twelve, he was sent to Ottery St. Mary Grammar School, a private institution kept by the Reverend George Coleridge, the poet's brother, to prepare promising students for Eton. Kinglake entered Eton in 1823. There he met two of the men who were to become his lifelong friends, John Savile and Eliot Warburton. When he left Eton for Cambridge in 1828, he did so ruefully, believing that the past five or six years were destined to be the happiest of his life.

At Cambridge he met Alfred Tennyson, Arthur Hallam, Richard Monckton Milnes, W. H. Thompson, Charles Buller, J. M. Kemble, and William Makepeace Thackeray, among others. He joined the Cambridge Union and participated in debates but did not lead in any of them. However, his quick wit and timely cogent comments left their

Alexander William Kinglake, circa 1863. Painting by Harriet M. Haviland (National Portrait Gallery).

mark. Fifty years later Milnes remembered him as a giant among them.

Kinglake received a B.A. in 1832 and, in accordance with his father's wishes, settled upon a career in law. He had thought of pursuing a military career, but financial considerations and shortsightedness prevented him from doing so. However, his interest in military affairs and his hankering for adventure endured.

In London he and his friend Warburton began to read for the bar under the tutorship of Bryan Procter, at whose home Thomas Carlyle, W. E. Forster, Charles Dickens, Robert Browning, James Russell Lowell, Abraham Hayward, and Thackeray were frequent visitors. Kinglake saw Thackeray often during the 1840s and 1850s, and Thackeray mentions him in his letters and diaries. One diary entry early in their acquaintance notes that Kinglake "is or says he is an atheist and tells everyone his opinion."

In the autumn of 1834 Kinglake and Savile, now Lord Pollington (Methley in *Eothen*), set out on a journey to the Near East; but business affairs cut short Pollington's tour, and he returned home from Smyrna while Kinglake continued on to Syria, Lebanon, the Holy Land, and Egypt. Upon his return Kinglake resumed his legal studies, but without much enthusiasm, and was called to the bar in 1837.

Kinglake made two attempts to turn his notes of the journey into a publishable account but abandoned the project in disgust. As he explained in the preface to *Eothen,* he could not express himself without a clear idea of his audience. When Warburton asked him for suggestions for his own visit, Kinglake hit upon the solution to his problem: since he was too shy to adopt the familiar tone with strange and casual readers, he decided to pretend that he was writing to Warburton. He set to work revising and polishing the manuscript, though by the time he deemed it ready for publication and found a publisher for it, Warburton had long gone on his journey.

Eothen; or, Traces of Travel Brought Home from the East was published in London in 1844 and in New York a year later. Kinglake was thirty-five; ten years had elapsed since the start of his journey. The manuscript was sent to several publishers before it was accepted by John Ollivier of Pall Mall, who agreed upon anonymity for the author but requested that he contribute to the cost of publication. John Murray, to whom it was sent first, rejected it because he did not like Kinglake's "wicked spirit of jesting at everything."

The book was a huge and instant success. It made its author, who did not remain anonymous for long, into a literary celebrity. It went into six editions in the following two years. The vast majority of reviews had high praise for the fresh, sparkling style and the charming personality behind it. Kinglake's style was not the only reason for the book's success, however. *Eothen* was a new kind of travel literature, characterized by informality and a subjective attitude. It was the first of a kind and transformed the conventional travelogue from a factual geographical guide into literature.

At the heart of *Eothen* (the word, as Gilbert Highet points out in his 1971 book *Explorations,* means "at dawn," not "from the East," as Kinglake thought) is the author's personality. In Kinglake's words in the preface, the work "conveys, not those impressions which ought to have been produced upon any 'well-constituted mind,' but those which were really and truly received at the time of his rambles, by a headstrong and not very amiable traveller whose prejudices in favor of other people's notions were then exceedingly slight. As I have felt, I have written."

The book is thus a collection of impressions—comic, touching, informative, amusing, and, above all, entertaining. The only justification for the choice of topics and incidents is the author's interest. The twenty-nine chapters recount his experiences as he traveled with a small band of attendants through Constantinople, to the country of the Troad, to Smyrna, Cyprus, and Beirut, where he called on the legendary Lady Hester Stanhope, "Queen of the Arabs," then to Palestine, where he visited Tiberias, Nazareth, and Jerusalem. He then crossed the Sinai desert from Gaza by camel to Cairo, which was being devastated by the plague at the time. He returned across the desert by way of Nablus and the Lake of Galilee to Damascus in Syria.

The topics of his epistolary-like essays range from the sublime to the ridiculous. The chapter titled "The Desert," for example, contains one of the best evocations of travel under the desert sun, while that on the Sphinx has been described as an ode. The chapter on Jerusalem details one of Kinglake's amusing experiences, in which a "congregation of fleas" feast on him in a Tiberias church, while the account of his sojourn in plague-ridden Cairo describes a grim and touching experience. In spite of the variety of topics and modes of treatment, the book is unified by the playful and amusing tone of its narrative. The beginning—Kinglake's enthusiastic observations on his first

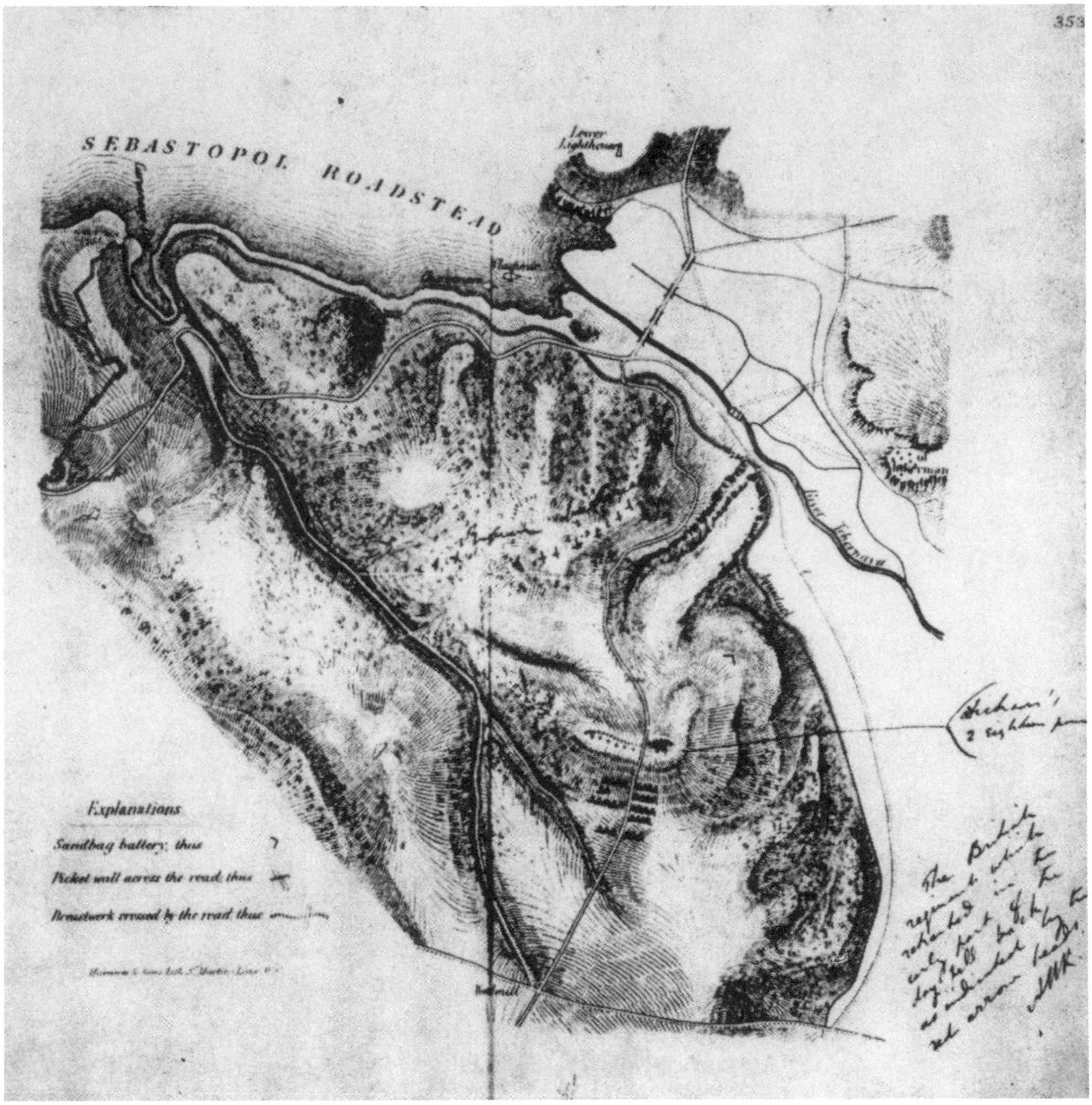

Annotations by Kinglake on a map of Sebastopol, where he went to observe the Crimean War firsthand (Layard Papers, The British Library)

night in the East, "free from the stale civilization of Europe"—and the ending—his thoughts as he leaves behind "an old and decrepit World" for the "kingdoms of the West"—form a natural and aesthetically satisfying frame for the work.

The influence of *Eothen* was considerable. His friend Warburton produced his *The Crescent and the Cross* within a year, Thackeray his *Notes of a Journey from Cornhill to Grand Cairo* in 1846, and Robert Curzon, another friend, his *A Visit to Monasteries in the Levant* in 1849. Jewett mentions Charles Doughty and T. E. Lawrence as other notable travelers who felt its power. Its impact was also evident in the United States, where George William Curtis's *Nile Notes of a Howadji* was published in 1851.

Although Murray had turned down *Eothen*, he invited Kinglake to submit other material which did not flout orthodoxy or go against the policy of the *Quarterly Review*. John Lockhart, editor of the *Quarterly*, had proposed to Kinglake that he write an article on "The Wrongs of Women" for the magazine. Kinglake countered by agreeing to write a piece on "The Rights of Women," which the *Quarterly* published in December 1844, in the same number which carried Warburton's review of *Eothen.* Kinglake's article is a review of six books, five of them by women: *Palm Leaves* (1844) by Milnes; *The Englishwoman in Egypt* (1844) by Mrs. Poole; *The Women of England* (1838) by Mrs. Ellis; *The Wives of England* (1843) by the same author; *Characteristics of Women* (1832) by Mrs. Jameson; and *The Romance of Biography; or, The Memoirs of Women Loved and Celebrated by Poets* (1837), also by Mrs. Jameson. Kinglake took Milnes to task for asserting that the institution of the Oriental harem provided a haven of security and repose for the male. He questioned Milnes's facts and chided him for abusing poetic license in presuming to describe life in a harem. The gently ironic tone, somewhat more serious, continues in Kinglake's remarks about the other volumes. He confesses to a good-humored suspicion of works written by women about women and is critical of their sanguine belief that everything can be accomplished by the exercise of authority. The integrated review is also a discussion of Kinglake's view of the characteristics of women and of the best conditions for the enhancement of their lives.

In response to Murray's invitation, Kinglake also submitted a review of Warburton's *The Crescent and the Cross,* which was published in the *Quarterly* in March 1845. Warburton's review of *Eothen* had praised the book highly for its style and humor but criticized it for "a puzzling and daring indifference to the prejudices of society," especially in the chapter on Jerusalem. Kinglake's review, titled "The French Lake" in reference to the Mediterranean and Napoleonic policy in the region, argued against Warburton's proposal that England seize Egypt to ensure its right of way through the Suez Canal and cited the failure of Napoleon's policy in the Near East as an example to be avoided.

In 1845 Kinglake visited Algeria and met Saint-Arnaud, then a colonel in the French Foreign Legion and later minister of war to Napoleon III and commander of French troops in the Crimean War. His favorable impression of Saint-Arnaud was later to change radically when he learned more about the Frenchman. The journal he kept during this trip was published for the first time as part of Gerald de Gaury's 1972 biography of Kinglake. Kinglake did no more writing in the decade following the "burst" of literary activity in the 1840s, apparently content to lead a fairly active social life while pursuing his legal profession. He became a member of the Traveller's Club and the Atheneum and at the latter spent much time in the company of fellow lawyer and writer Abraham Hayward.

Until England and France entered the Crimean War in 1854, it seemed that Kinglake's literary career was over. When he decided to go to the Crimea to observe the war firsthand, it was his interest in military affairs which impelled him to go. Kinglake caught up with the British force on its march to Sebastopol under the command of Lord Raglan. As Kinglake keenly observed Raglan's management of the war, the initial sympathy he felt for the commander grew into great admiration for his integrity, his wisdom, and his military ability. Though there is no sign that Kinglake intended to write about the war, after Raglan's death in 1856 Lady Raglan turned over to Kinglake all her husband's papers, assured that he would present a fair and accurate picture of the war. Thus began what Kinglake considered to be his life's work.

He did not, however, devote his entire time to writing his history. He ran for political office and was elected in 1857 to a seat in Parliament as the liberal member for Bridgewater. In 1869 he lost his seat when he was implicated in bribery charges brought against his agent, though he was later completely exonerated. Although from that time onward he concentrated on his book, in 1872 he did write an anonymous article for *Blackwood's Magazine* entitled "The Life of Madame Lafayette." The theme of the article is that an undue and mistaken observance of principles such as "Submit to the will of God" and "Obey the laws of your country" was the "very evil which unchained the hellhounds of the French Revolution."

Kinglake's *The Invasion of the Crimea: Its Origin, and an Account of Its Progress down to the Death of Lord Raglan* was published in eight volumes over a period of nearly twenty-five years, from 1863 to 1887. The first volume quickly went into several editions and generated much controversy.

Commentators for the London *Times* and the *Edinburgh Review* laid the blame for British misfortunes in the war on Lord Raglan and his staff and accused Kinglake of bias in favor of the commander. In 1863 Hayward published a pamphlet entitled *Mr. Kinglake and the Quarterlies* and signed simply "an Old Reviewer." Accusing the *Times* writers of misrepresentation, he rebutted their criticisms point by point in scathing language. Kinglake himself answered the criticisms made in the *Times* and the *Edinburgh Review* in the seventh volume of his history. He deplored reports, particularly in the *Times,* portraying Lord Raglan whiling away "his time in ease and tranquility among the relics of his army" and pointing to a time when he and his staff

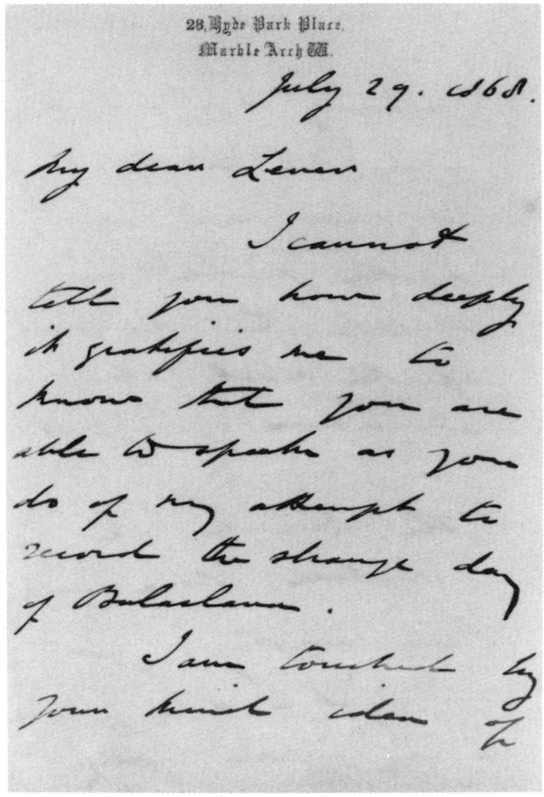

28, Hyde Park Place,
Marble Arch W.

July 29. 1868.

My dear Lever

I cannot tell you how deeply it gratifies me to know that you are able to speak as you do of my attempt to record the strange day of Balaclava.

I am touched by your kind idea of

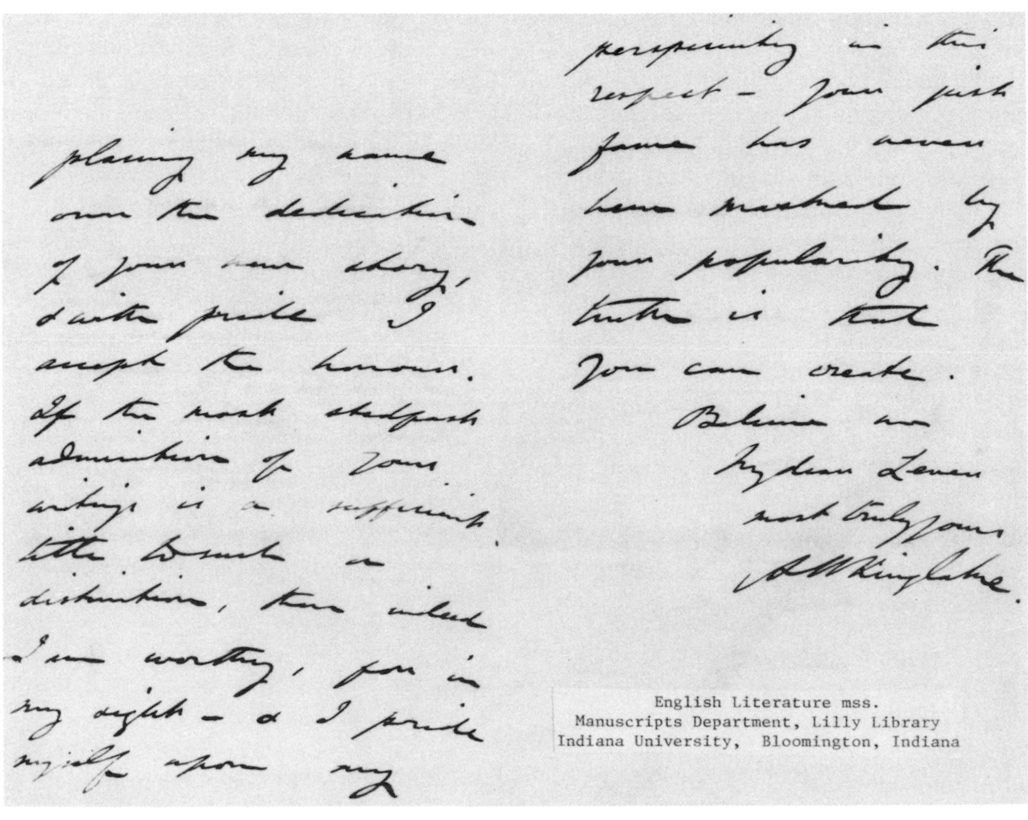

placing my name over the dedication of your new story, & with pride I accept the honour. If the most steadfast admiration of your writings is a sufficient title to such a distinction, then indeed I am worthy, for in my sight – & I pride myself upon my perspicuity in this respect – your just fame has never been marked by your popularity. The truth is that you can create.

Believe me
My dear Lever
most truly yours
A W Kinglake.

English Literature mss.
Manuscripts Department, Lilly Library
Indiana University, Bloomington, Indiana

Letter from Kinglake thanking Charles Lever for his favorable reaction to The Invasion of the Crimea *and expressing "steadfast admiration" for Lever's works (Lilly Library, Indiana University)* would "return with their horses, their plate and their china, their German cook, and several tons weight of official returns, all in excellent order, and the announcement that, the last British soldier being dead, they had left our position in the care of our gallant allies."

Despite the controversy provoked by Kinglake's treatment of his subject in *The Invasion of the Crimea,* his writing was accorded remarkable acclaim.

Kinglake's mastery of the language was as evident in his history as it had been in *Eothen.* The lucidity, the control, the grace, and the rhythms of his sentences were no less effective in the factual narrative than they were in the personal and lyrical *Eothen.* Sir Arthur Quiller-Couch, in fact, hailed Kinglake as one who "tamed that beautiful and dangerous beast, the English sentence." The style of *The Invasion of the Crimea,* however, is only one of its literary virtues. Although Kinglake was strictly bound to factual truth as a historian and as a gentleman, the history displays the imaginative vigor and narrative flair of the novelist. It is history presented as personal experience, not as dry fact. The work brings to life the personalities of the leading participants with acute and lively psychological analyses of their characters and motives. Kinglake uses dialogue to re-create dramatic scenes and sensuous details to give them immediacy. A number of volumes, and chapters within single volumes, make use of foreshadowing and suspense in serial-like fashion. Perhaps more effective than any of these devices in shaping and unifying the staggering amount of detail is Kinglake's underlying belief in the human will as a determining factor in the destiny of nations. Thus, much of the engrossing power of the narrative lies in Kinglake's skillful use of the conflict of wills between those in positions of power, as, for example, Czar Nicholas and Lord Stratford, dealt with in volume one, and the commanders involved in the Battle of Balaclava and the Charge of the Light Brigade, treated in volume five.

Several critics have pointed to deficiencies in the work: Kinglake's lack of perspective in presenting the minutest details of the action and in chronicling the hourly progression of some of the battles; the lack of proportion that results from the author's giving more space to some aspects of the war and not enough to others; the undue importance accorded the war as a historical event. Some have criticized Kinglake's style: the pace fails to vary and the author sometimes strains for grace and eloquence when these qualities are either unnecessary or inappropriate.

Kinglake spent the last twenty years of his life quietly in an apartment overlooking Hyde Park, walking usually to his clubs in Pall Mall. Friends he met there included Sir William Gregory, the Irish M.P.; Thomas Chenery, the Arabist and editor of the *Times;* Sir Edward Hamley, a general and military historian; and his most regular companion, Hayward. Although Kinglake admired women and had many friends among them, he never married. He became deaf in his later years and spent much of the time alone, reading military history or Mrs. Oliphant's novels, which he preferred to those of Dickens, Scott, Thackeray, and Bulwer-Lytton. He stopped going to his clubs in his eightieth year. He died on New Year's Day 1891 of gout and oral

"Not an M.P.," caricature of Kinglake by Adriano Cecioni, published in Vanity Fair, *2 March 1872 (Collection of Jerold J. Savory)*

cancer. Henry James gives this impression of him in his old age: "Old, deaf, delicate, distinguished, perfect, infinitely silent."

Whatever Kinglake's merits as a historian may have been, his talents as a writer seem unquestioned. His fame, however, rests almost solely on *Eothen,* which has become a classic of travel literature. His *Invasion of the Crimea,* which met with success and created heated controversy, seems largely forgotten. Even though he may not have fulfilled the promise of *Eothen* and, in retrospect, may have misdirected his talents, he managed to leave a body of work marked by literary excellence.

Biographies:

William Tuckwell, *A. W. Kinglake—A Biographical and Literary Study* (London: Bell, 1902);

Gerald de Gaury, *Travelling Gent.: The Life of Alexander Kinglake (1809-1891)* (London: Routledge & Kegan Paul, 1972).

References:

Geoffrey Bocca, "Lessons in English Literature from Sir Winston Churchill: 'More Kinglake,' " *Harper's,* 251 (September 1975): 70-71;

[Abraham Hayward], *Mr. Kinglake and the Quarterlies* (London: Privately printed, 1863);

Gilbert Highet, *Explorations* (New York: Oxford University Press, 1971);

D. G. Hogarth, Introduction to Kinglake's *Eothen* (Oxford & New York: Clarendon Press, 1910);

R. W. Jepson, Introduction to Kinglake's *Eothen* (London & New York: Longmans, Green, 1935);

Iran Bann Hassani Jewett, *Alexander William Kinglake* (Boston: Twayne, 1981);

Jan Morris, Introduction to Kinglake's *Eothen* (Oxford & New York: Oxford University Press, 1982), pp. iii-xvi;

Peter Quennell, "The Author of Eothen," in his *The Singular Preference* (New York: Viking, 1953), pp. 118-124;

Sir Arthur Quiller-Couch, *Adventures in Criticism* (New York: Putnam's/Cambridge: Cambridge University Press, 1925);

Kathleen M. Wilcox, *With Kinglake in the Holy Land* (London: Muller, 1967).

George Henry Lewes

(18 April 1817-30 November 1878)

Monika Brown

Pembroke State University

SELECTED BOOKS: *A Biographical History of Philosophy,* 4 volumes (London: Knight, 1845-1846); revised as *The Biographical History of Philosophy from Its Origin in Greece down to the Present Day,* 1 volume (London: Parker, 1857; New York: Appleton, 1857);

The Spanish Drama: Lope de Vega and Calderón (London: Knight, 1846);

Ranthorpe (London: Chapman & Hall, 1847; New York: Gottsberger, 1881);

Rose, Blanche, and Violet, 3 volumes (London: Smith, Elder, 1848); republished as *Three Sisters and Three Fortunes,* 1 volume (New York: Harper, 1848);

The Life of Maximilien Robespierre, with Extracts from His Unpublished Correspondence (London: Chapman & Hall, 1849; Philadelphia: Carey & Hart, 1849);

The Noble Heart: A Tragedy in Three Acts (London: Chapman & Hall, 1850; New York: French, 1855?);

Comte's Philosophy of the Sciences: Being an Exposition of the Principles of the Cours de Philosophie Positive of Auguste Comte (London: Bohn, 1853);

The Life and Works of Goethe, 2 volumes (London: Nutt, 1855; Boston: Ticknor & Fields, 1856);

Sea-Side Studies at Ilfracombe, Tenby, the Scilly Isles & Jersey (Edinburgh & London: Blackwood, 1858);

The Physiology of Common Life, 2 volumes (Edinburgh & London: Blackwood, 1859-1860; New York: Appleton, 1860);

Studies in Animal Life (New York: Harper, 1860; London: Smith, Elder, 1862);

Aristotle: A Chapter in the History of Science (London: Smith, Elder, 1864);

Problems of Life and Mind, First Series: The Foundations of a Creed, 2 volumes (London: Trübner, 1874-1875; Boston: Osgood, 1875);

On Actors and the Art of Acting (London: Smith, Elder, 1875; New York: Holt, 1878);

The Physical Basis of Mind, Being the Second Series of Problems of Life and Mind (London: Trübner, 1877; Boston: Osgood, 1877);

Problems of Life and Mind, Third Series, 2 volumes: volume 1, *The Study of Psychology;* volume 2, *Mind as a Function of the Organism; The Sphere of Sense and the Logic of Feeling; The Sphere of Intellect and the Logic of Signs* (London: Trübner, 1879; Boston: Osgood, 1879-1880);

The Principles of Success in Literature (San Francisco: Printed for Albert S. Cook, 1885); edited by T. Sharper Knowlson (London: Scott, 1898);

George Henry Lewes (photograph by Elliott and Fry)

Dramatic Essays, by Lewes and John Forster, edited by William Archer and Robert W. Lowe (London: Scott, 1896);

Literary Criticism of George Henry Lewes, edited by Alice R. Kaminsky (Lincoln: University of Nebraska Press, 1964).

PLAY PRODUCTIONS: *The Noble Heart,* Manchester, Theatre Royal, 18 February 1849; London, Olympic Theatre, 18 February 1850; New York, Bowery Theatre, 5 February 1851;

The Game of Speculation, as Slingsby Lawrence, adapted from *Mercadet,* an abridgment by Adolphe Philippe d'Ennery of Honoré de Balzac's *Le Faiseur,* London, Royal Lyceum Theatre, 2 October 1851;

A Chain of Events, by Lewes as Slingsby Lawrence and Charles Mathews, adapted from *La Dame de la Halle,* by Anicet Bourgeois and Auguste-Michel Masson, London, Royal Lyceum Theatre, 12 April 1852;

Taking by Storm!, as Frank Churchill, adapted from *Tambour battant,* by Adrien Decourcelle, Theodore Barrière, and Jules Lorin, London, Royal Lyceum Theatre, 3 June 1852;

A Strange History, by Lewes as Slingsby Lawrence and Mathews, adapted from *Marianne,* by Anicet-Bourgeois and Masson, London, Royal Lyceum Theatre, 29 March 1853;

The Lawyers, as Slingsby Lawrence, adapted from *Les Avocats,* by Philippe Dumanoir and L. F. Nicolai, London, Royal Lyceum Theatre, 19 May 1853; New York, Burton's Theatre, 19 August 1853;

Give a Dog a Bad Name, as Slingsby Lawrence, adapted from *Quand on veut tuer son chien,* London, Royal Lyceum Theatre, 18 April 1854;

Sunshine through the Clouds, as Slingsby Lawrence, adapted from *La Joie fait peur,* by Emile de Girardin, London, Royal Lyceum Theatre, 15 June 1854;

A Cozy Couple, by Lewes as Slingsby Lawrence and Mathews, adapted from *Le Village,* by Octave Feuillet, London, Royal Lyceum Theatre, 15 March 1855;

Buckstone's Adventures with a Polish Princess, as Slingsby Lawrence, London, Royal Lyceum Theatre, 29 June 1855;

Stay at Home, adapted from *Un Mari qui se derange,* London, Olympic Theatre, 11 February 1856;

Captain Bland, New York, Wallack's Theatre, 30 May 1864.

OTHER: *Selections from the Modern British Dramatists,* edited by Lewes, 2 volumes (Leipzig: Brockhaus, 1867);

Female Characters of Goethe, from the Original Drawings of William Kaulbach, explanatory text by Lewes (New York: Stroefer/Munich: Bruckmann, 1868).

PERIODICAL PUBLICATIONS: "Percy Bysshe Shelley," *Westminster Review,* 35 (April 1841): 303-344;

"Hegel's Aesthetics: Philosophy of Art," *British and Foreign Review,* 13 (March 1842): 1-49; republished as "The Inner Life of Art" in Lewes's *The Principles of Success in Literature* (1885);

"Errors and Abuses of English Criticism," *Westminster Review,* 38 (October 1842): 446-486;

"The Life and Works of Goethe," *British and Foreign Review,* 14 (March 1843): 78-135;

"Augustus Wilhelm Schlegel," *Foreign Quarterly Review,* 32 (October 1843): 160-181;

"Balzac and George Sand," *Foreign Quarterly Review,* 33 (July 1844): 145-162;

"The Rise and Fall of the European Drama," *Foreign Quarterly Review,* 35 (July 1845): 290-334;

"Recent Novels: French and English," including a review of *Jane Eyre, Fraser's Magazine,* 36 (December 1847): 686-695;

Review of *Vanity Fair,* by William Makepeace Thackeray, *Athenaeum* (12 August 1848): 794-797;

"Shakespeare's Critics: English and Foreign," *Edinburgh Review,* 90 (July 1849): 40-47;

"Currer Bell's *Shirley,*" *Edinburgh Review,* 91 (January 1850): 151-173;

"The Lady Novelists," *Westminster Review,* 58 (July 1852): 129-141;

Review of *Poems* (1853), by Matthew Arnold, *Leader,* 4 (26 November 1853): 1146-1147; *Leader,* 4 (3 December 1853): 1170-1171;

"Realism in Art: Recent German Fiction," *Westminster Review,* 70 (October 1858): 493-496;

"Novels of Jane Austen," *Blackwood's Edinburgh Magazine,* 86 (July 1859): 99-113;

"Criticism in Relation to Novels," *Fortnightly Review,* 3 (15 December 1865): 352-361;

"Mr. Darwin's Hypotheses," *Fortnightly Review,* new series 3 (1 April 1868): 353-373; new series 3 (1 June 1868): 611-628; new series 4 (1 July 1868): 61-80; new series 4 (1 November 1868): 492-509;

"Dickens in Relation to Criticism," *Fortnightly Review,* new series 17 (1 February 1872): 141-154;

"On the Dread and Dislike of Science," *Fortnightly Review,* new series 29 (1 June 1878): 805-815.

George Henry Lewes, assured of a place in literary history for his influence on the life and work of novelist George Eliot, left his own mark on mid-Victorian literature in several areas: as a versatile man of letters; as a thoughtful interpreter and popularizer of philosophy, biology, and psychology who made original contributions to all three fields; and especially as a literary theorist, critic, and biographer of wide range and considerable insight, not of the first rank but high in the second. Victorian readers of his nonfiction—about 250 periodical articles and sixteen books—found clear, lively, sometimes humorous expositions of an impressive range of subjects: Goethe and George Sand, Comte and Darwin, German aesthetics and French historiography, performances of actors and fallacies of spontaneous combustion. Lewes was also known as a novelist, a writer of stage plays, an actor, a public lecturer, the editor of several periodicals, and a researcher in physiology and psychology.

He wanted above all to be remembered for his contributions to philosophy and science, some of which are still recognized by historians of these fields. But even in his own day, more readers appreciated his literary criticism. Valued highly by Charlotte Brontë, Anthony Trollope, and Bernard Shaw, Lewes's critical work was largely ignored for the first half of the twentieth century, and remains all but unavailable outside Victorian periodicals. But since the work of Morris Greenhut in the late 1940s, most scholars who are familiar with Lewes's criticism have recognized its quality. Though he made some misjudgments by taking too scientific an approach, Lewes's ability to identify and analyze the best fiction and drama of many periods and countries, his early appreciation for literary realism, and his attempts to discover systematic philosophical principles for evaluating literature place him well above most reviewers of his age and of more recent times. Even his earliest writings reveal these abilities, which would help make his most enduring work, *The Life and Works of Goethe* (1855), a model critical biography. Recent studies of Lewes's writings have been valuable in identifying his essays (mostly published anonymously or pseudonymously), explaining his theories, and analyzing his responses to particular genres. But scholars are only beginning to find some of the deeper connections—among Lewes's interests and between his work and George Eliot's novels—that will help trace the intellectual development of this exceptional Victorian mind and evaluate fairly Lewes's contribution to English literature.

George Henry Lewes was born in London in 1817, the youngest of three sons of whom the older two died in early manhood. Literary interests ran in the family. A grandfather, Charles Lee Lewes, was a successful comic actor who created the role of Young Marlow in Oliver Goldsmith's *She Stoops to Conquer* (1773) and left behind his memoirs of the London stage (1805). John Lee Lewes, George Lewes's father, had published poetry and worked as a stage manager before dying young. When George Lewes was seven, his mother, born Elizabeth Ashweek, married Captain John Willim, who left little impression on her son. Lewes remained close to his mother throughout his life. Of his childhood experiences, he would best remember seeing the actor Edmund Kean perform.

After brief stays in Jersey and Brittany, Lewes received a classical education at a private school in the London suburb of Dulwich. Interested in philosophy but with, as he later admitted, "no very definite career before him," Lewes remained with his family in London from 1833 to 1838, working for a notary and a leather merchant, and studying medicine long enough to get an idea of physiology. He also met with a group of intellectual tradesmen, among them a Jew interested in Spinoza who served as the model for a character in Eliot's *Daniel Deronda* (1876). Before turning twenty Lewes had become a friend of Thomas and Jane Welsh Carlyle and the Leigh Hunt family, lectured on philosophy, and written a play about Italian poet Torquato Tasso, the last justified because he had himself already been "next to mad with love and its fallacies." Most of the two years from 1838 to 1840 Lewes spent in Germany, reading contemporary European literature and philosophy. In 1841 Lewes married nineteen-year-old Agnes Jervis, the attractive daughter of a liberal Staffordshire member of Parliament. The young couple, whom Jane Carlyle considered "a perfect pair of love-birds," enjoyed the society of London literary circles and had four sons: Charles (1842), Thornton (1844), Herbert (1846), and St. Vincent (1848). To support the family, Agnes did translations, and Lewes, with help from John Stuart Mill, published several books as well as many substantial articles in quarterlies such as the prestigious *Westminster Review*. Most of his lifelong interests were already in evidence.

Many of the critical essays Lewes wrote before 1845, the fruits of sustained study rather than simple reviews, show him defining the nature of art and the function of criticism. He planned his articles carefully and started each with a thought-provoking generalization. Dissatisfied with British critics who judged by personal or editorial prejudices, Lewes found in Hegel's aesthetics, which he introduced to English readers in an 1842 *British and Foreign Review* piece, his first and most enduring critical principles. Like Hegel, Lewes took literature seriously, and believed that "poetry" was to be found in any art that aroused emotions in the service of a "religious Idea," which to Lewes meant the moral ideals of the age. The function of the critic, then, as Lewes describes it in "Hegel's Aesthetics," is to identify these emotions and ideas and to evaluate how effectively the artist has carried them out. But he can only do so if he admits, with Hegel and Schlegel (the latter discussed in an 1843 article for *Foreign Quarterly Review*), that literature can be judged only by ideals of its own period and nation. Guided by these principles and by a Car-

Lewes, circa 1840, sketched by Anne Gliddon (National Portrait Gallery)

lylian commitment to honesty in expressing even unpopular opinions that he would later call "Sincerity," Lewes wrote appreciatively about moral ideals and artistic qualities in the poems of Shelley (*Westminster Review,* 1841), who was too often judged by his personal life, and he explained (in an 1845 *Foreign Quarterly Review* essay, "The Rise and Fall of the European Drama") the merits of Racine and Alfieri, whose tragedies were criticized for not resembling Shakespeare's. As he evaluated great literature, Lewes began to formulate some additional standards reflecting his scientific bent, insisting that critical judgments need supporting evidence, rejecting as simplistic such distinctions as ancient/modern and romantic/classical, and anticipating his later devotion to realism by praising Goethe's "*objective* tendency" and concreteness (*British and Foreign Review,* 1843).

If the Germans helped Lewes define his aesthetics, it was a Frenchman, Auguste Comte, who shaped his philosophy of knowledge. Much reading and some of his earlier articles provided the grounding for one of Lewes's two most successful books, *A Biographical History of Philosophy* (1845-1846). First published in an inexpensive self-education series, the book was shaped by Comte's philosophical system, whose main tenets Lewes learned from Mill and would accept, with reservations, throughout his life. Whereas modern religions, philosophies, and sciences can agree on nothing, Lewes explained in the introduction to a later edition, Comte offers a unified framework for man's quest for knowledge. In Comte's view, all areas of knowledge, from the physical world to human behavior and ethics, are governed by laws, which can be discovered by one method—Positive, scientific investigation—and used to improve human life. Before Positivism, man had to rely on earlier and inferior methods of investigation, the Theological and the Metaphysical. Lewes's *A Biographical History of Philosophy,* then, is the life story of Metaphysics, an outdated but necessary stage in man's intellectual evolution toward Positive inquiry. Thus even as Lewes introduces his readers to the lives and contributions of more than a hundred philosophers and schools—divided into two main groups, ancient and modern—he shows their methods repeatedly failing to answer their questions, by contrast to "the progressive development of Science," while ancient philosophy made progress only in ethics. Modern philosophy searched in vain for knowledge of "things *per se*" and "*ideas independent of experience*"; even the best minds, like Spinoza's, failed to recognize that the mind is not a "mirror" but a "partial creator of its own forms." As Lewes points out, however, modern philosophy does record the emergence of the only source of reliable knowledge, the scientific method.

With *A Biographical History of Philosophy,* Lewes, still in his twenties, established his reputation among his contemporaries. He was praised for his independence of mind, his clarity in explaining, and his lively approach, which for Frederic Harrison, in an 1878 obituary for the *Academy,* made philosophy "almost as exciting as a good novel." Partly because it was so readable, said the younger Positivist, the work "influenced the thought of the present generation almost more than any single book except Mr. Mill's *Logic.*" Lewes revised *A Biographical History of Philosophy* for a new edition, published in 1857; it was translated, and later republished, as a volume of John Lubbock's Hundred Best Books series until 1905. And if some university professors rejected it, its popularity with British students lasted into the 1930s.

Lewes's next few books, written for money, were less demanding and less memorable. He produced two novels—*Ranthorpe* (1847) and *Rose, Blanche, and Violet* (1848)—as well as *The Life of Maximilien Robespierre* (1849), intended for readers concerned about the revolutions of 1848. *Ranthorpe,* a partly autobiographical Bildungsroman written in 1842, impressed both Charlotte Brontë and Edgar Allan Poe, and it remains of interest for its descriptions of London bohemian life and for psychological similarities, noted by Barbara Smalley in her introduction to a 1980 republication, between some of its characters and characters in George Eliot's later novels. Though Lewes never wrote good fiction, his efforts made him more sensitive to the talents of others.

Reviews of novels make up a large proportion of Lewes's articles of the late 1840s and early 1850s, the period when he wrote much of his best criticism. Innovative artists force critics to rethink their standards, as he noted in an essay on Shakespeare (*Edinburgh Review,* 1849), and it is to Lewes's credit that he not only recognized in the nineteenth-century novel an important new art form but was able to identify its best practitioners and to use their novels to help him define appropriate standards of critical analysis and evaluation. By the time he reviewed Charlotte Brontë's *Jane Eyre* (*Fraser's Magazine,* 1847), Lewes had made "truth in the delineation of life and character," a faithfulness to common experience best realized in Jane Austen's novels, his primary criterion for deciding if a novel "rises into the first rank of literature." To Lewes

Drawing by William Makepeace Thackeray showing Agnes and George Henry Lewes at the piano while Thornton Hunt looks on (National Portrait Gallery). Thackeray signed the drawing with the small self-caricature at upper right.

the Positivist, who assumed a moral order underlying experience, this criterion of "truth," later called "realism," complemented rather than contradicted his earlier standards—artistic design, emotional impact, moral ideas, sincerity—which remained important to his criticism. That his concern for truth grew out of these earlier standards and his study of outstanding fiction is evident in his first substantial essay on the novel. In an 1844 article for *Foreign Quarterly Review,* Lewes set out to evaluate works by Balzac and George Sand (1844) for morality, artistic powers, and reader appeal, but in practice he largely equated all three criteria with truth to experience. Lewes went so far as to declare in his 1852 *Westminster Review* essay "The Lady Novelists" that all good literature "has *reality for its basis.*" His expanded critical standards, combined with a natural instinct for what constituted truth to experience, led to his best literary analyses of this period, whether he was finding the virtues of *Jane Eyre* and Thackeray's *Henry Esmond,* recognizing the mixed strengths and weaknesses of Brontë's *Shirley* and Thackeray's *Vanity Fair,* or noting resemblances of characterization that made Sophocles, Shakespeare, and Racine the greatest dramatists of their cultures. His criteria interfered with his appreciation for unusual poetry, like that of Keats and the early Browning, but not with his ability to recognize the genius of Melville's *Moby-Dick.*

Some of Lewes's literary articles of this time appeared in a new, radical paper, the *Leader,* of which he and his friend Thornton Leigh Hunt were joint editors. Among the articles Lewes wrote for this weekly, more than a hundred in all, the best-liked were his reviews of London stage performances. For these he invented a persona called Vivian, a rakish, satirical man-about-town in whose witty seriousness Bernard Shaw would find a kindred spirit. Vivian defined for his readers the various components that went into good acting and distinguished between what it meant to feel an emotion and to represent one on stage. In his *Leader* columns and in other articles, Lewes had no qualms about criticizing even the most admired actors of his time, including William Charles Macready and Charles Kean. And though he was exceptionally aware of Shakespeare's dramatic sense, he felt free to criticize the Bard's decisions.

Lewes also wrote on science and philosophy for the *Leader*. Some of these articles were expanded into a book, an introduction consisting of commentary and long translated passages to Comte's *Cours de philosophie positive* (1830-1842), and later writings. Lewes's *Comte's Philosophy of the Sciences* (1853) was often republished and shows just how much of Comte's system, including his social science and his hopes for art, Lewes accepted or at least respected. Lewes earned additional money during this time with yet another form of writing, stage plays—mostly comedies and melodramas adapted from the French, ostensibly by Slingsby Lawrence. Several of the plays, which some contemporaries preferred to the British plays running at the time, had long runs in London and put Lewes in the interesting position of reviewing his own work for the *Leader*.

The course that Lewes's personal life took during his thirties he would not have found true to life in a novel. During the late 1840s he traveled to the provinces soliciting backers for the *Leader,* acting in Dickens's cultural fundraising troupe (1847-1848) and in 1849 performing the roles of Shylock and of the hero of his original play *The Noble Heart*. While he was away, Agnes Lewes became attracted to Thornton Hunt, also married, and in 1850, the same year in which the Leweses' youngest son died, she bore Hunt a son. Lewes generously gave the baby his own name, thus appearing to condone his wife's adultery and losing his legal right to divorce her. But he stopped living with Agnes after she bore Hunt a second child in 1851. During this time, which Lewes later called a "very dreary *wasted* period," he was befriended by the social scientist Herbert Spencer, who encouraged his scientific interests and introduced him to Marian Evans. By late 1852 Lewes, the successful man of letters, was spending his evenings with Evans, the future George Eliot, then a thirty-three-year-old author of one translation and assistant editor of the *Westminster Review*. Drawn together by shared intellectual interests and loving natures, the pair scandalized Victorian society by taking off for Germany on 20 July 1854 and settling in London in 1855 as man and wife in all but law.

In 1855, at thirty-eight, Lewes published his masterpiece, *The Life and Works of Goethe,* a product of many years of reading and research. In analyzing the life and writings of the man whom Carlyle considered the best example of "the Hero as Literary Man," Lewes could for the first time exploit the full range of his knowledge, abilities, and experiences. Like Goethe, if not at his level, Lewes had read philosophy and written fiction and plays, studied science and worked in the theater, found moral ideals outside traditional religion, and even experienced happy, unhappy, and illicit love. Lewes's artistic sense shows in his choice of a structure for his work. In a chronological sequence of chapters, he develops a unifying theme: George Eliot called the work a "*natural history*" that revealed how Goethe's writings "were the outgrowth of his mind at different stages of its culture." Some chapters show appreciation for Goethe's versatility: "The Poet as a Man of Science," "The Theatrical Manager." Others reveal Lewes's psychological bent, his ability to select from Goethe's many experiences in his eighty-two years those which best illuminate the master's personality and his creations. Chapters not about themes or individual works are devoted to Goethe's main love affairs and to such influences as mental characteristics, the critic and philosopher Johann Gottfried von Herder, and Weimar in the eighteenth century. As a morally tolerant man, Lewes presented Goethe's life fairly. As a scientific inquirer, he could appreciate Goethe's greatness without idolizing him, question statements in Goethe's autobiography, and make fair use of letters and of interviews with people who knew Goethe. And as a lively prose stylist, he was able to reach audiences inaccessible to German scholars.

In the critical passages, Lewes effectively applied the knowledge and principles that informed his earlier responses to literature, while remaining open to special qualities in Goethe's art. Aside from *Faust,* part two, in which no realities appealed to his emotions, all of Goethe's major works are illuminated by his observations. Lewes's admiration for "truth to life," which in this work he terms "realist" and associates explicitly with scientific induction, helped him recognize Goethe's ability to write from personal experience and to make his characters live as individuals. Because in his literary criticism Lewes looked for reasons why a work appeals to the emotions, he recognized that *Faust,* part one, touches on all of human experience, and because he could find a moral vision behind immoral actions, he appreciated Goethe's novels. Lewes's knowledge of the drama enabled him to contrast Goethe's imagery and characterization with those of Shakespeare and Euripides, and though concern for artistic unity blinded Lewes to some of Goethe's manipulations of traditional genres, he recognized that *Faust,* part one, was not intended to be a formal tragedy.

As the first complete study of Goethe's life and works in any language, Lewes's book inevitably ran up against German scholarliness and Goethe veneration as well as English moral sensibilities. But overall the critical reception was favorable in both countries, and the work sold 900 copies in six weeks and 13,000 before the second edition came out in 1863. Carlyle, to whom the work was dedicated, wrote the author a letter proclaiming it "excellent"; Richard Holt Hutton, whose critical notice in the *National Review* was one of his own best essays, admired Lewes's criticism for its blend of appreciation and sensible judgment; and Anthony Trollope would call it "almost perfect" in his *Fortnightly Review* obituary for Lewes (1879). Chosen for Everyman's Library, it was the last of Lewes's works to go out of print. Today a great deal more is known about Goethe's life, but few of Lewes's insights have been disputed and *The Life and Works of Goethe* remains a respected early introduction to one of the greatest modern writers.

Soon after so successfully tracing the career of a literary genius, Lewes set about what would be his most important contribution to literature: encouraging and guiding another genius, the woman now calling herself Mrs. Lewes, who in 1855 had shown him an early attempt at writing fiction. In 1856, while the couple was at the seacoast collecting specimens for his newest project, he encouraged his companion, at this time a reviewer for the *Leader* and the *Westminster Review,* to "write a story." After following closely the progress of "Amos Barton," the first of Eliot's stories published as *Scenes of Clerical Life,* he negotiated for the anonymous publication in 1857 of all three scenes in *Blackwood's Magazine.* In 1859 the woman now writing as George Eliot produced her first novel, *Adam Bede,* creating no less of a sensation than did Darwin, in the same year, with his *On the Origin of Species.* By the end of her first decade as a novelist, George Eliot had given an enthusiastic public four additional novels: *The Mill on the Floss* (1860), *Silas Marner* (1861), *Romola* (1863), and *Felix Holt, The Radical* (1866). The resulting financial prosperity made possible more scientific work for Lewes, more travels to the country and the Continent for health and studies, a generous pension for Agnes Lewes, and a progressive education at the Hofwyl School in Switzerland for Lewes's three surviving sons. And in 1863 the Leweses, now both in their mid forties, settled comfortably into The Priory, a large home near Regent's Park, where they regularly entertained old friends and such luminaries as Trollope, Browning, Frederic Harrison, and T. H. Huxley.

The Priory, the London home Lewes shared with George Eliot from 1863 until his death in 1878

By this time George Eliot was far better known than George Lewes. Just how much of an impact he had on her novels is hard to judge: estimates vary from simple support to active collaboration. George Eliot herself was certain that she could not have written her novels without "the perfect love and sympathy of a nature that stimulates my own to healthful activity." Lewes handled all her practical affairs, praised in her writing the qualities he had advanced in his criticism, concealed unfavorable reviews, reassured her about her abilities in periods of doubt, and even made helpful suggestions about plot and character development. It is evident from her letters and essays that she respected his critical judgments and was either familiar with his criticism or already had similar views; in one letter she used phrases reminiscent of his to explain that her stories grow from a "psychological conception" of her characters, based on "what I *feel* to be *true*" to "human nature." In addition, many subjects that became part of the fabric of her novels—scientific research, human physiology and psychology, the culture and art of the Continent—she might never have learned as well on her own. Clearly Lewes created for the novelist not only a loving environment but also an intellectually stimulating and responsive one, where her powers flourished and advanced.

Even as he assisted his beloved "Polly," Lewes worked hard at biological research and writing, inspired by his study of Comte, his friendship with Spencer, and his interest in early theories of evolution. As recorded in his journals, he obtained a microscope, traveled to suitable locations, collected and dissected specimens, and read books by experts. Biological subjects, too, he made clear and lively for his readers, introducing familiar examples and analogies to clarify research findings and projecting his own confidence and enthusiasm. His articles in *Blackwood's* and in Thackeray's *Cornhill Magazine* (which Lewes helped to edit), along with the books that followed, gave Victorian readers a sense of how far science had come in explaining subjects such as marine life (*Sea-Side Studies at Ilfracombe, Tenby, the Scilly Isles & Jersey,* 1858), the human body and mind (*The Physiology of Common*

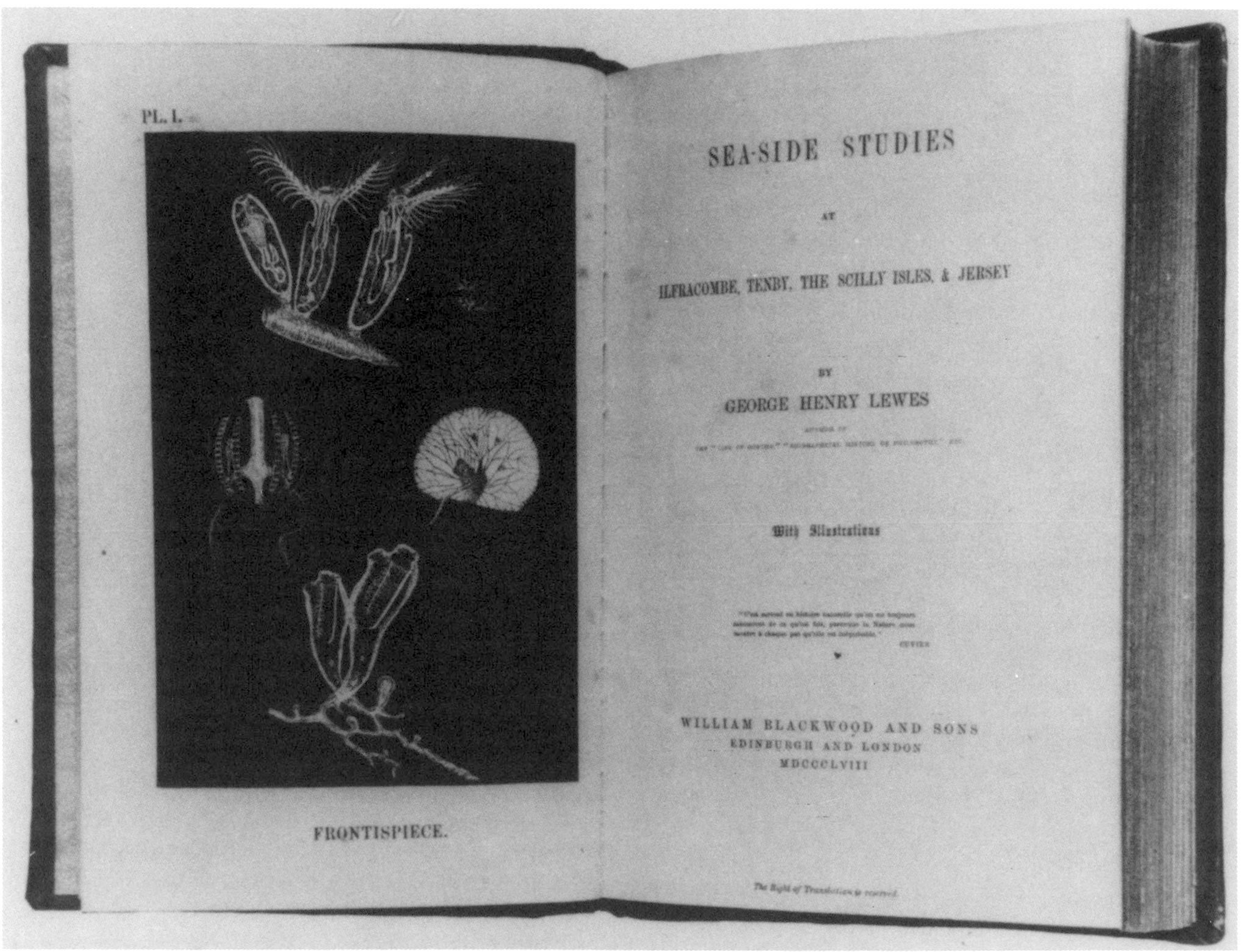

Frontispiece and title page for the volume Lewes described in 1876 as "the book of all my books which was to me the most unalloyed delight"

Life, 1859-1860), and animal physiology and evolution (*Studies in Animal Life,* 1860). T. H. Huxley sent an approving letter about the first of these books, but the most popular was *The Physiology of Common Life,* which, in its Russian translation (1861), was later mentioned in Dostoyevski's *Crime and Punishment* (1866) and helped spur the young Ivan Pavlov to abandon theology for physiology. In the early 1860s Lewes worked on a history of science, a counterpart to his revised history of philosophy, but only one section, *Aristotle: A Chapter in the History of Science* (1864), was published. No mere amateur, Lewes had a few papers read for him at conferences and is credited by modern historians of science with discoveries about the spinal cord, the functional identity of nerves, and muscle sensation.

In the late 1850s Lewes had also resumed writing criticism on a few subjects: fiction, actors and acting (the basis for a later book), and qualities that make good literature. In his articles, many of them for the *Fortnightly Review,* which he edited for its first year (1865-1866), Lewes's evaluation criteria, insights, and judgments resemble his earlier ones but also bear the marks of the new intellectual influences in his life. Closer reading of Comte, for whom art was an important agent of moral progress, along with his own study of psychology, made the former cultural relativist emphasize enduring standards for art and literature, most systematically in the six 1865 articles entitled "The Principles of Success in Literature" (published in book form in 1885, after his death). Study of Ruskin's third volume of *Modern Painters* (1856) and (in summer 1858) of the paintings in Munich and Dresden, as well as his admiration for George Eliot's novels, helped shape his new criterion for excellence: "high" or "idealized" realism. This concept Lewes first explained in "Realism in Art: Recent German Fiction" (*Westminster Review,* October 1858), using reasoning and examples reminiscent of Ruskin on Naturalism. Reality must in any case be adapted to its medium, Lewes observes in this piece, and some artists truthfully portray reality in "ideal" ways: great "emotional sensibility" can endow descriptions of ordinary life with emotional depth, a vivid imagination may give apparent reality to things that cannot really exist, and great genius, like that of Raphael in the Sistine Madonna, can reveal what is noblest in human nature. This last, for Lewes, is the highest form of art, and so the "antithesis" of "Realism" is "not Idealism, but *Falsism.*" The views presented here, also expressed at times by George Eliot, help explain why the two of them so valued her historical novel *Romola* and historical play *The Spanish Gypsy* (1868). They influenced Lewes's later literary judgments and were further explained in his articles on literary "success."

When the articles "The Principles of Success in Literature" appeared in 1865, they were presented to readers of the *Fortnightly Review* not as a theory of literature but as a self-help guide for aspiring authors. After declaring, with the Positivist's assurance, that "all Literature is founded upon psychological laws" that influence its appeal to readers, Lewes introduces three "principles"—Vision, Sincerity, and Beauty—which affect, respectively, man's intellectual, moral, and aesthetic sensibilities. In the long section on Vision, he brings together several related standards pertaining to the representation of reality in art: writing about what one has experienced, trying to see reality clearly, and presenting reality according to artistic principles such as distinctness, economy, and unity. Here Lewes also invokes psychological concepts of perception and imagination to explain why people see reality in different ways and why only the greatest artists can achieve the highest realism, "Idealism." Lewes's second principle, Sincerity, used earlier to defend Shelley and George Sand, requires both honesty in presenting one's own vision, however unpopular, and stylistic integrity, refusing to dress up one's thoughts in pretentious language. The final section, on Beauty, overlaps with the others and reads like an English-composition textbook: stylistic rules of Economy, Climax, and so on, mostly adapted from essays by other critics, are liberally illustrated with passages from Macaulay, Ruskin, and De Quincey.

The systematic way Lewes laid out his literary principles in the articles impressed some readers from the start, and alienated others. The methodical Trollope wanted to see the pieces republished as a book. Judged according to their intended purpose of advising authors, Lewes's articles do offer sensible advice for avoiding common pitfalls such as aiming too high or slavishly imitating others. When they were published in book form, after Lewes's death, it was because university professors, including Albert S. Cook of the University of California and Fred Newton Scott at Michigan, found them, in Scott's words, "suggestive and inspiring" for students. But those who seek in the articles a profound literary theory, an intelligent critic's last word, are often disappointed: Lewes too readily equates success and quality, draws more examples from painting and nonfiction than from imaginative literature, and seems to have let the criteria, in his late critical essays, interfere with his earlier appreciation for Charlotte Brontë and Henry Fielding. Lewes's formulation of his principles seems at least somewhat related to the fact that few of his later essays are as rich in insight as those of the 1840s and early 1850s. But even as literary theory, *The Principles of Success in Literature* put Lewes ahead of most mid-century critics: the first two principles did offer a coherent and in some respects original theory of realism. And Lewes's recognition of a higher realism led him to some valuable critical insights into the limitations as well as the merits of Jane Austen's novels (in an 1859 essay for *Blackwood's*) and into the imaginative powers of Scott (in *The Principles of Success in Literature*) and of Dickens (in an 1872 article in the *Fortnightly Review*).

Literary criticism was not especially important to Lewes in the last years of his life, which he devoted to his companion's work and reputation, to the fortunes of his children, and to his most ambitious intellectual undertaking. George Eliot was being plagued by worshipers, even before her masterpiece, *Middlemarch,* began to appear in 1871. Among Lewes's sons only the eldest, Charles, did well in life, working in the post office and delighting the Leweses with his wife and daughters. Things went poorly for the other two, settled on a farm in South Africa. Thornie returned to his father's home to die slowly and painfully in 1869, and Bertie, the youngest, died in 1875. In the 1870s, their health even worse than before, Lewes and George Eliot spent much time helping each other with their writing, traveled less, and reduced their social life. In 1876 they bought Witley Heights, a country estate next to that of the Tennysons.

Preparing for publication the three series of *Problems of Life and Mind* (1874-1879), underway since 1862, became Lewes's primary intellectual activity in his last few years. His "Key to All Psychologies," as he once called it, broke sufficient new ground to earn coverage in the *Encyclopedia of Philosophy* (1967) and to have had one volume, *The Study of Psychology,* republished in volume six of *Significant Contributions to the History of Psychology* (1977). Less accessible to contemporaries and less lively than his other writing, *Problems of Life and Mind* has often been ignored or deplored in literary studies of Lewes. But this project engaged both his and George Eliot's attention during a time when he was still writing some criticism and she was creating her most complex characters, and *Problems of Life and Mind* has rewarded a few scholars with new insights into the writings of both Lewes and George Eliot. Lewes intended, in Comtian terms, to turn psychology into a Positive science, but ran into logical difficulties that forced him to digress in even more ambitious directions. Thus the first series, boldly designated *The Foundations of a Creed* (1874-1875), not only explained the nature of scientific knowledge but also defined a new metascience, the study of abstractions such as Life, Mind, Cause, and Force which are important to all sciences and require data from many disciplines. This "empirical metaphysics," as explained by Jack Kaminsky in a 1952 article in *Journal of the History of Ideas,* allowed Lewes to deal scientifically with the apparent duality of body and mind; Lewes shows them to be different manifestations of a unified system of experiences. Only after demonstrating the unity of experience could Lewes proceed in the second series, *The Physical Basis of Mind* (1877), to describe physiological manifestations of mental experiences and, finally, to define the science of psychology, first its "nature, method, and scope" in *The Study of Psychology* (1879), volume one of the posthumously published third series, and then its laws in the final volume (1879). Lewes was an original psychologist because he studied thoughts and feelings by observing human behavior and because he believed that the human mind had evolved not only biologically but also socially, by the interaction of people in societies. This social component of mind, which George Eliot called "the supremely interesting element in the thinking of our time" and which Lewes saw as the basis of altruism, is important to her characters and to Lewes's responses to characters.

Another influence of Lewes's psychology on his criticism is evident in the only book for which he interrupted his work on *Problems of Life and Mind.* Based mainly on his *Pall Mall Gazette* articles of the 1860s, Lewes's *On Actors and the Art of Acting* (1875) has become enough of a theater classic to be republished in the 1960s. Lewes explained in the preface that he made an exception to his policy of not republishing critical articles because he was appalled by other critics' ignorance about acting as an art. Though the essays are primarily evaluations of actors from Edmund Kean in the 1830s to the Italian Tommaso Salvini in 1875, Lewes was also educating critics to recognize, as he had demonstrated in his *Leader* reviews, that many different factors influence their response to an actor's performance, including the quality of the play and the actor's physical traits. When Lewes explained at great length how many abilities and skills are

Lewes's grave, Highgate Cemetery, London

needed to portray an emotion on stage convincingly, he applied, as Joseph R. Roach, Jr., has pointed out in a 1980 *Theatre Journal* piece, concepts from his *The Physical Basis of Mind* and anticipated elements of Stanislavsky's famous "method" for actors. Similar concepts had been used to illuminate the "Principle of Vision" in Lewes's essays on literature. Other passages in *Problems of Life and Mind,* especially those on "moral types" in human character, have occasionally helped George Eliot's critics see new dimensions in her later characters, especially Will Ladislaw of *Middlemarch,* in whom many see an idealized Lewes.

Intellectually active to the end, Lewes continued producing *Fortnightly Review* essays on his favorite thinkers, including Darwin, Spinoza, and Comte. In his last article (1878) he lamented the theologians' "dread and dislike of science" and looked forward to a day when human ethics would be on a firm footing, after "science has fairly mastered the principles of moral relations." The science of his day could do little for him when he developed a serious intestinal illness, and on 30 November 1878, at the age of sixty-one, he died. George Eliot grieved in seclusion, revised the last series of *Problems of Life and Mind,* married the young lawyer John Walter Cross, and died soon after, also at sixty-one, in December 1880.

Lewes had left his mark on the people of his age, as a person and as a writer. From obituary notices and memoirs, it is evident that some of the personality traits that made him an ideal partner for George Eliot had been appreciated by his many friends. If his outward appearance was marred by a pockmarked face, shaggy hair, and unconventional dress—Jane Carlyle called him "the Ape"—Herbert Spencer found it "impossible to be dull in his company," and to John Morley his "sparkling good-humour" helped make evenings at The Priory "the high perfection of social intercourse." Trollope remembered his "vivacity," his "comic earnestness," and his storytelling ability. And if George Meredith wrote him off as a "mercurial little showman," even his strongest detractor, Eliza Lynn Linton, observed his talent for spreading "intellectual sunshine." Beyond his circle of friends Lewes reached and influenced a large audience through his contributions to many well-respected mid-Victorian periodicals and his successful books. Instead of preaching to his age in the manner of Carlyle and Ruskin, Lewes subtly educated his readers to accept Positivism, evolution, and physiological psychology by making these subjects clear and reasonable. As a critic, he fought all his life for standards of excellence against a tide of impressionistic reviewing, introduced in England the concept of realism, and, even earlier than Matthew Arnold, taught his public, by means of well-selected quotations, how to distinguish the best literature, that of Shakespeare and Goethe, Austen and Thackeray, from the mediocre fiction and drama of their day.

Today Lewes's writings remain readable, sometimes entertaining, and often thought-provoking. His versatility, which has sometimes lead to charges of dilettantism, actually is his great strength. As Fred Newton Scott noted near the beginning of the twentieth century, "No man, it is likely, will ever again find it possible" to do "brilliant" work in so many fields. Lewes was able to use his rich store of expertise to make connections among apparently disparate phenomena: body and mind, theatrical performance and literary creation, scientific induction and artistic realism, Shakespeare and Jane Austen. Unifying most of these diverse interests was a single theme: his interest in human emotions, especially in the noblest forms, and in their representation. Mostly unsuccessful at representing emotion himself, in his acting or in his novels and plays, Lewes studied emotion in acting, in the visual arts, in human sensation and behavior, and of course in literature. The emotions figure prominently in the works of most of his favorite philosophers—Spinoza, Hegel, and even Comte. Literature in which human emotions are central elicited his best criticism: nineteenth-century fiction, Shakespeare and Racine, Goethe and Shelley, and of course George Eliot's works; his most important misjudgments are of writers who are strongly aesthetic, such as Keats, or intellectual, such as Wordsworth and Browning.

Among twentieth-century readers, Lewes's theater criticism has found its appreciative audience, including John Gielgud; his contributions to science, philosophy, and psychology have received appropriate recognition; his role in shaping George Eliot's fiction, and even Charlotte Brontë's, is the subject of lively controversy. His literary criticism, however, is largely excluded from the anthologies and histories of criticism through which it could become widely known. Since the appearance in 1896 of William Archer's selection of Lewes's dramatic essays (in a volume that also included pieces by John Forster) and the last republication of *The Principles of Success in Literature* (1917), only a small volume of short excerpts, edited by Alice R. Kaminsky, has been published (in 1964). An annotated edition of perhaps twenty-five of Lewes's best writings on literature and aesthetics would help his critical writing find its audiences: historians of criticism and of rhetoric, devotees of some varieties of structuralism and reader-response criticism, teachers of literary masterpieces, and all who enjoy reading criticism that not only illuminates individual works but also challenges us to reflect on why imaginative literature is worth reading in our scientific age. Several twentieth-century scholars have ranked Lewes as the most significant British critic between Coleridge or William Hazlitt and Matthew Arnold. And if Arnold himself, in 1858, professed "a very high opinion of his literary judgment," if he was to Shaw an equal in criticism and to Trollope the "acutest critic" of his day, then surely today's Victorianists deserve exposure to the writings, and not just the life, of George Henry Lewes.

Letters:

The George Eliot Letters, 9 volumes, edited by Gordon S. Haight (New Haven: Yale University Press, 1954-1955, 1978; London: Oxford University Press, 1954-1956; London: Yale University Press, 1978).

Bibliographies:

William Baker, "G. H. Lewes and the *Penny* Cyclopaedia," *Victorian Periodicals Newsletter,* 7 (September 1974): 15-18;

Baker, *The George Eliot-George Henry Lewes Library: An Annotated Bibliography of Their Books at Dr. Williams's Library* (New York & London: Garland, 1977);

Baker, "Some Additions to George Henry Lewes's Bibliography," *Victorian Periodicals Review,* 12 (Fall 1979): 117-118.

Biographies:

Anna Theresa Kitchell, *George Lewes and George Eliot: A Review of Records* (New York: Day, 1933);

David Williams, *Mr. George Eliot: A Biography of George Henry Lewes* (London: Hodder & Stoughton, 1983; New York: Franklin Watts, 1983).

References:

Rosemary Ashton, *The German Idea: Four English Writers and the Reception of German Thought, 1800-1860* (Cambridge, London & New York: Cambridge University Press, 1980);

R. L. Brett, "George Henry Lewes: Dramatist, Novelist, and Critic," *Essays and Studies,* 11 (1958): 101-120;

A. K. Collins, "G. H. Lewes Revised: George Eliot and the Moral Sense," *Victorian Studies,* 21 (Summer 1978): 463-492;

Patrick Creevy, "The Victorian Goethe Critics: Notions of Greatness and Development," *Victorians Institute Journal,* 13 (1985): 31-57;

Franklin Gary, "Charlotte Brontë and George Henry Lewes," *PMLA,* 51 (1936): 518-542;

Morris Greenhut, "George Henry Lewes and the Classical Tradition in English Criticism," *Review of English Studies,* 24 (April 1948): 126-137;

Greenhut, "George Henry Lewes as a Critic of the Novel," *Studies in Philology,* 45 (July 1948): 491-511;

Greenhut, "G. H. Lewes's Criticism of the Drama," *PMLA,* 64 (June 1949): 350-368;

John Gross, *The Rise and Fall of the Man of Letters: Aspects of English Literary Life since 1800* (London: Weidenfeld & Nicolson, 1969);

Gordon S. Haight, *George Eliot: A Biography* (New York: Oxford University Press, 1968);

Edgar W. Hirshberg, *George Henry Lewes* (New York: Twayne, 1970);

Alice R. Kaminsky, *George Henry Lewes as Literary Critic* (Syracuse: Syracuse University Press, 1968);

Jack Kaminsky, "The Empirical Metaphysics of George Henry Lewes," *Journal of the History of Ideas,* 13 (June 1952): 314-332;

Harold Orel, *Victorian Literary Critics* (London: Macmillan, 1984);

Joseph R. Roach, Jr., "G. H. Lewes and Performance Theory: Towards a 'Science of Acting,' " *Theatre Journal,* 42 (October 1980): 312-328;

Daniel N. Robinson, Preface to *Significant Contributions to the History of Psychology, 1750-1920,* series A, volume 6 (Washington, D.C.: University Publications of America, 1977);

Diderik Roll-Hansen, "George Henry Lewes and His Critics," *English Studies,* 60 (1979): 159-165;

Marie U. Secor, "The Legacy of Nineteenth Century Style Theory," *Rhetoric Society Quarterly,* 12 (Spring 1982): 76-94;

W. M. Simon, *European Positivism in the Nineteenth Century: An Essay in Intellectual History* (Port Washington, N.Y. & London: Kennikat, 1972);

Barbara Smalley, Introduction to Lewes's *Ranthorpe* (Athens: Ohio University Press, 1980);

[James Sully] "George Henry Lewes," *New Quarterly Magazine,* 2 (October 1879): 356-376;

Hock Guan Tjoa, *George Henry Lewes: A Victorian Mind* (Cambridge & London: Harvard University Press, 1979);

Anthony Trollope, "George Henry Lewes," *Fortnightly Review,* new series 31 (1 January 1879): 15-24.

Papers:

The largest collection of Lewes material is at the Beinecke Rare Book and Manuscript Library at Yale, which has his manuscript journals (1856-1870), diaries (1869-1876), some letters, a notebook, a literary-receipts book, and manuscripts of several plays. Other letters are at the British Library.

Thomas Babington Macaulay

William F. Naufftus
Winthrop College

See also the Macaulay entry in *DLB 32, Victorian Poets Before 1850*.

BORN: Rothley Temple, Leicestershire, 25 October 1800, to Zachary and Selina Mills Macaulay.

EDUCATION: Trinity College, Cambridge, 1818-1822.

DEATH: Holly Lodge, Camden, 28 December 1859.

SELECTED BOOKS: *Pompeii: A Poem Which Obtained the Chancellor's Medal at the Cambridge Commencement, July 1819* (Cambridge, 1819);

Evening: A Poem Which Obtained the Chancellor's Medal at the Cambridge Commencement, July 1821 (Cambridge, 1821);

Lays of Ancient Rome (London: Longman, Brown, Green & Longmans, 1842; Philadelphia: Carey & Hart, 1843);

Critical and Miscellaneous Essays, 5 volumes (Philadelphia: Carey & Hart, 1842-1844);

Critical and Historical Essays, Contributed to the Edinburgh Review (3 volumes, London: Longman, Brown, Green & Longmans, 1843; 5 volumes, New York: White, Stokes & Allen, 1843);

The History of England from the Accession of James II, 5 volumes; volume 5 edited by Lady Hannah Trevelyan (London: Longman, Brown, Green & Longmans, 1848-1861; New York: Harper, 1849-1861);

Speeches, 2 volumes (New York: Redfield, 1853);

The Speeches of the Rt. Hon. T. B. Macaulay, Edited by Himself, 1 volume (London: Longman, Green, Brown & Longmans, 1854);

Biographical and Historical Sketches (New York: Appleton, 1857);

The Miscellaneous Writings of Lord Macaulay, edited by Thomas Flower Ellis, 2 volumes (London: Longmans, Green, Longman & Roberts, 1860);

Biographies by Lord Macaulay Contributed to the Encyclopaedia Britannica (Edinburgh: Black, 1860; New York: Macmillan, 1894);

Thomas Babington Macaulay in 1833. Portrait by S. W. Reynolds, Jr. (Collection of Mrs. Reine Errington).

The Indian Education Minutes of Lord Macaulay, edited by H. Woodrow (Calcutta, 1862);

Hymn by Lord Macaulay: An Effort of His Early Childhood, edited by L. Horton-Smith (Cambridge: Metcalf, 1902);

Marginal Notes, edited by George Otto Trevelyan (London: Longmans, Green, 1907);

Lord Macaulay's Legislative Minutes, edited by C. D. Dharker (London & New York: Oxford University Press, 1946);

Napoleon and the Restoration of the Bourbons: The Completed Portion of Macaulay's Projected "History of France, from the Restoration of the Bourbons to the Accession of Louis Philippe," edited by Joseph Hamburger (London: Longman, 1977; New York: Columbia University Press, 1977).

Collections: *The Works of Lord Macaulay. Complete,* edited by Lady Trevelyan, 8 volumes (London: Longmans, Green, 1866; New York: Appleton, 1866);

The Works of Lord Macaulay, Albany Edition, 12 volumes (London: Longmans, Green, 1898; New York: DeFau, 1898);

The Complete Works of Lord Macaulay, Bibliophile Edition, 20 volumes (Philadelphia: University Library Association, 1910).

PERIODICAL PUBLICATIONS: "The West Indies," *Edinburgh Review,* 41 (January 1825): 464-488;

"Milton," *Edinburgh Review,* 42 (August 1825): 304-346;

"Machiavelli," *Edinburgh Review,* 45 (March 1827): 259-295;

"Major Moody's Reports: Social and Industrial Capacities of Negroes," *Edinburgh Review,* 45 (March 1827): 245-267;

"Dryden," *Edinburgh Review,* 47 (January 1828): 1-36;

"History," *Edinburgh Review,* 47 (May 1828): 331-367;

"Hallam's *Constitutional History,*" *Edinburgh Review,* 48 (September 1828): 96-169;

"Mill's *Essay on Government:* Utilitarian Logic and Politics," *Edinburgh Review,* 49 (March 1829): 159-189;

"Bentham's Defence of Mill: Utilitarian System of Philosophy," *Edinburgh Review,* 49 (June 1829): 273-299;

"Utilitarian Theory of Government, and the 'Greatest Happiness Principle,'" *Edinburgh Review,* 50 (October 1829): 99-125;

"Southey's *Colloquies on Society,*" *Edinburgh Review,* 50 (January 1830): 528-565;

"Sadler's *Law of Population, and Disproof of Human Superfecundity,*" *Edinburgh Review,* 51 (July 1830): 297-321;

"Civil Disabilities of the Jews," *Edinburgh Review,* 52 (January 1831): 363-374;

"Moore's *Life of Lord Byron,*" *Edinburgh Review,* 53 (June 1831): 544-572;

"Croker's Edition of Boswell's *Life of Johnson,*" *Edinburgh Review,* 54 (September 1831): 1-38;

"Southey's Edition of the *Pilgrim's Progress,*" *Edinburgh Review,* 54 (December 1831): 450-461;

"Lord Nugent's *Memorials of Hampden,*" *Edinburgh Review,* 54 (December 1831): 505-550;

"Nares' *Memoirs of Lord Burghley*—Political and Religious Aspects of His Age," *Edinburgh Review,* 55 (April 1832): 271-296;

"Dumont's *Recollections of Mirabeau*—The French Revolution," *Edinburgh Review,* 55 (July 1832): 552-576;

"Lord Mahon's *War of the Succession,*" *Edinburgh Review,* 56 (January 1833): 499-542;

"Walpole's *Letters to Sir Horace Mann,*" *Edinburgh Review,* 58 (October 1833): 227-258;

"Thackeray's *History of the Earl of Chatham,*" *Edinburgh Review,* 58 (January 1834): 508-544;

"Sir James Mackintosh's *History of the Revolution,*" *Edinburgh Review,* 61 (July 1835): 265-322;

"Lord Bacon," *Edinburgh Review,* 65 (July 1837): 1-104;

"Life and Writings of Sir William Temple," *Edinburgh Review,* 68 (October 1838): 113-187;

"*Church and State* [by W. E. Gladstone]," *Edinburgh Review,* 69 (April 1839): 231-280;

"Sir John Malcolm's *Life of Lord Clive,*" Edinburgh Review, 70 (January 1840): 295-362;

"Ranke's *History of the Popes*—Revolutions of the Papacy," *Edinburgh Review,* 72 (October 1840): 227-258;

"Comic Dramatists of the Restoration," *Edinburgh Review,* 72 (January 1841): 490-528;

"The Late Lord Holland," *Edinburgh Review,* 73 (July 1841): 560-568;

"Warren Hastings," *Edinburgh Review,* 74 (October 1841): 160-255;

"Frederic the Great," *Edinburgh Review,* 75 (April 1842): 218-281;

"Madame D'Arblay," *Edinburgh Review,* 76 (January 1843): 523-570;

"Life and Writings of Addison," *Edinburgh Review,* 78 (July 1843): 193-260;

"Barère's *Memoirs,*" *Edinburgh Review,* 79 (April 1844): 275-351;

"The Earl of Chatham," *Edinburgh Review,* 80 (October 1844): 526-595;

"Essay on the Life and Character of King William III" (1822), edited by A. N. L. Munby, *Times Literary Supplement,* 1 May 1969, pp. 468-469.

Thomas Babington Macaulay was a public figure whose writings were inseparable from the rest of his career. His speeches made him one of the most important members of the House of Commons during the debates on the 1832 Reform Bill; his early essays for the *Edinburgh Review* were, for the most part, political polemic; and the minutes and penal code he wrote during his years as legislative member of the Supreme Council of the East India Company heavily influenced the course of education and law on the Indian subcontinent. The volumes of his essays collected from the *Edinburgh Review* were among the most popular books of the Victorian Age, making him for many modern critics the symbol of Victorian philistinism and, at the very least, a useful index of Victorian assumptions and tastes. But it is as a historian that he most vigorously survives today, generally sharing with Edward Gibbon the laurels as the British man of letters who most successfully combined the demands of narrative literature and historical truth.

In his historical essays and in his *The History of England from the Accession of James II* (1848-1861), Macaulay is a watershed figure. He is the last important British historian to look consciously to the Roman, Greek, and neoclassical historians for literary models—clearly imitating the narrative techniques and stylistic devices of Thucydides, Plutarch, Tacitus, Livy, Clarendon, and Hume. At the same time, he is a product of his own age, drawing parallels and lessons from contemporary events and indulging in Romantic sentiments and pictorial details. Finally, he looks forward to later trends in historical writing by giving the first distinguished examples of British social history, particularly in his famous third chapter of *The History of England*, with its overview of English society in 1685.

Throughout his works, Macaulay popularized—and became spokesman for—the so-called Whig view of history, a complex set of assumptions widely held in the nineteenth century and generally denigrated in the twentieth. This Whig view can be defined in several ways, but its chief ingredients were a belief that history in general, and modern Western history in particular, was essentially the record of progress; that historical figures should be praised for having furthered the cause of progress or blamed for having opposed it; and that the moderate reformers of the Whig party were usually the servants of progress, while both Tory reactionaries and dangerous radicals threatened civilization in various ways. Macaulay did not originate this set of ideas, and he would not always have endorsed them, but in a general way he popularized assumptions of this sort among his vast readership. It was Lord Acton, another Whig historian, who said that Macaulay's writings were "a key to half the prejudices of our age."

He was born on 25 October 1800 at his uncle's estate, Rothley Temple in Leicestershire, and raised in the Evangelical surroundings of Clapham Common, a London suburb where his father, Zachary Macaulay, was a prominent resident. The senior Macaulay was a prosperous merchant and shipowner involved in the African and East India trade, but his real interest was the abolition of slavery in the British Empire. Before his marriage he had served as the first governor of Sierra Leone, an African colony settled by freed slaves, and in later years he neglected his business firm, Macaulay and Babington, to devote his attention to editing the *Christian Observer*, the journal of the Evangelical abolitionists. Zachary Macaulay's wife, Selina Mills Macaulay, had been a student of the famous Evangelical educator Hannah More and spent most of her mature life raising her five daughters and four sons.

Thomas Macaulay, the eldest of these nine children, was an unusually precocious child who, at the age of ten, reminded Thomas DeQuincey's mother of Samuel Taylor Coleridge. During the two days the young Macaulay spent with her, he impressed her as a "Baby genius," but she was concerned that "he says such things that he will be ruined by praise." For the fact that he was not so ruined he could bestow his thanks on his father, who was always finding some cause for complaint—Tom Macaulay's handwriting was clumsy, his habits were slovenly, he was wasting time, he was reading novels, or he was falling into dangerous political opinions. Rather surprisingly, in view of his general combativeness, Macaulay revered his father and tried constantly to please him. He did not inherit the religious faith which had made his father's life emotionally satisfying, intellectually coherent, and socially useful, but he did inherit his father's reforming zeal—a zeal which made him a champion of Catholic and Jewish emancipation, of the abolition of both slavery and pocket boroughs, of the extension of the franchise, and of the extension of Western education and Western law to Britain's Indian empire.

At Cambridge the former child prodigy failed the mathematics tripos in 1822 but was otherwise a tremendous success. He won the Chancellor's Prize for English verse in 1819 and 1821, made his mark as an orator in the University Union, won a Craven scholarship in classics, and crowned his university career by being elected a fellow of Trinity College. During this time he also became a Whig and wrote a prize essay on the "Conduct and Character of William III." This essay, which was finally published in the *Times Literary Supplement* in 1969, was his most important undergraduate work because it first led him to consider seriously the work of the monarch who would eventually become the major figure in his *The History of England.* After leaving Cambridge, Macaulay read for the bar at Lincoln's Inn, spent as much time as possible with his family, and began his literary career in earnest by contributing regularly to *Knight's Quarterly Magazine.* These contributions included poetry, fiction, literary criticism, satires, and closet drama. They are now quite properly regarded as juvenilia, but in them Macaulay develops the ideas and the prose style that would soon make him the most popular writer for the *Edinburgh Review.* In *Knight's Quarterly Magazine* he advanced his notions on the nature of poetry in essays on Dante and Petrarch, made fun of an eminent Tory in his *Wellingtoniad,* and worked out his opinions on seventeenth-century English history in "A Conversation Between Mr. Abraham Cowley and Mr. John Milton, Touching the Great Civil War." Yet the differences between the articles in *Knight's Quarterly Magazine* and the *Edinburgh Review* essays are as interesting as their similarities are. The earlier pieces lack both the partisan bitterness and the almost insufferable arrogance that characterize Macaulay's *Edinburgh* reviews, a circumstance which suggests that Macaulay's *Edinburgh* essays owe some of their least attractive qualities as much to the editorial policies of the journal in which they appeared as to the personality of their author.

The *Edinburgh Review* was the quasi-official organ of the Whig party, and the period from 1825 to 1834—during which Macaulay wrote most of his reviews—was a politically acrimonious time preceding and following the passage of the Great Reform Bill of 1832. Arrogance and invective were characteristic of the *Edinburgh*'s reviewers as a group. In these years, Macaulay wrote twenty-seven articles—ostensibly book reviews but in fact wide-ranging essays on topics suggested, sometimes rather loosely, by the book under scrutiny. They are not today his most impressive writings, but they were the ones that established him both as a political and a literary figure. It was because of an article in the *Edinburgh Review* that Macaulay came to the attention of Lord Lansdowne, who in 1830 helped secure him a seat in Parliament through his pocket borough of Calne in Wiltshire, and it was through his three-volume collection *Critical and Historical Essays, Contributed to the Edinburgh Review* (1843) that Macaulay eventually reached the largest number of readers. The first essay (January 1825) was an abolitionist argument on the West Indies. This piece was followed by other purely political works, including a series of three attacks on James Mill and the Utilitarians in general. The general line of argument was that Mill was too theoretical and insufficiently pragmatic, that he reasoned from a priori notions rather than from observation of fact. These three essays are important in that they constituted one side of a debate between the Whig *Edinburgh Review* and the *Westminster Review,* the organ of the Benthamite Philosophical Radicals or Utilitarians. In his *Autobiography* (1873) John Stuart Mill recalls his own role in answering Macaulay's objections to his father's writings but also admits that the *Edinburgh* articles helped modify his faith in his father's views.

The three essays from this period that are still widely read today are "Milton" (August 1825); "Southey's *Colloquies on Society*" (January 1830); and "Croker's Edition of Boswell's *Life of Johnson*" (September 1831). "Milton," the essay which made Macaulay famous, is most notable for its mixed theory of progress. This theory argues that as men learn to think abstractly, they lose the ability to create the concrete images that are essential to great poetry: "Generalization is necessary to the advancement of knowledge; but particularity is indispensable to the creations of the imagination. In proportion as men know more and think more, they look less at individuals and more at classes. They therefore make better theories and worse poems." Macaulay appears to have no doubts about the beneficent nature of this change: the truth of poetry "is the truth of madness" and "poetry effects its purpose most completely in a dark age." The immediate purpose of this theory is to show Milton's greatness in producing great poetry in the polished seventeenth century, but it also suggests that Macaulay's much-maligned belief in progress was less simple than it is usually thought to be: the wealth and freedom of the modern world were worth more than the great poetry produced by the ancients, but he was hardly unaware of the drawbacks of the scientific, democratic, and industrial revolutions.

Most of the essay on Milton is concerned, however, with politics rather than poetry. In the 1820s and 1830s, Whig and Tory controversialists were in the habit of fighting over again the battles of the seventeenth century since it was felt that the issues of the Civil War were similar to those which eventually resulted in the 1832 Reform Bill and the

Thomas Flower Ellis, Macaulay's closest friend and editor of the posthumously published Miscellaneous Writings of Lord Macaulay *(Trinity College)*

rest of the reform legislation that was carried through or first proposed at this time—abolition of slavery in British colonies, Catholic Emancipation, the relief of Jewish Disabilities, Irish disestablishment, and the secularization of the universities. Tories praised Charles I, saw the Church of England in danger, and feared a return of the chaos and tyranny of the Civil War and Commonwealth. In his essay Macaulay follows the Whig tradition by damning Charles as a tyrant and Archbishop Laud as a bigot, making excuses for Cromwell and praising the Puritans in general and Milton in particular. Milton is seen as an ideal character because he shared the general Puritan characteristics of courage and hatred of tyranny and yet appreciated beauty as much as any Cavalier.

In his essay on Robert Southey's *Sir Thomas More; or Colloquies on the Progress and Prospects of Society* (1829), a recent work in which the poet laureate discussed political questions with the compliant ghost of More, Macaulay took up more obviously contemporary political questions. In keeping with the moderate reformist tradition of the Whig party, he condemns Southey both for the revolutionary opinions of his youth and the reactionary opinions of his old age. "He has passed from one extreme of political opinion to another, as Satan in Milton went round the globe, contriving constantly 'to ride with darkness.' Wherever the thickest shadow of the night may at any moment chance to fall, there is Mr. Southey." Much of the debate between Macaulay and Southey hinged on the question of whether material conditions were better or worse as a result of the industrial revolution. In his *Colloquies* Southey portrays the decay of rural England, the squalor of the new cities, and the unhealthiness of factory conditions. Macaulay cites statistics indicating greater life expectancy as well as greater material prosperity, and he ends with a peroration that is one of the best-known passages in all his works: "If any person had told the Parliament which met in terror and perplexity after the crash of 1720 that in 1830 the wealth of England would surpass all their wildest dreams . . . that London would be twice as large and twice as populous, and that nevertheless the rate of mortality would have diminished to half of what it then was, . . . our ancestors would have given as much credit to the prediction as they gave to *Gulliver's Travels*. Yet that prediction would have been true. . . . On what principle is it that, when we see nothing but improvement behind us, we are to expect nothing but deterioration before us?" And the "improvement behind us" has been produced, Macaulay concludes, by "the prudence and energy of the people" and not "the intermeddling of Mr. Southey's idol the omniscient and omnipresent State."

In this essay Macaulay acknowledges Southey's good intentions, and elsewhere he praises his talents as a writer, but his review of the Tory John Wilson Croker's 1831 edition of Boswell's *Life of Johnson* is clearly a personal attack. Almost half the essay is an assault on Croker's facts—"Indeed we cannot open any volume of this work in any place and turn it over for two minutes in any direction without finding a blunder"—or his explanatory notes—"He is perpetually telling us that he cannot understand something in the text which is as plain as language can make it." Had Croker been a supporter of parliamentary reform instead of one of its most inveterate, erudite, and eloquent opponents, presumably his shortcomings as an editor would have received less attention. Boswell himself is presented by Macaulay as a puzzling set of contradictions: "Without all the qualities which made him the jest and the torment of those among whom he lived, without the officiousness, the inquisitiveness, the effrontery, the toad-eating, the insensibility to all reproof, he never could have produced so excellent a book." Johnson is also depicted as a contradictory character: "He began to be credulous precisely at the point where the most credulous people begin to be skeptical. . . . He could discuss clearly enough the folly and meanness of all bigotry except his own."

Beyond their general Whig party line, several intellectual tendencies are apparent in these early essays. There is respect for empirical fact, and there is a matching suspicion for fine theories—both Southey's myth of a past golden age and Mill's myth of a rationally happy Utilitarian future. There are strong reactions to personalities, and the reactions to Milton and Johnson—writers long in their graves—are as strong as the reactions to Macaulay's contemporaries Croker and Mill. Finally, there is a clear tendency to find or create paradoxes: the theory of material progress and poetic decay in "Milton," the image of Southey's Miltonic voyage to the poles, and the presentation of Boswell and Johnson as bundles of contradictions. All of these characteristics would remain important throughout Macaulay's literary career.

The essay on Milton was something of a literary phenomenon. Macaulay's nephew George Otto Trevelyan later wrote in *The Life and Letters of Lord Macaulay* (1876) that "like Lord Byron, he awoke one morning to find himself famous." The modern reader who wonders what made the essays so popular must first consider Macaulay's prose style. "The more I think, the less I can conceive where you picked up that prose style," Francis Jeffrey wrote to Macaulay after receiving the manuscript of "Milton." The style varied. It could be urbane, witty, Augustan. It could be lushly sentimental or furiously indignant. It was, however, always clear, and this clarity was certainly a large part of Macaulay's appeal to the general reader. He took great pains with his writing so that the reader should have as little trouble as possible. His journal entry for 2 July 1850 is revealing: "My account of the Highlands is getting into tolerable shape. Tomorrow I shall begin to transcribe again, and to polish. What trouble these few pages will have cost me! The great object is that, after all this trouble, they may read as if they had been spoken off, and may flow as easily as table talk." In fact, as Hippolyte Taine says in the admiring chapter on Macaulay in his history of English literature (translated into English in 1871), "it seems as if he were making a wager with his reader, and said to him: Be as absent in mind, as stupid, as ignorant as you please. . . . I will repeat the same idea in so many different forms, I will make it sensible by such familiar and precise examples . . . that you cannot help being enlightened and convinced."

Such striving for clarity could, as Taine admits, become tedious, but it should be remembered that these essays were, to a certain extent, self-help works in a society where bookishness and literacy conferred status. As John Morley observed in the *Fortnightly Review* in 1876, Macaulay's "Essays are as good as a library . . . for a busy uneducated man, who has curiosity and enlightenment enough to wish to know a little about the great lives and great thoughts . . . that have marked the journey of man through the ages." And such a reader is taught to trust the writer. Macaulay writes as if there could be no doubt about the importance of his topics or about his own competence to pass judgment. Lord Melbourne is supposed to have remarked that he wished he were as sure of anything as Macaulay was of everything, but most of Macaulay's readers apparently thought his confidence justified. His most impressive intellectual gift was his memory, and he used this memory throughout his writings to dredge up an enormous range of highly specific examples and analogies to illustrate every point and support every argument he made. As Jane Millgate has suggested in *Macaulay* (1973), this is both reassuring and flattering to the reader. He is impressed by the writer's erudition and flattered by the writer's assumption that the reader shares this erudition, understands these allusions to literary works or historical events. When Macaulay says, as he does in his essay on the Anglo-Indian adventurer Robert Clive, that every schoolboy knows who strangled Atahualpa, the reader who finds himself innocent of this schoolboy knowledge may feel intimidated at first, but the context makes it clear that the strangler was a Spanish conqueror in the New World. So the busy, uneducated reader could take that hint and move on to the next paragraph, eventually working through a collection of essays that covers a wide range of topics.

The topics covered in Macaulay's early years with the *Edinburgh Review* include literary criticism on Dryden (January 1828) and Bunyan (December 1831) and character analyses of Byron (June 1831) and Machiavelli (March 1827). There is also a series of eight essays covering British history from the Reformation ("Nares' *Memoirs of Lord Burghley*—Political and Religious Aspects of His Age," April 1832) to the end of the Seven Years War ("Thackeray's *History of the Earl of Chatham,*" January 1834). The literary essays show more interest in an author's life and times than in his art; the historical essays repeatedly present the Whig view that the growth of liberty has been essential to the growth of British power, wealth, and culture. The essays on Horace Walpole (October 1833) and the Earl of Chatham, however, portray the mid-eighteenth century as a period of national degeneracy when old political ideals had decayed and new ones had not yet arisen to take their place. Macaulay did not think that progress was constant or inevitable any more than he thought it was the rule in all areas of human endeavor.

Several of the *Edinburgh Review* essays were very closely connected with speeches that he delivered in the House of Commons as member for Calne. The earliest of these was a January 1831 article, "Civil Disabilities of the Jews," arguing for admitting Jews to the vote and to all public offices. Macaulay advanced this idea in two parliamentary speeches as well as in the *Edinburgh Review* essay, but such laws were not passed until several decades later. Other reform measures were more immediately successful, with Parliament spurred on by the July 1830 French Revolution which brought down Charles X and ended the Bourbon dynasty.

Macaulay expressed an interest in writing an article for the *Edinburgh Review* on recent French political developments and spent the summer of 1831 traveling on the Continent and making notes. But Henry Brougham, an older and more established *Edinburgh* reviewer, claimed the subject as his own and Macvey Napier, the new editor, reluctantly granted this claim. The fragmentary essay which Macaulay did complete was lost for more than a century until it was discovered and published in 1977 as *Napoleon and the Restoration of the Bourbons*. It concludes with the events of 1815 rather than 1830 and consequently covers much of the same ground as Macaulay's July 1832 *Edinburgh Review* essay "Dumont's *Recollections of Mirabeau*—The French Revolution." Both essays develop the same theory of revolution: "We believe it to be a rule without exception, that the violence of a revolution corresponds to the degree of misgovernment which has produced that revolution." The subjects of Charles I were less oppressed than those of Louis XVI and were less vindictive as a result; the American subjects of George III were least violent of all because they were least oppressed.

A correct analysis of the nature of revolution seemed crucial because in the early 1830s, a revolution in England seemed a real possibility. The French Church and aristocracy had failed to prevent revolution, but Macaulay thought that the British Lords and Commons could do better. The French "would not have reform; and they had revolution. . . . They would not endure Turgot; and they were forced to endure Robespierre." This passage appears in both the essay on Mirabeau and Macaulay's second speech on the Reform Bill (5 July 1831). It is, in fact, the main theme that runs through the five Reform Bill speeches that he delivered between 2 March and 16 December 1831. In the 2 March speech, he warned the Commons to reform "now while the crash of the proudest throne of the Continent is still resounding in our ears." And again on 20 September he reminded the opponents of reform that the French aristocrats were "driven forth to exile and beggary, to cut wood in the back settlements of America, or to teach French in the school-rooms of London. . . . because they refused all concession till the time had arrived when no concession would avail."

Certainly the dangers seemed real and the business at hand momentous. In a letter to his friend and future editor Thomas Flower Ellis on 30 March 1831, Macaulay recorded his excitement during the vote on the first reading of the Reform Bill, which was won by the reformers by a margin of one. "It was like seeing Caesar stabbed in the Senate-House, or seeing Oliver taking the mace from the table; a sight to be seen once only, and never to be forgotten." When the votes were counted, "the jaw of Peel fell; and the face of Twiss was as the face of a damned soul; and Herries looked like Judas taking off his neck-tie for the last operation." Macaulay left the House, passing through crowds cheering and throwing their hats in the air, called a cab, "and the first thing the driver asked was, 'Is the bill carried?' 'Yes, by one.' 'Thank God for it, sir.' And away I rode to Gray's Inn." The comparisons with Caesar and Cromwell, as well as the conversation with the deferential cabby, suggest the sincere belief that England had just avoided a revolt of the lower classes, with resultant lawlessness and economic ruin. "Reform that you may preserve" had been the explicit or implied message of all Macaulay's speeches on the bill and was to become the main political theme of his *The History of England*. But the detail of Judas's neck-tie also suggests the author's obvious enjoyment of the fight. There were still some anxious moments ahead for Macaulay's party, but in the meantime, as the letter to Ellis continued, "as for me, I am . . . a lion."

The process of lionization involved invitations to Lord Grey's official residence at 10 Downing Street and also to Holland House, the seat of Lord Holland and unofficial headquarters of the Whig party. In a letter of 8 July 1831 to his sister Hannah, Macaulay described his reception at Downing Street: "Lady Holland . . . gave me a most gracious reception . . . and told me in her imperial decisive manner that had she talked with all the principal men on our side about my speech—that they all agreed that it was the best that had been made since the death of Fox. . . ." For a man who was only thirty years old, this praise was very flattering, but since Macaulay had neither wealth nor important family connections to help him rise in the world, such compliments had an even more important practical value.

The eventual passage of the Reform Bill meant that the pocket borough of Calne no longer had a seat in Parliament, but with Lord Lansdowne's continued support, Macaulay was appointed secretary to the Board of Trade at £1,200 per year and became Whig candidate for a new parliamentary seat in the industrial city of Leeds. Since the family firm of Macaulay and Babington was now near bankruptcy, the £1,200 and the additional lucrative offices which the government found for his father and brother were very gratifying to the promising politician. And one would expect him to have been supremely content when he won the Leeds election for the first reformed Parliament over the Tory Michael Sadler, whose theories on population he had earlier attacked with gusto in the *Edinburgh*.

Macaulay in 1832, when he stood successfully for the parliamentary seat of the newly enfranchised industrial borough Leeds. Drawing by I. N. Rhodes (British Library).

But on election night he was more intensely unhappy than he had ever been—and for reasons that almost nobody guessed until Sir George Otto Trevelyan's official biography of his uncle, *The Life and Letters of Lord Macaulay,* was published nearly half a century later. Macaulay's combativeness, his frequently expressed enthusiasm for common sense, and his glorification of material progress all tend to give the impression that he was a rather unemotional and insensitive man. The fact that he neither married nor carried on liaisons contributed to the same impression. His contemporary Walter Bagehot wrote, in an 1856 essay for the *National Review,* of his "inexperiencing nature . . . unalive to joys and sorrows," and twentieth-century critic Mario Praz described him, in *The Hero in Eclipse in Victorian Fiction* (1956), as a man with "a mind free of passion and emotion."

In fact, Macaulay was emotionally vulnerable. This side of his character can be seen in his dealings with his father, and surely the masculine aggressiveness of his public persona was to some extent a defense mechanism. On the night of the Leeds election, he was handed a letter informing him that one of his two favorite sisters, Margaret, was to be married, and suddenly he felt that the world had ended. "I am sitting in the midst of two hundred friends," he wrote to his other favorite sister, Hannah, "all glorying over the Tories, and thinking me the happiest man in the world. And it is all that I can do to hide my tears and to command my voice. . . . Dearest, dearest, girl, you alone are now left to me.—Whom have I on *earth* but thee— . . . But for you, in the midst of all these successes, I should wish that I were lying by poor Hyde Villiers. But I cannot go on. . . . But the separation from dear Margaret has jarred my whole temper. I am cried up here to the skies as the most affable and kind hearted of men, while I feel a fierceness and restlessness within me quite new and almost inexplicable."

This passage captures both the intensity of Macaulay's feelings and the fact that he managed to keep those feelings hidden from almost everybody who knew him. Indeed modern readers with a Freudian bias will find it easy enough to account for the fierceness and restlessness which Macaulay himself found inexplicable. Obviously Macaulay is an inviting target for the iconoclast. Some notion of his public image can be taken from the statement which Stephen Dedalus hears a priest make in *A Portrait of the Artist as a Young Man* (1916): "I believe that Lord Macaulay was a man who probably never committed a mortal sin in his life, that is to say, a deliberate mortal sin." A celibate Victorian sage widely believed to have been without stain or spot but inwardly tormented by incestuous passions is an appealing image for anybody bent on attacking Victorian respectability, and Macaulay's relationships with his demanding father and his two adoring young sisters were both tormented and decidedly peculiar. The examples of Wordsworth, Lamb, and any number of characters in Jane Austen's novels serve, however, as reminders that brothers and sisters were more often devoted to each other in early-nineteenth-century England than in most times and places. Conflicts between fathers and sons are common in any age, but the examples of Macaulay, John Stuart Mill, and Sir Edmund Gosse certainly suggest that being the son of a Victorian Evangelical or Utilitarian was a particularly uncomfortable situation. Presumably Macaulay's conflicts with his father had some role in creating his intense feelings for Margaret and Hannah—John Clive, in his biography *Macaulay: The Shaping of the Historian* (1973), suggests that the girls allowed him to play the role of father, supplanting Zachary Macaulay—and clearly his feelings for these sisters led him into a series of traumatic experiences in the period from 1832 to 1834.

After Margaret's marriage, Macaulay's sister Hannah became her brother's favorite and confidante. His political and literary careers continued to prosper. The Whigs remained in power after the 1832 elections, so Macaulay and his relatives continued to draw their salaries. He made a successful speech on the reform of the East India Company, advocating the appointment to the company's Supreme Council of one legislative member who would not be a company employee. When the position was later offered to him, at the recommendation of his old opponent James Mill, Macaulay was definitely grateful. This office carried an annual salary of £10,000—of which at least half could be saved—giving him the prospect of the kind of financial independence he desperately wanted. Without such resources he would need to depend on either his writing or on his political offices, offices which depended on his party's being in power and on his support of party policy. In 1832 he had nearly had to resign from the Board of Control over his disagreements with the government's cautious policy on the abolition of West Indian slavery. Luckily the government amended its bill so that he could support it, but such a resolution of conflict could hardly be counted on in the future.

Macaulay did decide to take the position in India, but the decision was painful. The prospect of leaving his family, his friends, his country, and his promising political career was daunting, but when Hannah consented to accompany him, he felt that his exile would be entirely bearable. And after a six-month ocean voyage and his arrival in Madras on 10 June 1834, he traveled enthusiastically across the subcontinent to meet with the governor-general, Lord William Bentinck, at Ootacamund. This trip, in which Macaulay was carried in a palanquin by native bearers, is recorded in a series of letters that show his appreciation for both the natural scenery and man-made monuments of India. The ruins of Seringapatam interested him because his uncle General Colin Macaulay had participated in the famous siege of 1798. The ruined courts reminded him of the college quadrangles at Oxford and Cambridge, the Indian jungles reminded him, as he wrote to his sister Margaret on 3 October 1834, of "the works of the great English landscape-gardeners," and a mountain view of the plain of Mysore moved him "almost to tears."

After this lyrical introduction to Indian life, Macaulay's situation deteriorated rapidly. When he arrived at Calcutta, he found that Hannah, like Margaret, was about to be "lost" to him through marriage to Charles Trevelyan, a young officer of the East India Company whom she had met during the voyage from England. In the shaping of Macaulay's personality, most biographers seem to give primary importance to the influence of Zachary Macaulay's paternal enormities, but the loss of his two favorite sisters was also crucial in the final forming of Macaulay's private life and consequently of his political and literary careers. For whatever reason, he never seems to have taken any step that could reasonably have led to marriage. His erotic impulses seem to have been sublimated, and his domestic affections were fully satisfied by his sisters. Obviously such arrangements do not last, all of which was clear enough to Macaulay after the sisters he had relied on had gone. As he wrote to Margaret on 7 December 1834, "Whatever I have suffered I have brought on myself. I have neglected the plainest lessons of reason and experience. . . . it is the tragical denouement of an absurd plot." In any event, he gave his full support to Hannah Macaulay's match and did his best not to let her realize how much the thought of her marriage made him suffer.

If his loss had consisted simply in his sisters' getting married, Macaulay might eventually have recovered. He moved in with the Trevelyans and, despite his considerable misgivings, the arrangement worked out well. He and Trevelyan became reasonably good friends, and when Hannah had children, he became a doting uncle. But shortly after the wedding, news arrived that Margaret had died of typhoid fever during the preceding August, four months before Macaulay had written the letter concerning Hannah's engagement. On 8 February 1835 he confessed to Thomas Flower Ellis that "I never knew before what it was to be miserable. . . . Even now, when time has begun to do its healing office, I cannot write about her without being altogether unmanned. That I have not altogether sunk under this blow I owe chiefly to literature. What a blessing it is to love books as I love them—to be able to converse with the dead and to live amidst the unreal." On 29 May he wrote again to Ellis, saying "my time is divided between public business and books. . . . My spirits have not yet recovered—I sometimes think they will never wholly recover—from the shock which they received five months ago." Fifteen years later, on 8 April 1849, Macaulay recorded in his journal a visit to Lichfield Cathedral. When he looked at a statue of some children, he "could think only of one thing; that, when last I was there, in 1832, my dear sister Margaret was with me, and that she was greatly affected. I could not command my tears, and was forced to leave our party and walk about by myself." Like the letter he wrote to Hannah on the election night at Leeds, the journal passage is striking for the intensity of the feelings it expresses and for Macaulay's effort to disguise them.

His initial reaction to Margaret's death was, as he suggested in the letter to Ellis, to bury himself in work and escapist reading. He did a great deal of important official work, but his extensive private reading was perhaps even more significant. At the end of 1835 he wrote to Ellis, saying that "the tremendous blow which fell upon me at the beginning of this year has left marks behind it which I shall carry to my grave. Literature has saved my life and my reason. Even now, I dare not, in the intervals of business, remain alone for a minute without a book in my hand. . . . I am half determined to abandon politics, and to give myself wholly to letters; to undertake some great historical work which may be at once the business and the amusement of my life." So the plan of *The History of England* emerged during this period—and in part at least because Macaulay had found literature so effective an escape from a pain that he found almost unbearable. When he told Ellis he was fortunate to be "able to converse with the dead and live amidst the unreal," he hit on the source of both much of his strength and much of his weakness as a writer.

George Otto Trevelyan has noted how Macaulay and Hannah talked about books in such a way that "a bystander would have supposed that they had lived in the times which the author treated, and had a personal acquaintance with every human being who was mentioned in his pages." Margaret Macaulay, in her journal for 30 March 1831, had recorded Macaulay's admission that he owed his accuracy in facts to his habit of "castle-building": a habit of imagining conversations between historical characters. "I am no sooner in the streets than I am in Greece, in Rome, in the midst of the French Revolution. Precision in dates, the day or hour in which a man was born or died, become absolutely necessary. A slight fact, a sentence, a word, are of importance in my romance." This comment suggests one reason behind his ability to write vivid historical narrative. But the habit he described to Ellis of conversing with the dead led to his developing violent prejudices about historical figures, prejudices which sometimes dis-

Macaulay's sister Hannah. She and Margaret Macaulay were his favorites, and, in the words of Macaulay's biographer John Clive, "it was these two younger sisters . . . upon whom alone was focused the strongly developed emotional side of his nature."

torted his understanding of historical evidence. Furthermore, the word *romance* suggests a certain escapist dimension often noted in Macaulay's historical writings. Escapist daydreams were particularly necessary to him during the painful first year in India, but they were important throughout his life. In a late letter to Ellis he wrote that he and Hannah "indulge[d] beyond any people I ever knew" in "the habit of building castles in the air" and that he thought it significant that the Greek term for this habit translated as "empty happiness."

In 1835, however, Macaulay was quite willing to settle for happiness of any kind. Escapist castle-building and reading (for example, one of Plutarch's lives in Greek or one of Calderón's plays in Spanish before breakfast each day plus heavy reading in the evenings) were supplemented by prodigious work during the day as legal member of the Supreme Council. In this capacity he produced two works of particular importance: the Minute on Indian Education and the Indian Penal Code. The former was perhaps the more important of the two because it decided the course of Indian higher education for at least 150 years. A considerable debate had been waged for years before Macaulay's arrival in India over the proper subjects for such education, with two schools of thought emerging. The Orientalists favored instruction in the Sanskrit and Arabic classics; the Anglicists argued for the English language as the medium of instruction. Instruction in the modern Indian vernacular languages was not considered a viable option by either party because it was believed that there was insufficient worthwhile reading matter available in these languages. Macaulay predictably supported the Anglicist position. Since Sanskrit and Arabic were as much "foreign" languages as English, Macaulay saw the issue as a simple one: "whether, when we can patronize sound philosophy and true history, we shall countenance, at the public expense, medical doctrines which would disgrace an English farrier—astronomy, which would move laughter in the girls at an English boarding-school—history, abounding with kings thirty feet high, and reigns thirty thousand years long—and geography, made up of seas of treacle and seas of butter." Hooghly College was consequently opened in Calcutta in 1836 as an English-language institution, and English remained the primary language of instruction in Indian schools (and eventually universities) throughout the British period and still plays an important role today. This fact has had incalculable effects on the spread of Western thought and national consciousness in India, and it is not surprising that Indian opinion has been divided over the merits of Macaulay's position.

The Indian penal code, like the education minute, has been criticized for its attempt to impose a new and foreign system on Indian life. This code was a much more substantial work than the minute—running with its notes to approximately 200 pages and being almost completely Macaulay's own work. The work was completed in May 1837, taking something under two years—compared with nine for the French Code Napoleon and three and one half for Livingstone's Code for Louisiana. Macaulay, by his own account, "changed the whole plan ten or twelve times" and yet had the vexation to find that it was not adopted in his lifetime. It was, however, adopted in 1860, providing a clear and compact guide for Indian civil servants, "the younger of whom," Trevelyan noted, "carry it about in their saddle-bags, and the older in their heads." But in 1837 the code seemed too radical and too simple, to take too little account of existing Indian laws. And Macaulay himself was not a popular public figure. He had helped pass two laws, which in combination caused him considerable trouble. The first was the "Black Act," which placed Englishmen outside Calcutta under the same courts as native Indians and was intensely resented by Anglo-Indians. Since the second law was the Censorship Act, which deregulated the Anglo-Indian press, this resentment was freely expressed. The physical climate of India seems never to have bothered Macaulay, and the political climate was an annoyance rather than a serious problem. He had been used to hostile journalists in England and had private sorrows that made Calcutta editorials seems insignificant, but he had not had a pleasant time in the East, and by the end of 1837 he was ready to leave. He had invested much of his princely salary and had inherited an additional £10,000 from his uncle General Macaulay, so his purpose in going to India had been accomplished; he need never worry about money again.

While in the East he had written two more essays for the *Edinburgh Review*, the first of which placed his life in considerable danger and the second of which has been similarly disastrous for his reputation. The first, "Sir James Mackintosh's *History of the Revolution*" (July 1835), was a review of Mackintosh's fragmentary history of the Glorious Revolution of 1688, as completed and edited by a certain Mr. Wallace. Wallace had appeared to be excessively critical of Mackintosh, and since Macaulay admired and liked Mackintosh, he attacked Wallace with what he later admitted was "an asperity . . . which ought to be reserved for offences against the laws of morality and honour." The review appeared in July 1835; when Macaulay returned to England three years later in the summer of 1838 (having spent the long sea journey home learning German), Wallace sent him an entirely serious challenge to a duel. Macaulay had no experience with firearms, but since the challenge had been made in a correct and gentlemanly manner, he saw no way out of a situation very likely to be fatal. Wallace was, however, persuaded to say that he had intended no disrespect to Mackintosh, Macaulay expressed regret that he had used excessive language as a result of having misunderstood Wallace's intention, and the confrontation was avoided.

The essay on Francis Bacon (July 1837), the other *Edinburgh Review* article from the Indian years, is one of Macaulay's best-known and most unfortunate writings. "Lord Bacon," wrote Walter Houghton in *The Victorian Frame of Mind* (1957), is the *locus classicus* of Victorian anti-intellectualism, and it has certainly had a major role in creating the popular image of its author as a complacent, insensitive, and belligerent boor. In depicting Bacon, the essay presents the most exaggerated of Macaulay's antithetical characters: "the difference between the soaring angel and the creeping snake was but the type of the difference between Bacon the philosopher and Bacon the Attorney-General . . . in one line the boldest and most useful of innovators, in another one the most obstinate champion of the foulest abuses." In Macaulay's essay Bacon's moral character is blackened, while his useful, practical, limited philosophy is praised as the basis for Western progress. Plato and other ancient philosophers "promised what was impracticable; they despised what was practicable; they filled the world with long words and long beards; and they left it as wicked as they found it," but Bacon's focus on the inductive method and on practical "fruit" has done a great deal "to make imperfect men comfortable." Thus Bacon becomes in Macaulay's hands a seventeenth-century Utilitarian who gave mankind the intellectual key to progress, with the result that "the books which have been written in the languages of Europe during the last two hundred and fifty years—translations from the ancient languages of course included,—are of greater value than all the books which at the beginning of that period were extant in the world." The important parenthetical clause about translations from the ancients is often unjustly overlooked by critics eager to pillory Macaulay, and these same critics tend erroneously to assume that he is describing his own tastes. In fact Macaulay himself read ancient literature (including Plato) without benefit of translations and generally preferred it to modern work. His statements in the Bacon essay are concerned with the books—including works on medicine and the natural sciences in general—that were of most value to most people, not simply to those people who had the advantages of the classical education that he himself had enjoyed. Furthermore, this essay was written in India when the author was miserably unhappy and even worried about losing his mind. His exaggerated praise of practical reason and reliable material progress should be seen in this context.

As soon as the threat of the duel with Wallace was out of the way, Macaulay set off for a long tour of France and Italy, leaving in October 1838 and returning in February 1839. In Italy he was vexed by the dirt and the corrupt officials but fascinated and invigorated by the classical associations. He passed scenes described by Livy and Tacitus and worked on his one collection of published poems, *Lays of Ancient Rome*. These poems, begun in India and eventually published in 1842, were attempts to reconstruct primitive Roman ballads which—the German historian Barthold Niebuhr had suggested—were the probable sources of Livy's stories in the early books of his *History*. Macaulay never took these poems very seriously, but they were widely read, and one—"How Horatius Kept the Bridge"—was memorized and declaimed by countless schoolboys over the next hundred years. In 1846 the book was already so widely circulated that the American historian Francis Parkman found a man reading it in the distinctly nonliterary setting of the Oregon Trail.

The Mackintosh essay, as well as the one on Sir William Temple (*Edinburgh Review*, October 1838) which he wrote shortly after returning from India, reflects Macaulay's lingering uncertainty about the future shape of his career. Mackintosh had so divided himself between politics and historical scholarship as to make no great figure in either field. Similarly Temple seemed to Macaulay to be culpably unable to stick to either politics or literature. Temple, he tells his readers, "avoided the great offices of the state with a caution almost pusillanimous . . . and while the nation groaned under oppression, or resounded with tumult and with the din of civil arms, amused himself by writing memoirs and tying up apricots." As this passage suggests, Macaulay was feeling the moral claims of public life at this point. While in India, he had written to his friend Ellis (30 December 1835) that the essence of a British political career seemed to be "pestiferous rooms, sleepless nights, aching heads, and diseased stomachs," but now he was more impressed by the demands which the embattled Whig party placed on his services. As late as 5 September 1839, the Duke of Wellington wrote to his friend Lady Wilson that Lord Melbourne "would prefer to sit in a Room with a Chime of Bells, ten Parrots and one Lady Westmoreland to sitting in Cabinet with Mr. Macaulay," but only fifteen days later, Macaulay, having been elected MP for Edinburgh, did join Melbourne's cabinet as secretary-at-war.

He held this position until the Whig ministry fell in July 1841. While in office he had the interesting task of interrogating a lunatic who had tried to assassinate Queen Victoria and the difficult duty of defending both government policy in the opium war with China and the military conduct of Lord Cardigan, the same Lord Cardigan who later led the Light Brigade to disaster at Balaclava. His speeches were as persuasive as the situations would permit, but he seems not to have been particularly upset when the fall of the Whigs released him from office. He had begun *The History of England* on 9 March 1839, right after returning from his Continental tour, and was really more interested in literary work than in politics. He was completing the *Lays of Ancient Rome* and continuing his work with the *Edinburgh Review.* Meanwhile *The History of England* was not getting enough attention, so he had plenty to do without trying to run the war office. He did not want to share the fate of Mackintosh, who never finished his history. On 12 July 1841 he took rooms in the Albany on Piccadilly, which, at different times, was also home to Byron and William Gladstone, and began to work on *The History of England* in earnest.

After his return from the Continental tour, he wrote twelve more essays for the *Edinburgh Review* before his determination to devote himself entirely to *The History of England* made him give up reviewing altogether after 1844. Two of the earliest of these essays were devoted to religious themes, one on the Church of England and the other on the papacy. The April 1839 criticism of Gladstone's *The State in Its Relations with the Church* (1838) is a useful reminder that the future Liberal prime minister was at this time a very conservative Tory and Tractarian who sought to make the British government a thoroughly Anglican institution. While Macaulay was entirely opposed to the idea of a religiously exclusive government, his essay is noteworthy for its courteous treatment of its opponent. The ad hominem attacks that had been part of Macaulay's earlier *Edinburgh Review* manner were part of the past. Perhaps Gladstone's erudition, amiable behavior, and obvious sincerity brought out Macaulay's generosity. Certainly Macaulay's own success was a factor. He was no longer an impecunious young man trying to fight his way into politics and journalism by savage attacks on eminent Tories such as Southey or Croker, nor was he a miserable exile in India venting his unhappiness in vilification of writers who had been dead for hundreds of years. He was financially independent; the Trevelyan family provided him with a good measure of the domestic happiness which he had thought lost forever; and he was about to reenter Parliament and become a minister. He could afford to treat young Mr. Gladstone generously. His other religious essay, an October 1840 review of Leopold von Ranke's *Ecclesiastical and Political History of the Popes,* published in English translation earlier that year, shows the same moderation and courtesy. He speaks of Ranke with respect and treats the rival claims of Protestantism and Catholicism fairly. He also helps define his notions about progress by making clear that he did not see religious truth to be progressive. "The ingenuity of a people just emerging from barbarism is quite sufficient to propound" the great problems of religious thought. "The genius of Locke or Clarke is quite unable to solve them."

From 1840 to 1842 three essays dealt with eighteenth-century figures who, in their combination of political and military leadership, look forward to William III in *The History of England.* Lord Clive (treated in conjunction with Sir John Malcolm's 1836 biography in January 1840) and Warren Hastings (the subject of an October 1841 piece) presumably interested Macaulay because he had been one of their successors in governing British India; Frederick the Great (April 1842) would, Macaulay thought, have an important role in *The History of England* since he had been England's chief ally in the Seven Years War. All three essays show Macaulay exulting in the heroic aspects of military narrative—however much he might in theory have detested war and attributed all solid human happiness to the fruits of quiet industry and the joys of the domestic hearth. In the Cambridge lectures that were posthumously published as *A Commentary on Macaulay's History of England* (1938), Sir Charles Firth observed that Macaulay "rejoiced like the war horse in *Job,* when he sniffed a battle afar off, a thing very becoming in a former Secretary at War." British troops in a thin red line overcoming hordes of bloodthirsty Marathas or the Prussian army withstanding the combined might of France, Austria, and Russia were clearly inspiring images for him—as inspiring as they could possibly have been to Kipling or Carlyle—despite Macaulay's relative reluctance to make excuses for the faults of military heroes.

In his 1960 essay "Macaulay: The Indian Years, 1834-38," the historian Eric Stokes remarked that the essays on Clive and Hastings show little sign that their author had lived in India, but his essays on Restoration comedy (January 1841), Fanny Burney, later Madame d'Arblay (January 1843), and Joseph Addison (July 1843) allowed Macaulay to write about the entirely congenial subject of literary life in the Restoration and eighteenth century. He had given up literary criticism because he was dissatisfied with his work—"I have never written a page of criticism of poetry, or the fine arts, which I would not burn if I had the power," he told McVey Napier in an 1838 letter. But he was quite at home discussing the lives and times of writers and including some consideration of their works, rather in the manner of Dr. Johnson's *Lives of the Poets* (1779-1781) but with an emphasis much more biographical and historical. The writers of this period were very real to Macaulay. His castle-building never apparently involved Indian sights or sounds, but he was imaginatively an intimate of Whitehall in the days of Charles II, of the coffeehouses in the days of Queen Anne, and of Dr. Johnson's circle in the days of George III. He insisted—in opposition to Charles Lamb—that the characters of William Wycherley's and Sir George Etheredge's plays were all too real reflections of the morals of their time. He defended Addison against the attacks of Alexander Pope and seized on Fanny Burney's ill-treatment as a lady-in-waiting to Queen Charlotte to express his indignation at the tyranny of George III.

In the early 1840s unauthorized collections of Macaulay's essays were being published in America and sold in Britain. Macaulay had decided in June 1842 not to republish his essays in an authorized edition because he did not want to be judged by them. "The public judges, and ought to judge, indulgently of periodical works," he wrote to Napier on 24 June. "They are not expected to be highly finished works. Their natural life is only six weeks." Essays, he noted, often contain errors and lack structure, but "all this is readily forgiven if there be a certain spirit and vivacity in the style." Republished articles, however, must meet a higher standard, and Macaulay was not at all sure that his would measure up to such a standard. By December, however, he had changed his mind: if he collected the essays himself, he could at least make sure that the texts were correct, that the least impressive essays were excluded, that the least justifiable passages of the remainder were revised, and that the royalties were paid to the author himself. The edition of *Critical and Historical Essays, Contributed to the Edinburgh Review,* which appeared in April 1843, was something of a publishing phenomenon. It sold out quickly and was succeeded by second, third, and fourth editions—which also sold out—and each year the public bought more copies than the year before. By 1876 Trevelyan claimed that the Longman edition alone had sold 120,000 copies, with 130,000 copies of individually published essays having been sold in the Traveler's Library series as well. Indeed, Trevelyan concluded, the British market for the essays "is so steady, and apparently so inexhaustible, that it perceptibly falls and rises with the general prosperity of the nation; and it is not too much to say that the demand for Macaulay varies with the demand for coal."

In this same year in which he collected his previously published essays from the *Edinburgh Review,* Macaulay made his last contribution to the journal. In April 1844 he indignantly denounced the "Jacobin carrion" Bertrand Barère and in October 1844 wrote his second essay dealing with William Pitt, the Earl of Chatham, narrating the vicissitudes of the statesman's later years. These last few essays on eighteenth-century soldiers, writers, and statesmen are among Macaulay's most successful, but he decided that if *The History of England* was ever to be completed, he would have to stop writing for the *Edinburgh Review.* As he wrote Napier on 6 December 1844, "but for the Review I should already have brought out two volumes at least. I really must make a resolute effort. Or my plan will end as our poor friend Mackintosh's ended." So a resolute effort was made, but while reviewing was now a thing of the past, politics was still a powerful distraction. Macaulay was still a member of Parliament and in July 1846 was persuaded to reenter the cabinet, this time as paymaster-general of the army in Lord John Russell's ministry. This position, he was relieved to discover, took up less of his time than he had expected, so progress on *The History of England* continued satisfactorily, and in July 1847 political distractions ended abruptly. To almost everybody's surprise, Macaulay lost both his place in the cabinet and his

"Unhappy ghosts wandering on the banks of Styx," sketch by John Doyle depicting the outcome of the 1847 elections to Parliament. Macaulay leads the defeated along the riverbank while John Bull as Charon takes the victors to their reward (British Library).

seat in the House of Commons in that month's general election.

Since this event constitutes the only serious career setback that Macaulay ever experienced, it calls for some explanation. Like many nationally prominent politicians, he had tended to neglect the voters of his own constituency. He rarely visited Edinburgh and seems to have thought that courting the voters was beneath his dignity. It never seems to have occurred to him to solicit their opinions, much less let those opinions have any effect on the speeches he gave or the votes he cast as their representative in Parliament. The single act which had apparently created most indignation among the Edinburgh electors was Macaulay's speech on 14 April 1845 supporting a Tory bill to almost triple the annual government grant to the Roman Catholic seminary at Maynooth in Ireland. He was always willing to attack what he saw as religious bigotry and was particularly unwilling to make any political accommodation on religious matters. In the Leeds election campaign of 1832, for example, a Methodist minister asked at a public meeting for a statement of Mr. Macaulay's religious creed. For his pains he was treated like a criminal. The candidate insisted that the questioner stand up and then replied that "I have heard with the greatest shame and sorrow the question that has been proposed to me; and with peculiar pain do I learn that this question was proposed by a minister of religion." After going on to denounce the luckless clergyman at length for what he called "this disgraceful inquisition," Macaulay said only that he was a Christian and then roundly scolded the audience for having applauded his answer.

Presumably Macaulay did not get the Methodist minister's vote in the Leeds election, and by July 1847 a large number of Edinburgh electors were concerned both by the religious policies of their M.P. and by his contemptuous dismissal of all such concerns as disgusting bigotry. The electors were not so obviously in the wrong as might now seem to have been the case. After all, Parliament routinely passed laws on religious matters, and Macaulay himself was not above being affected in his official actions by his religious biases. As paymaster-general, he had had the opportunity to award what he called "a tolerable piece of patronage," the chaplaincy of Chelsea Hospital. This position "would be an exceedingly pleasant situation for a literary man," he told Ellis, but "nothing shall induce me to take a Puseyite." The Puseyite (High Church Anglican) vote in Edinburgh was presumably small, and the electors did not have the advantage of reading Macaulay's private letters, but the Church of Scotland had recently split and Protestant passions were running high. The Maynooth speech had used the Scottish schism to point out that even established Protestant churches could not agree on doctrine and that only one of the contending parties within such churches could possibly be right. This idea could not but give offense, and the opposition was not above making full use of Macaulay's words in its attempt to unseat him. On 30 July 1847 he finished third in the poll, and that night he wrote some verse consoling himself with the thought that he had defied "a sullen priesthood and a raving mob" amid "hate's yell, and envy's hiss, and folly's bray." No doubt the defeat rankled, but the release from politics was welcome. He refused several offers to have his name put in nomination for other seats in Parliament and turned his full attention to *The History of England.* In November 1848 the students of Glasgow decided to show their superiority over the rival city of Edinburgh by electing Macaulay lord rector of their university, and, soon after, this vote of confidence was followed by the publication of the first two volumes of *The History of England from the Accession of James II.*

The History of England was the great, culminating work of Macaulay's career, the performance for which the *Edinburgh Review* articles had been merely rehearsals. In one of the earlier of those articles, simply called "History" and published in May 1828, he had set out his notions of how historians should write, and clearly many of these ideas were still among his shaping concepts in the 1840s when he wrote the first volumes of *The History of England.* After lamenting, in his most insufferable early *Edinburgh Review* manner, that "we are acquainted with no history which approaches to our notion of what a history ought to be," he reviewed the classic historians from Herodotus to Hume and found them all, to varying degrees, unsatisfactory. Herodotus thought like a child; Plutarch was a revolutionary fanatic. Thucydides was an impressive narrator but did not understand the importance of social history. Modern historians, such as Hume or Gibbon, were more analytical than the ancients, but they also failed to tell the truth. Herodotus, in Macaulay's opinion, "tells his story like a slovenly witness," while "Hume is an accomplished advocate" out to win a case. The ideal historian should be an impartial judge and should combine the literary art of the ancients with the modern understanding that political revolutions "are almost always the consequences of moral changes, which have gradually passed on the mass of the community, and which originally proceed far before their progress is indicated by any public measure." The failure to emphasize social, intellectual, and economic history was what Macaulay found most unsatisfactory in other historians. "He who would understand these things rightly must not confine his observations to palaces and solemn days. He must mingle in the crowds of the exchange and coffee-house. He must obtain admittance to the convivial table and the domestic hearth." The image of the historian walking about in a past age is clearly reminiscent of Macaulay's statements to his sister Margaret about castle-building, and there can be little doubt that already in 1828 he saw himself as the ideal historian who would give "to truth those attractions which have been usurped by fiction" and write a history that would be as popular and as sensitive to social details as Sir Walter Scott's Waverley Novels.

The *Edinburgh Review* essays had already met the standard of popularity, but they did not give their author the scope he needed for the kind of social history his theories required. The later ones were, he said, after the manner of Plutarch rather than Thucydides, biographies of great men rather than histories of a whole nation. When he came to *The History of England* itself, he confided to Ellis that at least he hoped to "produce something which shall for a few days supercede the last fashionable novel on the tables of young ladies," but in his journal he admitted that "I have tried to do something that may be remembered; I have had the year 2000, and even the year 3000, often in my mind."

The History of England was, however, firmly linked to the present, stretching from "the accession of King James the Second down to a time which is within the memory of men still living," as the opening page announced, linking the Glorious Revolution of 1688, which "brought the Crown into harmony with the Parliament," and the Great Reform Bill of 1832, "which brought the Parliament into harmony with the nation." In fact, *The History of England* is actually a fragment, ending with the death of William III in 1702, but the first two volumes, published in 1848, are a complete treatment of the Glorious Revolution in ten chapters. These volumes, and *The History of England* as a whole, are structured around a conflict between James II—representing the tyranny of Stuart absolutism and the superstition of Roman Catholic bigotry—and William III, representing constitutional monarchy and freedom of conscience. William is portrayed as brave, merciful, and wise; his life with Queen Mary is presented as an admirable example of domestic affection. James, meanwhile, is depicted as a coward, a sadist, a fool, and a lecher. Finally, James and his brother Charles II are seen as having made England an international nonentity under the control of Louis XIV; William, on the contrary, rallied Europe against the threat of French militarism and began the series of wars—stretching through the eighteenth century and finally ending only at Waterloo—by which England replaced France as the first nation of Europe.

William is a minor character until chapter seven. The first three chapters set the scene—describing the constitutional questions of the seventeenth century, sketching the characters of the major political figures of the period, and giving a vivid account of the state of the country at the accession of James in 1685. This account, the famous third chapter, is today the most frequently read section of *The History of England* and the one in which Macaulay tries hardest to demonstrate his assertion in the opening paragraphs of chapter one that "the history of our country during the last hundred and fifty years is eminently the history of physical, of moral, and of intellectual improvement." The physical improvement is perhaps the easiest kind to document, something Macaulay does throughout the third chapter—and elsewhere—whenever he can compare the seventeenth-century appearance of a town or a patch of countryside with its more attractive Victorian splendor. In Victorian London, for example, the Thames is spanned by "several bridges, not inferior in magnificence and solidity to the noblest works of the Caesars. In 1685, a single line of irregular arches, overhung by piles of mean and crazy houses, and garnished, after a fashion worthy of the naked barbarians of Dahomey, with scores of moldering heads, impeded the navigation of the river." Travel between towns was agonizingly slow, prohibitively expensive, and terribly dangerous. The towns themselves were dirty, small, unlit, and infested with beggars, bullies, and footpads, while huge tracts of countryside, totaling "a fourth part of England," had, in the last two centuries, been "turned from a wild into a garden."

Intellectual progress is illustrated both by the advancement of knowledge and by its spread. "Every bricklayer who falls from a scaffold, every sweeper of a crossing who is run over by a carriage, may now have his wounds dressed and his limbs set with a skill such as, a hundred and sixty years ago, all the wealth of a great lord like Ormond . . . could not have purchased." Nor was available knowledge as widespread in the seventeenth century as in the nineteenth. "Few knights of the shire had libraries so good as may now perpetually be found in a servants' hall, or in the back parlor of a small shopkeeper. An esquire passed among his neighbors for a great scholar, if Hudibras and Baker's Chronicle, Tarlton's Jests and the Seven Champions of Christendom, lay in his hall window among his fishing rods and fowling pieces." But most important of all was the moral inferiority of old England—the cruelty which had led even good masters to beat their servants, crowds to exult at public executions, politicians to seek each other's blood, and prisons to be "hells on earth." The seventeenth century was devoid of "that sensitive and restless compassion which has, in our own time, extended a powerful protection to the factory child, to the Hindoo widow, to the Negro slave . . . and which has repeatedly endeavored to save the life even of the murderer." The third chapter of *The History of England* has given much offense—both for its disparagement of the seventeenth-century clergy and gentry and for its apparent complacency concerning the Victorian scene in general and industrialism in particular. But the reduction of poverty, ignorance, and cruelty are admirable goals, and the chapter concludes with a clear expectation that life in Victorian England itself will seem very unsatisfactory when contrasted with life in the twentieth century.

The fourth chapter begins the narrative proper, showing James II proclaimed king and beginning his first steps toward imposing Roman Catholicism and royal absolutism. Chapter five describes the premature rebellions of the Earl of Argyle in Scotland and the Duke of Monmouth in southwestern England. Here Macaulay continues to contrast seventeenth-century poverty with Victorian prosperity. In his account of Argyle's followers sailing up the Clyde to Greenock, the reader is informed that this community was "then a small fishing village consisting of a single row of thatched hovels, now a great and flourishing port, of which the customs amount to more than five times the whole revenue which the Stuarts derived from the kingdom of Scotland." Similarly when the historian joins Monmouth in the steeple of Bridgewater parish church to survey the hostile royal army, he tells his audience how different the next day's battlefield of Sedgemoor looked in 1685. The sad fate of the rebels is the emotional high point of these early volumes. Argyle dies a heroic Protestant martyr prophesying deliverance for the country in the near future. Monmouth vainly begs for mercy from James, the cruel uncle whom he has wronged, and Judge Jeffreys descends on the rebellious counties to conduct sham trials both for rebels and for those completely harmless people who sheltered them. From here James goes on hubristically to impose ever greater tyrannies until the nobility, gentry, and clergy who had rallied to his cause against Monmouth are totally alienated. Now that the time is ripe, William descends upon England, is acclaimed by large numbers, and begins his advance on London, while more and more influential men desert King James. William does everything that a wise leader can do to guarantee the success of his cause, but his final victory is possible only because James is his own worst enemy. Merciless when victorious, he proves a coward when threatened and flees England, allowing Parliament to declare the throne vacant and to offer it to William and Mary.

As one might expect from the program laid out in the 1828 essay "History," Macaulay's narrative owes a good deal to such classical models as Tacitus, Plutarch, and Thucydides, but a stronger source of the history's popular appeal for its Victorian readers was its unmistakable series of biblical echoes. The Glorious Revolution was, among other things, a religious movement. William is the Protestant hero and the Deliverer. The martyred Earl of Argyle, with his premature uprising against James, serves as John the Baptist—a voice crying in the wilderness, beheaded by a tyrant, and prophesying the national salvation which he knows he will not live to see. Judge Jeffreys's victims are holy innocents, whose Christian piety and blameless lives are prominently emphasized, and William is clearly Christ-like. In the last chapter of volume two, for example, with the Revolution all but won and William triumphantly established in London, the new king tells a Dutch friend, "Here . . . the cry is all Hosannah today, and will, perhaps, be Crucify tomorrow."

To this religious appeal is added a patriotic one. William will not only lead England back to the greatness it had known under Elizabeth and Cromwell; he will also preserve the nation from the perils which beset so many European states in the mid-nineteenth century. The fact that the first part of *The History of England* appeared at the end of the revolutionary year 1848 allowed Macaulay to conclude it with his often-stated ideas about how chaos and barbarism could only be prevented by the timely adoption of reforms: "Now, if ever, we ought to be able to appreciate the whole importance of the stand which was made by our forefathers against the House of Stuart. All around us the world is convulsed by the agonies of great nations. Governments which lately seemed likely to stand during ages have been on a sudden shaken and overthrown. The proudest capitals of Western Europe have streamed with civil blood. . . . Meanwhile in our island the regular course of government has never been for a day interrupted. . . . And if it be asked what has made us to differ from others, the answer is that we never lost what others are wildly and blindly seeking to regain. It is because we had a preserving revolution in the seventeenth century that we have not had a destroying revolution in the nineteenth."

As the time of publication neared, Macaulay told his sister Hannah that "I have armed myself with all my philosophy for the event of a failure." The book was, after all, concerned with a period of British history that had never been considered particularly interesting, and there was always the danger that the author's partisan tone would alienate a great many readers. Furthermore, when Macaulay read a freshly printed copy of his own book along with a copy of Thucydides, he was reluctantly driven to the conclusion that the Greek historian's performance was, as he admitted in his journal, "much better than mine." The British reviewers and readers were, however, much more pleased with the book than its author was. By 4 December a second printing was called for, and by 12 December the author was told that "there has been no such sale since the days of *Waverley*." The second printing sold out almost as soon as it became available, and by 27 January 1849 the third printing was mostly gone. The early reviewers were universally flattering, with Tories rather unpredictably joining the Whig journals in praise of the Whig historian. Most remarkable, considering what Macaulay himself called the history's "insular spirit," was the fact that the work was also phenomenally popular in France and the United States. The author was more than a bit surprised by such enormous success but also clearly delighted, especially when he found a bookseller advertising Hume's Tory *History of England* (1754-1762) as being "highly valuable as an introduction to Macaulay."

By this time, he was already at work on volume three of his history. In August and September he took an extended trip to Ireland to examine the scenes of events which he would soon be describing, and except for similar trips to the Continent and occasional vacations in the countryside, his life was now centered in his study at the Albany and at the home of the Trevelyan family. In July 1852—without doing anything to advance his cause—Macaulay was returned to his old seat in Parliament by the contrite electors of Edinburgh, but almost immediately he suffered a heart attack which made it impossible for him to take a very active role in politics again. "Last July," he wrote in March 1853,

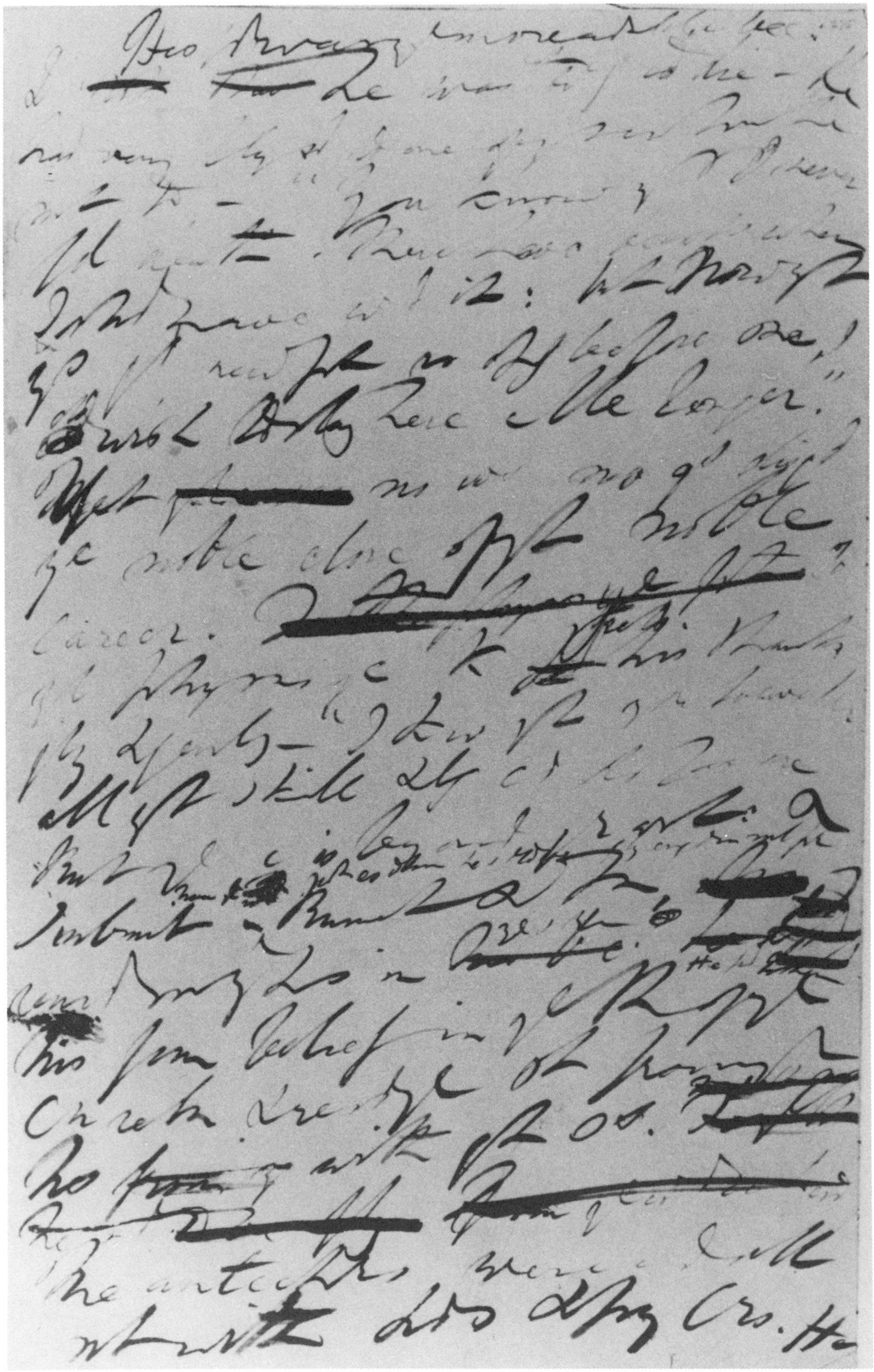

Page from the manuscript for volume five of Macaulay's The History of England *(by permission of the Trustees of The Pierpont Morgan Library)*

"I became twenty years older in a week." He did not suffer much pain and did not particularly fear death, but it was now necessary for him to avoid strenuous exertion, and he hated the thought of leaving *The History of England* after only two volumes. His original goal of reaching the 1832 Reform Bill was clearly now out of the question, but, he wrote in his journal, "I should be glad to finish William before I go."

The great honor done him by the Edinburgh electors was followed by others at home and abroad. In February he was elected to the French Institute and received the Prussian Order of Merit; in June he was awarded an honorary D.C.L. by Oxford University. In 1853 he also began the series of five brief biographies which he wrote during the next six years for the *Encyclopaedia Britannica.* The subjects were all drawn from the late-seventeenth century and the eighteenth century: John Bunyan, Francis Atterbury, Oliver Goldsmith, Samuel Johnson, and William Pitt the Younger. Johnson and Bunyan are subjects that he had already treated in *Edinburgh* reviews, and a comparison of these *Britannica* essays with Macaulay's earlier treatments of the same men shows him now adopting a less contentious persona and a less contrived prose style. These late essays are, in fact, much more in tune with *The History of England* than with the earlier reviews, and some desire to write more mature assessments of two of his favorite authors may have been Macaulay's main motive in doing the new pieces on Bunyan and Johnson. As for the others, it was now clear that *The History of England* was not likely to get far enough to allow Macaulay to deal with Atterbury, much less Goldsmith or the younger Pitt, so the essays gave him his one chance to assess men whom he found interesting and significant.

Nor were the essays for *Encyclopaedia Britannica* the only literary distraction from *The History of England* in these years. By 1853 a pirated American edition of Macaulay's speeches forced him to bring out his own collection. As with the collected essays ten years earlier, he omitted his least impressive performances, but while the essays had needed only minor corrections and occasional toning down, the speeches had to be almost entirely reconstructed. Macaulay's oral delivery in Parliament was so rapid that the official records in *Hansard's Parliamentary Debates* only furnished him with what he regarded as "hints" to assist him in rewriting the speeches from memory. And rewritten they were—as faithfully to the originals as their author could manage. But readers of the published speeches should be aware that the texts were prepared in 1853. In July 1853, for example, Macaulay spent a rainy day reconstructing his great speech of 5 July 1831 on the Reform Bill. Although he believed he had "made a speech very like the real one in language, and in substance exactly the real one," he was relying on memories that were twenty-two years old. During his trip to Ireland in 1849, he had found that he could still recite about half of *Paradise Lost,* suggesting that his memory was still strong, but it would be remarkable if the printed speeches did not include some improvements over the spoken ones. In any event, these texts are the best records available of Macaulay's parliamentary oratory, and like everything he wrote, they were well received. On the whole, however, he begrudged all the time the speeches took from *The History of England.* He knew that he could not live very many more years and was greatly relieved when volumes three and four finally appeared in December 1855.

The second installment of *The History of England* has generally been regarded as less impressive than the first, though it does contain some of Macaulay's best writing. Unfortunately, it has less obvious thematic and structural unity, and the central character of William III seems too uninteresting to carry the narrative. Volume three begins with a recasting of the Deliverer image, this time with the figure of Moses substituting for that of Christ. "From the time of the Exodus," Macaulay concedes, "the history of every great deliverer has been the history of Moses retold. Down to the present hour rejoicings like those on the shore of the Red Sea have ever been speedily followed by murmurings like those at the Waters of Strife." This passage signals the reaction which set in after the Revolution, with clergy and army having second thoughts about their desertion of King James, politicians renewing the partisan bickering which weakened England in its struggle with a unified, absolutist France, and the English people beginning to resent William's Dutch manners and Dutch favorites. Most urgent was the problem of Jacobite uprisings sweeping through the Scottish Highlands and overwhelming all of Ireland except for the two Protestant strongholds of Londonderry and Enniskillen.

The Irish and Scottish chapters of these volumes contribute the most vivid narratives. The relief of the siege of Londonderry, the Jacobite leader Claverhouse dying at the moment of victory at Killiecrankie in the Highlands, and William leading the charge that breaks the Jacobite resistance at the

Battle of the Boyne and opens the road to Dublin are dramatic, stirring events that Macaulay develops with obvious enthusiasm. The death of Queen Mary in 1694 gives him, in contrast, the material for a Victorian domestic tragedy. Mary is brave and devout, receiving the Eucharist, showing concern for her attendants' comfort, and attempting—when too weak to speak—"a last farewell of him whom she had loved so truly and entirely." William suffers "a series of fits so alarming that his Privy Councilors . . . were apprehensive for his reason and his life" and is finally carried "almost insensible" from the sickroom. The queen's death is mourned by the people, gloated over by scurrilous Jacobites, and honored by the king with the building at Greenwich of "the noblest of European hospitals"—now the Royal Naval College.

William is more consistently in the forefront of these volumes than in the earlier parts of *The History of England*, but much of his work consists of the unexciting task of coping with a Parliament which would rather engage in internal squabbles and in petty sniping at him than concentrate on the war with France. In the first two volumes of the history, the Whigs—for all their duly noted faults—are clearly superior to the Tories since they saw the danger of Stuart absolutism and recognized the fatuousness of the doctrines of divine right and passive obedience to the crown. In volumes three and four, however, the Tories are at least as good as the Whigs, reflecting both the politically untidy realities of the 1690s and a shift in Macaulay's own perspective. By the 1850s, according to Trevelyan, Macaulay had ceased to be a partisan in modern politics. He was still a "vehement ministerialist of 1698" but was progressively less enthusiastic about the Whigs as they metamorphosed into the Liberal party and seemed to be going beyond the reforms that he thought necessary. Also, Macaulay had cast the Whig Duke of Marlborough as the primary villain in volumes three and four of the history, as a traitor who gave important military secrets to the French and apparently planned to use his influence over the future Queen Anne to make himself the uncrowned ruler of England. The case against Marlborough seems today to have been convincingly refuted—as have Macaulay's vilifications of Claverhouse, William Penn, and others; and his wrong-headedness in these cases seems to reflect both the strong personal prejudices created by his habit of castle-building and his strong rhetorical need for villains to serve as foils to William.

William himself becomes a symbol of progress toward the end of volume four, when he is defeated by the French, under the Duke of Luxemburg, at Landen, his last major battle. "Never, perhaps, was the change which the progress of civilization has produced in the art of war more striking than on that day." William and Luxemburg were "two poor sickly beings who, in a rude state of society, would have been regarded as too puny to bear any part in combats," but "their lot had fallen on a time when men had discovered that strength of muscles is far inferior in value to strength of the mind." William's strength of mind had been such that he had created and maintained an alliance which had checked—though not vanquished—the hitherto invincible armies of France and saved Europe from the domination of an insolent tyrant. The fourth volume of *The History of England* concludes with the 1697 Treaty of Ryswick, in which France recognized its inability to impose its will on its enemies, and the final pages echo the last scenes and reflections in volume two. Macaulay describes the reception of the treaty in London with civic rejoicing like that which seven years earlier had welcomed the Deliverer to his new capital, and the achievements of the Revolution settlement are again summarized, beginning with military accomplishments and going on to the growth of freedom and the unprecedented prosperity of the economy. "Many signs," Macaulay concludes—in 1855 as in 1848—"justified the hope that the Revolution of 1688 would be our last Revolution."

When volumes three and four of *The History of England* were published, Macaulay worried that they might disappoint the tremendous expectations of the reviewers and readers and that they might fall short of what the earlier volumes had achieved in narrative excitement. He need not have concerned himself. The reviews were again highly favorable, and the sales soon surpassed those for the first volumes. Not surprisingly, the first two volumes now also had to be brought out in new editions to meet the new demand created by the success of volumes three and four. The phenomenal sales continued year after year so that by 1876 Trevelyan could claim that 140,000 copies of *The History of England* had been sold in Britain alone. Some idea of foreign sales can be taken from what Macaulay called "a most intoxicating letter" from Edward Everett in Massachusetts, saying that in America the history was outselling everything except the Bible.

The remainder of Macaulay's life was relatively comfortable and relatively quiet. In January 1856 he resigned his seat in Parliament, and in May he left the Albany and moved to Holly Lodge, Camden, where he began to take an interest in gardening. In August and September of the same year, he and Ellis took a tour of Italy, and in October he was back in London and working on volume five of the history. In 1857 Lord Palmerston's government raised him to the peerage as Baron Macaulay of Rothley, marking the first time in history that such an honor had been bestowed for literary achievement.

His health, however, continued to decline, and the work on *The History of England* was slower than ever. He completed three more chapters, managing—as he had hoped—to finish the saga of William. In February 1859 his brother-in-law Charles Trevelyan left England to take up an important new post in India, and in October Macaulay learned that Hannah would soon leave to join her husband. This news seems to have taken away his will to live. He died quietly in his study on 28 December 1859 while reading the current installment of his friend Thackeray's new novel *Lovel the Widower* in the *Cornhill Magazine*. His funeral was held in Westminster Abbey on 9 January 1860, and he was buried in the Poets' Corner.

When he died, his reputation was probably as high as it had ever been. Walter Bagehot compared him to Edmund Burke and lamented the fact that this great orator had departed without ever having addressed his new peers in the House of Lords. Thackeray bade farewell to both Macaulay and Washington Irving in an essay entitled "Nil Nisi Bonum," in which his recently deceased friends were described as the Gibbon and the Goldsmith of the nineteenth century. Having covered—in *The History of Henry Esmond, Esq.* (1852), *The English Humourists of the Eighteenth Century* (1853), and *The Four Georges* (1860)—much of the same historical ground as Macaulay, Thackeray was primarily impressed by the extent of Macaulay's reading, saying that the historian's head always reminded him of the dome of the British Museum, so full was it crammed with information: "He reads twenty books to write a single sentence." A two-volume posthumously published collection of Macaulay's miscellaneous writings (edited by Ellis, 1860) and the last three chapters of *The History of England* (edited by Hannah Macaulay Trevelyan, 1861) were eagerly received, and the first full-length bi-

"Thomas Babington Macaulay in His Study," painting by Edward Matthew Ward, 1853 (National Portrait Gallery)

ography, *The Public Life of Lord Macaulay* by the Reverend Frederick Arnold, appeared in 1862. But it was George Otto Trevelyan's official biography, *The Life and Letters of Lord Macaulay* (1876), which first showed the private side of Macaulay and increased his popularity by displaying his warm family life, his sensitivity, his considerable skill as a letter writer, and his numerous acts of private charity toward anyone who chose to ask him for money.

It was just as well that his private character should receive support at this time because his reputation as a writer was already in decline. In *Friendship's Garland* (1871), Matthew Arnold hailed him as "the Great Apostle of the Philistines" and described his once admired style in condescending terms: "the external characteristic being a hard metallic movement with nothing of the soft play of life, and the internal characteristic being a perpetual semblance of hitting the right nail on the head without the reality." The historian W. E. H. Lecky, in a 21 September 1876 letter to his wife, records a conversation in which he and Herbert Spencer agreed "about the especial atrocity of Macaulay, whose style 'resembles low organizations, being a perpetual repetition of similar parts.' " Meanwhile the accuracy of *The History of England* was under constant attack. As early as 1849, the now aged John Wilson Croker had attacked volumes one and two in the *Quarterly Review,* and a Mr. Churchill Babington of Cambridge University, in *Mr. Macaulay's Character of the Clergy* (1849), had disputed the low view taken in these volumes of the seventeenth-century Anglican parsons. W. E. Forster, in *William Penn and Thomas B. Macaulay* (1849), and Hepworth Dixon, in *William Penn: A Historical Biography* (1851), conclusively showed that Macaulay had been wrong in claiming Penn was an unscrupulous agent of James II—apparently because he had confused him with a certain George Penn. William Edmonstoune Aytoun, in an appendix to his *Lays of the Scottish Cavaliers* (1849), questioned Macaulay's picture of Claverhouse, and in 1861 a barrister named John Paget published *The New "Examen,"* a wide-ranging and convincing critique of several of Macaulay's major characterizations, particularly his vilification of Marlborough. By 1886 Edward A. Freeman, the eminent historian of the Norman Conquest, could say in *The Methods of Historical Study* that "I know that to run down Lord Macaulay is the fashion of the day" and to argue that the fashion had gone too far: "I can see Macaulay's great and obvious faults as well as any man; . . . but I cannot . . . speak lightly of one to whom I owe so much in the matter of actual knowledge, and to whom I owe more than to any man as the master of historical narrative." Similarly, such historians as Charles Firth (*A Commentary on Macaulay's History of England,* 1938), Herbert Butterfield (*George III and the Historians,* 1957), and Hugh Trevor-Roper (*Men and Events,* 1957) have all praised Macaulay's historical scholarship while acknowledging that it was far from infallible.

Both a popular and a scholastic audience remained for Macaulay throughout the late nineteenth century—even after much of the intelligentsia had turned away from his work. New editions of his books continued to appear, his much maligned prose style was studied diligently in countless classrooms, and William Minto gave him exhaustive attention in his 1887 *Manual of English Prose Literature.* Neither a few glaring factual errors nor the supposedly metallic and repetitive qualities of his style seem ever to have bothered Macaulay's general readers very much, and the Everyman's Library editions of his essays, poems, and *The History of England*—along with Oxford World Classics editions of the speeches and of Trevelyan's *Life and Letters of Lord Macaulay*—have kept virtually all of his works more or less constantly available in inexpensive editions. Macaulay's works were in print during years when most of the writings of Carlyle, Newman, Arnold, and Ruskin were not so readily available, a circumstance that presumably reflects the fact that Macaulay remained the most generally popular of the Victorian sages.

But clearly he has not been as widely read in the twentieth century as he was in the nineteenth, and probably this decline has less to do with style or character judgments than with changes in basic beliefs and assumptions. Macaulay's optimism, materialism, patriotism, "manliness," sentimentalism, and admiration for the middle classes became progressively less popular after World War I. So, in a 1929 letter to his brother, C. S. Lewis would record his disgusted discovery that Macaulay "developed his full manner as a schoolboy and wrote letters home from school which read exactly like pages out of the *Essays.* He was talking about the nature of government, the principles of human prosperity, the force of the domestic affections and all that junk at the age of fourteen." Later, Lytton Strachey, in *Portraits in Miniature* (1931), would dismiss the "preposterous optimism" that "fills his pages," and Mario Praz, in *The Hero in Eclipse in Victorian Fiction* (1956), would imagine Macaulay "greeting the advent of photography as an invention that would allow mankind to dispense with the services of men like Raphael and Titian" and thinking that "progress means to have one's whole dinner ready prepared in tins; progress is predigested food, the prefabricated house." Such comments, however, seem less criticisms of the mind and art of Thomas Babington Macaulay than visceral reactions against the pieties, beliefs, and technological achievements of bourgeois civilization.

Macaulay's influence is more difficult to trace than his reputation. Clearly his style was much imitated in his own day and for quite a few years after—as late as 1876, in the *Fortnightly Review,* John Morley lamented its baleful influence on all sorts of journalists who did not possess the great qualities which had redeemed Macaulay's own writings. The influence of his *The History of England* on the London chapters of Dickens's *A Tale of Two Cities* (1859), on Blackmore's *Lorna Doone* (1869), and most significantly on Thackeray's *History of Henry Esmond, Esq.* (1852) is clear to anyone who has read any of these novels with Macaulay in mind. And the distinguished historical works of his nephew George Otto Trevelyan and of his great-nephew George Macaulay Trevelyan, master of Trinity College, Cambridge, owe a great deal, both in conception and technique, to Macaulay's example. But the one later writer who resembles him most is Winston Churchill.

In *A Roving Commission: My Early Life* (1930), Churchill describes Macaulay's important role in gratifying the first stirrings of intellectual curiosity felt by the future prime minister when he was a young cavalry officer in India. During the hot afternoons in Bangalore, when most subalterns rested up for the evening's polo matches, he studied Gibbon and Macaulay in a belated attempt to come to terms with the world of ideas. "I had learnt The Lays of Ancient Rome by heart and loved them and of course I knew he had written a history; but I had never read a page of it. I now embarked on that splendid romance." Though Churchill found it hard to forgive the lies about his ancestor, the Duke of Marlborough, he "must admit" that he owed Macaulay "an immense debt upon the other side." The relationship between Churchill and Macaulay was much like that between Macaulay and Samuel Johnson. In each case the younger writer had a negative reaction to the personality of the older one, and yet these personalities all had a great deal in common: a gruff public manner guarding more tender private sensibilities, distinction as great talkers of a frequently pugnacious sort, and a tendency to personify for their respective generations the John Bull qualities of common sense, devotion to fair play, and love of a good fight—all combined rather improbably with extraordinary erudition. Surely Churchill's immense debt to Macaulay included some influence on Churchill's self-consciously archaic prose style, a style which Evelyn Waugh called sham Augustan and which is unlike that of any other modern politician. It also presumably included some lessons in how to tell a story. Despite the fact that Churchill's *Marlborough: His Life and Times* (1933-1938) was, in large part, an attack on Macaulay, an attempt in the author's words, "to fasten the label 'Liar' to his genteel coattails," it is just as biased—and just as convincing and engrossing—a version of English history as Macaulay's own. Similarly, Churchill's histories of the two world wars and of the English-speaking people are full of ideas and narrative techniques that could have been lifted from Macaulay's pages.

Certainly Churchill, a high political official who won the Nobel Prize for Literature, resembles Macaulay more closely than could any man of letters who had had no part in public life. Like Macaulay, he both wrote and made history, yet literary critics seldom think of either man as primarily a writer. Except for the *Lays of Ancient Rome* and Churchill's early novel *Savrola: A Tale of the Revolution in Laurania* (1900), neither wrote in belletristic modes, and literature has been redefined in the twentieth century to exclude the forms in which they (and Johnson) primarily worked. The Indian Penal Code, Churchill's letters and memos, and Johnson's dictionary are not the sort of thing often covered by English curricula, and even the speeches and historical works of Churchill and Macaulay are well outside the standard reading lists. In fact, Macaulay's eclipse as a writer probably owes as much to the kinds of writing he did as to the limitations of his style or to his unfashionable opinions.

In the first decades after Trevelyan's biography was published, several more books were written about Macaulay, but they were generally hostile or derivative. J. Cotter Morison's *Macaulay* (1882) in the English Men of Letters series and Richmond Croom Beatty's *Lord Macaulay, Victorian Liberal* (1938) are decidedly in the first category; Arthur Bryant's *Macaulay* (1932) is in the second. Almost nothing significant was written for the next thirty years, but beginning in 1968 and continuing into the 1980s, there has appeared an impressive series of articles, chapters of books, full-length studies, and new editions of Macaulay's previously unpublished work. This new interest in Macaulay presumably signals both the continuing strength of the interest in the Victorian world which he represents as well as any single writer can and a renewed respect for the rhetorical analysis of nonfictional prose as an enterprise quite as significant as the criticism of poetry, fiction, and drama. As Victorian studies and rhetorical criticism continue to broaden their appeal, we can expect to hear more about Thomas Babington Macaulay.

Letters:

The Letters of Thomas Babington Macaulay, edited by Thomas Pinney, 6 volumes (London: Cambridge University Press, 1974-1981).

Biographies:

Frederick Arnold, *The Public Life of Lord Macaulay* (London: Tinsley, 1862);

George Otto Trevelyan, *The Life and Letters of Lord Macaulay,* 2 volumes (London: Longman, 1876);

Arthur Bryant, *Macaulay* (London: Davis, 1932);

Richmond Croom Beatty, *Lord Macaulay, Victorian Liberal* (Norman: University of Oklahoma Press, 1938);

John Clive, *Macaulay: The Shaping of the Historian* (New York: Knopf, 1973).

References:

Walter Bagehot, "Mr. Macaulay," *National Review,* 2 (April 1856): 357-387;

J. W. Burrow, *A Liberal Descent: Victorian Historians and the English Past* (Cambridge: Cambridge University Press, 1981);

Herbert Butterfield, *History and Human Relations* (London: Collins, 1951);

Butterfield, "Reflections on Macaulay," *Listener,* 90 (13 December 1973): 826-827;

William Carleton, "Macaulay and the Trimmers," *American Scholar,* 19 (Winter 1949-1950): 73-82;

Winston S. Churchill, *Marlborough: His Life and Times,* volumes 1 and 2 (New York: Scribners, 1933);

Churchill, *A Roving Commission: My Early Life* (New York: Scribners, 1930);

Harry Hayden Clark, "The Vogue of Macaulay in America," *Transactions of the Wisconsin Academy,* 34 (1942): 237-292;

John Clive, "Macaulay, History, and the Historians," *History Today,* 9 (December 1959): 830-836;

Clive, "Macaulay's Historical Imagination," *Review of English Literature,* 1 (October 1960): 20-28;

Clive and Thomas Pinney, Introduction to *Thomas Babington Macaulay: Selected Writings,* edited by Clive and Pinney (Chicago: University of Chicago Press, 1972);

A. O. J. Cockshut, *Truth to Life: The Art of Biography in the Nineteenth Century* (London: Collins, 1974);

R. K. Das Gupta, "Macaulay's Writings on India," in *Historians of India, Pakistan and Ceylon,* edited by C. H. Philips (London: Oxford University Press, 1961), pp. 230-240;

E. S. de Beer, "Macaulay and Croker: The Review of Croker's Boswell," *Review of English Studies,* 10 (1959): 388-397;

Sir Charles Firth, *A Commentary on Macaulay's History of England* (London: Macmillan, 1938);

David Fong, "Macaulay: the Essayist as Historian," *Dalhousie Review,* 51 (Spring 1971): 27-40;

Fong, "Macaulay and Johnson," *University of Toronto Quarterly,* 40 (Fall 1970): 38-48;

G. S. Fraser, "Macaulay's Style as an Essayist," *Review of English Literature,* 1 (October 1960): 9-19;

Peter Gay, "Macaulay," in his *Style in History* (New York: Basic Books, 1974);

Peter Geyl, "Macaulay in his Essays," in his *Debates With Historians* (London: Batsford, 1955), pp. 19-34;

William E. Gladstone, "Lord Macaulay," *Quarterly Review,* 142 (July 1876): 1-50;

John R. Griffin, *The Intellectual Milieu of Lord Macaulay* (Ottawa: University of Ottawa Press, 1965);

Joseph Hamburger, *Macaulay and the Whig Tradition* (Chicago: University of Chicago Press, 1976);

David Knowles, *Lord Macaulay, 1800-1859* (Cambridge: Cambridge University Press, 1960);

George Levine, *The Boundaries of Fiction: Carlyle, Macaulay, and Newman* (Princeton: Princeton University Press, 1968);

William Madden, "Macaulay's Style," in *The Art of Victorian Prose,* edited by George Levine and Madden (New York: Oxford University Press, 1968), pp. 127-151;

Jane Millgate, "Father and Son: Macaulay's *Edinburgh* Debut," *Review of English Studies,* 21 (May 1970): 159-167;

Millgate, "History versus Fiction: Thackeray's Response to Macaulay," *Costerus,* new series 2 (1974): 43-58;

Millgate, *Macaulay* (London: Routledge & Kegan Paul, 1973);

Millgate, "Macaulay at Work: an Example of his Use of Sources," *Cambridge Bibliographical Society Transactions,* 5 (1970): 90-98;

William Minto, *Manual of English Prose Literature* (Boston: Ginn, 1887);

Peter Morgan, "Macaulay on Periodical Style," *Victorian Periodicals Newsletter,* 1 (January 1968): 26-27;

J. Cotter Morison, *Macaulay* (London: Macmillan, 1882);

John Morley, "Macaulay," *Fortnightly Review,* new series 112 (April 1876): 494-513;

A. N. L. Munby, *Macaulay's Library* (Glasgow: Jackson, 1966);

Terry Otten, "Macaulay's Critical Theory of Imagination and Reason," *Journal of Aesthetics and Art Criticism,* 28 (Fall 1969): 33-43;

John Paget, *The New "Examen"* (Edinburgh & London: Blackwood, 1861);

G. R. Potter, *Macaulay* (London: Longmans, Green, 1959);

Mario Praz, "Macaulay," in his *The Hero in Eclipse in Victorian Fiction* (London: Oxford University Press, 1956), pp. 102-117;

William H. Rogers, "A Study in Contrasts: Carlyle and Macaulay as Book Reviewers," *Florida State University Studies,* no. 5 (1952): 1-9;

Bernard Semmel, "T. B. Macaulay: The Active and Contemplative Lives," in his *The Victorian Experience: The Prose Writers* (Athens: Ohio University Press, 1982), pp. 22-46;

Gerald Sirkin and Natalie Sirkin, "The Battle of Indian Education: Macaulay's Opening 'Salvo' Newly Discovered," *Victorian Studies,* 14 (June 1971): 407-428;

Vincent E. Starzinger, *Middlingness: Juste Milieu Political Theory in France and England 1815-48* (Charlottesville: University Press of Virginia, 1965);

Leslie Stephen, "Macaulay," in his *Hours in a Library,* volume 3 (London: Smith, Elder, 1879), pp. 279-324;

Eric Stokes, "Macaulay: The Indian Years, 1834-38," *Review of English Literature,* 1 (October 1960): 41-50;

Lytton Strachey, "Macaulay," in his *Portraits in Miniature and Other Essays* (London: Chatto & Windus, 1931);

Martin Svaglic, "Classical Rhetoric and Victorian Prose," in *The Art of Victorian Prose,* edited by George Levine and William Madden (New York: Oxford University Press, 1968);

William M. Thackeray, "Nil Nisi Bonum," *Cornhill Magazine,* 1 (February 1860): 129-134;

George Macaulay Trevelyan, *Clio, a Muse and Other Essays Literary and Pedestrian* (London: Longmans, Green, 1913);

Trevelyan, "Macaulay and the Sense of Optimism," in his *Ideas and Beliefs of the Victorians* (London: Sylvan Press, 1949);

Hugh Trevor-Roper, Introduction to Macaulay's *Critical and Historical Essays* (New York: McGraw-Hill, 1965);

Trevor-Roper, "Macaulay and the Glorious Revolution," in his *Men and Events* (New York: Harper, 1957);

Jack Valenti, "Macaulay and his Critics," in his *The Bitter Taste of Glory: Nine Portraits of Power and Conflict* (New York: World, 1971);

Ronald Weber, "Singer and Seer: Macaulay on the Historian as Poet," *Papers on Language and Literature,* 3 (Summer 1967): 210-219;

Edwin Yoder, Jr., "Macaulay Revisited," *South Atlantic Quarterly,* 63 (1964): 542-551.

Papers:

The most important collection of Macaulay's papers is at Trinity College, Cambridge; it includes juvenilia, several hundred letters, and the eleven volumes of the unpublished journal which Macaulay kept from 1838 to 1859. The British Library has the manuscripts for five *Edinburgh Review* essays. Two more manuscripts for *Edinburgh Review* articles are at New York's Pierpont Morgan Library, as are large portions of the manuscript for the fifth volume of *The History of England.* An important collection of Macaulay family papers is at the Huntington Library, San Marino, California, and official papers by Macaulay are at several locations: the Public Record Office and the India Office Library in London and the West Bengal Record Office in Calcutta.

Harriet Martineau

(12 June 1802-27 June 1876)

Gillian Thomas
Saint Mary's University

See also the Martineau entry in *DLB 21, Victorian Novelists Before 1885.*

SELECTED BOOKS: *Devotional Exercises for the Use of Young Persons* (London: Hunter, 1823; Boston: Bowles, 1833);

Addresses with Prayers and Original Hymns for the Use of Families and Schools (London: Hunter, 1826);

Principle and Practice; or, The Orphan Family (Wellington: Houlston, 1827; New York: Printed for W. B. Gilley, 1828);

The Rioters; or, A Tale of Bad Times (London: Houlston, 1827);

Mary Campbell; or, The Affectionate Granddaughter (Wellington: Houlston, 1828);

The Turn Out; or, Patience the Best Policy (London: Houlston, 1829);

The Essential Faith of the Universal Church Deduced from the Sacred Records (London: Printed for the Unitarian Association, 1831; Boston: Bowles, 1833);

Five Years of Youth; or, Sense and Sentiment (London: Printed for Harvey & Darton, 1831; Boston: Bowles & Greene, 1832);

Sequel to Principle and Practice (London: Printed for Houlston, 1831);

Illustrations of Political Economy (25 monthly parts, London: Fox, 1832-1834; 8 volumes, Boston: Bowles, 1832-1835);

The Faith as Unfolded by Many Prophets: An Essay Addressed to the Disciples of Mohammed (London: Printed for the Unitarian Association, 1832; Boston: Bowles, 1833);

Providence as Manifested through Israel (London: Printed for the Unitarian Association, 1832; Boston: Bowles, 1833);

Poor Laws and Paupers (4 volumes, London: Fox, 1833-1834; 1 volume, Boston: Bowles, 1833);

Christmas-Day; or, The Friends (London: Printed for Houlston, 1834);

Illustrations of Taxation, 5 volumes (London: Fox, 1834);

Harriet Martineau, circa 1835

The Children Who Lived by the Jordan. A Story (Salem, Mass.: Landmark, 1835; London: Green, 1842);

The Hamlets (Boston: Munroe, 1836);

Miscellanies, 2 volumes (Boston: Hilliard, Gray, 1836);

Society in America, 3 volumes (London: Saunders & Otley, 1837);

How to Observe Morals and Manners (London: Knight, 1838; New York: Harper, 1838);

My Servant Rachel, A Tale (London: Houlston, 1838);

Retrospect of Western Travel (3 volumes, London: Saunders & Otley, 1838; 2 volumes, New York: Lohman, 1838);

Deerbrook: A Novel (3 volumes, London: Moxon, 1839; New York: Harper, 1839);

The Martyr Age of the United States of America (Boston: Weeks, Jordan & Otis Broaders/New York: Taylor, 1839; Newcastle upon Tyne: Printed for the Emancipation and Aborigines Protection Society, 1840);

The Playfellow: A Series of Tales (4 volumes, London: Knight, 1841-1843; 1 volume, London & New York: Routledge, 1883);

The Hour and the Man: A Historical Romance (3 volumes, London: Moxon, 1841; 2 volumes, New York: Harper, 1841);

Life in the Sick-Room: Essays by an Invalid (London: Moxon, 1844; Boston: Bowles & Crosby, 1844);

Dawn Island: A Tale (Manchester: Gadsby, 1845);

Letters on Mesmerism (London: Moxon, 1845); republished as *Miss Martineau's Letters on Mesmerism* (New York: Harper, 1845);

Forest and Game-Law Tales, 3 volumes (London: Moxon, 1845-1846);

The Billow and the Rock (London: Knight, 1846);

The Land We Live In, by Martineau and Charles Knight, 4 volumes (London: Knight, 1847);

Eastern Life, Present and Past (3 volumes, London: Moxon, 1848; 1 volume, Philadelphia: Lea & Blanchard, 1848);

Household Education (London: Moxon, 1849; Philadelphia: Lea & Blanchard, 1849);

History of England during the Thirty Years' Peace 1816-46 (2 volumes, London: Knight, 1849; 4 volumes, Philadelphia: Porter & Coates, 1864);

Two Letters on Cow-Keeping, by Harriet Martineau, Addressed to the Governor of the Guiltcross Union Workhouse (London: Charles Gilpin/Edinburgh: Black/Dublin: J. B. Gilpin, 1850);

Introduction to the History of the Peace from 1800 to 1815 (London: Knight, 1851);

Letters on the Laws of Man's Nature and Development, by Martineau and Henry George Atkinson (London: Chapman, 1851; Boston: Mendum, 1851);

Letters from Ireland (London: Chapman, 1852);

Guide to Windermere, with Tours to the Neighbouring Lakes and Other Interesting Places (Windermere: Garnett/London: Whittaker, 1854);

A Complete Guide to the English Lakes (Windermere: Garnett/London: Whittaker, 1855);

The Factory Controversy: A Warning Against Meddling Legislation (Manchester: Printed by A. Ireland for the National Association of Factory Occupiers, 1855);

A History of the American Compromises (London: Chapman, 1856);

Sketches from Life (London: Whittaker/Windermere: Garnett, 1856);

British Rule in India: A Historical Sketch (London: Smith, Elder, 1857);

Corporate Tradition and National Rights: Local Dues on Shipping (London: Routledge/Manchester: Dinham, 1857);

Guide to Keswick and its Environs (Windermere: Garnett/London: Whittaker, 1857);

The "Manifest Destiny" of the American Union (New York: American Anti-Slavery Society, 1857);

Suggestions towards the Future Government of India (London: Smith, Elder, 1858);

Endowed Schools of Ireland (London: Smith, Elder, 1859);

England and Her Soldiers (London: Smith, Elder, 1859);

Health, Husbandry and Handicraft (London: Bradbury & Evans, 1861); republished in part as *Our Farm of Two Acres* (New York: Bunce & Huntingdon, 1865);

Biographical Sketches (London: Macmillan, 1869; New York: Leopoldt & Holt, 1869);

Harriet Martineau's Autobiography, with Memorials by Maria Weston Chapman (3 volumes, London: Smith, Elder, 1877; 2 volumes, Boston: Osgood, 1877);

The Hampdens: An Historiette (London: Routledge, 1880).

OTHER: *Traditions of Palestine,* edited by Martineau (London: Longman, Rees, Orme, Brown & Green, 1830); republished as *The Times of the Saviour* (Boston: Bowles, 1831);

The Positive Philosophy of Auguste Comte Freely Translated and Condensed, 2 volumes (London: Chapman, 1853; New York: Appleton, 1854).

PERIODICAL PUBLICATION: "Letter to the Deaf," *Tait's Edinburgh Magazine,* new series 1 (April 1834): 174-179.

Harriet Martineau's "somewhat remarkable" life, her controversial books and essays, and her strongly held convictions on such diverse matters as slavery, woman's rights, farming, medicine, and religion were frequent subjects of comment among the major figures of the Victorian literary world. Almost everyone of note in literary circles on both sides of the Atlantic had something to say about "Miss Martineau," yet few twentieth-century readers are familiar with her writings.

Martineau's brother James, who encouraged her to write her first work, a piece for the Monthly Repository *entitled "Female Writers of Practical Divinity." Portrait by G. F. Watts.*

Like many Victorian writers and intellectuals, she left an account of a grim childhood. The sixth of eight children of bombazine manufacturers, Thomas and Elizabeth Rankin Martineau, Harriet Martineau was reared according to what she described in her *Autobiography* (1877) as the "taking-down system." She was offered little sympathy either for her intense childhood fears or for the multitude of physical symptoms which plagued her in her early years. When she began to become deaf at the age of twelve her family insisted that she was merely inattentive, "and ever (while my heart was breaking) they told me that 'none are so deaf as those that won't hear.' " Only three years later, when the deafness that was to be lifelong had become almost total, did her family accept it as fact.

Despite their emotional austerity, her early surroundings were intellectually stimulating. Her family's home was in Norwich, a provincial town with a history of intellectual activity. Their religious denomination was Unitarian, an influential sect with a large membership and a tradition of vigorous debate on theological and philosophical matters. Furthermore, her family were in favor of girls receiving an education, though one that would be pursued at home rather than at school and which would take second place to sewing. Evidently a precocious child, she read Milton enthusiastically at the age of seven. In her *Autobiography* she records that "there was hardly a line in *Paradise Lost* that I could not have instantly turned to . . . and when my curtains were drawn back in the morning, descriptions of heavenly light rushed into my memory." By the time she was fourteen she was an avid student of what was to become a lifelong preoccupation: Political Economy—the classical economic and social theory which formed the basis of Utilitarian philosophy.

Martineau's younger brother James was the first to encourage her to write. As consolation for the loss of his close companionship when he returned to college, he suggested that she occupy herself by writing an article for the Unitarian journal *Monthly Repository*. In 1820 she wrote an essay entitled "Female Writers of Practical Divinity" and submitted it under the pseudonym V of Norwich. The following month her eldest brother was reading the *Repository* aloud to the family. He expressed admiration for the piece by V of Norwich, and when he questioned his sister about why she did not join in his praises she burst out,"I never could baffle any body. The truth is that paper is mine." As she recalled in her *Autobiography*, "He then laid his hand on my shoulder, and said gravely (calling me 'dear' for the first time) 'Now, dear, leave it to other women to make shirts and darn stockings; and do you devote yourself to this.' I went home in a sort of a dream, so that the squares of the pavement seemed to float before my eyes. That evening made me an authoress."

She was sufficiently encouraged to begin her first published book, *Devotional Exercises for the Use of Young Persons* (1823), and began a novel, which she later abandoned, in the style of popular novelist Robert Plumer who attracted a large readership by his novel *Tremaine* (1825), an attempt to combine philosophy with fiction. The final collapse of the family's fortune in 1829, three years after the deaths of her father and her eldest brother, left her "destitute;—that is to say, with precisely one shilling in my purse." This absolute loss of "gentility" proved fortuitous, compelling Martineau to find some means of supporting herself and her mother and aunt.

Happily for Martineau, she was prevented by her deafness from pursuing the usual shabby-genteel woman's occupation of "governessing." Instead, she planned to earn money by doing fancy

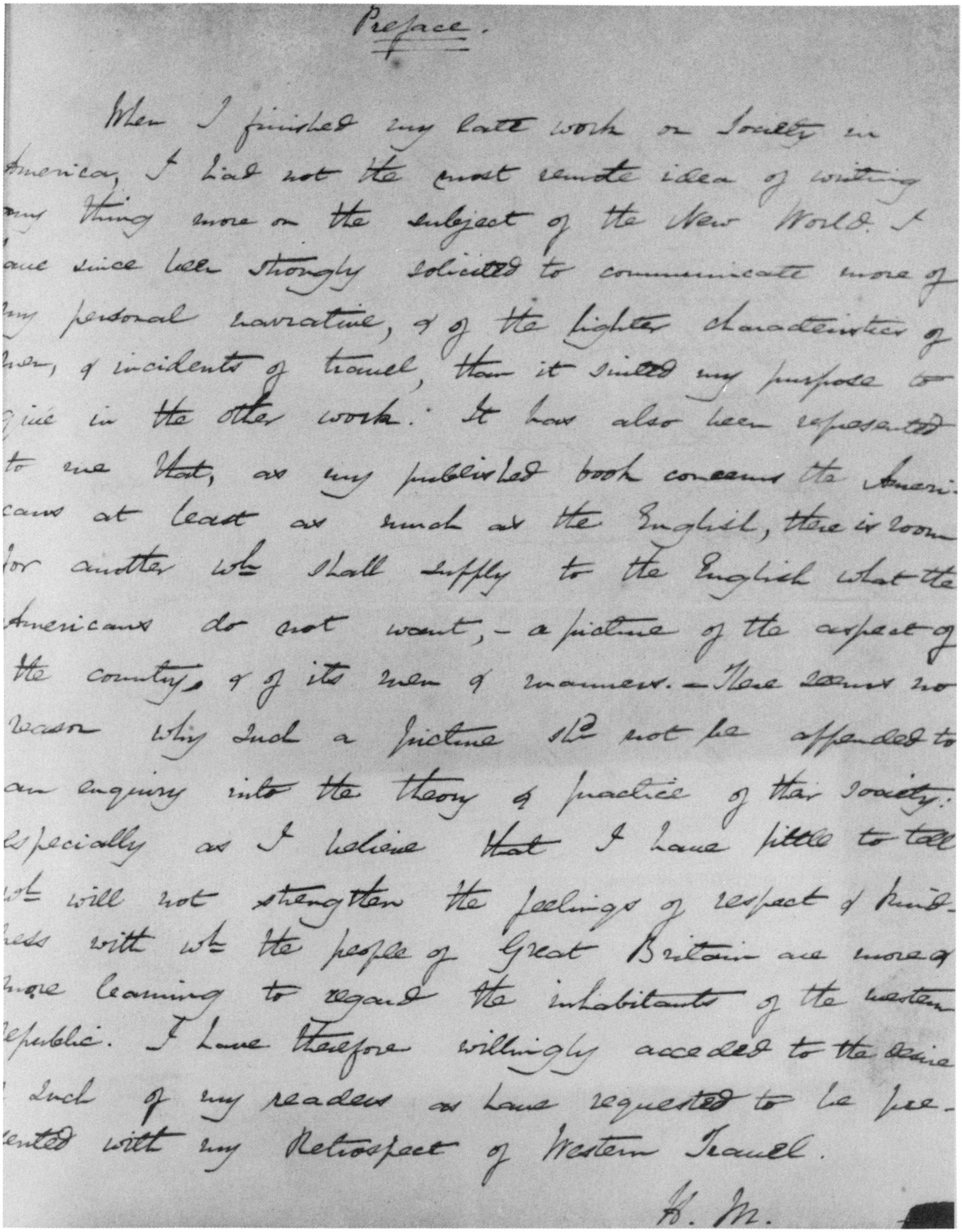

Preface.

When I finished my late work on Society in America, I had not the most remote idea of writing any thing more on the subject of the New World. I have since been strongly solicited to communicate more of my personal narrative, & of the lighter characteristics of men, & incidents of travel, than it suited my purpose to give in the other work. It has also been represented to me that, as my published book concerns the Americans at least as much as the English, there is room for another wh. shall supply to the English what the Americans do not want, — a picture of the aspect of the country, & of its men & manners. — There seems no reason why such a picture shd not be appended to an enquiry into the theory & practice of their society: especially as I believe that I have little to tell wh. will not strengthen the feelings of respect & kindness with wh. the people of Great Britain are more & more learning to regard the inhabitants of the western Republic. I have therefore willingly acceded to the desire of such of my readers as have requested to be presented with my Retrospect of Western Travel.

H. M.

Page from the manuscript for Retrospect of Western Travel, *Martineau's 1838 account of her visit to the United States (Lilly Library, Indiana University)* needlework by day and using all her remaining waking hours to write, thus establishing a lifelong pattern of extending her working hours late into the night and rising early in the morning. W. J. Fox, the new editor of the *Monthly Repository,* offered her fifteen pounds a year for book reviews and invited her to send him "two or three tales, such as his 'best' readers would not pass by." Since Fox's encouragement included payment as well as praise, she decided to travel to London, hoping to begin a literary career in earnest. Since she had no connections in the literary world, her stay did not result in any firm offers of work. Nevertheless, she hoped to find enough work undertaking "proof-correcting and other literary drudgery" to allow her the opportunity to pursue more ambitious literary projects. Suddenly, however, she received "peremptory orders" from her mother summoning her home to Norwich. Pressure from relatives had evidently persuaded Martineau's mother that the notion of a "literary career" was hopelessly unrealistic and that her daughter's only option was "to pursue,—not literature but needlework."

The sharpness of her disappointment was slightly softened when she learned that the *Repository* was offering three small prizes for essays "by which Unitarianism was to be presented to the notice of Catholics, Jews and Mohammedans." Although the prize money involved was small, she wrote essays on all three subjects and found, when, with her mother's permission, she again visited London, she had won all three prizes. She interpreted this news as confirmation that "authorship was my legitimate career" and embarked on a more ambitious project, a set of didactic tales, each of which illustrated a basic principle of Utilitarian theory. After initial difficulty in finding a publisher for *Illustrations of Political Economy,* the series, which appeared in twenty-five parts from 1832 to 1834, became a huge success and the young woman from Norwich found herself "lionized" in literary London.

Martineau's tales quickly made her the subject of controversy. Her series of didactic stories was attacked in an unsigned review in the *Quarterly Review* by John Wilson Croker, who was enraged that "unfeminine and mischievous doctrines on the principles of social welfare" should be promulgated by a woman, "a *female Malthusian.* A *woman* who thinks child-bearing a *crime against society!* An *unmarried woman* who declares against *marriage!!*" The popular success of the series, however, enabled her to suspend her hectic writing schedule and travel to America.

Although her American travels resulted in two books, *Society in America* (1837) and *Retrospect of Western Travel* (1838), unlike many other English writers of the period, she does not appear to have planned the journey with the express purpose of producing a book. She was intrigued with the idea of testing her ideas of Political Economy against the institutions of a society which seemed to contrast sharply with those of the Old World. She had also publicly criticized slavery, and she wanted an opportunity to observe it at first hand.

Her return to England in 1836 was the beginning of three years of intense activity during which she produced her novel *Deerbrook* (1839) as well as her books of American travels before she became seriously ill during a European tour. The cause of her illness seems to have been a uterine tumor which caused severe pain because of the pressure it exerted on other organs, and the prescribed cure was the standard one for ailing Victorian women—rest. She moved to Tynemouth to be within reach of her physician brother-in-law, Thomas Greenhow, as well as to avoid the constant demands of life in London.

Despite her illness, her five years in Tynemouth were productive. She wrote *Life in the Sick-Room* (1844), a remarkable account of her experiences as an invalid which explores extensively the psychological impact of prolonged illness. She also wrote what many critics consider her most outstanding work of fiction. *The Crofton Boys,* one of four short children's novels published together under the title *The Playfellow* (1841-1843), is one of the first sensitive accounts of adolescent psychology in fiction intended for a young audience. Martineau was amused to receive letters from schoolboys convinced from the authenticity of her account that she must be one of them.

Respite from her five years of chronic illness came only at the price of dissension. On the recommendation of several friends Martineau agreed to be mesmerised to see if she could obtain relief from her symptoms. Her physical problems began to recede after a series of hypnotic trances induced first by two mesmeric practitioners and later by her maid Jane. However, Martineau's family interpreted the improvement in her health as an indication of disloyalty to her physician brother-in-law. When gossip about the origin of her cure extended to discussion in the press, Martineau wrote her own version of the story, "Six Letters on Mesmerism," published in the *Athenaeum* in 1844 and as a book the following year. She was distressed to find that the letters appeared in the *Athenaeum* accompanied

The Knoll, Ambleside, Martineau's home in the Lake District where she spent the last thirty years of her life. Drawing by Claude Harrison.

by editorial notes attempting to discredit the mesmeric cure. Worse was to follow when her brother-in-law had a pamphlet published entitled *A Medical Report of the Case of Miss H----M------*, giving a detailed gynecological explanation of her symptoms. Though remarkably free of prudery in such matters, Martineau was appalled to find such a medical account of her problems "In a shilling pamphlet—not even written in Latin—but open to all the world!"

More controversy followed her first published work after she had made a full recovery. She had recently met Henry George Atkinson, who, though thirteen years her junior, shared many of the same views and interests. This friendship resulted in their collaboration on *Letters on the Laws of Man's Nature and Development,* published in 1851. Though Atkinson's writing suggests that his intellect was much inferior to Martineau's, in the letters she assumes the role of pupil, apparently accepting the muddleheaded Atkinson as a mentor and setting aside her usual trenchant analysis. The published letters caused a furor, not because of their fuzzy thinking, but because they seemed to define a philosophical position which would later become known as agnosticism. Even the freethinking George Eliot thought the letters "the boldest I have seen in the English language" but, nonetheless, "studiously offensive."

In the meantime Martineau had marked her complete return to health by establishing herself in 1846 in her own newly built house, The Knoll, at Ambleside in the Lake District. Rejecting the prospect of a "hackney coach and company life" of the kind she might fall into in London, she thought the Lake District ideal as a place to establish "a house of my own among poor improvable neighbours, with young servants whom I might train and attach to myself; with pure air, a garden, leisure, solitude at command, and freedom to work in peace and quietness." Furthermore, Ambleside gave her neighbors such as Wordsworth and Matthew Arnold who shared her literary and intellectual interests.

In many respects this phase of her life was both the most contented and the most productive. She took an immense interest in the running of her household with its tiny farmstead and made both the frequent subject of books and essays, most notably *Health, Husbandry and Handicraft* (1861). She wrote a popular history of her own time, *History of England During the Thirty Years' Peace 1816-46* (1849), contributed to Dickens's periodical *Household Words,* and wrote regular and influential articles for the *Daily News.* She traveled in the Middle East and wrote *Eastern Life, Present and Past* (1848) recounting her travels. She also revised and collected a number of the articles she had written for the *People's Journal* into a single volume, *Household Education* (1849), which called for a more liberal approach to education based more on the child's needs and abilities than on the parent's authority. When, after ten years of relief, her ill-health began to recur, she embarked on her most important work, her *Autobiography,* in order to ensure that her own version of events would be recorded before her death.

Despite deteriorating health, she lived for nearly twenty more years and continued to be politically active. When she received Florence Nightingale's telegram, "Agitate, Agitate for Lord de Gray in place of Sir G. Cornewall Lewis," the unabashedly partisan Martineau devoted her next *Daily News* editorial to promoting Nightingale's candidate for the War Ministry. Much more controversial was her cooperation with Florence Nightingale and Josephine Butler in the Ladies' National Association for the repeal of the Contagious Diseases Acts. Parliament had begun considering the Contagious Diseases Bill in 1864. Intending to reduce the incidence of venereal disease in the military, the bill permitted forcible medical examinations of any woman in a military town on the suspicion that she might be a prostitute. No evidence was required and no appeal permitted; nor were men to be subject to medical examination. Despite the lobbying of Martineau and others, the bill not only became law, but its scope was widened to include the whole country. Martineau was vociferous in her opposition to the acts and her name headed the list of the one hundred twenty-eight influential women who signed the "Appeal to the Women of England," published as a letter in the *Daily News* on 31 December 1869. During the next two years it became evident to the ruling Liberals that there was significant public opposition to the Contagious Diseases Acts, and they appointed a royal commission, which recommended amendment of the acts. Though the final repeal of the acts was not completed until ten years after Martineau's death, her efforts were widely considered instrumental in bringing about their demise.

Although increasingly saddened by the deaths of friends and contemporaries, Martineau faced her own death philosophically with, as she put it in her *Autobiography,* "no reluctance whatever to pass into nothingness, leaving my place in the universe to be filled by another."

Martineau, circa 1867 (National Portrait Gallery)

There can be no doubt, judging by the frequency with which her contemporaries referred to her, that Harriet Martineau ranked in their minds as a figure of considerable stature. While some, John Stuart Mill, for example, plainly found her personally disagreeable, others, including George Eliot, admired her character as well as her writing. In a letter Eliot remarked of Martineau that "After all she is a *trump*—the only English woman that possesses thoroughly the art of writing." Even when the two were no longer on good terms Eliot expressed a desire to write "an admiring appreciation" of Martineau as an obituary, assuming that Eliot outlived her.

Of Martineau's fiction perhaps only *The Crofton Boys* has retained its appeal. *Deerbrook* is of interest to students of nineteenth-century fiction for its similarities to Jane Austen's writing as well as for its remarkable portrait of electoral corruption in a provincial setting. In Martineau's travel writing the modern reader is likely to appreciate most the sense of indefatigability and fearlessness that the author conveys, though the books on American travels also contain some interesting observations on the psychology of slavery, and *Eastern Life, Present and Past* is one Martineau's most reflective works, with its sensitive examination of the impact of early scriptural studies on the imagination.

Martineau's most influential writings in her own time were her works of popular education. Indeed, when in 1853 Martineau prepared her own obituary for the *Daily News,* she wrote that "she could popularize, while she could neither discover nor invent." In *Household Education,* one of her most frequently republished nonfiction works, she drew upon her own early unhappy childhood experiences in order to outline what she considered a sound method of education. One of the great strengths of her work is her ability to generalize and derive insights from her own experience. This skill is most evident in her early essay "Letter to the Deaf" and in *Life in the Sick-Room.* Similarly, her practical experience forms the basis for advice on domestic matters in *Health, Husbandry and Handicraft.* All these works are animated by a spirit of optimism and an apparently boundless faith in education as a means of social change and reform.

Harriet Martineau's *Autobiography* remains by far her most significant work and one of the most absorbing examples of nineteenth-century autobiographical writing. It is full of powerful evocations of the sensory world of childhood, her deft sketches of people, and observant commentaries on mores of her own times. Although her views, in particular her feminism and her agnosticism, were often in advance of those of her contemporaries, it is as a superb observer and reporter of her own times that Harriet Martineau is best remembered.

Letters:

Elisabeth Sanders Arbuckle, ed., *Harriet Martineau's Letters to Fanny Wedgwood* (Stanford, Cal.: Stanford University Press, 1983).

Bibliography:

Joseph B. Rivlin, *Harriet Martineau: A Bibliography of Her Separately Printed Books* (New York: New York Public Library, 1947).

Biographies:

Vera Wheatley, *The Life and Work of Harriet Martineau* (London: Secker & Warburg, 1957);

R. K. Webb, *Harriet Martineau: A Radical Victorian* (London: Heinemann, 1960);

Valerie Kossew Pichanick, *Harriet Martineau: The Woman and Her Work, 1802-1876* (Ann Arbor: University of Michigan Press, 1980).

References:

Mitzi Myers, "*Harriet Martineau's Autobiography:* The Making of a Female Philosopher," in *Women's Autobiography: Essays in Criticism,* edited by Estelle C. Jelinek (Bloomington: Indiana University Press, 1980);

John Cranstoun Nevill, *Harriet Martineau* (London: Muller, 1943);

Valerie Kossew Pichanick, "An Abominable Submission: Harriet Martineau's Views on the Role and Place of Women," *Women's Studies,* 5, no. 1 (1977): 13-32;

Gillian Thomas, *Harriet Martineau* (Boston: G. K. Hall, 1985).

Frederick Denison Maurice

(29 August 1805-1 April 1872)

E. Cleve Want
Texas A&M University

SELECTED BOOKS: *Eustace Conway; or, The Brother and Sister,* anonymous, 3 volumes (London: Bentley, 1834);

Subscription No Bondage, or the Practical Advantages Afforded by the Thirty-nine Articles as Guides in all the Branches of Academical Education, as Rusticus (Oxford: Parker/London: Rivington/ Cambridge: Deighton, 1835);

Letters to a Member of the Society of Friends, by a Clergyman of the Church of England, 12 parts (London: Darton, 1837); republished as *The Kingdom of Christ: Or, Hints on the Principles, Ordinances, and Constitution of the Catholic Church in Letters to a Member of the Society of Friends,* 3 volumes (London: Darton & Clark, 1838); revised as *The Kingdom of Christ; Or, Hints to a Quaker Respecting the Principles, Constitution, and Ordinances of the Catholic Church* (London: Rivington, 1842); republished under original title (New York: D. Appleton/ Philadelphia: G. S. Appleton, 1843);

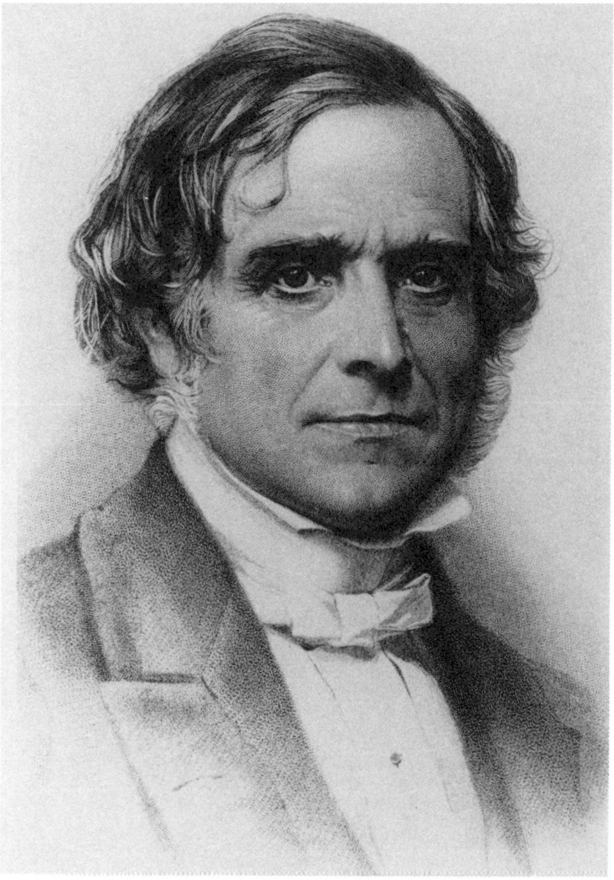

Frederick Denison Maurice. Engraving by F. Holl from a portrait by Lowes Dickinson.

Has the Church, or the State, the Power to Educate the Nation? A Course of Lectures (London: Rivington, 1839);

Reasons For Not Joining a Party in the Church: A Letter to the Ven. Samuel Wilberforce, Archdeacon of Surrey; Suggested By the Rev. Dr. Hook's Letter to the Bishop of Ripon, on the State of Parties in the Church of England (London: Rivington, 1841);

On Right and Wrong Methods of Supporting Protestantism: A Letter to Lord Ashley Respecting a Certain Proposed Measure for Stifling the Expression of Opinion in the University of Oxford (London: Parker, 1843);

The Epistle to the Hebrews: Being the Substance of Three Lectures Delivered in the Chapel of the Honourable Society of Lincoln's Inn, on the Foundation of Bishop Warburton, with a Preface Containing a Review of Mr. Newman's Theory of Development (London: Parker, 1846);

The Religions of the World and Their Relations to Christianity, Considered in Eight Lectures Founded by the Right Hon. Robert Boyle (London: Parker, 1847);

The Lord's Prayer: Nine Sermons Preached in the Chapel of Lincoln's Inn in the Months of February, March, and April (London: Parker, 1848; Philadelphia: Hooker, 1852);

The Prayer-Book Considered Especially in Reference to the Romish System: Nineteen Sermons Preached in the Chapel of Lincoln's Inn (London: Parker, 1849);

The Church a Family: Twelve Sermons on the Occasional Services of the Prayer-Book Preached in the Chapel of Lincoln's Inn (London: Parker, 1850);

The Old Testament: Nineteen Sermons on the First Lessons for the Sundays from Septuagesima Sunday to the Third Sunday After Trinity, Preached in the Chapel of Lincoln's Inn (London: Parker, 1851); revised with a new preface as *The Patriarchs and Lawgivers of the Old Testament: A Series of Sermons Preached in the Chapel of Lincoln's Inn* (Cambridge: Macmillan, 1855; London & New York: Macmillan, 1890);

The Prophets and Kings of the Old Testament: A Series of Sermons Preached in the Chapel of Lincoln's Inn (Cambridge: Macmillan, 1853; Boston: Crosby, Nichols/New York: Francis, 1853);

Theological Essays (Cambridge: Macmillan, 1853; New York: Redfield, 1854);

The Word "Eternal," and the Punishment of the Wicked: A Letter to the Rev. Dr. Jelf, Canon of Christ Church, and Principal of King's College (Cambridge: Macmillan, 1853; New York: Francis/Boston: Crosby, Nichols, 1854);

The Doctrine of Sacrifice Deduced from the Scriptures: A Series of Sermons (Cambridge: Macmillan, 1854);

Lectures on the Ecclesiastical History of the First and Second Centuries (Cambridge: Macmillan, 1854);

The Unity of the New Testament: A Synopsis of the First Three Gospels and of the Epistles of St James, St Jude, St Peter, and St Paul to Which Is Added a Commentary on the Epistle to Hebrews (Cambridge: Macmillan, 1854; London: Parker, 1854; Boston: Lee & Shepard/New York: Dillingham, 1879);

Learning and Working. Six Lectures Delivered in Willis's Rooms, London, in June and July, 1854. The Religion of Rome, and Its Influence on Modern Civilization. Four Lectures Delivered in the Philosophical Institution of Edinburgh, in December, 1854 (Cambridge: Macmillan, 1855);

The Gospel of St. John. A Series of Discourses (Cambridge: Macmillan, 1857; London & New York: Macmillan, 1888);

The Epistles of St. John: A Series of Lectures on Christian Ethics (Cambridge: Macmillan, 1857);

What Is Revelation? A Series of Sermons on the Epiphany; to Which Are Added Letters to a Student of Theology on the Bampton Lectures of Mr. Mansel (Cambridge & London: Macmillan, 1859);

Sequel to the Inquiry, What Is Revelation? In a Series of Letters to a Friend; Containing a Reply to Mr. Mansel's "Examination of the Rev. F. D. Maurice's Strictures on the Bampton Lectures of 1858" (Cambridge & London: Macmillan, 1859);

The Claims of the Bible and of Science. Correspondence Between a Layman and the Rev. F. D. Maurice on Some Questions Arising Out of the Controversy Respecting the Pentateuch (London: Macmillan, 1863);

The Gospel of the Kingdom of Heaven; A Course of Lectures on the Gospel of St. Luke (London: Macmillan, 1864; London & New York: Macmillan, 1893);

The Conflict of Good and Evil in Our Day: Twelve Letters to a Missionary (London: Smith, Elder, 1865);

The Commandments Considered as Instruments of National Reformation (London: Macmillan, 1866);

Casuistry, Moral Philosophy, and Moral Theology: An Inaugural Lecture, Delivered in the Senate House, Cambridge, on Tuesday, December 4, 1866 (London: Macmillan, 1866);

The Workman and the Franchise; Chapters From English History on the Representation and Education of the People (London & New York: Strahan, 1866);

The Conscience: Lectures on Casuistry, Delivered in the University of Cambridge (London & Cambridge: Macmillan, 1868);

Social Morality: Twenty-One Lectures Delivered in the University of Cambridge (London & Cambridge: Macmillan, 1869; London & New York: Macmillan, 1893).

Although Frederick Denison Maurice is appropriately remembered as the spiritual founder of the Cambridge "Apostles," an early editor of the *Athenaeum,* a founder of Queen's College, an influential preacher, a cofounder of Christian Socialism, the mentor of Charles Kingsley, and a founder and principal of the Working Men's College, he was fundamentally a theologian who became active in other areas because he saw and accepted the implications of his theology. However, as a theologian he is singularly difficult to classify. He in fact abhorred party divisions in the church and attempted always to convince his readers of the implicit unity of all humanity. He was uniquely aware of the artificial divisions that separate human beings and fragment a species that should regard itself as a family.

Maurice's convictions grew out of the unusually tense family situation in which he grew up. Born in 1805 in Normanstone, near Lowestoft, in Suffolk, he was the only surviving son in a family of eight sisters. His father, the Reverend Michael Maurice, was a broad-minded and tolerant Unitarian minister whose wife, Priscilla Hurry Maurice, and children eventually abandoned Unitarianism for either the Baptist or Anglican church. The religious gulfs among the family members sharing the same household grew so large that they were able to communicate their convictions on such subjects only in lengthy letters. Michael Maurice tried to shield young Frederick from the influence of his older sisters; the result was that his sisters could not speak to him of their beliefs, and his father chose not to speak of his. As Frederick Maurice wrote to his older son in an autobiographical letter of 1866, "These years were to me years of moral confusion and contradiction." But he was also impelled by this difficult situation to resolve the tensions he must have breathed with the air of the household: "The very word Unity has been haunting me from my cradle. . . . It has been associated with Theology from my cradle."

Having chosen the bar as his potential profession, he entered Cambridge University in 1823, matriculating first at Trinity College and later at Trinity Hall. While at Cambridge he assumed the leadership and set the tone for the famed "Apostles" and began his literary career as one of the editors of the *Metropolitan Quarterly Magazine.*

During the long vacation of 1826 he went to London to study law and then returned to Cambridge for his examination and took a first class in civil law. However, since he was unwilling to subscribe to Anglican doctrine, he did not receive a degree. Returning to London, Maurice became a participant in the London Debating Society, where he made the acquaintance of John Stuart Mill, with whom he found areas of both common ground and sharp disagreement. In 1828 he edited the *Athenaeum* and along with John Sterling, a close friend from his Cambridge period, wrote extensively for it, setting the tone for its long, distinguished run.

As Torben Christensen (*Origin and History of Christian Socialism 1848-54,* 1962), Olive J. Brose (*Frederick Denison Maurice,* 1971), and Frank Mauldin McClain (*Maurice: Man and Moralist,* 1972) have demonstrated, the year 1828 culminated in a time of personal crisis for Maurice. His lone published novel, *Eustace Conway,* which appeared unsigned in 1834, is the most valuable evidence available for determining how and why he turned from a projected legal and political career to a clerical and theological one. The novel, at least partially autobiographical, features a central character who is first attracted to utilitarianism, then German transcendentalism, and finally a form of Christianity which is depicted as more realistic about human nature than the under- or over-valuation of it in the current philosophies. Eustace is led toward acknowledgment of man's utter dependency upon, and consequent need for, God, a condition he shares with all human beings. Without trust in God, a human being is doomed to insecurity and alienation because he perceives his fellow human beings as threats rather than as creatures with whom he can identify as brothers. These ideas are more fully and clearly stated in his later writings.

It is hardly surprising that the author of *Eustace Conway* resolved to seek ordination in the Church of England, believing it would soon be disestablished in the wave of reform engulfing England in the early 1830s. To this end he entered upon a secondary undergraduate career—at Oxford this time, where his close associates included William E. Gladstone. Following his graduation and ordination, Maurice served several years at a country curacy in Bubbenhall, where in 1835 he produced, under the pseudonym of Rusticus, his first theological book, *Subscription No Bondage,* in which he argued for an interpretation of the Thirty-nine Articles as a basis on which inquiry and learning could take place free from theological superstitions. Also in *Subscription No Bondage* he called on Anglicans to recognize the positive values of other religious groups and to explore the grounds of unity that lay among them. Doing so, Maurice maintained, would bring about an awakening within Anglicans of the implications of their own beliefs.

These ideas are more fully developed in the stages of what began as a series of letters to a Quaker friend (published in twelve parts in 1837) and became *The Kingdom of Christ* (1838), greatly revised in the second edition (1842), one of Maurice's most enduring works. In *The Kingdom of Christ* he defines his vision of the Catholic (that is, Universal) church not so much against such bodies as the Quakers, whose belief that Christ is in every man he applauded, as against the High Church emphasis of the Oxford Movement, which he saw as a contraction of the Catholic church rather than a revival of it. In Brose's view Maurice also "demonstrated that the principles of Fox, Luther, and the Unitarians were 'too strong, too vital, to bear the imprisonment' of their respective systems. But he had also endeavored to counteract the prevalent view of the times that all institutional religions and churches were dying out. . . . In his discussion of religious awakenings, idealist philosophic trends, and the implications for society lurking in the French Revolution, he affirmed that they all signified partial, tentative gropings toward a spiritual and universal society." In part two of *The Kingdom of Christ,* Maurice contrasts what he conceives of as the Catholic church to the "Romish System."

In 1835 Maurice had accepted the position of chaplain to Guy's Hospital in London, taking up

Maurice in 1846, the year he became chaplain of Lincoln's Inn. Drawing by Samuel Laurence (National Portrait Gallery).

residency in January 1836. For most of the remaining years of his life Maurice was intimately involved with the life of the capital city, preaching, teaching, writing, and engaging in the intellectual life of the city and the period. His literary acquaintances included Mill, Thomas Carlyle, and, later, Alfred Tennyson.

On 7 October 1837 Maurice married Anna Barton, the sister-in-law of his friend John Sterling, who officiated at the wedding. The marital relationship was a close one, and Maurice acknowledged Anna as late as 1870 as knowing "the secrets of the true Churchmanship better than any of my male acquaintances, and oh, how much better than I did." McClain states that much of Maurice's best work, especially *The Kingdom of Christ,* was the product of their years together and that through her knowledge of German she helped introduce him to continental theology. Two children were born of this union—John Frederick Maurice (1841-1912), the later biographer of his father, and Edmund Maurice (1843-1926). Anna died of tuberculosis on 25 March 1845 after nursing her sister and John Sterling through the terminal stages of the illness the previous year. Maurice was left to raise their two sons with the help of his sister Priscilla.

From 1840 a professor of English literature and modern history at King's College, London, Maurice was made a professor of theology there in 1845 and chaplain of Lincoln's Inn in 1846. By virtue of these positions as well as through his writings, Maurice became a major influence on the younger generation and was widely read and respected as a theologian and as a person.

With the outbreak of revolution on the Continent and the threat of upheaval in England in 1848, Maurice became active along with Charles Kingsley and John Malcolm Ludlow in the Christian Socialist Movement, especially providing an intellectual basis in his publications in *Politics for the People,* which he edited with Ludlow, *Tracts on Christian Socialism,* and the *Christian Socialist.* The movement was intended to provide a safety valve for an explosive situation and to encourage open and direct discussion rather than armed conflict. In his publications associated with the movement, Maurice again found occasion to lament the parties and factions that were rampant and to exhort the nation to build on mutual interests. His goal was no less to make Christians conscious of social responsibilities than to make Socialists aware of common ground with Christian theology properly understood.

In the midst of the Christian Socialist furor Maurice married Georgiana Hare, the half sister of Julius Hare, who had been a mentor of Maurice at Cambridge and remained a friend until his death in 1855. Georgiana had been a close friend to Anna, Maurice's first wife. The wedding took place on 4 July 1849 during one of her frequent bouts of illness. A habitual invalid, she was often bedridden following even moderate exertion, yet outlived her husband by eighteen years. Ludlow and others viewed her as a debilitating influence on Maurice.

As a result of his Christian Socialist activities, Maurice was assailed in the religious press as one who subverted Christian faith and associated with infidels. The controversy caused Dr. Richard William Jelf, the principal of King's College, to question Maurice's activities, acquaintances, and beliefs. Maurice's *Theological Essays* (1853) brought to a head the confrontation with the religious press and the owners of King's College. Growing out of a long desire to reach out to Unitarians especially, the book was based on a series of sermons he had delivered at Lincoln's Inn during Lent and Easter of that year. The attacks against it centered on the concluding essay, entitled "On Eternal Life and Eternal Death," in which Maurice asserted that the Greek word *aiónios* (rendered by the word *eternal* in English translations) meant in the New Testament context a quality beyond time rather than the more commonly understood "everlasting" or "unending." Thus according to Maurice, the terms *eternal life* and *eternal death* in the New Testament applied to life in the presence or absence of God rather than to unending bliss or unending punishment.

The fact that the religious press in denouncing Maurice identified him as professor of theology at King's College caused Jelf and the college council to fear repercussions on the college. When they called for Maurice's resignation and he refused, they declared his professorial chairs vacant in November 1853. Maurice's activity in higher education was by no means at an end, however. He was a founder of Queen's College for women in 1848, principal from 1848 to 1854, and professor of history and theology during the same period. He resumed his position as professor from 1858 to 1866, when he moved to Cambridge.

In 1854 Maurice delivered six lectures published the following year as *Learning and Working.* His purpose was to encourage interest in adult education and to raise money for the founding of the Working Men's College, which took place in October of that year. In his lectures, Maurice criticized the higher education of his time as an extension of the rote instruction of children. He advocated that higher education be addressed to adults and have as its goal the realization of freedom and order in morally responsible beings. One of his most successful undertakings, the Working Men's College had among its early instructors John Ruskin, Dante Gabriel Rossetti, and Thomas Hughes.

By the late 1850s the religious scene in Great Britain had shifted sufficiently that Maurice found new forms of religious orthodoxies and heterodoxies to contend with. His controversies with philosopher and theologian Henry Longueville Mansel over the nature of revelation and with Bishop John William Colenso on the nature of scripture revealed Maurice attempting a middle ground between rigid literalism and what he saw as analysis destructive of religious faith. The controversy between Maurice and Mansel was essentially over what Mansel termed "the laws and limits of religious thought"—whether the nature of God is in any way knowable to human beings. It began with the publication of Mansel's pamphlet *Man's Conception of Eternity: An Examination of Mr. Maurice's Theory of a Fixed State out of Time* (London: Parker, 1854) during the controversy over Maurice's *Theological Essays.* Maurice responded in the preface to *The Patriarchs and Lawgivers of the Old Testament* (1855). Their debate continued in Mansel's *The Limits of Religious Thought Examined in Eight Lectures Delivered Before the University of Oxford, in the Year 1858, on the Bampton Foundation* (Oxford: Murray, 1858), Maurice's *What Is Revelation? A Series of Sermons on the Epiphany; to Which Are Added Letters to a Student of Theology on the Bampton Lectures of Mr. Mansel* (1859), Mansel's *An Examination of the Rev. F. D. Maurice's Strictures on the Bampton Lectures of 1858* (London: Murray, 1859), and Maurice's *Sequel to the Inquiry, What Is Revelation? In a Series of Letters to a Friend; Containing a Reply to Mr. Mansel's "Examination of the Rev. F. D. Maurice's Strictures on the Bampton Lectures of 1858"* (1859).

The London college founded by Maurice in October 1854

To Mansel, an absolute and infinite God was inaccessible to the limited human mind and thus should not be subject to speculation. The best human beings could hope for was what he called "regulative truths," which guide behavior but do not reveal God's nature. He held the Bible to be an inspired body of such truths, giving authoritative rules for human conduct.

Maurice objected to Mansel's view both of the nature of God and of the Bible. However inadequate human language may be to describe or define God, he maintained, direct knowledge of God—which he equated with eternal life—was possible and was the subject of Biblical teaching. To abandon this living faith and to reduce the Bible to a body of rules was, to Maurice, to misunderstand the Bible totally. Mansel remarked at one point that he and Maurice were speaking different languages, but Maurice seems not to have understood that they were using the term *knowledge* in very different senses—Mansel as a philosophical concept and Maurice in the Biblical sense of intimate acquaintance. At any rate he saw Mansel's position as a dangerous one against which he must prophesy. To many, however, Maurice appeared simply abusive and vehement.

Maurice's controversy with Colenso was briefer and less acrimonious but no doubt more personally painful to him, for the two men had earlier been cordial friends. In 1853 Colenso had dedicated a volume of sermons to Maurice and defended him against attacks in the religious press.

As Bishop of Natal in southern Africa, Colenso had begun a translation of Genesis into Zulu for the natives, and in trying to answer their obviously sincere questions as to the truth of the material, he concluded that much of the Pentateuch was not historical but was the production of a period much later than that of Moses. Indeed, he concluded that Moses's own historicity was dubious and that Joshua was a legendary figure. He applied his considerable mathematical skills to a study of such concerns as the size of the tabernacle and the camp in the wilderness and concluded that the Biblical numbers did not support a literalist interpretation. He believed that God's word could be "heard in the Bible, by all who humbly and devoutly listen for it," although he did not consider it God's word in any literal sense.

The first three volumes of Bishop Colenso's *The Pentateuch and Book of Joshua Critically Examined* (London: Longman, 1862-1879) were published in late 1862 and 1863 and caused an immediate uproar, calls for his resignation, and even an unsuccessful attempt to depose him. Maurice, quite shocked at Colenso's approach to Biblical criticism, responded in *The Claims of the Bible and of Science. Correspondence Between a Layman and the Rev. F. D. Maurice on Some Questions Arising Out of the Controversy Respecting the Pentateuch* (1863). He professed to have no quarrel with historical criticism of the Bible in principle nor with denial of Mosaic authorship of the Pentateuch, but questioned whether inconsistencies or inaccuracies in the texts invalidated the accounts of God's actions in history any more than inconsistencies and inaccuracies in Herodotus invalidated the historicity of the Persian Wars. To Maurice, Colenso had fallen into the same trap as many believers in verbal inspiration. Both demanded a literal accuracy in the Bible quite foreign to the mind-set of the ancient Hebrew world.

In 1866 Maurice was elected to the Knightbridge Professorship of Casuistry, Moral Theology and Moral Philosophy at Cambridge—an appropriate action by his first alma mater. The move to Cambridge obligated Maurice to bring much of his London activity to an end, though he remained principal of the Working Men's College. His last years were peaceful and free of controversy.

Among the last of Maurice's writings to be published in his lifetime were two series of lectures delivered at Cambridge. In *The Conscience: Lectures on Casuistry, Delivered in the University of Cambridge* (1868), the first of these series to appear, Maurice returned to his lifelong theme of the importance of social relationships. He emphasized the necessity and the inseparability of one's self-consciousness (the "I") and one's moral consciousness (the "ought") and held that only through a link with God as the "living Guide" can the brotherhood of all be realized.

In the second series, *Social Morality: Twenty-One Lectures Delivered in the University of Cambridge* (1869), Maurice urged the importance of human relationships with the mutual obligations as the education of both self-consciousness and moral consciousness. These relationships begin in the home and include those of husband-wife, parent-child, sibling-sibling, and master-servant. They extend outward to relationships within the nation, which Maurice saw as a community held together by mutual interest and need in contrast to an empire ruled by brute force. Ultimately his focus was a universal human society. Human beings would despair at their own dependency and the aloofness of the power of creation unless that power is seen as a Fatherly Will who in the Son of God and of Man revealed not rules but a person in whom God has suffered with his creatures. The Spirit of God—the Spirit of Truth—operates continually in the present to penetrate the gloom and reveal a loving

Right, Maurice standing in front of Thomas Carlyle in a preliminary sketch for Ford Madox Brown's painting Work, *shown below. The painting, exhibited in London in 1865, represents all the varieties of labor and was inspired by the writings of Carlyle. Maurice and Carlyle are the "brain-workers" (City Art Galleries, Manchester).*

God and redeemed humanity. Maurice concluded his work with the conviction that when we realize that we are members of one another and that injury to one is injury to all,

> So there will be discovered beneath all the politics of the Earth, sustaining the order of each country, upholding the charity of each household, a City which has foundations, whose builder and maker is God. It must be for all kindreds and races; therefore with the Sectarianism which rends Humanity asunder, with the Imperialism which would substitute for Universal fellowship a Universal death, must it wage implacable war. Against these we pray as often as we ask that God's will may be done in Earth as it is in Heaven.

Maurice's health failed in 1871, and he died at Cambridge on Easter Monday, 1 April 1872.

Maurice's most consistent target was the emphasis on humanity's damnation rather than on salvation and deliverance. Somewhat in the vein of such Romantic poets as William Blake, he considered much contemporary theology as an absolute perversion of true teaching. His son reports that a common saying of his was that "the young men of his day would not believe in the Devil that was presented to them as God and therefore called themselves Atheists." In *Eustace Conway,* the protagonist is told to "strive to emancipate your brethren; not by telling them how evil their institutions *are,* how evil society *is,* (you have found that that belief has begotten despondency in you), but by telling them how virtuous and great they *may be.*" Maurice was under no illusions as to the health of the Church of England or of English society. He believed, however, that improvement lay neither in a smug status quo nor in ill-conceived plans to destroy it.

Maurice in his lifetime was both extravagantly praised and extravagantly criticized, often on grounds of partisanship. Julius Hare, a mentor, close friend, and later brother-in-law, considered him the greatest mind since Plato. Leslie Stephen, who wrote the influential entry on Maurice in the *Dictionary of National Biography,* once said of him in a private letter, "Of all the muddleheaded intricate futile persons I ever studied, he was the most utterly bewildering." Maurice's unorthodox (at least by the standards of his own time) writings and actions were bound to make this paradoxically shy and modest person a center of controversy, and unbiased estimates of him were few in his lifetime.

In the twentieth century a more balanced estimate of him has emerged. Although Maurice was largely neglected in the period between the two world wars, since 1945 he has been the object of much study and writing in the fields of church history, education, literature, political theory, and, especially, theology. Maurice will never again be a household word, but his writings still have power to influence later generations in a world yet faced by many of the conflicts and problems in theology and human relationships he struggled so long and hard to resolve.

Bibliographies:

G. J. Gray, Bibliography, in *The Life of Frederick Denison Maurice Chiefly Told in His Own Letters,* edited by Frederick Maurice, 2 volumes (London: Macmillan, 1884; New York: Scribners, 1884)—bibliography appears in second and subsequent editions only;

Peter Allen and E. Cleve Want, "The Cambridge 'Apostles' as Student Journalists: A Key to Authorship in the *Metropolitan Quarterly Magazine* (1825-6)," *Victorian Periodicals Newsletter,* 6 (December 1973): 26-33.

Biographies:

Frederick Maurice, ed., *The Life of Frederick Denison Maurice Chiefly Told in His Own Letters,* 2 volumes (London: Macmillan, 1884; New York: Scribners, 1884);

C. F. G. Mastermann, *Frederick Denison Maurice* (London & Oxford: Mowbray, 1907);

Florence Higham, *Frederick Denison Maurice* (London: SCM Press, 1947).

References:

Peter Allen, *The Cambridge Apostles: The Early Years* (Cambridge: Cambridge University Press, 1978);

Allen, "F. D. Maurice and J. M. Ludlow: A Reassessment of the Leaders of Christian Socialism," *Victorian Studies,* 11, no. 4 (1968): 461-482;

Anglican Theological Review, 54 (October 1972), issue devoted to articles based on papers read at the American Maurice Centenary Conference, 1972;

Olive J. Brose, *Frederick Denison Maurice: Rebellious Conformist* (Athens: Ohio University Press, 1971);

Torben Christensen, *The Divine Order: A Study in F. D. Maurice's Theology* (Leiden: Brill, 1973);

Christensen, *Origin and History of Christian Socialism 1848-54* (Aarhus: Universitetsforlaget, 1962);

W. Merlin Davies, *An Introduction to F. D. Maurice's Theology* (London: S.P.C.K., 1964);

Claude Jenkins, *F. D. Maurice and the New Reformation* (London: S.P.C.K., 1938);

Henry Longueville Mansel, *An Examination of the Rev. F. D. Maurice's Strictures on the Bampton Lectures of 1858* (London: Murray, 1859);

Mansel, *The Limits of Religious Thought Examined in Eight Lectures Delivered Before the University of Oxford, in the Year 1858, on the Bampton Foundation* (Oxford: Murray, 1858);

Mansel, *Man's Conception of Eternity: An Examination of Mr. Maurice's Theory of a Fixed State out of Time* (London: Parker, 1854);

C. F. G. Mastermann, *John Malcolm Ludlow the Builder of Christian Socialism* (Cambridge: Cambridge University Press, 1963);

Frank Mauldin McClain, *Maurice: Man and Moralist* (London: S.P.C.K., 1972);

Mary Louise McIntyre, "Deliverance: Notes on a Sermon, 'The Absolution' delivered by F. D. Maurice at Lincoln's Inn on December 10, 1848," *Historical Magazine of the Protestant Episcopal Church,* 54 (March 1985): 51-66;

H. Richard Niebuhr, *Christ and Culture* (New York: Harper & Row, 1951);

Schubert M. Ogden, *Christ Without Myth: A Study Based on the Theology of Rudolf Bultmann* (New York: Harper & Row, 1961);

John F. Porter and William J. Wolf, *Toward the Recovery of Unity: The Thought of Frederick Denison Maurice* (New York: Seabury Press, 1964);

Arthur Michael Ramsey, *F. D. Maurice and the Conflicts of Modern Theology* (Cambridge: Cambridge University Press, 1951);

Bernard M. G. Reardon, *From Coleridge to Gore: A Century of Religious Thought in Britain* (London: Longman, 1971);

Charles Richard Sanders, *Coleridge and the Broad Church Movement: Studies in S. T. Coleridge, Dr Arnold of Rugby, J. C. Hare, Thomas Carlyle and F. D. Maurice* (Durham: Duke University Press, 1942);

Alec R. Vidler, *F. D. Maurice and Company: Nineteenth Century Studies* (London: SCM Press, 1966);

Vidler, *The Theology of F. D. Maurice* (London: SCM Press, 1948); republished as *Witness to the Light: F. D. Maurice's Message For Today* (New York: Scribners, 1948);

H. G. Wood, *Frederick Denison Maurice* (Cambridge: Cambridge University Press, 1950).

Papers:

There are substantial collections of Maurice's papers at the British Library (in the Kingsley, Gladstone, and Macmillan collections); the Cambridge University Library (in the Ludlow and Maurice collections); the Working Men's College, London (Muniments Room); King's College, London (Relton Library); and the Huntington Library, San Marino, California.

Henry Mayhew

(25 November 1812-25 July 1887)

Anne Humpherys
Lehman College, City University of New York

See also the Mayhew entry in *DLB 18, Victorian Novelists After 1885.*

BOOKS: *The Wandering Minstrel: A One-Act Farce* (London: Miller, 1834; Philadelphia: Turner, 1836);

"But however"—: A Farce in One Act, by Mayhew and Henry Baylis (London: Chapman & Hall, 1838);

What to Teach and How to Teach It: So that the Child May Become a Wise and Good Man, Part I (London: Smith, 1842);

The Prince of Wales's Library: No. I—The Primer (London: Illuminated Magazine, 1844);

The Greatest Plague of Life; or, The Adventures of a Lady in Search of a Good Servant, by Mayhew and Augustus Mayhew (London: Bogue, 1847; London & New York: Routledge, 1859);

The Good Genius That Turned Everything into Gold; or, The Queen Bee and the Magic Dress, by Mayhew and Augustus Mayhew (London: Bogue, 1847);

Whom to Marry and How to Get Married! or, The Adventures of a Lady in Search of a Good Husband, by Mayhew and Augustus Mayhew (London: Bogue, 1847-1848; New York: New World, 1848);

The Image of His Father; or, A Tale of a Young Monkey, by Mayhew and Augustus Mayhew (London: Hurst, 1848; New York: Harper, 1848);

The Magic of Kindness; or, The Wondrous Story of the Good Huan (London: Darton, 1849; New York: Harper, 1849);

Acting Charades; or, Deeds Not Words, by Mayhew and Augustus Mayhew (London: Bogue, 1850);

The Fear of the World; or, Living for Appearances, by Mayhew and Augustus Mayhew (New York: Harper, 1850); republished as *Living for Appearances* (London: Blackwell, 1855);

Low Wages: Their Causes, Consequences, and Remedies, parts 1-4 (London: Woodfall, 1851);

London Labour and the London Poor, Nos. 1-63 (volume 1 and parts of volumes 2 and 3, London: Woodfall, 1851-1852; 4 volumes [volume 4 by Mayhew and others], London: Griffin, Bohn, 1861-1862; New York: Dover, 1968);

Henry Mayhew

1851; or, The Adventures of Mr. and Mrs. Sandboys and Family, who came up to London to 'enjoy themselves,' and to see the Great Exhibition, by Mayhew and George Cruikshank (London: Bogue, 1851);

The Story of the Peasant-Boy Philosopher; or, A Child Gathering Pebbles on the Sea Shore (London: Bogue, 1854; New York: Harper, 1855);

The Wonders of Science; or, Young Humphry Davy (London: Routledge, 1855; New York: Harper, 1856);

The Rhine and Its Picturesque Scenery (London: Bogue, 1856; New York: Bangs, 1856);

The Great World of London, Parts 1-9 (London: Bogue, 1856); completed by John Binny as *The Criminal Prisons of London and Scenes of Prison Life* (London: Griffin, Bohn, 1862);

The Upper Rhine: The Scenery of Its Banks and the Manners of Its People (London: Routledge, 1858; London & New York: Routledge, Warne & Routledge, 1860);

Young Benjamin Franklin; or, The Right Road through Life (London: Blackwood, 1861; New York: Harper, 1862);

The Boyhood of Martin Luther (London: Low, 1863; New York: Harper, 1864);

German Life and Manners as Seen in Saxony at the Present Day (2 volumes, London: Allen, 1864);

Report Concerning the Trade and Hours of Closing Usual among the Unlicensed Victualling Establishments at Certain So-Called "Working Men's Clubs" (London: Judd, 1871);

Mont Blanc: A Comedy in Three Acts, by Mayhew and Athol Mayhew (London: Privately printed, 1874);

The Unknown Mayhew, edited by E. P. Thompson and Eileen Yeo (New York: Pantheon, 1971);

Voices of the Poor, edited by Anne Humpherys (London: Cass, 1971).

OTHER: *Figaro in London,* volumes 4-8, edited by Mayhew (London: Strange, 1835-1839);

The Comic Almanac, edited by Mayhew (London: Bogue, 1850-1851);

"On Capital Punishments," in *Three Papers on Capital Punishment* (London: Cox & Wyman, 1856);

The Shops and Companies of London and the Trades and Manufactories of Great Britain, parts 1-7, edited by Mayhew (London: Strand, 1865);

London Characters, second edition, includes contributions by Mayhew (London: Chatto & Windus, 1874).

PERIODICAL PUBLICATIONS: "Labour and the Poor," letters 1-82, London *Morning Chronicle,* 19 October 1849-12 December 1850;

"The Great Exhibition," parts 1-9, Edinburgh *News and Literary Chronicle,* 1851.

Henry Mayhew's reputation as a pioneering nineteenth-century social historian has been as uneven as his career itself. In actual time, Mayhew's important work took up only eight years of a long forty-year working life, and even during those eight years he was engaged in conducting his investigations for only four. Not a little of what is impressive about his career, in fact, lies in the quality and quantity of work he produced in such a short time, none of it, however, finished.

In his twenties and thirties, Mayhew was known as part of a group of popular journalists whose usually precarious livelihoods came from the emerging comic press and the popular stage. Little of what Mayhew produced during these years is significant in itself, though he played an important role in the development of the satirical press in the early Victorian period by giving a generally responsible tone to *Figaro in London* and *Punch,* both of which he helped found. But in 1849, in the course of a more or less conventional reporting job for the *Morning Chronicle* (after the *Times* probably the most important daily in England), he found his subject, his style, and, ultimately, his fame.

For three years Mayhew, an apparently indolent man who seems to have had considerable trouble finishing projects, worked at an astonishing rate, producing hundreds of interviews of thousands of words with London's underpaid skilled and unskilled workers, as well as with many more men, women, and children who existed on the margins of society—the restless, the inventive, and, to their contemporaries, the alien population of street sellers, finders, petty criminals, and itinerant entertainers. But after this intense three-year period was brought to a sudden halt, ostensibly by a lawsuit, Mayhew never regained his enthusiasm or his will to work, except for a brief six months or so in 1856 when he conducted a survey of the London prisons, completed for publication by John Binny as *The Criminal Prisons of London and Scenes of Prison Life* (1862).

The initial interviews of the skilled and unskilled workers that Mayhew conducted for the *Morning Chronicle* in 1849-1850 made his contemporary reputation as reformer, writer, and humanitarian. But this reputation was as short as was his serious working life. Though he lived until 1887, after 1860 he passed into an obscurity which was so complete that his works were not available again until the 1950s when Peter Quennell edited a series of selections from *London Labour and the London Poor,* a work of several volumes that began to appear in 1851. In 1955, when the London County Council decided to honor him with a blue plaque on the house where he had lived with his brother Alfred, they did so mainly for his role as a founder of *Punch,* a magazine in whose beginning he did have a solid role but with which his association lasted only two years. In the 1960s and 1970s, scholarly interest in urban history, in working-class literature, and in the issues of social history brought Mayhew's major work back into prominence, and its stature has been increasing ever since. Mayhew's social histories—his contributions on the skilled and unskilled poor for the *Morning Chronicle* (republished in various selected forms in the 1970s) and his *London Labour and the London Poor* (republished in full in the 1960s)—are now standard texts in nineteenth-century British studies.

Probably due to the erratic nature of his career, the biographical material on Mayhew is relatively thin. It consists of a few anecdotes handed down by his early journalistic companions, a disappointingly uninformative "biography" by his son (who also chose to honor his father only for his role in the early days of *Punch*), and a few family stories recounted by descendants of his brothers. There are a number of small details about his personal life to be deduced from his published work, but the sum total of all this information really raises more questions than it answers about the puzzling and contradictory personality of the man.

The story begins on 25 November 1812 when Mayhew was born one of seventeen children and the fourth of seven sons of a successful London solicitor, Joshua Dorset Joseph Mayhew, and his wife, Mary Ann Fenn Mayhew. Mayhew's father had the reputation of being something of a tyrant. In the late 1840s Henry Mayhew and his youngest brother Augustus satirized him in a bitter comic poem, "A Respectable Man," in which they ran down the list of his faults: hypocrisy, penuriousness, temper, and capriciousness.

Nonetheless Henry Mayhew apparently had a traditional early childhood. His family recognized his intellectual potential; Mayhew later recalled that his father expected that he, Henry, could become lord chancellor of England. His father did the best he could for his brilliant son, sending him to one of the top secondary schools in the country, Westminster. But the educational regime at that school was uncongenial to Mayhew's interests and temperament; after a number of years there, he ran away at the age of fifteen, and for the rest of his life continued to criticize the rote method and the classical curriculum at that school.

When, after this, he said he wanted to be a research chemist, his father offered him an apprenticeship to an apothecary, one of the few ways a boy could learn science in early Victorian England. Mayhew however did not take his father's offer. Instead he went as a midshipman to India, where his older brother Alfred was working with the East India Company. Mayhew's stay there was not long either, for in the late 1830s, when he was in his late teens, he was back in London, where he worked in his father's office and embarked on a program of self-education in natural science with his one-pound-a-week allowance. With his old school friend Gilbert à Beckett, he also entered the bohemian world of journalism and light drama, where he eventually was to discover his true vocation.

Joshua Mayhew had wanted all his sons to be solicitors as he was, and, as each son reached his majority, he was duly apprenticed to his father and the cost of his apprenticeship deducted from his future portion of his father's estate. But only the third son, Alfred, became a solicitor, and as a reward, when his father died in 1858, Alfred was given the bulk of the £50,000 estate. For his part, during the 1830s Henry Mayhew set up a laboratory in the house of his brother Alfred, now returned from India, and later in his own quarters in various parts of London. He seems to have read voraciously and to have mastered the fundamentals of natural science. (He later claimed to have discovered a dye similar to our aniline dyes.) Altogether, his scientific education was a significant achievement, and it led Mayhew to have a high—perhaps too high—estimate of the value of "self-help" in education. This self-training in chemistry also had an important effect on Mayhew's conception of scientific method, which he later tried to introduce into his social surveys, as he said in an October 1850 speech, "for the first time, I believe, in the world."

The other half of his life during this period, however, was equally important in preparing him for these major works. Following a debacle while working at his father's office in the early 1830s (Mayhew forgot to file some important papers and nearly caused his father to be arrested at his own dinner table), Mayhew escaped to Paris, where he met the already well-known writer Douglas Jerrold, himself avoiding creditors, and the young William Makepeace Thackeray, also trying to live cheaply. Out of this association, after all three apparently settled their affairs and returned to London, grew a close-knit, creatively supportive, happy-go-lucky circle of friends and acquaintances in the world of London journalism and light drama. They wrote for and founded many comic journals and joined together in writing farces and burlettas for the popular stage as well; Mayhew himself wrote the successful *The Wandering Minstrel* (1834) and with Henry Baylis *"But however"*— (1838). He also collaborated on works with Mark Lemon and others. These dramatic works, all unpublished, have no lasting importance.

Journalism was to be the source of Mayhew's major contributions to the literature of his time, even though of the many endeavors of Mayhew and his group during this period, only one, *Punch,* became spectacularly successful. The brain child apparently of Mayhew, the magazine began in 1841 under the joint leadership of Mayhew, Mark Lemon, and Stirling Coyne, but most of their talented friends wrote for it. Mayhew is generally credited with establishing the venerable magazine's tone of genial social criticism. He edited the magazine for a short time after its beginning, but new publishers in 1842 felt that he was not completely dependable, and from 1842 on Mark Lemon was the sole editor. Mayhew continued his association with *Punch* until March 1846, but he was gradually moving away from his old friends of the 1830s and early 1840s. He joined with many of them in Dickens's celebrated amateur theatrical of Ben Jonson's *Every Man in His Humour* in 1845, but his diminishing connection with *Punch,* his bankruptcy, and other problems seem to have loosened the ties to his old circle.

At this time in his life and indeed throughout it, Mayhew was a man of sanguine temperament, an apparently inexhaustible supply of ideas, and a totally indolent nature. He was a gay but irresponsible companion, unable to follow through on many promises and plans. This combination of talent and temperament plagued him all his life and contributed to many of the frustrations and uncompleted projects that define his life and work.

Shortly after his ouster from the editorship of *Punch,* Mayhew, undoubtedly needing money and also looking for an outlet for his more "philosophical" ideas, began on his own a two-pronged publishing venture concerned with education. Using the popular serial-part format, in 1842 Mayhew brought out one monthly number of a theoretical work, *What to Teach and How to Teach It,* and in 1844 followed it with the first (and only) number of the practical example, *The Prince of Wales's Library: No. I—The Primer,* both of which deal with common theories of education and stress the need to emphasize practical subjects and to enable the student to learn through experience rather than by the rote learning common at the time. Neither serial was completed.

Mayhew was married in 1844 at the age of thirty-two to Jane Jerrold, the oldest daughter of his friend Douglas Jerrold and nineteen at the time of her marriage. They subsequently had a son and a daughter, Athol and Amy. Throughout his life, except for the handful of years when he was doing his major social surveys, Mayhew was always on the brink of financial disaster. Such a life had to be difficult for his family, and there were a number of separations between Mayhew and his wife, one only three years after their marriage, but none permanent until later in the 1860s. Jane Mayhew took good care of her undependable husband, doing his correspondence, dealing with his creditors, being the amanuensis for his books. It could not have been an easy life for her, however, and the difficulties and problems she faced were probably the reason for the break in relations after 1850 that occurred between her father, Douglas Jerrold, and her husband.

Mayhew's marriage was the highlight of his personal life during the 1840s, even as his designation as metropolitan correspondent for the *Morning Chronicle* at the end of 1849 marked the beginning of his most significant work. Between these two events, however, was an unmitigated disaster: bankruptcy in 1846. This event probably drove his wife back to her father for a while and finished Mayhew's standing with his own father, who effectively cut him out of his will.

The fiasco was characteristic of Mayhew's happy-go-lucky attitude toward life. Upon marrying Jane Jerrold, with his usual buoyancy of spirit and carelessness about details, he bought and furnished a beautiful home for his bride at a cost way beyond his means. He was encouraged to do so, apparently because he expected to make a lot of money on a new publishing scheme he was entering into with an unreliable publisher, Thomas Lyttleton Holt. The project was the *Iron Times,* a daily journal to be made up exclusively of railroad news. The newspaper failed, however, in 1846, and Holt went bankrupt, followed very closely by Mayhew himself, who escaped going to jail only because there had been a recent change in the law.

After the bankruptcy Mayhew joined with Augustus for three years in writing a series of six novels. "The Brothers Mayhew," as they were called on the title pages, wrote these novels in a spirit of conventional light satire, and they managed to get some of the best illustrators—such as H. K. Browne or Phiz, Kenny Meadows, and George Cruikshank—to provide the plates. The novels include *The Greatest Plague of Life* (1847), *The*

Good Genius That Turned Everything into Gold (1847), *Whom to Marry and How to Get Married!* (1847-1848), *The Image of His Father* (1848), *The Magic of Kindness* (1849), and *The Fear of the World* (1850). The Brothers Mayhew also produced in 1850 a Christmas book, *Acting Charades,* for family parties. Of the fictional works, *The Greatest Plague of Life* and *Whom to Marry and How to Get Married!* are probably the best, though even these works have mainly historical interest now. In these two books the Brothers Mayhew gently satirized the pretensions of middle-class women. These comic novels are similar in spirit to what is reputed to be Mayhew's most famous contribution to *Punch,* a joke based on a well-known advertisement for furniture: "Worthy of Attention. Advice to Persons about to Marry,—Don't."

Also at this time Mayhew began his major work. In late August or September 1849, in his role as journalist, Mayhew made a visit for the *Morning Chronicle* to Jacob's Island, a slum south of the Thames. He went there because the recent murderous outbreak of cholera in London (14,000 people had died of the disease in the preceding year in London alone) had been particularly bad in this neighborhood, which housed a large number of tanning operations and which had, a decade before, been made infamous by Dickens in *Oliver Twist.* In 1849, though no one knew how cholera spread, there was a sense that since the worst outbreaks seemed to be in the slums, it must have something to do with filth, bad sanitary conditions, even overcrowding. Mayhew's assignment apparently was to look around and see what he could turn up about the conditions amid which the area's inhabitants lived.

Cover for one of the weekly numbers of Mayhew's best-known work

What Mayhew found in that visit to Jacob's Island shocked him profoundly, and the subsequent report he wrote for the *Morning Chronicle* was the genesis of his famous articles on the lot of the poor and his work as a social historian. Almost immediately after Mayhew's description of Jacob's Island was published, the newspaper announced a forthcoming major series entitled "Labour and the Poor," which was to survey the condition of the lower classes all over England. They sent special reporters to manufacturing towns such as Manchester and Leeds and others to rural agricultural counties, including Dorset and Cambridgeshire. Mayhew was appointed "Metropolitan Correspondent" to report from London.

In the course of the following year, from 19 October 1849 through 12 December 1850, the *Morning Chronicle* published eighty-two articles (or "letters" as they were called) by the metropolitan correspondent. In the beginning they appeared three times a week, alternating with letters from the manufacturing and rural districts. After January, however, the *Morning Chronicle* was committed to using a great deal of its space for publishing verbatim accounts of the debates in Parliament, and Mayhew's articles eventually appeared only once a week. But his articles had grown in length in the previous months because he included longer and longer interviews with the various working people he met during his investigations. At the height of his production for the *Morning Chronicle,* a letter could run as many as eight full-length columns.

The readers of these articles were very enthusiastic about them. People wrote laudatory letters and sent donations to a special "Labour and the Poor Fund" which at one time contained £869; there did not seem to be a single newspaper in the country that did not comment on the series, nearly all favorably and many enthusiastically. Mayhew became an instant expert, in demand as a speaker by both middle-class philanthropic groups and working men's pressure groups alike. What these readers were responding to were the same details that modern readers find so powerful in Mayhew's work, namely the pictures of working conditions and day-to-day lives of many individual men and women who struggled amid great hardship to be decent and generous. The survey was not inclusive; Mayhew covered only the clothing workers extensively and most of the space was given to the destitute "slop" or pieceworkers. But the impact went beyond these limits, for Mayhew was able to suggest a common humanity in London's workers that his readers generalized if he assiduously did not.

Mayhew evolved his method for reporting the working histories of his informants during the first two months of his work. Space was naturally limited in a newspaper, and Mayhew had to make some choices about what material to present and how to present it. His "scientific" model led him to devote an increasing amount of space to what he called the "data" for his investigation of the condition of the poor, namely the specific details gleaned from interviews with the workers themselves. But his method involved artistic choices, for Mayhew gave the information in a running narrative as though each informant were telling the uninterrupted story of his life. Mayhew eliminated his questions—though they are usually deducible—to save space and put the material in the first person. Though he made various stabs in the following years at using these "facts" to generate a theory of low wages, he never did get to any fully articulated hypothesis beyond the insistence that supply and demand did not work favorably for many workers and that piecework was devastating to the rate of pay for all workers.

The working arrangement Mayhew had with the *Morning Chronicle* did not last. He and the editors had differences over editorial practices which grew ever more exacerbated, and Mayhew finally quit as metropolitan correspondent almost exactly one year after his first articles had appeared. The quarrel was ostensibly over economic theory. The *Chronicle* editorially was a strong supporter of the benefits of free trade to all classes of society. A number of the working people Mayhew interviewed expressed opinions contrary to this position and Mayhew himself came to think it was incorrect. But the *Morning Chronicle* cut these comments out of Mayhew's reports, later justifying the practice as simple elimination of a "hacknied commonplace."

Mayhew was understandably irritated by these editorial depredations in his work, particularly since his purpose in his investigations, he said, was to determine "scientifically" the truth about the condition of the lower classes through an impartial examination of all the evidence. Such an examination was impossible if the *Morning Chronicle* editors insisted on editing out all the evidence on one side. The coup de grace was an argument between Mayhew and the editors over an article, written by another journalist and published in October 1850, praising one of the big ready-to-wear tailoring firms which was a big advertiser in the *Morning Chronicle*. Mayhew was angered by this article because this firm, the Nicholl Brothers of Regent Street, was among those he considered the worst employers with regard to the wages of their pieceworkers. Mayhew was afraid readers of the laudatory article, which was published anonymously as was all journalism during this period, might think it was by him.

Sometime during this final breakup of the *Chronicle* series, Mayhew made the arrangements for his next project, the one by which nearly all twentieth-century readers know him—*London Labour and the London Poor*. In the beginning Mayhew saw this work as a continuation of his *Chronicle* investigations into "Those that Will Work, Cannot Work, and Will Not Work" in London. The format of the new publication was a serial like that of the earlier *What to Teach and How to Teach It*. It appeared in installments of about eighteen pages from December 1850 through February 1852, a total of sixty-three issues. The page numbers of each part were consecutive so that the various numbers could be bound together and sold as a single volume.

Despite his intentions, Mayhew was not able to complete his *Chronicle* surveys in *London Labour and the London Poor;* indeed he was not even to begin them again. Instead the whole of his efforts for the next year and two months was devoted to an increasingly detailed survey of the "street folk," the men, women, and children who sold different types of food and articles in the streets and also those who collected the various street refuse either to sell again or to cart away. It is on these interviews, these "street biographies" as Mayhew called them, that his modern reputation was made, for to the twentieth-century reader the peculiarity and fecundity of mid-nineteenth-century London street life is as fascinating as it is unreachable through almost any means other than Mayhew's surveys.

Mayhew followed the same format in these interviews that he had developed at the *Morning Chronicle*. He omitted his questions and cast each "biography" in the first person so that it seems his informants tell the stories of their lives and describe the nature of their "work" in their own words, though clearly each interviewed street seller is responding to Mayhew's probing, sensitive, and imaginative questions. The range of these biographies is both astonishing and delightful, covering everything from regular costermongers to the more arcane collectors of "pure" (dogs' dung, used in tanning), discarded cigar butts (to be reprocessed into "new" cigars), loose pieces of coal dropped off barges in the shallows of the Thames (collected by children called "mud larks"), and so on. In addition Mayhew includes intermittent digressions on the lives and tricks of street patterers—who had to talk people into buying sheets printed with ballads and popular songs or other unusual items—the blind, the Irish, and the petty criminal types who inhabited low lodging houses in the slums, and the refuse collectors and river dredgers. The human spectacle in Mayhew's work is rich and full if narrowly representative in terms of the overall working class.

At the same time that Mayhew was engaged in this, his major work, he had other projects in hand. He edited the *Comic Almanac* for 1850-1851 and planned a new novel, "The Shabby Fammerly," with Augustus Mayhew. He also undertook two simultaneous and quite different assignments in connection with the Great Exhibition of the Industry of All Nations in 1851. On the one hand, in collaboration with the artist George Cruikshank, once a month from January through September he brought out a nine-part comic novel, *1851; or, The Adventures of Mr. and Mrs. Sandboys and Family*. . . . On the other hand, as a reporter in May-July of 1851, he did a series of nine articles critically commenting on the various displays at the Exhibition. Also in November and December of 1851, again as his own publisher, he produced four numbers of a projected nine-part "philosophical" treatise on political economy, *Low Wages: Their Causes, Consequences, and Remedies*, in which he proposed to codify his theories that piecework drove wages down and workers deserved a greater share of the profit generated by their work. Potentially these explanations and theories of Mayhew's could have provided an important qualification of the laissez-faire economic theory that dominated English political thought at the time. But the work was abandoned and its circulation in any case must have been miniscule since even the British Library does not have a copy of it.

Mayhew's flurry of activity lasted only two years. In February 1852 he had a falling out with the printer of *London Labour and the London Poor* over financial arrangements. The printer seized all the unsold copies of the work, including a number not yet distributed; he then got an injunction to prevent Mayhew from selling any more copies of the work. There were various court appearances and some negotiations, but nothing came of them, and this was the end of *London Labour and the London Poor* for another four years.

For these four years there is little record of Mayhew's activity. He was clearly in financial trouble after the failure of *London Labour and the London Poor*. As he had after his bankruptcy the decade before, he embarked on a series of books which he hoped would sell. This time, rather than the novels he had written earlier with Augustus Mayhew, he produced two children's books, both biographies of scientists whose lives were meant as models of self-help and self-education for young boys. In 1854 *The Story of the Peasant-Boy Philosopher*, the biography of Owen Ferguson the astronomer, was published and the next year saw *The Wonders of Science; or, Young Humphry Davy*. Though well-intentioned, these works do not have a successful balance between information and narrative, and it is hard to imagine that any child, even the most serious Victorian youth, ever found them enjoyable.

As another measure in his effort to right his financial situation, for about two years (1854-1855) Mayhew and his family went to Germany, where they could live more cheaply than in England and, in the time-honored tradition, also avoid his creditors.

Early in 1856, however, Mayhew was back in London. Perhaps his children's books did well enough to justify a return; but Mayhew also had a number of new projects that augured well for him. Not only did he have enough material gleaned from his stay in Germany to produce two travel books, but he had also reached some kind of agreement with David Bogue, a former publisher of his, who was going to finance him in a new survey of London and also republish the previously published numbers of *London Labour and the London Poor* (the lawsuit with the original publisher being in the process of settlement) in two volumes and enable Mayhew, with the help of his brother Augustus, to research the street entertainers for a third volume.

DOCTOR BOKANKY, THE STREET HERBALIST.

[*From a Daguerreotype by* BEARD.]

"Now then for the Kalibonca Root, that was brought from Madras in the East Indies. It 'll cure the tooth-ache, head-ache, giddiness in the head, dimness of sight, rheumatics in the head, and is highly recommended for the ague; never known to fail; and I've sold it for this six and twenty year. From one penny to sixpence the packet. The best article in England."

LONG-SONG SELLER.

"Two under fifty for a fardy'!"

[*From a Daguerreotype by* BEARD.]

THE STREET-SELLER OF NUTMEG-GRATERS.

[*From a Daguerreotype by* BEARD.]

THE LUCIFER MATCH GIRL.

From a Daguerreotype by BEARD

Illustrations for Mayhew's London Labour and the London Poor

The first product of Mayhew and Bogue's new association was the survey *The Great World of London,* published in monthly parts beginning in March of 1856. It was to be a broad survey of London life and occupations but after the first number it became a survey of the various London prisons. Mayhew was temperamentally and creatively unable to work on a large scale. His genius was for detail, and, as with *London Labour and the London Poor* which quickly turned from a survey of all those who do, can't, and won't work to a minutely detailed history of the street folk, the general panorama of *The Great World of London* soon became a particularized survey of London prisons, their history, disciplines, and day-to-day routines. The work was thorough in its treatment of these matters and gave Mayhew an opportunity to express his humane judgments on the psychological brutality of most of the prison regimes in London (which differed widely according to the prison involved). But he was not allowed to speak to the prisoners and was thus forced to rely on official statements and analyses. There is, however, little in his survey of prisons that could not be found elsewhere.

The more Mayhew took on the more he found to do. The year 1856 contrasts sharply with the previous two years. While conducting research on the London prisons for *The Great World of London* he also produced his first travel book, *The Rhine and Its Picturesque Scenery.* He was asked to address the committee working to abolish capital punishment and his thoughtful speech on that subject was subsequently published by the committee. He was involved again in free-lance journalism, writing for Henry Vizetelly's cheap daily the *Illustrated Times.* He continued his interest in working-class concerns by supporting various plans for inexpensive and accessible entertainments for the lower classes. He also stage-managed several unusual gatherings of parolees and "swell mobsmen" (con men who dressed as gentlemen) to gather information for his ongoing investigations of prisons and criminal life.

Despite the variety of activity, Mayhew's major hopes were undoubtedly fastened on the two-part project with Bogue. Such hopes were soon to be completely and finally crushed, for Bogue died very suddenly (he was only forty-four) and both *The Great World of London* and the plans for the completion of *London Labour and the London Poor* were stopped in mid sentence. Bogue's death marked the end of Mayhew's career as a social investigator of the working class in London. He never picked up his pen on their behalf again. The reasons are complex; they have to do with his personality—his irresponsibility and his difficulty of finishing his work—and also the fact that public interest in his subjects was no longer there. Readers cared less about revelations of low wages and poor working conditions than they had in the late 1840s. Mayhew's "street biographies" had always had less appeal for his contemporaries than for modern readers, partly because the circulation of *London Labour and the London Poor* was small and also because the street folk were not as pathetic, not as easy to patronize as were the subjects of the *Morning Chronicle* investigations. This mixture of personal and social causes plus some plain bad luck in Bogue's death ended Mayhew's career as a social historian less than ten years after it had begun. Lacking his subject of labor and the poor, Mayhew never again did any significant writing during the long thirty years left in his life.

Mayhew went back to earlier enterprises but none was long lasting. In 1857 he and Augustus Mayhew began to publish serially the novel *Paved with Gold,* but Henry Mayhew did not stay with the project beyond five numbers, and on the 1858 publication of the novel in book form, Augustus received sole credit. Henry Mayhew returned to his earliest activity, the drama, by putting together a comic review in which he spoke about his work on *London Labour and the London Poor.* He imitated various street people, and a friend played the piano and sang humorous songs. This review had some success in London, it seems, and in the summer it made the rounds of the watering spots. But in Brighton, Mayhew was driven off the stage when he saw his father grimly sitting in the front row. After Joshua Mayhew chastised him for "compromising the respectability of his family by continuing so 'degrading' a pursuit," Mayhew abruptly abandoned the project. This may have been one of the last encounters between Mayhew and his father, for Joshua Mayhew died the following year.

Mayhew tried a little of everything in the following years. He produced another travel book, *The Upper Rhine,* in 1858 and edited the paper the *Morning News* for a short time in 1859. He wrote another children's book, *Young Benjamin Franklin* (1861), and then went to Germany again.

Mayhew later said he went to Germany to research a book on Martin Luther and indeed in 1863 his last children's book, *The Boyhood of Martin Luther,* was published. It is equally likely, however, that the trip was motivated by his precarious financial situation, as before. His wife and children went with him and the family lived for two or three

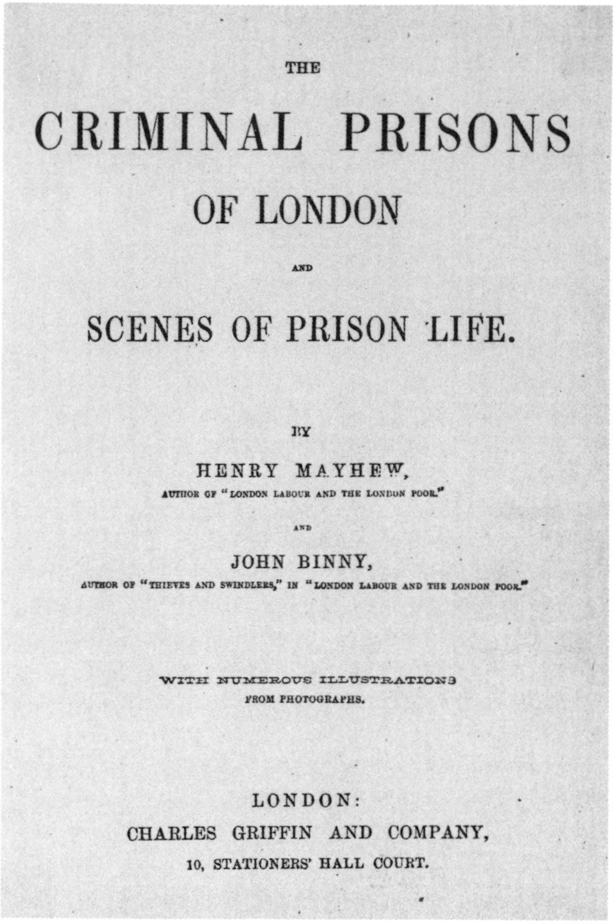

THE

CRIMINAL PRISONS

OF LONDON

AND

SCENES OF PRISON LIFE.

BY

HENRY MAYHEW,

AUTHOR OF "LONDON LABOUR AND THE LONDON POOR."

AND

JOHN BINNY,

AUTHOR OF "THIEVES AND SWINDLERS," IN "LONDON LABOUR AND THE LONDON POOR."

WITH NUMEROUS ILLUSTRATIONS

FROM PHOTOGRAPHS.

LONDON:

CHARLES GRIFFIN AND COMPANY,

10, STATIONERS' HALL COURT.

Title page for Mayhew's survey of London jails completed by John Binny for publication in 1862

years in Eisenach. Either just before he left or while he was away, *London Labour and the London Poor* finally reached the form in which it has come down to modern readers. In 1861 three volumes, identical to the 1851 text, were published in book form; a fourth volume, written by other authors except for the first thirty-seven pages, and *The Criminal Prisons of London and Scenes of Prison Life,* the last 140 pages written by John Binny, appeared the next year. There seems to have been little if any critical interest in *The Criminal Prisons,* and in 1865 a cheap reprint of the four volumes of *London Labour and the London Poor* appeared with hardly a remark in the press.

The mid 1860s saw the last of Mayhew's work. In 1864 he produced a final book on Germany, the two-volume *German Life and Manners as Seen in Saxony at the Present Day,* based on his stay a few years before. This work is, like his other two books on Germany, prejudiced and ill-tempered in its evaluation of the Germans. Mayhew was not happy in Germany; being there made him fiercely pro-English, and the complacency of his view of his own country in these books is as surprising, coming from the author of "Labour and the Poor," as his attacks on everything German are painful to read.

The next year for several months he edited a monthly journal entitled the *Shops and Companies of London,* a survey of various skilled industries in London. Though it might appear at first that in this project he had returned to the subject of labor in London, he was interested only in the management view of each of the trades and as a result the various reports are little more than advertising specials.

Records of Mayhew's activity after 1865 are again quite scarce. He suggested various projects in the late 1860s and early 1870s but none seems to have materialized. He is reported by one source to have been a correspondent in 1870 at Metz during the first major engagement of the Franco-Prussian War. He edited one issue of *Only Once a Year,* a cheap and insignificant miscellany, and investigated working men's clubs for licensed victuallers who were worried about the competition. His reputation for fairness and good investigative reporting was thus still intact, but he made nothing out of it. Some of his earlier pieces in the *Morning Chronicle* and in *London Labour and the London Poor* were republished unchanged in *London Characters,* a volume of sketches by several authors which appeared in 1874. For his final publication he returned to the mode of his first: he and his son wrote a play in 1874, *Mont Blanc,* based on a French farce, which was not a success on the stage.

How Mayhew managed to live in these later years of his life is not known. Presumably he continued to have the one pound a week his father left him in his will. Perhaps that was all he had. His wife sometime in the years after 1865 moved in with her daughter and son-in-law, and, though Mayhew visited Sundays for dinner, the separation was permanent. He was not with his wife when she died in 1880. Mayhew himself died in near total obscurity in 1887, leaving an "estate" totaling ninety pounds, ten shillings, by today's standards about five hundred dollars. His work on labor and the poor at mid century was almost as completely forgotten as was the author himself when he died.

This neglect lasted for almost a hundred years, although Mayhew always had a kind of underground reputation with students of the Victorian period. With the publication of Peter Quennell's selections (*Mayhew's London,* and *May-*

hew's Characters, 1951), his reputation began to grow, and in the 1970s Mayhew became a well-known Victorian writer again. Critical opinion has generally been enthusiastic about the picture of street life that emerges from *London Labour and the London Poor,* and, since 1971, when E. P. Thompson and Eileen Yeo edited the first selections of articles on "Labour and the Poor" from the *Morning Chronicle* in *The Unknown Mayhew,* the author has received praise for his depiction of working-class London life.

But there have also been reservations expressed, both in Mayhew's own time and in recent years, about the accuracy of both the general picture and the specific details. Some readers have suspected Mayhew of "doctoring" details to make them more lively, more sensational, or more pathetic. Another type of reservation is that expressed by Gertrude Himmelfarb, who sees Mayhew as the prime exponent of the view of the poor as an alien race. Himmelfarb herself sufficiently distrusts the reliability of Mayhew's reported interviews not to have used them in her book *The Idea of Poverty* (1984), though she quotes Mayhew's comments extensively.

The issue of Mayhew's accuracy can never be resolved with complete satisfaction. What went on at the interviews or afterward when Mayhew wrote up the reports will never be known. If, however, one takes his surveys as a whole—as he surely intended that his readers should—and resists the temptation to place undue weight on individual statements or "facts" his work can stand as a vitally important historical document. Mayhew himself went to great lengths to assure the general accuracy of his survey—lengths far in excess of standard Victorian procedures even for parliamentary investigations. He tried to have a variety of workers in different categories of an industry tell their stories and give figures. He held large meetings at which many workers in the same trade gave testimony. He did not, because his work was unfinished, ever point out discrepancies or attempt to account for any particular differences in statistics or evidence, which is why one must be cautious about his details. But he seemed convinced that the various informants confirmed one another's reports more than they contradicted them. There are typographical errors in all the accounts, and in some cases Mayhew was undoubtedly careless or misinformed. But overall, the accuracy of the picture of the life and work of the poor and the marginal in mid-Victorian London that emerges from reading the whole of Mayhew's social surveys is as reliable as it is powerful.

References:

James Bennett, *Oral History and Delinquency. The Rhetoric of Criminology* (Chicago & London: University of Chicago Press, 1981), pp. 11-64, 265-274;

John L. Bradley, Introduction to *Selections from "London Labour and the London Poor"* (London: Oxford University Press, 1965);

Gertrude Himmelfarb, "The Culture of Poverty," in her *The Idea of Poverty. England in the Industrial Age* (New York: Knopf, 1984), pp. 312-356;

Anne Humpherys, *Henry Mayhew* (Boston: G. K. Hall, 1984);

Humpherys, *Travels into the Poor Man's Country: The Work of Henry Mayhew* (Athens: University of Georgia Press, 1977);

Athol Mayhew, *A Jorum of Punch* (London: Downey, 1895);

F. B. Smith, "Mayhew's Convict," *Victorian Studies,* 22 (Summer 1979): 431-448;

M. H. Spielman, *The History of "Punch"* (New York: Cassell, 1895);

E. P. Thompson, "Mayhew and the 'Morning Chronicle,' " in *The Unknown Mayhew,* edited by Thompson and Eileen Yeo (New York: Pantheon, 1971), pp. 11-50;

Eileen Yeo, "Mayhew as a Social Investigator," in *The Unknown Mayhew,* edited by Thompson and Yeo (New York: Pantheon, 1971), pp. 51-95.

John Stuart Mill

Eugene R. August
University of Dayton

John Stuart Mill

BIRTH: Pentonville, London, 20 May 1806, to James and Harriet Burrow Mill.

MARRIAGE: 21 April 1851 to Harriet Hardy Taylor.

DEATH: Avignon, France, 7 May 1873.

BOOKS: *A System of Logic, Ratiocinative and Inductive, Being a Connected View of the Principles of Evidence, and The Methods of Scientific Investigation* (2 volumes, London: Parker, 1843; revised, 1846; 1 volume, New York: Harper, 1846; revised again, 1851, 1856, 1862, 1865, 1868, 1872);

Essays on Some Unsettled Questions of Political Economy (London: Parker, 1844);

Principles of Political Economy, with Some of Their Applications to Social Philosophy, 2 volumes (London: Parker, 1848; Boston: Little & Brown, 1848; revised, 1849, 1852, 1857, 1862, 1865, 1871);

On Liberty (London: Parker, 1859; Boston: Ticknor & Fields, 1863);

Thoughts on Parliamentary Reform (London: Parker, 1859; revised and enlarged, 1859);

Dissertations and Discussions, Political, Philosophical, and Historical. Reprinted Chiefly from the Edinburgh and Westminster Reviews (4 volumes: volumes 1-2, London: Parker, 1859; volumes 3-4, London: Longmans, Green, Reader & Dyer, 1867, 1875; 5 volumes, Boston: Spenser, 1864-1868);

Considerations on Representative Government (London: Parker, Son & Bourn, 1861; New York: Harper, 1862);

Utilitarianism (London: Parker, Son & Bourn, 1863; revised, 1864, 1867, 1871; Boston: Small, 1887);

Auguste Comte and Positivism (London: Trübner, 1865; Philadelphia: Lippincott, 1866);

An Examination of Sir William Hamilton's Philosophy and of the Principal Philosophical Questions Discussed in His Writings (1 volume, London: Longmans, Green, Longman, Roberts & Green, 1865; 2 volumes, Boston: Spencer, 1866; revised, 1867, 1872);

Inaugural Address Delivered to the University of St. Andrews, Feb. 1st, 1867 (London: Longmans, Green, Reader & Dyer, 1867; Boston: Littell & Gay, 1867);

England and Ireland (London: Longmans, Green, Reader & Dyer, 1868);

The Subjection of Women (London: Longmans, Green, Reader & Dyer, 1869; Philadelphia: Lippincott, 1869);

Chapters and Speeches on the Irish Land Question (London: Longmans, Green, Reader & Dyer, 1870);

Autobiography (London: Longmans, Green, Reader & Dyer, 1873; New York: Holt, 1873);

Three Essays on Religion (London: Longmans, Green, Reader & Dyer, 1874; New York: Holt, 1874);

Early Essays by John Stuart Mill, edited by J. W. M. Gibbs (London: Bell, 1897);

The Spirit of the Age, edited by Frederick A. von Hayek (Chicago: University of Chicago Press, 1942);

Mill on Bentham and Coleridge, edited by F. R. Leavis (London: Chatto & Windus, 1950; New York: Stewart, 1951);

Prefaces to Liberty: Selected Writings of John Stuart Mill, edited by Bernard Wishy (Boston: Beacon, 1959);

John Mill's Boyhood Visit to France; being a Journal and Notebook Written by John Stuart Mill in France, 1820-21, edited by Anna Jean Mill (Toronto: University of Toronto Press, 1960);

Essays on Literature and Society, edited by J. B. Schneewind (New York: Collier Books, 1965);

Literary Essays, edited by Edward Alexander (Indianapolis: Bobbs-Merrill, 1967);

The Nigger Question, by Thomas Carlyle, and *The Negro Question,* by John Stuart Mill, edited by Eugene R. August (New York: Appleton-Century-Crofts, 1971);

Essays on Poetry, edited by F. Parvin Sharpless (Columbia: University of South Carolina Press, 1976).

Collection: *Collected Works of John Stuart Mill,* edited by John M. Robson and others, 25 volumes, ongoing (Toronto: University of Toronto Press, 1963-).

OTHER: *The Rationale of Judicial Evidence, From the Mss. of Jeremy Bentham,* edited with a preface by Mill, 5 volumes (London: Hunt & Clarke, 1827);

James Mill, *Analysis of the Phenomenon of the Human Mind, with Notes Illustrative and Critical by Alexander Bain, Andrew Findlater, and George Grote,* edited with additional notes by John Stuart Mill, second edition, 2 volumes (London: Longmans, Green, Reader & Dyer, 1869);

Four Dialogues of Plato, including the "Apology" of Socrates, translations and notes by Mill, edited by Ruth Borchardt (London: Watts, 1947).

Like many aspects of John Stuart Mill's life and work, his literary artistry remains a subject of enduring interest and lively disagreement. Few people would now question Mill's importance as spokesman for the humane liberal tradition in the history of ideas, although considerable controversy still flares over the nature and value of his views upon such topics as individual liberty, epistemology, Utilitarian ethics, sexual and racial equality, economic theory, and religious belief. Similarly, the question of Mill's prose artistry is far from settled.

From the day in 1873 when Thomas Carlyle in a letter to his brother John dismissed Mill's *Autobiography* as the life history of a steam engine to the recent characterization of Mill in a widely used anthology of literature as the "least literary of the important Victorian prose writers," some readers have insisted that Mill's prose is almost entirely devoid of art. Mill has been seen by these readers as a frosty rationalist without a tincture of the poet, his prose being notable chiefly for its utilitarian starkness. Other readers, however, have pointed to the extraordinary power of many of Mill's writings. In particular, the ability of these works to influence people's ideas, attitudes, and lives suggests that logic alone is insufficient to account for their impact. Thomas Hardy's citing *On Liberty* (1859) as a cure for despair is but one of many examples of Mill's influence. Also, a number of studies in the past twenty years have convincingly traced the interweaving of imagery, metaphor, and even symbol with ratiocination in many of Mill's major texts. In the view of the authors of these pieces, Mill is one

Mill's father and mentor, James Mill. Drawing by Joseph Slater dated 1831.

of the great Victorian sages, subtly blending argument and art, not just to win a debate but also to alter his readers' perceptions of reality and to move them powerfully to live and act on those new perceptions.

Nearly all commentators, including Mill himself, agree that his life and thought were decisively shaped by his father's forceful personality and by the extraordinary education which Mill received at his hands. James Mill, a Scotsman making his way precariously in the world of London journalism, had married Harriet Burrow in 1805. A year later, John Stuart Mill was born, the first of nine children produced by what proved to be an ill-sorted union between a dynamically intellectual male and an apparently well-meaning but ineffectual female. A disciple and protégé of the Utilitarian philosopher and reformer Jeremy Bentham, James Mill chose to educate his eldest son at home, making the boy's mind a showpiece of what empirical and logical methods could produce if they were untrammeled by social and religious preconceptions. Mill's *Autobiography* (1873) provides a memorable account of this remarkable venture in Benthamite instruction. James Mill began early, teaching Greek to his son when the boy was three. During the next four years, the young Mill also studied mathematics and read widely in English books (especially histories), reporting on his reading to his father during their vigorous walks together. Between the ages of eight and fourteen, Mill studied Latin, geometry, algebra, differential calculus, experimental science, logic, and economics. Although not excluded, fiction and poetry were not strong elements in this Utilitarian education. The primary aim of the training was to enable the boy to think for himself by using empirical and rational means to arrive at truth.

Mill's education had both advantages and liabilities which manifested themselves in his later life and in his writings. At fourteen he had acquired the equivalent of a university education, as well as techniques for continuing self-learning throughout his life. His father's Benthamite bias gave Mill an unusually clearheaded and independent way of looking at controversial matters, in addition to an enthusiastic commitment to liberal reforms as a way of bettering human society. But his education at home also retarded his physical and emotional growth. Because he was kept from the "corrupting" influence of children his own age, his ability to play was arrested and his motor skills remained underdeveloped. Although Mill was not physically punished, his father's impatience and withering scorn crippled the boy's self-esteem and left him feeling unloved: the psychosexual damage evident in Mill's later life probably derives from these years of stern tutelage. According to the *Autobiography,* the tendency of his education to foster analysis at the expense of feeling also caused Mill problems in later years. Because he feared he could not love his father, inexpressiveness became second nature to Mill: high seriousness and moral indignation were the dominant modes of his personality, to the detriment of playfulness and joy.

Many characteristics of Mill's prose reflect this education. The voice in his writings is always erudite and rational; the language is more abstract than concrete. All of his major works are directed toward what Mill in the *Autobiography* called "the improvement of mankind," and the discussion in these works is conducted with unmistakable seriousness and moral purpose. The fervor of Mill's mission is often the dominant emotion in his writings, an emotion often conveyed as a strong sense of dedication and urgency. Any emotion in his writings, however, usually lies beneath the surface of a prose that seemingly acknowledges no strong feeling. Similarly, the figurative elements of his language lie embedded in a predominately rational structure. Mill's muted language is at the opposite extreme from the dazzling blend of imagery and sound in such characteristic Carlylian works as *Sartor Resartus* (1836) and *Past and Present* (1843). Nevertheless, as if in defiance of his unpoetic education, Mill's prose exhibits an identifiable imaginative dimension.

Locale may also have played a part in shaping Mill's personality. He grew up in London, mostly in Westminster in a house located in Queen Square (now Queen Anne's Gate) and maintained with financial help from Jeremy Bentham, who lived nearby. During the summer months, Bentham sometimes hosted the Mills in the country, especially at Ford Abbey in Devonshire, a rural retreat memorialized by a uniquely poetic sentence in Mill's *Autobiography*. In 1820 Mill at fourteen went to stay for nearly a year in southern France with Jeremy Bentham's brother Samuel and his family, where he acquired a taste for French language and politics, botany, and mountain scenery. It is tempting to see Westminster (a center of London radicalism) as stimulating Mill's liberal and logical tendencies, while Ford Abbey and the Pyrenees nurtured his more romantic and affective ones. Significantly, in the latter part of his life, Mill divided his year between London and Avignon.

Mill's fifteenth through his twentieth years were dominated by his commitment to becoming the "reformer of the world" (to use his term from the *Autobiography*), the rational activist that his father and Jeremy Bentham had hoped for. Upon Mill's return to England in 1821, his formal education was completed by his reading of a French redaction of one of Bentham's treatises. This important event fixed the principle of utility ("it is the greatest happiness of the greatest number that is the measure of right and wrong") as the capstone of Mill's moral vision. Mill now had a humanistic religion to fill the place of the theological one he never had. Fired by youthful enthusiasm, he began a program of self-education, joined and formed debating societies, and was present at the founding of the *Westminster Review*. A Benthamite periodical, the *Westminster* was designed to advance such "philosophical radical" views as the need for more representative government, greater freedom of public discussion, economic and social reforms to combat population growth and poverty, and the use of associationist psychology as a means of improving education and humanity's moral qualities. Mill himself began to publish in these years—first, letters to journals on controversial topics, and later a full-scale article in the *Westminster*, "Periodical Literature: Edinburgh Review" (1824). A continuation of his father's exposé of the tepidly liberal arguments and assumptions of the Whig *Edinburgh Review*, young Mill's article seethes with zealous denunciation, including some strictures on the moral tone of Shakespeare and Sir Walter Scott. In these years Mill also began working under his father at the East India House (where the younger Mill was to continue in employment until 1858). In addition, he undertook the involved task of preparing for publication the convoluted manuscript of Bentham's *Rationale of Judicial Evidence*, published in five volumes in 1827.

Utilitarian philosopher Jeremy Bentham, whose principles James Mill followed in educating his son. Portrait by H. W. Pickersgill (National Portrait Gallery).

In the midst of this activity, Mill in 1826 suffered what he later described as an excruciating "mental crisis." According to Mill's *Autobiography*, the onset of the crisis was his sudden discovery that crusading for radical causes was not enough. The greatest-happiness principle, ironically, was producing no happiness for one of its most zealous advocates. Left depressed and desperate by this realization, young Mill dragged through the winter of 1826-1827 until he found himself moved to tears by reading a passage from Jean François Marmontel's *Mémoires d'un père* (1804). Reinvigorated by this evidence of feeling within himself, Mill gradually began to recover. Eventually he came to fault his education for emphasizing analysis while neglecting emotion. In art, especially in the poetry of Wordsworth, young Mill began to find the needed resources for replenishing his feelings. The combination of rural, often mountainous, scenery and placid emotion in Wordsworth's poems provided the therapy for helping Mill to exorcise the mental gloom into which he had slipped.

Mill's account of the mental crisis as a turning point in his life has been echoed by later biographers. Some, however, have added interesting speculations of their own about its causes. Overwork, the absence of love, emotional repression have all been cited, in addition to the notion that the breakdown was partly the result of a suppressed death-wish directed by Mill against his father. The crucial passage in Marmontel, it has been pointed out, deals with a son's response to his father's death, and Mill's physical and emotional collapse at his own father's death in 1836 has not escaped notice. Whatever the causes, the mental crisis of 1826 transformed Mill personally and philosophically. Although he always adhered to basic Benthamite positions, his mental crisis sent him seeking for what he termed "many-sidedness" as opposed to his father's philosophic rigidity. In the process, he transformed the greatest-happiness principle into a more complex concept of humanity's moral development. He also transformed himself from the youthful zealot of Benthamism into a more eclectic thinker and a more humane philosopher who valued poetry as well as logic.

The 1830s were marked by Mill's continuing search for many-sidedness, by the formation (amid considerable emotional distress) of the most enduring attachment of his life, and by a series of essays which reflect his intellectual and personal odyssey. These essays, many interesting in their own right, culminate at the end of the decade in two literary masterworks, "Bentham" and "Coleridge."

Attempting to correct what he described as the "half-philosophy" of his Benthamite education, Mill sought the other half of the truth from exponents of political conservatism and idealist epistemology. By the time Bentham died in 1832, Mill was already listening half sympathetically to the Romantic poet and transcendentalist philosopher Mill called his "completing counterpart," Samuel Taylor Coleridge. Mill was also listening so attentively to the Scots "mystic" Thomas Carlyle and to the Saint-Simonian advocate Gustave d'Eichthal that each half believed that he had enlisted Mill as a disciple. Certainly when Thomas and Jane Welsh Carlyle moved to London in 1834, Mill's friendly visits to their Chelsea home were as regular as the local church bells.

Mill's true allegiance, however, lay elsewhere. In 1831 he met Harriet Hardy Taylor, the wife of an affable London merchant and the mother of their three children. As Mill and Harriet Taylor's feelings for each other grew more intense in 1832, the emotional pressure on them and her husband John Taylor mounted. Friends and family tried to dissuade Mill, but he steadfastly refused advice. Eventually, Harriet Taylor separated from her husband, living as his wife in name only, while he continued generously to support her. In deference to his feelings, Harriet Taylor and John Stuart Mill kept their relationship platonic, although they continued to see each other regularly and sometimes traveled together with her children. Once arrived at, this arrangement continued for years, only to be altered by John Taylor's death in 1849.

During the 1830s while Mill was seeking philosophic many-sidedness, his relationship with Harriet Taylor apparently contributed to his interest in poetry and renewed his respect for liberty. In

Harriet Taylor about seven years before her marriage to Mill (British Library of Political and Economic Science)

"The Spirit of the Age," a series of five essays published in seven installments under the pseudonym A. B. in the *Examiner* early in 1831, Mill's conservative enthusiasm had reached the point where he was capable of questioning the value of liberty of thought. At one point in the series—a lively dissection of current social unrest which stresses the need for philosophers who can reach beyond half-truths—Mill argues that because the mass of people in the age grasp only half-truths, it is pernicious to encourage them to assert their liberty of thought and to discard authority. This view of liberty is reversed dramatically, however, in the *Monthly Repository,* in an essay "On Genius," signed Antiquus, published more than a year later (October 1832) and presumably written after Mill's meeting with Harriet Taylor. After defining genius as simply the ability to know reality through one's own mental efforts, Mill in this essay extols thinking for oneself rather than relying upon authority. Apparently, Harriet Taylor's influence upon Mill was both early and decisive.

Of significance to students of literature are Mill's developing thoughts on poetry, perhaps best seen in four essays written during the 1830s, the first two using the pseudonym Antiquus—"What Is Poetry?" (1833), "The Two Kinds of Poetry" (1833), a review of Tennyson's poems (1835), and a review of Carlyle's *The French Revolution* (1837). (In 1859 Mill confused matters somewhat by revising the first two essays for publication in *Dissertations and Discussions,* combining them as a unit titled "Thoughts on Poetry and Its Varieties"; the views of poetry in the two essays, however, seem incompatible and represent different stages of Mill's developing formulation of poetry's nature and function.) Read in sequence, the four texts show Mill working out a justification of poetry against Bentham's contention that the poet betrays rational truth by "stimulating our passions and exciting our prejudices."

First published in the *Monthly Repository* (January 1833), "What Is Poetry?" defines poetry as feeling expressing itself in art—verse, music, painting, and so on. The poet, then, *is* truthful—to his feelings. But in the process of this justification, the essay practically denies poetry an audience: "eloquence is *heard,* poetry is *over*heard." Although Mill says that the poet may later display his artistry and thus reach an audience, he sets forth a view of poetry that has the effect of placing the poet *as poet* in isolation, cutting him off from the practical world of public affairs.

"The Two Kinds of Poetry" (*Monthly Repository,* October 1833) attempts to extend Mill's perception of poetry, and in the process it emerges as a far more important essay whose ideas echo throughout many of Mill's later works. Using associationist psychology, it argues that in the mind of the poet ideas are linked synchronously by emotion, whereas in a thinker's mind ideas are linked "in mere casual order," chronologically or successively. The essay then discriminates between a naturally poetic mind (like Shelley's) and a cultivated but not naturally poetic mind (like Wordsworth's). In the first, poetry overflows spontaneously; in the latter, thought is tinged or overlaid with emotion. Mill ironically adapts Wordsworth's definition of poetry from the preface to *Lyrical Ballads* (1798) to describe Shelley, not Wordsworth, as poet. (Shelley is accorded this accolade most likely because of Harriet Taylor's preference for his work.) The essay goes on to posit the ideal of a poet-philosopher, that is, a poetic mind which has acquired logical and scientific culture.

The readers of the *Monthly Repository* where Mill's two essays on poetry appeared were not inimical to poetry, but when Mill reviewed two volumes of Tennyson's early poetry in the *London Review* (July 1835), he was defending the utility of poetry for a largely Benthamite audience. To do so, he argues that the noblest end of genuine poetry is raising human beings toward the perfection of their nature. In discussing the poems, he acutely identifies Tennyson's natural poetic ability as shown in his powerful evocation of feeling through imagery and symbol, through what later generations would call an objective correlative. Mill also astutely notices that Tennyson is cultivating logic and science as well as poetry, and he predicts that by continuing with this labor Tennyson stands a chance of becoming a poet-philosopher such as Mill advocates.

In some ways, Mill's July 1837 review of Carlyle's *French Revolution* in the *London and Westminster Review* (the new title for the merged *London Review* and the *Westminster Review*) was a repayment for friendship, insights, and a debt of another sort. After deciding that he could not publicly reveal his disbelief in Christianity, Mill had earlier abandoned his own plans to write a history of the revolution, and when Carlyle announced his intention to attempt the subject, Mill lent him books, ideas, and encouragement. Having spent five months writing book one of the history, Carlyle lent the manuscript to Mill. Somehow, while in Mill's possession, it was accidentally burned as scrap paper, probably by a maid. When a badly shaken Mill broke the news to him, Carlyle magnanimously comforted Mill as best as he could and immediately began rewriting the lost book one. He graciously assented to Mill's heartstricken offer of temporary financial help. When the book was published, Mill hailed it in an early review, afterwards congratulating himself that he had thereby prevented the bewildered and hostile misreadings it would most likely have received in the press. But Mill's praise of *The French Revolution* was not mere flattery or atonement; he was a man of too much integrity for that. The review clearly states his metaphysical and political differences with Carlyle, but argues that the book's greatness lies beyond such matters in its poetry, that is, in its ability to re-create the feelings that accompanied historic events. Calling Carlyle's book an epic poem, Mill asserts that it is thus all the more accurate as history. Once again, Mill is expertly "selling" the utility of poetry to a Benthamite audience.

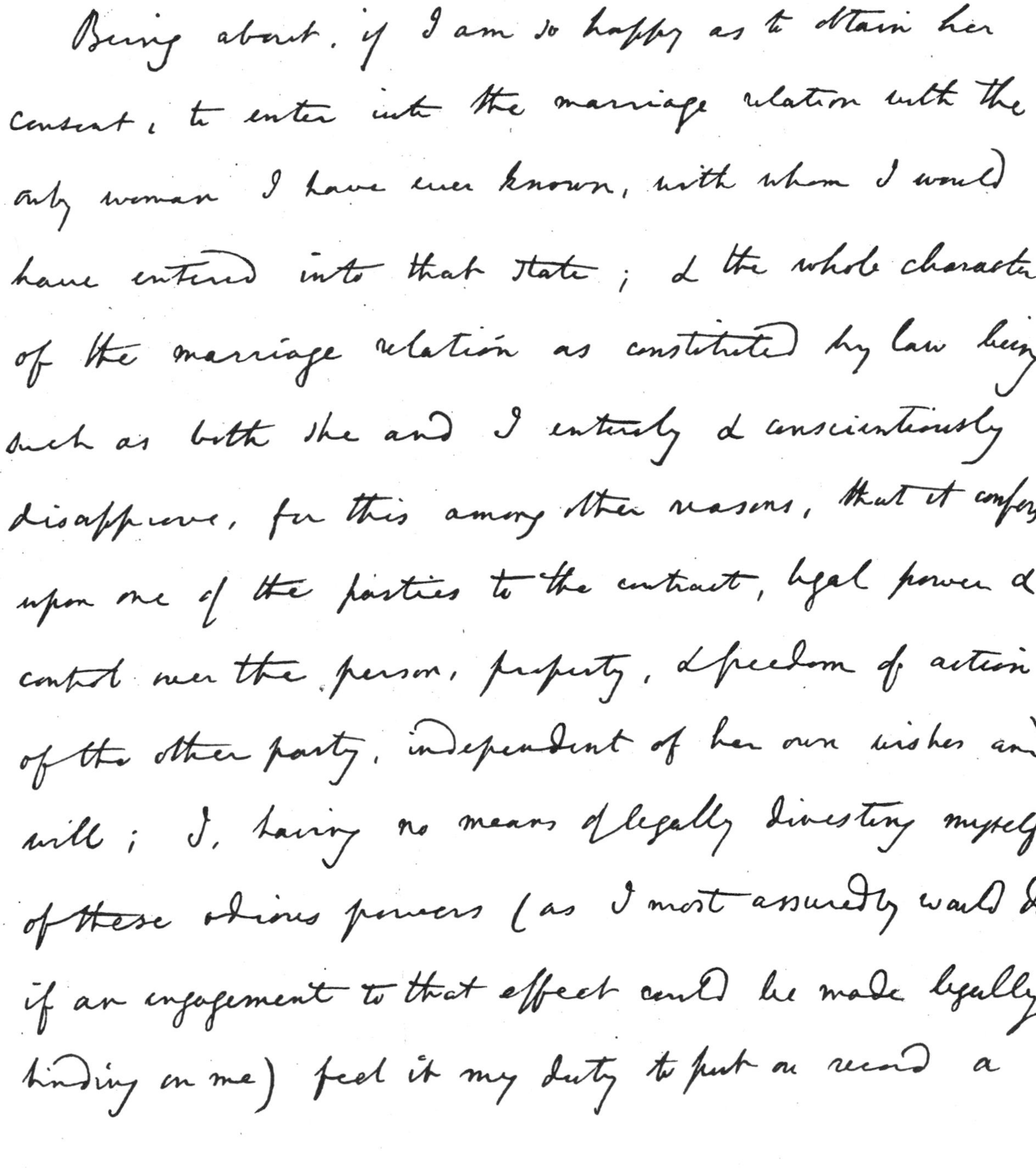

Being about, if I am so happy as to obtain her consent, to enter into the marriage relation with the only woman I have ever known, with whom I would have entered into that state; & the whole character of the marriage relation as constituted by law being such as both she and I entirely & conscientiously disapprove, for this among other reasons, that it confers upon one of the parties to the contract, legal power & control over the person, property, & freedom of action of the other party, independent of her own wishes and will; I, having no means of legally divesting myself of these odious powers (as I most assuredly would do if an engagement to that effect could be made legally binding on me) feel it my duty to put on record a

*Mill's statement, written the month before his marriage to Harriet Taylor, protesting legal rights conferred on men by Victorian marriage laws (*The Letters of John Stuart Mill*, edited by Hugh Elliot, 1910)*

formal protest against the existing law of marriage, in so far as conferring such powers; and a solemn promise never in any case or under any circumstances to use them. And in the event of marriage between Mrs Taylor and me I declare it to be my will and intention, & the condition of the engagement between us, that she retains in all respects whatever the same absolute freedom of action, & freedom of disposal of herself and of all that does or may at any time belong to her, as if no such marriage had taken place; and I absolutely disclaim & repudiate all pretension to have acquired any *rights* whatever by virtue of such marriage.

J. S. Mill.

6th March 1851

Mill's journey toward many-sidedness is charted significantly in other writings of the 1830s, in particular "Civilisation" (*London and Westminster Review,* 1836) and "Poems and Romances of Alfred de Vigny" (*London and Westminster Review,* 1838). Unfortunately, two potentially valuable essays have been lost, namely Mill's two reviews of Robert Browning's *Pauline.* Given a copy of the poem in 1833, Mill wrote a review which proved too long for its intended publication in the *Examiner,* and its revised version, intended for *Tait's Edinburgh Magazine,* never appeared in print. Although neither version of Mill's review is extant, the copy of *Pauline* containing his marginal comments and final negative appraisal of the poem has survived. In 1833 this copy had unluckily found its way back to Browning. Although the question of its impact upon the young poet is much debated, many scholars believe that Mill's commentary jolted Browning sufficiently to make him avoid similar subjective displays in future poems.

Mill's search for many-sidedness in the 1830s bore its most impressive fruit in two essays, "Bentham" (1838) and "Coleridge" (1840), both published in the *London and Westminster Review,* of which Mill was now the proprietor. In a famous introduction to a 1950 republication of the two essays, F. R. Leavis described them as "classical" documents which constitute essential reading for the student of Victorian literature. But while Leavis saw the essays as background material for "real" literature (such as George Eliot's novels), more recent critics would argue that the essays themselves are "real" literature.

The rhetorically impressive proems which open both essays contrast Bentham and Coleridge as the two seminal minds of the age, the two men who had most influenced the practical and speculative character of the times. In Mill's estimation, they are the teachers of the teachers; they have shaped the minds of the intellectuals of the age. Bentham and Coleridge are depicted as representative of two types of mind—the one logical, analytical, and precise; the other intuitive, comprehensive, and suggestive. They are almost archetypal opposites—the progressive versus the conservative, the skeptic versus the believer, the empiricist versus the transcendentalist. They are each other's "completing counterpart," accurate in what they affirm, wrong-headed in what they deny. Because each holds half the truth, it is necessary for those who desire wholeness to bring together the two men's visions. In these two impressive essays, Mill shows the way to achieving such a synthesis.

"Bentham" and "Coleridge" provide vivid examples of Mill's rhetorical ability to shape his text to fit his purpose and his audience. To broaden the outlook of doctrinaire liberal readers, the essays encourage a critical assessment of the limitations of Benthamism, while pointing to the positive insights which can be culled from a conservative school of thought such as Coleridge represents. Mill's purpose was no doubt reinforced by his personal awareness of the shortcomings of Benthamite thought and practice. While Mill clearly affirms in the essays his allegiance to Utilitarianism and duly notes its value, "Bentham" has the effect of stressing the limitations of the man and his thought, while "Coleridge" emphasizes the positive aspects of Germano-Coleridgean conservatism.

In "Bentham," the more rhetorically complex and personal of the essays, anticlimax dominates the discussion. Creatively borrowing language, imagery, metaphors, and allusions from Carlyle's review in *Fraser's Magazine* (May 1832) of John Wilson Croker's edition of *The Life of Samuel Johnson,* Mill's essay creates an elaborate picture of Bentham as father-teacher-hero-god figure; it then shows Bentham's inadequacies in all these roles. No distinction is made between the man and his philosophy: the successes and failures of the one are the successes and the failures of the other. Much about Bentham is praised—his questioning spirit, his challenge to custom-encrusted authority, his moral integrity in the face of intimidation, his introduction of precision into philosophic and social inquiry, his attacks upon vague generalizations and prejudices, his reforms of law. But the text continually assails his failures—his narrowness of vision, his failure to learn from earlier thinkers, his lack of historical perspective, his simplified views of happiness and human nature, his too-easy dismissal of ideas he could not grasp, his preposterous rejection of poetry. In the end, Bentham's achievements seem largely overwhelmed by his absurd failures. When "Bentham" created such a run on the *London and Westminster Review* that a second printing was called for, Mill added a footnote at the end of the essay depicting his subject as an irresponsible child, a final damning touch to his portrait of Bentham as man and thinker.

If "Bentham" was designed to stir a more critical attitude toward Utility among philosophical radicals, "Coleridge" was designed to foster a more sympathetic inquiry into conservative thought. The essay openly declares Mill's allegiance to Utilitarian

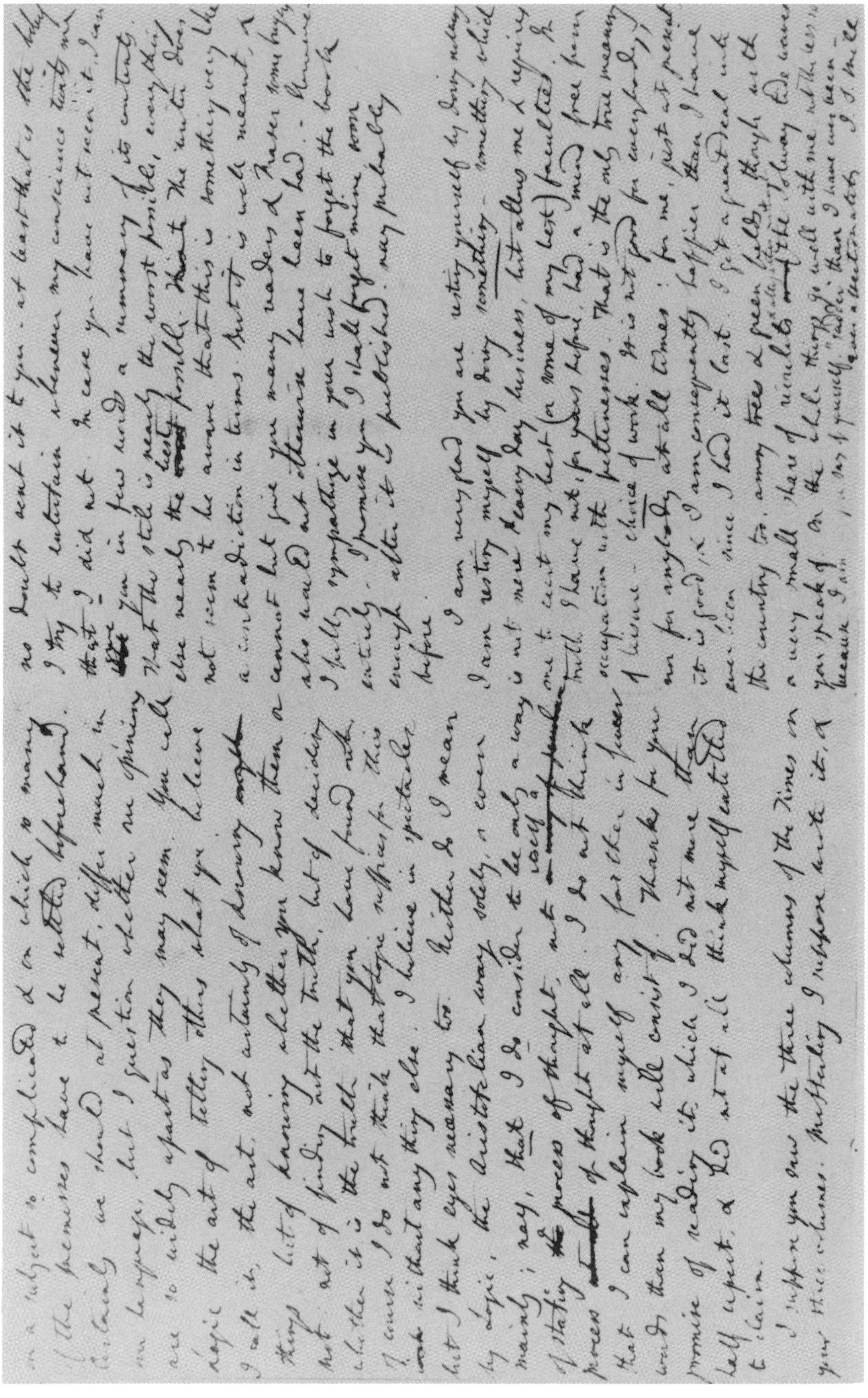

in a subject so complicated & on which so many
of the premisses have to be settled beforehand.
Certainly we should at present, differ much in
our language, but I question whether our opinions
are so widely apart as they may seem. You call
Logic the art of telling others what you believe
I call it, the art, not certainly of knowing ~~[illegible]~~
things but of knowing whether you know them or
not: not of finding out the truth, but of deciding
whether it is the truth that you have found out.
Of course I do not think that Logic suffices for this
~~[illegible]~~ without anything else. I believe in spectacles
but I think eyes necessary too. Neither do I mean
by Logic, the Aristotelian way solely, or even
mainly; nay, that I do consider to be only a way
of stating ~~the~~ process of thought, not itself a ~~[illegible]~~
process ~~[illegible]~~ of thought at all. I do not think
that I can explain myself any farther in fewer
words than my book will consist of. Thanks for your
promise of reading it, which I did not more than
half expect, & did not at all think myself entitled
to claim.

I suppose you saw the three columns of the Times on
your three volumes. Mr Sterling I suppose wrote it, &
no doubt sent it to you - at least that is the belief
I try to entertain whenever my conscience tells me
that I did not. In case you have not seen it, I can
give you in few words a summary of its contents.
That the style is nearly the worst possible, everything
else nearly the ~~[illegible]~~ best possible. ~~[illegible]~~ The writer does
not seem to be aware that this is something very like
a contradiction in terms. But it is well meant, &
cannot but give you many readers & Fraser some buyers
who would not otherwise have been had. - However
I fully sympathize in your wish to forget the book
entirely. I promise you I shall forget mine soon
enough after it is published: nay probably
before.

I am very glad you are resting yourself by doing nothing
I am resting myself by doing something - something which
is not mere everyday business, but allows me & requires
me to exert my best (or some of my best) faculties. In
truth I have not, for years before, had a mind free from
occupation with pettinesses. That is the only true meaning
of leisure - choice of work. It is not good for everybody,
nor for anybody at all times: for me, just at present
it is good, & I am consequently happier than I have
ever been since I had it last. I get a great deal into
the country too, among trees & green fields, though with
a very small share of rivulets [illegible] the Solway tide waves
you speak of. On the whole things go well with me, not the less so
because I am [illegible] "sadder" than I have ever been [illegible]
J. S. Mill

From a letter to Thomas Carlyle dated 8 August 1837, in which Mill explains his concept of "Logic," noting, "Certainly we should at present, differ much in our language, but I question whether our opinions are so widely apart as they may seem" (by permission of the Trustees of The Pierpont Morgan Library) reformers, disagrees with Coleridge's a priori metaphysics, and summarily disqualifies Coleridge's views on political economy. But most of the essay is devoted to a sympathetic survey of eighteenth-century conservative thought, showing how it operated as a corrective to the excesses of liberals and revolutionaries, and as a repository for insights which they chose to overlook. "Coleridge" is built on a pattern of thesis-antithesis-synthesis; eighteenth-century radicalism yields to eighteenth-century conservatism which in turn leads to possible nineteenth-century synthesis. When the essay focuses specifically on Coleridge's thought, it is to emphasize its value for liberal reformers. It shows that Bentham questioned institutions from the outside (so to speak), while Coleridge entered into their origins, purposes, and spirit, asking whether they were now fulfilling their original social functions. If not, they should be reformed; only if they were beyond reform should they be eliminated. Coleridge saw that institutions often provided for important human needs and that abolishing them, as radicals often heedlessly advocated, could cause more harm than good. Mill finds in Coleridge a worthy critic of Protestant bibliolatry, or worship of the letter of the Bible. Coleridge justified the existence of a national church only if it performed an educative function for society. Even Utilitarians, Mill argues, cannot complain of a conservative philosopher who teaches that the "outward" object of virtue is "the greatest producible sum of happiness of all men." The aim of "Coleridge" is to demonstrate that a Tory philosopher, while operating as a conservator of truths which Tories have forgotten or which liberals have never known, must often be a better liberal than liberals are themselves.

Writing of Bentham and Coleridge, Mill remarks in "Coleridge": "Whoever could master the premises and combine the methods of both, would possess the entire English philosophy of his age." This passage provides the clue to the image of himself which Mill creates in the essays. Rhetorically, in these essays Mill has found his characteristic voice, the voice of the whole philosopher who is able to transcend partial truths and achieve a comprehensive vision of reality. With minor variations, this is the voice in all of Mill's major writings.

During the 1840s the promise of Mill's earlier career came to fruition in two monumental works which established his reputation in England, *A System of Logic* (1843) and *Principles of Political Economy* (1848). While scholars in other disciplines have explored the significance of both works, literary critics have bestowed upon neither text the kind of attention which they have paid to Carlyle's writings on social conditions, Ruskin's on art and economics, and Newman's on religion. Yet both of Mill's works would repay literary analysis, for both are at one level polemical writings designed to persuade an audience through argument and imaginative rhetorical strategy. Both works project a vision of the world as flawed but improvable through rational means.

The most cautiously written of all Mill's works, *A System of Logic* began to take shape at least as far back as 1830, and the published work went through eight carefully revised editions in Mill's lifetime. Among his purposes was that of strengthening the claims of experiential philosophy by systematizing and validating its methods of observation, reasoning, and experimenting. In the process, *A System of Logic* both implicitly and explicitly undercuts transcendentalist assumptions. Although presented (perhaps somewhat disingenuously) as a neutral guide to rational processes which can be used by both a priori and experiential thinkers, *A System of Logic* is—and was perceived to be—an attack upon intuitionism. Part of the book's surprising popularity in Victorian times no doubt resulted from its being seen as a particularly weighty installment in "the omnipresent debate" (to borrow the title of Wendell V. Harris's 1981 book) between empiricism and transcendentalism in nineteenth-century England.

In this extensive survey of logic, book one clears the ground with a glance at the language used for naming and for formulating propositions. Mill seemingly skirts the issue of intuitive knowledge by ruling it outside the scope of logic: logic, he argues, is concerned not with how we know but how we judge what we think we know. Book two is devoted to deductive reasoning, including a close review of the syllogism. Although interesting, Mill's efforts here are not strikingly original, deduction having already received considerable examination and development from the time of Aristotle onward. By contrast induction was a comparatively neglected topic; consequently, the heart of *A System of Logic* is found in book three, an extensive and often original attempt to establish the means by which inductive reasoning can approximate an exact science. As Mill explains his position, validating inductive methods is imperative for three reasons: induction is crucial to any philosophy based upon experience, it is necessary for building reliable generalizations (and hence necessary for accurate deductive reasoning), and it is the method essential to modern science. Book four examines concerns which are "subsidiary" to induction (including, again, naming and philosophical language), and book five enjoyably enumerates the various fallacies which disrupt logic. Of most interest to students of literature is perhaps book six, "On the Logic of the Moral Sciences." Mill begins by addressing a question which deeply troubled him: does scientific predictability of human behavior negate free will? If so, then human liberty is an illusion. Mill, however, concludes that individual choice is one of the determinants of behavior. Hence human choice is possible, and it matters. After wrestling with this demon, Mill investigates the validity of various methodologies in the social sciences. The final chapter of *A System of Logic,* "Of the Logic of Practice, or Art; Including Morality and Policy," discusses what Mill calls "Art" or the knowledge of duties, practical ethics, or morality. Art proposes the ends for which Science clarifies the means. Every art requires a first principle of conduct, and (without attempting to justify his choice) Mill announces his own to be Utility—the greatest-happiness principle. But he adds a characteristic twist to this Benthamic goal: the greatest happiness of the greatest number can be best achieved by the individual's cultivation of an ideal nobility of character which must sometimes sacrifice immediate happiness or pleasure. The book which began as a dry treatise on logic concludes with a vision of the coming moral improvement of humanity.

Although at several points in the book Mill insists that *A System of Logic* is nonpolemical, the detached objectivity in the early part of book one yields increasingly to argumentative skirmishes with various opponents, especially intuitionists. If *A System of Logic* does not entirely rule out intuitive insights, it narrowly limits the field to which they can be legitimately applied. By the end of the work, intuitionism seems to have been so circumscribed as to be rendered irrelevant to most human concerns. *A System of Logic,* then, bubbles with controversies, and Mill's rhetorical skill in handling opponents deserves greater attention than it has received. Moreover, the persona or image of the "speaker" Mill creates in the book develops imaginatively throughout the work. The depersonalized logician of book one is gradually humanized through several stages into the final chapter's prophet of human moral regeneration. Even in a work as abstruse as *A System of Logic,* Mill operates as an imaginative writer.

His next major work, the encyclopedic *Principles of Political Economy,* came at the end of a decade of social concern about economic matters. The "hungry forties" in Victorian England, capped by the horrors of the Irish potato famine, left political leaders and common readers equally eager for information about the "laws" of economic matters. Like *A System of Logic, Principles of Political Economy* is a large-scale work, designed to render a recondite science understandable to a mass audience. Its massive five books describe the laws of production, the methods of distribution, exchange and value, the impact of social progress on production and distribution, and the role of government in fostering a nation's economic well-being. By stressing that the laws of production are fixed but those of distribution are not, *Principles of Political Economy* opened the door for considerable speculation about the wisdom of many accepted economic practices. Even more than *A System of Logic,* Mill's 1848 work shows him at his best as theoretician, popularizer, and polemicist. Amid the abstract theorizing, the book includes concrete illustrations of economic life from around the world and throughout history. In a series of fascinating images, it gives the reader a view of political economy that is at once panoramic and specific. Images of primitive pastoral societies, utopian communities, ryots working on Indian farms, industrial laborers toiling in British factories, desperate Irish cottiers facing rack rent and eviction, thriving American farms, and so on, bring the subject of political economy into human focus. Mill also engages once again in lively debate of controversial issues; he denounces, for example, English economic practices in Ireland, he suggests alternatives, and in later editions of *Principles of Political Economy* he inveighs against the British government's failures to act upon them.

An important clue to Mill's rhetorical method is contained in the book's full title, *Principles of Political Economy, with Some of Their Applications to Social Philosophy.* Mill, in short, is operating as both "Scientist" and "Artist." He is both describing economic laws and evaluating various economic practices in terms of a morality which posits the greatest happiness of the greatest number as its ultimate goal. Thus, *Principles of Political Economy* is also a polemical work, arguing the value of economic systems in terms of Mill's revised Utilitarian ethic. At one level, then, the book is an impassioned argument for means to improve the human lot. Once again, its rhetoric, which has been largely ignored by literary scholars, deserves at least as much attention as has been devoted to Mill's change of heart about socialism.

Three sections in *Principles of Political Economy* merit special mention for their enduring interest. The chapter "Of the Stationary State" pictures a time, dreaded by earlier theorists, when societies can no longer expand economically. Mill, however, argues that—provided population is held in check—such a state need not be feared; indeed, it is to be desired. With the necessaries of life easily taken care of, humans will be able to devote their energies to the art of living, to self-cultivation. "It is scarcely necessary to remark," Mill makes a point of remarking, "that a stationary condition of capital and population implies no stationary state of human improvement." By arguing for population control, Mill shows himself a forerunner of modern ecologists: it would be catastrophic for the human spirit, he points out, for every last acre of earth to be utilized to support a vast population. With places of natural beauty and solitude lost or greatly reduced in number, individuals will lack a crucial resource for nurturing their characters.

The following chapter, "On the Probable Futurity of the Labouring Classes," is perhaps the most famous section of *Principles of Political Economy*. It predicts that eventually workers will reject upper-class paternalism in favor of their own autonomy. Ruskin, whose animosity toward *Principles of Political Economy* was great, perhaps saw himself as one of the paternalistic sentimentalists rebuked in this chapter. Also this chapter, which originally rejected socialist schemes, was transformed in later editions (at Harriet Taylor's insistence) into an endorsement of them. As might be expected, considerable discussion has been generated among scholars about the history and implications of these changes. In the fifth book of *Principles of Political Economy*, which addresses the topic of government's legitimate role in economic matters, Mill discusses whether state-organized economies or free-enterprise systems better serve the cause of human improvement; he concludes that the preferable system is whichever one allows the greater room for individual liberty. Mill insists that, except when required by a greater good, laissez-faire or nonintervention by government "should be the general practice."

During the 1840s, as the relationship between Mill and Harriet Taylor deepened, the indignant feminism they shared increasingly influenced their thought, if not always their behavior. However radical their ideas, both contrived to live as conventionally as possible under the circumstances. Both withdrew from social life to a considerable extent, no doubt to quiet the gossip circulating about them. Harriet Taylor separated from her husband's bed but not his board, and Mill continued to live with his mother and sisters while forbidding any discussion of Harriet in his presence. In 1849, when John Taylor died of cancer, Harriet was genuinely distressed and went into a respectable period of mourning. Ever the indulgent husband, John Taylor had provided handsomely in his will for his wife's financial future, and Harriet apparently had no ideological qualms about accepting money from a husband whom she had estranged during his lifetime. Although both Mill and Harriet Taylor spent the next two years grumbling about the degenerate state of conventional matrimony, in April 1851 they slipped off to Melcombe Regis and were quietly married at the Register Office there. Later Mill went so far as to suggest that the two agnostics should remarry in a church ceremony. Before the civil ceremony Mill had written out a formal protest rejecting any legal rights which the marriage would confer upon him; Harriet Taylor wrote out no similar document absolving her future husband from the responsibilities which the marriage would impose upon him. Their marriage seems to have been less a partnership of equals than an acting out of chivalric male worship of the woman on the pedestal, and in this way it actually reflected certain Victorian ideals. Similarly, in retrospect the feminism that energized their social indignation often seems less a search for gender equality than an angry program designed to bolster female power by stressing the wrongs done to women and by ignoring the burdens imposed upon men and the problems faced by both sexes together. The quality of this feminism was to influence Mill's later writings, especially *The Subjection of Women*.

The announcement of his intended marriage proved to be the breaking point between Mill and his family, the separation being largely of his doing. Apparently feeling that his mother and siblings had received news of the impending nuptials with insufficient enthusiasm and respect, Mill heaped abuse on them and resolutely refused their attempts at reconciliation. Always touchy on the subject of Harriet Taylor, Mill could be vindictive when sufficiently aroused.

During their seven and a half years of married life, the couple lived quietly at Blackheath, crystallizing their thoughts in a series of works which, when published, would permanently establish Mill's fame as a thinker and writer. Although evidence is scanty, these works apparently originated in husband-and-wife conversations, were written down by him, revised by her, and rethought by both as time went on. Whatever the circumstances of composition, *On Liberty* (1859), *Utilitarianism* (1863), most of the *Autobiography* (1873), "Nature," and "Utility of Religion" (the last two published in *Three Essays on Religion,* 1874) were written during these years. Plans for other works were mapped out; these were published after Harriet Mill's death as *Considerations on Representative Government* (1861), *Auguste Comte and Positivism* (1865), and *The Subjection of Women* (1869).

Plagued by poor health, both John and Harriet Mill often resorted to travels on the Continent, together or separately. In 1858, just after Mill had retired from East India House, the couple set off for southern France. Along the way, Harriet Mill was taken ill and died on 3 November 1858. Emotionally devastated, Mill purchased a house within sight of the cemetery in Avignon where she was buried. For the rest of his life he spent several months of every year in southern France and often meditated for hours at her grave. Harriet Taylor Mill had become nothing less than his sacred muse in the Religion of Humanity.

No aspect of Mill studies elicits greater controversy than his relationship with Harriet Taylor. There is still little agreement about her as a person, about how and what she contributed to Mill's thought, and about whether that contribution was beneficial. In the *Autobiography* and elsewhere Mill's encomiums on his wife as a paragon of intellect and virtue are stated in such extravagant terms as to almost invite disbelief. In his 1960 book H. O. Pappe has written of the Harriet Taylor "myth," and numerous critics would agree that her saintly character and intellectual brilliance were largely figments of Mill's imagination. Others, however, would not. Commentators on Harriet Taylor range from those who depict her as Mill's intellectual equal and partner to those who depict her as a would-be bluestocking without original ideas. She has been seen by some as a liberated woman who defied Victorian conventions, by others as a pampered female who manipulated two gullible males into catering to her every whim. The destruction—at her wish—of most of her correspondence with Mill has complicated attempts to assess her character and mind. That she contributed in some way to Mill's work is clear enough, but the nature of that contribution remains uncertain despite admirable biographical and textual research in recent years. Even when the contribution is clearly established—as in the laboring-class chapter of *Principles of Political Economy*—its value remains hotly contested. Of the numerous attempts to assess Harriet Taylor's influence, perhaps the most intriguing and controversial is Gertrude Himmelfarb's 1974 book expressing her view of "the other John Stuart Mill" whose balanced thought was skewed by Harriet into radicalism, especially in *On Liberty* and *The Subjection of Women.*

Three months after Harriet Mill's death, Mill saw to it that *On Liberty* was published. The book was, in some special way, their joint production, and Mill refused to alter it once "her all but unrivalled wisdom" was no longer there to advise him. *On Liberty* was immediately hailed as a classic, a status which it enjoys to this day despite numerous critical reservations about it. Unlike many of Mill's other works, *On Liberty* has drawn the attention of literary scholars who have analyzed its skillful weaving of argument and art. Written in Mill's most energetically cogent style, the book is both a lucid argument and a rallying cry defending the civil liberty of the individual against the pressures of the state and mass society. Coming across *On Liberty* at a bookseller's, Charles Kingsley read it through at once and insisted that it had made him "a clearer-headed, braver-minded man on the spot." Many another reader has had a similar experience. The impact of *On Liberty* on Western thought and law, as well as on personal convictions, is surely enormous.

The book opens with a historical survey of the conflict between liberty and authority. Images of struggle are effectively deployed to convey a sense of dire confrontation between forces of good and evil. Mill understood that the old conflicts between rulers and populace were being replaced by a new conflict between governments of the masses and the individual. Even in democracies, the majority can become the despot that rules minorities and individuals. To defend individual liberty, Mill defines "one very simple principle" which it is the purpose of the entire book to expound: "the sole end for which mankind are warranted, individually or collectively, in interfering with the liberty of action of any of their number, is self-protection." Only to prevent harm to others can an individual's actions be legitimately restrained by the state, society, or other individuals. This principle requires that, barring harm to others, the individual be allowed to exercise freedom of conscience and opinion, freedom of thought and expression, and freedom to live life as he or she sees best. In the initial chapter of *On Liberty* Mill has defined—as succinctly as anyone has—what in fact is the guiding political principle of genuinely free societies throughout the world.

Mill and his stepdaughter, Helen Taylor, circa 1865 (Radio Times Hulton Picture Library)

Chapter two is a vigorous defense of freedom of thought and discussion. In it Mill argues forcefully that such freedom needs to be permitted for three reasons. First, if an opinion is true, prohibiting it denies its truth to humanity. Second, even if an opinion is in error, it may contain a portion of the truth which it would be pernicious to silence. Third, even if an opinion is entirely false, allowing it into the marketplace of ideas prevents truth from ossifying into dead dogma. A truth being defended is a truth kept alive. The text of the chapter gets well beyond the bare bones of this argument, however, as Mill introduces controversy and vividly recreates historical and hypothetical examples of truth's being suppressed by force. Today, its defense of freedom of discussion remains pertinent and controversial. However, even for some twentieth-century readers sympathetic to the principle of freedom of speech, *On Liberty* can raise troubling questions, perhaps most thoughtfully articulated by Edward Alexander in his "post-holocaust" retrospect of Mill's liberalism in *The Victorian Experience: The Prose Writers* (1982), edited by Richard A. Levine.

Chapter three, "Of Individuality, as One of the Elements of Well Being," is at the heart of *On Liberty* and remains a classic document in Western liberal thought. It is also among the most rhetorically powerful texts Mill ever wrote. Here, Mill combines his defense of liberty with his ethical goal of the improvement of humanity. Only freedom to live as one decides is best, he argues, can produce humanity's moral development. Having the "right" way imposed upon the individual by force necessarily stunts the individual's moral growth. This chapter argues not only for "negative freedom" from coercion but also for "positive freedom" to find one's own best mode of human development. Determined to move readers by feeling as well as to convince them by logic, Mill employs a wide range of rhetorical strategies in this chapter, most notably the strikingly contrasted images of painful constriction and spontaneous energy, of mechanical deadness and natural growth. Memorable images include pollarded trees, a stagnant Dutch canal versus the magnificent outpouring of Niagara, and the painfully bound feet of a Chinese lady. In this chapter, tolerance is not enough: Mill urges a joyous acceptance of everyone's individuality as a potential path toward the overall improvement of the human race.

A stirring discourse on the tendency of government and society to interfere with the individual, chapter four excoriates the near universal tendency of people to mistake their customs and preferences for cosmic laws. Citing examples, Mill skillfully moves from cases of irrational persecution which readers can easily recognize as such, to cases of persecution which they are likely to have countenanced. By doing so, rhetoric and logic are shrewdly deployed to achieve that most difficult of tasks—awakening the audience to awareness of its own intolerance. The fifth and final chapter presents briefly some situations in which government may legitimately interfere with individual liberty. The final pages of the work, however, are saved for another vigorous defense of freedom, thus concluding *On Liberty* with a rousing peroration.

Shortly after his wife's death, Mill had felt himself paralyzed by grief. But soon he began to revive, and indeed the 1860s were like a second spring in his life. His stepdaughter, Helen Taylor, now assumed her mother's role as his source of feminine inspiration, and agitation for a new reform bill reawakened his youthful zest for political skirmishes. During the 1860s Mill produced some of his most thought-provoking work, and—improbably enough—he was elected to Parliament.

The first work resulting from Mill's renewed interest in politics was his *Considerations on Representative Government,* apparently written mostly during 1860. The book crystallizes Mill's mature thinking on how to maximize the benefits of the new democracies while limiting their potential liabilities. Compared with the fiery rhetoric of *On Liberty, Considerations on Representative Government* is a mellow work. But like nearly everything else Mill wrote it generates its own interest through its display of an incisive mind probing pertinent questions. And it too has its lively polemical passages. It begins with theory, tying political matters to ethical concerns: characteristically, Mill argues that representative government is usually best because it is conducive to the improvement of humanity. The mass of people should elect their leaders, but the business of government is best left to those leaders and not to the populace itself. Although the book's suggestions were anything but foregone conclusions in 1860, a number of them have since proven to be valuable components of democratic structures (for example, extension of the franchise to all tax-paying adults, woman suffrage). Other suggestions may seem quaintly reactionary (for example, opposition to the secret ballot, a plan for allowing extra votes to more educated people). Still other suggestions remain intriguing possibilities, at least in the United States (for example, limited campaign spending).

Of considerable importance to later moralists, Mill's next major work—*Utilitarianism,* published in 1863—is a compact volume which derives much of its interest from Mill's effort to accomplish a great deal in relatively few pages. *On Liberty* is the exposition of a single principle, but the aims of *Utilitarianism* are many and diverse. Because the pleasure-pain ethic of Utility was often derided in the early nineteenth century as "sensualism" and "pig philosophy," Mill adopts a tone of high seriousness in this volume, usually maintaining a loftiness which appealed enormously to Victorian earnestness. As much as he can, Mill aims at a nonpartisan discussion; usually he refrains from overt objections to intuitionist ethics and strives for an impartiality above party divisions. In addition, Mill attempts to align the old-style Benthamite calculations of pleasures and pains with his own new-style utility directed toward the moral development of the individual and the race.

In *Utilitarianism* Mill attempts a number of such compressed reformulations which for some readers raise more questions than they answer. For example, he argues that in calculating pleasures the quality of the pleasure affects its quantity, that is, the "higher" pleasures of the more fully developed person outrank the "lower" pleasures of the ignorant sensualist. "It is better to be a human being dissatisfied than a pig satisfied," Mill writes, "better to be Socrates dissatisfied than a fool satisfied." The appeal that such a doctrine would have had to Victorian audiences is unquestionable, although the philosophic issues it raises are considerable. A similar problem arises when Mill attempts to provide supporting evidence for the idea that happiness is an ultimate good. Such ultimate aims, as Mill had pointed out in *A System of Logic,* do not admit of the usual kinds of logical proof; the best that one can do is offer "considerations" to the reason in order to elicit its assent. The "consideration" offered here is that happiness is desired; therefore, it is desirable. Likewise, because each individual desires his own happiness, the general happiness of the human race is also desirable. The chain reaction of disagreement and defense which this passage has set off is perhaps best left to professional moralists, but the student of literature should note how adroitly this same passage links "happiness" with "virtue." Mill's little book on Utilitarianism not only instigated an ongoing debate over ethical principles but also achieved its rhetorical goal of winning a wider respect for Utility among philosophers and lay readers alike.

The year 1865 saw the publication of two books by Mill, each an assessment of another thinker's work. The books are as different as the two men they evaluate. *Auguste Comte and Positivism* is a compact work for a popular audience; *An Examination of Sir William Hamilton's Philosophy* is exhaustive and ponderous. The book on Comte resembles Mill's earlier, lively essay on Bentham; that on Hamilton resembles a mammoth sequel to *A System of Logic.* As in "Bentham," *Auguste Comte and Positivism* employs anticlimax first to exalt and then to degrade Comte's work. This pattern fit Mill's experience of Comte's thought. He owed much to Comte's earlier writings with their discussion of the three stages of history, the concept of altruism, the methodology of sociology, and the Religion of Humanity. But Comte's later work with its advocacy of despotism was a devastating denial of all that Mill held dear. In Mill's book, fulsome praise of Comte's *Cours de philosophie positive* (1830-1842) is followed by a catalogue of his absurdities in constructing a repressive Religion of Humanity with himself as Grand Pontiff. A favorable estimate of Comte's contribution to the philosophy of science is followed by an outrageous account of his totali-

THE LADIES' ADVOCATE.
MRS. BULL. "LOR, MR. MILL! WHAT A LOVELY SPEECH YOU *DID* MAKE. I DO DECLARE I HADN'T THE SLIGHTEST NOTION WE WERE SUCH MISERABLE CREATURES. NO ONE CAN SAY IT WAS *YOUR* FAULT THAT THE CASE BROKE DOWN."

Cartoon published in Punch, *1 June 1867, after Mill's unsuccessful attempt to amend the Reform Bill, giving voting rights to women*

tarian utopia. As in "Bentham," the worst that can be said is left until last, and the text's final word is, significantly, "ridiculous." In *An Examination of Sir William Hamilton's Philosophy* Mill at last offers a full-scale critique of intuitionism through the study of one of its leading nineteenth-century practitioners. Although the book is overtly polemical, the controversy usually fizzles—except in a few memorable passages such as the one which takes issue with one of Hamilton's disciples, Henry Mansel, on the nature of God's goodness. Part of the problem may be that Hamilton, at least as this book presents him, seems hardly worth the extensive effort made to refute him. To many readers, it may seem that Mill spends most of his time flogging a dead horse. The examination of Hamilton, however, should not be underestimated, for it is the capstone of Mill's quarrel with what he regarded as the most potentially dangerous philosophy of his day. Nor should it be ignored, for it contains Mill's more mature views on several crucial philosophic questions.

In 1865, the same year that his critiques of Comte and Hamilton were published, Mill was invited to stand for Parliament as Liberal member for Westminster. Although he attached some extraordinary conditions to his consent and conducted a most unorthodox campaign, he was elected. His term in Parliament deserves closer attention than it has yet received, if only for fuller accounts of his involvement in three important events. First, his participation in the tumultuous debates over the 1867 Reform Bill needs to be clarified. (Mill introduced an amendment to extend voting rights to women; although defeated, the amendment won seventy-three votes.) Second, his involvement in debates over the Irish question warrants closer scrutiny. (Mill's 1868 pamphlet *England and Ireland* succinctly presents his views on how wiser British rule could alleviate Irish troubles.) And, finally, his full role in the recall and prosecution of Gov. Edward John Eyre of Jamaica needs to be chronicled. When unrest among island blacks had erupted in violence at Morant Bay, government troops under Eyre retaliated by killing and imprisoning hundreds of blacks. With dubious legality, Eyre also executed a black leader who had been one of his most outspoken critics. Although Mill's effort to prosecute Eyre for murder was unsuccessful, he effectively expressed in speeches and letters the outrage of humanitarians against Eyre's conduct. (Mill's condemnation of racism can be seen in his 1850 essay "The Negro Question," a stinging reply to Carlyle's racist tract, "Occasional Discourse on the Negro Question," published in 1849. Both appeared in *Fraser's Magazine.*)

Despite the distractions of Westminster politics, Mill took time off between parliamentary sessions to write one of his most magisterial works, the *Inaugural Address Delivered to the University of St. Andrews* (1867). Elected to an honorary post at the Scottish University, Mill was obliged to deliver a lecture on a subject relevant to university concerns. As his topic he chose the nature and value of a liberal education, and for the address he wrote one of the most impressive accounts of what a university education can be. Ironically, this tribute came from a man who had never gone to college. Like John Henry Newman's *Idea of a University, Defined and Illustrated* (1873) (with which it can be compared without embarrassment), Mill's *Inaugural Address* envisions an ideal university as a goal toward which actual universities can strive: "Let us try what conscientious and intelligent teaching can do, before we presume to decide what cannot be done." Taking an authoritative overview of the various educational disciplines in his speech, Mill discourses on the contribution which each makes toward the formation of a well-educated mind—and by extension toward the ultimate improvement of humanity. The sweep of Mill's intellect is superbly displayed as he demonstrates not only his understanding of what Newman called "the circle of the sciences" but also his judicious balancing of the various disciplines. At the outset of the address Mill rejects the notion that universities exist primarily for professional training: "Men are men before they are lawyers, or physicians, or merchants, or manufacturers; and if you make them capable and sensible men, they will make themselves sensible lawyers or physicians." Beginning with the study of language and literature, Mill goes on to consider the role of the sciences in the university, the emergence of the social sciences, and the value of mathematics, logic, ethics, politics, jurisprudence, aesthetics, and religious studies. The aim of the university is to nourish the whole person by providing an outline of human knowledge in many disciplines, by fostering an understanding of scientific methodologies and an appreciation of the arts, and by disciplining moral awareness. Mill's persona in the address is that of "the imperial intellect" which has taken all knowledge as its province and has achieved a wisdom transcending partial views: it is perhaps Mill's most successful depiction of the whole philosopher who combines Science and Art. Although parliamentary duties delayed Mill's visit to St. Andrews for over a year and although the address reportedly took three hours to deliver, students cheered Mill enthusiastically, especially his defense of the university as a place of free thought. Although not as well known as some of his other works, the inaugural address provides a brilliant epitome of Mill's thought, and it remains a stimulating challenge to later generations of educators and students alike.

In the 1868 election Mill was not returned to Parliament, voters apparently being disenchanted with some of his more quixotic endeavors. Losing no time, however, Mill—with Helen Taylor by his side—took on his next challenge, a drive to obtain woman suffrage. To help create an atmosphere propitious to the cause, Mill decided to publish *The Subjection of Women,* which had been in manuscript for nearly a decade. An exceptionally passionate attempt to consolidate the feminist feeling and to sway public opinion, *The Subjection of Women,* which appeared in 1869, was greeted with extreme responses of outrage and adulation. Reactions to the book remain similarly divided to this day.

Like *On Liberty* (to which it might be considered a sequel), *The Subjection of Women* sets out to argue one principle, "a principle of perfect equality" between the sexes. Mill knew his rhetorical task was a formidable one: he had to dislodge from his audience's deepest feelings the "intuition" that the socially prescribed roles for women and men were "natural" ones. To win his case, he summoned his most impassioned arguments and subtle imagery. In the book Mill surveys the legal position of women, especially wives, in Victorian England and finds it analogous to that of slaves. Mill argues for equal opportunity for women in education and the professions, debunking the notion that women were intellectually inferior to men or incapable of handling positions of public authority. The final chapter focuses on the increase in human talent

"A Feminine Philosopher," caricature of Mill published in Vanity Fair, *29 March 1873 (Collection of Jerold J. Savory)*

Portrait by G. F. Watts painted shortly before Mill's death in 1873 (National Portrait Gallery)

available to society when women are permitted to compete with men outside the home. Mill utilizes numerous rhetorical devices to win reader assent. Most notably, he depicts belief in male dominance as a form of idolatry left over from barbaric ages: it is, Mill writes, "as if a gigantic dolmen, or a vast temple of Jupiter Olympius, occupied the site of St. Paul's and received daily worship, while the surrounding Christian churches were only resorted to on fasts and festivals." As in *On Liberty*, in *The Subjection of Women* Mill uses contrasting images of the "natural" and the "artificial" and depicts history as a battle between authority and liberty, with the gradual victory of liberty ensuring the present drive for women's emancipation. As a part of this historical vision, the text includes considerable master-slave language to reinforce the concept of the legal position of wives in Victorian England. In terms which might describe an idealized version of his relationship with his wife, Mill envisages a new union of emancipated women and men working together as equals.

Predictably, *The Subjection of Women* has been hailed by feminists of both sexes. But some recent partisans, including Susan Brownmiller in her introduction to the 1971 edition of Mill's book, have faulted a few of its positions, especially Mill's chivalric attitude toward women and his traditional view of family breadwinning: "In an otherwise just state of things, it is not, therefore, I think, a desirable custom, that the wife should contribute by her labour to the income of the family." Those readers, such as John Gordon in *The Myth of the Monstrous Male and Other Feminist Fables* (1982), who have more serious reservations about *The Subjection of Women* find in it many of the recurrent excesses of which radical feminist literature is often accused—the chip-on-the-shoulder stridency that generates more heat than light, the exaggerated analogy between the situation of women and the oppression of blacks, the reduction of the history of the sexes to the battle of the sexes, and the simplistic stereotyping of women as helpless victims and of men as monstrous oppressors. Even more problematic is Mill's effort in *The Subjection of Women* to address women's concerns in a vacuum, without making an equal effort to understand the social pressures and disabilities experienced by men. Keenly alive to what the Victorian age called "The Woman Question," Mill perhaps never recognized and formulated "The Man Question"—to say nothing of "The Man and Woman Question."

Despite Mill's best efforts for woman suffrage, the movement faltered, partly because of increasing resistance and partly because of internal dissension among its partisans. Mill, however, had other interests to engage his attention, including additional work on his *Autobiography* and other writings. In his mid sixties, as his health began to decline, Mill became increasingly sunny in disposition, although little of his amiableness can be glimpsed in the somewhat grim portrait which G. F. Watts painted in 1873. Shortly after the portrait was completed, Mill and his stepdaughter, Helen Taylor, set off once again for Avignon. He always seemed happiest being near his wife's grave, now marked by a marble mausoleum engraved with another of Mill's elaborate tributes to her. Early in May, Mill caught a chill after an extended walking tour, and his condition worsened rapidly. He died on 7 May 1873 and was buried beside his wife. But even after death, Mill continued to be a figure of controversy, especially as additional works appeared in print under Helen Taylor's supervision.

Of the works published posthumously, the most important is his *Autobiography*. In the 1850s when much of "the Life" was written Mill envisioned it at the head of a collection of his works, and today most scholars consider it an indispensable introduction to his life and thought. Besides being a crucial social and personal document, Mill's *Autobiography* is an artistic reconstruction of his life which dramatizes his intellectual and moral development. Because manuscripts, as well as other materials, have survived for both the early draft written in the 1850s and the later, extended version completed in 1870, the *Autobiography* offers readers a rare glimpse of one of Mill's works in the process of creation. The Toronto edition of Mill's works, which began to appear in 1963, provides an invaluable service by carefully annotating and printing the parallel passages of the two manuscript versions on facing pages, thereby allowing readers to see at a glance how Mill and Harriet Taylor altered his original wording. The question of multiple authorship in the *Autobiography* has been carefully explored in Jack Stillinger's 1983 article "Who Wrote Mill's Autobiography?" in *Victorian Studies*. The early draft includes material which the Mills later suppressed, and the final version demonstrates the kind of material which they wanted to appear in the "official" life. The early draft is more personal; the completed *Autobiography* is more polished. As John M. Robson has noted in a 1965 article for *College Composition and Communication,* there is a shift from the "private" to the "public" voice between the two texts.

In the opening paragraph of the *Autobiography* Mill sets up a tripartite pattern which anticipates the book's structure. He lists three reasons for writing his life: first, to record for an age interested in education an account of his own unique tutelage; second, to record for an age of transition the successive stages of his mental and moral development; and third, to acknowledge the debts which his development owes to others. Those to whom Mill is indebted are classified into three groups: those who are well known, those who are less well known, and the "one to whom most of all is due, one whom the world had no opportunity of knowing." (This "one," the reader learns later, is Mill's wife.) The paragraph's tripartite pattern introduces an autobiography which presents Mill's life in three significant phases: his Benthamic education and youthful activism overseen by his father, his acquisition of broader emotional and intellectual insights during his mental crisis and the subsequent search for many-sidedness, and the achievement of full philosophic vision during his evolving relationship with Harriet Taylor Mill. This last phase of Mill's life is also divided into three sections: his intimate friendship with her, their marriage, and the communion of their spirits after her death. Mill's life is thus presented as a mental and spiritual journey, a philosophic *commedia* in which the hero begins in a loveless *inferno,* struggles through a *purgatorio* of mental crisis and striving for fuller knowledge, and enters into a *paradiso* of philosophic vision and activity presided over by a Beatrice whose powers transcend death.

Mill's account of his childhood education and youthful zealotry is marked by irony and anticlimax. James Mill's impressive achievement in educating his son is constantly undercut by details of the father's inadequacies and the drawbacks of the education. The *Autobiography* presents Mill's father as a harsh, unloving man whose emotional failures considerably undermined his accomplishment in educating his son. Repeatedly, the text stresses the moral harm done to both father and son by James Mill's failure to cultivate emotion, especially benevolent and compassionate feelings—in a word, love. Likewise, Mill presents his own radical activism as remarkable but somehow mechanical; it is rooted in no deep ability to feel and love. The inadequacy of Mill's early education becomes clear during the second phase of his life. The young Mill asks himself: "Suppose that all your objects in life were realized; that all the changes in institutions

The mausoleum at St. Véran, near Avignon, burial place of John Stuart and Harriet Taylor Mill

and opinions which you are looking forward to, could be completely effected at this very instant: would this be a great joy and happiness to you?" When an "irrepressible self-consciousness" honestly answers "No!" the youth is left desolate. Clearly, man cannot live by Utilitarian reform alone. During his mental crisis young Mill is assisted by a series of guides (including Wordsworth, John Sterling, and Carlyle) who lead him toward fuller philosophic vision. It is only in the third phase of his life, however, that Mill encounters his ultimate guide, Harriet Taylor, a "natural poet" seeking surer intellectuality. In the final section of the *Autobiography* Harriet and John Mill develop together toward genuine philosophic wisdom.

Although Mill describes himself as someone who grew up without religion, he uses religious language in the *Autobiography* to recount his life as a sacred quest. Indeed, this language helps to explain the embarrassed and incredulous reactions of some readers to Mill's portrait of his wife's mind and character, for the *Autobiography* presents her as a secular saint in the Religion of Humanity, a Victorian Beatrice who survives death to remain an inspiration to her lover. Those who can accept Mill's vision of his wife or who are persuaded by the text to suspend their disbelief are obviously better prepared to accept the myth of Mill's life as presented in the *Autobiography*. Those who question whether the "real" or "historical" Harriet Mill can be reconciled with the exalted portrait of her in the *Autobiography* have trouble with this myth. There is no avoiding the issue. After dramatizing the state of helpless despondency into which Harriet's death throws him, Mill depicts how her inspiration has reinvigorated his life and thought. As Helen Taylor assumes her mother's role as Mill's feminine inspiration, it is as if Harriet has been reincarnated in her daughter. Helen Taylor becomes Harriet's apotheosis, and Mill's life flourishes under her guidance. The latter pages of the *Autobiography* recount a series of episodes, each constructed upon a tripartite pattern: an announcement that Mill has a duty to perform, an account of the crisis enjoining that duty, and a statement of his success in performing it. Whether puncturing the dangerously inflated reputation of Sir William Hamilton or talking sense to Hyde Park demonstrators, he succeeds unexpectedly, but behind these successes lies the guidance of Harriet-Helen. When at last the various crises have subsided, Mill's "memoir" closes with a paragraph radiating a quiet joy and contentment. The *commedia* is completed.

The second of Mill's major works published posthumously was *Three Essays on Religion* (1874), composed of "Nature," "Utility of Religion," and "Theism." The first two essays were written in the early 1850s, the third between 1868 and 1870. The three essays were not intended to form a unit, as Helen Taylor remarked in her introductory notice, and some readers have considerable difficulty reconciling the views expressed in them. For a student of literature, however, the essays are perhaps best approached as three reports from a questioning mind groping its way from angry skepticism to tentative affirmation. In this view of them, the essays form another variant of the pattern of conversion so familiar in Victorian poetry and prose. "Nature" approximates Mill's everlasting no, "Utility of Religion" his center of indifference, and "Theism" the everlasting yea—or at least a qualified version of it. One cannot help but notice, in any event, that the passionate antagonism toward supernatural belief in "Nature" and "Utility of Religion" mellows in "Theism" into quiet acceptance of "imaginative hope" concerning immortality and the goodness of God.

Containing some of the most vivid denunciations Mill ever wrote, "Nature" castigates any morality based upon a maxim enjoining humanity to "follow nature." Spectacularly violent imagery depicting nature on a rampage is used to heap scorn upon those who have urged humanity to follow such a model. "In sober truth," Mill declares indignantly, "nearly all the things which men are hanged or imprisoned for doing to one another are nature's everyday performances." From one angle, the essay represents one more expression of Victorian revulsion against the lingering Romantic tendency to worship nature; from a broader perspective, it is a biting reply to ethical prescriptions through the ages which have urged people to imitate a vaguely defined "nature." It is certainly one of the angriest depictions of "Nature red in tooth and claw" produced during Victorian times. In ringing tones, Mill proclaims that if humanity intends to improve at all its only hope is to reject entirely the insane practices of nature. (It is, incidentally, intriguing to consider how this view of nature can be reconciled with Mill's impassioned plea for the preservation of natural wilderness in the "Stationary State" chapter of *Principles of Political Economy* or with the depiction of nature as a benevolent moral force in chapter two of the *Autobiography*, a chapter apparently written around the same time that "Nature" was.) The essay is a fervent refusal to worship nature and nature's God when their doings are so patently vicious.

The tone of "Utility of Religion" is only slightly less hostile in its assessment of supernatural religion. Indeed, the first part of the essay might be better titled "The Un-Utility of Religion," for it argues that belief in the supernatural is not essential for genuine morality. According to this essay, widespread acceptance of moral practices, early education, and the individual's desire to win public approval can affect ethical behavior even better than fear of hell or hope of heaven. The tone of the essay softens somewhat when Mill grants that in the past supernatural beliefs did help to keep common humanity moral, but in the latter part of the essay he argues that such supernaturalism is no longer credible to thinking people and that the Religion of Humanity can serve even better by holding up models of human behavior for others to follow: "the idea that Socrates, or Howard or Washington, or Antoninus, or Christ would have sympathized with us, or that we are attempting to do our part in the spirit in which they did theirs, has operated on the very best minds, as a strong incentive to act up to their highest feelings and convictions." As progress makes life more gratifying for greater numbers of people, humanity will be able to surrender more easily its hope of immortal life. "Utility of Religion" thus represents something of a midpoint between the fierce nay-sayings of "Nature" and the cautious yeas of "Theism."

After the fierce polemics of the two previous essays, the quiet rationalism of "Theism" is almost startling. Calmly setting out to review the grounds of theistic belief, in the essay Mill dispassionately examines some of the more common arguments for the existence of God. He rejects nearly all, giving only qualified support to a version of the argument from design in the universe. Propped by this thin support, the essay argues that monotheism is compatible with objective evidence. Mill eventually justifies belief in a God of limited powers who calls humanity to assist in the struggle against evil. Finally, because the evidence for and against belief in immortality is inconclusive, Mill argues that thinking people may legitimately indulge in the "imaginative hope" that human life survives death. For those who feel that Mill betrayed the apparent atheism of his earlier writings, "Theism" is seen as the last infirmity of a noble mind. For others—including Gertrude Himmelfarb in *On Liberty and Liberalism* (1974)—the essay represents a candid expression of a mind at last gathering the courage of its own beliefs. In any event, after the rhetorical storms of "Nature" and "Utility of Religion," "Theism" resembles a haven of quiet questioning and cautious affirmation.

While the debate over Mill's status as prose artist is likely to continue, additional literary analyses of his writings should help to clarify how his prose manages to achieve the strong effects it often does. Just as scholars in other disciplines have examined how Mill was able to blend Utilitarian logic and moral passion to create a philosophy of human improvement, literary scholars need to examine more deeply how he was able to fuse rational argument and imaginative artistry to create some of the most memorable prose statements of the Victorian age.

Letters:

Earlier Letters, 1812-1848, edited by Francis E. Mineka, 2 volumes (Toronto: University of Toronto Press, 1963);

Later Letters, 1849-1873, edited by Mineka and Dwight N. Lindley, 4 volumes (Toronto: University of Toronto Press, 1972).

Biographies:

Alexander Bain, *John Stuart Mill: A Criticism, with Personal Recollections* (London: Holt, 1882);

Michael St. John Packe, *The Life of John Stuart Mill* (New York: Macmillan, 1954);

Bruce Mazlish, *James and John Stuart Mill: Father and Son in the Nineteenth Century* (New York: Basic Books, 1975).

References:

Susan Hardy Aiken, "Scripture and Poetic Discourse in *The Subjection of Women,*" *PMLA,* 98 (May 1983): 353-373;

Edward Alexander, "John Stuart Mill: A Post-Holocaust Retrospect," in *The Victorian Experience: The Prose Writers,* edited by Richard A. Levine (Athens: Ohio University Press, 1982), pp. 83-111;

Alexander, *Matthew Arnold and John Stuart Mill* (New York: Columbia University Press, 1965);

Eugene R. August, *John Stuart Mill: A Mind at Large* (New York: Scribners, 1975);

August, "Mill as Sage: The Essay on Bentham," *PMLA,* 89 (January 1974): 142-153;

August, "Mill's *Autobiography* as Philosophic *Commedia,*" *Victorian Poetry,* 11 (Summer 1973): 143-162;

Rise B. Axelrod, "Argument and Strategy in Mill's *The Subjection of Women,*" *Victorian Newsletter,* no. 46 (Fall 1974): 10-14;

James R. Bennet, "Mill, Francis W. Newman, and Socialism: Mill's Two Argumentative Voices," *Mill News Letter,* 2 (Fall 1966): 2-7;

Richard A. Cherwitz and James W. Hilkins, "John Stuart Mill's *On Liberty:* Implications for the Epistemology of the New Rhetoric," *Quarterly Journal of Speech,* 65 (February 1979): 12-24;

Alan Donagan, "Victorian Philosophical Prose: J. S. Mill and F. H. Bradley," in *The Art of Victorian Prose,* edited by George Levine and William Madden (New York: Oxford University Press, 1968), pp. 53-72;

John B. Ellery, *John Stuart Mill* (New York: Twayne, 1964);

Andrew Griffin, "The Interior Garden of John Stuart Mill," in *Nature and the Victorian Imagination,* edited by U. C. Knoepflmacher and G. B. Tennyson (Berkeley: University of California Press, 1977), pp. 171-186;

John Grube, "*On Liberty* as a Work of Art," *Mill News Letter,* 5 (Fall 1969): 2-6;

Wendell V. Harris, "The Warp of Mill's 'Fabric' of Thought," *Victorian Newsletter,* no. 37 (Spring 1970): 1-7;

F. A. Hayek, *John Stuart Mill and Harriet Taylor* (Chicago: University of Chicago Press, 1951);

Gertrude Himmelfarb, *On Liberty and Liberalism: The Case of John Stuart Mill* (New York: Knopf, 1974);

Gordon D. Hirsch, "Organic Imagery and the Psychology of Mill's *On Liberty,*" *Mill News Letter,* 10 (Summer 1975): 3-13;

Nels Juleus, "The Rhetoric of Opposites: Mill and Carlyle," *Pennsylvania Speech Annual* (September 1960): 1-7;

F. R. Leavis, Introduction to *Mill on Bentham and Coleridge* (London: Chatto & Windus, 1950); republished as *On Bentham and Coleridge,* by John Stuart Mill (New York: Harper, 1962);

Glenn K. S. Man, "Structure and Narration in Mill's *Autobiography,*" *Revue de l'Université d'Ottawa,* 51 (April-June 1981): 304-314;

Charles Matthews, "Argument Through Metaphor in John Stuart Mill's *On Liberty,*" *Language and Style,* 4 (Summer 1972): 221-228;

James McDonnell, "Success and Failure: A Rhetorical Study of the First Two Chapters of Mill's *Autobiography,*" *University of Toronto Quarterly,* 45 (Winter 1976): 109-122;

Emery Neff, *Carlyle and Mill: An Introduction to Victorian Thought,* revised edition (New York: Columbia University Press, 1952);

H. O. Pappe, *John Stuart Mill and the Harriet Taylor Myth* (Melbourne: Melbourne University Press, 1960);

Keith Rinehart, "John Stuart Mill's *Autobiography:* Its Art and Appeal," *University of Kansas City Review,* 19 (1953): 265-273;

John M. Robson, "John Stuart Mill," in *Victorian Prose: A Guide to Research,* edited by David J. DeLaura (New York: Modern Language Association, 1973), pp. 185-218;

Robson, "Mill's 'Autobiography': The Public and the Private Voice," *College Composition and Communication,* 16 (February 1965): 97-105;

Robson and Michael Laine, eds., *James and John Stuart Mill: Papers of the Centenary Conference* (Toronto: University of Toronto Press, 1976);

Alan Ryan, *John Stuart Mill* (New York: Pantheon Books, 1970);

David R. Sanderson, "Metaphor and Method in John Stuart Mill's *On Liberty,*" *Victorian Newsletter,* no. 34 (Fall 1968): 22-25;

J. B. Schneewind, ed., *Mill: A Collection of Critical Essays* (Garden City: Doubleday, 1968);

F. Parvin Sharpless, *The Literary Criticism of John Stuart Mill* (The Hague: Mouton, 1967);

Thomas Woods, *Poetry and Philosophy: A Study in the Thought of John Stuart Mill* (London: Hutchinson, 1961).

Papers:

Important collections of Mill letters and papers are in the Mill-Taylor collection, British Library of Political and Economic Science, London School of Economics; at the National Library of Scotland; at the Keynes Library, King's College, Cambridge; and in the John Stuart Mill Collection at the Yale University library. The manuscript of the *Autobiography* is located at the Columbia University Library, and the early draft of the *Autobiography* is at the library of the University of Illinois, Urbana-Champaign. The copy of Robert Browning's *Pauline* with Mill's annotations is in the Forster and Dyce Collection at the Victoria and Albert Museum. The early draft of *A System of Logic* and the only known manuscript of *Principles of Political Economy* are located at the Pierpont Morgan Library. The press-copy manuscript of *A System of Logic* is at the British Library. Mill's will is at Somerset House, London.

John Henry Newman

James Forsythe Hazen
University of Nevada

photograph by Lewis Barraud

See also the Newman entries in *DLB 18, Victorian Novelists After 1885,* and *DLB 32, Victorian Poets Before 1850.*

BIRTH: London, England, 21 February 1801, to John and Jemima Fourdrinier Newman.

EDUCATION: B.A., Trinity College, University of Oxford, 1820; fellow (1822) and tutor (1826), Oriel College, University of Oxford.

AWARDS AND HONORS: Doctor of Divinity (Rome), 1850; Honorary fellow, Trinity College, Oxford, 1878; Cardinal, Roman Catholic Church, 1879.

DEATH: Birmingham, England, 11 August 1890.

SELECTED BOOKS: *St. Bartholomew's Eve; A Tale of the Sixteenth Century: in Two Cantos,* anonymous, by Newman and J. W. Bowden (Oxford: Munday & Slatter, 1818);

Suggestions Respectfully Offered to Certain Resident Clergymen of the University in Behalf of the Church Missionary Society, by a Master of Arts (Oxford: Cooke, 1830);

Memorials of the Past (Oxford: King, 1832);

The Arians of the Fourth Century: Their Doctrine, Temper and Conduct, Chiefly as Exhibited in the Councils of The Church, between AD 325 and AD 381 (London: Rivington, 1833; New York: Catholic Publication Society, 1882);

Tracts for the Times, by Members of the University of Oxford, anonymous, nos. 1-3, 6-8 by Newman and R. H. Froude; nos. 10, 11, 15 by Newman and Sir W. Palmer; nos. 19-21, 31, 33, 34, 38, 41, 45, 47, 71, 73, 74 by Newman and B. Harrison; nos. 75, 76, 79, 82, 83, 85, 88, 90 by Newman, 6 volumes (London: Rivington/Oxford: Parker, 1833-1841);

Parochial Sermons (6 volumes, London: Rivington/Oxford: Parker, 1834-1836; 2 volumes, New York: D. Appleton/Philadelphia: G. S. Appleton, 1843);

Elucidations of Dr. Hampden's Theological Statements (Oxford: Baxter, 1836);

Lyra Apostolica, anonymous, by Newman, John William Bowden, Richard Hurrell Froude, John Keble, Robert Isaac Wilberforce, and Isaac Williams (Derby, U.K.: Mozley/London: Rivington, 1836; New York: D. Appleton/Philadelphia: G. S. Appleton, 1844);

Lectures on the Prophetical Office of the Church, Viewed Relatively to Romanism and Popular Protestantism (London: Rivington/Oxford: Parker, 1837);

Lectures on Justification (London: Rivington, 1838);

The Church of the Fathers, anonymous (London: Rivington, 1840);

The Tamworth Reading Room: Letters on an Address Delivered by Sir Robert Peel Bart. M.P. on the Establishment of a Reading Room at Tamsworth, by Catholicus, Originally Published in the Times, *and Since Revised and Corrected by the Author* (London: Mortimer, 1841);

A Letter Addressed to the Rev. R. W. Jelf D.D., Canon of Christ Church, in Explanation of No. 90 in the Series Called the Tracts for the Times, by the Author (Oxford: Parker/London: Rivington, 1841);

An Essay on the Miracles Recorded in the Ecclesiastical History of the Early Ages (Oxford: Parker/London: Rivington, 1843);

Sermons Bearing on Subjects of the Day (London: Rivington/Oxford: Parker, 1843; New York: D. Appleton/Philadelphia: G. S. Appleton, 1844);

Sermons, Chiefly on the Theory of Religious Belief, Preached before the University of Oxford (London: Rivington/Oxford: Parker, 1843);

Plain Sermons by Contributors to the "Tracts for the Times," volume 5, anonymous (London: Rivington, 1843);

An Essay on the Development of Christian Doctrine (London: Toovey, 1845; New York: D. Appleton/Philadelphia: G. S. Appleton/Cincinnati: Derby, Bradley, N.d.);

Loss and Gain, anonymous (London: Burns, 1848); republished as *Loss and Gain; or, the Story of a Convert* (Boston: Donahoe, 1854);

Discourses Addressed to Mixed Congregations (London: Longman, Brown, Green & Longmans, 1849; Boston: Donahoe, 1853);

Lectures on Certain Difficulties Felt by Anglicans in Submitting to the Catholic Church (12 parts, London: Burns & Lambert, 1850; 1 volume, New York: Office of New York's Freeman's Journal, 1851);

Christ upon the Waters: A Sermon Preached on Occasion of the Establishment of the Catholic Hierarchy in this Country (Birmingham, U.K.: Maher/London: Burns & Lambert, 1850);

Lectures on the Present Position of Catholics in England, Addressed to the Brothers of the Oratory (London: Burns & Lambert, 1851);

Discourses on the Scope and Nature of University Education, Addressed to the Catholics of Dublin, 11 parts (Dublin: Duffy, 1852); revised and republished with *Lectures and Essays on University Subjects* (1859) as *The Idea of a University Defined and Illustrated* (London: Pickering, 1873);

The Second Spring: A Sermon Preached in the Synod of Oscott, on Tuesday July 13th 1852 (London, Dublin & Derby: Richardson, 1852);

Verses on Religious Subjects, anonymous (Dublin: Duffy, 1853);

Callista: A Sketch of the Third Century, anonymous (London: Burns & Lambert, 1856; New York & Boston: Sadlier, 1856);

The Office and Work of Universities (London: Longman, Green, Longman & Roberts, 1856);

The Mission of St. Philip Neri: An Instruction, Delivered in Substance in the Birmingham Oratory, January, 1850, and at Subsequent Times (N.p., 1857);

Sermons Preached on Various Occasions (London: Burns & Lambert, 1857; New York: Catholic Publication Society, 1887);

Lectures and Essays on University Subjects (London: Longman, Brown, Green, Longman & Roberts, 1859);

Mr. Kingsley and Dr. Newman: A Correspondence on the Question Whether Dr. Newman Teaches that Truth Is No Virtue? (London: Longman, Green, Longman, Roberts & Green, 1864);

Apologia pro Vita Sua: Being a Reply to a Pamphlet Entitled "What, Then, Does Dr. Newman Mean?" (8 parts, London: Longman, Green, Longman, Roberts & Green, 1864; 1 volume, New York: Appleton, 1865); revised as *History of My Religious Opinions* (London: Longman, Green, Longman, Roberts & Green, 1865);

The Dream of Gerontius (London: Burns & Oates, 1865; New York: Catholic Publication Society, 1885);

A Letter to the Rev. E. B. Pusey, D.D., on His Recent Eirenicon (London: Longmans, Green, Reader & Dyer, 1866; New York: Kehoe, 1866);

The Pope and the Revolution: A Sermon Preached in the Oratory Church Birmingham on Sunday October 7 1866 (London: Longmans, Green, Reader & Dyer, 1866);

Verses on Various Occasions (London: Burns & Oates, 1868; Boston: Donahoe, 1868);

An Essay in Aid of a Grammar of Assent (London: Burns & Oates, 1870; New York: Catholic Publication Society, 1870);

Two Essays on Scripture Miracles and on Ecclesiastical (London: Pickering, 1870);

Essays Critical and Historical, 2 volumes (London: Pickering, 1871);

Historical Sketches, 3 volumes (London: Pickering, 1872-1873);

Discussions and Arguments on Various Subjects (London: Pickering, 1872);

Tracts Theological and Ecclesiastical (London: Pickering, 1874);

A Letter Addressed to His Grace the Duke of Norfolk on Occasion of Mr. Gladstone's Recent Expostulation (London: Pickering, 1875; New York: Catholic Publication Society, 1875);

The Via Media of the Anglican Church, Illustrated in Lectures, Letters, and Tracts Written between 1830 and 1841; with a Preface and Notes, 2 volumes (London: Pickering, 1877);

Two Sermons Preached in the Church of St. Aloysius, Oxford on Trinity Sunday 1880 (Oxford: Privately printed, 1880);

Lead, Kindly Light. Illustrated (Boston: Roberts, 1884);

The Development of Religious Error (London: Burns & Oates, 1886);

On a Criticism Urged against a Catholic Doctrine (Birmingham: Billing, 1889);

My Campaign in Ireland, Part I: Catholic University Reports and Other Papers, edited by Neville (Aberdeen: Privately printed, 1896);

Sermon Notes of John Henry Cardinal Newman, 1849-1878, edited by Fathers of the Birmingham Oratory (London: Longmans, Green, 1913);

John Henry Newman: Autobiographical Writings, edited by Henry Tristram (London: Sheed & Ward, 1956; New York: Sheed & Ward, 1957);

Faith and Prejudice and Other Unpublished Sermons of Cardinal Newman, edited by Charles Stephen Dessain (New York: Sheed & Ward, 1956); republished as *Catholic Sermons of Cardinal Newman* (London: Burns & Oates, 1957);

On Consulting the Faithful in Matters of Doctrine, edited by John Coulson (London: Chapman, 1961);

The Philosophical Notebook of John Henry Newman, 2 volumes, edited by Edward Sillem (Louvain: Nauwelaerts, 1969-1970);

The Theological Papers of John Henry Newman on Faith, and Certainty, edited by J. Derek Holmes (Oxford: Clarendon Press, 1976);

The Theological Papers of John Henry Newman on Biblical Inspiration and on Infallibility, edited by Holmes (Oxford: Clarendon Press, 1979).

Collection: *Works of John Henry Newman,* Uniform Edition, 41 volumes (London: Longmans, Green, 1908-1918).

OTHER: *Select Treatises of S. Athanasius, Archbishop of Alexandria, in Controversy with the Arians,* translated by Newman (Oxford: Parker/London: Rivington, 1843); revised with *Historical Tracts of S. Athanasius* (1843), 2 volumes (London: Pickering, 1881);

Historical Tracts of S. Athanasius, Archbishop of Alexandria, translated by Newman (Oxford: Parker/London: Parker, 1843); revised with *Select Treatises of S. Athanasius* (1843), 2 volumes (London: Pickering, 1881).

"Forty years ago," wrote Matthew Arnold in 1883, "when I was an undergraduate at Oxford, voices were in the air there which haunt my memory still." One of those voices was that of John Henry Newman preaching from the pulpit of St. Mary's Church: "Who could resist the charm of that spiritual apparition, gliding in the dim afternoon light through the aisles of St. Mary's, rising into the pulpit, and then, in the most entrancing of voices, breaking the silence with words and thoughts which were a religious music—subtle, sweet, mournful?" Arnold's recollection in his essay "Emerson" is an apt tribute, for it suggests the personality and magnetism of the man while also noting the quality both of his words and of his thoughts. Eloquent in speech and writing, Newman also had something distinctive and powerful to say. He said it not for the specialists in theology or philosophy or ecclesiastical history or educational theory but for the ordinary educated man, and thus he belongs in the ranks of the great prose writers of the Victorian era, with Macaulay, Carlyle, Mill, Ruskin, and Arnold himself, men in communion with the whole intelligent and thoughtful public of their day.

Newman in person seemed to many a "spiritual apparition," yet he was also a natural leader of men, a planner of campaigns, an able editor, a practical and even shrewd churchman, a scholar, an enthusiastic amateur violinist, a poet, a novelist, a great literary stylist, and a dangerous opponent in controversy. In him were combined an acuteness of intellect and a devoutness of religious faith seldom found together in a single person. In *The Idea of a University Defined and Illustrated* (1873) he wrote the ablest argument of modern times for the pure "culture of the intellect" as the end and aim of university education, while in the *Apologia pro Vita Sua* (1864), in his sermons, and in his other religious writings, he argued with equal force and conviction that reason by itself is insufficient to guide the total life of man, that an assent to Christian truth is a moral, if not an intellectual, imperative. He believed passionately in reason, and in scientific inquiry, yet disdained that intellectual detachment which in the end believes nothing.

His long life of nearly ninety years divides in two at the year 1845 when he was converted to the Roman Catholic Church. During his Anglican period his search for a mode of faith satisfying both to heart and mind led him from the Calvinist religion of his adolescence to the High Church Anglo-Catholicism of the Oxford Movement and the *Tracts for the Times* (1833-1841). When this movement toward a "second Reformation" of the Church of England failed in its purpose, Newman turned to the Roman Catholic Church, for which he became from 1845 until his death in 1890 a leading representative in the Protestant world. For the modern reader Newman's life is the story of a highly intellectual man who was also a man of strong religious faith, and the story of a Roman Catholic priest and cardinal who was also a product of Protestant culture. Newman's writings address readers of all religious persuasions, or none, with an appeal deriving from that sense of the common elements in all human experience suggested by the motto he adopted as cardinal: *Cor ad cor loquitur* (heart speaks to heart).

John Henry Newman was born in London on 21 February 1801, the eldest of six children of John Newman, a banker, and Jemima Fourdrinier Newman. Newman's younger brother, Francis William Newman, became a well-known English freethinker and socialist, and was in later days professor of Latin at the University of London. Two of his sisters married into the Mozley family; his niece, Anne Mozley, was Newman's first biographer. The third sister and youngest child, Mary, was the family favorite; her early death at age nineteen was a loss which Newman felt all his life. Newman's childhood was, however, in general a happy one; his father was a tolerant and genial man of business, his mother handsome and affectionate, his brothers and sisters lively and individual. In religion the Newmans were conventionally Anglican, neither High Church nor Evangelical.

Newman's own strongly religious character revealed itself early. In his *Apologia pro Vita Sua,* the intellectual autobiography he wrote in 1864, Newman recalls the otherworldly bent of his mind as a boy: "I thought life might be a dream, or I an Angel, and all this world a deception." This intuition had the effect of "confirming me in my mistrust of the reality of material phenomena, and making me rest in the thought of two and two only absolute and luminously self-evident beings, myself and my Creator." To that Creator, and to His work in the world, Newman from early youth felt his life consecrated. That work might well be "missionary work among the heathen"; in any case it would involve a celibate life: "it would be the will of God that I should lead a single life." He took great delight in reading the Bible, but "I had no formed religious convictions till I was fifteen."

In fact, although for Newman the existence of his Creator was "luminously self-evident," he was, even as a boy, fascinated by the literature of religious skepticism. While a student in Dr. Nicholas's school at Ealing (1808-1816), Newman read Thomas Paine's tracts "against the Old Testament" (probably *The Age of Reason*) and "found pleasure in thinking of the objections which were contained in them." He read David Hume's "Of Miracles," a famous attack on the credibility of alleged supernatural occurrences. "Also," Newman recalls in the *Apologia,* "I recollect copying out some French verses, perhaps Voltaire's, in denial of the immortality of the soul, and saying to myself something like 'How dreadful, but how plausible!' " In later years, Newman's deep understanding of, and sometimes startling openness to, the tradition of religious skepticism caused the agnostic T. H. Huxley to claim that he could put together a good "primer of infidelity" using Newman's writings alone. In any case, Newman learned early in life that Christianity in his day was under attack by formidable philosophical opponents whose arguments could not be ignored.

In the last year of his schooling at Ealing, in the autumn of 1816, Newman at age fifteen "fell under the influences of a definite Creed." This creed was the Evangelical protestantism of one of his teachers, the Reverend Walter Mayers, who, in addition to his personal influence, put into Newman's hand several books, "all of the school of Calvin," notably *The Force of Truth* (1779) by Thomas Scott. While Newman in time threw off utterly the Calvinist idea of predestination (referring to it in the *Apologia* as a "detestable doctrine"), he retained all his life an essentially Calvinist sense of the willfulness and rebelliousness of raw human nature. From Scott too he learned "that fundamental truth of religion," the doctrine of the Holy Trinity. Newman admired the unworldliness of Scott, and also his maxim "Growth the only evidence of life."

Newman's Evangelical and Calvinist period (1816 to about 1825) thus left on his mind some lasting impressions and even doctrines. But he also came at this time upon a very different kind of religious thought and writing, ecclesiastical history, which was to dominate his mind at least until the time of his conversion to the Roman Catholic Church in 1845. In the autumn of 1816 he read Joseph Milner's *History of the Church of Christ* (five volumes, 1795-1809) and "was nothing short of enamoured of the long extracts from St. Augustine, St. Ambrose, and the other Fathers which I found there." Newman was at the threshold of what he later saw as an "intellectual inconsistency," admiring the Fathers of the Roman Church while at the same time, as a Protestant, needing to maintain that Rome was in error. The dilemma was intensified at the time (1816 or so) by Newman's reading the *Dissertations on the Prophecies* (1754-1758) of Thomas Newton, which affirmed, in accord with Protestant belief, that the Pope of Rome was no less than "the Antichrist predicted by Daniel, St. Paul, and St. John."

In the *Apologia pro Vita Sua* Newman says little about his undergraduate years at Oxford. He took up residence at Trinity College in June of 1817 and graduated B.A. in 1820, not yet twenty years of age. His temper was not suited to the undergraduate life of the university at that period, which consisted too much of upper-class idleness and dissipation. He showed distinct promise as a student but failed to earn a first-class degree. Determined to succeed despite this disappointment, Newman remained at Oxford, receiving pupils on private tuition and preparing to stand for a fellowship at Oriel, the most intellectually vigorous college of the university. This fellowship he won on 12 April 1822, a day which he "ever felt the turning-point of his life, and of all days most memorable."

Being a fellow of Oriel College, Oxford University, brought him into contact with the ideas and personalities which dominated the middle years of his life and gave it its purpose and direction. In particular, Newman came under the influence of Richard Whately and Edward Hawkins, both about ten years older than he and also fellows of Oriel. They weaned Newman away from his Calvinism, alerted him to the dangers inherent in an exclusive reliance upon the Bible, and convinced him of the importance of the historical Church in guiding the religious life, what Newman called the "doctrine of Tradition." From another fellow of Oriel, William James, Newman learned another doctrine of the Anglican Church, that of the apostolic succession, a traditional part of the Church's creed but not much in evidence at the time, and certainly not in Evangelical circles.

Richard Whately, a fellow at Oriel College with Newman whose ideas, Newman wrote, "had a gradual, but a deep effect on my mind," providing him with the basis of the Oxford Movement

Of the Oriel group, Richard Whately was perhaps the most important influence on Newman at this stage. Newman later wrote that Whately opened his mind and taught him to think. Whately was a staunch opponent of Erastianism (named for Thomas Erastus, a Swiss theologian who looked upon the Church as merely a department of the State). Whately's anti-Erastian position affirmed that the Church was itself a "substantive body or corporation" and that "Church and State should be independent of each other." Interference of the Church in temporal affairs, or of the State in spiritual affairs, was a "profanation of Christ's kingdom." Furthermore "The clergy . . . ought not to be the hired servants of the Civil Magistrate." These ideas, some of which Newman repeats in Whately's own words, "had a gradual, but a deep effect on my mind." They were, in fact, the foundation of the Oxford Movement which Newman was to lead from 1833 to 1841.

On Trinity Sunday, 13 June 1824, Newman was ordained deacon in the Anglican Church and became curate of St. Clement's Church, Oxford.

He felt the tremendous significance of his ordination, writing in his journal: "It is over. I am Thine, O Lord; I seem quite dizzy and cannot altogether believe and understand it; . . . I have the responsibility of souls on me to the day of my death." He took up the arduous work of ministering to his parish, organizing worship, visiting the sick, raising money and preaching two sermons a week. He preached for the first time on 23 June 1824, on the text "Man goeth forth to his work and to his labour until the evening." He had himself found his own work and labor. In May of 1825 he was advanced from deacon to priest in the Anglican Church.

In the meantime Newman continued his intellectual work as a fellow of Oriel College. With Hawkins's help he received a commission from the *Encyclopedia Metropolitana* to write an article on Cicero, another on Apollonius of Tyana, and a third on miracles, his first publications. The income from these writings was a helpful supplement to his salary as curate of St. Clement's, which was forty-five pounds a year. He assisted Whately in the composition of his *Elements of Logic* (1826), a standard text for many years. He served for a time as vice-principal of St. Alban Hall and was appointed tutor of Oriel College in 1826. These accomplishments, and the appointment as tutor, gave Newman a new sense of his powers. "I began to be known. I preached my first University Sermon. . . . I came out of my shell."

The full emergence of Newman from his shell came about through his contact with two other men of Oriel, John Keble and Richard Hurrell Froude. The latter, brother of the historian James Anthony Froude, Newman met in 1826; he became Newman's closest friend from this time until his early death from tuberculosis in 1836. In Newman's words, Froude "was a man of the highest gifts, truly many-sided, . . . brimful and overflowing with ideas and views. His opinions arrested and influenced me, even when they did not gain my assent. He professed openly his admiration of the Church of Rome, and his hatred of the Reformers. . . . He felt scorn of the maxim 'The Bible and the Bible only is the religion of Protestants'; and he gloried in accepting Tradition as a main instrument of religious teaching."

If Froude's eyes were turned toward Rome, John Keble's contemplated the United States. He saw there a branch of the Anglican Church utterly independent of the state, and he admired what he saw. Of all Newman's friends at this period, Keble was most concerned about what the dependence of the Anglican Church on the State might mean for the spiritual authority of the Church. He was in that sense the true father of the Oxford Movement. Like Newman, Keble united intellectual power with a simplicity and depth of religious devotion. He had been a brilliant student and tutor of Oriel from 1817 to 1823, but, as Newman beautifully phrased it, "Having carried off as a mere boy the highest honours of the University, he had turned from the admiration which haunted his steps" to live the simple life of a country priest. In 1827 Keble's *The Christian Year* was published, a collection of short poems designed to inculcate a religious sense of the passing days and weeks of time. It was enormously popular. August 24 is not August 24, it is St. Bartholomew's Day—to see it and other days in this way is to live the Christian year. In Newman's words, "Keble struck an original note and woke up in the hearts of thousands a new music, the music of a school, long unknown in England."

As the 1820s drew to a close and Newman approached his thirtieth year, he had shaped a good part of his mature intellectual, theological,

Richard Hurrell Froude, a contemporary and close friend at Oriel who, in Newman's words, "was a man of the highest gifts, truly many-sided, . . . brimful and overflowing with ideas and views. His opinions arrested and influenced me, even when they did not gain my assent" (engraving by Edward Robinson based on the drawing by George Richmond).

and ecclesiastical position. While retaining something of the ardor and fervency of the Evangelical style in religion, Newman had abandoned an exclusive reliance upon Scripture in favor of the "doctrine of Tradition," he had felt the importance of an apostolic succession in that tradition, and he had embraced the idea of the Church as a body or corporation separate from the State and having its own powers, works, and need of self-governance. He had warmed to the "new music" of saintly Keble's devotionalism and had been strongly attracted to the Romanizing of Froude.

Newman began work on his first full-length book, *The Arians of the Fourth Century* (1833), in 1828. The Arians (followers of Arius) denied the divinity of Christ and were condemned by the Nicene Council (325 A.D.). Newman sought to explore the origin and history of this heresy, and thereby to understand how and why unorthodox doctrines came into being, why they lasted as long as they sometimes did, and how in the end the Church dealt with them.

In chapter one, Newman sketches the state of the Christian Church at a crucial stage of its development, far enough removed in time from the days of Christ's own teaching for the oral tradition of the Apostles to have lost some of its earlier force, yet not having reached the stage at which an exact written statement of its creed had been formed. In these circumstances it was almost inevitable that heretical doctrines would spring into being, especially in view of the vigorous philosophical and theological schools of Judaism, Neo-Platonism, Gnosticism, and Eclecticism which surrounded and influenced the Church. Newman considers it likely, in fact, that the first "Arian" was not Arius himself but rather one Paulus, bishop of Antioch, who owed his position in that city at least in part to the patronage of its queen, Zenobia, a Jewess "by birth or creed."

In an effort to please her, Paulus raised questions about the divinity of Christ, which in short order resulted in his own removal as bishop, but which, once raised, created doubts in other minds. In the absence of a written statement of the creed, Christians seemed at liberty to interpret the Holy Scripture as they wished. And when Arius appeared on the scene (Newman's chapter two), it was precisely to raise questions about the interpretation of Scripture. When St. John, for example, writes of "the only begotten Son," what do the words "begotten" and "Son" mean? Do they not imply a time when the Son was not, and thus that He was not coeternal with the Father? And even a certain inferiority on the part of the Son in relation to the Father, a Glory yet a "lesser Glory"? It is perfectly true that had Arius looked at other passages of Scripture, for example, Prov. 8:27 ("When He established the heavens, there was I"), which implies the coeternity of the Son, he might have thought differently. But, as Newman says disdainfully of Arius and his followers, "The mere words, Father and Son, were all they wanted of revealed authority; they professed to do all the rest for themselves."

The Council of Nicea (Newman, chapter three), the first ecumenical council of the Catholic Church of Christ, was assembled at Nicea in 325 A.D. mainly to deal with the issues raised by Arius and to promulgate in writing the doctrine of orthodoxy. From 225 to 300 representatives of the Church attended the council, only 13 to 22 of whom were Arians. Discussion was open; Arius was questioned and heard; in the end, most of his followers recanted; Arius himself was banished to Illyria, but not excommunicated. The Council promulgated the Nicene Creed, the definitive statement of the Christian Church on the doctrine of the Trinity, slightly amplified by a later council in 381 A.D.

Nevertheless, Arius continued to preach his heretical doctrine and to convince others. An able politician, he secured the support of secular power in the various cities where he lived and preached; his return to higher position in the Church was prevented only by his early death. In the remaining chapters of his book (four, five, and six) Newman gives an account of the later manifestations of his doctrine and of the councils assembled to put or keep it down.

For Newman, the history of Arianism had several points of importance. First, it revealed the tendency of the Church to tolerate diverse ideas, especially when they involved very difficult points of doctrine, up to the point at which they began to provoke a crisis—only then does it formulate its definitive creed. Second, the Arian controversy illustrated the dangers inherent in what might be called the Protestant principle of every man's reading and interpreting Scripture for himself. Sooner or later a dizzying variety of interpretations will emerge, and the individual believer is no more competent to decide among them than he is competent to work out for himself the principles of Newton's laws of gravitation. An authoritative interpretation is needed, and who can make it better than the whole wisdom of the Church assembled in such a meeting as the Nicene Council? On this score, Newman's study of the Arians reinforced his doctrine of Tradition. Third, the alliance of both Paulus, the first "Arian," and Arius himself, with secular power, and the way in which such alliances tended to keep alive an erroneous way of thinking even after the Church had pronounced upon it, showed Newman the dangers of secular interference in religious matters and thus reinforced his conviction that the Church is properly itself a corporate body independent of the State.

All three of these lessons had a bearing on the drama of the Oxford Movement. In the *Apologia pro Vita Sua,* Newman introduces this important episode of his life with the following sentence: "While I was engaged in writing my work upon the Arians, great events were happening at home and abroad, which brought out into form and passionate expression the various beliefs which had so gradually been winning their way into my mind." Though Newman was himself in temper and belief a conservative, he was living in an age of change and reform. In 1828 the English Parliament repealed the Test Act of 1673 (which required holders of public office to belong to the Anglican Church). In 1829 the Catholic Emancipation Act granted Roman Catholics specifically the right to sit in Parliament, provided they took an oath barring the Pope from interfering in British domestic affairs. In 1832 the First Reform Act lessened the property qualification for voters and broadened the franchise to include much of the middle class.

Whatever the political wisdom or unwisdom of these acts, they seemed to Newman, Keble, and their friends to threaten the position of the Anglican Church. If, in a country with an established Church headed by the King and governed by Parliament, non-Anglicans could be elected to that Parliament, did this not mean that control of the national Church was, or could be, in the hands of politicians who might not even belong to it? Confirmation of this nightmare came quickly, when, in February 1833, the Parliament began debate on a bill for the suppression of the Irish sees, which proposed to abolish ten of the eighteen Anglican bishoprics in Ireland (a predominantly Catholic country). Since this bill originated in the Parliament, not in the Church, it was, in Newman's view, a clear encroachment of the State upon the Church and needed to be resisted.

During the eight months preceding the passage of this last bill in August 1833, Newman was out of the country, traveling in Italy and Sicily, recuperating from his labors on the Arians book and accompanying Hurrell Froude as he fought the tuberculosis gradually taking his life. The two

John Keble, whose sermon "National Apostasy," preached 14 July 1833, launched the Oxford Movement (Warden and Fellows of Keble College)

friends followed the Parliamentary debates on the Irish bill in the English newspapers and became increasingly enraged by the apparent inability of the Church to resist this assault. In Rome, Newman told a fellow Englishman, "We have a work to do in England." On 9 July, Newman arrived home. Five days later, on Sunday, 14 July 1833, John Keble preached his famous sermon at Oxford under the title "National Apostasy," and the Oxford Movement was born.

The most inflammatory thing about Keble's sermon on "national apostasy" was its title. The sermon itself quietly, but clearly, made its central point: the nation was denying the faith of its own Church, whose origin was supernatural and whose historical development was apostolic, by allowing its secular Parliament to rule that Church. What was to be done? As early as the spring of 1833, Keble, Hurrell Froude (who had returned from the

Mediterranean before Newman), William Palmer, Arthur Perceval, Hugh Rose, and others had formed an association in defense of the Church. The idea was to keep in communication with one another and to write letters of protest (signed by all) to the bishops in an effort to rally the Church as a whole.

When Newman arrived in July, however, he wittily argued that "Living movements do not come of committees, nor are great ideas worked out through the post, even though it had been the penny-post." He favored communicating with the nation at large through a series of tracts on the subjects in dispute, addressed to the entire Anglican clergy of the land and to laymen. Newman's plan was adopted by the little group at Oxford. He himself wrote the first tract in September 1833, which became number one of a series of ninety (Newman wrote or coauthored about thirty altogether). Under the general title of *Tracts for the Times* these were published periodically from 1833 to 1841 and gave to the Oxford Movement its other name, the Tractarian Movement.

Tract number one, written by Newman but published without his signature, was entitled *Thoughts on the Ministerial Commission* (that is, the Parliamentary body which had just abolished the Irish bishoprics). It called upon ordinary clergymen to rally behind their bishops in protesting the encroachment of the State upon the Church (the bishops were making no such protest, but Newman's aim was to move them by inflaming the lower clergy, which would then force the bishops to act). Tract two was also focused on the Irish problem: "You cannot help what has been done in Ireland, but you may protest against it. You may as a duty protest against it in public and private; you may keep a jealous watch on the proceedings of the nation, lest a second act of the same kind be attempted."

In tract three Newman spelled out what that "second act" might be: "Attempts are making to get the liturgy altered." There had been talk in Parliament, and in certain Evangelical quarters of the Church, of revising *The Book of Common Prayer* so as to make it acceptable to believers of many theological parties, even perhaps to Unitarians. This third tract was the first to broaden the basis of the Movement beyond the Irish issue into a wider protest against the pervasive "liberal" reforms (or, as Newman saw them, signs of laxity and indifferentism on important points of doctrine) being contemplated by the Church.

Although the immediate stimulus to the Movement was its response to the Parliamentary actions cited above, Newman and his allies intended no less than a total revitalization of the Anglican Church. The Church was seen to be in a perilous position, assaulted from without by the growing forces of secularism and unbelief and weakened from within by a tendency to compromise its historical position and even its doctrine. The Church was to be rescued from its own weakness. As Newman put it in the *Apologia:* "She must be dealt with strongly, or she would be lost. There was need of a second reformation." The way back to authority and truth for the Anglican Church lay not in compromise with secularism, with political power, with Protestant dissent, or with Rome, but rather in a reassertion of what the Church had been and still could be.

Tracts continued to pour forth from the little group at Oxford, and by the end of 1833 twenty tracts had been published, printed in London, and distributed to bookshops throughout the land. They enjoyed a brisk sale; letters of congratulations and support arrived at Oxford in large numbers; the issues raised by the Tractarians were widely discussed in the newspapers and periodicals of the day. There were occasional attacks, too, largely on the alleged Romanizing tendency of the tracts.

Near the end of 1833, the Movement drew to it an important new adherent, Edward Bouverie Pusey, canon of Christ Church, Oxford, and Regius professor of Hebrew at the University of Oxford. He wrote tract eighteen, *Thoughts on the Benefits of the System of Fasting Enjoined by our Church,* and signed it with his initials. Fasting by Anglicans was nearly a forgotten practice at that date; Pusey reminded his readers that the Prayer Book not only encourages but "enjoins" the regular use of self-denial as part of the Christian life. In content the tract was important, but the initials E.B.P. appended to it were even more important. In Newman's words, "Froude and I were nobodies"; most of the Tractarians were young and unknown men of the Church (with the exception of Keble). Pusey, on the other hand, was a leading figure of the established Church, well-known and widely respected. Because of him, the Movement became known under a third label, Puseyism.

In 1834 twenty-seven tracts appeared, bringing the total to forty-seven. Tracts thirty-eight and forty-one introduced into Newman's polemical writing the concept of the Anglican Church as the *via media,* the middle way between Protestantism and the Roman Church. The Protestant reformers

Edward Bouverie Pusey, canon of Christ Church, who joined the Oxford Movement in 1833 and succeeded Newman as leader (Warden and Fellows of Keble College)

(Luther, Calvin, and others) had broken away from the original, catholic or universal, Church of Christ by denying its Tradition and relying solely on Holy Scripture and on "justification by faith" (Newman's critique of this latter concept was worked out in his *Lectures on Justification* of 1838). The Roman Church, on the other hand, had added too much in the way of doctrine and practice to the primitive Church. Only the Anglican Church preserved the true spirit of the original; what it lacked in universality and catholicity (being confined largely to one nation), it made up for in being apostolic, that is, faithful to the primitive church of the apostles. This theme was developed not only in tracts thirty-eight and forty-one, both entitled *Via Media,* but also in the *Lectures on the Prophetical Office of the Church* published in 1837 and in articles printed in the *British Critic,* for which Newman served ably as editor from 1838 to 1841. All of this was traditional Anglican doctrine, but Englishmen of Newman's time were so accustomed to thinking themselves Protestants that the idea of the *via media,* of the Church holding itself aloof both from Protestantism and from Rome, seemed novel, revolutionary, and even bigoted in the 1830s. For Newman it was the crucial, overall conception; when, sometime later, he abandoned it, his conversion to Rome came almost immediately.

"But the Tracts," R. W. Church wrote in *The Oxford Movement* (1891), "were not the most powerful instruments in drawing sympathy to the Movement. Without Mr. Newman's four o'clock sermons at St. Mary's the Movement might never have gone on, certainly would never have been what it was. While men were reading and talking about the Tracts they were hearing the sermons, and in the sermons they heard the living meaning and reason and bearing of the Tracts. . . ." Before the Oxford Movement began, Newman had left his curacy of St. Clement's to become vicar of St. Mary's, Oxford, the university church (1828). There, both before and during the Movement, he preached many of his greatest sermons. His style was quiet and untheatrical, but the force of his personality and words enchanted and compelled every audience he addressed.

The first volume of his sermons was published in 1834; further volumes appeared throughout the following decade, reaching a total of nine during his Anglican period: *Parochial Sermons* (six volumes), *Plain Sermons, Sermons, Chiefly on the Theory of Religious Belief,* preached at Oxford, and *Sermons Bearing on Subjects of the Day,* all published between 1834 and 1843. During his Roman Catholic period (1845-1890), he produced *Discourses Addressed to Mixed Congregations* (1849), and *Sermons Preached on Various Occasions* (1857). In an age when sermons were frequently published and widely read, Newman's seemed transcendent. Literary figures as diverse as Matthew Arnold, George Eliot, and Edward FitzGerald admired them greatly; William Makepeace Thackeray declared them the best ever written.

Sermons preached during the Tractarian period (1833-1841) often addressed subjects raised in the tracts. Thus "Tolerance of Religious Error" (December 1834) argues that, although love is unquestionably the "first and greatest" of Christian commandments, we are not bidden to love the heretic. St. Paul, in Titus 3:10, tells us to "reject" him, and St. John, to "receive him not into your house" (2 John 9-10). Yet we are living in a time, Newman argues, when the very idea of heresy or of religious error has come to seem obsolete or even "uncharitable": "We are over-tender in dealing with sin and sinners. We are deficient in jealous custody of the revealed Truths which Christ has left us." Christianity has become too much a matter of feelings only, we must remember that God is not only Love, He is also "a consuming fire" (Heb. 12:29). "I wish I saw," Newman says, "any prospect of this element of zeal and holy sternness springing up among us, to temper and give character to the languid, unmeaning benevolence which we misname Christian love. I have no hope of my country till I see it."

In chapter two of the *Apologia pro Vita Sua*, Newman states the three central principles of the Oxford Movement: "First was the principle of dogma: my battle was with liberalism; by liberalism I mean the anti-dogmatic principle and its developments. . . . from the age of fifteen, dogma had been the fundamental principle of my religion: I know no other religion; I cannot enter into the idea of any other sort of religion; religion, as a mere sentiment is to me a dream and a mockery." For Newman religion was always a matter of fact and truth; being a Christian meant, among other things, knowing and believing the creed of the Church. Insofar as the Anglican Church seemed prepared to neglect or deny such traditional doctrines as the authority of its own apostolic succession, the requirement of fasting, and even the Trinity, it was taking a wrong course. Second was the doctrine of the "visible church, with sacraments and rites which are the channels of invisible grace. I thought that this was the doctrine of Scripture, of the early Church, and of the Anglican Church." By "visible" Church, Newman meant the Church as a corporate body or institution existing in the world, founded by Christ, and not subservient to any national state, secular power, parliament, or king. This principle was the immediate cause of the Oxford Movement (when the Parliament abolished the ten Irish bishoprics). The third principle was opposition to the Roman Church. Writing as a Catholic in 1864, Newman was careful to say that this principle he has "utterly renounced and trampled upon." But at the time of the movement, in accord with Anglican doctrine, "I thought the Church of Rome was bound up with the cause of Antichrist by the Council of Trent" (which condemned the Protestant reformers of the sixteenth century). Though his friend Froude was remarkably friendly to the Roman Church, and even Keble had written "Speak *gently* of our sister's fall" in *The Christian Year,* Newman well understood that any attempt to revitalize the Anglican Church was bound to support and justify its separation from Rome.

As the Movement matured, Newman's thoughts became increasingly fixed on this third and, for him, least agreeable of its principles. In the *Via Media* tracts he had worked to define the precise relationship between the Anglican and the Roman Churches. He regretted the historical separation and present state of noncommunion between them. As an Anglican he felt obliged to explain and justify the separation, but could he do this? Was there good reason for it? The later tracts written by Newman show his effort to deal with these questions (Tract 71, *On the Controversy with the Romanists*) but also his growing conviction that there was so much ground common to them that the separation was hard to justify (Tract 75, *On the Roman Breviary*). This latter tract "frightened my own friends," he later wrote, because of its warmth toward Rome.

During the later years of the Tractarian period, Newman occasionally took what he called "hits" from Rome, sudden but powerful moments of feeling that the Roman Church was in the right after all, that the via media was an empty concept, a "paper religion," that the Anglican Church was simply in a state of schism. An article by the Catholic bishop Nicholas Wiseman entitled "The Anglican Claim" (in the *Dublin Review,* August 1839) quoted the famous words of St. Augustine responding to the Donatist heresy: *securus judicat orbis terrarum* (he judges rightly who speaks for the whole world). These words rang in Newman's ears for months, suggesting the thought that Anglicanism was no via media but simply another small schismatic sect.

Finally, in February 1841, in the famous tract ninety (*Remarks on Certain Passages in the Thirty-Nine Articles*), Newman got to the very heart of Anglican doctrine, the most widely known and familiar statement of its creed. Readers of the *Via Media* tracts, and certainly those of tract seventy-five, had wondered, "How can you manage to sign the Articles? They are directly against Rome." The extent to which the Articles were "against Rome" Newman sought to explore in tract ninety. In brief, Newman reached the conclusion that the Thirty-Nine Articles were not really a Protestant statement at all; there was as much in them contradicting Luther, Calvin, and the reformers as there was contradicting Rome. The Articles were capable of a Catholic interpretation.

This view of things was a bombshell. A "tumult broke out against my Tract," a "storm of indignation . . . throughout the country"; "I was denounced as a traitor." Even old friends such as

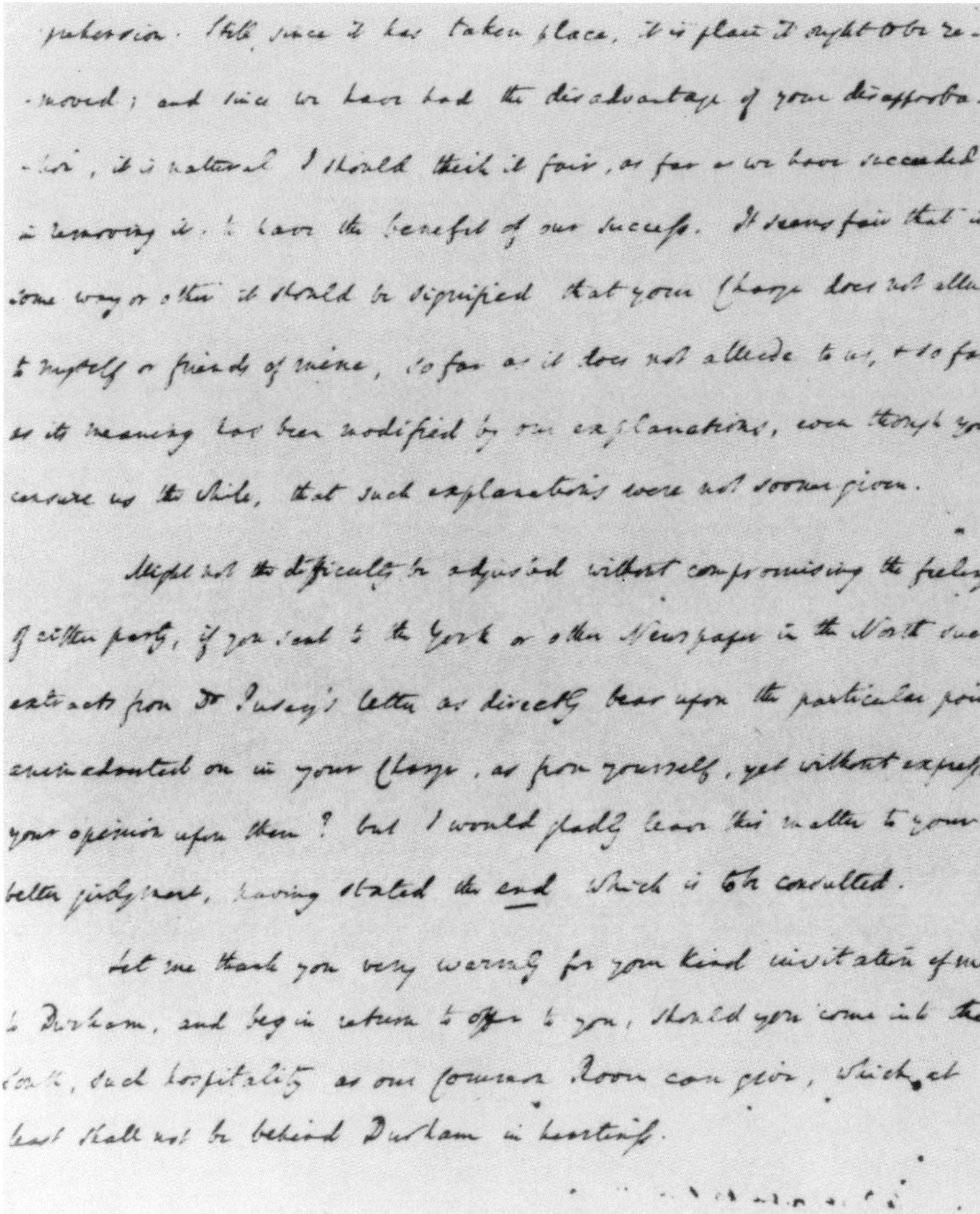
pulsion. Still, since it has taken place, it is plain it ought to be re-
-moved; and since we have had the disadvantage of your disapproba-
-tion, it is natural I should think it fair, as far as we have succeeded
in removing it, to have the benefit of our success. It seems fair that in
some way or other it should be signified that your Charge does not allude
to myself or friends of mine, so far as it does not allude to us, & so far
as its meaning has been modified by our explanations, even though you
censure us the while, that such explanations were not sooner given.

Might not the difficulty be adjusted without compromising the feelings
of either party, if you sent to the York or other Newspaper in the North such
extracts from Dr Pusey's letter as directly bear upon the particular points
animadverted on in your Charge, as from yourself, yet without expressing
your opinion upon them? but I would gladly leave this matter to your
better judgment, having stated the end which is to be consulted.

Let me thank you very warmly for your kind invitation of me
to Durham, and beg in return to offer to you, should you come into the
South, such hospitality as our Common Room can give, which at
least shall not be behind Durham in heartiness.

Letter from Newman, dated 13 October 1837, to the Reverend George Townsend, followed by a letter from Edward Bouverie Pusey. The letters represent Newman's and Pusey's responses to a petition presented by the conservative Townsend, an opponent of Catholic emancipation who later traveled to Italy in an effort to convert the Pope (by permission of the Trustees of The Pierpont Morgan Library).

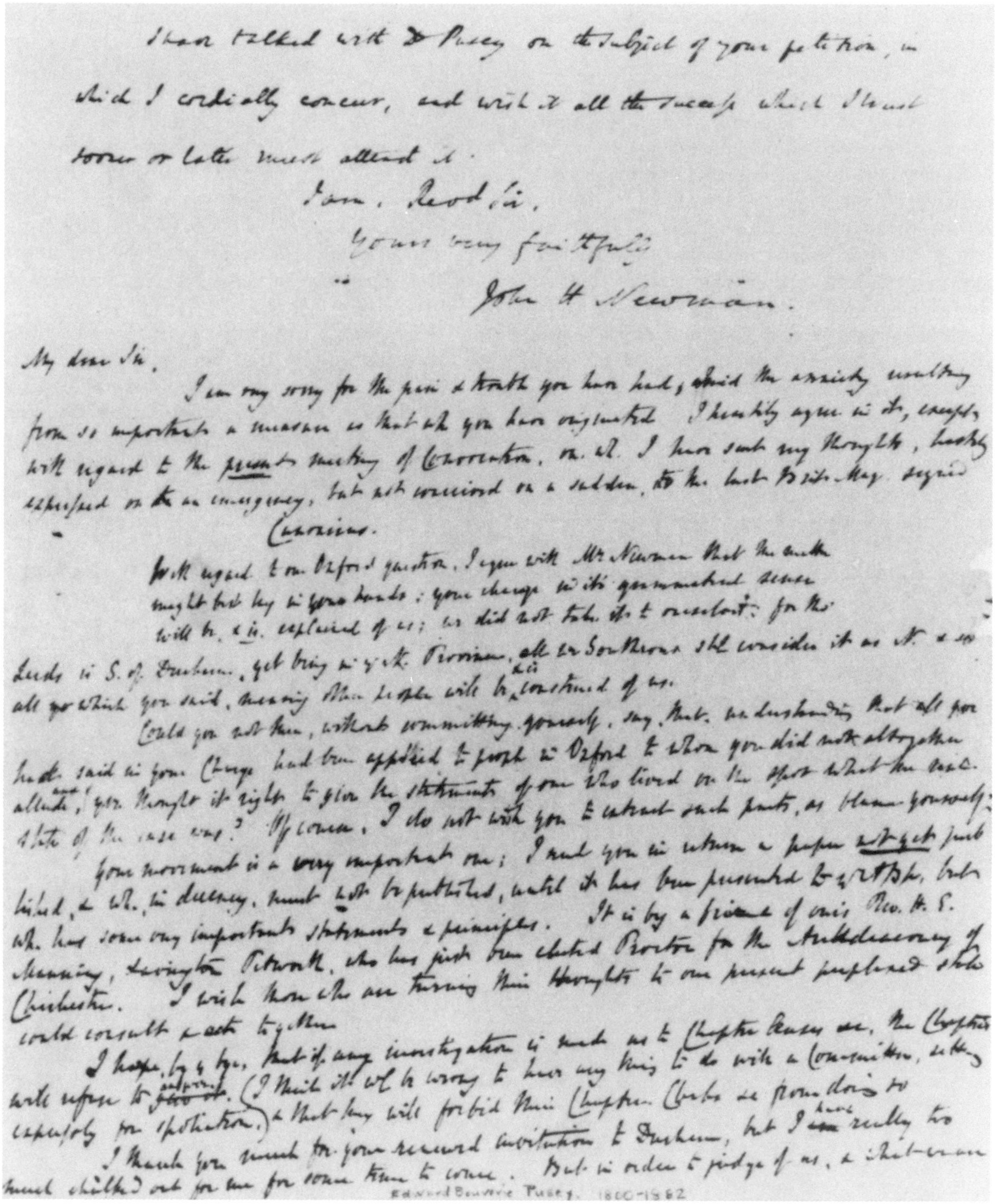

I have talked with Dr Pusey on the subject of your petition, in which I cordially concur, and wish it all the success which I trust sooner or later must attend it.

I am, Revd Sir,

Yours very faithfully

John H Newman.

My dear Sir,

I am very sorry for the pain & trouble you have had, amid the anxiety resulting from so important a measure as that wh you have originated. I heartily agree in it, except with regard to the present meeting of Convocation, [illegible] I have sent my thoughts, hastily expressed on the an emergency, but not conceived on a sudden, to the [illegible]

[illegible]

With regard to our Oxford question, I agree with Mr Newman that [illegible] ... your charge [illegible]

[illegible]

Could you not then, without committing yourself, say, that, understanding that all you had said in your Charge had been applied to people in Oxford to whom you did not altogether allude, you thought it right to give the statements of one who lived on the spot [illegible]

Your movement is a very important one; [illegible]

[illegible]

I wish those who are turning their thoughts to our present perplexed state could consult & act together.

I hope, by & bye, that if any investigation is made as to Chapter [illegible]

I thank you much for your renewed invitation to Durham, but I have really too much chalked out for me for some time to come. [illegible]

Edward Bouverie Pusey, 1800-1882

Pusey and Keble were made uneasy by the Romish tendency of Newman's thinking; a few younger disciples broke with the Movement. But many of the Tractarians were in fact more drawn to Rome than Newman himself was at this stage, and he always insisted that his chief purpose in writing tract ninety was to keep them in the Anglican fold.

But tract ninety was the last of the *Tracts for the Times*. For eight years Newman and his friends had been interpreting the Anglican Church in ways they knew would not be congenial to many of their colleagues and superiors. Newman always felt that if his own bishop censured the tracts, or gave signs of definite disapproval, he would be bound in conscience to quit. Such censure came in March 1841; the bishop of Oxford instructed Newman to discontinue the tracts and to make it publicly known that this was done in compliance with his wish. Other bishops throughout the land repudiated the tracts as well, and it was clear that no appeal to them would be helpful.

Newman resigned his place in the Movement. In the spring of 1842 he left Oxford to take up residence in the tiny village of Littlemore, about three miles from Oxford, where he had bought ten acres of land some years before, and where his mother and sisters had lived for a time after the death of Newman's father in 1824 (his mother died in 1836). At Littlemore, Newman had helped establish a new parish church and for many years had served both it and St. Mary's in Oxford. He managed the meager parish funds with a careful hand and was beloved of his parishioners. In 1840 he had thought of building a kind of monastery at Littlemore, a place of retreat for anyone in need of withdrawal from the world. By 1842 he was himself much in need of such withdrawal. The bitter end of his role in the Oxford Movement had proved to Newman (though not to others) that there was no place in the priesthood of the Church of England for men who saw it as he did. In 1843 he resigned his orders and gave the last, and one of the most beautiful, of his Anglican sermons, "The Parting of Friends."

His heart was tending toward the Roman Church, as Froude's had done, but his intellect held him back. In the three years he spent at Littlemore (1842-1845), Newman pondered the great intellectual obstacle to his conversion: the additions of doctrine and practice which the Roman Church had made to the primitive, apostolic church. He began work on what has been called "his greatest contribution to religious thought," *An Essay on the Development of Christian Doctrine* (1845). The idea that Christian doctrine had developed over the centuries, and would continue to develop, was not a novel

Oriel College and, in the background, St. Mary's, Oxford. Newman was elected a fellow of Oriel in 1822; in 1828, five years before the Oxford Movement began, he became vicar of St. Mary's.

one in theological history, but it had an acute pertinence to Newman's dilemma during the period 1842-1845. The claim of the Anglican Church to be the true Church of Christ rested upon its apostolicity, its fidelity to the creed and ritual of the primitive church. The Roman Church had erred in adding too much to that creed and ritual (for example, the doctrines of transubstantiation, the supremacy of the Pope, the veneration of the Virgin Mary). If it could be determined that these additions were not "corruptions" (the common Anglican term of abuse for them) but "developments" of primitive doctrine and practice, the basis of Anglican protest against Rome would disappear.

Part one of Newman's book is a general discussion of the idea of doctrinal development. The Revealed Truth of Christianity makes its appearance in the world in the same way that any new idea does (the "divine right of kings," for example, or "the rights of man"), and for the full comprehension, explication, and application of it, time is required: "the highest and most wonderful truths, though communicated to the world once for all by inspired teachers, could not be comprehended all at once by the recipients." He quotes the poet George Crabbe: "Truth is the daughter of time." What is commonly called the development of doctrine is no more than a gradual unfolding and elucidation of what was received at the beginning. True, this process of elucidation is subject to human error; corruption as well as true development of the original teaching is possible (in the case of the Arian heresy, for example). The problem then becomes how to distinguish "doctrinal developments" from "doctrinal corruptions."

This problem is the subject of part two of *An Essay on the Development of Christian Doctrine*. Newman suggests seven "notes" or qualities of the genuine "development" of an idea: preservation of its type, continuity of its principles, power of assimilation, logical sequence, anticipation of its future, conservative action upon its past, and chronic vigor. Newman's discussion of the first of these, "Preservation of its Type," is by far the longest (over 100 pages) and takes for illustration this startling description of the Christian Church "commonly called Catholic": "There is a religious communion claiming a divine commission, and holding all other religious bodies around it heretical or infidel; it is a well-organized, well-disciplined body; it is a sort of secret society binding together its members by influences and engagements which it is difficult for strangers to ascertain. It is spread over the known world.... It is a natural enemy to governments external to itself; it is intolerant and engrossing, and tends to a new modeling of society; it breaks laws, it divides families. It is a gross superstition; it is charged with the foulest crimes; it is despised by the intellect of the day; it is frightful to the imagination of the many." Show this description, Newman says, to a man of the first centuries of our era, to a man of the thirteenth century, or to a man of the nineteenth: "Each knows at once, without asking a question, who is meant by it." Newman thus demonstrates in this ingenious rhetorical device that the Catholic Church as a whole, with all its doctrines and practices, has indeed "preserved its type." It is seen as one recognizable thing even by its enemies, and in the earliest as well as in the latest stages of its development.

In the later chapters of part two, Newman analyzes and illustrates the other "Notes" of true development of doctrine. Under the heading of "Logical Sequence," for example, he suggests that, although the Roman doctrines of pardons, penances, and purgatory have not found acceptance in the Protestant or even the Anglican Church, they are logically sequential from the doctrine of baptism, which all Christians embrace. The sacrament of baptism is held to remit the sins of the past, but what of those committed after the sacrament is administered? Pardons and penances fill an obvious need and also derive logically from the principle underlying baptism, namely, that sins may be remitted. And the doctrine of purgatory (often the object of Protestant denunciation) is too but a logical development of this same principle, since it is sometimes impossible (as in the case of murder or sudden death) to obtain the remission of sins during life (chapter nine). In like manner, Newman argues in favor of such Roman doctrines as the resurrection of the flesh, the value of a virgin life, the cult of saints and angels, and the veneration of the Blessed Virgin, under the heading of the various "Notes" of true development.

Perhaps the most arresting passage in all of *An Essay on the Development of Christian Doctrine* is the close of part one entitled "The Papal Supremacy." Here Newman examines, within the framework of the developmental theory, that Roman institution against which, above all, the Anglican Church had set itself from the beginning. How does it now appear, in the light of the theory? Is the papacy a true development or a corruption?

In short, it is a true development because it preserves the type of the original Christian community. So long as Jesus himself lived on earth, He was, of course, the infallible source of revealed truth; upon his death, his apostles became that source. So long, in turn, as those apostles lived, "Christians knew that they must live in unity, and they were in unity." But as the Christian community grew in numbers and spread itself over the world, and as time passed, "divergent courses" needed to be reconciled. When priests disagreed, they deferred to their bishops, and when bishops disagreed, they deferred to the Bishop of Rome, the successor of St. Peter: thus the papacy emerged. This development was both "natural" and "true" since it restored the original hierarchy of Jesus' own ministry. Newman sums up: "If the whole of Christendom is to form one Kingdom, one head is essential; at least this is the experience of eighteen hundred years." To this idea, Newman further shows, the early Fathers gave additional support by acknowledging the authority of Rome from a very early date: St. Clement, St. Ignatius of Antioch, St. Ireneaus, and many others. He quotes them, and concludes: "More ample testimony for the Papal Supremacy, as now professed by Roman Catholics, is scarcely necessary than what is contained in these passages. . . ."

In writing *An Essay on the Development of Christian Doctrine* Newman made his most significant contribution to theology and also resolved his own personal religious dilemma. "I had begun my Essay on the Development of Doctrine in the beginning of 1845," Newman wrote in the *Apologia pro Vita Sua,* "and I was hard at it all through the year till October. As I advanced, my difficulties so cleared away that I ceased to speak of 'the Roman Catholics,' and boldly called them Catholics. Before I got to the end, I resolved to be received, and the book remains in the state in which it was then, unfinished." On 3 October 1845, Newman resigned his fellowship at Oriel, and on 9 October was received into the Roman Catholic Church by Father Dominic of the Passionist Order. Immediately before and after the event, Newman wrote a flurry of letters to friends, family, and former Tractarians informing them of his admission "into what I believe to be the one and only fold of the Redeemer" (letter to Pusey, 8 October 1845).

Newman's conversion distressed many of his friends, pleased others (a good many of these followed him into the Catholic Church), and created a sensation in England. John Henry Newman of Oriel College, Oxford, leader of the Tractarian Movement, probably the best-known Anglican religious leader of his time, a convert to Rome! His move was a fatal blow to the Oxford Movement, and, as both Benjamin Disraeli and William E. Gladstone said, an immeasurable calamity for the Church of England as a whole. From the point of view of the Roman Church in England, on the other hand, Newman's conversion was a windfall whose proportions were equally hard to estimate. In the late months of 1845 Newman was warmly welcomed into the Church by his old acquaintance Nicholas Wiseman (whom he had met in Rome in 1833), now his bishop. There was some fear, at the beginning, that the new convert, an eminent man, might prove difficult and demanding. Wiseman saw at once that this would not be so and wrote to a fellow "old" Catholic: "He opened his mind completely to me; and I assure you the Church has not received, at any time, a convert who has joined her in more docility and simplicity of faith than Newman."

In October of 1846 Newman went to Rome, where, after a period of study and training, he was ordained priest on 30 May 1847. He received a commission from Pope Pius IX to introduce into England the institution of the Oratory. Bearing this commission, he arrived home in England on Christmas Eve of 1847. The next fifteen years proved to be, however, the most difficult of Newman's life. In the eyes of many Englishmen what Newman had done seemed a betrayal of the nation and its Church. His behavior throughout the years of the Oxford Movement seemed duplicitous, as if Newman were all along heading for Rome and had only seemed to be an ardent Anglican. For English Catholics, on the other hand, Newman seemed a great "catch" but also somehow untrustworthy in view of his controversial history.

Newman's life as a Catholic priest in England centered on the religious community of the Oratory in Birmingham, which he founded officially on 1 February 1848 and served the rest of his days, a service interrupted only by his residence in Dublin as rector of the Catholic University of Ireland in the mid 1850s. As an institution, the Oratory is a small group of secular priests (Newman thought the ideal number to be about twelve) organized under a rule developed by themselves and living together with a larger number of lay brothers and novices. The Oratorians hear confessions, celebrate the mass and carry out other pastoral duties, but they are also free to teach in the schools often attached to an Oratory, to study and to write. The Oratory, originally founded in Rome in the sixteenth century by St. Philip Neri, was ideally suited to the temper of Newman and of many of the converts who followed him, being semimonastic yet informal and independent. A London Oratory was

The Birmingham Oratory, founded by Newman in 1848

founded in 1849, with Newman's friend F. W. Faber at its head. The Birmingham Oratory was, after the Oxford years, Newman's second home.

Other projects of Newman's early years as a Catholic were too often frustrated. A new translation of the Catholic Bible was begun but never finished, because Bishop Wiseman learned of a similar undertaking in the United States and withdrew his support. An English translation of an Italian *Lives of the Saints,* to be brought out by members of the Birmingham Oratory, was begun in 1847 but soon abandoned when the Catholic hierarchy judged the Italian work too insistent on the subject of miracles to gain a friendly reception in England. Wiseman's advice that Newman should expose the renegade Dominican friar Giacinto Achilli resulted in a painful and prolonged trial for libel (1852); Newman lost and was forced to pay the expenses of the court, amounting to £14,000. The London *Times* proclaimed the trial a gross miscarriage of justice, but Newman suffered prolonged and adverse publicity. Small wonder that Newman's novel about conversion, *Loss and Gain* (1848), described as *The Story of a Convert* on the title page for the third edition, should bear the title it does. (His other novel, *Callista: A Sketch of the Third Century,* was published in 1856.)

On the other hand, Newman's public lectures in 1850 and 1851 were among his most successful ventures. At the London Oratory, in the late spring of 1850, Newman delivered his *Lectures on Certain Difficulties Felt by Anglicans in Submitting to the Catholic Church* and had them published as a book in July. Addressed to his friends and associates in the Oxford Movement, these lectures argue that "Communion with the Roman See" was "the legitimate issue of the religious movement of 1833." This, as we have seen, was true for Newman himself and for about a hundred Anglicans involved in the Movement, but most Tractarian sympathizers, including Keble and Pusey most notably, remained in the Anglican Church even after the collapse of Tractarianism. Newman's lectures were designed to deal with the doubts and hesitations of these lingerers. The first seven lectures attack the Anglican Church with verve, humor, and cutting "hits"; the last five deal with many of the objections to Catholic teaching and practice Newman had earlier analyzed and overcome in *An Essay on the Development of Christian Doctrine.*

In the first lectures Newman hits hard at the Anglican Church. The failure of the Oxford Movement to reform the Church proved that it was, after all, merely "a department of Government, or a function or operation of the State." Its "Prayer-Book is an Act of Parliament of two centuries ago, and its cathedrals and its chapter-houses are the spoils of Catholicism." It cannot be a guardian of orthodoxy, since it is purely and simply the creature of Parliament, and as such it is "as little bound by what it said or did formerly, as this morning's newspaper by its former numbers." These biting phrases are characteristic of the brilliancy and aggressive mood of all the lectures, which delighted not only the Catholics of Newman's London audience but many Protestants as well (especially Dissenters, who had their own disagreements with the Anglican Church). A number of important conversions followed, and in August of 1850 Rome conferred upon Newman the honorary degree of Doctor of Divinity.

On 29 September 1850 Pope Pius IX formally restored the Roman Catholic hierarchy in England, a country which had since 1673 been considered a missionary field by the Roman Church and whose priests and bishops had worked under the supervision of the College of Propaganda at Rome. The restoration was greeted by much of the English public and press as if it were a declaration of war, as if the Legions of Julius Caesar were on the march again in the nineteenth century. It was popularly called "the Papal Aggression," and the controversy which ensued was a graphic reminder to Newman and to all English Catholics of how prejudiced against Rome their countrymen were. The *Times* vehemently criticized the Pope's act; the prime minister, instead of attempting to calm the waters, sided with popular indignation; protest meetings were held all over the land; the Pope was burned in effigy; priests were pelted with mud and stones; windows were broken in Catholic chapels and even in the houses of Catholic laymen. Newman, attempting to draw some of the popular wrath upon himself and away from his superiors, preached a powerful sermon, "Christ upon the Waters" (27 October 1850), on the occasion of the installation of William Ullathorne as the first Roman bishop of Birmingham. In July of 1852, also on the subject of the return of Catholicism to England, Newman preached the most beautiful of his Catholic sermons, "The Second Spring."

Newman in 1851, six years after his conversion to Catholicism. Painting by M. R. Giberne (Birmingham Oratory).

Responding to the outcry over "the Papal Aggression," Newman, in the summer of 1851, delivered his *Lectures on the Present Position of Catholics in England* to the brothers of the Birmingham Oratory. They were published in book form that same year. These lectures, whose subject he was now in a position to feel keenly, are, like those of 1850, among the liveliest and most immediately engaging of his public utterances, mixing as they do a mordant wit, an abundance of illustration and anecdote, and a tone alternately abusive, pitying, and stern. His purpose is the public exposure of prejudice, that prejudice felt by ordinary (and sometimes not so ordinary) Protestant Englishmen against the Roman Catholic Church, its monks, nuns and priests, its Pope, its history, and its converts. At times Newman amusingly and wittily exposes the crude prejudices of John Bull on these subjects; at other times, the tone darkens, as he contemplates the tremendous weight and wide prevalence of that prejudice, which had grown in England since the time of Henry VIII and which had been so forcibly illustrated by the events of the previous nine months.

He begins in lecture one ("Protestant View of the Catholic Church") with the fine anecdote of the Lion and the Man: the Lion visits the splendid house of the Man, observing everywhere upon its walls pictures of himself. The Man says he should be pleased, see how important you are to me! The Lion points out that all the pictures show the defeat and degradation of the Lion: here defeated by Samson, there groveling in a cage, elsewhere butchered by a gladiator or yoked in harness to pull the emperor's chariot. The Lion's final comment points the moral: "Lions would have fared better, had lions been the artists." In Newman's telling, the Lion is the Catholic Church, the house is England, and the Man is John Bull. The man can paint the lion however he pleases, for the house is his and he is the artist. In England there is an established Protestant Church supported by taxation, governed by Parliament, and headed by the king; the very meaning of "protestant" is protest against Rome. Is it any wonder that in such a country, with an established Church so founded, hostility to Rome should be so virulent and so long-lasting?

The hostile Protestant view of Rome amounts to what Newman calls the Protestant Tradition, and in subsequent lectures he unfolds the workings of that tradition. "By tradition is meant," he wittily says, "what has ever been held, as far as we know, though we do not know how it came to be held, and for that very reason think it true, because else it would not be held." To the prejudiced mind the facts are irrelevant, because the momentum of tradition always carries the day. What does it matter that the French Protestant historian François Guizot tells us that the Roman Church in the early Middle Ages was "the salvation of Christianity"? We will still believe, because it is a popular Protestant tradition, that the Church at that era was "most darkened and corrupted." What does it matter that a firsthand, impartial, and distinguished witness such as Joseph Blanco White assures us that the Jesuits of Spain "toiled without pecuniary reward, and were equally zealous in promoting devotional feelings both among their pupils and the people at large"? We shall still believe, because tradition tells us, that the Jesuit body is "the pattern of all that is evil." And what does it matter that the German historian Johann Neander, a Protestant, writes warmly of the Catholic monks of earlier centuries as the very types of "love and charity" and as making important contributions to the agricultural science of Western Europe? We shall still believe them, on the contrary, to be "the very types and emblems of laziness, uselessness, ignorance, stupidity, fanaticism, and profligacy" because that is what Protestant Tradition tells us.

In lecture seven ("Assumed Principles the Intellectual Ground of the Protestant View"), Newman takes up a typical Protestant objection to the Catholic Church: "our belief in the miracles wrought by the relics and the prayers of the saints." Such belief, Protestants say, is a "self-evident absurdity," yet what is the basis for so saying? Protestants believe in the Incarnation just as Catholics do, and the Incarnation is the supreme miracle of all: "No miracle can be so great as that which took place in the Holy House of Nazareth; it is indefinitely more difficult to believe than all the miracles of the Breviary, of the Martyrology, of Saints' lives, of legends, of local traditions, put together." Surely it is inconsistent to accept this supreme miracle and to deny all or most others. Yet Catholics are continually abused by Protestants for "believing in miracles."

The Protestant view is rooted in ignorance about the Roman Church; it feeds upon "fable"; it rejects as unwholesome food all "true testimony"; it perpetuates itself through the ordinary mechanisms of prejudice. Blanco White's critical but fair-minded account of the Roman Church soon went out of print and was forgotten, while the sensational and "blasphemous fiction" of Maria Monk, her *Awful Disclosures,* was an immediate best-seller in 1836 and remained in wide circulation as Newman spoke in the summer of 1851. Why do Protestants read and believe such trash? In addition to the weight of Tradition, there is also a psychological cause: "Something or other men must fear, men must loathe, men must suspect, even if it be to turn away their minds from their own inward miseries." And the very extravagance of such anti-Catholic fictions as Monk's *Awful Disclosures* itself causes a kind of belief: "The reader says, 'It is so shocking, it must be true; no one could have invented it.' "

Newman's account of the present position of Catholics in England is a dark one. There seems little prospect that the Protestant view will change in the short run. All that Catholics can do is attempt to get themselves and their faith better known, for the root cause of prejudice is ignorance; the position of the Church in England can only improve with each increase of general understanding about it. For the longer term, Newman's faith assures him that "The Maker of all, and only He, can shiver in pieces this vast enchanted palace in which our lot is cast; may He do it in His time!"

One obstacle to the improvement of the position of Catholics in Great Britain was the lack of higher education for them. The great universities at Oxford and Cambridge were Protestant institutions, while the University of London, and the Queen's colleges established in Ireland at Galway and Cork, were purely secular. Many Catholics felt the need for a genuine Catholic university of the kind the Belgians had created in the University of Louvain. The logical place was Ireland, with its large Catholic population, but the university would,

One of the first photographs ever taken of Newman, London, 1861 (Birmingham Oratory)

it was hoped, attract students from all of Great Britain. Archbishop Paul Cullen, primate of Ireland, acting under the authority of a papal bull, invited Newman in April of 1851 to design and lead such an institution, to be called the Catholic University of Ireland, and to give a series of lectures on the subject. Newman accepted the presidency of the as yet nonexistent university in November of 1851 and he remained actively involved in trying to get it going for several years. Some students were enrolled and classes taught, but the project ultimately came to nothing, and Newman resigned in 1858.

Newman's lectures of 1852, however, are a classic statement of the nature and purposes of liberal education. The nine "discourses" delivered in Dublin (and published in eleven parts that year) are the heart of *The Idea of a University Defined and Illustrated.* They appear as part one of the book ("University Teaching"); part two ("University Subjects") is composed of ten further essays and lectures written from 1854 to 1858 and published originally as *Lectures and Essays on University Subjects* (1859). The first four "discourses" take up the sensitive question of the place of theology in the university curriculum. Newman well understood that some members of his audience supported the purely secular universities at Cork and Galway, while others meant by the phrase "Catholic university" an institution devoted primarily to religious training. Neither of these is, in Newman's view, a proper university. The latter, which seeks primarily a moral objective, contradicts the basic purpose of a university, which is to foster "the culture of the intellect." The former, the purely secular university having no chair of theology at all, is for Newman "an intellectual absurdity" because, while professing in its designation "university" to be concerned with universal or total knowledge, it excludes at the outset one branch of knowledge "which, to say the least, is as important and as large" as any other, theology.

This point Newman argues out in detail in discourse two under the title "Theology a Branch of Knowledge," one of the most energetic and challenging of all the lectures. The target here is that "Liberalism" in religion which, as we have seen, it had been Newman's constant mission to oppose, that "Liberalism" which held "that Religion consists, not in knowledge, but in feeling or sentiment," that "Liberalism" which warmly proclaims its belief in God but "does not think that any thing is known or can be known for certain, about the origin of the world or the end of man." Such is, Newman suggests, the general belief of the religion of the day, but, he asks, what is the difference between saying that there is no God and saying that *nothing whatever* can be known about Him? If you believe the latter, "how do you differ from Hume or Epicurus?" He well knew that his audience, Christians all, considered themselves very different from Hume and Epicurus, and that his points had been made: theology is a branch of knowledge and must be part of a university curriculum.

In discourse four Newman explores a further danger in omitting theology from university teaching: the other branches of knowledge will usurp its place. Economics (in Newman's day called "political economy") will give us "economic man" and insinuate, without necessarily intending to do so, that his economic interests and purposes are the only ones that matter. Biology will give us "biological man," and so on. No Christian believes that either physical health alone or economic well-being alone is the total purpose of man's life, yet these studies pursued without reference to theology tend to inculcate such belief and encroach upon a domain in which they have no authority. For this reason too, the study of theology is essential in an institution devoted to universal truth.

That theology was for Newman not only an essential but in fact the chief and most important branch of knowledge he does not quite say. Theology involves knowledge of the supernatural world, the other branches of knowledge the natural. For him the former is more important than the latter, undoubtedly, but so far as university studies are concerned, the two realms are simply distinct. Unlike other religious men of the nineteenth century, Newman was never disturbed in his faith by the development of the Darwinian theory of evolution or by other scientific accounts of the natural world. This theme he treats more fully in his lecture on "Christianity and Physical Science" in part two of *The Idea of a University.*

Having established in the first four discourses the place of theology in a true university, Newman gets to the overall aim of education in discourse five, "Knowledge Its Own End." The kind of knowledge of concern in a university is not "useful" in the ordinary sense; it is not acquired to be used for some further purpose, but is in itself an end: "Knowledge is capable of being its own end. Such is the constitution of the human mind, that any kind of knowledge, if it really be such, is its own reward." Knowledge "is an object, in its own nature so really and undeniably good, as to be the compensation of a great deal of thought in the compassing, and a great deal of trouble in the attaining." It does not bring wealth or honor with it. Nor does it bring virtue: "Knowledge is one thing, virtue is another." "There is a physical beauty and a moral: there is a beauty of person, there is a beauty of our moral being, which is natural virtue; and in like manner there is a beauty, there is a perfection, of the intellect." This, and only this, a university seeks to develop.

Despite the intrinsic merit and public success of his speaking and writing in these years, however, Newman felt throughout the 1850s somewhat frustrated and unfulfilled. He never doubted the wisdom and rightness of his conversion, but was he serving his new and beloved Church as well as he was able? Too many projects had come to nothing: the Bible translation, the *Lives of the Saints,* the Catholic University of Ireland. His brief editorship of the Liberal Catholic periodical the *Rambler* (in 1859) propelled him into the middle of a continuing controversy between "liberal" Catholics and the more "conservative" hierarchy. The last thing Newman needed, as a recent convert, was to be identified with any specific "party" of his new Church, but his sympathy with Catholic liberals such as Lord Acton in England and Ignaz Döllinger in Germany often put him in this position. His own article, "On Consulting the Faithful in Matters of Doctrine," published in the *Rambler* in 1859, was delated to Rome on a charge of heresy, though the charge was soon dropped. At the same time, Newman regretted keenly the loss of his Anglican friends and felt at times that his conversion had been too abrupt and unexplained. Perhaps what was needed, for his new friends, his old, and for himself, was a plain statement in full of what he had done and what he was.

But Newman was not accustomed to writing about himself. An occasion, a provocation, was needed to bring forth in full the project he had vaguely in mind. That occasion came to him, almost, as he later thought, by an act of Providence. On 30 December 1863, Newman received in the mail a copy of *Macmillan's* magazine for January 1864. The anonymous sender had marked a passage in a book review signed with the initials C.K.: "Truth for its own sake, had never been a virtue with the Roman clergy. Father Newman informs us that it need not, and on the whole ought not to be; that cunning is the weapon which Heaven has given to the Saints wherewith to withstand the brute male force of the wicked world which marries and is given in marriage." The passage was brief, but a clear insult, attacking at once Newman's own truthfulness and that of the Roman clergy in general; it even impugned Newman's manhood in a vague but malicious phrase. It was also quite public, printed in a magazine of wide circulation.

Newman protested the "grave and gratuitous slander" in a note to the editors of *Macmillan's* and soon found himself in correspondence with C.K., who turned out to be Charles Kingsley, professor of modern history at Cambridge, chaplain to the Queen, and a very well-known novelist of the day. Failing to get from Kingsley a definite apology or retraction, Newman published the correspondence (as he had told Kingsley he would, and as Kingsley said he had "every right" to do) in the form of a pamphlet: *Mr. Kingsley and Dr. Newman: A Correspondence on the Question Whether Dr. Newman Teaches that Truth Is No Virtue?* (31 January 1864). The battle was joined, and continued through the spring, as Kingsley responded with a pamphlet of his own under the title *"What, Then, Does Dr. Newman Mean?"* and Newman replied with two further pamphlets in April. The Newman-Kingsley controversy created a sensation that spring, and those who followed it generally felt that Newman had the better of it, in wit, in clarity, and in truth. As the *London Review* observed, Kingsley had simply "lost his temper" and had given a "furious answer in forty pages to Father Newman's single sheet."

Skillful and total as Newman's victory in the controversy with Kingsley was, he still felt that Kingsley's question "What does Dr. Newman mean?," though impudently and maliciously asked in the context of controversy, might be given a larger meaning and a full reply. Newman wrote rapidly, in April and May of 1864, what is now known as his *Apologia pro Vita Sua.* It first appeared as a series of seven pamphlets with a separately published appendix, was published as a book that same year (one year later in the U.S.), became known under a new title, *History of My Religious Opinions* in the revised edition of 1865, and reached its final form in the edition of 1886. The early editions address Kingsley and the controversy; the later ones assume more and more the shape of a spiritual and intellectual autobiography.

Newman about the time of his Apologia pro Vita Sua *(Birmingham Oratory)*

The five chapters of the *Apologia pro Vita Sua* treat the stages of Newman's life as he conceived them in 1864, the first being titled "History of My Religious Opinions to the Year 1833." Chapters two and three tell the story of the Oxford Movement, four the transition years at Littlemore, the writing of *An Essay on the Development of Christian Doctrine,* and Newman's conversion to the Roman Catholic Church in 1845. The writing is often moving, occasionally witty, always lucid and candid; Newman's account of his earlier friends and associates at Oriel College, and in the Oxford Movement, as well as that of his opponents, is always generous, respectful, and honest. The book is not an autobiography in the full sense of the word, being rather, as he proclaimed it, a history of his "religious opinions" and intellectual development.

The final chapter of the *Apologia,* chapter five, is titled "Position of My Mind since 1845" and is a brief but powerful statement of Newman's own fundamental position. He begins with the startling acknowledgment that "every article of the Christian Creed, whether as held by Catholics or by Protestants, is beset with intellectual difficulties; and it is simple fact, that, for myself, I cannot answer these difficulties." But "Ten thousand difficulties do not make one doubt, as I understand the subject; difficulty and doubt are incommensurate." A man may have great difficulty solving a mathematical problem, but this does not cause him to doubt that there is a correct solution to it. Thus on the great central question of religion, Newman makes the following, nearly paradoxical declaration: "Of all points of faith, the being of a God is, to my own apprehension, encompassed with most difficulty, and yet borne in upon our minds with most power."

But, he continues, his own internal certainty of "the being of a God" seems challenged or even contradicted when "I look out of myself into the world of men, and there I see a sight which fills me with unspeakable distress. . . . I look into this living busy world, and see no reflexion of its Creator." Instead he sees "the many races of man, their starts, their fortunes, their mutual alienation, their conflicts . . . their aimless courses, their random achievements . . . the tokens so faint and broken of a superintending design, . . . the disappointments of life, the defeat of good, the success of evil, physical pain, mental anguish, the prevalence and intensity of sin, the pervading idolatries, the corruptions . . . that condition of the whole race, so fearfully yet exactly described in the Apostle's words, 'having no hope and without God in the world.' "

How can these facts be reconciled with the existence of a God? "I can only answer, that either there is no Creator, or this living society of men is in a true sense discarded from His presence. . . . And so I argue about the world;—*if* there be a God, *since* there is a God, the human race is implicated in some terrible aboriginal calamity. It is out of joint with the purposes of its Creator." Thus the doctrine of what is "theologically called original sin becomes to me almost as certain as that the world exists, and as the existence of God."

Given the terrible power and prevalence of what is "theologically called original sin," and reading the signs of its influence upon the human world around him, how can the believer maintain his equally powerful, nearly spontaneous and instinctive, belief in the being of a God? Reason alone cannot perform this task; in theory, and "correctly exercised," perhaps it could. But "actually and historically" the tendency of "unaided reason" is "towards a simple unbelief in matters of religion," and such unbelief is in fact the trend of the times. Education cannot reverse this trend; nor can a splintered Protestantism, ever dividing itself into more and more warring sects; nor even can Holy Scripture: "a book, after all, cannot make a stand against the wild living intellect of man."

"Supposing then it be the Will of the Creator to interfere in human affairs, and to make provisions for retaining in the world a knowledge of Himself, so definite and distinct as to be proof against the energy of human scepticism," what would that provision be? Clearly the Catholic Church of Christ, founded by God himself, existing in unbroken continuity for 1800 years, spread throughout the world and "retaining in the world" that "knowledge" of Him who founded it. Only in this living institution is to be found an adequate counterweight to that "original sin" which ever threatens to keep mankind from knowing and obeying its Creator.

The *Apologia pro Vita Sua* was, from its first publication in 1864, a resounding success. It not only vindicated Newman from Kingsley's original charge but also brought him, almost overnight, to a position of public influence and favor. The candor, the fairness, the generosity of Newman's pages won nearly universal praise, and his careful account of the reasons for, and the history of, his conversion to the Roman Church made that conversion seem different, more intelligible than it had seemed to the casual, and more or less prejudiced, view of Protestant and English eyes. A wave of conversions to Rome (including that of the poet Gerard Manley Hopkins) followed the publication of the *Apologia.* Letters of congratulations, of support, and of spiritual inquiry came to Newman from America, from India, from around the world. The publication in 1865 of his most compelling poem, "The Dream of Gerontius," also contributed to Newman's worldwide celebrity at this period. He rapidly became a better-known, and in many quarters a more highly regarded, spokesman for English Catholicism than most of his ecclesiastical superiors. Adopting this role to some extent, Newman responded in 1866 to his old friend Pusey's 1865 pamphlet *Eirenicon* ("reunion") with another entitled *A Letter to the Rev. E. B. Pusey.* Warmly sharing Pusey's hope that a reunion of the Anglican and Roman Churches could be worked out, Newman nevertheless had to chastise Pusey for holding too much traditional Protestant prejudice and misunderstanding about the Church of Rome for his proposals to be immediately practicable. His "olive branch" had been "launched as from a catapult," Newman wrote, in view of Pusey's strong criticisms of such Roman doctrines as Papal Infallibility and the Immaculate Conception of Mary. The prospect of a reunion seemed a long way off.

Newman felt it was now time, in the late 1860s, to address directly the most fundamental religious issue of the age, the question of belief itself. For him personally "the being of a God" had always been an undoubted "first principle" of thought and action, yet he had always recognized that the general trend of his time was toward unbelief. He had for a long time wanted to answer the challenge of this trend but had hesitated to do this, feeling that an inadequate or flawed analysis of faith and reason would be worse than none at all. Certain of his sermons preached from 1826 to 1843 had dealt with the "theory of religious belief" and had been published in a volume in 1843. Now in the late 1860s, and with the success of the *Apologia pro Vita Sua* upon him, Newman began *An Essay in Aid of a Grammar of Assent* (1870).

This work is the most difficult and technical of Newman's writings, employing, especially in its earlier chapters, the terminology of formal logic Newman had worked with when assisting Whately on his *Elements of Logic* in 1826. Thus part one of the essay is entitled "Assent and Apprehension" and deals with several ways in which we may hold, apprehend, or entertain propositions: we may "doubt" them, we may "infer" their truth from a given body of evidence, or we may "assent" absolutely to their truth. For the proposition "Free trade is a benefit," for example, we may be uncertain whether it is true or not (doubt), we may infer its truth from other truths ("free trade keeps down prices" or "free trade makes more goods available") and thus accept its truth conditionally upon them (inference), or we may be absolutely and unconditionally convinced of its truth (assent). Some philosophers, John Locke, for example, argued that all knowledge of the external world is inferential (inferred from a given body of evidence more or less strong); its truth is more or less probable depending on the quality and amount of the evidence, and is in no case certain.

Newman, however, quarrels with Locke on just this point, arguing that it is untrue to our experience to suggest that we do not "assent" to any proposition absolutely but always regard it as more or less "probable." The proposition "Great Britain is an island," for example, we do not hold in any conditional way, we do not regard it as "very probably true"—we regard it as absolutely true, we assent to it. We may not be able to produce on demand all our reasons for so believing—indeed, over time, we tend to forget the reasons for our most fundamental beliefs. Nevertheless, a convergence of probabilities amounts to a certitude, and we are certain that Great Britain is an island in the same way that we are certain of our own existence. Thus "assent," defined as the absolute and unconditional acceptance of a proposition about matters of fact, is not merely a theoretical possibility. It is a reality of everyday life, an operation or posture of the mind in every way as valid as "doubt" or "inference."

In the sphere of religion "assent" is of preeminent importance, since most men do not accept the truths of Christianity conditionally, or by drawing careful, logical "inferences" from such "evidence" as is available. Professional theologians may proceed in this way—inferring from the "design" of nature the existence of an intelligent Creator, for example—but the average religious person does not. His assent to religious truth is not "notional" (that is, inferential, intellectual, abstract) but "real" (that is, experiential and concrete).

For Newman such "real assent" comes about through the ordinary man's experience of Conscience. In arguing out this point (chapter five) Newman produces the most controversial passage of his "grammar." He assumes, as a "first principle," that "we have by nature a conscience" in the same way that we have by nature a memory, an imagination, a faculty of reasoning. When we do a good thing, we feel pleasure and approbation, when we do a bad thing, we feel pain and blame. And, Newman argues, "in this special feeling, which follows on the commission of what we call right or wrong, lie the materials for the real apprehension of a Divine Sovereign and Judge." Thus "the phenomena of Conscience, as a dictate, avail to impress the imagination with the picture of a Supreme Governor, a Judge, holy, just, powerful, all-seeing, retributive." In this sense, Conscience "is the creative principle of religion, as the Moral Sense is the principle of ethics."

Newman's suggestion that Conscience, the voice of God in man, is the "creative principle of religion" is the most striking and original feature of *An Essay in Aid of a Grammar of Assent.* Together with his analysis and defense of the reality of "assent" as a phenomenon both of everyday life and of the religious life, it stands out as the most challenging assertion of the book. Many readers find his analysis of both these things logically unsatisfying, but considered as a psychological account of the origin and nature of faith in the believing mind, it seems at least biographically authentic. Newman had always been fascinated with Bishop Joseph Butler's argument, in *The Analogy of Religion* (1736), that "probability is the guide of life" and that the probabilities both of natural and of revealed religion favored belief. Yet he also felt that one's assent to religious truth had to be, and was, rooted in something more than a sense of its "probability." In chapter one of *Apologia pro Vita Sua* he had argued that "probabilities which did not reach to logical certainty, might suffice for a mental certitude." In *An Essay in Aid of a Grammar of Assent* he attempted to work out more fully the logical basis of such "mental certitude," to demonstrate "the logical cogency of faith." The book did not enjoy the warm reception given the *Apologia.* Catholic theologians found its terminology unorthodox; unbelievers found it philosophically flawed. Newman himself was not satisfied with it, although some recent philosophers of religion and of language have found in its pages a valuable reassessment of the ancient opposition between reason and faith.

While Newman was writing *An Essay in Aid of a Grammar of Assent,* a new theological controversy broke out, concerning the Infallibility of the Pope. As early as 1864 Pope Pius IX had spoken of calling a new General Council of the Church, the first since the Council of Trent in 1545. In 1867 the Vatican Council was formally announced, to take place one or two years hence. It was widely understood, though not formally proclaimed, that some defi-

Newman in Rome, 1879. Behind Newman to his immediate left is Father William Neville, who served Newman as companion and amanuensis during the cardinal's last years (Brompton Oratory, London).

nition of Papal Infallibility would be called for. As the Vatican Council approached, the Church was plunged into controversy between those who sought to define Infallibility in its most extreme form (in terms of a direct revelation to the Pope which made consultation with the Church in general unnecessary) and those who, like Newman, saw the authority of the Pope in more traditional terms (involving a consultation with the Church and careful consideration of Scripture and apostolic tradition).

Newman himself was invited to attend the Council. He declined on grounds of ill-health, but his opinion on the subject was sought by many bishops in England, France, and Germany who were to attend. Although he himself believed there was an Infallibility lodged in the Church, he also believed a formal promulgation and definition of the doctrine was premature, reminding one of his correspondents that the Church pondered the doctrine of the Immaculate Conception for several centuries before defining it formally in 1854. By contrast, the current proceedings of 1867-1870 were altogether too hasty. In the end, the definition of Papal Infallibility by the Vatican Council of 1870 was moderate rather than extremist, and Newman, as he wrote to a friend, was "pleased at its moderation—that is, if the doctrine in question is to be defined at all."

Newman correctly anticipated that almost any formula of Papal Infallibility would be misunderstood and mocked in the Protestant world and would, at least in England, set back rather than advance the Catholic cause. In 1874 no less a figure than William E. Gladstone, former prime minister and a leading Anglican layman, launched a sharp attack on the Vatican decrees of 1870, suggesting that, through them, Catholics had lost their mental and their moral freedom to the point that they could no longer be considered trustworthy subjects of the State. Newman's response to this onslaught was his *Letter Addressed to His Grace the Duke of Norfolk* (1875), his last major work of controversial writing. In discussing the question of the "civil allegiance" of Roman Catholics (an issue raised, American readers may recall, during the presidential campaign of John F. Kennedy in 1960), Newman makes an important point in his very title, for the

Duke of Norfolk was both a Roman Catholic and a peer of the realm, a man whose patriotism could scarcely be questioned even by Gladstone.

In the letter, Newman, writing at age seventy-four, displays a verve, cogency, and logical force undiminished by his years. He won a decisive victory over Gladstone, who withdrew the main charge of his own pamphlet shortly after Newman's had appeared. Newman makes two central points in his letter, each of which is decisive. Together they are devastating to Gladstone's argument, which was, in essence, that Catholics had given their "consciences" into the hold of a "foreign Power" and thus could not be trusted as citizens of England. In the first place, Newman responds in section five of the letter ("Conscience"), conscience, in the Catholic view, is inalienable. It cannot be given to another person, not even the Pope; it is not the "creation of man," it is the "voice of God" implanted "in the intelligence of all His rational creatures." Its authority is supreme, and should it "come into collision with the word of a Pope," it is to be followed "in spite of that word."

In the second place, such collisions cannot really occur, since the domain of conscience is conduct, action, "something to be done or not done," while the domain of Papal Infallibility is "speculative truth" and "abstract doctrine." The Pope is "not infallible in his laws, nor in his commands, nor in his acts of state, nor in his administration, nor in his public policy." He is not infallible when he commands a particular individual to do or not to do a particular thing. In short, since the Pope is not infallible in that very domain of "conduct" with which "conscience" is concerned, no "dead-lock . . . can take place between conscience and the Pope."

The skirmish with Gladstone was the last important battle of Newman's career, though in the fifteen years of life remaining to him he wrote a few periodical essays, including a controversial one, "On the Inspiration of Scriptures," published in *Nineteenth Century,* February 1884. Throughout the 1870s Newman spent a good deal of time in the revision and republication of his earlier writings as part of the collected edition of his works. As he approached and passed his own seventy-fifth birthday, many of his old friends and fellow Oratorians were dying, notably Father Ambrose St. John in 1875, Newman's closest friend in his later years. Just before Christmas in 1877 Newman received word of his election as the first honorary fellow of Trinity College, Oxford (his undergraduate college), and returned there, where he had not set foot since 1846, to receive the honor and accept the congratulations of old friends.

In the spring of 1878, Pope Pius IX died and was succeeded by the more liberal and intellectual Pope Leo XIII. It was rumored that Newman would be made a cardinal. In the following year the rumor became a fact, and the aged Newman traveled to Rome to receive the cardinal's hat (May 1879), and thence home to scenes of public celebration in London and Birmingham, for the honor was seen as both a triumph for Newman and a compliment to England. The popular view of the Roman Church in England had changed markedly since the days of the "Papal Aggression" thirty years before, partly as a consequence of Newman's own conversion and writing. Newman felt deeply the honor of the cardinalate, telling his friends at the Oratory that "the cloud is lifted from me for ever." Through the last decade of his life, Newman lived quietly at Rednal near Birmingham, continuing most of his duties at the Oratory and its attached school, though his health began to fail in 1886. He died quietly on Monday, 11 August 1890.

Newman's intellectual and literary legacy is diverse and rich. His collected *Works* occupy forty volumes, his *Letters and Diaries* an additional thirty-one. Neither his poetry nor his two novels are of the highest order, but his *Apologia pro Vita Sua* is a great spiritual and autobiographical statement, standing beside the *Confessions* of St. Augustine and the *Pensées* of Pascal. His *Essay on the Development of Christian Doctrine* and his *Essay in Aid of a Grammar of Assent* are distinct contributions to theology and religious thought. *The Idea of a University* is an assured classic of educational theory. Many of his sermons are among the finest in English, rivaled only by those of John Donne. As a controversial writer Newman reveals his personality and talent most engagingly, especially in the *Tracts for the Times, Lectures on the Present Position of Catholics in England,* and in *A Letter Addressed to His Grace the Duke of Norfolk.*

Newman was a powerful and persuasive defender of religious faith in a period of growing unbelief. Although he left the Anglican Church, the Oxford Movement, which he inspired and led, has had a lasting influence on its development. After his conversion in 1845, Newman contributed immeasurably to knowledgeable and sympathetic understanding of the Roman Catholic Church in the English-speaking world. The award of the cardinalate in 1879 presaged the important influence Newman's ideas would have on the development of the Church in the twentieth century. The Second

Newman a few weeks before his death (Birmingham Oratory)

Vatican Council of 1962-1965, devoted to an *aggiornamento,* or "updating," of Catholicism, was said to be Cardinal Newman's Council because his ideas about the Church in the modern world, about conscience, about the development of doctrine, and about the role of the laity and the bishops affected the deliberations profoundly. Pope John XXIII cited Newman's *Lectures on Certain Difficulties Felt by Anglicans in Submitting to the Catholic Church* in calling the council, and Pope Paul VI praised Newman's life as "an itinerary, the most toilsome, but also the greatest, the most meaningful, the most conclusive, that human thought ever travelled during the last century, indeed one might say during the modern era, to arrive at the fullness of wisdom and of peace."

Letters:

Letters and Correspondence of John Henry Newman During his Life in the English Church, with a Brief Auto-Biography, edited by Anne Mozley, 2 volumes (London & New York: Longmans, Green, 1890);

Correspondence of John Henry Newman with John Keble and Others, 1839-1845, edited by Fathers of the Birmingham Oratory (London & New York: Longmans, Green, 1917);

The Letters and Diaries of John Henry Newman, edited by Charles Stephen Dessain, Ian Ker, Thomas Gornall, and others (London: Nelson, 1961-1972; Oxford: Clarendon Press, 1973-).

Bibliographies:

Vincent F. Blehl, S.J., *John Henry Newman: A Bibliographical Catalogue of His Writings* (Charlottesville: University Press of Virginia, 1978);

John R. Griffin, *Newman: A Bibliography of Secondary Sources* (Front Royal, Va.: Christendom Publications, 1980).

Biographies:

Wilfrid Ward, *The Life of John Henry Cardinal Newman, Based on His Private Journals and Correspondence,* 2 volumes (New York & London: Longmans, Green, 1912);

Maisie Ward, *Young Mr. Newman* (New York: Sheed & Ward, 1948);

Louis Bouyer, *Newman: His Life and Spirituality,* translated by J. Lewis May (London: Burns & Oates, 1958);

Meriol Trevor, *Newman,* 2 volumes (London: Macmillan, 1962; New York: Doubleday, 1962-1963);

William Robbins, *The Newman Brothers* (Cambridge: Harvard University Press, 1966);

Charles Stephen Dessain, *John Henry Newman* (London: Nelson, 1966);

Brian Martin, *John Henry Newman: His Life and Work* (London: Chatto & Windus, 1982).

References:

Josef L. Altholz, *The Liberal Catholic Movement in England* (London: Burns & Oates, 1962);

Brand Blanshard, *Reason and Belief* (New Haven: Yale University Press, 1975);

Vincent F. Blehl, "The Patristic Humanism of John Henry Newman," *Thought,* 50 (September 1975): 266-274;

Blehl and Francis X. Connolly, eds., *Newman's "Apologia": A Classic Reconsidered* (New York: Harcourt, Brace, 1964);

Thomas S. Bokenkotter, *Cardinal Newman as an Historian* (Louvain: Nauwelaerts, 1959);

William E. Buckler, "Newman's *Apologia* as Human Experience," *Thought,* 39 (Spring 1964): 77-88;

Arthur B. Calkins, "John Henry Newman on Conscience and the Magisterium," *Downside Review,* 87 (October 1969): 358-369;

James M. Cameron, "The Night Battle: Newman and Empiricism," *Victorian Studies,* 4 (December 1960): 99-117;

Owen Chadwick, *From Bossuet to Newman: The Idea of Doctrinal Development* (Cambridge & New York: Cambridge University Press, 1957);

Chadwick, *Newman* (London: Oxford University Press, 1983);

R. W. Church, *The Oxford Movement* (London & New York: Macmillan, 1891); edited by Geoffrey Best (Chicago: University of Chicago Press, 1970);

John Coulson, *Newman and the Common Tradition* (Oxford: Clarendon Press, 1970);

Coulson, ed., *The Rediscovery of Newman: An Oxford Symposium* (London: Sheed & Ward, 1968);

A. Dwight Culler, *The Imperial Intellect* (New Haven: Yale University Press, 1955);

David J. DeLaura, *Hebrew and Hellene in Victorian England: Newman, Arnold and Pater* (Austin: University of Texas Press, 1969);

DeLaura, ed., Newman's *Apologia pro Vita Sua,* Norton Critical Edition (New York: Norton, 1968)—includes critical essays;

John R. Griffin, "The Radical Phase of the Oxford Movement," *Journal of Ecclesiastical History,* 27 (January 1976): 47-56;

Charles Frederick Harrold, *John Henry Newman: An Expository and Critical Study of His Mind* (London: Longmans, Green, 1945);

Christopher Hollis, *Newman and the Modern World* (Garden City: Doubleday, 1968);

John Holloway, *The Victorian Sage* (New York: Norton, 1965);

Walter E. Houghton, *The Art of Newman's "Apologia"* (New Haven: Yale University Press/London: Oxford University Press, 1945);

D. G. James, *The Romantic Comedy* (London: Oxford University Press, 1948);

Edward F. Jost, "Newman and Liberalism: The Later Phase," *Victorian Newsletter,* no. 24 (Fall 1963): 1-6;

Edward E. Kelly, S.J., "Newman, Vatican I and II, and the Church Today," *Catholic World,* 202 (February 1966): 291-297;

Terence Kenny, *The Political Thought of John Henry Newman* (London: Longmans, Green, 1957);

I. T. Ker, ed., Introduction to Newman's *The Idea of a University* (Oxford: Oxford University Press, 1976);

Americo D. Lapati, *John Henry Newman* (New York: Twayne, 1972);

George Levine, *The Boundaries of Fiction: Carlyle, Macaulay, Newman* (Princeton: Princeton University Press, 1968);

Hugh A. MacDougall, *The Acton-Newman Relations* (New York: Fordham University Press, 1962);

Damian McElrath, O.F.M., "Richard Simpson and John Henry Newman: *The Rambler, Laymen and Theology,*" *Catholic Historical Review,* 52 (January 1967): 509-533;

E. R. Norman, *Church and Society in England: 1770-1970* (Oxford: Clarendon Press, 1976);

Marvin R. O'Connell, *The Oxford Conspirators* (London: Macmillan, 1969);

Robert Pattison, "John Henry Newman and the Arian Heresy," *Mosaic,* 11 (Summer 1978): 139-153;

Linda H. Peterson, "Newman's *Apologia pro Vita Sua* and the Traditions of the English Spiritual Autobiography," *PMLA,* 100 (May 1985): 300-314;

Jouett L. Powell, "Cardinal Newman on Faith and Doubt: The Role of Conscience," *Downside Review,* 99 (April 1981): 137-148;

H. H. Price, *Belief* (London: Allen & Unwin, 1969);

Alvan S. Ryan, ed., *Newman and Gladstone: The Vatican Decrees* (Notre Dame: University of Notre Dame Press, 1962);

Robin Selby, *The Principle of Reserve in the Writings of John Henry Cardinal Newman* (Oxford: Clarendon Press, 1975);

Basil A. Smith, *Dean Church: The Anglican Response to Newman* (New York: Oxford University Press, 1958);

Philip Snyder, "Newman's Way with the Reader in *A Grammar of Assent*," *Victorian Newsletter*, no. 56 (Fall 1979): 1-6;

Roderick Strange, *Newman and the Gospel of Christ* (Oxford: Clarendon Press, 1981);

T. C. F. Stunt, "John Henry Newman and the Evangelicals," *Journal of Ecclesiastical History*, 21 (January 1970): 65-74;

Martin J. Svaglic, "Charles Newman and His Brothers," *PMLA*, 71 (June 1956): 370-385;

Svaglic, "John Henry Newman: The Victorian Experience," in *The Victorian Experience: The Prose Writers*, edited by Richard A. Levine (Athens: Ohio University Press, 1982);

Svaglic and Charles Stephen Dessain, "John Henry Newman," in *Victorian Prose: A Guide to Research*, edited By David J. DeLaura (New York: Modern Language Association, 1973);

Svaglic, ed., Introduction to Newman's *Apologia pro Vita Sua* (Oxford: Clarendon Press, 1967);

G. B. Tennyson, "Tractarian Aesthetics: Analogy and Reserve in Keble and Newman," *Victorian Newsletter*, no. 55 (Spring 1979): 8-10;

Thomas Vargish, *Newman: The Contemplation of Mind* (Oxford: Clarendon Press, 1970);

Jan H. Walgrave, *Newman the Theologian*, translated by A. V. Littledale (New York: Sheed & Ward, 1960);

John H. Wildman, "Newman in the Pulpit: The Power of Simplicity," *Studies in the Literary Imagination*, 8 (Fall 1975): 63-75;

Basil Willey, *Nineteenth Century Studies* (London: Chatto & Windus, 1949);

Raymond Williams, *Culture and Society: 1780-1950* (New York: Columbia University Press, 1958).

Papers:

The archives of the Birmingham Oratory, Birmingham, England, contain nearly all of Newman's papers: letters, journals, private diaries, historical, philosophical, and theological papers, and unpublished sermons.

A. Welby Pugin

(1 March 1812-14 September 1852)

Michael Bright
Eastern Kentucky University

A. Welby Pugin, sketched by Joseph Nash

SELECTED BOOKS: *A Letter to A. W. Hakewill, Architect, in Answer to His Reflections on the Style for Rebuilding the Houses of Parliament* (Salisbury: Privately printed, 1835);

Contrasts; or, A Parallel between the Noble Edifices of the Fourteenth and Fifteenth Centuries, and Similar Buildings of the Present Day; Shewing the Present Decay of Taste: Accompanied by Appropriate Text (London: Privately printed, 1836; revised and enlarged, London: Dolman, 1841);

An Apology for a Work Entitled "Contrasts"; Being a Defence of the Assertions Advanced in That Publication, Against Various Attacks Lately Made Upon It (Birmingham: Privately printed, 1837);

The True Principles of Pointed or Christian Architecture: Set Forth in Two Lectures Delivered at St. Marie's, Oscott (London: Weale, 1841);

The Present State of Ecclesiastical Architecture in England (London: Dolman, 1843);

An Apology for the Revival of Christian Architecture in England (London: Weale, 1843);

Glossary of Ecclesiastical Ornament and Costume, Compiled and Illustrated from Ancient Authorities and Examples (London: Bohn, 1844);

Floriated Ornament: A Series of Thirty-one Designs (London: Bohn, 1849);

Some Remarks on the Articles Which Have Recently Appeared in the "Rambler" Relative to Ecclesiastical Architecture and Decoration (London: Dolman, 1850);

An Earnest Address, on the Establishment of the Hierarchy (London: Dolman, 1851);

A Treatise on Chancel Screens and Rood Lofts, Their Antiquity, Use, and Symbolic Signification (London: Dolman, 1851).

Near the end of his brief life, A. Welby Pugin remarked that he had done the work of a hundred years in forty. The greater part of this work was devoted to his architectural practice and the design of more than a hundred buildings, the most notable being the new Houses of Parliament, whose elevations and ornamentation he designed for Sir Charles Barry. The lesser part of his extraordinary productivity consisted of an advocacy of the Gothic Revival in his polemical writings, but if less time and energy were spent on these books than on the buildings, they did have more influence, and Pugin himself commented near the end of his life that his writings more than anything else had revolutionized the taste of England. England's renewed taste for medieval architecture, first apparent in Horace Walpole's Strawberry Hill and in William Beckford's Fonthill Abbey, had developed rapidly by

Pugin's time, but in these still early stages of the Gothic Revival knowledge of medieval architecture was superficial and the architects of neo-Gothic buildings generally copied the forms of ancient models with little understanding of underlying principles. Pugin revolutionized taste by explaining the principles of architectural design, and, further, in claiming that only pointed architecture fully embodied these principles, he provided the intellectual basis for making Gothic architecture a serious cause instead of just one more style in the architect's repertoire. More ambitiously, he meant to rescue architecture and its related decorative arts from stylistic confusion and structural dishonesty.

The only child of Augustus Charles Pugin, a French émigré, and Catherine Welby Pugin, Augustus Welby Northmore Pugin was born in London on 1 March 1812. As a boy he attended Christ's Hospital, and, after completing his studies there, he entered his father's office to prepare himself for a career in architecture. He proved such an apt pupil that in 1827, when he was only fifteen years old, he was commissioned to design furniture for Windsor Castle. His next important job was stage scenery for the ballet *Kenilworth* in 1831. These early endeavors in Gothic design foretokened his later work in the Gothic Revival, even as his purchase of a boat at about this time indicated the other great love of his life—sailing. "There is nothing worth living for," he once told a friend, "but Christian Architecture and a boat."

In 1831 Pugin married Anne Garnet, who died giving birth to their daughter, Anne, the following year. The death of his wife was followed by that of his father in the same year and by the death of his mother in 1833. Shortly after his mother's death, Pugin married Louisa Burton, who would bear five children, the eldest of whom (Edward Welby) succeeded to his father's architectural practice. In 1835 Pugin moved from London to Salisbury, and there his career began in earnest. He built for himself his first house, he began working for Charles Barry on the competition designs for the new Houses of Parliament, and he converted to Catholicism, a bold and courageous act at the time. Henceforth, religion and architecture were inseparable elements in Pugin's life: "I feel perfectly convinced," Pugin wrote at about the time of his conversion, "the Roman Catholic Church is the only true one, and the only one in which the grand and sublime style of church architecture can ever be restored."

Pugin's first exposition of this belief was *Contrasts; or, A Parallel between the Noble Edifices of the Fourteenth and Fifteenth Centuries, and Similar Buildings of the Present Day; Shewing the Present Decay of Taste: Accompanied by Appropriate Text* (1836). In the second paragraph of this book Pugin set forth the golden rule of architecture upon which all of his later arguments were to rest: "the great test of Architectural beauty is the fitness of the design to the purpose for which it is intended. . . ." The rule was not original with Pugin, variations of it having appeared from Vitruvius to eighteenth-century French architectural theorists, but by using it to attack shams and the impropriety of neoclassical architecture, Pugin gave it an importance that was to make it the one inviolable principle of nineteenth-century architecture. The second argument in *Contrasts* that became a common theme in his later books was that revived classical architecture, from the time of the Reformation to the present, disregarded the equation of design and purpose, and should therefore be abandoned in favor of Gothic architecture, which alone was capable of embodying the principle in England.

The caustic and withering style of *Contrasts* betokened the rhetoric of Pugin's later works: Henry VIII is described as a "merciless tyrant," his daughter, Elizabeth, is "that female demon," and Archbishop Cranmer is "perfidious and dissembling." In other writings Pugin called neoclassical architecture "the Pagan Monster" and referred to the architect James Wyatt as "this monster of architectural depravity—this pest of cathedral architecture." In using such vituperative and contumelious language as this, Pugin risked offending some of his readers to promote his cause, but, as he later wrote in *The Present State of Ecclesiastical Architecture in England* (1843), "It is only by depicting modern deformities in forcible language that we can hope for their being remedied. Milk-and-water men never effect anything; they deserve drowning in their own insipid compositions." There could be no namby-pamby mincing of words in the crusade to deliver Christian architecture; for Pugin, the time required an English Jeremiah, a nineteenth-century Savonarola, a Carlylian hero as artist. Pugin could be as abrasive in his dealings with clients as he was in his writings, but with his family and friends he was jovial, good-natured, and possessed of bonhomie. He was, in short, a man whose strong opinions and feelings made him a dangerous enemy, a valuable ally.

Beginning with the premise that purpose determines architectural design, Pugin proceeds in *Contrasts* to show that climate, customs, and especially religion are the determinants of architectural styles. This argument leads him to the conclusion that Christianity produced pointed architecture and, therefore, that only in pointed architecture can the doctrines of Christianity be embodied. That is, returning to the major premise, if the design must suit the purpose, then only pointed architecture meets the purpose of Christian churches. By this line of thought Pugin brings together religion and architecture (he ordinarily referred to the Gothic style as "Christian" or "Catholic"), and in combining them he is able to argue that classical architecture, which he usually called "pagan" because it too had originated from religious purposes, is entirely inappropriate for churches. Because classical architecture had been revived at the time of the Reformation, Pugin at first blamed Protestantism for the downfall of pointed architecture, but he came to realize that this theory did not account for what happened in Catholic countries. Therefore, in the second edition of *Contrasts* (1841), he revised his explanation to show that there was first a decay in Christianity, the two effects of which were Protestantism and "the revived pagan principle." These two effects, in turn, accounted for the mutilation of English churches, principally during the sixteenth and seventeenth centuries, and for the introduction of pagan elements in both English churches and those in Catholic countries. The rest of the text records Pugin's chronicle of the desecrations of English churches from the time of Henry VIII and Edward VI to the present.

The title of the book more accurately describes the illustrations than the text, for each plate contrasts a medieval building or architectural feature with a modern one, and each contrast illustrates the superiority of the old over the new. In keeping with Pugin's association of religion and architecture, the contrasts also illustrate the moral superiority of the old. For example, the master of the medieval poorhouse dispenses alms, whereas the master of the modern poorhouse holds a whip and manacles; the poor resident in the old receives a dignified Christian burial, but in the new he is carted off for dissection by medical students. The technique of contrasting former and modern times is similar to that used by Robert Southey in his *Colloquies* (1829) and Thomas Carlyle in *Past and Present* (1843), and the association between morality and architecture looks forward to works by John Ruskin and William Morris. Anticipating his own later writings is Pugin's belief that pointed architecture can be restored only by comprehending its principles, not by copying its forms, for even as pointed architecture had originally developed in response to religious principles, so now could it be revived only by working from those principles. If the design was to fit the purpose, the purpose must first be understood.

In 1837 Pugin made one of his frequent trips to the Continent and also began lecturing at St. Marie's College, Oscott (near Birmingham), where he was appointed professor of ecclesiastical antiquities. Two of his lectures at Oscott, probably delivered in 1838 or 1839, were published in 1841 as *The True Principles of Pointed or Christian Architecture*. Less controversial than *Contrasts*, which had established Pugin as the foremost champion of the Gothic cause, *The True Principles of Pointed or Christian Architecture* had a profounder and longer lasting influence. Having declared in *Contrasts* the importance of going beyond the copying of forms to the understanding of principles, Pugin now explained what those principles were, and this he does in the opening paragraph: "The two great rules for design are these: *1st, that there should be no features about a building which are not necessary for convenience, construction, or propriety; 2nd, that all ornament should consist of enrichment of the essential construction of the building*. The neglect of these two rules is the cause of all bad architecture of the present time."

Pugin's exposition of these fundamental rules is basically a restatement of his comment in *Contrasts* about design following from purpose. In explaining the rules Pugin first shows how construction is determined by materials—whether they be stone, metal, or wood—and how, in turn, structural requirements determine architectural features. He demonstrates, for example, how the strength of stone allowed medieval architects to build exceedingly high buildings, how the lateral pressure of the walls of these buildings called for buttresses, and how these buttresses, required for structure, were ornamented. One type of buttress ornament was the pinnacle, which had in itself the functional purposes of adding weight to the buttress and of throwing off rain and the symbolic purpose of suggesting the Resurrection by its vertical lines. Instead of exposing, and ornamenting, structure, classical architecture dishonestly conceals it, in the manner, for example, of St. Paul's Cathedral with its screen to hide the buttresses.

After discussing how convenience and construction determine architectural features, Pugin takes up propriety, by which he means that "*the external and internal appearance of an edifice should be illustrative of, and in accordance with, the purpose for which it is destined.*" Here again is the correlation

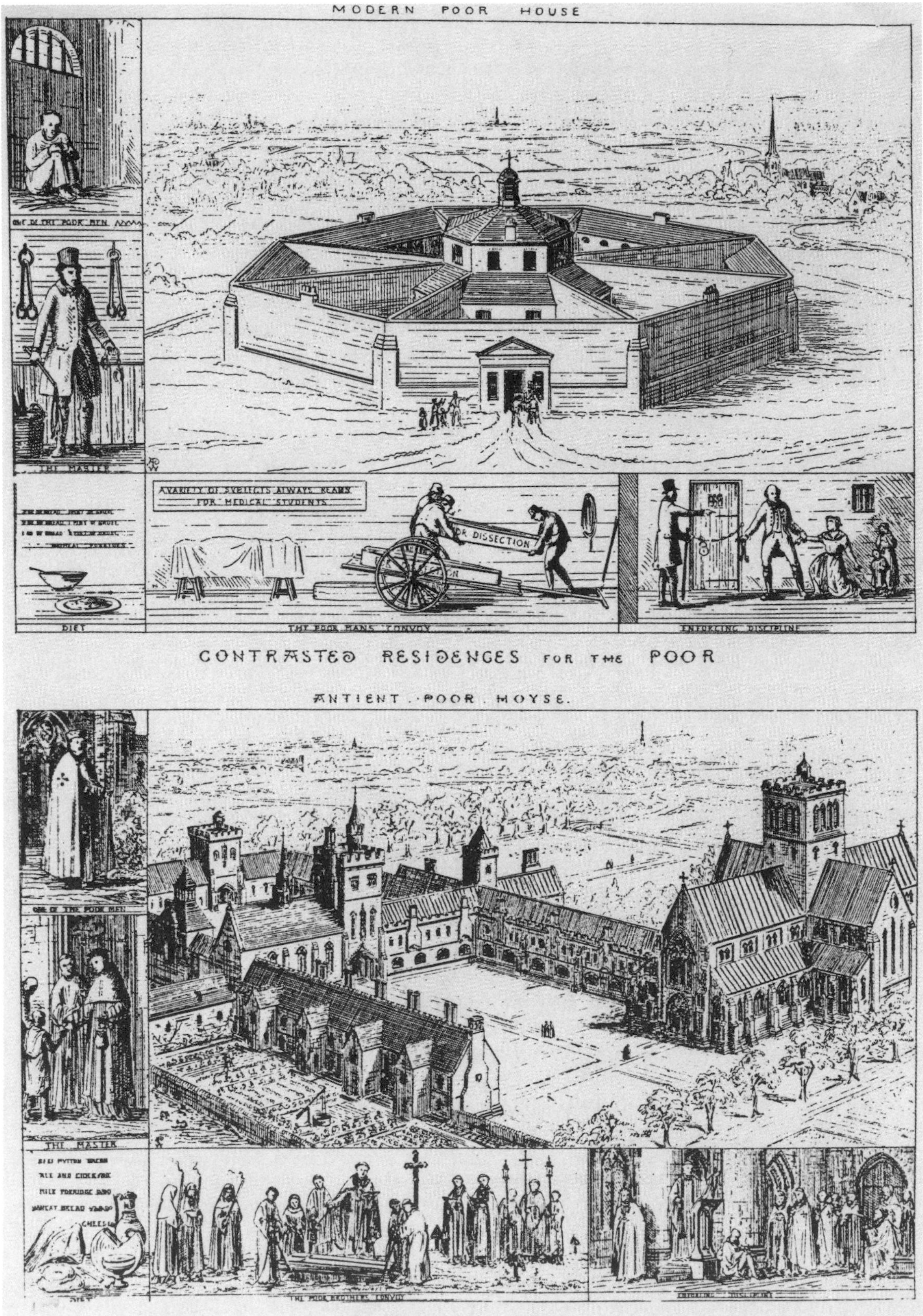

Illustrations by Pugin for his 1836 book, Contrasts, *in which he attempts to demonstrate the architectural, as well as the moral, superiority of the old over the new*

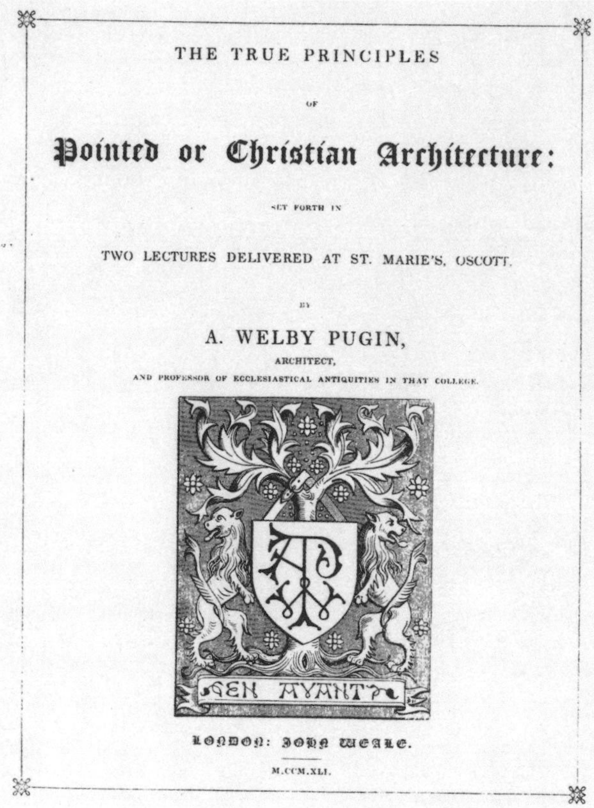
THE TRUE PRINCIPLES

OF

Pointed or Christian Architecture:

SET FORTH IN

TWO LECTURES DELIVERED AT ST. MARIE'S, OSCOTT.

BY

A. WELBY PUGIN,

ARCHITECT,

AND PROFESSOR OF ECCLESIASTICAL ANTIQUITIES IN THAT COLLEGE.

EN AVANT

LONDON: JOHN WEALE.

M.CCM.XLI.

Frontispiece and title page decorated with Pugin's armorial insignia for the volume in which he explains the "two great rules for design"

between purpose and design. Pugin proves this architectural law by discussing three categories of buildings: ecclesiastical, collegiate, and domestic and civil. He returns to his argument that classical architecture, having arisen as the expression of paganism, is inappropriate for churches, and that only pointed architecture, having developed as the expression of Christianity, can illustrate by its appearance the Christian purpose of the church. Furthermore, Italian architecture is inappropriate for English houses because of the difference in the climates of Italy and Great Britain, and the castellated style is absurd for modern houses, which need no fortifications. The most expedient way to ensure that the appearance of a building reveals its purpose is for the architect to design the plan before the elevation; this method, moreover, lessens the possibility of including features for effect rather than for function. If, however, an architect starts with the elevation and designs it for symmetry, he may include features that have no use other than to achieve a balanced impression. This approach to building violates Pugin's first great rule for design, that there should be no unnecessary features about a building, and it produces buildings that Pugin deplores as dishonest, as shams. For Pugin a little truth was better than a great fiction, and in championing what he liked to call "the real thing," he exerted a powerful influence on the moral sensibilities of his contemporaries. A reporter for the London *Times,* writing three years after Pugin's death, commented that Pugin "first exposed the shams and concealments of modern architecture. . . . it was he who first showed us that our architecture offended not only against the laws of beauty, but also against the laws of morality."

By the time Pugin produced *The True Principles of Pointed or Christian Architecture* and the second edition of *Contrasts* in 1841, he had moved his family from Salisbury to Chelsea, London, had established a growing architectural practice, and had written for the *Dublin Review* an article that was incorporated two years later in *The Present State of Ecclesiastical Architecture in England* (1843). This book, comprising two articles from the *Dublin Review* of May 1841 and February 1842, begins with a description of mistakes made in modern churches and then explains how churches ought to be built. In his explanation Pugin demonstrates how such features as chancels, porches, altars, and towers developed from religious doctrine and practice, all in accordance with the rule that purpose determines design and that plan precedes elevation. On the basis of this rule Pugin once again attacks unnecessary features designed to create a uniform elevation, describing them as artificial and deceptive, lacking picturesque variety.

The second half of the book is quite different from the first in that it focuses on the internecine rivalry which had evolved between the Catholic and Protestant factions of the Gothic Revival during the interim between May 1841 and February 1842. On the one hand, Pugin was gratified that men at Oxford and Cambridge were doing so much to advance the Revival; indeed, he was chagrined that Anglicans were doing far more than Catholics. On the other hand, these Protestants had begun to claim exclusive rights to the Revival and to impugn Catholics. Faced with this situation, the churchman got the better of the architect, and Pugin appropriated the claim of exclusivity by maintaining that only Catholics could revive the ecclesiastical architecture of the Middle Ages. In his argument in *The Present State of Ecclesiastical Architecture in England,* Pugin uses his cardinal rule of purpose determining design as the major premise. The minor premise is that medieval churches were designed according to Catholic purposes, and the conclusion is that if the design of modern churches is to be true to ancient examples, then the purposes must be true to Catholic doctrine. Having established these points, Pugin then demonstrates how Anglican worship is incompatible with Gothic churches by concentrating on the sacrament of Communion and the related architectural features of the chancel, altar, and rood screen. Pugin concludes that "it is quite impossible for any man who abides in the Anglican Church, as she is at present constituted, to *build a Catholic church and use it afterwards.*" Given the absolute incompatibility of Protestant doctrine and Catholic architecture, Anglican ecclesiologists and architects must abandon "*either the Common Prayer or the ancient models.*" Pugin suggests the proper choice between the two alternatives in the last sentence of the book, in which he writes of "the holy work of England's conversion."

An Apology for the Revival of Christian Architecture in England was published in 1843, the same year as *The Present State of Ecclesiastical Architecture in England,* but was written later and reveals a far more conciliatory attitude toward Anglicans. As a matter of fact, in the new work Pugin reverses himself and argues that medieval church architecture is perfectly suitable for Anglican worship. Perhaps Pugin realized that controversy within the ranks was jeopardizing the Gothic Revival and that the real enemy was classical paganism, but whatever his reason, he justifies his change of mind by saying that if Anglican practice is at variance with medieval design, Anglican canons and rubrics demand no other kind. The critical architectural problem, as Pugin perceives it in his "Apology," is that the neoclassical style had finally gone bankrupt after four centuries of domination and left a vacancy which architects sought to fill with all sorts of alien and exotic styles. This anarchic state of things Pugin condemns as the "*carnival* of architecture," the final consequence of the inconsistency of design that had arisen with the introduction of pagan art during the Renaissance.

Applying once more the rule of architecture upon which all of his writings are founded, Pugin defines an inconsistent design as one in which "the purpose or destination of the building" has not "formed the ground-work of the composition." The solution to the problem of consistency is Gothic architecture, for it alone is in perfect accord with the religion, climate, and customs of England. Against the charge that present conditions in England are very different from those that had produced the pointed style in the Middle Ages, Pugin argues that the primary determinants of architectural design—religion, climate, laws, and customs—remain basically the same. Besides, architects should not attempt to reproduce medieval buildings exactly but should work on the principles of medieval architects, thereby gaining a flexibility that can accommodate new materials, techniques, and purposes. Builders, Pugin writes, "should neither cling pertinaciously to ancient methods of building, solely on the score of antiquity, nor reject inventions because of their novelty, but try both by sound and consistent principles, and act accordingly." Steam engines, for example, should be used for sawing stone and timber and for lifting heavy materials; iron may be used for structural ties. Thus, machines and new material are to be employed as long as they do not encroach on the domain of art. Throughout the book Pugin defends medieval architecture as the only style appropriate for all buildings and all times, Anglican as well as Catholic, civil as well as ecclesiastical, modern as well as ancient. Only the revival of Christian

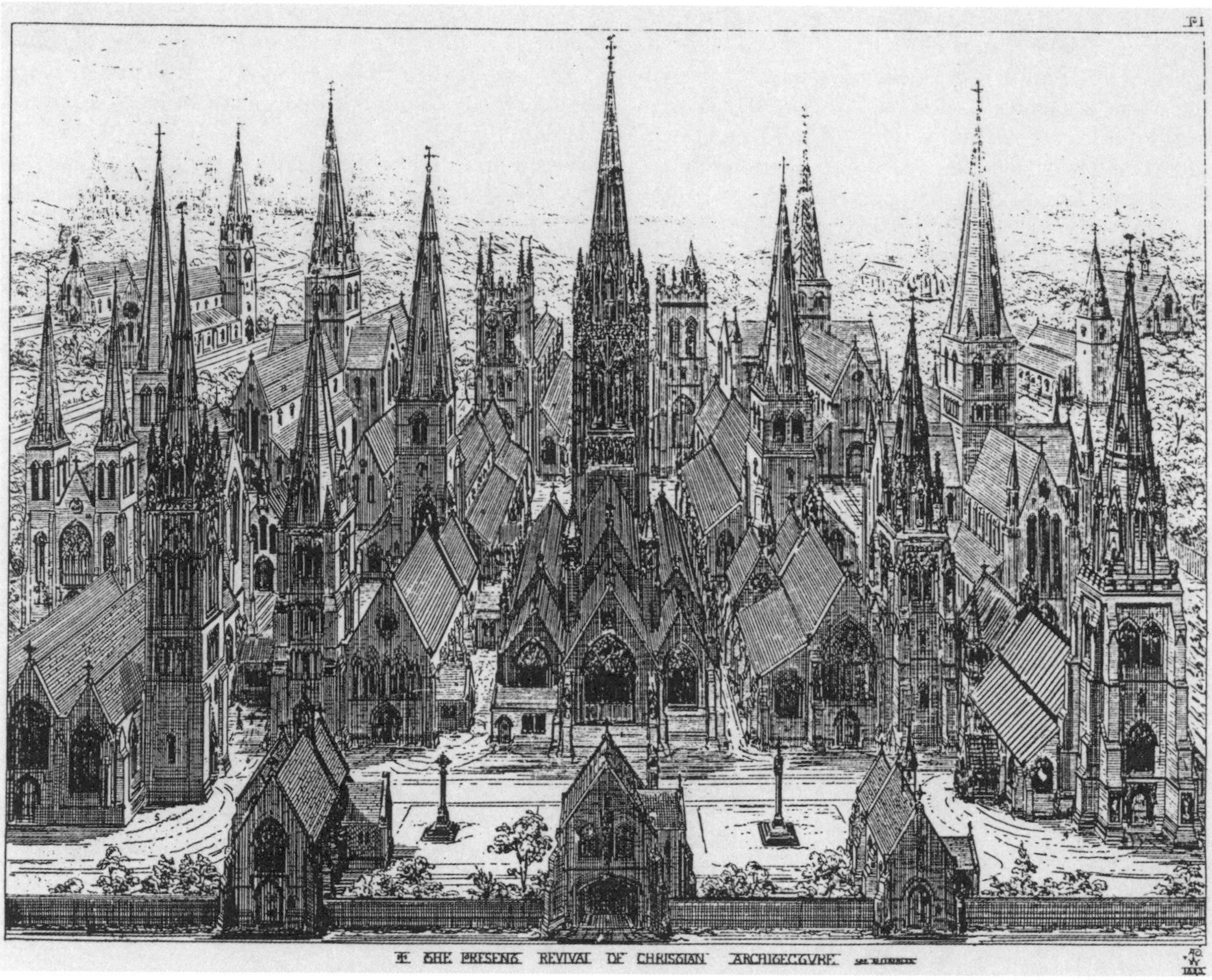

Drawing by Pugin depicting various churches he had designed, used as the frontispiece to his Apology for the Revival of Christian Architecture in England

architecture can, he asserts, deliver England from the chaotic carnival of modern times.

After 1843 Pugin produced the splendidly illustrated *Glossary of Ecclesiastical Ornament and Costume* (1844), as well as a number of articles and short books, but *An Apology for the Revival of Christian Architecture in England* is his last important statement on building and design. In 1844 Pugin moved into a house he had built for himself at Ramsgate, and next to the house he built a church, dedicated to St. Augustine. The same year Louisa Burton Pugin, his second wife, died. In the few years remaining of his brief life, he resumed work with Barry on the new Houses of Parliament and continued to design buildings in his own right. Increasingly, during the last part of his career, he devoted his energies to architectural furnishings—metalwork, tiles, stained glass, furniture, and so forth. In 1848 he married his third wife, Jane Knill, with whom he subsequently had two children. The Medieval Court at the Great Exhibition of 1851 was Pugin's last major enterprise, for early in the next year he began to suffer what he described as "nervous fever" and which he attributed to exhaustion from having done the work of a hundred years in forty. He became more unsettled, was subject to hallucinations, and finally was committed to Bethlehem Hospital, London. After treatment there and in another hospital, his wife returned him home, but a few days later, on 14 September, he died of apoplexy. He was buried in his own church on 21 September 1852.

Pugin's intolerance of any religion but Roman Catholicism and of any architecture but Gothic prompted such people as John Ruskin and John Henry Newman to charge him with fanaticism and bigotry, and even today some readers resent Pugin's zeal. Others, Sir George Gilbert Scott among them, forgave the faults of genius and acknowledged the great contribution Pugin had made in awakening people to the failures of modern architecture and in laying the theoretical foundation for the Gothic Revival. If Gothic architecture did not become the single, universal style for England, nor the style from which a future architecture would evolve, and if England did not return to Catholicism as Pugin had hoped, the many Revival buildings that adorn the cities and towns of England testify to the partial success of Pugin's efforts. His greater and more enduring contribution was to architecture as a whole rather than to the Gothic Revival in particular, for by setting forth principles, by demanding the correspondence of purpose and design, and by decrying shams, Pugin provided rules as appropriate to the Greek as to the Gothic, to the twentieth century as to the nineteenth. For this contribution he was acclaimed in his own time, and for this contribution he is esteemed today as the most important English architectural theorist of his century.

Biographies:

Benjamin Ferrey, *Recollections of A. N. Welby Pugin, and His Father, Augustus Pugin* (London: Stanford, 1861);

Michael Trappes-Lomax, *Pugin: A Mediaeval Victorian* (London: Sheed & Ward, 1932);

H. E. G. Rope, *Pugin* (Hassocks: Pepler & Sewell, 1935);

Denis Gwynn, *Lord Shrewsbury, Pugin and the Catholic Revival* (London: Hollis & Carter, 1946).

References:

Margaret E. Belcher, " 'The Church of Our Fathers': A. W. N. Pugin and Daniel Rock," *Southern Review,* 15 (November 1982): 321-333;

Michael Bright, "A Reconsideration of A. W. N. Pugin's Architectural Theories," *Victorian Studies,* 22 (Winter 1979): 151-172;

Kenneth Clark, *The Gothic Revival: An Essay in the History of Taste* (London: Constable, 1928);

Charles L. Eastlake, *A History of the Gothic Revival* (London: Longmans, Green, 1872);

Henry-Russell Hitchcock, *Early Victorian Architecture in Britain,* 2 volumes (New Haven: Yale University Press, 1954);

James Patrick, "Newman, Pugin, and Gothic," *Victorian Studies,* 24 (Winter 1981): 185-207;

Nikolaus Pevsner, *Some Architectural Writers of the Nineteenth Century* (Oxford: Clarendon Press, 1972);

Phoebe Stanton, *Pugin* (London: Thames & Hudson, 1971);

Stanton, "Pugin: Principles of Design versus Revivalism," *Journal of the Society of Architectural Historians,* 13 (October 1954): 20-25;

Stanton, "The Sources of Pugin's *Contrasts,*" in *Concerning Architecture,* edited by Sir John Summerson (London: Lane/Penguin Press, 1968);

Paul Waterhouse, "The Life and Works of Welby Pugin," *Architectural Review: For the Artist and Craftsman,* 3 (1897-1898): 167-175, 211-221, 264-273; 4 (1898): 23-27, 67-73, 115-118, 159-165;

Alexander Wedgwood, *A. W. N. Pugin and the Pugin Family* (London: Victoria and Albert Museum, 1985);

Wedgwood, *Catalogue of the Drawings Collection of the Royal Institute of British Architects: The Pugin Family* (Farnborough: Gregg International, 1977).

Papers:

Pugin's most important drawings and papers are in London, in the RIBA (Royal Institute of British Architects) Drawings Collection and at the Victoria and Albert Museum Library.

Edward Bouverie Pusey
(22 August 1800-16 September 1882)

Donald S. Armentrout
University of the South

SELECTED BOOKS: *An Historical Enquiry into the Probable Causes of the Rationalist Character Lately Predominant in the Theology of Germany,* 2 volumes (London: Rivington, 1828, 1830);

Remarks on the Prospective and Past Benefits of Cathedral Institutions, in the Promotion of Sound Religious Knowledge, Occasioned by Lord Henley's Plan for Their Abolition (London: Roake & Varty, 1833);

Tracts for the Times, by Members of the University of Oxford, nos. 18, 66-70, 77, 81 by Pusey, 6 volumes (Oxford: Parker/London: Rivington, 1833-1841);

Subscription to the Thirty-Nine Articles; Questions Respectfully Addressed to Members of Convocation on the Declaration Proposed as a Substitute for the Subscription to the Thirty-Nine Articles (Oxford: Printed by W. Baxter, 1835);

An Earnest Remonstrance to the Author of the "Pope's Pastoral Letter to Certain Members of the University of Oxford:" With a Postscript, Noticing the Edinburgh Review, and Other Pamphlets, and an Appendix on Apostolical Succession (London: Printed for J. G. & F. Rivington, 1836); republished, without postscript and appendix, as *Tracts for the Times,* no. 77;

Plain Sermons by Contributors to the "Tracts for the Times," volume 3 (London: Rivington, 1841);

The Articles Treated on in Tract 90 Reconsidered and Their Interpretation Vindicated in a Letter to The Rev. R. W. Jelf (Oxford: Parker, 1841);

A Letter to His Grace the Archbishop of Canterbury, on Some Circumstances Connected With the Present Crisis in the English Church (Oxford: Parker, 1842);

The Holy Eucharist: A Comfort to the Penitent (Oxford: Parker/London: Rivington, 1843; New York: Harper, 1843);

A Course of Sermons on Solemn Subjects Chiefly Bearing on Repentance and Amendment of Life, Preached in St. Saviour's Church, Leeds, During the Week After Its Consecration on the Feast of S. Simon and S. Jude, by Pusey and others, edited by Pusey (Oxford: Parker, 1845);

Sermons During the Season from Advent to Whitsuntide (Oxford: Parker, 1848);

The Royal Supremacy Not an Arbitrary Authority But Limited by the Laws of the Church, of Which Kings Are Members (Oxford: Parker, 1850);

The Church of England Leaves Her Children Free to Whom to Open Their Griefs. A Letter to the Rev. W. U. Richards (Oxford: Parker, 1850);

A Letter to the Right Hon. and Right Rev. the Lord Bishop of London, in Explanation of Some Statements Contained in a Letter by the Rev. W. Dods-

Edward Bouverie Pusey (drawing by the Reverend Edward Kilvert)

worth (Oxford & London: Parker, 1851);

The Doctrine of the Real Presence, As Contained in the Fathers, from the Death of S. John the Evangelist to the Fourth General Council, Vindicated, in Notes on a Sermon "The Presence of Christ in the Holy Eucharist," Preached A.D. 1853, Before the University of Oxford (London: Parker, 1855);

The Councils of the Church from the Council of Jerusalem, A.D. 51, to the Council of Constantinople, A.D. 381, Chiefly as to Their Constitution, but also as to Their Objects and History (Oxford: Parker, 1857);

The Real Presence of the Body and Blood of Our Lord Jesus Christ, the Doctrine of the English Church, with a Vindication of the Reception by the Wicked and of the Adoration of Our Lord Jesus Christ, Truly Present (Oxford: Parker, 1857);

The Minor Prophets, with a Commentary Explanatory and Practical and Introductions to the Several Books (Oxford: Parker, 1860);

Daniel the Prophet. Nine Lectures Delivered in the Divinity School of the University of Oxford (Oxford & London: Sold by John Henry & James Parker, 1864; New York: Funk & Wagnalls, 1885);

Nine Sermons, Preached Before the University of Oxford, and Printed Chiefly Between A.D. 1843-1855 (Oxford: J. Henry & J. Parker, 1865);

The Church of England a Portion of Christ's One Holy Catholic Church, and a Means of Restoring Visible Unity. An Eirenicon, in a Letter to the Author of "The Christian Year" (Oxford: Parker, 1865; New York: Appleton, 1866);

First Letter to the Very Rev. J. H. Newman, D.D. An Explanation Chiefly in Regard to the Reverential Love Due the Ever-Blessed Theokotos, and the Doctrine of Her Immaculate Conception; with an Analysis of Cardinal de Turrecremata's Work on the Immaculate Conception. Eirenicon, Part II (Oxford: Sold by J. Parker/London: Rivington, 1869);

Is Healthful Reunion Possible? A Second Letter to the Very Rev. J. H. Newman, D.D. Eirenicon, Part III (Oxford: Sold by J. Parker/London: Rivington, 1870);

Sermons Preached Before the University of Oxford Between A.D. 1859-1872 (Oxford: James Parker, 1872);

Lenten Sermons, Preached Chiefly to Young Men at the Universities, Between A.D. 1858-1874 (Oxford: Parker, 1874);

On the Clause "And the Son," in Regard to the Eastern Church and the Bonn Conference: A Letter to the Rev. H. P. Liddon (Oxford: Parker/New York: Pott, Young, 1876);

Parochial and Cathedral Sermons (London: Sold by Parker & Rivington, 1882);

Private Prayers, edited by H. P. Liddon (London: Rivington, 1883; New York & London: Longmans, 1917).

OTHER: *A Library of the Fathers of the Holy Catholic Church, Anterior to the Division of the East and West,* translated by members of the English Church, edited by Pusey, John Henry Newman, John Keble, and Charles Marriott, 50 volumes (Oxford: Parker/London: Rivington, 1838-1885).

Edward Bouverie Pusey was second only to John Henry Newman as a leader of the Tractarian, or Oxford, Movement in the Church of England, a movement that began on 14 July 1833, when John Keble, professor of poetry, preached his Assize Sermon, titled "National Apostasy," at St. Mary's Church, Oxford. The convocations of Canterbury and York, the provincial assemblies of the clergy of the Church of England, had not met since 1717 when, in 1833, Parliament passed the Irish Temporalities Bill, which reduced the number of bishoprics in Ireland. Keble charged in his sermon that with the passage of the bill the State was interfering with the apostolic rights of the Church. In 1834, Pusey joined the Oxford Movement by writing Tract 18, *Thoughts on the Benefits of the System of Fasting, Enjoined by Our Church,* the first of the movement's *Tracts for the Times* to bear the signature of its author. Pusey's importance as a Tractarian is, in part, reflected by the fact that the movement was frequently called "Puseyism" and by Newman's assertion that, with Tract 18, "He at once gave to us a position and a name." Pusey wrote only eight of the ninety *Tracts for the Times,* but after Newman joined the Roman Catholic church in 1845, Pusey became the Oxford Movement's undisputed leader.

Pusey was born at Pusey, a small village in Berkshire, about twelve miles southwest of Oxford, on 22 August 1800 to the Honorable Philip Bouverie Pusey, the youngest son of Jacob Bouverie, first Viscount Folkestone, and Lady Lucy Sherard, the widow of Sir Thomas Cave. Philip Bouverie had changed his last name to Pusey as a condition of succession to the Pusey estate.

In 1807 Pusey was sent to a school at Mitcham in Surrey to prepare for Eton, where he went in 1812. In October 1817 he became a private student of Dr. Edward Maltby, later bishop of Durham. He matriculated at Christ Church, Oxford, in 1819, and in 1824 was elected fellow at Oriel College, Oxford, where he became associated with John Henry Newman and John Keble. He received his B.A. in 1822 and his M.A. in 1825. From 1825 to 1827, Pusey studied at Göttingen, Berlin, and Bonn, where he became acquainted with many leading German scholars. At both Oxford and in Germany, he studied Hebrew, Arabic, and other Semitic languages.

Pusey was ordained to the diaconate on Trinity Sunday, 1 June 1828, at the Cathedral Church of Christ in Oxford, by Charles Lloyd, bishop of Oxford. On 12 June of that year he married Catharine Maria Barker. Of their four children, only his youngest daughter survived him. Catharine Pusey died on 26 May 1839. He was ordained to the priesthood on 23 November 1828, at the Parish Church of Cuddesdon by Bishop Lloyd. Near the end of 1828 the Duke of Wellington, then prime minister, named him regius professor of Hebrew at Oxford and canon of Christ Church, an office he held until his death on 16 September 1882. As professor of Hebrew he became a leading scholar of oriental languages.

Soon after his return to England in June 1827, Pusey published the first part of his two-volume *An Historical Enquiry into the Probable Causes of the Rationalist Character Lately Predominant in the Theology of Germany* (1828, 1830), an answer to "The State of Protestantism in Germany," a series of four lectures given by Hugh James Rose, who also later became a member of the Oxford Movement. Rose, of Trinity College, Cambridge, argued that Protestantism in Germany had lost its hold on the fundamentals of the Christian faith, especially those doctrines which concern the person of Jesus Christ, and he maintained that most German scholars rejected the authority of scripture and relied on reason alone to determine doctrine. He argued that German rationalism would not have an impact on English Christianity because the doctrine of the Church of England was safeguarded by such formularies as the Thirty-Nine Articles and the *Book of Common Prayer* and because of its episcopal form of church government, with bishops in apostolic succession.

Pusey responded that the doctrine of the Church of England could easily be subverted by a rationalism similar to that which had emerged in Germany, and he argued that German rationalism was the result of a "dead orthodoxism," the reliance on mere forms and phrases of orthodox Christianity, without concern for the spiritual realities they are intended to convey. Maintaining that this condition descended from seventeenth-century Lutheran scholasticism, he argued that the eighteenth-century pietism of Philip Jacob Spener and August Hermann Francke was an effort to combat it. Ironically Pusey so phrased his sympathetic treatment of German Pietism that he was widely understood to be advocating rationalism as well. Though he tried at length to correct the misunderstanding in a second volume, published in 1830, the result did not satisfy him, and he forbade its reprinting during his lifetime.

While at first a political liberal, Pusey gradually came to fear liberalism and its impact on the Church. After the first Reform Bill was passed by the House of Lords on 7 June 1832, it was assumed that the Reformed Parliament, which was to meet early in 1833, would first attempt to reform the Church. In this context Robert Eden, Lord Henley, wrote *A Plan of Church Reform, with a Letter to the King,* a pamphlet calling for Church reform, especially the redistribution of cathedral endowments. Pusey responded to Henley with *Remarks on the Prospective and Past Benefits of Cathedral Institutions* (1833), arguing that Henley had overlooked the services which cathedral clergy had rendered to the English Church in the past. Stating that the cathedrals had been "the nurseries of most of our chief divines, who were the glory of our English name: in them these great men consolidated the strength which has been so beneficial to the Church," he felt they must continue to be centers of learning and of clerical education.

Realizing that the Church had to be defined and defended as a divine institution, he allied himself with the Tractarians, who had begun to insist on the divine right of ecclesiastical government. Newman took the lead in September 1833, when he published the first of the *Tracts for the Times,* which was a vigorous assertion of apostolic succession.

In Tract 18, *Thoughts on the Benefits of the System of Fasting, Enjoined by Our Church,* which appeared in January 1834, Pusey outlined the Christian duty of fasting. Though fasting was at times enjoined by the Church, Pusey considered it a protection against the slothful and worldly habits which are so agreeable to mankind's natural selfishness. For him regularity in fasting was as essential as regularity in church attendance and in reading the daily lessons ordered by the Church, because it made it easier for the Christian to practice a self-denying charity. He urged the restoration of Friday absti-

The major figures of the Oxford Movement: Henry Edward Manning, Edward Bouverie Pusey, John Henry Newman, and John Keble (Bodleian Library, Oxford)

nence because it impressed on one, week by week, the memory of Jesus' suffering.

Tract 66, *On the Benefits of the System of Fasting Prescribed by Our Church: Supplement to Tract XVIII* (1834), was Pusey's response to questions raised about Tract 18 in a letter addressed to the editor of the *British Magazine*. Pusey expanded his discussion about fasting and argued against the claim that it was "Popish," insisting that fasting was a practice of the Primitive Church. Pusey's most significant writing for the Oxford Movement, *Scriptural Views on Holy Baptism,* which was published in three parts (Tracts 67-69) between August and October 1835, argues for the centrality of baptism in the life of the Christian and for the doctrine of baptismal regeneration. Many Protestants at the time viewed the sacraments of baptism and the Holy Eucharist merely as symbols of what Christ had done for them and as signs of His love. Baptism had become but a sign of God's favor and the Eucharist but a remembrance of the death of Christ. By contrast for Pusey and the other Tractarians the sacraments were the vehicles of divine grace, and the efficacy of the sacraments depends on the apostolic succession of those who administer them.

In Tract 68 Pusey maintained that baptismal regeneration was taught in the scriptures and by the early Church and asserted, "Baptismal regeneration, as connected with the Incarnation of our Blessed Lord, gives a depth to our Christian existence, an actualness to our union with Christ, a reality to our sonship to God, an interest in the presence of our Lord's glorified Body at God's right hand, a joyousness amid the subduing of the flesh, an overwhelmingness to the dignity conferred on human nature, a solemnity to the communion of saints who are the fullness of Him Who filleth all in all, a substantiality to the indwelling of Christ, that to those who retain this truth the school which abandoned it must needs appear to have sold its birthright." Believing that the infant receives the remission of original guilt and the adult the remission of actual sins, Pusey also proposed a rigorous doctrine of the forgiveness of postbaptismal sins. Never clearly defining regeneration, he believed that with the decline of faith in the grace of baptism had come a waning of the sense of the grievousness of postbaptismal sin. While forgiveness in baptism is free, full, instantaneous, and universal, Pusey asserted, it is essential for the holiness of the Church that those who have forfeited their baptismal forgiveness must live a life of repentance in order to earn slow, partial, and gradual forgiveness. This is essential for the holiness of the Church. Tract 70 is the *Notes to the Scriptural Views of Holy Baptism.*

In 1836 Pusey published *An Earnest Remonstrance to the Author of "The Pope's Pastoral Letter,"* (republished as Tract 77), a response to *A Pastoral Epistle from His Holiness the Pope to Some Members of the University of Oxford, Faithfully Translated from the Original Latin* (1836), written by Charles Dickinson, a chaplain of Archbishop Richard Whately. Dickinson claimed that the pope admired the Oxford Movement and frequently quoted from the Tracts, making the Oxford Movement appear to be similar to Roman Catholicism. Pusey argued against this charge, claiming that Dickinson had in effect indicted some of the greatest Anglican theologians.

In his last Tract, *Catena Patrum IV: Testimony of Writers in the Later English Church to the Doctrines of the Eucharistic Sacrifice, with an Historical Account of the Changes Made in the Liturgy as to the Expression of That Doctrine* (Tract 81), which appeared in 1837, Pusey called on the English Church to recover the idea that Christ is truly and efficaciously sacrificed in the Eucharist. He also apologized for the English Reformers' failure to express adequately the doctrine of Eucharistic sacrifice.

Since the issuing in 1563 of the Thirty-Nine Articles of Anglican faith, to which the clergy was required to subscribe, there had been controversy. When the provost at Oxford University suggested that students could simply "declare assent" to the Thirty-Nine Articles, Pusey answered him with *Subscription to the Thirty-Nine Articles; Questions Respectfully Addressed to Members of Convocation on the Declaration Proposed as a Substitute for the Subscription to the Thirty-Nine Articles* (1835). He argued that declaration is less than subscription, which was essential to maintain allegiance to the teaching of the Church.

The Tractarians were devoted to the Fathers of the Church and believed that the norm for the Church's life and theology was the period before the split of 1054 between the Roman Catholic church in the West and the Orthodox Eastern church. Wanting to make the teaching of the Church Fathers available to Englishmen in their own language, they prepared *A Library of the Fathers of the Holy Catholic Church, Anterior to the Division of the East and West* (1838-1885), hoping to impress upon them that the Anglican branch of the Catholic church was founded upon scripture and the agreement of the undivided Church and that her authority was not based on the opinions of individual teachers, who might and did differ, but on the teaching held by all, in all times and all places. This was the motivation for the publication of *A Library of the Fathers.* From 1836 until his death, Pusey assisted in the publication of these fifty volumes, writing prefaces and translating texts.

On 25 January 1841 Newman published Tract 90, *Remarks on Certain Passages in the 39 Articles,* in which he argued that Anglicanism agreed with true Roman Catholicism and that the Thirty-Nine Articles agreed with the Decrees of the Council of Trent. The bishop of Oxford intervened and the publication of the Tracts was suspended. Pusey defended Newman with his *The Articles Treated on in Tract 90 Reconsidered and Their Interpretation Vindicated in a Letter to The Rev. R. W. Jelf.* Identifying his position with Newman's, Pusey maintained that the Articles must be read in conformity with and subordination to the teaching of the Catholic church, and he argued that the criticisms of the Catholic church contained in the Thirty-Nine Articles were of the Roman Catholic church of the sixteenth century and not of the undivided Church before 1054. He willingly agreed that some of the Roman Catholic doctrines that arose in the Middle Ages—such as the existence of purgatory and the rise of the cult of the Virgin Mary—were corruptions of the teachings of the early Church Fathers, but he asserted that on many major points of theology there was agreement.

With the publication of Tract 90, many believed that the Tractarians were trying to move the Church of England toward a Roman Catholic position. Pusey addressed the charge with *A Letter to His Grace the Archbishop of Canterbury, on Some Circumstances Connected With the Present Crisis in the English Church* (1842). Recognizing the existence in England of a tendency toward Rome, he contended that it was not the result of the *Tracts for the Times* but was due largely to the recent growth of the Roman Church in England and to the longing for visible unity of the Church. This tendency, he argued, could be controlled by emphasizing the blessings which were connected with membership in the Church of England and by criticizing Roman Catholic practices such as the denial of the Eucharist cup to the laity and the cult of the Virgin Mary.

On 14 May 1843 Pusey preached a sermon in Christ Church, Oxford, later published as *The Holy Eucharist: A Comfort to the Penitent* (1843), in which he once again drew on the teachings of the early Church Fathers to express his views on the sacrament of communion. Although he did not advocate the Roman Catholic doctrine of transubstantiation, many of his listeners, unfamiliar with Early Church teachings, believed that he had done so, and in June the vice-chancellor of Oxford suspended him from preaching at Oxford for two years.

In 1850 Pusey defended the apostolic rights of the English Church in *The Royal Supremacy Not an Arbitrary Authority But Limited by the Laws of the Church, of Which Kings Are Members,* a response to the Gorham Judgment, in which civil authorities had intervened in Church matters. In 1847 the bishop had refused to institute G. C. Gorham to a living he had been presented in Exeter, alleging that Gorham was heterodox on baptismal regeneration. Gorham appealed to the Judicial Committee of the Privy Council, which ruled in his favor. Like the other Tractarians, Pusey believed in the authority and independence of the Church, and, shocked by the ruling, he argued that the Privy Council could not make doctrine and that the kings of England were laymen subject to the laws of the Church. He maintained that bishops derive their authority not from the Crown but from their Sees.

In *The Church of England Leaves Her Children Free to Whom to Open Their Griefs* (1850) Pusey expanded on ideas he had expressed in an 1846 sermon, "The Entire Absolution of the Penitent," in which he claimed that priests in the Church of England had the power to grant absolution. In his

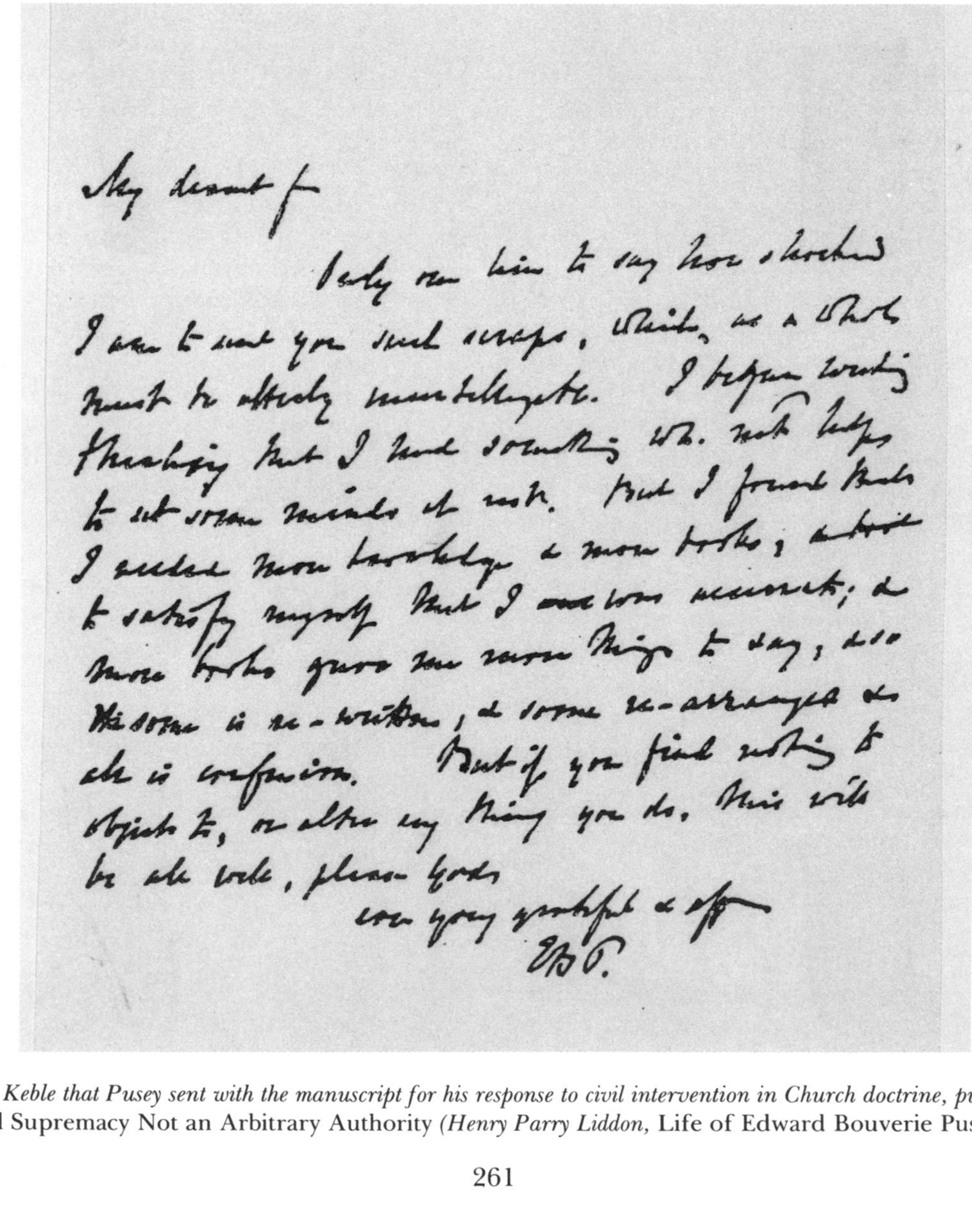

My dearest K

I only now have to say how ashamed I am to send you such scraps, which, as a whole must be utterly unintelligible. I began writing flowingly but I had something wh. took long to set some minds at rest. But I found that I needed more knowledge & more books, in order to satisfy myself that I was accurate; & more books gave me more things to say; also this some is re-written, & some re-arranged & all is confusion. But if you find nothing to object to, or alter any thing you do, this will be all well, please God

ever your grateful & aff

EBP.

Letter to John Keble that Pusey sent with the manuscript for his response to civil intervention in Church doctrine, published in 1850 as The Royal Supremacy Not an Arbitrary Authority *(Henry Parry Liddon,* Life of Edward Bouverie Pusey, D.D., *1898)* book Pusey argued that members of the Church of England are free to choose their own confessors, an established Tractarian belief, and he also maintained that the power of absolution was not limited to bishops but was given to every priest in his ordination.

On 24 September 1850 Pope Pius IX issued a bull by which England was constituted an ecclesiastical province of the Roman Catholic church with one archbishop and twelve suffragan bishops. Calling this bull the "papal aggression," Bishop Blomfield of London and others claimed that Pusey's writings had promoted it. Pusey responded to these criticisms with *A Letter to the Right Hon. and Right Rev. the Lord Bishop of London* (1851), his clearest justification of the Oxford Movement and the most complete account and defense of his teaching and practice. He defended absolution as a sacrament, the Eucharist as a propitiatory sacrifice, the objective reality of Jesus' presence in the Eucharist and the adoration of that presence, the devotion to Jesus' five wounds, and the counsels of perfection—the higher forms of service and devotion to which all are not called.

Pusey continued to write about the Holy Eucharist, which was central to the theology and devotion of the Tractarians. In an 1853 sermon preached at Christ Church, "The Presence of Christ in the Holy Eucharist," which he expanded with notes into *The Doctrine of the Real Presence, As Contained in the Fathers, from the Death of S. John the Evangelist to the Fourth General Council* (1855). Pusey stated that the Church and its sacraments are extensions of the incarnation. The Church is the tangible, historical link between the incarnation and the believer, the historical mediator of salvation, and the sacrament of the Holy Eucharist conveys the objective presence of Jesus Christ to the believer. Arguing that the objective presence of Jesus Christ results from the consecration, while the outward elements of bread and wine remain, Pusey sought a position between Roman Catholic transubstantiation and Zwinglian memorialism, quoting the Church Fathers extensively to illustrate his view. He also argued that God's grace and the believer's salvation come principally through this sacrament and that the efficacy of the sacrament depended upon the apostolic succession of those who administered it.

Pusey's study of the early Church councils led to the publication in 1857 of his *The Councils of the Church from the Council of Jerusalem, A.D. 51, to the Council of Constantinople, A.D. 381, Chiefly as to Their Constitution, but also as to Their Objects and History*. It is not a complete account of all the general and provincial councils from the apostles to Theodosius, but a review of their constitutions and actions intended to elucidate the point that matters of doctrine were always decided by bishops, the successors of the Apostles and the teaching authority of the Church. He therefore criticized the Protestant Episcopal church in the United States for permitting lay representation in Church councils.

In his last major work on the Eucharist, *The Real Presence of the Body and Blood of Our Lord Jesus Christ, the Doctrine of the English Church, with a Vindication of the Reception by the Wicked and of the Adoration of Our Lord Jesus Christ, Truly Present* (1857), Pusey took a clearly High Church view of the Eucharistic presence of Christ. Contending that the body and blood of Christ was present in the form of bread and wine, and that this doctrine was embodied in the English Church formularies, Pusey argued that the wicked, who take, eat, and drink the body and blood of Christ unworthily, do so to their condemnation and do not discern Christ's presence.

Pusey insisted that biblical study was the best antidote to lax theology, heresy, and rationalism, and his years of Old Testament scholarship came to fruition in the 1860s. *The Minor Prophets* (1860), the only published part of a planned series called "The Holy Bible, with a Commentary Explanatory and Practical and Introductions to the Several Books, by Clergymen of the Church of England," is a technical study which did not gain wide acceptance and which has been replaced by later studies. *Daniel the Prophet* (1864), an effort to address the Higher Criticism of the day, presents a conservative position with regard to dating and interpreting the text. While this volume is a significant piece of scholarship, Pusey is remembered more for his historical and ecclesiological studies than his biblical studies.

Pusey and the other Tractarians were interested in the reunion of all Christianity, but their greatest ecumenical commitment was to unite the Anglican and the Roman Catholic churches. In 1864 Pusey received a letter from Henry Edward Manning, a former Tractarian who was received into the Roman Catholic church in 1851. Answering Manning's charge that the Church of England was not a true Church but rather was a "cause and spring of unbelief," Pusey wrote the first part of his *Eirenicon, The Church of England a Portion of Christ's One Holy Catholic Church, and a Means of Restoring Visible Unity* (1865). Demonstrating the great amount of doctrine held in common by the Church

"High Church," caricature of Pusey published in Vanity Fair, *2 January 1875 (Collection of Jerold J. Savory)*

of Rome and the Church of England, Pusey reasserted his old contention that the quarrel of the English Church was not with the authoritative faith of Rome as defined by the Council of Trent, but with the popular system of unauthorized beliefs and practices, such as devotion to the Virgin Mary and indulgences. Claiming that late medieval abuses and corruptions were the "church-dividing" issues, he compared the Eastern Churches and the Church of England in their denial of papal supremacy, and suggested that the English Church could be the medium appointed by God for the reunion of Rome with the East, as well as with those Protestants who accept the ecumenical creeds.

Newman, who had become a Roman Catholic in 1845, answered Pusey, claiming that he exaggerated Roman Catholics' devotion to Mary. Pusey responded with *Eirenicon, Part II, First Letter to the Very Rev. J. H. Newman* (1869) in which he explained that he did not derogate the honor due to Mary but challenged popular claims made for her. He urged reverential love for Mary because she was *theotokos,* the God-bearer, as stated at the Council of Ephesus in 431. He also quoted much of Cardinal Juan de Turrecremata's treatise *De Veritate Conceptionis B. Virginis* (1547), rejecting the Immaculate Conception, which Pope Pius IX had proclaimed as dogma in the bull "Ineffabilis Deus" on 8 December 1854.

Pusey was hopeful that the twentieth ecumenical council, Vatican Council I, convoked by Pius IX to meet in 1869-1870, would clarify certain Roman Catholic teachings, such as those on purgatory, the deuterocanonical books, and Roman supremacy, now being discussed as papal infallibility. In this context he wrote *Eirenicon, Part III, Is Healthful Reunion Possible? A Second Letter to the Very Rev. J. H. Newman* (1870) and sent copies to many of the bishops who attended the council. Much of this book was a response to criticisms leveled against his first two *Eirenicons,* though Pusey did add an extended discussion of the claim of infallibility and concluded that history did not support the idea. On 18 July 1870 when the Vatican Council passed the constitution "Pastor Aeternus," which claimed that the Pope was infallible when he spoke *ex cathedra* on issues of faith and morals, Pusey was disappointed in the council's decision, which ended his hopes for "healthful reunion" with Rome. When *Eirenicon, Part III* was republished in 1876 he changed the title to *Healthful Reunion as Considered Possible Before the Vatican Council.*

Pusey called these three works *Eirenicon* ("reunion"). Three responses to different but related issues of Roman Catholicism and the reunion of the Church, they exhibited Pusey's deep commitment to the unity of the Church, his refusal to follow Newman into Roman Catholicism, and his vast knowledge of Church history.

Pusey's last significant book was *On the Clause "And the Son" in Regard to the Eastern Church and the Bonn Conference* (1876). Reunion conferences between Old Catholics (those who rejected papal infallibility), Anglicans, and the Eastern Church were held at Bonn in 1874 and 1875. A major topic of discussion was the *Filioque* clause of the Nicene Creed, which proclaimed that the Spirit proceeds from the Father and the Son, a clause included in the Western forms of the Creed but not in the Eastern forms. Fearful that the conferences would reach agreement on a formula which excluded the

Filioque clause, and aware that the American delegates favored its exclusion, Pusey argued that to drop the *Filioque* clause would be to surrender the position for which the Western Church had fought for centuries. Pusey granted that the clause was not in the original creed and that its earliest recorded use was at the Council of Toledo in 589, but he argued that its insertion was essential to guard against unecclesiastical spiritualism. Pusey's treatise is still the fullest discussion of this clause, both historically and doctrinally, but it was too technical to be widely appreciated.

Edward Bouverie Pusey died at Ascot Priory in Berkshire on 16 September 1882 having maintained to the end that the English Church was Catholic, but not Roman, and Reformed, but not Protestant. Author of the most significant justifications of the Oxford Movement, he was buried in the cathedral at Oxford.

Letters:

John O. Johnson and W. C. E. Newbolt, eds., *Spiritual Letters of Edward Bouverie Pusey* (London: Longmans, Green, 1898).

Biographies:

Henry P. Liddon, *Life of Edward Bouverie Pusey, D.D.*, edited and prepared for publication by J. O. Johnson and Robert J. Wilson, 4 volumes (London: Longmans, Green, 1893-1897);

George W. E. Russell, *Dr. Pusey* (London: A. R. Mowbray, 1907).

References:

William S. Bricknell, ed., *The Judgement of the Bishops upon Tractarian Theology* (Oxford: J. Vincent, 1845);

Yngve Brilioth, *The Anglican Revival: Studies in the Oxford Movement* (London & New York: Longmans, Green, 1925);

Edward G. K. Browne, *History of the Tractarian Movement* (Dublin: J. Duffy, 1856);

Owen Chadwick, ed., *The Mind of the Oxford Movement* (Stanford: Stanford University Press, 1967);

Richard W. Church, *The Oxford Movement: Twelve Years, 1833-1845* (London: Macmillan, 1892);

Christopher H. Dawson, *The Spirit of the Oxford Movement* (London: Sheed & Ward, 1834);

Augustus B. Donaldson, *Five Great Oxford Leaders: Keble, Newman, Pusey, Liddon and Church* (London: Rivington, 1900);

Geoffrey Faber, *Oxford Apostles: A Character Study of the Oxford Movement* (Baltimore: Penguin, 1954);

Eugene R. Fairweather, ed., *The Oxford Movement*, Library of Protestant Thought (New York: Oxford University Press, 1964);

Charles C. Grafton, *Pusey and the Church Revival* (Milwaukee: Young Churchman, 1902);

William H. Hutchinson, ed., *The Oxford Movement: Being a Selection from Tracts for the Times* (London: Walter Scott, 1906);

Edmund A. Knox, *The Tractarian Movement, 1833-45* (London & New York: Putnam's, 1933);

James C. Livingston, "The Oxford Movement and Anglo-Catholicism," in his *Modern Christian Thought: From the Enlightenment to Vatican II* (New York: Macmillan, 1971);

William H. Mackean, *The Eucharistic Doctrine of the Oxford Movement: A Critical Survey* (London & New York: Putnam's, 1933);

Marvin R. O'Connell, *The Oxford Conspirators: A History of the Oxford Movement* (New York: Macmillan, 1969);

Sidney L. Ollard, *The Anglo-Catholic Revival, Some Persons and Principles* (Milwaukee: Morehouse, 1925);

Ollard, *A Short History of the Oxford Movement* (Milwaukee: Morehouse, 1915);

John H. Overton, *The Anglican Revival* (New York: Herbert S. Stone, 1898);

Vernon F. Storr, *The Development of English Theology in the Nineteenth Century* (London & New York: Longmans, Green, 1913).

John Ruskin

Charles T. Dougherty
University of Missouri at St. Louis

BIRTH: London, 8 February 1819, to John James and Margaret Ruskin.

EDUCATION: A.B., Oxford University, 1842; M.A., 1843.

MARRIAGE: 10 April 1848 to Euphemia Gray; annulled 15 July 1854.

DEATH: Coniston, 20 January 1900.

SELECTED BOOKS*: *Salsette and Elephanta: A Prize Poem* (Oxford: Vincent, 1839);

Modern Painters, 5 volumes (London: Smith, Elder, 1843-1860; volumes 1-2, New York: Wiley & Putnam, 1847-1848; volumes 3-5, New York: Wiley, 1856-1860);

The Seven Lamps of Architecture (London: Smith, Elder, 1849; New York: Wiley, 1849);

Poems. J. R. Collected 1850 (London: Privately printed, 1850);

The King of the Golden River; or, The Black Brothers: A Legend of Stiria (London: Smith, Elder, 1851; New York: Wiley, 1860);

Notes on the Construction of Sheepfolds (London: Smith, Elder, 1851; New York: Wiley, 1851);

Examples of the Architecture of Venice, Selected, and Drawn to Measurement from the Edifices (London: Smith, Elder, 1851);

Pre-Raphaelitism (London: Smith, Elder, 1851; New York: Wiley, 1851);

The Stones of Venice, 3 volumes (London: Smith, Elder, 1851-1853; New York: Wiley, 1851-1860);

Giotto and His Works in Padua (3 parts, London: Printed for the Arundel Society, 1853-1860; 1 volume, New York: Scribners, 1899);

Lectures on Architecture and Painting Delivered at Edinburgh in November 1853 (London: Smith, Elder, 1854; New York: Wiley, 1854);

The Opening of the Crystal Palace, Considered in Some of its Relations to the Prospects of Art (London: Smith, Elder, 1854; New York: Alden, 1885);

Notes on Some of the Principal Pictures Exhibited in the Rooms of the Royal Academy: 1855 (London: Smith, Elder, 1855);

The Harbours of England (London: Gambart, 1856);

Notes on Some of the Pictures Exhibited in the Rooms of the Royal Academy, and the Society of Painters in Water Colours, No. II—1856 (London: Smith, Elder, 1856);

Notes on the Turner Gallery at Marlborough House, 1856 (London: Smith, Elder, 1857);

The Political Economy of Art, Being the Substance (with additions) of Two Lectures delivered at Manchester, July 10th and 13th, 1857 (London: Smith,

John Ruskin, 1882

* This list excludes revised and enlarged editions.

Elder, 1857; New York: Wiley & Halsted, 1858);

Notes on Some of the Principal Pictures Exhibited in the Rooms of the Royal Academy and the Society of Painters in Water Colours, No. III—1857 (London: Smith, Elder, 1857);

Catalogue of the Turner Sketches in the National Gallery (London: Privately printed, 1857);

The Elements of Drawing in Three Letters to Beginners (London: Smith, Elder, 1857; New York: Wiley & Halsted, 1857);

Catalogue of the Sketches and Drawings by J. M. W. Turner, R.A., Exhibited in Marlborough House in the Year 1857-8 (London: Privately printed, 1857);

Notes on Some of the Principal Pictures Exhibited in the Rooms of the Royal Academy, the Old and New Societies of Painters in Water Colours, the Society of British Artists, and the French Exhibition, No. IV—1858 (London: Smith, Elder, 1858);

Cambridge School of Art. Mr. Ruskin's Inaugural Address Delivered at Cambridge, Oct. 29, 1858 (Cambridge: Deighton, Bell/London: Bell & Daldy, 1858);

The Oxford Museum, by Ruskin and Henry W. Acland (London: Smith, Elder/Oxford: Parker, 1859);

The Unity of Art. By John Ruskin, Esq., M.A. Delivered at the Annual Meeting of the Manchester School of Art, February 22nd, 1859 (Manchester: Printed by Thos. Sowler, 1859);

The Two Paths: Being Lectures on Art, and its Application to Decoration and Manufacture, Delivered in 1858-9 (London: Smith, Elder, 1859; New York: Wiley, 1859);

The Elements of Perspective Arranged for the Use of the Schools and Intended to be Read in Connexion with the First Three Books of Euclid (London: Smith, Elder, 1859; New York: Wiley, 1860);

Notes on Some of the Principal Pictures Exhibited in the Royal Academy, the Old and New Societies of Painters in Water Colours, the Society of British Artists, and the French Exhibition. No. V—1859 (London: Smith, Elder, 1859);

"Unto this Last": Four Essays on the First Principles of Political Economy (London: Smith, Elder, 1862; New York: Wiley, 1866);

Sesame and Lilies: Two Lectures Delivered at Manchester in 1864 (London: Smith, Elder, 1865; New York: Wiley, 1865);

The Ethics of the Dust: Ten Lectures to Little Housewives on the Elements of Crystallisation (London: Smith, Elder, 1866; New York: Wiley, 1866);

The Crown of Wild Olive: Three Lectures on Work, Traffic, and War (London: Smith, Elder, 1866; New York: Wiley, 1866);

Time and Tide, By Weare and Tyne. Twenty-five Letters to a Working Man of Sunderland on the Laws of Work (London: Smith, Elder, 1867; New York: Wiley, 1868);

First Notes on the General Principles of Employment for the Destitute and Criminal Classes (London: Privately printed, 1868);

The Queen of the Air: Being a Study of the Greek Myths of Cloud and Storm (London: Smith, Elder, 1869; New York: Wiley, 1869);

Lectures on Art Delivered Before the University of Oxford in Hilary Term, 1870 (Oxford: Clarendon Press, 1870; New York: Wiley, 1870);

Fors Clavigera: Letters to the Workmen and Labourers of Great Britain (96 letters, London: Printed for the author by Smith, Elder, 1871-1884; 8 volumes, Orpington: George Allen, 1871-1884; New York: Wiley, 1880-1886);

Munera Pulveris: Six Essays on the Elements of Political Economy (London: Printed for the author by Smith, Elder, 1872; New York: Wiley, 1872);

Aratra Pentelici: Six Lectures on the Elements of Sculpture, Given Before the University of Oxford in Michaelmas Term, 1870 (London: Printed for the author by Smith, Elder, 1872; New York: Wiley, 1872);

The Relation between Michael Angelo and Tintoret: Seventh of the Course of Lectures on Sculpture Delivered at Oxford, 1870-71 (London: Printed for the author by Smith, Elder, 1872; New York: Alden, 1885);

The Eagle's Nest: Ten Lectures on the Relation of Natural Science to Art, Given Before the University of Oxford in Lent Term, 1872 (London: Printed for the author by Smith, Elder, 1872; New York: Wiley, 1873);

The Sepulchral Monuments of Italy: Monuments of the Cavalli Family in the Church of Santa Anastasia, Verona (London: Arundel Society, 1872);

The Nature and Authority of Miracle (N.p.: Privately printed, 1873);

Love's Meinie: Lectures on Greek and English Birds (3 parts: lectures 1-2, Keston: George Allen, 1873; New York: Wiley, 1873; lecture 3, Orpington: George Allen, 1881; 1 volume, Orpington: George Allen, 1881);

Ariadne Florentina: Six Lectures on Wood and Metal Engraving, With Appendix (7 parts: lecture 1, Keston: George Allen, 1873; lectures 2-6 and appendix, Orpington: George Allen, 1874-

1876; 1 volume, Orpington: George Allen, 1876);

The Poetry of Architecture: Cottage, Villa, etc. To Which Is Added Suggestions on Works of Art, as Kata Phusin (New York: Wiley, 1873); republished as *The Poetry of Architecture: Or, The Architecture of the Nations of Europe Considered in its Association with Natural Scenery and National Character,* as Ruskin (Orpington: George Allen, 1893);

Val d'Arno: Ten Lectures on the Tuscan Art Directly Antecedent to the Florentine Year of Victories, Given Before the University of Oxford in Michaelmas Term, 1873 (Orpington: George Allen, 1874; New York: Alden, 1885);

Mornings in Florence: Being Simple Studies of Christian Art, for English Travellers (6 parts, Orpington: George Allen, 1875-1877; 1 volume, New York: Wiley, 1877; Orpington: George Allen, 1885);

Proserpina: Studies of Wayside Flowers, While the Air was Yet Pure Among the Alps, and in the Scotland and England which My Father Knew (10 parts, Orpington: George Allen, 1875-1886; parts 1-6 republished in 1 volume, 1879; New York: Alden, 1885);

Notes on Some of the Principal Pictures Exhibited in the Rooms of the Royal Academy: 1875 (Orpington: George Allen/London: Ellis & Bond, 1875);

Deucalion: Collected Studies of the Lapse of Waves, and Life of Stones (8 parts, Orpington: George Allen, 1875-1883; parts 1-3, 2 volumes, New York: Wiley, 1875-1877; parts 1-6, 1 volume, Orpington: George Allen, 1879);

Guide to the Principal Pictures in the Academy of Fine Arts at Venice, Arranged for English Travellers, 2 parts (Venice, 1877; Orpington: George Allen, 1882-1883);

St. Mark's Rest. The History of Venice, Written for the Help of the Few Travellers Who Still Care About Her Monuments (6 parts, including appendix and two supplements, Orpington: George Allen, 1877-1884; 1 volume, 1884; New York: Wiley, 1884);

The Laws of Fésole: A Familiar Treatise on the Elementary Principles and Practice of Drawing and Painting (4 parts, Orpington: George Allen, 1877-1879; New York: Wiley, 1877-1879; 1 volume, Orpington: George Allen, 1879; New York: Wiley, 1879);

Notes by Mr. Ruskin on His Drawings by the late J. M. W. Turner, R.A. (London: Elzevir Press, 1878);

Notes by Mr. Ruskin on Samuel Prout and William Hunt, Illustrated by a Loan Collection of Drawings Exhibited at the Fine Art Society's Galleries (London: Fine Art Society, 1879);

Letters Addressed by Professor Ruskin, D.C.L., to the Clergy on the Lord's Prayer and the Church, edited by F. A. Malleson (N.p.: Privately printed, 1879);

Elements of English Prosody for Use in St. George's Schools. Explanatory of the Various Terms Used in "Rock Honeycomb" (Orpington: George Allen, 1880);

Arrows of the Chace, Being a Collection of Scattered Letters Published Chiefly in the Daily Newspapers, 1840-1880 (2 volumes, Orpington: George Allen, 1880; New York: Wiley, 1881);

"Our Fathers Have Told Us." Sketches of the History of Christendom for Boys and Girls Who Have Been Held at Its Fonts, Part I: The Bible of Amiens (5 parts, Orpington: George Allen, 1880-1885; 1 volume, 1885; New York: Alden, 1885);

The Art of England: Lectures Given in Oxford (6 parts, Orpington: George Allen, 1883-1884; 1 volume, 1884; New York: Wiley, 1884);

The Pleasures of England: Lectures Given in Oxford (4 parts, Orpington: George Allen, 1884-1885; 1 volume, New York: Wiley, 1885);

The Storm-Cloud of the Nineteenth Century: Two Lectures Delivered at the London Institution, February 4th and 11th, 1884 (2 parts, Orpington: George Allen, 1884; 1 volume, 1884; New York: Wiley, 1884);

On the Old Road: A Collection of Miscellaneous Essays, Pamphlets, Etc., Etc., Published 1834-1885, 2 volumes, edited by Alexander Wedderburn (Orpington: George Allen, 1885);

Praeterita: Outlines of Scenes and Thoughts Perhaps Worthy of Memory in My Past Life (28 parts, Orpington: George Allen, 1885-1889; 3 volumes, Orpington: George Allen, 1886-1889; New York: Wiley, 1886-1889);

Dilecta: Correspondence, Diary Notes, and Extracts from Books, Illustrating Praeterita, 3 parts (Orpington: George Allen, 1886-1900);

Verona and Other Lectures, edited by W. G. Collingwood (Orpington: George Allen, 1894; New York & London: Macmillan, 1894);

Lectures on Landscape, Delivered at Oxford in Lent Term, 1871 (Orpington: George Allen, 1897);

The Diaries of John Ruskin, edited by Joan Evans and J. H. Whitehouse, 3 volumes (Oxford: Oxford University Press, 1956-1959);

The Brantwood Diary of John Ruskin, edited by Helen Gill Viljoen (New Haven: Yale University Press, 1970).

Collection: *The Works of John Ruskin,* Library Edition, edited by E. T. Cook and Alexander Wedderburn, 39 volumes (London: George Allen/New York: Longmans, Green, 1903-1912).

John Ruskin was the most influential art critic to write in England between the death of Sir Joshua Reynolds in 1792 and the publications of Clive Bell and others around 1914. It is not, in fact, too much to say that his is the most important body of art criticism in the English language. It is a useful exercise to read all of his books, in order, year by year, for in a real sense Ruskin's bibliography is his biography. He wrote every day except Sunday and published everything he wrote except his diary and some hundreds of personal letters, and he wrote it all so well that he is acknowledged to be one of the great masters of English prose.

Ruskin was also a hardworking, "hands-on" art critic. He was not a painter or a sculptor; he was a critic, and he knew the difference. Besides producing a stream of books on art and artists, he taught drawing, wrote textbooks, reviewed shows, organized museums and galleries, collected paintings, gave public lectures, promoted new artists, wrote guidebooks, catalogued collections, and, finally, served as the first professor of fine art at Oxford. His architectural studies were the results of arduous observation of the details of Italian Gothic cathedrals, which demanded hours of climbing on ladders and scaffolding. He illustrated most of his own books with meticulous drawings, and, after 1871 when he established in Orpington, Kent, a publishing house named for and operated by his longtime associate George Allen, he became his own publisher.

It is probable that Ruskin worked so hard because he combined a Puritan conscience with a love of beauty that was immediate and sensual. He passionately loved natural scenery and painting, but he believed that God did not approve of rich, idle young men who indulged their passions. He knew that if he were to enjoy his rapture of the eyes in this fallen world, he would have to labor and to do good works. He did both.

Ruskin was the only child of John James and Margaret Ruskin, a Scottish couple who had married late in life. His father was a prosperous sherry merchant, whose work required frequent trips to the Continent and regular calls at the houses of the landed gentry in England. Before the development of the museums, the galleries in these houses were the repositories of most of the important paintings in Great Britain, and John James Ruskin became a knowledgeable connoisseur. His son traveled with him on occasion from the time that he was six years old, and he thus became a precocious art critic.

Margaret Ruskin, in contrast, had scant interest in the arts. She was an unbending Evangelical. Almost from infancy young Ruskin read the Bible at his mother's knee, straight through, "hard names and all," as he said, over and over. He read Scott and Homer and learned the elements of Latin, but he had no toys and no playmates and was severely disciplined. John Ruskin attended a day school occasionally and was sometimes taught by a tutor, but his education was eccentric and irregular. In 1836, however, he qualified as a gentleman-commoner and thus was admitted without examination to Christ Church College, Oxford.

He began serious writing immediately. In 1837 and 1838 he published under the pseudonym Kata Phusin (According to Nature) a series of four articles entitled "The Poetry of Architecture" in the *Architectural Magazine.* It was a study of how cottages and villas in England, France, and Switzerland fit with their surroundings and related to the national characteristics of the inhabitants. The articles were well received and were a remarkable achievement for an eighteen-year-old.

In 1839 Ruskin received the prestigious Newdigate Prize for poetry at Oxford. The next year, however, he dropped out of the university because of illness and traveled on the Continent. In 1841, at home, he wrote *The King of the Golden River* for a girl who was visiting his parents. This classic fairy tale, which has been constantly in print since it was first published in 1851, contains in its allegory the germ of much of Ruskin's later social thought. The girl was Euphemia Gray, who, seven years later, became his bride.

In 1842 Ruskin returned to Oxford, took his examinations, and graduated. He immediately began work on a book to defend his favorite painter, J. M. W. Turner. Turner had been a famous, well-established painter for forty years. In his later years he changed his manner of painting and therefore had been subjected to harsh criticism, but he scarcely needed the young Ruskin to defend him. Ruskin, however, plunged into the controversy. In 1843, the year he received an Oxford M.A., he produced volume one of *Modern Painters,* a work which was to extend to five volumes and to occupy him for seventeen years. The volume was published with the signature "a Graduate of Oxford." The argument of this volume is, first, that a painting ought to be true to life, and, second, that Turner's

Ruskin's parents, John James and Margaret Ruskin. Portraits by Henry Raeburn and James Northcote.

paintings were more nearly true than were those of the landscape painters of the previous two centuries.

The assertion that a painting ought to be true to life was made against the theory of Sir Joshua Reynolds and the practice, as Ruskin perceived it, of Claude, Poussin, and Salvator Rosa. Reynolds had argued that a painter should not paint the accidental qualities of a specific object, but rather that he should strive to present "the ideal form" of a natural object. This was common doctrine in the eighteenth century. Ruskin had no patience with this thinking. He was bound to nature by the scientific bias of his time. As a traveler with his parents, he had been raised in the tradition of view-hunting. He loved nature with all his Evangelical fervor because God had made it. Because he lived in the age of Wordsworth, he saw nature as a source of beneficent influences, and he had recently come to admire the abstract forms which he found in nature. He believed that it was immoral to paint nature falsely under the delusion that one could improve upon her, and he believed that it was immoral to use nature simply as a vehicle for showing one's prowess as a painter.

The second part of his argument, that Turner painted nature more accurately than did his predecessors, is the longer part of the volume. He divides nature into categories: color, light and shade, space, clouds, mountains, water, and vegetation. In each category he describes some examples of natural scenery, then shows the accuracy of Turner's painting. It is Ruskin's descriptions, his word-painting, that give this volume its distinction, though some of the prose seems too ornate even for Victorian taste. The weakness of the volume lies in its logic because the validity of Ruskin's argument rests entirely upon the accuracy of his vision. The first installment of *Modern Painters* was praised and condemned, but no one doubted that a major new writer had appeared on the London scene. Ruskin's work was savagely attacked in an unsigned review by John Eagles for *Blackwood's Magazine:* "Self-convicted of malice, he has not the slightest suspicion of his ignorance. . . ." It fared little better in a two-part review by George Darley, also unsigned, in the *Athenaeum:* "[This work] is just not blasphemous

St. Mark's Cathedral and the Ducal Palace drawn by Ruskin at age sixteen, when he made his first trip to Venice (The Brantwood Trust, Coniston)

because it is crack-brained." In contrast, volume one of *Modern Painters* was praised by Walt Whitman in the *Brooklyn Eagle* and by reviewers for the *Weekly Chronicle*, the *Churchman*, and *Gentleman's Magazine*. The critic for *Fraser's Magazine* called it "perhaps the most remarkable book which has ever been published in reference to art. . . ."

In 1844 Ruskin did some reading in art history and spent time at the Louvre. The next year he made his first trip to the Continent without his parents. He went to visit the scenes which Turner had painted, but in northern Italy he discovered the great religious and historical painters of the Renaissance. He was overwhelmed by what he saw, and especially by the canvases of Tintoretto.

He returned to England, and, after five months of concentrated writing, Ruskin's *Modern Painters*, volume two, was published in 1846. The first volume had been concerned with Truth in art, the second was concerned with Beauty. It is the shortest of the five volumes. The subject is difficult and this volume is principally interesting as the record of the attempt of an Evangelical of distinct Puritan cast to come to terms with the sensuous appeal of beauty in art. It was published along with the third edition of the first volume, both by "a Graduate of Oxford."

By this time Ruskin knew much more about art than he had at the beginning of his project. He now knew that art had a history, that the Turner controversy was but an episode in that history, and that the idea of Truth in art was a much simpler concept when dealing with landscape than when looking at a religious painting. It was ten years before he resumed work on *Modern Painters*.

On 10 April 1848 John Ruskin married Euphemia Gray. About this time he also turned his attention to architecture. After a tour of the cities of Normandy, he produced in 1849 *The Seven Lamps of Architecture*. This work was an application of the principles of *Modern Painters* to architecture. It differed from the earlier volumes in that for Ruskin Truth in architecture meant something like an integration of form, function, and site rather than conformity to an exterior object. *The Seven Lamps of Architecture* was the first of his volumes to be illustrated. Ruskin was a superb draughtsman and he drew and sketched all the illustrations himself, a practice he was to continue. This was also Ruskin's first volume published under his own name.

Ruskin was beginning to suspect that there was a connection between the quality of the art produced at a certain time and place and the quality of the culture out of which it came, and he needed a new argument. Two volumes of *Modern Painters* had not succeeded in winning popular taste away from the Old Masters. He perceived that this taste had been corrupted by the Renaissance, though it would not be easy to make the case that the period that produced Michelangelo, da Vinci, and Raphael had a corrupting influence because their great genius had obscured their faults. Ruskin believed that their mastery of and concentration upon technique led the viewer to contemplate not nature, or man, or God, but the artist himself. It was a self-conscious art, corrupted by pride of technique. To make his case for the relationship of art and culture and against the Renaissance, Ruskin decided to discuss architecture rather than painting. Architecture is the more social art. Individual genius does not come into play in the way that it does in painting; architecture involves many workmen, and the great buildings serve social purposes.

Ruskin chose Venice as his laboratory. He spent the winter of 1849-1850 there with his young wife. While she reveled in the brilliant society of the Austrian occupation, he toiled feverishly on high ladders and scaffolding, sketching in loving detail the decorative devices of these great buildings which he believed were inevitably to be lost to increasing industrial pollution or to slip beneath the waves. Volume one of *The Stones of Venice* was published in 1851. It is a technical introduction to architecture. A building is an artificial arrangement of stones, and Ruskin leads readers through the process, from the quarry to the foundation, the walls and the roof.

The same year, 1851, Ruskin's pamphlet entitled *Pre-Raphaelitism* was published. It was a defense of a group of young London artists, including John Everett Millais, Edward Burne-Jones, William Holman Hunt, and Dante Gabriel Rossetti, who called themselves the Pre-Raphaelite Brotherhood (PRB). They were trying to break the bondage of Renaissance tradition and they strove to paint with meticulous accuracy. Their shows were viciously attacked and Ruskin threw his by-now-considerable weight on their side. He defended their theory and practice, but most of the pamphlet was concerned, once more, with the paintings of Turner. Since Turner's paintings were not at all like those of the PRB, Ruskin felt obliged to explain how he could admire both styles.

The Ruskins returned to Venice for a full year in 1851 and 1852, and in 1853 the final two volumes of *The Stones of Venice* were published. In the second volume Ruskin describes and pays tribute to the Byzantine churches of early Venice and shows their superiority to pagan art. Then, in a passage that is one of the most widely republished and quoted in all Ruskin, he turns to his consideration of Gothic architecture. He concludes the excellence of Gothic architecture lies in the way its builders solved structural problems and in the way they ornamented the buildings, but especially in the manner in which the structures, by their very irregularity, reflect a civilization whose workers were free to express themselves in their work. The contrast with the life of the factory worker in the new industries of England was evident: "You must either make a tool of the creature, or a man of him. You cannot make both."

The *Communist Manifesto* had appeared in 1848; in 1850 Karl Marx arrived in London, where he worked at the British Museum writing *Das Kap-*

Euphemia Gray Ruskin, drawn by Ruskin in 1848 or 1850 (Ashmolean Museum, Oxford). They were married 10 April 1848.

William Bell Scott, Ruskin, and Dante Gabriel Rossetti, 1863 (Picture Post Library). Ruskin had defended the paintings of Rossetti and others of the Pre-Raphaelite Brotherhood in his 1851 pamphlet Pre-Raphaelitism.

ital. A workers' revolution was in the air. Young militants seized upon Ruskin's words. "The Nature of the Gothic," a chapter in volume two of *The Stones of Venice,* was published separately and distributed as a pamphlet. Ruskin had become an important social commentator.

Volume three of *The Stones of Venice* was subtitled *The Fall.* It is an account of the Renaissance architecture of Venice. In Ruskin's view, Venice had abandoned her religious fervor; she then lost her preeminence as a trading nation and a sea power, and her architecture fell to the ministry of pride and luxury. The parallel with Great Britain was clear. It too was a great sea power and trading nation which was losing its religious fervor. For the English there were sermons in *The Stones of Venice.*

Ruskin's work was still receiving bad reviews from the established quarterlies, but he continued to receive praise from the more popular press. The *Times* gave *The Stones of Venice* a very long, generally favorable review in three installments. Ruskin was clearly a force on the London scene. His work on architecture is written in the same Latinate prose as *Modern Painters.* As in that work, the sentences are long and complex, with many subordinate clauses, self-conscious rhythms, alliterations, the suspension of the predicate, and other devices of classical rhetoric. The opening sentences of *The Stones of Venice* serve as an example: "Since first the dominion of men was asserted over the ocean, three thrones, of mark beyond all others, have been set upon its sands: the thrones of Tyre, Venice, and England. Of the First of these great powers only the memory remains; of the Second, the ruin; the Third, which inherits their greatness, if it forget their example, may be led through prouder eminence to less pitied destruction." Ruskin's powers of description are brought to bear on buildings and city streets instead of on natural scenery, but the work is more orderly, more under control than is *Modern Painters. The Stones of Venice* is probably the finest study of a great city ever written.

From Shakespeare to Thomas Mann, Venice has fascinated writers from what Byron called "the moral North." Ruskin's passionate response to this seductive city and the frantic, even maniacal, pace of his work may also have had personal roots. In 1854 his wife successfully sued for an annulment of their marriage on the grounds that it had never been consummated. The decree was granted on 15 July 1854. Almost exactly one year later, on 3 July 1855, she married John Everett Millais, one of the Pre-Raphaelite painters whom Ruskin had befriended.

The episode had no visible effect on Ruskin's public life and work. He does seem, however, to have sought ways to be more effective in the practical order and to reach a broader audience. He met Dante Gabriel Rossetti in 1854. Turner had died in 1851 and it occurred to Ruskin that there might be more merit in helping a live artist than in defending a dead one. Therefore, for several years he did what he could to lift Rossetti's financial burdens so that he would be free to paint.

He also began to teach drawing at the Working Men's College and, in 1855, began to write annual reviews of the paintings hung each year at the Exhibition of the Royal Academy. These pamphlets, meant to be sold to visitors entering the gallery, were published for five years, until 1859; a final one appeared in 1875.

In 1856 Ruskin produced volumes three and four of *Modern Painters.* One reads volume three with a sense of continuity, not from volume two, but from *The Stones of Venice.* In the ten years since the second volume of *Modern Painters* had appeared, Ruskin had seen many more paintings, especially in Italy, and had learned much. He maintained steadfastly his general argument that a great painter looks at what he paints through the eyes of love, thus sees it truly and paints it truly. A bad painter paints out of pride, or self-love. Ruskin now understood, however, that there were great painters who made no attempt to paint external nature accurately—Italian primitives like Giotto, for example. Therefore, he devoted the first part of the volume to distinguishing between good and bad use of the imagination to create "ideal" images. He had also learned that people, even in Europe, have not always seen Nature in the same way, that landscape has a history. The second part of *Modern Painters,* volume three, traces the history of landscape from Homer to Turner.

Volume four contains additional essays on Turner, a long technical discussion of the geology of mountains, and two chapters on the effects of mountains on people who live in them and visit them. These chapters carry forward brilliantly the eighteenth-century concept of the picturesque.

The opinions of the reviewers of this volume were consistent with most of those expressed concerning earlier volumes. However, Ruskin continued to have strong support in the more popular journals. George Eliot, in a review of volume three for the *Westminster,* wrote, "he who teaches . . . with such power as Mr. Ruskin's, is a prophet for his generation"; of the third and fourth volumes she declared, "[they] contain, I think, some of the finest writing of the age."

As an extension of his teaching, in 1857 Ruskin produced a textbook, *The Elements of Drawing in Three Letters to Beginners.* His study of Venice had reaffirmed his conviction that there was a connection between a society and the art it produces. He was beginning to believe that British society was in such a wretched state that little advancement in the arts was possible. If he were to reform the taste of his countrymen in art, he would have first to reform the society. All his writing on art, he suspected, may have been a waste of time.

From this time forward almost all of his writings were either public lectures or magazine articles, as he reached for a larger public. These new formats are reflected in Ruskin's radical change in style. The periodic sentences of the longer books are gone, replaced with sentences of simple structure and limpid clarity. Ruskin's shift to lectures and periodical pieces also created problems for bibliographers because the works were published at the time they were written and then gathered into books which appeared sometimes many years later, and with different titles.

An example is the two lectures Ruskin delivered in 1857 on "The Political Economy of Art." In these addresses he identified the troubles of British society as liberalism in religion and laissez-faire capitalism. The great industrial town of Manchester was the seat of both, so he gave his lectures there. He tried to talk to businessmen about art in terms that they would understand. How does one identify a good artist? How much should one pay him? Why should businessmen collect art? Why should they try to help preserve the art being destroyed by war in Italy? The lectures were printed in an inexpensive edition immediately and were published again, with additions, under the title "*A Joy for Ever,*" in 1880. Newspapers carried full accounts of the lectures and most took the view that Mr. Ruskin should stay away from social questions and confine himself to art.

The year 1858 was a decisive one in Ruskin's life. Turner had died in 1851 and left nineteen thousand sketches, drawings, and paintings to the nation. Ruskin had been named executor and trustee of Turner's estate. Although he did not function during the prolonged litigation that followed, he did survey and catalogue the bulk of these pictures. When he had finished, he was tired of Turner; and he perceived that Turner had severe limitations. He concluded that Turner was still the greatest landscape painter who had ever lived and probably the greatest painter England could produce, but the great Venetians had captured Ruskin.

He also dated from 1858 the loss of his Evangelical faith. He did not cease to be a Christian, and he did not move toward Catholicism, but he did abandon the sectarian views of his childhood. He also abandoned some of the arguments that supported the first two volumes of *Modern Painters.* In fact, he was beginning to wonder whether there was any use in landscape painting at all. Perhaps it is better to look at real scenery than at a painting, and, if it seemed desirable to record accurately a scene, the camera was now available.

In 1859 Ruskin wrote another textbook, *The Elements of Perspective,* and he set about finishing *Modern Painters.* He no longer had enthusiasm for the project, but his father was proud of his work on art. In 1858 Ruskin had been elected an honorary scholar at Christ Church, Oxford. This was a great distinction; he was clearly succeeding in his career as an art critic, and his father did not want him to abandon this career for the rough-and-tumble world of public controversy over political and social matters.

To please his father, Ruskin plunged forward and published volume five of *Modern Painters* in

An 1853 drawing of Ruskin's wedding to Euphemia Gray by John Everett Millais (Victoria and Albert Museum). In 1854 Euphemia Ruskin had the marriage annulled; the following year she married Millais. In Millais's drawing the ghostly figure behind the groom is Ruskin's grandfather, John Thomas Ruskin, who committed suicide in 1817.

1860. It is one of the most challenging books to come out of Victorian England. Because he had lost his enthusiasm for landscape, Ruskin concentrated on Turner's paintings of mythological subjects, and, because he had given up his conventional religious beliefs, he was able to bring a freshness and vitality to his reading of the ancient myths. The result is a notable Christian statement about art as the Light of the World, the Redeemer from darkness and chaos.

In the same year, as a series of magazine articles, Ruskin produced *"Unto this Last,"* his most successful incursion into the field of political economy. Before looking at the argument of this series, however, it is useful to consider the titles of his three principal works on the subject together: *"Unto this Last," Munera Pulveris,* and *The Crown of Wild Olive.*

Ruskin's fundamental insight in these works was that capitalism, guided by the economic theory of the time, defined man as a selfish being who presumably acts always in his own interest. More than that, in Ruskin's view, this selfishness is perceived not as an evil in man's fallen nature but as a positive good. Ruskin points out that nineteenth-century England represents the only culture that has ever exalted selfishness as a virtue. All other cultures in all other times have perceived it to be a vice. *"Unto this Last"* takes its title from Matthew 20:14. *Munera Pulveris* (A Little Dust) finds its title in an obscure Ode by Horace, the principal Roman poet after the death of Vergil, who died a few years before the birth of Christ.

The Crown of Wild Olive is a series of three lectures delivered in different cities in 1864 and

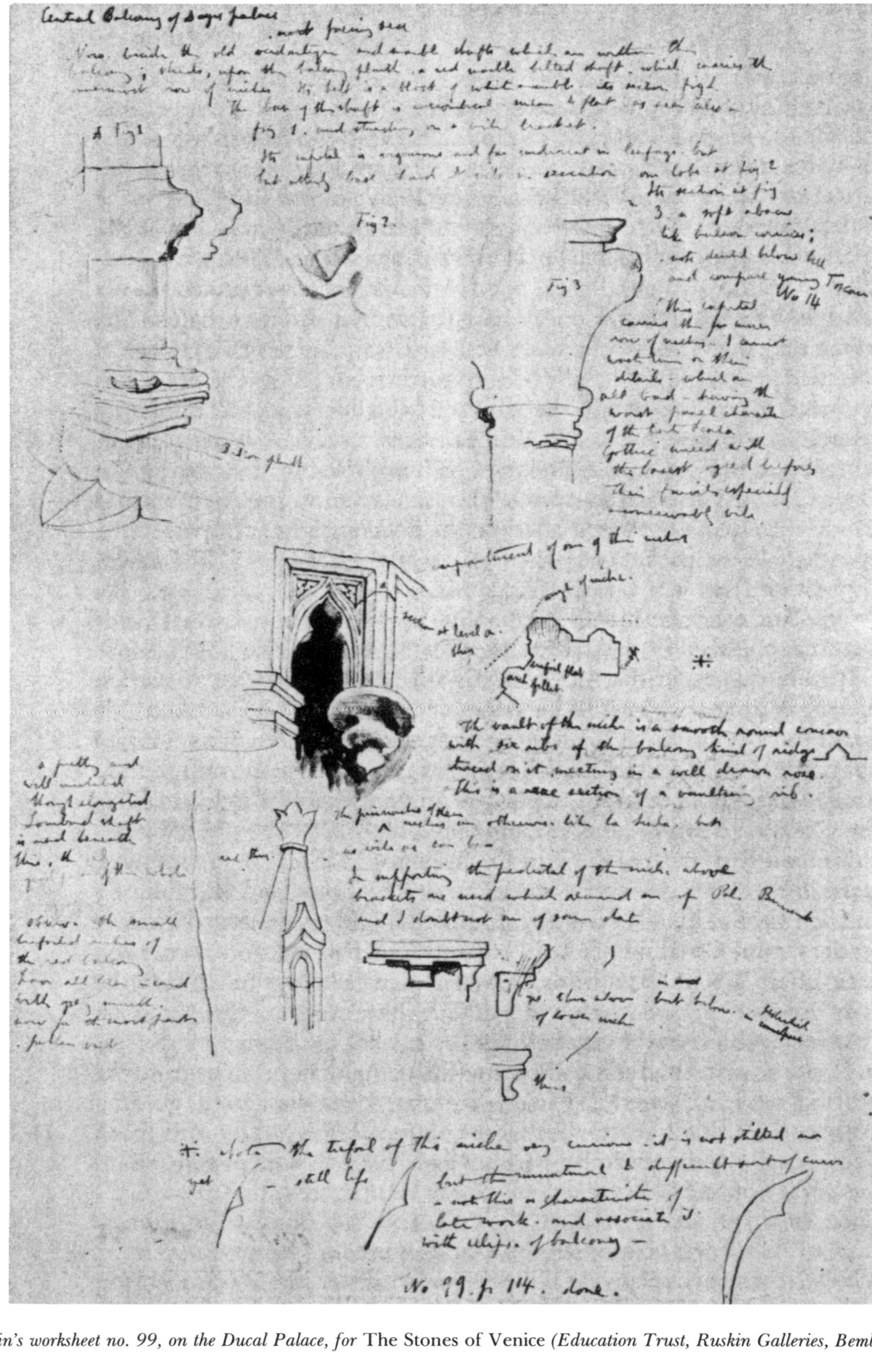

Ruskin's worksheet no. 99, on the Ducal Palace, for The Stones of Venice *(Education Trust, Ruskin Galleries, Bembridge)*

Self-caricature by Ruskin (by permission of the Trustees of The Pierpont Morgan Library)

professional man was. *"Unto this Last"* was published in four articles in consecutive issues of *Cornhill Magazine* and *Harper's New Monthly Magazine* (New York) in 1860, before the series was stopped by the editor. The essays were gathered into a book in 1862 and a second edition appeared in 1877.

The articles caused a fierce outcry when they first appeared, but the volume has been one of Ruskin's most frequently republished and most influential books. Written in a clear, straightforward prose, the articles lay out a theory of a just wage and a just price, exalting the merchant as a person who devotes his life to supplying the needs of his community.

In 1862 and 1863 Ruskin published a sequel to *"Unto this Last"* under the heading "Essays on Political Economy." They appeared in four issues of *Fraser's Magazine,* and, once again, the editor halted the series. Gathered into a volume, *Munera Pulveris,* in 1872, these pieces attack the law of supply and demand as a way of determining wages and prices and attempt to redefine elementary economic concepts such as wealth, value, and money.

In 1864 Ruskin's father died. In December of that year he delivered two lectures, one week apart, at the Town Hall in Manchester. The two lectures, "Of Kings' Treasuries" and "Of Queens' Gardens," were published together the following year under the title *Sesame and Lilies.* The first lecture was delivered in connection with a fund-raising effort to establish a library, an occasion that allowed Ruskin to move away from the subjects that had occupied him for twenty years.

He had tried to change people's taste in art; he had tried to point the way toward a reformation in society itself. The first Manchester lecture provided an opportunity to step back from controversy—and to talk about books. Bad books are a terrible waste of time, he said, but good books are precisely the most precious possessions of a nation. The wisdom and moral training found in good books are essential to the stability of the state.

The occasion of the second lecture was to raise funds for schools and Ruskin addressed himself to the education of women. If man needed wisdom and moral strength, what did women need? His answer was that women needed to learn the same things that men did (with the exception of theology!) and that their training should issue in the virtues of justice and mercy. The ideal kingdom would then be ruled by men and women, kings and queens, of strong character, fortified by the virtues of wisdom, justice, and charity.

1865. The third lecture, "War," was privately printed in 1866, the year that the complete volume was published. A fourth lecture, "The Future of England," was delivered in 1869 and added to the 1873 edition. In these lectures Ruskin offers a choice of pagan or Christian ethics. If the ostensibly Christian businessmen of England need a reason for abandoning their economic theories and replacing them with justice and charity, Ruskin promises them that their reward will be eternal life in Heaven. He knows that his audience may well regard this kind of talk as frothy nonsense to be listened to with patience only on Sunday morning and so pursues his point: if eternal life is not a sufficient reward, do these things as the ancient Romans did them—that you may be honored among your friends. Let your reward be a crown of wild olive placed upon your head. This is, of course, the ironic message of a man who has despaired of ever conveying his message to the middle class.

Ruskin wanted to reach that class because he was a member of it. His father was a merchant who loved the arts and was an honorable man. Ruskin wanted to show that a merchant who cared about his employees and felt a responsibility toward the community could be held in honor the way a

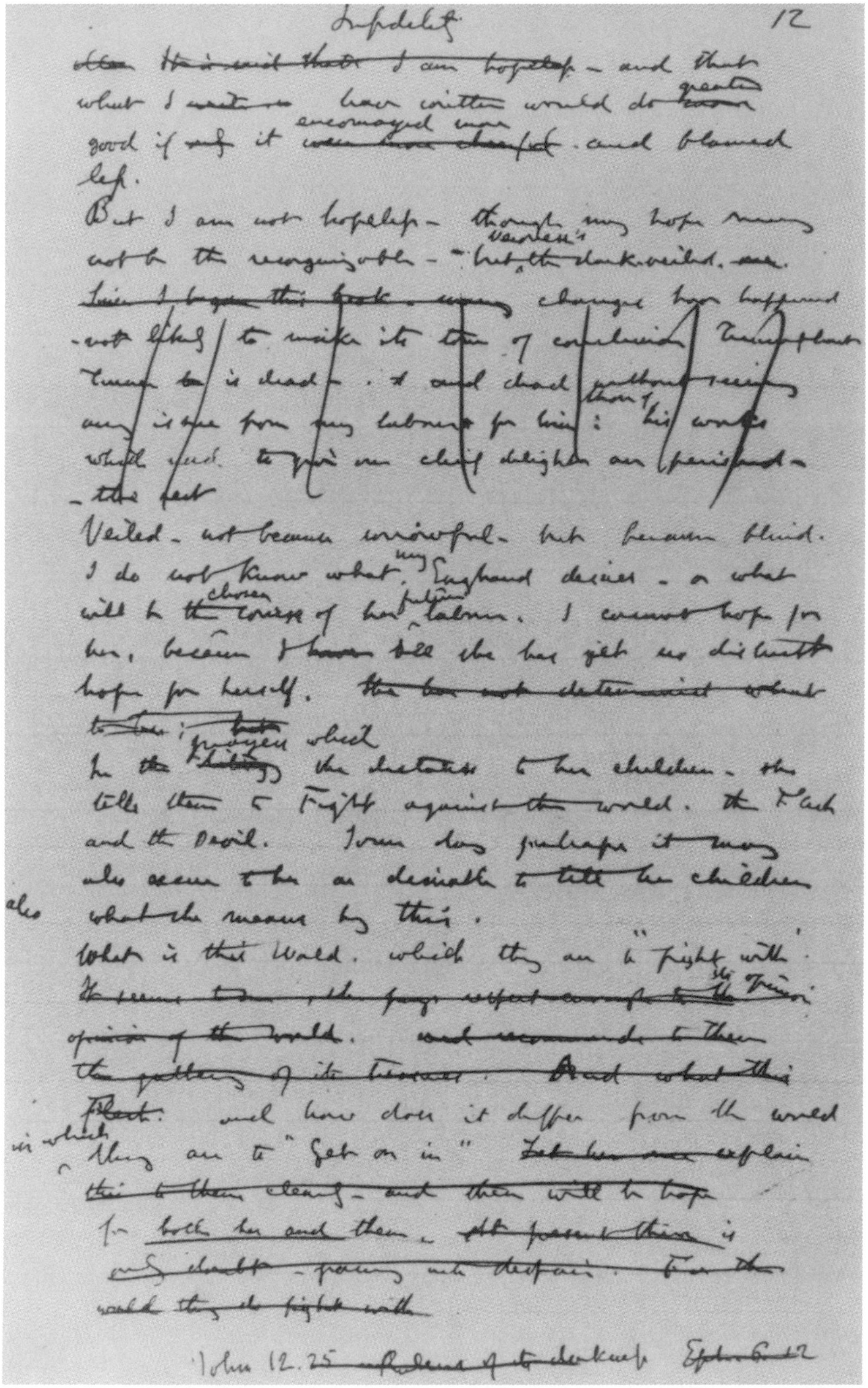

Infidelity 12

– and that what I have written would do greater good if it encouraged more – and blamed less.

But I am not hopeless – though my hope may not be the recognizable – but the dark-veiled.

Veiled – not because sorrowful – but because blind. I do not know what my England desires – or what will be the chosen course of her future labour. I cannot hope for her, because till she has got no distinct hope for herself.

In the prayer which she dictates to her children – she tells them to Fight against the world. the Flesh and the Devil. Some day perhaps it may also occur to her as desirable to tell her children also what she means by this.

What is that World. which they are to "fight with".

and how does it differ from the world in which they are to "Get on in"

for both her and them.

John 12.25

Page from the manuscript for the final chapter of Modern Painters, *volume five (by permission of the Trustees of The Pierpont Morgan Library)*

Drawing by Ruskin of Rose La Touche, the young Irish girl, thirty years his junior, to whom he proposed marriage in 1866 (Education Trust, Ruskin Galleries, Bembridge)

The lectures represent a tendency that surfaced in the later chapters of *Modern Painters,* volume five. When Ruskin studied Turner's paintings of mythological subjects, he began to organize his own thoughts in mythic terms. He had begun to see Turner as a painter of the fallen world and all art as a struggle to overcome the chaos of that world. The great Venetians, he believed, strove mightily to achieve the redemption of that world but, because their religion was ultimately false, they failed. "Of Kings' Treasuries" is an account of human wisdom, the best that can be achieved in the fallen world, the world of the Old Testament, of King Solomon. "Of Queens' Gardens" presents a Garden of Eden, where woman, or the female principle, presides over the world of the New Testament, redeemed by Love and ruled by Christ.

Sesame and Lilies was Ruskin's most popular work. It went through twenty editions in forty years and is still republished from time to time. In 1868 he delivered a third lecture, this time in Dublin, which was added to the 1871 edition of *Sesame and Lilies.* He had become a very popular lecturer. More than two thousand tickets were sold to this lecture, "On the Mystery of Life and its Arts." The address is, in some ways, a sad one, for Ruskin had concluded that neither literature nor art really mattered very much. But there is no bitterness in this conclusion. He simply says that man's efforts might be better spent in feeding the hungry, clothing the naked, and housing the shelterless—those things upon which, according to Matthew's Gospel, we shall finally be judged.

Going to Ireland to deliver the lecture must have been a bittersweet occasion for Ruskin. In 1858 he had begun giving drawing lessons to a nine-year-old Irish girl named Rose La Touche. Rose was beautiful, sickly, and talented, and Ruskin, over the next six or seven years, fell hopelessly in love with her. On her seventeenth birthday, when he was forty-seven, he proposed marriage. Rose asked him to wait until she was twenty-one, or at least until she reached nineteen, to which Ruskin agreed. Her parents, however, were understandably concerned. It was not only Ruskin's age but also his former marriage and his new irreligion that distressed them. They did what they could to break off the relationship and the resulting uncertainty deeply troubled Ruskin for the next ten years until, in 1875, at the age of twenty-seven, Rose died. Her memory haunted Ruskin for the rest of his life.

In 1865 Ruskin was invited to address the Royal Institute of Architects on the study of architecture in the schools. These practicing architects regarded him as an unpractical theorist, but it is significant that they did invite him to address them. He told them that they had taken but half his message. He had freed them from the tyranny of classical art, and they had achieved the ugliness of Gothic without its freedom. Beginning in 1865 he also published "The Cestus of Aglaia," a collection of articles on the laws of art, which appeared in the *Art Journal.*

Since 1857 Ruskin had been visiting a girls' school at Winnington Hall, Cheshire. It is clear that Ruskin enjoyed these visits with the girls, who were a pleasant change from his students at the Working Men's College. The result of his time at Winnington Hall was *The Ethics of the Dust* (1866), a series of ten lectures, more or less about mineralogy, in the form of a dialogue with a group of girls. Public reception of Ruskin's book was mixed. A reviewer of *The Ethics of the Dust* in *Saturday Review,* 30 December 1865, found it "whimsical, incongruous, and silly beyond all measure." The critic for the *Guardian,* 21 February 1866, reported that "Mr. Ruskin appears to unusual advantage; playful, allegorical, and dramatic as well as instructive."

Ruskin remained in the thick of British intellectual life. In 1867 he was invited to give the Rede Lecture at Cambridge, where he received an honorary degree. The address, entitled "On the Relation of National Ethics to National Arts," was a summary of previous writings and remarks. After a brief period of discouragement, Ruskin plunged into the serious study of mythology which had its beginnings in *Modern Painters,* volume five, and *Sesame and Lilies.* He knew Max Müller, at Oxford, and he knew the work of James Fergusson. His objective was to use primitive myths of earth and air as a way of perceiving the natural world as it appeared to ancient man. To understand this primitive view of nature and then to trace its development as it is reflected in the development of mythologies would be, Ruskin reasoned, a way to understand contemporary man's relation to nature.

It was evident that this kind of learning would have expanded enormously Ruskin's understanding of landscape painting, and he regretted that he had not had these insights when he had written *Modern Painters,* volume two, especially the chapters on "Typical Beauty." He produced *The Queen of the Air: Being a Study of the Greek Myths of Cloud and Storm* in 1869. It was to have been followed by a companion volume on Greek earth myths, but this work was never completed. The 1869 volume is vintage Ruskin—discursive and filled with brilliant insights—and it was also well received. Carlyle wrote Ruskin on 17 August 1869: "No such Book have I met with for long years past"; the critic for the *Westminster Review,* October 1869, similarly offered praise: "we are inclined to call this the most brilliant and successful piece of interpretation to which any set of Hellenic myths have been subjected in England since the discoveries of philologists have set interpreters on the right road." In a private letter Ruskin said of it, "It is the best I ever wrote; . . . it is the most useful and careful piece I have done."

In Ruskin's principal economic books, *Unto this Last, Munera Pulveris,* and *The Crown of Wild Olive,* he had developed a devastating criticism of capitalism. He contradicted its theories and exposed the miserable lives of the working people that had been its fruit. These studies were collections of articles and lectures designed for the middle class, the winners in the economy. In 1867, however, Ruskin sought another audience—the working man. He wrote twenty-five letters addressed to "a Working Man of Sunderland" which were published over a period of two months in newspapers in two of the great industrial cities, Leeds and Manchester. In the same year they were collected in a book entitled *Time and Tide.* In these letters Ruskin showed himself to be close to the thought of Thomas Carlyle, Matthew Arnold, and the Christian Socialists. That is, he was profoundly critical of capitalism, its injustices and the squalor in which the poor were forced to live, but he drew back from supporting communist or socialist revolutions. As a group, these Victorian thinkers urged instead the moral reformation of owners and workers in order to bring about a just society. They mistrusted the mob and bureaucracy alike and saw this conversion as society's hope.

In 1868 a Mr. Felix Slade bequeathed a sum of money for the endowment of Slade professorships in fine art at the universities of Oxford and Cambridge and at University College, London. Ruskin was the unanimous choice of the electors to fill the chair at Oxford. He gave his inaugural lecture in February 1870 and began a period of intense activity. He delivered twelve courses of lectures at Oxford, all of which were published. He organized the university's art collection. He started a drawing school. He saw himself as a kind of professor of beauty, so he lectured and wrote on botany, on geology, and on ornithology. He founded a museum. He wrote guidebooks for the use of travelers in Florence and Venice.

Ruskin took rooms at Corpus Christi College and worked actively with the students. On one occasion he involved the young Alfred Milner, Arnold Toynbee, and Oscar Wilde, among others, in an arduous road-building project. It was his view that strong and healthy young men of the upper classes, instead of playing games, should try manual labor. He thought that they might get just as much exercise and, at the same time, learn about life. In spite of this activity at the university, Ruskin did not abandon his commitment to social reformation. During the years of his professorship he produced one pamphlet per month addressed to the working men of England. These ninety-six "letters" were eventually published together in the multivolumed *Fors Clavigera* (1871-1884). He also involved himself in practical projects—cleaning the streets, selling tea at honest prices, and the forming of his Guild of St. George.

A chronological account of his writing during this period is impossible because he worked on

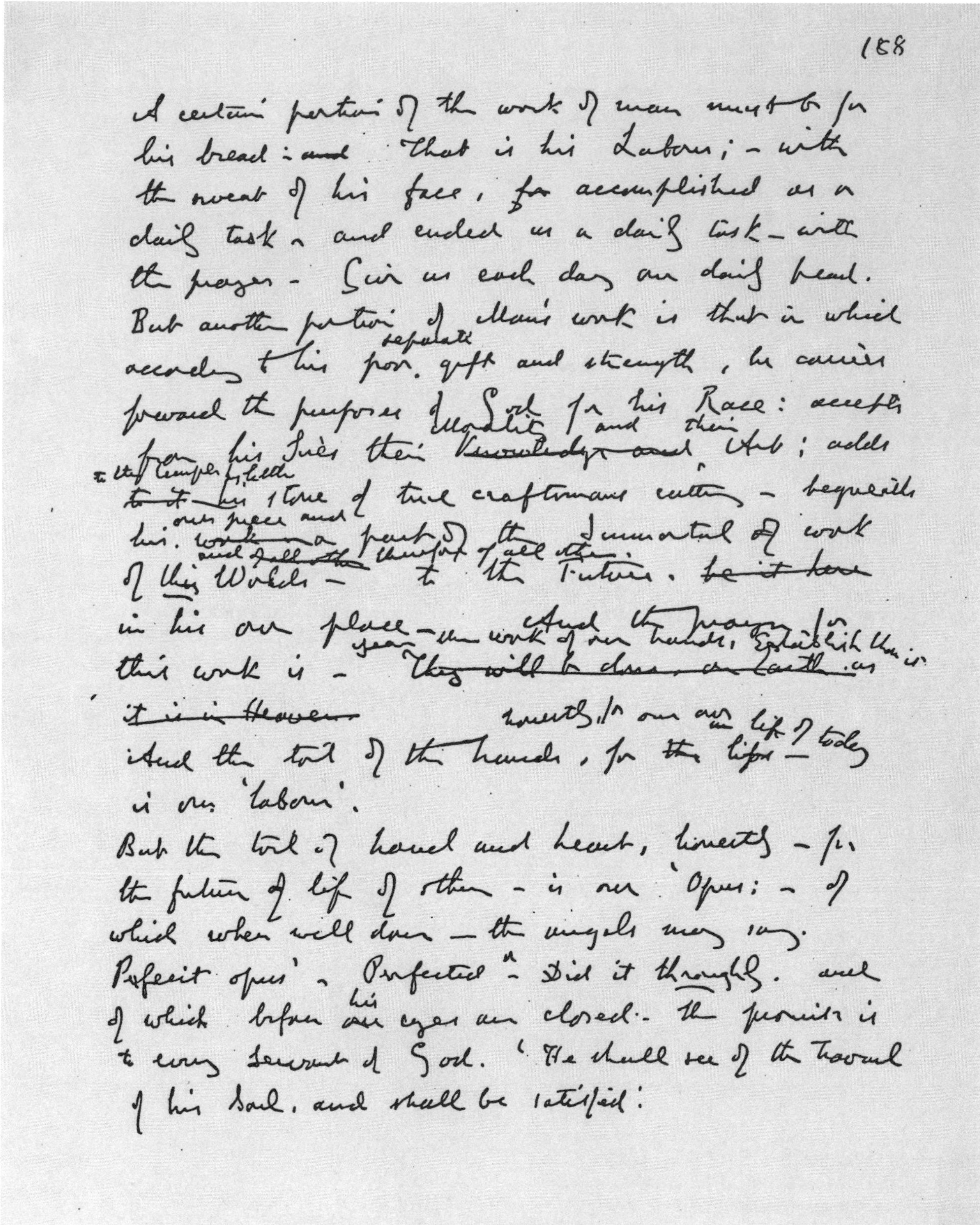
158

A certain portion of the work of man must be for his bread: — That is his Labour; — with the sweat of his face, be accomplished as a daily task — and ended as a daily task — with the prayer — Give us each day our daily bread.

But another portion of Man's work is that in which according to his separate pow. gift and strength, he carries forward the purposes of God for his Race: accepts from his Sires their Morality and their Art; adds to the temple of the ... his stone of true craftsman's cutting — bequeaths his own place and a part of the immortal of work of this World — to the Future.

in his own place — And the prayer for this work is — ... as it is in Heaven.

And the toil of the hands, for the life — for our own life of today is our 'Labour'.

But the toil of hand and heart, honestly — for the future of life of others — is our 'Opus'; — of which when well done — the angels may say. 'Perfecit opus' — "Perfected" — Did it thoroughly. and of which before his eyes are closed — the promise is to every Servant of God. 'He shall see of the travail of his Soul, and shall be satisfied.'

Page from the manuscript for Fors Clavigera, *Ruskin's series of ninety-six "letters" to the working men of England (W. G. Collingwood,* The Life and Work of John Ruskin, *1893)* everything at once. "Head too full, and don't know which to write first," he wrote in his diary in 1872. In 1875 he calculated that he had seven large books in press at the same time. His mother died in 1871, at the age of ninety; Rose La Touche died in 1875. It is not surprising that Ruskin suffered a severe physical and mental collapse in 1878.

Ruskin served three three-year terms as professor of fine arts, from 1870 to 1879. His lectures were models of orderly presentation in which he undertook to distill the work of a lifetime for systematic presentation to students. He later remarked that the "lectures were the most important piece of my literary work done with unabated power, best motive, and happiest concurrence of circumstance." At Oxford he had found, again, a new audience. He did not give up on the working class; he continued to address them on economic and social matters, but he had decided, as he put it in his inaugural lecture, that the sons of the nobility and gentry were best able to love landscape. This remark may have been designed to encourage his students, but he was noting a phenomenon that more recent history confirms. The love of landscape is an urban phenomenon. It coincides with the rise of great industrial cities. The laborer struggling to plow a field or to haul a load over a mountain does not enjoy the view, and people, in truth, come to treasure natural beauty only as they are in danger of destroying it. Ruskin, however, surmised that a love of beauty developed only in homes where the arts were honored, where music and the fine arts flourished. He also believed that love of landscape required a sense of history, an awareness of the human life that has passed over a scene.

In his second lecture at Oxford, "The Relation of Art to Religion," he wrestled once more with what for him were difficult questions. First, what role does religion play as a cause of art? Second, what effect does art have upon religion? His answer to the first question was simple: religious inspiration does not directly affect art. The second problem was more difficult, and in his attempt at resolution Ruskin's Evangelical heritage surfaces. Religious painting, Ruskin holds, does realize and make concrete religious doctrine, and this is good, but it also circumscribes the religious event in place and time. This is one of the two standard objections to religious art. The other is temptation to idolatry.

He continued his series of inaugural lectures with "The Relation of Art to Morals" and "The Relation of Art to Use." In the first he asserted that immorality was the love of chaos and the love of self. All bad art comes from these misguided allegiances. Morality is the love of life, of order, and of something outside the self. All good art, assuming, of course, technical competence, flows from these moral instincts. The second of these lectures can be summarized in Ruskin's phrase: "[Art] gives Form to knowledge and Grace to utility." The second series of Oxford lectures delivered in the fall term 1870, published as *Aratra Pentelici* (1872), are devoted to sculpture. In these Ruskin began with consideration of a breakfast plate, its structure and decoration, and developed a full series of addresses on Greek and Florentine sculpture, contending in a magnificent summary that "Art is the contest of life with clay."

These first two series of lectures were delivered to large audiences, including many from outside the university. In the spring 1871 term, however, Ruskin changed his forum. For this series on landscape he limited attendance to students enrolled in his course so that his work on art might be integrated into the university studies. Because he addressed a smaller gathering he was able to

Ruskin in 1874, photographed by Lewis Carroll

distribute examples of art and lift his own burden of having to prepare so many formal lectures directed toward large audiences. The spring 1871 talks were not published until many years later, as *Lectures on Landscape* (1897). The thesis of this volume is that nature is only significant in terms of its relation to human life. An interest in nature that is limited to its colors and its forms, or to the science of it, is inferior. An erupting volcano is significant, not because of its aesthetic qualities and not because it exemplifies principles of evaporation and gravity, but because it is dangerous and lethal to men.

The series of ten lectures which Ruskin delivered in the spring term 1872, and had published that year as *The Eagle's Nest,* is as subtle and complicated as anything he ever wrote. His intention was to show the place of art in the university program by relating it to the end of a university. He argues that it is the place of art to serve knowledge. It records and makes vivid the passions of men. Great art records the "right things" so that, paradoxically, the art will be forgotten as men are led to contemplate those right things. *Val D'Arno* (1874), a collection of the fall 1873 lectures, is a series of studies of Tuscan art in relation to the history of Florence. The lectures deal mainly with architecture and are not much different from Ruskin's writing in *The Stones of Venice* except that they develop no broad social thesis.

In the spring of 1874 Ruskin went abroad, but he returned for the fall semester and offered a series of lectures which were published under the title "The Aesthetic and Mathematical Schools of Art in Florence," first collected in the Library Edition of his works. In these talks Ruskin distinguishes between those who draw the appearance of things and those who draw from measurements. He taught the latter as a beginner's technique, but always regarded it as just that. In his explanation of what he calls the aesthetic school, his position is not far from that of the impressionists, who were flourishing by this time in Paris, and even in London.

During his university years, Ruskin also began work on a number of technical studies. They include *Ariadne Florentina* (1873-1876) and *The Laws of Fésole* (1877-1879), which are about engraving and drawing. He also produced *Love's Meinie* (1873), *Deucalion* (1875-1883), and *Proserpina* (1875-1886), on ornithology, geology, and botany. Ruskin's approach to natural history was, first, to look carefully at an object, and then to attempt to discover what had been thought about it by wise men throughout history. Hence a vital part of Ruskin's studies of natural objects is his investigations of the myths that had grown up around those objects. While he was at the university Ruskin also prepared notes and prefaces for new editions of *Modern Painters* and of *The Stones of Venice.*

In 1878 Ruskin suffered his severe breakdown. In letter number seventy-nine of *Fors Clavigera,* dated 18 June 1877, Ruskin had made some adverse comments on one of Whistler's paintings. Whistler sued for libel and the case came to trial in 1878. Ruskin was not well enough to attend, and he lost the case. The jury found for Whistler, but awarded him only one farthing in damages. Ruskin used the verdict as an occasion to resign his professorship in 1879. This episode marked the virtual end to his public life. He did, however, continue to produce the pamphlets published as *Fors Clavigera* until 1884. The literary interest in these "letters" comes from the fact that they contain a vein of ironic writing as rich as any to be found in Victorian England. Ruskin's target is the merchants who had been deaf to his calls to honor and to conscience.

After 1879 Ruskin gave much money and what energy he had to the Guild of St. George. This group which he founded was to be a kind of commune. The members were to farm, do light manufacturing, and educate their children according to the principles which he had laid down. Although attempts were made by zealous followers to begin such enterprises as far away as Australia and the United States, the project never really got off the ground, though the guild did successfully establish a small educational museum in Sheffield.

In 1883 Ruskin accepted reappointment to his professorship at Oxford. His lectures, published as *The Art of England* (1883-1884), are appreciations of whatever he could find to praise in contemporary British art. He praised Sir Edwin Landseer, Hunt, Rossetti, and some illustrators of children's books. It was his own practice, and he urged it upon all who heard him, to buy only the work of living artists.

Ruskin developed in his last years a keen awareness that the new industrialism was polluting the air and the water and thus ruining the architecture and the frescoes that had survived for centuries. In 1884 he delivered a lecture entitled "The Storm-Cloud of the Nineteenth Century" in which he complained that the atmosphere had changed during his lifetime. The lecture is elegantly structured and supported, but it was ridiculed at the time. Ruskin was a keen and practiced observer of light and clouds and it is now clear that he was

Ruskin's study at Brantwood, the Coniston country home he purchased in 1871

correct in his concerns. To save what he could, Ruskin turned to the writing of historical sketches. One of the best is *"Our Fathers Have Told Us"* (1880-1885), or *The Bible of Amiens* as it is known, a full exposition of the cathedral at Amiens. He produced *St. Mark's Rest* (1877-1884) and *The Pleasures of England* (1884-1885) in the same vein. They represent his attempts to get at the root myths and legends of Christian Europe, and thus of Christian art.

Ruskin began to produce his autobiography, *Praeterita,* in 1885, and it appeared intermittently until 1889. It is a charming, if selective, account of his life. It does not, for example, mention his marriage, but it more than fulfills Ruskin's promise in the subtitle to provide an "Outline of Scenes and Thoughts Perhaps Worthy of Memory in My Past Life." Ruskin had frequent attacks of both physical and mental illness between 1879 and 1889. In 1871 he had bought a country home, Brantwood, at Coniston which he occupied when his schedule permitted. In 1889 he finally retired there and lived quietly, in the care of a young relative, until his death on 20 January 1900.

Ruskin's early works, in the 1840s, were vigorously attacked in the established journals, while the newer, more moderate journals were often favorable. Often a reviewer simply reflected his own estimate of Turner, rather than of Ruskin. However, Ruskin was reviewed widely and, while still in his twenties, he was clearly a strong presence in the rather limited world of art criticism. In the 1850s his valiant defense of the Pre-Raphaelites cost him dearly in the art world, but *The Stones of Venice* was an achievement too massive to dismiss. His works were reviewed in a range of publications, from prominent quarterlies to daily newspapers. Reviews were mixed, but Ruskin was a powerful cultural influence all over England. The 1860s were the years of his lectures on social and economic subjects. Most of the press attacked him as a man out of his field, but he had his defenders, and he had a large popular following. His tenure as professor of fine art at Oxford, at least until his breakdown in 1878, must be judged as a brilliant success.

As the century closed, Ruskin's reputation as an art critic declined. The Pre-Raphaelites fell out of favor and, although he had only championed them because they were the best painters working at the time in England, Ruskin's reputation suffered with theirs. He had missed the impressionist developments in France, and the rise of the art-for-art's-sake school made Ruskin's work seem out of date.

In spite of the magnificent Library Edition, which appeared from 1903-1912, Ruskin, along with many Victorian writers, was no longer widely read by the early twentieth century. When he was read at all, it was for his social criticism. He influenced Gandhi, Tolstoy, and many members of the early British Labour Party. In the United States, where a cigar was named in his honor, he was remembered as a friend of the working man.

Important studies of Ruskin began to appear again in the 1930s and 1940s. Much of this interest was stimulated by new information about his marriage, his loves, and his breakdown. Some of this information was simply sensational, but much of it was genuinely illuminating. Since 1950 there has been a steady stream, in both England and the United States, of biographies, studies, and editions of individual works. Though the most recent academic work on Ruskin is vigorous, much of it follows paths already marked. Studies based on Ruskin's economic, social, or political views are still scarce, although Robert Hewison's 1981 collection of critical essays by various hands contains a number of contributions in this area.

Ruskin and his lifelong friend Henry Acland at Brantwood, August 1893

Jeanne Clegg's *Ruskin and Venice* (1981) is a narrowly focused, very competent study of the absolutely central episode in Ruskin's life and work—the four years he spent in Venice living out his marriage and writing *The Stones of Venice*—but *Modern Painters* continues to attract most of the scholars. Elizabeth K. Helsinger's *Ruskin and the Art of the Beholder* (1982) is a valuable work in which the author traces the shifts of aesthetics and criticism that occurred in England during Ruskin's lifetime and shows his relationship to these changes, some of which he reflected and some of which he caused. Helsinger also brings to Ruskin criticism some of the insights into the role of the reader and viewer of a work of art that have been developed by recent literary criticism. Gary Wihl's *Ruskin and the Rhetoric of Infallibility* (1985) attempts to impose a large pattern on Ruskin's criticism. This task has always proved difficult and is never entirely successful, but this study has the merit of dealing with many works that are usually neglected. A more recent volume which approaches in a fruitful way the challenge of finding order in Ruskin's thought is Paul L. Sawyer's *Ruskin's Poetic Argument: The Design of the Major Works* (1985). A less traditional approach which is stimulating but offers its own difficulties is Jay Fellows's *Ruskin's Maze: Mastery and Madness in His Art* (1981). Two recent collections of essays on Ruskin offer a similar contrast. Robert E. Rhodes and Del Ivan Janik's *Studies in Ruskin* (1982) is a festschrift honoring Professor Van Akin Burd, the editor of several volumes of Ruskin letters. The essays follow the lines of traditional scholarship. John Dixon Hunt and Faith Holland's *The Ruskin Polygon: Essays on the Imagination of John Ruskin* (1982), in contrast, explores less-well-trodden paths.

It is in biography that we may expect important developments. There was a spate of Ruskin biographies between 1949 and 1954; then there was a pause for twenty years. During these years scholars devoted their energies to the editing and publishing of the diaries and of the great bulk of Ruskin's letters. Now that this material is available, new biographers will be able to take full advantage of these sources.

Two solid new biographies have appeared, John Dixon Hunt's *The Wider Sea: A Life of John Ruskin* (1982) and Tim Hilton's *John Ruskin: The Early Years* (1985), the first part of a projected two-volume work. In summary, Ruskin's reputation has risen with the general increase in interest in Victorian literature. He has no popular following anymore, but those who have ranged widely through his books can assert that his is a blazing genius of the Victorian age.

Letters:

Hortus Inclusus: Messages from the Wood to the Garden, Sent in Happy Days to the Sister Ladies of the Thwaite, Coniston, edited by Albert Fleming (Orpington: George Allen, 1887; New York: Wiley, 1887);

Letters of John Ruskin to Charles Eliot Norton, edited by Charles Eliot Norton, 2 volumes (Boston & New York: Houghton, Mifflin, 1905);

John Ruskin's Letters to Francesca and Memoirs of the Alexanders, edited by Lucia Gray Swett (Boston: Lothrop, Lee & Shepard, 1931);

The Gulf of Years: Letters from John Ruskin to Kathleen Olander, edited by Rayner Unwin (London: Allen & Unwin, 1953);

Ruskin's Letters from Venice, 1851-1852, edited by John L. Bradley (New Haven: Yale University Press, 1955);

Letters of John Ruskin to Lord and Lady Mount-Temple, edited by Bradley (Columbus: Ohio State University, 1964);

Dearest Mama Talbot, edited by Margaret Spence (London: Allen & Unwin, 1966);

The Winnington Letters, edited by Van Akin Burd (Cambridge: Harvard University Press, 1969);

Ruskin in Italy: Letters to His Parents, 1845, edited by Harold I. Shapiro (Oxford: Clarendon Press, 1972);

Sublime and Instructive, edited by Virginia Surtees (London: Joseph, 1972);

The Ruskin Family Letters, edited by Burd, 2 volumes (Ithaca & London: Cornell University Press, 1973);

John Ruskin and Alfred Hunt, edited by Robert Secor (Victoria, B.C.: University of Victoria, 1982);

The Correspondence of Thomas Carlyle and John Ruskin, edited by George Allan Cate (Stanford: Stanford University Press, 1982).

Bibliographies:

Thomas J. Wise and James P. Smart, *A Complete Bibliography of the Writings in Prose and Verse of John Ruskin, LL.D.,* 2 volumes (London: Privately printed, 1893);

Kirk H. Beetz, *John Ruskin: A Bibliography, 1900-1974* (Metuchen, N.J.: Scarecrow Press, 1976).

Biographies:

W. G. Collingwood, *The Life and Work of John Ruskin,* 2 volumes (London: Methuen, 1893);

E. T. Cook, *The Life of John Ruskin,* 2 volumes (London: Allen, 1911);

Derrick Leon, *Ruskin: The Great Victorian* (London: Routledge & Kegan Paul, 1949);

Peter Quennell, *John Ruskin: The Portrait of a Prophet* (New York: Viking, 1949);

Joan Evans, *John Ruskin* (London: Cape, 1954);

John L. Bradley, *An Introduction to Ruskin* (Boston: Houghton Mifflin, 1971);

John Dixon Hunt, *The Wider Sea: A Life of John Ruskin* (New York: Viking, 1982);

Tim Hilton, *John Ruskin: The Early Years* (New Haven: Yale University Press, 1985).

References:

Joan Abse, *John Ruskin, The Passionate Moralist* (New York: Knopf, 1981);

Quentin Bell, *Ruskin* (Edinburgh: Oliver & Boyd, 1963);

A. C. Benson, *Ruskin: A Study in Personality* (London: Smith, Elder, 1911; New York: Putnam's, 1911);

John L. Bradley, ed., *Ruskin: The Critical Heritage* (London: Routledge & Kegan Paul, 1984);

Van Akin Burd, "Another Light on the Writing of *Modern Painters,*" *Publications of the Modern Language Association,* 68 (September 1953): 755-763;

Burd, "Background to *Modern Painters:* The Tradition and the Turner Controversy," *Publications of the Modern Language Association,* 74 (June 1959): 254-267;

Burd, "Ruskin's Defense of Turner: The Imitative Phase," *Philological Quarterly,* 37 (October 1958): 465-483;

Burd, "Ruskin's Quest for a Theory of Imagination," *Modern Language Quarterly,* 17 (March 1956): 60-72;

Kenneth Clark, *Ruskin at Oxford* (Oxford: Clarendon Press, 1947);

Jeanne Clegg, *Ruskin and Venice* (London: Junction Books, 1981);

Charles T. Dougherty, "Of Ruskin's Gardens," in *Myth and Symbol,* by Northrop Frye, L. C. Knights, and others (Lincoln: University of Nebraska, 1963), pp. 141-151;

Dougherty, "Ruskin's Moral Argument," *Victorian Newsletter,* no. 9 (Spring 1956): 4-7;

Dougherty, "Ruskin's Views on Non-Representational Art," *College Art Journal,* 15 (Winter 1955): 112-118;

John T. Fain, *Ruskin and the Economists* (Nashville: Vanderbilt University Press, 1956);

Jay Fellows, *Ruskin's Maze: Mastery and Madness in His Art* (Princeton: Princeton University Press, 1981);

Raymond E. Fitch, *The Poison Sky: Myth and Apocalypse in Ruskin* (Athens: Ohio University Press, 1982);

Kristine Ottesen Garrigan, *Ruskin on Architecture* (Madison: University of Wisconsin Press, 1973);

Katharine Gilbert, "Ruskin's Relation to Aristotle," *Philosophical Review,* 49 (1940): 52-62;

Sister Mary Dorothea Goetz, *A Study of Ruskin's Concept of the Imagination* (Washington, D.C.: Catholic University of America Press, 1947);

Frederic Harrison, *John Ruskin* (New York: Macmillan, 1902);

Elizabeth K. Helsinger, *Ruskin and the Art of the Beholder* (Cambridge: Harvard University Press, 1982);

Robert Hewison, *John Ruskin: The Argument of the Eye* (Princeton: Princeton University Press, 1976);

Hewison, ed., *New Approaches to Ruskin: Thirteen Essays* (London: Routledge & Kegan Paul, 1981);

J. A. Hobson, *John Ruskin: Social Reformer* (Boston: Estes, 1898);

John Dixon Hunt and Faith Holland, eds., *The Ruskin Polygon: Essays on the Imagination of John Ruskin* (Manchester: Manchester University Press, 1982);

Sir William James, *John Ruskin and Effie Gray* (New York: Scribners, 1947);

Henry Ladd, *The Victorian Morality of Art* (New York: Long & Smith, 1932);

George P. Landow, *The Aesthetic and Critical Theories of John Ruskin* (Princeton: Princeton University Press, 1971);

Landow, "Ruskin's Refutation of False Opinions Held Concerning Beauty," *British Journal of Aesthetics,* 8 (1968): 60-72;

Landow, "Ruskin's Versions of 'Ut Pictura Poesis,' " *Journal of Aesthetics and Art Criticism,* 26 (1968): 521-528;

David Larg, *John Ruskin* (London: Davis, 1932);

Alice Meynell, *John Ruskin* (New York: Dodd, Mead, 1900);

Robert E. Rhodes and Del Ivan Janik, eds., *Studies in Ruskin* (Athens: Ohio University Press, 1982);

John D. Rosenberg, *The Darkening Glass* (New York: Columbia University Press, 1961);

Rosenberg, "Style and Sensibility in Ruskin's Prose," in *The Art of Victorian Prose,* edited by George Levine and William Madden (New York: Oxford University Press, 1968), pp. 177-200;

Paul L. Sawyer, *Ruskin's Poetic Argument: The Design of the Major Works* (Ithaca: Cornell University Press, 1985);

James Clark Sherburne, *John Ruskin, or the Ambiguities of Abundance* (Cambridge: Harvard University Press, 1972);

William Smart, *A Disciple of Plato* (Glasgow: Wilson & McCormick, 1883);

Roger B. Stein, *John Ruskin and Aesthetic Thought in America, 1840-1900* (Cambridge: Harvard University Press, 1967);

Francis G. Townsend, "John Ruskin," in *Victorian Prose: A Guide to Research,* edited by David J. DeLaura (New York: Modern Language Association, 1973);

Townsend, *Ruskin and the Landscape Feeling: A Critical Analysis of His Thought During the Crucial Years of His Life, 1843-1860* (Urbana: University of Illinois Press, 1951);

Helen Gill Viljoen, *Ruskin's Scottish Heritage* (Urbana: University of Illinois Press, 1956);

Donald Wesling, "Ruskin and the Adequacy of Landscape," *Texas Studies in Literature and Language,* 9 (1967): 253-272;

J. Howard Whitehouse, *Vindication of Ruskin* (London: Allen & Unwin, 1950);

Gary Wihl, *Ruskin and the Rhetoric of Infallibility* (New Haven: Yale University Press, 1985);

R. H. Wilenski, *John Ruskin* (London: Faber & Faber, 1933).

Papers:

The Ruskin papers are scattered, but the major repositories are the Pierpont Morgan Library, in New York; the Beinecke Rare Book and Manuscript Library, at Yale University; the Ruskin Gallery at Bembridge School, Isle of Wight; and the John Rylands Library, Manchester.

Samuel Smiles

(23 December 1812-16 April 1904)

William B. Thesing
University of South Carolina

BOOKS: *Physical Education; or, the Nurture and Management of Children, Founded on the Study of Their Nature and Constitution* (Edinburgh: Oliver & Boyd, 1838; London & New York: Scott, 1905);

History of Ireland and the Irish People under the Government of England (London: Strange, 1844);

Railway Property: Its Conditions and Prospects (London: Wilson, 1849);

The Life of George Stephenson, Railway Engineer (London: Murray, 1857; revised and enlarged, London: Murray, 1857; Boston: Ticknor & Fields, 1858); revised and enlarged again as *The Lives of George and Robert Stephenson*, volume 3 of *Lives of the Engineers* (1862); enlarged again as *The Life of George Stephenson and of His Son Robert Stephenson; Comprising also a History of the Invention and Introduction of the Railway Locomotive* (London: Murray, 1868);

Self-Help; with Illustrations of Character and Conduct (London: Murray, 1859; Boston: Ticknor & Fields, 1860);

Workmen's Earnings, Strikes, and Savings (London: Murray, 1861);

Lives of the Engineers, with an Account of Their Principal Works: Comprising also a History of Inland Communication in Britain (3 volumes, London: Murray, 1861-1862; enlarged, 5 volumes, 1874);

Industrial Biography: Iron-Workers and Tool-Makers (London: Murray, 1863; Boston: Ticknor & Fields, 1864);

Lives of Boulton and Watt. Principally from the original Soho MSS. Comprising also a History of the Invention and Introduction of the Steam-Engine (London: Murray, 1865; Philadelphia: Lippincott, 1865);

The Huguenots; Their Settlements, Churches and Industries in England and Ireland (London: Murray, 1867; New York: Harper, 1867);

Character: A Book of Noble Characteristics (London: Murray, 1871; New York: Harper, 1872);

The Huguenots in France after the Revocation of the Edict of Nantes. With a Visit to the Country of the Vaudois (London: Strahan, 1873; New York: Harper, 1874);

Thrift: A Book of Domestic Counsel (London: Murray, 1875; New York: Harper, 1875);

Life of a Scotch Naturalist: Thomas Edward, Associate of the Linnean Society (London: Murray, 1876; New York: Harper, 1876);

Robert Dick: Baker of Thurso, Geologist and Botanist (London: Murray, 1878; New York: Harper, 1879);

George Moore: Merchant and Philanthropist (London & New York: Routledge, 1878);

Duty; with Illustrations of Courage, Patience, and Endurance (London: Murray, 1880; New York: Harper, 1880);

Samuel Smiles, portrait by Sir George Reid (National Portrait Gallery)

Men of Invention and Industry (London: Murray, 1884; New York: Harper, 1885);

Life and Labour; or, Characteristics of Men of Industry, Culture, and Genius (London: Murray, 1887; New York: Harper, 1888);

Jasmin: Barber, Poet, Philanthropist (London: Murray, 1891; New York: Harper, 1892);

A Publisher and His Friends. Memoir and Correspondence of the Late John Murray, with an Account of the Origin and Progress of the House, 1768-1843, 2 volumes (London: Murray, 1891);

Josiah Wedgwood, F.R.S.: His Personal History (London: Murray, 1894; New York: Harper, 1895);

Autobiography of Samuel Smiles, LL.D., edited by Thomas Mackay (London: Murray, 1905; New York: Dutton, 1905).

OTHER: Samuel Smiles, Jr., *A Boy's Voyage Round the World: Including a Residence in Victoria, and a Journey by Rail across North America,* edited by Smiles (London: Murray, 1871; New York: Harper, 1874);

James Nasmyth, Engineer, An Autobiography, edited by Smiles (London: Murray, 1883; New York: Harper, 1884).

Asa Briggs, the twentieth-century social critic and historian who has devoted the most attention to Samuel Smiles, sums up Smiles's general significance best: "Every society has its propagandists who try to persuade their fellow-citizens to develop a special kind of social character which will best serve the needs of the day. In mid-Victorian England one of the most important propagandists was Samuel Smiles, described by the editor of the *Autobiography* as 'the authorized and pious chronicler of the men who founded the industrial greatness of England.' . . . Where Carlyle meditated on the abbot Samson, Smiles told his stories—true stories of men like Josiah Wedgwood, William Lee, James Brindley, and George Stephenson. He saw that the everyday work of applied science had its romance, and he found his heroes among the engineers, the inventors, and the enterprisers." In addition to his contributions to industrial biography, he is remembered for the "gospel of work" that he propounded in *Self-Help* (1859), a guidebook to success and "getting on" that attained worldwide popularity in the Victorian period. As Asa Briggs points out, the sales of *Self-Help* "far exceeded those of the great nineteenth-century novels." Smiles is also of interest and importance because he touched so many spheres of Victorian life. At one time or another during his long life he was a biographer, essayist, historian, doctor, journalist, editor, social reformer, railway secretary, popular moralist and lecturer, and continental traveler.

He was born at Haddington, near Edinburgh, Scotland, on 23 December 1812, one of eleven children of Janet Wilson and Samuel Smiles, who was for many years a paper maker but in later life a general merchant. He was educated at Haddington grammar school, but on 6 November 1826, he began a five-year apprenticeship to a firm of medical practitioners in his native community. When one of the partners, Dr. Lewins, moved to Leith in 1829, Smiles accompanied him. He was allowed to attend classes during the early hours of the day at Edinburgh University, where he matriculated in late 1829. When his apprenticeship expired, he moved to Edinburgh and studied medicine. Although he and his family were deeply affected by the death of the elder Smiles during an 1832 cholera epidemic spread by poor sanitary conditions, Smiles nonetheless was able through diligent effort to earn his medical diploma on 6 November 1832. Even though the competition was intense in Haddington, he decided to work there as a general surgeon for a time. He complained that he answered calls from only the most impoverished and remote patients in the area. Soon he began devoting his time to delivering public lectures on chemistry and health conditions. He also contributed to weekly newspaper columns. His first published volume, which he financed, was *Physical Education; or, the Nurture and Management of Children, Founded on the Study of Their Nature and Constitution* (1838). Smiles realized that he needed to leave his native town in order to make a viable career. In the spring of 1838 he toured Europe. At Leyden he was examined and secured a specialized medical certificate. By the fall of 1838 he was back in England and later he recorded in his *Autobiography* (1905) his vivid first impressions of London: "I need not go through the sights I saw during my first visit to London. But it was not the 'sights' I saw, but the enormous size of London, that impressed me. I had been brought up in a country town where I knew everybody, even the cocks and hens running about the streets. Now I was in a great city of some three millions of people, where I was only a stray unit, knowing nobody. The busy throng of the streets, the rush of life through the thoroughfares, the tide of human necessity which rolled along from day to day, could not fail to excite my sense of wonder. London was a new world, unlike everything I had before seen, or even imagined. It filled my mind, and took possession of my being."

However, as he came in closer contact with the urban masses, he had some reservations: "I did not much admire the London crowd. They seemed loafers and idlers, not working men. . . . I kept clear of the crowd, and looked after my pockets." He soon took a trip to northern England to pay a memorable visit to Ebenezer Elliott, the Sheffield iron merchant and radical poet known as "The Corn-Law Rhymer." Smiles was named editor of the radical *Leeds Times* in November 1838. For the next decade, he was a political activist for liberal causes. He promoted working-class education, worked for an extension of the franchise and for the anti-corn-law movement. Throughout the 1840s he lectured to working-class audiences. Nevertheless, he refused to support the Chartist movement because he feared that it might incite violence. In 1842 he resigned as editor of the *Leeds Times* and devoted his full energies to popular writing and lecturing for the next three years.

On 7 December 1843, Smiles married Sarah Anne Holmes, the daughter of a Leeds contractor. Although she served as a faithful companion until her death in 1900, Smiles, with typical Victorian reticence, devoted only one paragraph of his *Autobiography* to his married life: "I never regretted my marriage. My wife and I were altogether united through life. I obtained a cheerful and affectionate companion, and I hope that she obtained a devoted and equally affectionate husband. But these are things over which we draw the curtain. The happiness of married life cannot be babbled about to all the world." The couple produced two sons and three daughters. Toward the end of 1845 Smiles was appointed assistant secretary of the Leeds and Thirsk railway. He maintained an association with various railway enterprises for the next two decades, his employment surviving many mergers and reorganizations. From 1854 to 1866 he served as secretary of South Eastern Railway; from 1866 to 1871 he was president of the National Provident Institution.

Smiles's literary writings are most usefully divided into four categories: inspirational and didactic collections of essays about the proper conduct of life; biographies of men of invention, industry, and science; history and travel books; and memoirs. *Self-Help* was the first of several didactic and inspirational books by Smiles. Although it had been rejected by six publishers, when John Murray brought it out in 1859 it quickly became Smiles's most-popular and best-known work. Its underlying philosophy is the principle of individualism: unless there is self-motivation and exertion, no law or institution can be of effective assistance. In fact, actions by these external agencies may even be hurtful or enfeebling. To Smiles, the function of government was restrictive; its primary service was to protect life, liberty, and property. "There is no power of law," he writes, "that can make the idle man industrious, the thriftless provident, or the drunken sober; though every individual can be each and all of these if he will, by the exercise of his own free powers of actions and self-denial." Smiles, however, warns against the mistake of looking for sudden or great turns in fortune. By presenting hundreds of capsule biographies, he shows how distinction and improvement can be attained through long-term discipline, patience, and perseverance. In his own words, "Success . . . can only be achieved through industry, practice, and study. . . ."

Surprising to some readers is Smiles's tendency to downplay the notion of "genius." In typical fashion, he musters quotations from various sources to arrive at a consensus definition of what he means by the term: "Some have even defined genius to be only common sense intensified. A distinguished teacher and president of a college spoke of it as the power of making efforts. John Foster held it to be the power of lighting one's own fire. Buffon said of genius—it is patience. . . . Newton said: 'If I have done the public any service, it is due to nothing but industry and patient thought.'" Smiles's brief biographical sketches—often stories of those who rose from humble origins to attain success through self-exertion—cover men in a wide range of disciplines and professions: Michael Faraday and Sir Humphry Davy, scientists; Joseph Brotherton, politician; Robert Dick, baker, geologist, and botanist; Sir Robert Peel and Lord Brougham, statesmen; and Edward Bulwer-Lytton and Sir Walter Scott, authors. All of these figures, and dozens more, serve as examples of the achievement of success through steady, continuous labor. In the twelve chapters of *Self-Help,* Smiles's method does not vary. As John L. Bradley concisely observes in a 1959 essay: "In writing *Self-Help* Smiles employs three devices over and over, in chapter after chapter, to command the reader's attention. These are: economy of style; aphorism; and 'capsule' biography strongly flavored with anecdote. . . . His style throughout is flat, plain, direct, uncomplicated by metaphor or simile." Bradley further analyzes the "clear narrative line" of Smiles's anecdotes and his "succinctly and plainly put" aphorisms, such as "The path of success in business is usually the path of common sense." Many readers found Smiles's writing to be simple, direct, and entertaining. Others found his anecdotes inspirational models for self-improvement.

Contemporary critical response to the book was mixed. The critic for *Chambers's Journal* called it "a handy and amusing volume" and recommended it "as a present for youth." The reviewer for *Macmillan's Magazine* criticized Smiles's notion of "self-culture" as a concept which might lead to social isolation and selfishness. The notice in *Tait's Edinburgh Magazine* was the most critical. The reviewer complained that the book was "worldly" in spirit and "shallow"; it "teaches superficial views of life, and its realities. . . . [and] places too much value on monetary achievements, . . . too little on moral triumphs." The popular reception of *Self-Help* was overwhelmingly positive. As Kenneth Fielden points out in a 1968 piece, "Self-Help took its place amongst, and provided the impetus for, many movements displaying both the hopes and fears of middle-class Britons." *Self-Help* was not, however, limited to a middle-class British audience: in the author's lifetime it sold a quarter of a million copies and was translated into seventeen languages, including all of the major languages of Europe and Asia. Besides its holding a secure place on the list of best-selling Victorian publications, there is much evidence that the book worked actual changes in readers' lives. Many wrote Smiles directly to thank him for saving them from the "slide downward." One gentleman testified that "*Self-Help* has been of extraordinary service to me. I have repeatedly gained hope and courage from its aphorisms and brave sentences; and with them I have tried to encourage others." The most exotic evidence of Smiles's popular, worldwide influence is the inscription of various mottoes from the book on the palace walls of an Egyptian khedive. When a visiting Englishman asked the khedive's architect if the quotations on the walls were from the Koran, he replied that they were "principally from Smeelis. . . . They are from his *Self-Help;* they are much better than the texts from the Koran."

After the immense popular success of *Self-Help,* Smiles produced four sequel volumes of essays that expanded upon similar themes and were offered to an admiring public as guides to conduct. In *Character: A Book of Noble Characteristics* (1871) Smiles uses many examples from books and life stories to define the features and circumstances of good character. He devotes extended discussion to domestic surroundings and the important contributions of women working at home in their "true sphere." Chapter nine, "Companionship in Marriage," defines different types of husbands and wives and makes an interesting distinction between "brain-women" and "heart-women." Other chapters use examples of great men to demonstrate the need for self-discipline and good temper. *Thrift: A Book of Domestic Council* (1875) turns saving money into a moral duty to be practiced by all levels of society: "It is an acquired principle of conduct. It involves self-denial. . . . Wealth is obtained by labour, it is preserved by savings and accumulations. . . . Let no man say he cannot economise." Several chapters are devoted to the workings of specific Victorian institutions that encouraged saving, such as the Friendly Benefit Societies and Penny Banks. Chapter twelve of *Thrift,* "Living Beyond Means," criticizes middle-class conformity. In *Duty; with Illustrations of Courage, Patience, and Endurance* (1880) Smiles discusses the nature of community as well as social and economic relations between, for example, employer and employee. That Smiles himself recognizes a continuity (in ideas and format) among his five books on conduct is clear from the opening words of his preface to *Life and Labour; or, Characteristics of Men of Industry, Culture, and Genius* (1887): "The following work has been written on the lines of *Self-Help* and *Character.*" Contrasts between rural and urban society in Great Britain are discussed in several chapters of *Life and Labour.* Chapter eight opens with an observation that reveals Smiles's basic anti-urban bias: "Great towns do not necessarily produce great men. On the contrary the tendency of life and pursuits in great towns is rather to produce small men." Generally, Smiles expresses his preference for the close, supportive network of the village community.

The second category of Smiles's prose writing from 1855 to 1895 is biography. His first major success was *The Life of George Stephenson, Railway Engineer* (1857). Just as *Self-Help* was a culmination of a decade of lecturing, so too the biography of Stephenson marked a culmination of more than a decade of study and firsthand railway experience on Smiles's part. As part of his avocation, Smiles gathered firsthand and secondhand information on the development of the railway system in Great Britain. He became more and more intrigued by the singular success of George Stephenson, originally an engine wright at a colliery near Newcastle. For several years Stephenson's son discouraged Smiles's writing because he felt that there would not be sufficient interest in a whole book about his father's life.

An 1880 photograph of Smiles with his daughter-in-law Lucy and his grandchildren John, Harry, Lily, and Aileen

In the biography Smiles shows how the elder Stephenson "through industry and perseverance" worked out the practical adaptation of steam power to locomotion on railroads. By the end of 1815 Stephenson was ahead of all competitors in the field of locomotive invention. However, his greatest challenge came with the establishment of the Liverpool and Manchester Railway. To read the history of this controversial struggle is to learn much about British social history and Victorian reactions to industrialization in general. And yet, Smiles does not lose sight of the individual triumph of this inventor of the "Travelling Engine" on 6 October 1829: "The entire performance excited the greatest astonishment amongst the assembled spectators; the directors felt confident that their enterprise was now on the eve of success, and George Stephenson rejoiced to think, that, in spite of all false prophets and fickle counsellers, his locomotive system was now safe." Smiles follows Stephenson's life story to his death in 1848. Thus, many of the positive and negative features of early railway development are revealed in the biography: from the excitement of "abridging distance, bringing nations into closer communication, and enabling them more freely to exchange the products of their industry" to the "disastrous" fraud and folly of "railway enterprizes and speculations." In the end, Stephenson is hailed as a model of "the power of *Perseverance*" and Smiles optimistically celebrates the glory of Victorian industrial progress: Britain's railways are "the most magnificent system of public intercommunication that has yet been given to the world." Smiles's first full-length biography received favorable reviews. The critic for the *Westminster Review* called it "a solid, pleasant and useful book." The *London Review* notice conveyed a similar, if qualified, enthusiasm: the reviewer hailed it as a tribute to "the common working talent of mankind," but he argued that Smiles exaggerated Stephenson's originality as an inventor.

Smiles expanded his treatment of industrial heroes in his three-volume *Lives of the Engineers, with an Account of Their Principal Works* (1861-1862). In this composite work the struggles and accomplishments of several pioneers of technical progress are detailed: James Brindley, father of English canals; Thomas Telford, first president of the Institute of Civil Engineers; John Rennie, builder of Waterloo Bridge in London; and John Smeaton, the first professional engineer. These volumes are of interest for an understanding of the history of transportation technology, the art of the engineer, and the changes in Victorian industrial society. *Industrial Biography: Iron-Workers and Tool-Makers* (1863) was less of a popular success; it treated important developments in machine tools and iron working.

Smiles was often asked to write biographies of contemporary industrial figures. He turned down many such requests, preferring to write about subjects that interested him. Often his time for composition was limited: "I wrote in the evenings, mostly after six. . . . with my children playing about me." In 1878 he produced a biography of George Moore, a merchant and philanthropist; the same year he recounted the fascinating life story of Robert Dick, a Scottish baker, geologist, and botanist. As late as the 1890s, he was still compiling books on figures that interested him or served as exemplars of his doctrine of self-help. Thus, *Jasmin: Barber, Poet, Philanthropist* appeared in 1891 and the important study *Josiah Wedgwood, F.R.S.: His Personal History* in 1894. Writing of *Jasmin,* the *Athenaeum* reviewer criticized Smiles's talents as a literary critic: "Dr. Smiles seems scarcely at home in poetry." Critics generally applauded Smiles's decision to return to writing the life history of a self-taught, persevering journeyman potter who became an industrialist of world renown in the Wedgwood biography.

A third and minor category of Smiles's writing is history and travel literature. Smiles planned to get married in late 1843 and was looking for ways to augment his income. A publishing office in Leeds asked him to write a guide to Ireland, though, as he admitted in his autobiography, he was scarcely qualified for this task: "This was an entirely new field of work. I looked into the materials for such a history. Unfortunately, they were not very numerous. . . . I must confess that it was written too hurriedly, and scarcely deserved the success it obtained." *History of Ireland and the Irish People under the Government of England* was published in 1844. Although the *Athenaeum* reviewer praised the book's "honesty and impartiality" and the fact that Smiles's "sympathies are on the side of the oppressed," other critics found the book to be shallow and stereotypical in its descriptions of the Irish people and their supposed lack of achievements. Smiles also wrote two studies of the Huguenots. After collecting information, visiting historical sites, corresponding with descendants, and delivering several lectures on the subject, he produced *The Huguenots; Their Settlements, Churches and Industries in England and Ireland* in 1867. Smiles was attracted to this neglected but courageous religious group because he admired their "high standard of character." He praised the Huguenot refugees for their "unusual virtue, . . . unusual vigour and determination." Likewise, he found their modern descendants to be clever and conscientious. The book sold almost 10,000 copies; however, as Smiles himself admitted in his autobiography, "It was nothing like so successful as some of my other books. . . ." A subsequent work, *The Huguenots in France after the Revocation of the Edict of Nantes,* appeared in 1873. In this book Smiles offers descriptions of the port of La Rochelle, the towns of Moulins, Vichy, Lyons, and Dauphiny, and the Swiss canton of Vaudois—all places associated with the history of the Huguenots.

The memoir is the fourth and final category of Smiles's literary career. For many years he worked to compile the two-volume tribute to John Murray *A Publisher and His Friends* (1891). Of the effort, which he began in 1879, Smiles said: "It involved a great deal of labour—reading the correspondence of that celebrated publishing house for nearly three quarters of a century—from the times of Drs Langhorne and Johnson to Hallam, Borrow, and Head, who appeared as authors in comparatively recent years." Smiles made extracts from the letters and thereby narrated the development of the professional lives of the first and second John Murrays and evolution of the distinguished publishing firm. Toward the end of a decade of work on this project, Smiles added an introduction on

"Self-Help," a drawing of Smiles published in Vanity Fair, *14 January 1882 (Collection of Jerold J. Savory)*

the history of publishing and bookselling; he had accumulated a final manuscript of 2,000 pages. Critics for many influential journals, including the *Athenaeum, Edinburgh Review,* and *Westminster Review,* hailed the work as one of Smiles's most important efforts. The *Atlantic* reviewer pinpointed the book's larger significance: "[it] is extraordinary for the breadth and diversity of its literary information. Murray himself is the central figure, and the story is of his transactions with authors. It is a work of the memoirs of trade, with a leading attention to the financial fortunes of literature. There is much about profit and loss, the prices paid, the avarice of authors. . . ." The reviewer also praised the book's treatment of general-interest topics, such as bookmaking in the Victorian period and the history of Murray's *Quarterly Review.* At different times in his life and especially during his final years, Smiles worked on the story of his own life. The *Autobiography of Samuel Smiles, LL.D* was edited by his friend Thomas Mackay and published posthumously in 1905. As Mackay writes in his preface, Smiles presents his life as "one of great contentment and of continuous industry." His book is of historical value in its descriptions of middle-class professional and domestic life in Victorian society. In some passages, Smiles offers apologies and retorts. He defends his own honor in a railway embezzlement scandal that occurred while he worked as railway secretary for the company involved. He also defends his brand of cheerful optimism and answers critics who claim that he prompted a sordid reverence for material success. Although the reviewer for the *Bookman* complained that the autobiography lacked candor and depth, most readers would agree with the judgment of the London *Times* critic: "It is an excellent autobiography, characteristically vigorous, cheerful, encouraging and wholesome." The book is an invaluable and fairly balanced source for information concerning Smiles's life and opinions as well as public reactions to his various works.

In the final decades of his life, Smiles was forced to slow the pace of his activity to some degree. In November 1871 he suffered a paralytic stroke that was disabling for almost a year. He spent some time traveling in Italy, France, and Norway. In 1878 Edinburgh University awarded him the honorary degree of LL.D. Four years after the death of his wife, Smiles died at his residence at Kensington, on 16 April 1904, at the age of ninety-one. He was buried at Brompton Cemetery underneath a large plain stone with the inscription "Samuel Smiles, author of Self-Help."

Beginning with a centenary edition of *Self-Help,* published with an introduction by Asa Briggs in 1958, there has been a slight but steady revival of critical and historical interest in Smiles during the second half of the twentieth century. Asa Briggs emphasizes Smiles's desire for social reform; Ira Bruce Nadel in his *Biography: Fiction, Fact and Form* (1984), values Smiles's contributions to the genre of short analytic biographies, especially his *Lives of the Engineers.* A. O. J. Cockshut in *Truth to Life* (1974) offers a detailed and reasoned defense of Smiles's ideas; he stresses the importance of understanding "the tension between his individualism and his strong and sincere sense of social responsibility." Nina Auerbach in *Woman and the Demon*

(1982), offers some original remarks from the perspective of feminist criticism: "It is suggestive that in Samuel Smiles's *Character,* quasi-religious hymns to this attribute consistently give way to apparently digressive exaltations of noble womanhood. Though he never links womanhood and character explicitly—he seems squeamishly to feel that the two are incompatible—they are associated in the dual focus of his book." It is to be expected that as such interest and controversy grows, more of his works will be republished and discussed in the years ahead.

Biography:

Aileen Smiles, *Samuel Smiles and His Surroundings* (London: Hale, 1956).

References:

Nina Auerbach, *Woman and the Demon: The Life of a Victorian Myth* (Cambridge: Harvard University Press, 1982), pp. 193-195;

John L. Bradley, "Samuel Smiles' *Self-Help:* Forgotten Centenary," *Victorian Newsletter,* no. 16 (Fall 1959): 23-25;

Asa Briggs, "A Centenary Introduction," in Smiles's *Self-Help* (London: Murray, 1958), pp. 7-31;

Briggs, "Samuel Smiles and the Gospel of Work," in his *Victorian People* (Chicago: University of Chicago Press, 1972), pp. 116-139;

A. O. J. Cockshut, *Truth to Life: The Art of Biography in the Nineteenth Century* (London: Collins, 1974), pp. 105-124;

Kenneth Fielden, "Samuel Smiles and Self-Help," *Victorian Studies,* 12 (December 1968): 155-176;

J. F. C. Harrison, "The Victorian Gospel of Success," *Victorian Studies,* 1 (December 1957): 155-164;

Ira Bruce Nadel, *Biography: Fiction, Fact and Form* (New York: St. Martin's, 1984), pp. 18-30.

Papers:

About one thousand letters from, to, and relating to Samuel Smiles, Smiles's account book, and other family papers are in the Archives Department, Central Library, Leeds.

Alexander Smith

(31 December 1829-5 January 1867)

D. W. Thomas
Central Washington University

See also the Smith entry in *DLB 32, Victorian Poets Before 1850.*

BOOKS: *Poems* (London: Bogue, 1853; Boston: Ticknor, Reed & Fields, 1853);

Sonnets on the War, by Smith and Sydney Dobell (London: Bogue, 1855);

City Poems (Cambridge: Macmillan, 1857; Boston: Ticknor & Fields, 1857);

Edwin of Deira (Cambridge: Macmillan, 1861; Boston: Ticknor & Fields, 1861);

Dreamthorp: A Book of Essays Written in the Country (London: Strahan, 1863; Boston: Tilton, 1864);

Alfred Hagart's Household (Boston: Ticknor & Fields, 1865; 2 volumes, London & New York: Strahan, 1866);

A Summer in Skye (2 volumes, London: Strahan, 1865; 1 volume, Boston: Ticknor & Fields, 1865);

Miss Oona McQuarrie: A Sequel to Alfred Hagart's Household (Boston: Ticknor & Fields, 1866);

Last Leaves: Sketches and Criticisms, edited by Patrick Proctor Alexander (Edinburgh: Nimmo, 1868);

A Life-Drama, City Poems, Etc., edited by R. E. D. Sketchley (London: Scott, 1901);

The Poetical Works of Alexander Smith, edited by William Sinclair (Edinburgh: Nimmo, 1909).

OTHER: John Bunyan, *Divine Emblems; or, Temporal Things Spiritualised,* preface by Smith (London: Bickers, 1864);

Robert Burns, *The Poetical Works of Robert Burns,* edited with a biographical memoir by Smith, 2 volumes (London & Cambridge: Macmillan, 1865); enlarged as *Poems, Songs, and Letters, Being the Complete Works of Robert Burns* (Philadelphia: Lippincott, 1868; London: Macmillan, 1879);

John W. S. Hows, *Golden Leaves from the American Poets,* introductory essay, "American Poetry," by Smith (London: Warne, 1866).

Alexander Smith was an aspiring poet who, his highly acclaimed early work soon discredited and ridiculed as "spasmodic," turned to prose in the hope of finding a new literary career. In doing so, he incorporated into his new work many of the characteristic features of his verse, and the largely favorable responses of contemporary readers testified to the growing popularity of this prose before his early death. Generally forgotten or remembered only as a "spasmodic" curiosity today, Smith managed to leave a small but significant body of prose which both explains his theoretical conceptions and demonstrates his critical understanding of the familiar essay as a literary form.

Born in his parents' thatched house in Kilmarnock, southwest of Glasgow, Alexander Smith

Alexander Smith

was the first of several children. But because no law required that births in Scotland be recorded until 1854, and perhaps because the Smiths were dissenters whose parenthood would not have been documented in parochial records, no formal notice exists of the boy's birth in the last hours of 1829. Years later an obituary erroneously cited 1830 as the year of his birth, but the newspaper's subsequent correction of that date never quite managed to overtake the error: though Smith's friends who wrote of him all cite 1829 as his birth-year, many standard nineteenth- and twentieth-century reference works have continued to perpetuate the mistake.

Alexander Smith's father Peter was a pattern designer of calico prints and sewed muslins; his mother, Helen Murray Smith, a gentle and thoughtful woman whose deep love for her son was returned in what biographer Thomas Brisbane calls "one of the noblest instances of reciprocal affection that has ever been manifested in the family circle." A proud Highlander herself, Mrs. Smith and another neighborhood lass fed young Smith's imagination with tales drawn from Ossianic legends, thus nurturing the naturally shy and sensitive boy's love for stories. In these he learned to find a comforting realm of experience amidst the adversities that he and his family faced. Peter Smith's struggle, for example, to provide for his family necessitated the repeated moving of their home back and forth between Kilmarnock and Paisley, where Smith's sporadic schooling allowed him to begin learning to read. There, too, both Smith and his younger sister were stricken with a fever which ultimately killed her and profoundly affected the young Smith. A partial paralysis of the right side of his face caused a lifelong squint to his right eye, and his shock at his sister's death fostered a strain of melancholy that attracted him to such early reading as Leigh Hunt's essay on "Deaths of Little Children," John Bunyan's *Pilgrim's Progress,* and Henry Wadsworth Longfellow's "Footsteps of Angels"—and a melancholy that underlies virtually all of his later works as a poet and essayist.

Near the end of the 1830s, continued hard times drove the family to Glasgow, where Smith enjoyed, for about two years, the only formal education he was to receive. He did well, but his family's thoughts of training such a promising student for the Secessionist ministry were soon sacrificed when the boy had to begin learning his father's trade by working in a warehouse. In the mornings and evenings, however, Smith resorted to reading—just as he had after his sister's death—to escape the solitude and drabness of his impoverished working-class life and long factory hours. He read extensively and eclectically: Scott and James Fenimore Cooper had been his favorite novelists, but the English poets became his "chiefest friends"—especially Byron and Wordsworth, but later Keats, Shelley, and Tennyson. Inspired by travel narratives and Cooper's novels, the sixteen-year-old pattern tracer eventually composed his first long poem, "Black Eagle," about an American Indian warrior. Although he felt this to be "unworthy of preservation" and soon destroyed it, he continued to write much shorter verse, poetic scraps which he had begun composing during his brief school days.

In 1846 some Glasgow boys working in the warehouses and several university students formed a Saturday night literary club, the Addisonian Society, whose aim was to provide a forum for debates about books and for the writing and reading of essays. Smith was soon invited to join, and his first contribution, a personal essay he had been required to compose and read to the club, stunned the others. In Brisbane's words, "The essay from its beginning took the members by surprise, and they listened unto the close with fixed silence and increasing admiration. When the essayist sat down, no one felt disposed to speak. Criticism was disarmed. . . . The appearing of 'A Life Drama' [Smith's astonishingly successful first long poem published in 1853] did not make a more profound sensation on the public than the reading of his first essay did on the society that night. He had been previously almost silent as a member, but they had now discovered his ability, and he was tacitly by all placed first in membership." Smith later wrote and read essays on such literary figures as Addison, Keats, Burns, and Ebenezer Elliott. From being a group, as Brisbane put it, "in danger of becoming an arena of wranglers" before the presentation of Smith's first essay, the club seemed to shift its orientation: "The ablest members' hearts were made to glow with unwonted warmth in laudable emulation, and the writing of essays became henceforth a serious, earnest, and arduous affair."

Smith himself also benefited from membership in the society, for through it he ended the relative solitude in which he had been living while working as a pattern designer. He made close friendships with other members who shared personal interests with him and could expand his own limited knowledge and range of experience. Brisbane, for example, regularly accompanied him on pleasant weekend rambles along the Clyde, as did Hugh Macdonald—a poet, author of travel books, and amateur naturalist whose botanical lessons, like the excursions, helped ensure that Smith would learn to write as he does in all his most vivid descriptive work: "with his eye on the object," as critics of his earliest poetry were to demand.

Equally important, the Society aroused and encouraged Smith's ambition to write for an audience, despite his powerful native taciturnity. Brisbane recalls how Smith's habitual reticence, even after the two had become very close friends, made so startling his revelation of all his poetry manuscripts and of his oddly pained apprehensions about wishing to become a poet. "It is with a feeling of humiliation I make this confession," Smith told Brisbane—by letter, even, rather than face to face—in first acknowledging his literary aspirations. That he maintained such extreme humility throughout his life was also evident in his response to the tremendous acclaim his first book elicited. When he happened to see in a bookstore window a large handbill advertising "A Life Drama, by Alexander Smith, the Glasgow Poet," he immediately sent to the bookseller a courteous note asking that the notice be removed, because it offended his sense of modesty. Smith himself fondly recalled much later what his membership in the Addisonian Society had done for him: "I know I derived much benefit from it," he reflected just before his death. "Through its means I was first stimulated to composition, and had my latent powers roused to action."

The products, and the promise, of Smith's "latent powers" first appeared during 1850 in the "Poet's Corner" of the Glasgow *Evening Citizen,* where these pseudonymously published poems by Smith Murray drew little attention but left their author much encouraged. Through the help of George Gilfillan, an influential critic and spiritual patron of aspiring new poets, a selection of manuscript poems Smith had submitted in 1851 with hopes of receiving some advice was soon being publicized in Gilfillan's eulogizing articles in the *Eclectic Review, London Critic,* and *Hogg's Instructor.* Such an eagerly expectant audience was thus created for Smith's *Poems* (1853) that this first book was in a fourth London edition by 1855. In America, where, as Smith's later editor and memorialist Patrick Proctor Alexander recalled, "Smith's works were always more widely circulated than at home," records indicate that sales of the Boston editions reached 10,000 "in a few months."

Astonished by this success and the fame it so suddenly brought, Smith happily decided to forgo working as a pattern designer and, with the £100 he had received for his book, decided to take a trip to England with his friend John Nichol. British readers he met lionized him much as his fellow Scots had, but Smith maintained his characteristic humility and was pleased to be able to meet such influential literary and intellectual figures as Harriet Martineau, Philip J. "Festus" Bailey, Herbert Spencer, and George Henry Lewes. Returning to Glasgow after spending a week with the Duke of Argyle at Inverary, he assumed the editorship of the *Glasgow Miscellany,* a short-lived journal which failed when in 1854 Smith left to pursue further opportunities for the development of his literary career.

The secretaryship of the University of Edinburgh had fallen vacant, and, with the help of influential new friends, Smith was elected to the position—one which, at a starting annual salary of £150, promised him the first real security he had known. He moved to Edinburgh to assume his new duties early in 1854 and later in that year saw his essay on the life and work of William Cowper appear in the eighth edition of the *Encyclopaedia Britannica.* Smith's knowledge of literary figures and their work as well as his ability to present it earned him other encyclopedia assignments, including pieces in *Mackenzie's Biographical* and *Chambers's,* "the Editor of the last of which . . . used to say that, for neat, felicitous, carefully-condensed work on the prescribed conditions, . . . he had no such literary contributor" as Smith, one friend recalled. By Alexander Nicolson's account in an 1867 article for *Good Words,* just as Smith had in Glasgow, he soon "became the centre of a warmly-attached circle of friends, chiefly connected with literature and art"—a small society called the Raleigh Club, which met weekly in Edinburgh to share social and intellectual conversation.

In the summer of 1854, however, William Edmondstoune Aytoun's *Firmilian,* a brilliant lampoon of the "Spasmodic" excesses of poetry like Smith's "Life-Drama," signaled a change in critical tastes which, along with subsequent charges in a letter published in the *Athenaeum* that his poetry was replete with plagiarism, ended his career as a poet almost as suddenly as it had begun. As one of Smith's university colleagues, Aytoun was an amiable man who encouraged Smith to write prose for journals and even offered to help him place such work with *Blackwood's Magazine.* Smith wrote one long critical essay entitled "Scottish Ballads" which appeared among others by eminent scholars in *Edinburgh Essays, 1856,* and through the later 1850s he published several others. But he continued to seek recognition as a poet, having collaborated with Sydney Dobell on a small book, *Sonnets on the War* (1855), which brought little attention and, perhaps more important, little of the recompense Smith soon had reason to seek. After marrying Flora Macdonald of Ord, Skye, in the spring of 1857, he settled in a cottage at Wardie, in the northern part of Edinburgh. From here he still hoped to supplement his university income and meet his growing financial responsibilities chiefly through writing poetry. The disappointing reception of both *City Poems* (1857) and *Edwin of Deira* (1861), however, forcibly convinced him that he must turn to prose if his literary efforts were to add sufficiently to his income.

So after 1861 Smith wrote diligently, contributing familiar essays, criticism, some fiction, and, stubbornly, some occasional poetry to such magazines as *North British Review, Museum, West of Scotland, Argosy, Quiver, Temple Bar,* and *Good Words.* Much of this writing is certainly the best of Smith's prose, and, like the earlier "Scottish Ballads" and *Blackwood's* essays, it was eventually collected or rewritten for incorporation into his books—the first of which from this second phase of his career was *Dreamthorp* (1863).

Subtitled *A Book of Essays Written in the Country,* this collection is purportedly written by an old man from Dreamthorp, an inland village which is Smith's imaginative re-creation of Linlithgow, just west of Edinburgh. The initial essay, "Dreamthorp," establishes a narrative framework by generally describing the apparently timeless, slow-to-change village, the simple and unhurried lives of its inhabitants, and the often melancholy pastoral atmosphere which pervades everything. Two recurrent themes which characterize virtually all of Smith's prose are introduced: the aged narrator and his fellow villagers are ever conscious of the imminence of death, which they deeply respect, and they are all actively interested in the world of imaginative literature.

Such themes and moods provide the only hints of unity there are in *Dreamthorp,* for the narrative framework established by the first essay is almost immediately dropped: the ability to organize and unify a lengthy work had never been Smith's forte. Speaking of his poetry, he acknowledged his own "vagrancy" or "want of severity in the outline of substantial forms," and his prose volumes also display this looseness. What "Dreamthorp" promises is a collection of the old man's essays about his placid life and reflections on literary matters as he "ripen[s] for the grave," but subsequent essays fail to sustain Smith's premise. "On the Writing of Essays," the second piece in the collection, is more a theoretical study of a literary form than the familiar essay which its opening leads one to expect. And the narrator of "A Lark's Flight" seems not to be an old man: he relates details of an execution he witnessed during his boyhood "more than twenty years ago."

In fact, the book's primarily critical studies, such as "William Dunbar" or "Geoffrey Chaucer," are interspersed with familiar essays, such as "On Death and the Fear of Dying" and the widely anthologized "A Lark's Flight." At times the technical or critical is gracefully infused with the familiar—as in "Men of Letters," "A Shelf in My Bookcase," or the opening pages of "On the Writing of Essays." In this last essay the old man argues that life in Dreamthorp affords ample matériel for his essays and then offers an extensive theoretical conception of the genre—of its origins, development, styles, and literary ends—which, to quote Richard Murphy's "Alexander Smith on the Art of the Essay" (1948), many modern critics have found to be "the best definition of the personal essay": "The essay, as a literary form, resembles the lyric," insists Smith's aged persona, "in so far as it is moulded by some central mood.... Give the mood, and the essay, from the first sentence to the last, grows around it as the cocoon grows around the silkworm.... It is not the essayist's duty to inform, to build pathways through metaphysical morasses, to cancel abuses, any more than it is the duty of the poet to do these things. Incidentally he may do something in that way, just as the poet may, but it is not his duty.... The essayist is a kind of poet in prose, and if questioned harshly as to his uses, he might be unable to render a better apology for his existence than a flower might."

This exposition of "mood" rather than of information, as well as the "egotism" which Smith also declares essential to the essayist's art, reflects the poetic, impressionistic nature of his own critical work. His predilection for figurative devices contributes to his subjectivity in such critical discourse as "On the Writing of Essays," and it is also evident—often in a style which some readers found too florid—in his familiar essays. Although his poetry had been lauded for its creation of mood, critics had belabored his verse for its inability to sustain a unified line of thought. But his turn to prose serendipitously freed him to be "playing at fast and loose with himself and his reader," as he insisted in *Dreamthorp* that the essayist must. The essay thus proved more amenable than poetry to Smith's talents: his abundant (often overabundant) use of imagery, frequently rhythmic cadences, and vivid evocation of mood were familiar poetic strengths whose incorporation into his essays recalled to his readers the charm of Charles Lamb's prose. Only two months after the appearance of *Dreamthorp* in June 1863, a sixth run of 1,000 copies was in press, and a second edition appeared the following year.

Also in 1864 appeared the first of two editions of works for which Smith wrote prefatory essays. The least-known of anything he wrote, his preface to Bunyan's *Divine Emblems* actually discusses that work only in the last two and a half paragraphs. The rest voices his appreciation of Bunyan, as man and as author of such works as *The Pilgrim's Progress* and *Grace Abounding*—especially of Bunyan's allegorizing imagination, which the former pattern de-

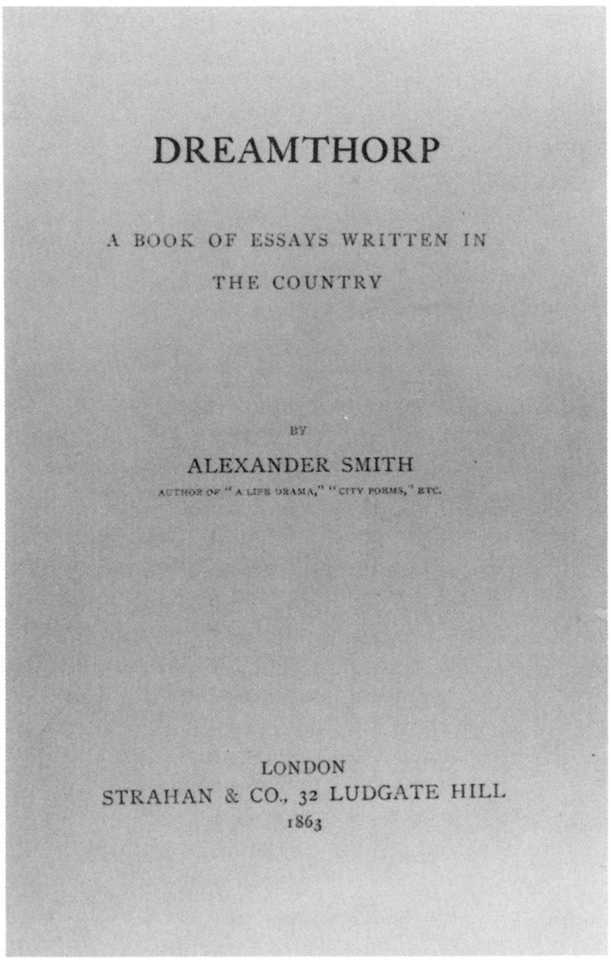
DREAMTHORP

A BOOK OF ESSAYS WRITTEN IN THE COUNTRY

BY

ALEXANDER SMITH

AUTHOR OF "A LIFE DRAMA," "CITY POEMS," ETC.

LONDON
STRAHAN & CO., 32 LUDGATE HILL
1863

Title page for Smith's first collection of familiar essays, narrated by an old man who lives in the imaginary village of Dreamthorp, where everything is "unhurried, quiet, moss-grown, and orderly"

signer sympathetically compares to that of the more genteel, well-educated Edmund Spenser. "American Poetry," Smith's introductory essay to the British edition of *Golden Leaves from the American Poets* (1866), understandably does not aim to assess critically the work of all the poets included in John W. S. Hows's extensive anthology. After briefly correlating some general features of American history and culture with literary qualities which Smith felt were distinctive in American poetry, he reviews the lives, literary reputations, and works of Bryant, Longfellow, Poe, Holmes, and Lowell—those whom he saw as the five greatest American poets, "gathering up and embodying in themselves the characteristics of all the others." Both of these prefaces demonstrate Smith's impressionistic critical disposition and the rather Carlylian presumption expressed in several *Dreamthorp* essays: that a writer's life and personality are invariably revealed in his work, most particularly in his style.

Smith's belief in this intimate connection between a writer's life and his art, his personality and his work, is most evident in his biographical memoir of Burns. Published in 1865 as the preface to Macmillan's Golden Treasury edition of *The Poetical Works of Robert Burns,* this essay incorporated much of what the young Smith had written on Burns in an 1852 Addisonian Society paper. Smith also edited the Burns volume, a task that yielded his most extensive and systematic critical work; he found the editing unpleasant, the work on the glossary boring and time-consuming. The memoir itself, however, offers a sensitive reading of Burns's life and work, and in several respects it represents the best of Smith's biographical and critical essays. Such predecessors as John Lockhart, John Wilson, and Thomas Carlyle had published biographical studies of Burns, but the affection and understanding which Smith had for his fellow Ayrshire-born poet lent his essay a sympathetic tone that distinguished it from the earlier works. Smith's edition, with his preface, was republished in 1868 when Burns's letters were added to the work, now designated the Globe Edition and entitled *Poems, Songs, and Letters, Being the Complete Works of Robert Burns.* Both editions were republished, the latter quite frequently: it remained in print well into the twentieth century.

Smith's efforts on the Burns edition, however, were but part of what made 1865 such an exhausting yet productive year, for in the January number of *Good Words* he had begun to publish monthly installments of a largely autobiographical novel, *Alfred Hagart's Household* (1865). He had planned this as a short, one-volume work, but it proved so popular that the magazine publisher coaxed him to extend it through a second volume. Smith found serial publication extremely taxing—the September installment was postponed until October while he and his family took their much-needed August vacation. But he was so gratified by the reception of his first novel that, had his health permitted, "it was in this field," as his friend Patrick Proctor Alexander insisted, "that his next and more serious effort would have been made."

Other friends remarked that Smith's health had begun to fail under the strains of his writing and his work at the university sometime during 1865. But despite his occasional "giddiness" and "strange nervous distemperatures" which they saw as symptoms of an "over-wrought brain," his second major prose work, *A Summer in Skye,* also appeared later that year. The Hebridean island of Skye had been his wife's home, and the Smiths had annually spent several summer weeks there with Flora Smith's father, Charles Macdonald, who provided a model for the patriarchal Mr. McIan in Smith's book. Through these repeated provincial vacations, Smith had come to know Skye and its inhabitants well, and his curious two-volume collection about the island was published during what was to be his last visit there.

A pastiche of interpolated tales, occasional poetry, and essays, as well as sketches of provincial characters, folkways, and historical events, *A Summer in Skye* is a loosely organized but pleasant, often humorous recounting of the work-wearied urban narrator's reinvigorating summer, his trip from Edinburgh to Skye, his sojourn on the island, and his journey back to Glasgow and, finally, Edinburgh. But Smith did not intend for readers to regard his work simply as a guidebook or travel narrative: he sought to provide "little useful information," for his aim, similar to that of the *Dreamthorp* essays, was, as he described it, "simply to record the impression which the Island, with its weather, its scenery, its people, and its peculiar spiritual atmosphere had, during many visits, made on my own mind."

Most contemporary reviewers, and even some of Smith's friends, complained of its extremely long, apparently digressive opening and closing sections describing Edinburgh and Glasgow. What such reviewers condemned as the "laborious" and "positively exasperating" incorporation of such "pages of padding and twaddle" veined with "passages which startle by the vividness of their painting" revealed an inability to focus and unify an extended literary work, the familiar charge which critics of Smith's earlier books had voiced. The sections on Edinburgh and Glasgow certainly slow the pace of the narrative, but their leisurely tone also reveals Smith's ambivalent attitudes toward the cities where he had first found success and was continuing to pursue it as a mature writer. And the contrast between the narrator's pre- and post-vacation impressions of everyday Edinburgh in these sections—the latter impression enhanced by his reading of Ossianic translations "breathing the very soul of the wilderness [he] had lately left"—betokens one of Smith's main themes: "Something of Edinburgh melted into my remembrance of Skye—something of Skye was projected into actual Edinburgh. Thus is life enriched by ideal contrast and interchange."

The clusters of epigrammatic sentences and the florid, strained imagery which characterize all of Smith's earlier work are still evident throughout *A Summer in Skye,* and its sketches and familiar essays are not such integral, polished pieces as those of *Dreamthorp.* Nevertheless, many twentieth-century readers have continued to feel that Smith's

book does provide a thorough and authentic portrait of Skye's scenery, people, and provincial life. Because its setting and topical references are distinctively Scotch rather than English, like those of *Dreamthorp, A Summer in Skye* has perhaps never been as appealing to sizeable English or American audiences. At least, it has been republished much less frequently than *Dreamthorp* in the twentieth century and remains not as well known as Smith's earlier volume.

Despite poor health that persisted through the winter of 1865 and eventually prevented Smith from returning to Skye for vacation in August 1866, he continued to write diligently for magazines. Five of the essays later collected in the posthumous *Last Leaves: Sketches and Criticisms* (1868) appeared from December 1865 to September 1866, and three installments of fiction were published in July 1866 under the title "The M'Gillowies of M'Gillowie." When Smith resumed his university duties that fall, however, his fatigue and weakened condition finally forced him to bed with gastric fever on 20 November. This condition was soon complicated by diphtheria and gradually developed into typhoid fever. Just after his thirty-seventh birthday, Smith died at home on 5 January 1867. Five days later he was buried in Warriston cemetery, and many of his friends erected as their tribute a memorial cross with the simple inscription, "Alexander Smith, Poet and Essayist."

Last Leaves: Sketches and Criticisms, a collection of nine essays and two poems, was compiled and published in April 1868 with a memoir of Smith by his close friend Patrick Proctor Alexander. Most of the essays are primarily critical or theoretical studies, and, like the familiar essays "Winter" and "An Essay on an Old Subject" in this volume, many reiterate ideas Smith had examined earlier in *Dreamthorp* or *A Summer in Skye*. "Essayists, Old and New," for example, assesses the contemporary social implications and literary consequences of the prominence of magazines and then outlines, from Montaigne's time, the historical evolution of the essay, the magazines' preeminent literary form. Echoes of *Dreamthorp*'s "On the Writing of Essays" also resound in *Last Leaves*'s "Literary Work," which offers a striking foreshadowing of some of the Aesthetic Movement's conceptions of art, of its materials and its uses or values. Similarly, "On Dreams and Dreaming" prefigures some psychological conceptions of the relation between dreams, wish-fulfillment, and personality—ideas either modified or much more fully elaborated by Freud in his later studies. In all, the work posthumously collected in *Last Leaves* ranges from Smith's earliest piece on "Scottish Ballads" (1857) to "Sydney Dobell" (1866), one of his last-published essays on his friend and fellow "Spasmodic" poet.

As one might expect, these essays reveal little that is new about Smith's talent as a prose writer, although Patrick Proctor Alexander selected the best of Smith's uncollected essays as a memorial to him. Reviewers—even while voicing once again their familiar judgments on the opulent imagery, the fatiguing clusters of epigrams, and the occasionally startling, vividly concrete representations of abstract ideas—seemed, in the words of the critic for the *London Review,* "more than willing . . . to take Alexander Smith as we find him in this and other prose volumes, as an essayist of real and special powers—indolent, meditative, introspective, brooding in tender twilight of reverie over thoughts that touch our common humanity, fond of books and art, fond of the leaves and the hot sunshine, yet all the while darkly haunted by the thought of death." In the two years following Smith's death, the book appeared in three editions but has not been republished since then, even though it includes several significant essays from his canon.

Unfortunately dismissed as a "Spasmodic" writer after his poetry had initially received enthusiastic acclaim, Alexander Smith found in prose another avenue for his literary aspirations. As a historian or theoretical critic of the essay, he revealed a sensitivity to its possibilities as a literary form and a well-informed understanding of its evolutionary development. With hard work and through the revelation of his own quite un-Spasmodic personality—quiet, honest, unassuming, tolerant, and good-humored—in his essays, he managed to cultivate for his prose an audience that was growing at the time of his death. But in part, the brevity of his career as an essayist, during which his best literary work was produced, made it unlikely that numerous contemporary readers and writers would perpetuate the memory of one who had died so young, especially one who had lived as reticently as he. Smith was no Byron.

A more obvious reason for his obscurity as a prose writer, however, lies in the kind of essay he wrote so well. The familiar essay was his métier, and even his critical prose—aside from his encyclopedia articles—was generally infused with impressionistic responses, with the personality of Alexander Smith. Writing prose in a time of fermenting social change and intellectual growth, contemporary masters like Carlyle, Arnold, Mill,

Newman, Darwin, and others addressed pressing topical issues and raised controversial new ideas in expository, often polemic, prose that differs in matter, manner, and purpose from Smith's. Those who knew the man all remarked his unusually intolerant, "obstinate antipathy" for controversy and "metaphysical" speculation, and Smith's prose habitually avoids topics which evoke such responses. Instead, his dreamily reflective essays on such universal and familiar subjects as death and dying, books and the literary imagination, and the beauty and timeless patterns of nature reveal Alexander Smith as a man whose essential human concerns, and whose aims as a prose writer, were primarily to give pleasure, not to inform or persuade. Despite the relative obscurity of Smith's prose works, they demonstrate significant links in the historical development of the familiar essay from the Romantic Charles Lamb to such later Victorians as Robert Louis Stevenson and the Aesthetics.

Biography:

Thomas Brisbane, *The Early Years of Alexander Smith, Poet and Essayist* (London: Hodder & Stoughton, 1869).

References:

Herbert B. Grimsditch, "Alexander Smith: Poet and Essayist," *London Mercury,* 12 (July 1925): 284-294;

John Hogben, Introduction to Smith's *Dreamthorp* (New York: Kennerly, 1907), pp. vii-lii;

Richard Murphy, "Alexander Smith: Man of Letters," Ph.D. dissertation, University of Pittsburgh, 1939;

Murphy, "Alexander Smith on the Art of the Essay," in *If by Your Art: Testament to Percival Hunt,* edited by Agnes Lynch Starrett (Pittsburgh: University of Pittsburgh Press, 1948), pp. 239-250;

James Ashcroft Noble, "Mr. Stevenson's Forerunner," *Yellow Book: An Illustrated Quarterly,* 4 (January 1895): 121-142;

Mary Jane W. Scott, "Alexander Smith: Poet of Victorian Scotland," *Studies in Scottish Literature,* 14 (1979): 98-111;

Stephen Henry Thayer, "Alexander Smith," *Andover Review,* 15 (February 1891): 163-172;

Hugh Walker, Introduction to Smith's *Dreamthorp, with Selections from "Last Leaves"* (London: Oxford University Press, 1914), pp. v-xxv.

William Makepeace Thackeray

(18 July 1811-24 December 1863)

Marilyn Naufftus Karlson

See also the Thackeray entry in *DLB 21, Victorian Novelists Before 1885.*

BOOKS: *Flore et Zéphyr: Ballet Mythologique par Théophile Wagstaffe* (London: Mitchell, 1836);

The Yellowplush Correspondence, as Charles J. Yellowplush (Philadelphia: Carey & Hart, 1838);

Reminiscences of Major Gahagan, as Goliah O'Grady Gahagan (Philadelphia: Carey & Hart, 1839);

An Essay on the Genius of George Cruikshank (London: Hooper, 1840);

The Paris Sketch Book, by Mr. Titmarsh, 2 volumes (London: Macrone, 1840; New York: Appleton, 1852);

Comic Tales and Sketches, Edited and Illustrated by Mr. Michael Angelo Titmarsh, 2 volumes (London: Cunningham, 1841);

The Second Funeral of Napoleon, in Three Letters to Miss Smith of London; and The Chronicle of the Drum, By Mr. M. A. Titmarsh (London: Cunningham, 1841); republished as *The Second Funeral of Napoleon, by M. A. Titmarsh and Critical Reviews* (New York: Lovell, 1883);

The Irish Sketch Book, by M. A. Titmarsh (2 volumes, London: Chapman & Hall, 1843; 1 volume, New York: Winchester, 1843);

Jeames's Diary (New York: Taylor, 1846);

Notes of a Journey from Cornhill to Grand Cairo, by Way of Lisbon, Athens, Constantinople, and Jerusalem, Performed in the Steamers of the Peninsular and Oriental Company, by Mr. M. A. Titmarsh (London: Chapman & Hall, 1846; New York: Wiley & Putnam, 1846);

Mrs. Perkins's Ball, by Mr. M. A. Titmarsh (London: Chapman & Hall, 1847);

Vanity Fair: A Novel without a Hero (19 monthly parts, London: Bradbury & Evans, 1847-1848; 2 volumes, New York: Harper, 1848);

The Book of Snobs (London: Punch Office, 1848; New York: Appleton, 1852);

Our Street, by Mr. M. A. Titmarsh (London: Chapman & Hall, 1848);

The Great Hoggarty Diamond (New York: Harper, 1848); republished as *The History of Samuel Titmarsh and the Great Hoggarty Diamond* (London: Bradbury & Evans, 1849);

The History of Pendennis. His Fortunes and Misfortunes, His Friends and His Greatest Enemy (23 monthly parts, London: Bradbury & Evans, 1848-1850; 2 volumes, New York: Harper, 1850);

William Makepeace Thackeray (Boston Public Library)

Doctor Birch and His Young Friends, by Mr. M. A. Titmarsh (London: Chapman & Hall, 1849; New York: Appleton, 1853);

Miscellanies: Prose and Verse, 8 volumes (Leipzig: Tauchnitz, 1849-1857);

The Kickleburys on the Rhine, By Mr. M. A. Titmarsh (London: Smith, Elder, 1850; New York: Stringer & Townsend, 1851);

Stubbs's Calendar; or, The Fatal Boots (New York: Stringer & Townsend, 1850);

Rebecca and Rowena: A Romance upon Romance, by Mr. M. A. Titmarsh (London: Chapman & Hall, 1850; New York: Appleton, 1853);

The History of Henry Esmond, Esq., a Colonel in the Service of Her Majesty Q. Anne, Written by Himself (3 volumes, London: Smith, Elder, 1852; 1 volume, New York: Harper, 1852);

The Confessions of Fitz-Boodle; and Some Passages in the Life of Major Gahagan (New York: Appleton, 1852);

A Shabby Genteel Story and Other Tales (New York: Appleton, 1852);

Men's Wives (New York: Appleton, 1852);

The Luck of Barry Lyndon: A Romance of the Last Century, 2 volumes (New York: Appleton, 1852-1853);

Jeanne's Diary, A Legend of the Rhine, and Rebecca and Rowena (New York: Appleton, 1853);

Mr. Brown's Letters to a Young Man about Town; with The Proser and Other Papers (New York: Appleton, 1853);

Punch's Prize Novelists, The Fat Contributor, and Travels in London (New York: Appleton, 1853);

The English Humourists of the Eighteenth Century: A Series of Lectures Delivered in England, Scotland, and the United States of America (London: Smith, Elder, 1853; New York: Harper, 1853);

The Newcomes. Memoirs of a Most Respectable Family, Edited by Arthur Pendennis Esqre (23 monthly parts, London: Bradbury & Evans, 1853-1855; 2 volumes, New York: Harper, 1855);

The Rose and The Ring; or, The History of Prince Giglio and Prince Bulbo: A Fireside Pantomine for Great and Small Children (London: Smith, Elder, 1855; New York: Harper, 1855);

Miscellanies: Prose and Verse, 4 volumes (London: Bradbury & Evans, 1855-1857);

Ballads (Boston: Ticknor & Fields, 1856);

Christmas Books (London: Chapman & Hall, 1857; Philadelphia: Lippincott, 1872);

The Virginians: A Tale of the Last Century (24 monthly parts, London: Bradbury & Evans, 1857-1859; 1 volume, New York: Harper, 1859);

The Four Georges: Sketches of Manners, Morals, Court and Town Life (New York: Harper, 1860; London: Smith, Elder, 1861);

Lovel the Widower (New York: Harper, 1860; London: Smith, Elder, 1861);

The Adventures of Philip on His Way through the World; Shewing Who Robbed Him, Who Helped Him, and Who Passed Him By (3 volumes, London: Smith, Elder, 1862; 1 volume, New York: Harper, 1862);

Roundabout Papers (London: Smith, Elder, 1863; New York: Harper, 1863);

Denis Duval (New York: Harper, 1864; London: Smith, Elder, 1867);

Early and Late Papers Hitherto Uncollected, edited by J. T. Fields (Boston: Ticknor & Fields, 1867);

Miscellanies, Volume IV (Boston: Osgood, 1870);

The Orphan of Pimlico; and Other Sketches, Fragments, and Drawings, with notes by A. I. Thackeray (London: Smith, Elder, 1876);

Sultan Stork and Other Stories and Sketches (1829-44), Now First Collected, edited by R. H. Sheppard (London: Redway, 1887);

Loose Sketches, An Eastern Adventure, Etc. (London: Sabin, 1894);

The Hitherto Unidentified Contributions of W. M. Thackeray to Punch, with a Complete Authoritative Bibliography from 1845 to 1848, edited by M. H. Spielmann (London & New York: Harper, 1899);

Mr. Thackeray's Writings in the "National Standard" and the "Constitutional," edited by W. T. Spencer (London: Spencer, 1899);

Stray Papers: Being Stories, Reviews, Verses, and Sketches 1821-47, edited by Lewis S. Benjamin as Lewis Melville (London: Hutchinson, 1901; Philadelphia: Jacobs, 1901);

The New Sketch Book: Being Essays Now First Collected from the "Foreign Quarterly Review," edited by R. S. Garnett (London: Rivers, 1906);

Thackeray's Contributions to the "Morning Chronicle," edited by Gordon N. Ray (Urbana: University of Illinois Press, 1955).

Collections: *The Works of William Makepeace Thackeray,* Library Edition, 22 volumes (London: Smith, Elder, 1867-1869);

The Works of William Makepeace Thackeray, Biographical Edition, 13 volumes (London: Smith, Elder, 1898-1899);

The Works of William Makepeace Thackeray, edited by Lewis S. Benjamin as Lewis Melville, 20 volumes (London: Macmillan, 1901-1907);

The Oxford Thackeray, 17 volumes (London: Oxford University Press, 1908);

The Works of William Makepeace Thackeray, Centenary Biographical Edition, 26 volumes (London: Smith, Elder, 1910-1911).

William Makepeace Thackeray is best known for his novel *Vanity Fair,* with its attack on pretension and hypocrisy and its intriguing character Becky Sharpe. A few of his other novels are still read—*Henry Esmond, The Newcomes, Pendennis,* and *Barry Lyndon*—as is his children's story *The Rose and the Ring.* Unfortunately, the nonfiction that makes up a substantial and entertaining segment of his work is now largely ignored, though Thackeray's nonfiction offers much the same appeal as his fiction. In essays as well as novels, we have the company of genial but often satirical narrators and a range of villainous, foolish, amusing, and sometimes admirable characters. In his movement back and forth from essayist to serial novelist, Thackeray made no abrupt changes but improved gradually with the mellowing effects of age and experience. His purpose and themes remained constant. His intent was always to root out humbug, cant, sham, and snobbery. On a larger scale he wanted to tell the truth, and the major truth he saw was that few individuals were genuinely great but many pretended to greatness. He tried to make people see themselves realistically—quite ordinary small beer rather than fine wine—and be content.

Thackeray, the only child of Richmond and Anne Becher Thackeray, was born in Calcutta, India, on 18 July 1811. His father, a successful revenue collector for the East India Company, died four years later, and at the age of six Thackeray was sent to England without his mother. There he was shifted around among inadequate schools and his odd antique Anglo-Indian relatives until his mother returned to England in 1819 as Mrs. Henry William Carmichael-Smyth. She and his stepfather gave him the nurturing he had missed and eventually sent him to a new school, Charterhouse, from 1822 to 1828. At Charterhouse he rejected the brutality reflected in Greek grammar lessons that began with teaching the word for "I thrash." Such lessons, as well as two fights in which his nose was broken, taught him to distinguish himself more for kindness to smaller boys than for scholarship. However, the beauty of Charterhouse, the sense of living history it gave him, and the lasting friendships with John Leech and others who encouraged him to draw and write were more useful than lessons, and Thackeray's memories of his experiences at the school softened with age.

In 1829 he entered Trinity College, Cambridge. There also the friendships that he formed—with Alfred Tennyson and Edward FitzGerald among others—stimulated his literary interests. He helped create a periodical, the *Snob,* edited its sequel, the *Gownsman,* and wrote for both. As he became more involved in literary and social pursuits, he paid less attention to his studies and began to spend alarming amounts of money. In 1830 he left Cambridge without a degree and with a £1,500 gambling debt; numerous trips to Germany and France in the next four years were meant to help him decide on a profession. He considered many possibilities—diplomacy, translating, and the law—and actually spent a year at the Middle Temple, but, wherever he went, he concentrated more on literary and social life than on hard work.

In 1833, at the age of twenty-one, he bought a weekly, the *National Standard and Journal of Literature, Science, Music, Theatricals, and the Fine Arts,* and made himself the Paris correspondent. Then financial disaster struck: in a bank failure he lost almost all that remained of his patrimony. He hauled down the financially untenable *National Standard* and diligently set to work in Paris to become an artist. Art, however, turned out to be his love rather than his talent, although he eventually illustrated many of his own works. In Paris he divided his efforts between art and writing, and he fell in love with a young Irish girl, Isabella Shawe. To improve his financial situation, in 1836 he became the Paris correspondent for the *Constitutional and Public Ledger,* a new radical newspaper his stepfather had helped create. In August Thackeray and Isabella Shawe were married; in June 1837 they had their first child, Anne, and in July the *Constitutional* ceased publication.

In the decade that followed, Thackeray experienced both overwhelming personal loss and professional recognition. When Isabella Shawe married Thackeray, she was a timid, immature girl. After their second child, Jane, died at eight months of age in 1839, Isabella became unable to cope with the demands of life. A third child, Harriet, born in May 1840, added happiness and more strain. Finally, on a trip to Ireland that September, Isabella Thackeray's increasing insanity became clear when she tried to drown herself. Thackeray severely taxed his resources to cure her but finally had to confine her permanently in 1842. The family life he had always prized was over. Instead he had to struggle with poverty, despair, and loneliness, frequently being separated even from his daughters. During this time he found support in

Sketch by Thackeray, circa 1838, of his wife, Isabella Shawe Thackeray, and their first child, Anne (Collection of Mrs. Richard Fuller)

his family and friends and gained new depth as a man and writer, evident in the gentle melancholy and emphasis on endurance that marked his later works. What he lost in love at home he gained in the charity he later defined in lectures as an essential characteristic of the great humorists.

During this ordeal, he earned money by writing whenever he could; he produced a large amount of work and gradually established a reputation that rivaled Dickens's. He wrote much travel literature and fiction, culminating in *Vanity Fair* (1847-1848), worked on an incomplete biography of French statesman Charles Maurice de Talleyrand, and contributed to over a dozen magazines and newspapers. His first major publication was *The Paris Sketch Book* (1840), a collection of essays and tales published under the pseudonym Michael Angelo Titmarsh. It compares badly to his later work; nonetheless, his sense of the ludicrous is strong and finds ample material in the "owl-like solemnities" of George Sand, Jacques Louis David, and others. Several of Thackeray's commentaries on the cultural life of France gave his views on the function of art and literature. He writes of fiction as being as true as history and of the instructive power of the novelist, attitudes that affected the shape of his novels and essays. He also emphasizes the importance of the commonplace as the proper realm of art and literature and rejects the "bloated, unnatural, stilted, spouting, sham sublime." In *The Paris Sketch Book* Thackeray advocates a return to the natural and true, demanding that each artist or writer develop his own talents and vision rather than imitate predecessors "whose ideas fit us no more than their breeches."

A small volume including *The Second Funeral of Napoleon, in Three Letters to Miss Smith of London; and The Chronicle of the Drum* was published in 1841. *The Chronicle of the Drum,* a poem, reviews French history from the middle of the eighteenth century through Napoleon's fall. *The Second Funeral of Napoleon,* in prose, begins where *The Chronicle of the Drum* leaves off and is an account of the disinterment of Napoleon's body at St. Helena, its transport to Paris, and its burial there. Although often strongly satirical, this work contained autobiographical scenes of English family life that made it Thackeray's own favorite among his writings for years.

Besides the volumes of observations on France, Thackeray wrote two full-length travel books and numerous essays based on his travels. He had originally intended to write a book about Ireland in 1840, but after that disastrous trip he postponed work on it until he was on a solitary tour in 1842, which resulted in *The Irish Sketch Book,* published in 1843. He again used the Titmarsh pseudonym, but for the first time his own name appeared on one of his works, on the dedication page. In *The Irish Sketch Book,* Thackeray filters his account of Ireland through the persona of Titmarsh—a reflective and good-natured though crotchety Londoner to whom creature comforts matter (he prefers not to pursue "the picturesque under umbrellas"). He complains endlessly about the dirt, begging, boasting, improvidence, and crippling partisanship; but he finds the Irish more intelligent, good-natured, and moral than the English, and at one point considers thrashing an English snob for abusing an Irish innkeeper. Ireland, as he portrays it, is a land of contradictions, where dirty beggars are terrified of clean poorhouses, where piety and brutality coexist, where everything is "poor, mean, and yet somehow cheerful," where the scenery is "just like the Irish melodies—sweet, wild, and sad even in the sunshine." Although *The Irish Sketch Book* is rambling and repetitious, Titmarsh's itinerary provides a clear plan for the book, a structure lacking in the hodgepodge of tales and essays that make up *The Paris Sketch Book.* Titmarsh himself moves into a central role with a more fully developed character—more vulnerable and, although still judgmental, more self-deprecating and less superior than in the previous work.

The Irish Sketch Book took two years of planning and effort; by comparison, the trip on which Thackeray based his *Notes of a Journey from Cornhill to Grand Cairo* (1846) was the result of a momentary lark. Thackeray had always been fascinated by the East, so during dinner one evening he accepted an invitation to take a ten-week tour by way of Spain, Gibraltar, and Athens to such stops as Smyrna, Constantinople, Rhodes, Syria, Jerusalem, and Cairo. Almost immediately he left on a trip that reflects an exhilaration lacking earlier. In his *Notes* on the journey we again have the impression of an idiosyncratic, often insular and satirical narrator, who is blind to architectural wonders such as those in Athens or Cairo but delighted by more human wonders—the people he sees and the places he visits that seem to bring Dulcinea, Ali Baba, or paintings by Murillo vividly to life.

Although much of Thackeray's known journalism is of little interest, he wrote many fine essays and reviews. His most polished work as a reviewer was written for the *Morning Chronicle.* Thackeray's reviews are lively, engaging, energetic, and often highlighted by his love of absurdities. Like the best nineteenth-century review essays, they frequently go beyond the book under scrutiny to offer insights into the times. In a review of Dickens's *Cricket on the Hearth* (*Morning Chronicle,* 24 December 1845) he describes the panorama of London at Christmas; in an essay on *Coningsby* (*Morning Chronicle,* 13 May 1844) he shows the impression Disraeli made on his contemporaries ("fancy a prophet delivering heavenly messages—with his hair in papers"); and in a piece on Arthur P. Stanley's *Life and Correspondence of Dr. Arnold* (*Morning Chronicle,* 3 June 1844), he expresses the reverence for Thomas Arnold felt by a generation that had learned firsthand of the need for educational reform. In some reviews, Thackeray provides a look into a more distant past, into the "pleasant, curious

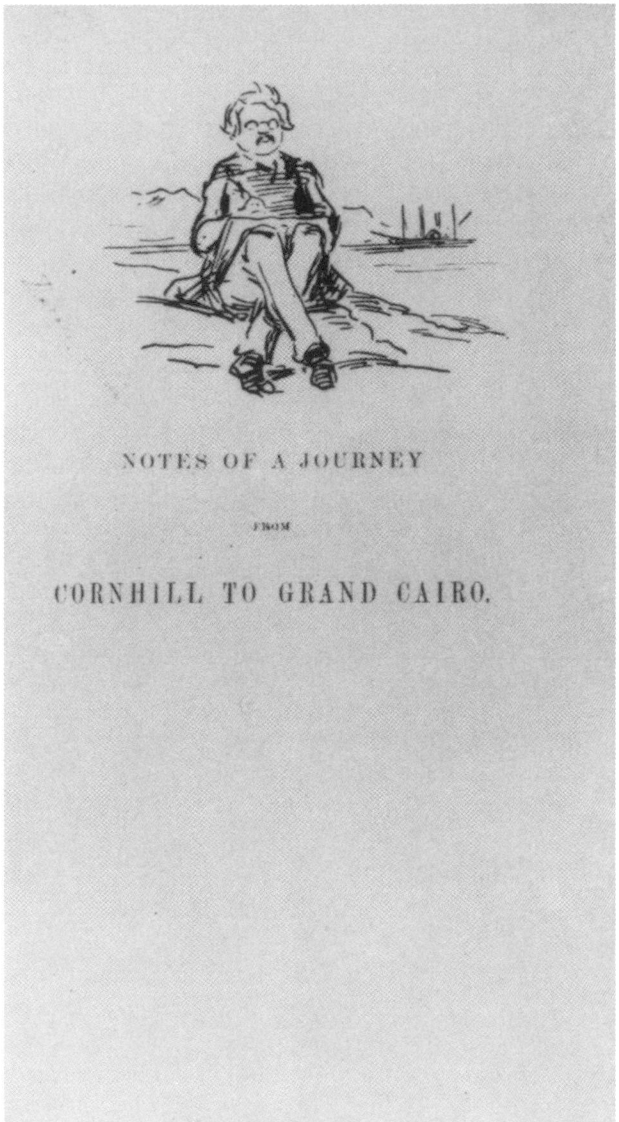

Self-portrait by Thackeray on the half-title for his 1846 travel book (Henry W. and Albert A. Berg Collection of English and American Literature, New York Public Library, Astor, Lenox and Tilden Foundations)

gossip [of] careless volumes" that awaken "disreputable old ghosts" from the eighteenth century. In these pieces he points out plenty that is trivial enough to laugh at yet serious enough to convey a melancholy moral, as he would do in his later lectures. Thackeray also makes several judgments that implicitly reveal his own aims as a writer. In a review of Gilbert Abbot à Beckett's *The Comic Blackstone* (*Morning Chronicle,* 31 December 1845) he describes the limits and abilities of "writers of fun": "it is something to be *Mercutio* if you can't be *Romeo*—to be a gentleman, if not a hero—to have a shrewd, kindly, wit without the least claim to be a sublime genius or a profound philosopher." In another, concerning Disraeli's *Sybil* (*Morning Chronicle,* 13 May 1845), he asserts that the novelist should limit himself to "morals and manners" rather than "algebra, religion, political economy, or other abstract science." And he ignores the boundaries between history and fiction, as he often does in his works: he writes, in a review of Douglas Jerrold's *Mrs. Caudle's Curtain Lectures* (*Morning Chronicle,* 26 December 1845), of "real living personages in history, like Queen Elizabeth, or Sancho Panza," and discusses nonfiction as if it were the work of playwrights in which "a hundred old acquaintances from the dead world arise and play their parts."

In addition to his reviews, Thackeray's journalism included fiction and nonfiction for *Fraser's Magazine* and *Punch.* Unlike the anonymous *Morning Chronicle* contributions, these usually appeared under pseudonyms that became narrative personas—Titmarsh, the Fat Contributor, George Savage Fitzboodle, Fitz-Jeams de la Pluche, Mr. Brown, Mr. Spec, Dr. Solomon Pacifico. The essays range from occasional somber pieces to considerations of gastronomic delights to art criticism to literary parodies to mock histories. The satire is often strong but is at its best in "The Snobs of England, by One of Themselves," which appeared in *Punch* in 1846 and 1847 and was published as *The Book of Snobs* in 1848.

Like *Vanity Fair,* written almost simultaneously, *The Book of Snobs* examines through the eyes of a narrator the hypocrisy that results from the emphasis on money and position in English society. In Thackeray's college days *snob* had been a slang designation for society's lower elements; he redefined it as a moral term. For Thackeray, "He who meanly admires mean things" is a snob, and almost everyone qualifies. Thackeray's narrator, Mr. Snob, provides a long list of aristocratic, city, country, military, and university snobs. What could become a wearisome exercise, however, remains sufficiently light-handed to be enjoyable. The humorous names in Thackeray's character sketches often indicate the shortcomings to be satirized: the virtuous, majestical, and proud Lady Susan Scraper scrapes together enough money to maintain footmen, carriage, and charities but not enough to provide ample food for her daughters; the Rev. Tom Sniffle cares for the poor and writes well-intentioned, vapid sermons until Lady Fanny Brandyball turns his head and he becomes the pretentious Rev. T. D'Arcy Sniffle; young De Mogyns (formerly

Cover for the 1848 collection of satirical essays first published in Punch *as "The Snobs of England, by One of Themselves"*

Muggins) dreams of a nonexistent poetic past as he "sleeps in white kid gloves, and commits dangerous excesses upon green tea." In these caricatures Thackeray repeatedly shows how honest human values are thrown aside for false status. To some critics, such as J. T. Y. Greig, in *Thackeray: A Reconsideration* (1950), this method is an exasperating exercise in finding snobbery everywhere. According to Gordon N. Ray, *The Book of Snobs* "deserves a place on the shelves between [Thomas Carlyle's] *Past and Present* and [Matthew Arnold's] *Culture and Anarchy*" for its analysis of the effects of materialism on English society, and the prominent place a sampling of Snob papers is given at the end of the most recent collection of Thackeray's journalism, *Drawn from Life: The Journalism of William Makepeace Thackeray* (1984), indicates their continuing appeal. At the time of their first appearance, this *Punch* series gave Thackeray his first great popular success.

With the success of *Vanity Fair* (1847-1848), Thackeray gained professional, social, and financial security. His other major novels followed: *Pendennis, Henry Esmond,* and *The Newcomes.* A naturally gregarious man, he enjoyed, as he put it, being "lionised," and he was often invited into the homes of influential people. His social life included an increasingly important bond with Jane Brookfield, the wife of his old friend William Brookfield. Thackeray had met her in 1842, and as their friendship grew it periodically strained his relationship with her husband until the couple finally broke with Thackeray in 1851, shortly after he had begun writing *The History of Henry Esmond, Esq.* The bitterness of the break was responsible for shaping much of that novel; it also made more attractive the lecture tours he had planned to earn back his patrimony for his wife and daughters.

Thackeray's two lecture series, published in book form as *The English Humourists of the Eighteenth Century* (1853) and *The Four Georges* (1860), have much in common: they were written as if they were conversations with old friends about the eighteenth century, they were financial and popular successes in England, Scotland, and America, and they furnished material for *Henry Esmond* and *The Virginians* (1857-1859). Although these lectures compress a lifetime of voracious reading, Thackeray's love of the eighteenth century goes back to his boyhood days when he lived in his great-grandmother's house, where whist, quadrilles, and sedan chairs were still part of the routine and when he had a guardian who had been a friend of Sheridan and Burke. Thackeray always wanted to view history at this personal level, close enough in time to touch the people who had lived through it, and ordinary enough to see what the great and not-so-great had in common. When he contemplated exalted figures, he preferred to examine their human quirks and qualities. Even at the tender age of nine he showed this leveling tendency during a visit to the Royal Yacht, where he observed "the bed on which his Royal Highness snores," as his mother reported in a letter to his grandmother (3 February 1820). Later his interest in writing Talleyrand's biography grew out of meeting Talleyrand's personal secretary. In *The English Humourists of the Eighteenth Century,* he judges his subjects by asking whether we would have liked to have lived with them, and in the first lecture of *The Four Georges,* he reaches into the past through his old friend Mary Berry, born in 1765: "as I took [her] hand," he tells us, he thought of "how with it I held on to the old society of wits and men of the old world." Thackeray studied and wrote biography and history like a novelist, concentrating on men rather than movements and instinctively keeping an eye open for the telling personal detail. In *The English Humourists of the Eighteenth Century,* Thackeray discusses Jonathan Swift, William Congreve, Joseph Addison, Richard Steele, Matthew Prior, John Gay, Alexander Pope, William Hogarth, Tobias Smollett, Henry Fielding, Laurence Sterne, and Oliver Goldsmith. Although Thackeray's lectures were well received in 1851, some of his judgments have angered later critics. In countering Thomas Carlyle's "Hero as Man of Letters," Thackeray shows his habitual distrust of greatness. He treats the satiric genius of Swift as frightening, and even the gentler isolation of Addison is attractive to Thackeray only when Addison succumbs to "a certain weakness for wine" or assumes the humble posture of prayer. Thackeray emphasizes personal weaknesses in his discussions of "poor Congreve" and "Harry Fielding" and turns Thomas Babington Macaulay's unheroic portrait of Steele (*Edinburgh Review,* July 1843), always "sinning and repenting," into that of a flawed Christian hero whose "faults and careless blunders [are] redeemed . . . by his sweet and compassionate nature." The author of *The Book of Snobs,* "by One of Themselves," believed that the writer was brother to his reader and partook of the same sins. Thus, it is not strange that he approvingly evokes Steele with the words "Let us love . . . one another, brother—God knows we have need of love and pardon."

The English Humourists of the Eighteenth Century displays, in technique and theme as well as in detail, some of the important features of Thackeray's novels. In fact, in *Henry Esmond* Thackeray portrays several of the humorists from the lectures and uses scenes, dialogue, and descriptions, often with only slight changes in wording. As early as *The Paris Sketch Book* he had claimed that novels were truer than histories, and in his lecture on Steele he asserts: "a volume of Dr. Smollett, or a volume of the *Spectator* . . . carries a greater amount of truth in solution than the volume which purports to be all true. Out of the fictitious book I get the expression of the life of the time; of the manners, of the movement, the dress, the pleasures, the laughter, the ridicules of society—the old times live again, and I travel in the old country of England. Can the heaviest historian do more for me?"

It is not surprising then that Thackeray occasionally ignores facts (such as Steele's industriousness) that are inconvenient to his versions of

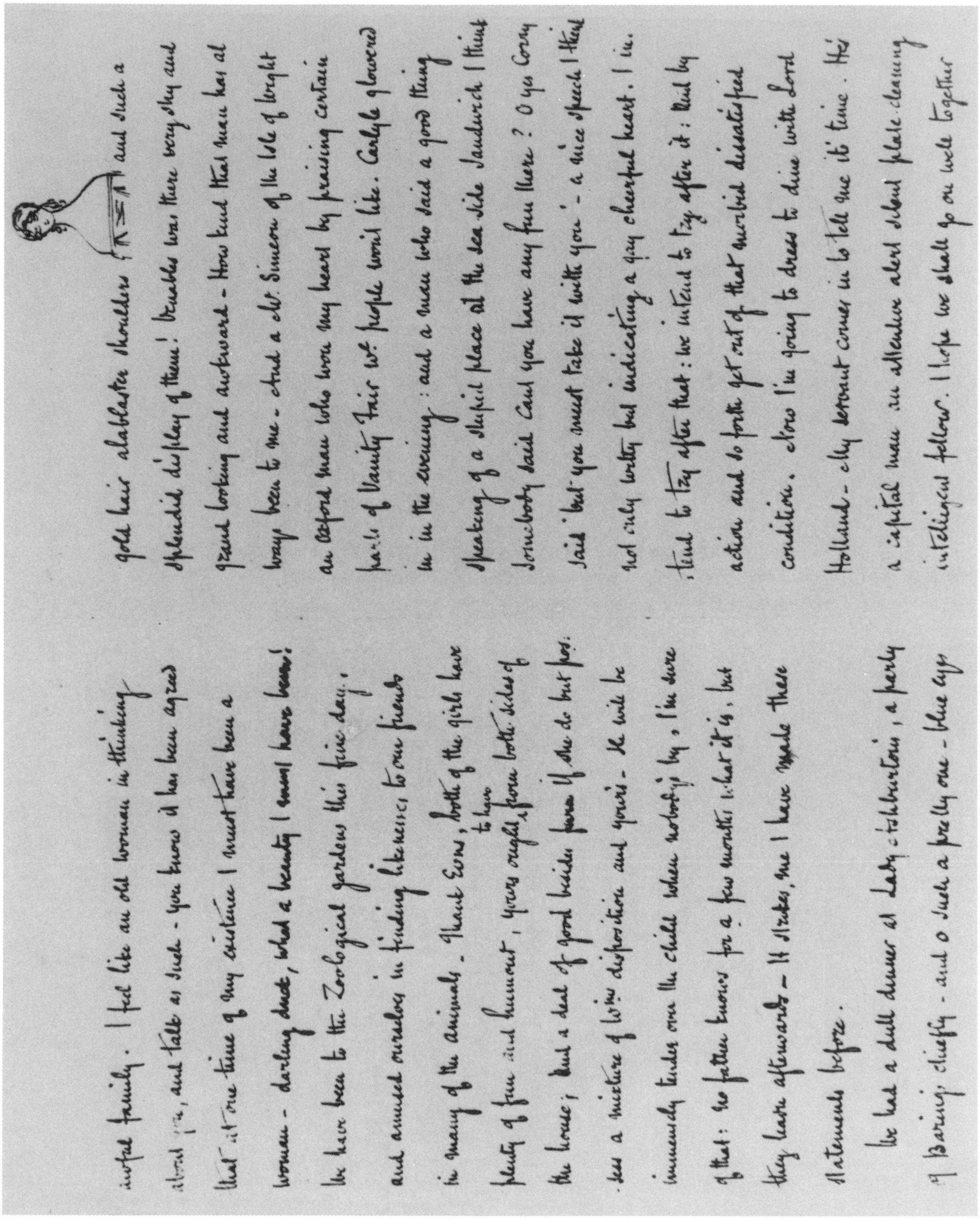
awful family. I feel like an old woman in thinking about you, and talk as such - you know it has been agreed that at one time of my existence I must have been a woman - darling duck, what a beauty I must have been! We have been to the Zoological gardens this fine day, and amused ourselves in finding likenesses to our friends in many of the animals. Thank Evns, both of the girls have plenty of fun and humour, yours ought to have from both sides of the house; and a deal of good besides from If she do but possess a mixture of Wm disposition and yours - He will be immensely tender over the child when nobody's by, I'm sure of that: no father knows for a few months what it is, but they learn afterwards - It strikes me I have made these statements before.

We had a dull dinner at Lady Ashburton's, a party of Barings chiefly - and o such a pretty one - blue eyes gold hair alablaster shoulders and such a splendid display of them! Venables was there very shy and grand looking and awkward - How kind that man has always been to me - And a Mr. Simeon of the Isle of Wight an Oxford man who won my heart by praising certain parts of Vanity Fair wh. people wont like. Carlyle glowered in in the evening: and a man who said a good thing speaking of a stupid place at the sea side Sandwich I think Somebody said Cant you have any fun there? O yes Corry said 'but you must take it with you' - a nice speech I think not only witty but indicating a gay cheerful heart. I intend to try after that: we intend to try after it: and by action and so forth get out of that morbid dissatisfied condition. Now I'm going to dress to dine with Lord Holland - My servant comes in to tell me it's time. He's a capital man an attentive alert silent plate cleaning intelligent fellow. I hope we shall go on well together

March 1850 letter from Thackeray to Jane Brookfield, the wife of his friend William Brookfield. Thackeray's bond with Mrs. Brookfield brought about the end of his relationship with the couple in 1851 (by permission of the Trustees of The Pierpont Morgan Library).

the humorists, just as a novelist controls details that are out of keeping with his view of his characters. Yet the anger his judgments have generated is based not only on his exaggerations and inaccuracies but also on the stylistic skill with which he delivers them. He sums up his judgment of Swift, for instance, not with a list of factual accomplishments but with a powerful metaphor: "Treasures of wit and wisdom, and tenderness, too, must that man have had locked up in the caverns of his gloomy heart, and shone fitfully to one or two whom he took in there. But it was not good to visit that place." In his few criticisms of Addison, Thackeray depends less on statement than on depiction of significant gestures and stances: "I don't think the great Mr. Addison liked young Mr. Pope, the Papist, much; I don't think he abused him. But when Mr. Addison's men abused Mr. Pope, I don't think Addison took his pipe out of his mouth to contradict them." Even minor details of physical description are chosen by the novelist's eye: Steele's "inked ruffles, and claret-stains on his tarnished lace coat" emphasize Thackeray's unheroic portrait.

His skill as a stylist is also the key to his recreation of the times, which generally met with praise from his contemporaries. For this he depends on a plethora of anecdotes that he develops into minor scenes and on long, descriptive lists, as in his discussion of Hogarth: "We look, and see pass before us the England of a hundred years ago—the peer in his drawing-room, the lady of fashion in her apartment, foreign singers surrounding her, and the chambers filled with gewgaws in the mode of that day; the church, with its quaint florid architecture and singing congregation; the parson with his great wig, and the beadle with his cane. . . ." His intense enjoyment of incidents from the daily lives and favorite works of the humorists proved infectious, and, as John Henry Newman and others acknowledged, Thackeray revived the taste for these works of the eighteenth century and changed the minds of many Victorians who had turned away from them.

In *The Four Georges,* a series of lectures (delivered in 1855) about the first four Hanoverian monarchs, Thackeray's intention was not to write a history analyzing politics, diplomacy, constitutional developments, or economics, for "We are not the Historic Muse, but her ladyship's attendant, tale-bearer, *valet de chambre.*" Thackeray's aims as a lecturer mirror those he had as a novelist: the subtitle of his lectures, *Sketches of Manners, Morals, Court and Town Life,* covers precisely those matters he described in his *Morning Chronicle* reviews and elsewhere as the business of the novelist. In *The Four Georges* Thackeray refers to the great writers and painters of the day—Fielding, Richardson, Burke, Johnson, Boswell, Goldsmith, and Sir Joshua Reynolds. Among the sources he uses are many diaries and letters, particularly those of George Selwyn and Fanny Burney. He is usually descriptive rather than analytic, discussing how men lived rather than why they acted as they did; when he does speculate, he concentrates on personality or talks about how general movements manifest themselves in the domestic lives of kings and courts. His effort is more to bring life to the past than to understand it, to give a vivid panorama rather than a profound study, to "peep here and there," as he says, at the Georges and their court and to "amuse . . . with the result of many a day's and night's pleasant reading."

In addition to the life of the times of the Georges, Thackeray examines the character of each of the monarchs. Generally the result is a picture inimical to the cult of aristocracy and "king-worship." Thackeray portrays George I as "not a lofty monarch . . . but not a hypocrite" and George II as "gross, low, and sensual." George IV becomes a symbol of snobbery and the sham sublime in a denunciation that uses a clothing metaphor to indicate Thackeray's contempt for George IV's superficiality: "I try and take him to pieces, and find silk stockings, padding, stays, a coat with frogs and a fur collar, a star and blue ribbon, a pocket-handkerchief prodigiously scented, one of Truefitt's best nutty brown wigs reeking with oil, a set of teeth and a huge black stock, underwaistcoats, more underwaistcoats, and then nothing." Thackeray's treatment of George III, his love for his family, and his struggle with insanity, however, is sympathetic, probably because of Thackeray's own experience with his wife's illness.

Unlike many of his other trips, Thackeray's lecture tours of the United States in 1852-1853 and 1855-1856 did not result in a major work of nonfiction. His novel *The Virginians* is his only major work inspired by his American experiences, and its slow pace reflects the strain that touring put on his health. The book lost money for the publisher, and Thackeray felt his novelistic powers were depleted when in 1859 publisher George Smith invited him to edit and write for a new periodical, the *Cornhill Magazine.* Thackeray made a success of the opportunity. The first number broke records with a sale of 120,000 copies, and its unusually high average of 85,000 sales must have owed much to its con-

Thackeray's drawing of the house at 2 Palace Green, Kensington, which he purchased in 1860 (Collection of Mr. W. T. D. Ritchie)

tributors, including Alfred Tennyson, Anthony Trollope, Elizabeth Barrett Browning, John Ruskin, and Matthew Arnold. Thackeray, however, had not the hardness necessary to be an editor and resigned the "thorn-cushioned editorial chair" in 1862.

Although his novels *Lovel the Widower, The Adventures of Philip,* and *Denis Duval* were serialized in *Cornhill Magazine,* his major contributions were his familiar essays, the *Roundabout Papers,* published in book form in 1863. They stand in relation to the rest of his nonfiction much as *Henry Esmond* does to his other novels, notable for their tone of autumnal melancholy. Each of these strongly autobiographical works is largely structured by the narrator's reminiscence of youth in old age. As Esmond looks at his new Castlewood in his old age, past and present, near and far merge as they do in the *Roundabout Papers* when the narrator looks at Tunbridge Wells Common and sees not just the scene before his eyes but also the scene as it was in his youth; he hears a peal of bells and the sound takes him back to his great-grandmother's house; he feels as if he is alive both in 1860, working at his desk, and in 1828, listening to chimes at midnight in Antwerp. History and fiction also fuse as Thackeray portrays Esmond or Mr. Roundabout in conversation with the humorists he had studied in his lectures. The *Roundabout Papers,* however, has a sense of playfulness and whimsy missing in *Henry Esmond;* the occasional mock-heroic speech and the friendly, conversational tone also help modify the force of Thackeray's satire, still present though not as pervasive as in the earlier works. He praises more than he disparages, finding the true gentlemanly ideal in his departed friends Washington Irving and Macaulay, "the Goldsmith and Gibbon of our time." He takes up the familiar themes of the joys of reading novels, but now he has a greater appreciation for works of history and greater generosity toward such novelists as Alexandre Dumas père than he showed in *The Paris Sketch Book.* His musings on childhood and on the passing of life and even his brief glimpse of poverty indicate a degree of compassion in *The Irish Sketch Book.* And in the paper entitled "Small-Beer Chronicle," Thackeray returns to a habitual theme: "All CLARET *would be port if it could*"; men try to "portify" themselves when they should enjoy the pleasures of being *ordinaire.* These essays, however, are

Thackeray's port, not his *ordinaire*, and have received some of the highest praise from critics, Saintsbury suggesting it as the best introduction to Thackeray and Las Vergnas calling it his "favorite book."

Thackeray ended his years in a style pleasing to him. The *Cornhill Magazine* had brought him considerable wealth. In 1860 he bought a house at 2 Palace Green, Kensington, in the old court section, rebuilt it in red brick according to his eighteenth-century ideals, and initiated another revival of the fashions of the previous century. After Macaulay's death, George Smith proposed that Thackeray continue Macaulay's *History of England* through Queen Anne's reign; Thackeray planned to do so, as he put it in a letter of May 1862, with "an old green and an old palace and magnificent trees before the windows at w^h^ I write." His stepfather had died, but his mother and two daughters were with him in his house, and his elder daughter's first signs of becoming a successful writer (Anne Thackeray's first piece was published in the May 1850 issue of *Cornhill*) confirmed her father's longstanding pride in her. In November 1863 Thackeray contributed his last "Roundabout Paper" to *Cornhill Magazine,* and on Christmas Eve 1863 he died, leaving the wonderfully fresh but incomplete manuscript for *Denis Duval,* which was published posthumously with the new year.

Throughout his life Thackeray had a lively wit, quick and sometimes impatient. His criticisms of art, literature, and society were based on the value of adhering to the natural and abandoning pretension, snobbery, and the sham sublime. From the beginning of his career he emphasized the ordinary as worthwhile and pointed to imitation of those with wealth or position as the source of human misery. While his satire exposed bitter truths, he found gentle antidotes in humility and love. As he redefined *snob* in moral terms, so did he redefine *humor* as "wit and love," and even *gentleman:* "without love, I can fancy no gentleman." In fact, morality for Thackeray was largely defined by love, and the standard by which he wrote is perhaps best summarized in his comment at the end of *The Book of Snobs:* "if Fun is good, Truth is still better, and Love best of all."

Letters:

The Letters and Private Papers of William Makepeace Thackeray, edited by Gordon N. Ray, 4 volumes (London: Oxford University Press, 1945-1946).

Bibliographies:

Gordon N. Ray, "Thackeray and 'Punch': 44 Newly Identified Contributions," *Times Literary Supplement,* 1 January 1949;

Henry S. Van Duzer, *A Thackeray Library* (Port Washington, N.Y.: Kennikat, 1965);

Edward M. White, "Thackeray's Contributions to *Fraser's Magazine,*" *Studies in Bibliography,* 19 (1966): 67-84;

Dudley Flamm, *Thackeray's Critics: An Annotated Bibliography of British and American Criticism 1836-1901* (Chapel Hill: University of North Carolina Press, 1967);

John C. Olmsted, *Thackeray and His Twentieth-Century Critics: An Annotated Bibliography, 1900-1975* (New York & London: Garland, 1977).

Biographies:

Lionel Stevenson, *The Showman of Vanity Fair: The Life of William Makepeace Thackeray* (New York: Scribners, 1947);

Gordon N. Ray, *Thackeray: The Uses of Adversity, 1811-1846* (New York: McGraw-Hill, 1955);

Ray, *Thackeray: The Age of Wisdom, 1847-1863* (New York: McGraw-Hill, 1958);

Ann Monsarrat, *An Uneasy Victorian: Thackeray the Man, 1811-1863* (New York: Dodd, Mead, 1980).

References:

Albert I. Borowitz, "Why Thackeray Went to See a Man Hanged," *Victorian Newsletter,* no. 48 (Fall 1975): 15-21;

Edwin R. Clapp, "Critic on Horseback," *Sewanee Review,* 38 (July-September 1930): 286-300;

Costerus, special Thackeray issue, new series 2 (1974);

John W. Dodds, *Thackeray: A Critical Portrait* (New York: Oxford University Press, 1941);

Dodds, "Thackeray in the Victorian Frame," *Sewanee Review,* 48 (October-December 1940): 466-478;

Dennis Douglas, "Thackeray and the Uses of History," *Yearbook of English Studies,* 5 (1975): 164-177;

Spencer L. Eddy, Jr., *The Founding of "The Cornhill Magazine"* (Muncie, Ind.: Ball State University Press, 1970);

Judith L. Fisher, "The Aesthetic of the Mediocre: Thackeray and the Visual Arts," *Victorian Studies,* 26 (Autumn 1982): 65-82;

J. T. Y. Greig, *Thackeray: A Reconsideration* (London: Oxford University Press, 1950);

Harold Strong Gulliver, *Thackeray's Literary Apprenticeship* (Valdosta, Ga.: Southern Stationery and Printing, 1934);

Edgar F. Harden, "The Writing and Publication of Thackeray's *English Humourists*," *Papers of the Bibliographical Society of America*, 76, no. 2 (1982): 197-207;

Raymond Las Vergnas, *W. M. Thackeray: L'Homme, le Penseur, le Romancier* (Paris: Librairie Ancienne Honoré Champion, 1932);

Charles Mauskopf, "Thackeray's Concept of the Novel: A Study of Conflict," *Philological Quarterly*, 50 (1971): 239-252;

Lidmila Pantůčková, *W. M. Thackeray as a Critic of Literature* (Brno, Czechoslovakia: Purkyne University Press, 1972);

Ralph Wilson Rader, "Thackeray's Injustice to Fielding," *Journal of English and Germanic Philology*, 56 (April 1957): 203-212;

George Saintsbury, *A Consideration of Thackeray* (London: Oxford University Press, 1931);

Elizabeth Segel, "Thackeray's Journalism: Apprenticeship for Writer and Reader," *Victorian Newsletter*, no. 57 (Spring 1980): 23-27;

M. H. Spielmann, *The History of "Punch"* (London: Cassell, 1895);

Miriam M. H. Thrall, *Rebellious "Fraser's": Nol York's Magazine in the Days of Maginn, Thackeray, and Carlyle* (New York: Columbia University Press, 1934);

Geoffrey Tillotson and Donald Hawes, eds., *Thackeray: The Critical Heritage* (London: Routledge & Kegan Paul, 1968);

Eva Beach Touster, "The Literary Relationship of Thackeray and Fielding," *Journal of English and Germanic Philology*, 46 (October 1947): 383-394;

Anthony Trollope, *Thackeray* (London: Macmillan, 1879);

Charles Whibley, *Thackeray* (New York: Dodd, Mead, 1903).

Papers:

Manuscripts for Thackeray's published and unpublished nonfiction are held by the Houghton Library and the Widener Library at Harvard University, the New York Public Library, the Huntington Library, the Fales Library at New York University, the Pierpont Morgan Library, the Princeton University Library, the Glasgow University Library, the British Library, the Rosenbach Foundation Library, and the Humanities Research Center at the University of Texas, Austin.

Victoria

(24 May 1819-21 January 1901)

Richard Tobias
University of Pittsburgh

BOOKS: *Leaves from the Journal of Our Life in the Highlands, from 1848 to 1861: To Which are Prefixed and Added Extracts from the Same Journal Giving an Account of Earlier Visits to Scotland, and Tours in England and Ireland, and Yachting Excursions,* edited by Arthur Helps (London: Privately printed, 1867; London: Smith, Elder, 1868; New York: Harper/Chicago: Griggs, 1868; enlarged, London: Smith, Elder, 1877);

More Leaves from the Journal of a Life in the Highlands, from 1862 to 1882 (London: Smith, Elder, 1884; New York: Harper, 1884);

Leaves from a Journal: A Record of the Visit of the Emperor and Empress of the French to the Queen and of the Visit of the Queen and H.R.H., the Prince Consort, to the Emperor of the French, 1855 (London: Privately printed, 1888); with an introduction by Raymond Mortimer (London: Deutsch, 1961; New York: Farrar, Straus & Cudahy, 1961);

The Girlhood of Queen Victoria: A Selection from Her Majesty's Diaries Between the Years 1832 and 1840, 2 volumes, edited by Viscount Escher (New York: Longmans, Green/London: Murray, 1912).

Queen Victoria with her oldest daughter, Victoria, Princess Royal. This picture, taken in 1844 or 1845, is the first photograph of the Queen (by gracious permission of Her Majesty the Queen).

The woman who gave her name to a great age of English prose was herself competent in the craft. Unfortunately, her daughter Beatrice destroyed her major work, the 122 volumes of journal that she kept all her life (the last entry is 6 January 1901, two weeks before her death). She often wrote 2,500 words a day, the equivalent of a novel a month. The journal survives only in extracts Beatrice copied in blue notebooks before she consigned the rest to a fire. Victoria's most recent biographer, Cecil Woodham-Smith, says that "Her style of writing, far from literary, was admirably vivid; characters leap alive from the pages. She was honest, the leading characteristic of her nature; she did not write to justify herself, or to explain but poured with vehemence, enthusiasm, passion, sometimes with violence, but never with rancour, everything she had done, observed and experienced during the course of the day." That judgment may not be entirely accurate for her earliest journal, from 1830 to 1840, prepared under the watchful eye of her mother, Duchess of Kent, and Baroness Lehzen, her governess. Two volumes have been culled from this early journal under the title *The Girlhood of Queen Victoria,* published in 1912.

Other fragments of the full journal have been published. In her lifetime Victoria arranged for commercial publication of two volumes, *Leaves from the Journal of Our Life in the Highlands* (1868) and *More Leaves from the Journal of a Life in the Highlands*

(1884), and a third, *Leaves from a Journal* (1888), was privately printed.

Additional fragments survive in Charles Grey's 1867 biography, *The Early Years of His Royal Highness the Prince Consort,* prepared under "the direction of Her Majesty the Queen." The complete 122-volume record would have been an incomparable personal report of a woman at the heart of her age, writing with power, persuasion, and skill.

In her journal and letters, the Queen demonstrates the most important characteristic of a successful writer: the compelling need to communicate. Victoria's nurse reported that the two-year-old child was "inclined to be obstinate and self-willed." In her letters to her ministers and to her children she is indeed commanding. Victoria knew that her judgments mattered, and in her writings she communicated her will to ministers, children, relatives, and sometimes seemed, in the journal entries, to work toward these judgments. As readers, we are fascinated, but accidental, observers.

The Queen's etching of Prince Albert at the time of their marriage (by gracious permission of Her Majesty the Queen)

No person was ever so deliberately conceived and educated as Victoria. She was born and bred to rule Great Britain. Her grandfather, George III, had fifteen children, but because of the Royal Marriage law requiring membership in a Protestant confession, royal status, and approval by the cabinet, few of his children found wives. Instead they found mistresses or made morganatic marriages. William IV had ten illegitimate children by an actress, Mrs. Jordan (née Dorothy Phillips), but no children survived from his marriage to his consort Queen Adelaide. The Prince of Wales, who became George IV, sired a daughter, Charlotte, but Charlotte died in childbirth in 1817. There was no grandchild to succeed. Therefore, Edward, fourth son and Duke of Kent, exiled his mistress to Paris and sought a German wife who would meet the requirements of the Royal Marriage law. He found Victoire, Princess of Saxe-Coburg and Dowager Princess of Leiningen. She was Protestant and she was certified of royal birth. Her brother Leopold fathered Princess Charlotte's stillborn child. Dutifully, the new Duchess of Kent became pregnant, but a particular difficulty obtruded. The Duke of Kent was so in debt that his creditors required him to live cheaply on the Continent rather than in London where his extravagance consumed his Parliamentary income. The Duchess of Kent, eight months pregnant, was bundled into a carriage and taken halfway across Europe so that her child could be born on English soil. Early in the morning of 24 May 1819 (just two weeks after Keats had written his "Ode to a Nightingale"), the Duchess delivered a daughter who was named Alexandrina Victoria. The name was not English; King William IV tried to persuade the Duchess to change the name to Elizabeth or Charlotte. The Duke of Kent, having played his part in the dynastic comedy, left the scene. He died on 23 January 1820, when his daughter was not quite eight months old. For the rest of her life, Victoria sought to replace that father. Much of her writing reveals her search for a surrogate, especially after she ascended the throne on 20 June 1837.

A number of men tried to be surrogate fathers to Victoria. The first attempt, by her father's military equerry and her mother's confidential adviser, Sir John Conroy, failed. Near the end of her life, an attempt by William Gladstone also failed. Although the Queen was small (under five feet; she is called "the little Queen" in the memoirs of her prime minister Lord Melbourne), she was not malleable. Her uncle Leopold, husband of the dead Princess Charlotte, advised her, but when he became King of the Belgians, their relationship was necessarily limited to an exchange of letters. Melbourne, her first prime minister, treated her as if she were a much-loved daughter. Throughout her reign she tended to look upon her ministers—the Duke of Wellington, Sir John Peel, and Benjamin Disraeli, for example—as fathers, but none could match the influence of Albert, who came to her side in 1839. After Albert's death, a trusted Scottish servant, John Brown, gave her the emotional support of a strong male figure. Aside from her half-sister, Princess Feodora, she never had a close woman friend, a person with whom she could speak frankly and openly. She quarreled with her mother and her governess Baroness Lehzen. Her court women were helpful, but they were selected and kept because they accepted her obstinancy and willfulness without question. Her writing, except for the letters to children, shows a woman trying to be sovereign and a woman much in need of counsel and advice.

On 26 August 1819 a far and apparently dissociate event occurred. Albert, Duke of Saxe-Coburg-Gotha, was born in his native principality in Germany, and the marriage of the two first cousins was planned. Albert's father was brother to the Duchess of Kent. Victoria and Albert met once in childhood without being impressed with each other. Victoria loved amusement, and on first sight Albert did not appear sufficiently amusing. When they met again on 10 October 1839, she fell in love; on 15 October she asked him to marry her. The wedding took place on 10 February of the following year. They had nine children and set the character of the age. Their children and grandchildren occupied royal palaces from London to Moscow. Their daughters carried the genetic defect that caused grandsons to be victims of hemophilia, the bleeding disease, of which their son Leopold died. The marriage was the climactic event in her life; Albert was the father and lover that she needed. He guided, advised, instructed. When he died on 14 December 1861, she thought her life had ended. She lived for another forty years, but much of her thought was for what he would have done, whether he would have approved. She spent forty years creating monuments for him.

Her first book is, in part, a memorial to Albert. She made the extracts from the journal she published in 1867 as *Leaves from the Journal of Our Life in the Highlands* with Arthur Helps, himself a minor Victorian prose writer, as editor. The book was privately printed for the Royal family, and Helps corrected her grammar and spelling. Because he feared that copies of the book might reach the public and become the source of published extracts that would not please the Queen, he persuaded her to agree to commercial publication in 1868, by Smith, Elder, the same firm that published the Brontë sisters and George Eliot. Although she protested "that she had no skill whatever in authorship," she was pleased with the book, the favorable reviews, and the two-thousand-pound profit earned by the sale of thirty thousand copies in the "cheap edition." Disraeli is supposed to have flattered her by murmuring, "We authors, ma'am," at an appropriate moment. Some in her family were reticent in commenting on the book; others complained. Clearly, the seeds of the family plan to make sure that the 122 volumes of the journal would never reach the public had been sowed. Victoria, they believed, revealed herself too much.

Her literary adviser and editor Arthur Helps reported in his preface that Victoria permitted publication of her *Leaves from a Journal of Our Life in the Highlands* in order to heal any "abrupt severance of class from class." The Queen wished, he continued, to support "a full community of interests, a constant exchange of good offices, and a kindly respect felt and expressed by each class . . . in the great brotherhood that forms a nation." In short, she hoped that book would strengthen her reign and reinforce her objectives as sovereign. When Victoria was a girl, her mother had traveled with the young princess from one end of England to another each summer, following the tradition of Royal Progresses, or tours by which English monarchs presented themselves to their people. William IV looked askance at the pretense of the tours, but the Duchess of Kent wanted the nation to see its future ruler. Victoria's *Leaves from the Journal of Our Life in the Highlands* is itself a kind of progress, a presentation of royal life and ambitions. The book was an agency of Victoria's government, for in it she displays for the nation the model wife, mother, sovereign, and court.

A second motive for the publication of *Leaves from the Journal of Our Life in the Highlands* was to preserve, and possibly even to sanctify, the memory

The Queen and Prince Consort, photographed by Roger Fenton at Buckingham Palace, 30 June 1854 (Victoria and Albert Museum)

of Albert for the royal children and the nation. Princess Beatrice was only five when her father died. Young Albert, the Prince of Wales (who became Edward VII when he assumed the throne in 1901), would benefit, the Queen believed, from reminders of his father's virtues. Victoria's subjects complained that she mourned too much and too long; the book, she hoped, would prove that she mourned justly. The Queen's portrayal of Albert in the journal shows the paterfamilias and royal adviser on holiday hunting, hiking, and enjoying the landscape. He was the one who eased the Queen's cares; he was a devoted servant, brave, energetic, and always on call. Historians now see evidence that Albert indeed worked himself to death for the Queen; in *Leaves from the Journal of Our Life in the Highlands* he is a man on a needed holiday. If the first demand of good prose, as Walter Pater says in his essay "Style," is a compelling and difficult subject, then Victoria had that subject in Albert, whom she strove to depict not only as fit consort (she wanted his title to be King Consort) but also as a hero in his own time.

Leaves from the Journal of Our Life in the Highlands has a third message in the ideal world which Victoria and Albert found in Scotland. Scotland, unlike London, was peaceful, and the air was pure. Its inhabitants, according to Victoria, were "simple, dear, devoted." In the Scotland of the journal, the Queen shrinks from "the world and all its irritating trials, noises, troubles and frivolities." Victoria had read the Scottish writers Sir Walter Scott and Mrs. Oliphant, and often her journal reflects the romance of their novels. For example, when Lord Breadalbane presented his Highlanders in full regalia, it seemed to the Queen "as if a great chieftain in olden feudal times was receiving his sovereign. It was princely and romantic." In Victoria's eyes, her Scots servants Grant and John Brown were "perfect—discreet, careful, intelligent, attentive, ever ready to do what is wanted; and [Brown], particularly, is handy and willing to do everything and anything, and to overcome every difficulty, which makes him one of my best servants anywhere." They were models of behavior, worthy of imitation by the prime ministers and members of the Cabinet, royal children, journalists, and subjects with whom the Queen had to contend at home. Modern, but still feudal, Scotland seemed to preserve in amber the medievalism which lent so much character to writing, architecture, and even ordinary pleasures in Victoria's time.

The Queen found the work of preparing *Leaves* and *More Leaves from the Journal of a Life in the Highlands,* published in 1884, therapeutic. The first book aided her difficult recovery from Albert's death, and she reported that after finishing the second book she was more fit for her onerous tasks. A third book, *Leaves from a Journal,* virtually unknown until 1961, contains her account of the 1855 visit of Napoleon III to England and the Queen and Prince Consort's return visit to France. According to Raymond Mortimer in his introduction to the 1961 edition, this portion of the journal was privately printed in 1888, the year after she celebrated her jubilee of fifty years on the throne, in a form nearly identical to the Queen's manuscript. In *Leaves from a Journal* Victoria reports the adulation of the crowds and the flattery of Napolean III. As in the earlier published accounts Albert plays an important role as the Queen describes the figure that Albert cut in France. The French were more willing to grant him precedence and to recognize him as her equal in all but name.

The 1866 engraving used as the frontispiece for the second published collection of extracts from the Queen's journal

There was, in addition to the three journal volumes, another book. After the death of John Brown, Victoria wrote a biography of him. *More Leaves from the Journal of a Life in the Highlands* had been dedicated to him, but she wanted to leave some further mark of his influence. She wrote a portion of the biography covering the years from 1849 to 1865. Her object was, as she put it in a letter, to "show by her gratitude and friendship that Brown was 'a gt deal more' than a devoted servant." Her advisers were appalled, but none had the courage to dissuade the Queen from publishing, even privately, as she at first planned. The Dean of Windsor finally said firmly that publication would be "most undesirable," and the manuscript was destroyed. The biography must have been a singular document, and it would be of great interest. Brown was a servant, but he was a Scot with firm notions, the kind of commanding presence that Victoria needed. Although there were jokes about Brown and his role in the Queen's household, there is no firsthand record of their relationship, no biography that, in Victoria's words, might force "false biographies & Lives [to] fall into the background & vanish altogether." By "false" biographies, she meant any version of her life that she did not command. From all the available evidence, Victoria was always discreet; her greatest indiscretion was to send Brown sentimental greeting cards.

Victoria's largest extant body of writing is her correspondence with her ministers. The nine volumes of *The Letters of Queen Victoria* (1907-1930) are a selection offering both sides of the correspondence in addition to extracts from her journals. In these volumes, one can see Victoria planning strategies and developing convictions. In letters written when Albert was her private secretary, one can distinguish a Teutonic thoroughness and logic added to her style. In many letters, the Queen guards her political role zealously and uses the power of language to extend her influence on the government and the nation. Victoria writes with simplicity and

Queen Victoria with John Brown, the Scottish servant to whom she dedicated More Leaves from the Journal of a Life in the Highlands *(photograph by G. W. Wilson, Balmoral, 1863)*

directness. The "very decided will of her own" that Countess Cowper attributed to Victoria is evident in her official letters. She wrote to Palmerston, her foreign secretary, that he "sent to her drafts to approve when the originals have already been sent away. . . . Perhaps Lord Palmerston would look into this and rectify these mistakes." Palmerston did learn and later when he became her prime minister he was most careful about consulting her. She battled constantly with her ministers when she thought her will was overlooked or ignored. She sometimes persuaded them; they sometimes persuaded her. She always spoke, as she put it, "plainly out." In her correspondence with the wily Palmerston, she emerges as sensible, intelligent, and sensitive. She worried, for example, about the propriety of underground subversion in European capitals. She sometimes sought to protect her relatives on the Continent from the machinations of Liberal English governments. Sometimes she curbed Palmerston, and always she was watchful to keep him within some measure of order.

The richest examples of Victoria's writing, however, are to be found in her letters to her daughter Victoria—Vicky—Crown Princess of Prussia. Nearly eight thousand letters survive written by the two women. Victoria encourages, advises, monitors, queries, and debates with Vicky. The Crown Princess was an equal adversary. Often Vicky seems the superior writer—with more open intelligence, more wide experience, and possibly a more tragic view of experience than Victoria, who assumed that the will to do good would make sure that good would come. In the letters to her daughter Victoria discussed the difficulty of childbirth, rearing children, and pleasing husbands and relatives. She reported having been shocked (her favorite spelling was *schocked*) when a woman of her court "valsed" when she was seven months pregnant. Vicky needed help in educating her wayward and difficult son who became Kaiser Wilhelm, especially when Bismarck himself arranged to send the boy to a military school where Prussian values would be instilled. Victoria's letters have the vigor, simplicity, and conviction that mark her as a writer. Above all in her letters she is direct. She told the Crown Princess that Albert, Prince of Wales, was dull; she explained to parents of one grandchild that the child was ugly. When the Prince of Wales reported that his friends were shocked that he appeared so infrequently in *More Leaves from the Journal of a Life in the Highlands,* the Queen replied by citing the four times that he was mentioned. She told the Prince that he should read the book himself and not count on his friends to report to him. He would have figured in the account more often, the Queen concluded, "had he not refused so many invitations to Balmoral." She made a palpable hit. The Prince of Wales preferred the lights of London to the gloom of the family's castle, Balmoral, in Scotland.

The letters to Vicky constitute an extended dramatic monologue. She was experienced enough to be conscious of herself as a Queen, but her direct judgments of Gladstone, whom she disliked, Bismarck, whom she feared, and even her willful grandson who became Kaiser Wilhelm have been strikingly born out by subsequent events. There is, therefore, an accidental yet satisfying irony in reading her words. In her letters and journal she reveals that she read more history than novels, and she preferred poetry to prose. She liked Tennyson's poems, but thought Mrs. Browning's *Aurora Leigh* coarse. She was not the slightest sympathetic to the cause of women, but she admired Florence Nightingale and wished that she might serve in some

The Royal Family, May 1857. Left to right: Prince Alfred, Prince Albert, Princess Helena, Princess Alice and (in front of her) Prince Arthur, Queen Victoria holding Princess Beatrice, Victoria, Princess Royal (behind the Queen), Princess Louise, Prince Leopold, and Edward, Prince of Wales (by gracious permission of Her Majesty the Queen).

humble and self-sacrificing way herself. She read all of Macaulay's *History of England,* was not shocked, as were some, by George Eliot's *Adam Bede,* and thought Charlotte Brontë's *Jane Eyre* "admirably written."

Elizabeth Longford concludes her 1964 biography of Queen Victoria with ten pages aiming to "convey the richness of her contradictions," and indeed perhaps the only safe way to summarize her age is to list its many, confusing, and rich contradictions. It was typical of her age that she produced 122 volumes of journals, and it was also typical that her literary executor destroyed the record she so carefully made. Had those journals survived we would have an even more contradictory, though richer, picture of an age, and a richer heritage of a striking, particular, and surprising human being and writer.

Letters:

The Letters of Queen Victoria: A Selection from Her Majesty's Correspondence Between the Years 1837 and 1861, edited by Arthur Christopher Benson and Viscount Escher, 3 volumes (London: Murray, 1907; New York: Longmans, Green, 1907);

The Letters of Queen Victoria, Second Series: A Selection from Her Majesty's Correspondence and Journal Between the Years 1862 and 1885, edited by George Earle Buckle, 3 volumes (London: Murray, 1926-1928; New York: Longmans, Green, 1926-1928);

The Letters of Queen Victoria, Third Series: A Selection from Her Majesty's Correspondence and Journal Between the Years 1886 and 1901, edited by Buckle, 3 volumes (London: Murray, 1930-1932; New York: Longmans, Green, 1930);

Further Letters of Queen Victoria, from the Archives of the House of Brandenburg-Prussia, edited by Hector Bolitho (London: Butterworth, 1938); republished as *Letters of Queen Victoria, from the Archives of the House of Brandenburg-Prussia* (New Haven: Yale University Press, 1938);

Regina vs. Palmerston: The Correspondence Between Queen Victoria and Her Foreign and Prime Minister, 1837-1865, edited by Brian Connell (Garden City: Doubleday, 1961);

Dearest Child: Letters Between Queen Victoria and the Princess Royal 1858-61, edited by Roger Fulford (London: Evans, 1964; New York: Holt, Rinehart & Winston, 1965);

Dearest Mama: Letters Between Queen Victoria and the Crown Princess of Prussia, 1861-1864, edited by Fulford (London: Evans, 1968; New York: Holt, Rinehart & Winston, 1969);

Dear and Honoured Lady: The Correspondence between Queen Victoria and Alfred Tennyson, edited by Hope Dyson and Charles Tennyson (London: Macmillan, 1969; Rutherford, N.J.: Fairleigh Dickinson University Press, 1971);

Your Dear Letter: Private Correspondence of Queen Victoria and the Crown Princess of Prussia, 1865-1871, edited by Fulford (London: Evans, 1971; New York: Scribners, 1971).

Biographies:

Giles Lytton Strachey, *Queen Victoria* (London: Chatto & Windus, 1921; New York: Harcourt, Brace, 1921);

Elizabeth Longford, *Victoria, R.I.* (London: Weidenfeld, 1964); republished as *Queen Victoria: Born to Succeed* (New York: Harper & Row, 1965);

Cecil Woodham-Smith, *Queen Victoria from her Birth to the Death of the Prince Consort* (London: Hamilton/New York: Knopf, 1972).

References:

David Duff, *Victoria Travels: Journeys of Queen Victoria between 1830 and 1900, with Extracts from Her Journal* (London: Muller, 1970);

Charles Grey, *The Early Years of His Royal Highness the Prince Consort* (London: Smith, Elder, 1867; London: Harper, 1867);

Giles St. Aubyn, "Queen Victoria as an Author," *Essays by Diverse Hands: Being the Transactions of the Royal Society of Literature,* edited by John Guest, new series 38 (1975): 127-142.

Papers:

Queen Victoria's papers are in the Royal Archives at Windsor Castle.

Books for Further Reading

Alexander, Edward. *Matthew Arnold and John Stuart Mill.* New York: Columbia University Press, 1965.

Alexander. *Matthew Arnold, John Ruskin, and the Modern Temper.* Columbus: Ohio State University Press, 1973.

Altick, Richard D. *The English Common Reader: A Social History of the Mass Reading Public, 1800-1900.* Chicago: University of Chicago Press, 1957.

Altick. *Victorian People and Ideas.* New York: Norton, 1973.

Brantlinger, Patrick. *The Spirit of Reform: British Literature and Politics, 1832-1867.* Cambridge: Harvard University Press, 1977.

Briggs, Asa. *The Age of Improvement.* London & New York: Longmans, Green, 1959.

Brinton, Crane. *English Political Thought in the Nineteenth Century.* Cambridge: Harvard University Press, 1949.

Buckley, Jerome. *Victorian Poets and Prose Writers.* New York: Appleton-Century-Crofts, 1977.

Buckley. *The Victorian Temper: a Study in Literary Culture.* Cambridge: Harvard University Press, 1951.

Burn, W. L. *The Age of Equipoise: a Study of the Mid-Victorian Generation.* New York: Norton, 1964.

Cockshut, A. O. J. *The Art of Autobiography in 19th and 20th Century England.* New Haven: Yale University Press, 1984.

Cockshut. *Truth to Life: The Art of Biography in the Nineteenth Century.* New York: Harcourt Brace Jovanovich, 1974.

Dale, Peter Allan. *The Victorian Critic and the Idea of History: Carlyle, Arnold, Pater.* Cambridge: Harvard University Press, 1977.

DeLaura, David J. *Hebrew and Hellene in Victorian England: Newman, Arnold, and Pater.* Austin: University of Texas Press, 1969.

DeLaura. *Victorian Prose: A Guide to Research.* New York: Modern Language Association of America, 1973.

Fleishman, Avrom. *Figures of Autobiography: the Language of Self-Writing in Victorian and Modern England.* Berkeley: University of California Press, 1983.

Gibbons, Tom. *Rooms in the Darwin Hotel: Studies in English Literary Criticism and Ideas, 1880-1920.* Nedlands: University of Western Australia Press, 1973.

Gross, John. *The Rise and Fall of the Man of Letters: A Study of the Idiosyncratic and the Humane in Modern Literature. Literary Life Since 1800.* New York: Macmillan, 1969.

Harris, Wendell V. *The Omnipresent Debate: Empiricism and Transcendentalism in Nineteenth Century English Prose.* DeKalb: Northern Illinois University Press, 1981.

Himmelfarb, Gertrude. *Victorian Minds.* New York: Knopf, 1968.

Holloway, John. *The Victorian Sage.* London: Macmillan, 1953.

Hough, Graham. *The Last Romantics.* London: Duckworth, 1949.

Houghton, Walter E. *The Victorian Frame of Mind, 1830-1870.* New Haven & London: Yale University Press, 1957.

Knights, Ben. *The Idea of the Clerisy in the Nineteenth Century.* Cambridge: Cambridge University Press, 1978.

Levine, George. *The Boundaries of Fiction: Carlyle, Macaulay, Newman.* Princeton: Princeton University Press, 1968.

Levine, George, and William A. Madden, eds. *The Art of Victorian Prose.* New York: Oxford University Press, 1968.

Levine, Richard A., ed. *The Victorian Experience: the Prose Writers.* Athens: Ohio University Press, 1982.

Lucas, John, ed. *Literature and Politics in the Nineteenth Century.* London: Methuen, 1971.

Morgan, Peter F. *Literary Critics and Reviewers in Early Nineteenth-Century Britain.* London: Croom Helm, 1983.

Neff, Emery E. *Carlyle and Mill: An Introduction to Victorian Thought,* revised edition. New York: Columbia University Press, 1926.

Orel, Harold. *Victorian Literary Critics: George Henry Lewes, Walter Bagehot, Richard Holt Hutton, Leslie Stephen, Andrew Lang, George Saintsbury and Edmund Gosse.* New York: St. Martin's, 1984.

Orel, and George Worth, eds. *The Nineteenth-Century Writer and his Audience: Selected Problems in Theory, Form, and Content.* Lawrence: University of Kansas Publications, 1969.

Siebenschuh, William R. *Fictional Techniques and Factual Works.* Athens: University of Georgia Press, 1983.

Starzyk, Lawrence J. *The Imprisoned Splendor: a Study in Early Victorian Critical Theory.* Port Washington, N.Y.: Kennikat, 1977.

Tillotson, Geoffrey. *Criticism and the Nineteenth Century.* London: Athlone, 1951.

White, Robert B., Jr. *The English Literary Journal to 1900.* Detroit: Gale Research, 1977.

Williams, Raymond. *Culture and Society, 1780-1950.* New York: Columbia University Press, 1958.

Wilson, Harris W., and Diane Long Hoeveler. *English Prose and Criticism in the Nineteenth Century: A Guide to Information Sources.* Detroit: Gale Research, 1977.

Wolff, Michael, ed. *The Victorian Periodical Press: Samplings and Soundings.* Leicester: Leicester University Press, 1982.

Contributors

Donald S. Armentrout	*University of the South*
Eugene R. August	*University of Dayton*
Michael Bright	*Eastern Kentucky University*
Monika Brown	*Pembroke State University*
Ian Campbell	*University of Edinburgh*
Joan Corwin	*Evanston, Illinois*
Sidney Coulling	*Washington and Lee University*
James Diedrick	*Albion College*
Charles T. Dougherty	*University of Missouri at St. Louis*
James Forsythe Hazen	*University of Nevada*
Winifred Hughes	*Princeton, New Jersey*
Anne Humpherys	*Lehman College, City University of New York*
Marilyn Naufftus Karlson	*Augusta, Georgia*
Clinton Machann	*Texas A&M University*
Carolyn Matalene	*University of South Carolina*
Kathleen McCormack	*Florida International University*
William F. Naufftus	*Winthrop College*
Stephen Pulsford	*University of South Carolina*
Michael Shelden	*Indiana State University*
G. B. Tennyson	*University of California, Los Angeles*
William B. Thesing	*University of South Carolina*
D. W. Thomas	*Central Washington University*
Gillian Thomas	*Saint Mary's University*
R. K. R. Thornton	*University of Newcastle upon Tyne*
Richard Tobias	*University of Pittsburgh*
Ned Toomey	*Central Washington University*
E. Cleve Want	*Texas A&M University*

Cumulative Index

Dictionary of Literary Biography, Volumes 1-55
Dictionary of Literary Biography Yearbook, 1980-1985
Dictionary of Literary Biography Documentary Series, Volumes 1-4

Cumulative Index

DLB before number: *Dictionary of Literary Biography,* Volumes 1-55
Y before number: *Dictionary of Literary Biography Yearbook,* 1980-1985
DS before number: *Dictionary of Literary Biography Documentary Series,* Volumes 1-4

A

Ashton, Winifred (see Dane, Clemence)
Asimov, Isaac 1920- DLB-8
Atheneum Publishers....DLB-46
Atherton, Gertrude 1857-1948....DLB-9
Atkins, Josiah circa 1755-1781....DLB-31
Atkins, Russell 1926- DLB-41
The Atlantic Monthly Press....DLB-46
Atwood, Margaret 1939- DLB-53
Aubert, Alvin 1930- DLB-41
Aubin, Penelope 1685-circa, 1731....DLB-39
Auchincloss, Louis 1917- DLB-2; Y-80
Auden, W. H. 1907-1973....DLB-10, 20
Audio Art in America: A Personal Memoir....Y-85
Austin, Alfred 1835-1913....DLB-35
Austin, Mary 1868-1934....DLB-9
The Author's Apology for His Book (1684), by John Bunyan....DLB-39
An Author's Response, by Ronald Sukenick....Y-82
Authors and Newspapers Association....DLB-46
Authors' Publishing Company....DLB-49
Avalon Books....DLB-46
Avison, Margaret 1918- DLB-53
Avon Books....DLB-46
Ayckbourn, Alan 1939- DLB-13
Aytoun, William Edmondstoune 1813-1865....DLB-32

B

Babbitt, Natalie 1932- DLB-52
Babcock, John [publishing house]....DLB-49
Bache, Benjamin Franklin 1769-1798....DLB-43
Bacon, Delia 1811-1859....DLB-1
Bacon, Thomas circa 1700-1768....DLB-31
Badger, Richard G., and Company....DLB-49
Bage, Robert 1728-1801....DLB-39
Bagehot, Walter 1826-1877....DLB-55
Bagnold, Enid 1889-1981....DLB-13
Bailey, Francis [publishing house]....DLB-49
Bailey, Paul 1937- DLB-14
Bailey, Philip James 1816-1902....DLB-32
Baillie, Hugh 1890-1966....DLB-29
Bailyn, Bernard 1922- DLB-17
Bainbridge, Beryl 1933- DLB-14
The Baker and Taylor Company....DLB-49
Baker, Walter H., Company ("Baker's Plays")....DLB-49
Bald, Wambly 1902- DLB-4
Balderston, John 1889-1954....DLB-26
Baldwin, James 1924- DLB-2, 7, 33
Baldwin, Joseph Glover 1815-1864....DLB-3, 11
Ballantine Books....DLB-46
Ballard, J. G. 1930- DLB-14
Ballou, Robert O. [publishing house]....DLB-46
Bambara, Toni Cade 1939- DLB-38
Bancroft, A. L., and Company....DLB-49
Bancroft, George 1800-1891....DLB-1, 30
Bancroft, Hubert Howe 1832-1918....DLB-47
Bangs, John Kendrick 1862-1922....DLB-11
Bantam Books....DLB-46
Banville, John 1945- DLB-14
Baraka, Amiri 1934- DLB-5, 7, 16, 38
Barber, John Warner 1798-1885....DLB-30
Barbour, Ralph Henry 1870-1944....DLB-22
Barclay, E. E., and Company....DLB-49
Bardeen, C. W. [publishing house]....DLB-49
Baring, Maurice 1874-1945....DLB-34
Barker, A. L. 1918- DLB-14
Barker, George 1913- DLB-20
Barker, Harley Granville 1877-1946....DLB-10
Barker, Howard 1946- DLB-13
Barker, James Nelson 1784-1858....DLB-37
Barker, Jane 1652-1727?....DLB-39
Barks, Coleman 1937- DLB-5
Barlow, Joel 1754-1812....DLB-37
Barnard, John 1681-1770....DLB-24
Barnes, A. S., and Company....DLB-49
Barnes, Djuna 1892-1982....DLB-4, 9, 45
Barnes, Margaret Ayer 1886-1967....DLB-9
Barnes, Peter 1931- DLB-13
Barnes, William 1801-1886....DLB-32

C

D

E

G

H

I

J

K

L

M

N

Q

R

S

T

U

V

W

Y

Z